Little Lulu®

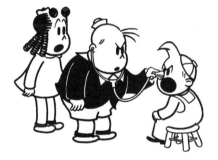

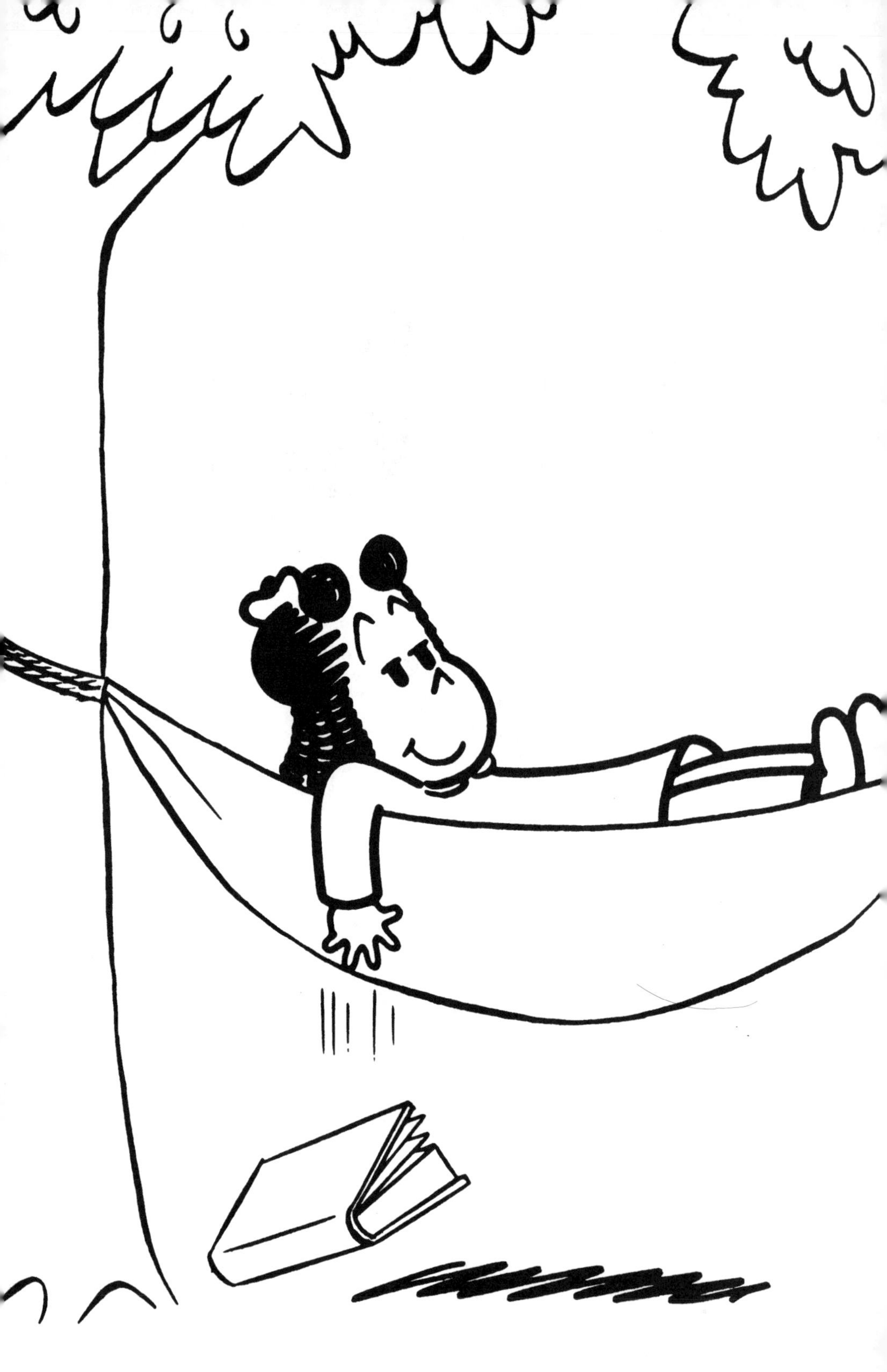

Little Lulu®

The Expert

Story and Art
John Stanley
and
Irving Tripp

Based on the character
created by
Marge Buell

DARK HORSE BOOKS®

Publisher
Mike Richardson

Editor
Dave Marshall

Collection Designer
Krystal Hennes

Art Director
Lia Ribacchi

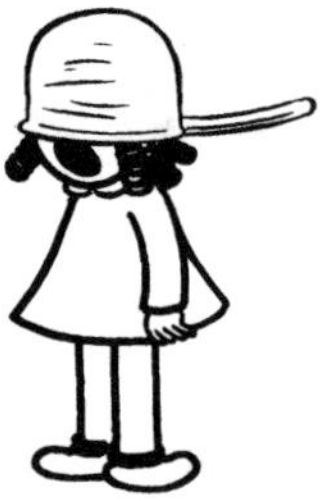

Published by
Dark Horse Books
A division of Dark Horse Comics, Inc.
10956 SE Main Street
Milwaukie, OR 97222

darkhorse.com

Little Lulu ® Vol. 18: The Expert

The comic on pages 198 to 211 was originally intended for issue twenty-six of Marge's *Little Lulu* but was never published.

First edition: January 2008
ISBN 978-1-59307-687-0

1 3 5 7 9 10 8 6 4 2
Printed in the United States of America

A note about Lulu

Little Lulu came into the world through the pen of cartoonist Marjorie "Marge" Henderson Buell in 1935. Originally commissioned as a series of single-panel cartoons by *The Saturday Evening Post*, Lulu took the world by storm with her charm, smarts, and sass. Within ten years, she not only was the star of her own cartoon series, but a celebrity spokesgirl for a variety of high-profile commercial products.

Little Lulu truly hit her stride as America's sweetheart in the comic books published by Dell Comics starting in 1945. While Buell was solely responsible for Lulu's original single-panel shenanigans, the comic-book stories were put into the able hands of comics legend John Stanley. Stanley wrote and laid out the comics while artist Irving Tripp provided the finished drawings. After a number of trial appearances in Dell Comics, Lulu's appeal was undeniable, and she was granted her very own comic-book series, called *Marge's Little Lulu*, which was published regularly through 1984.

This volume contains every comic from issues eighty-two through eighty-seven of *Marge's Little Lulu*.

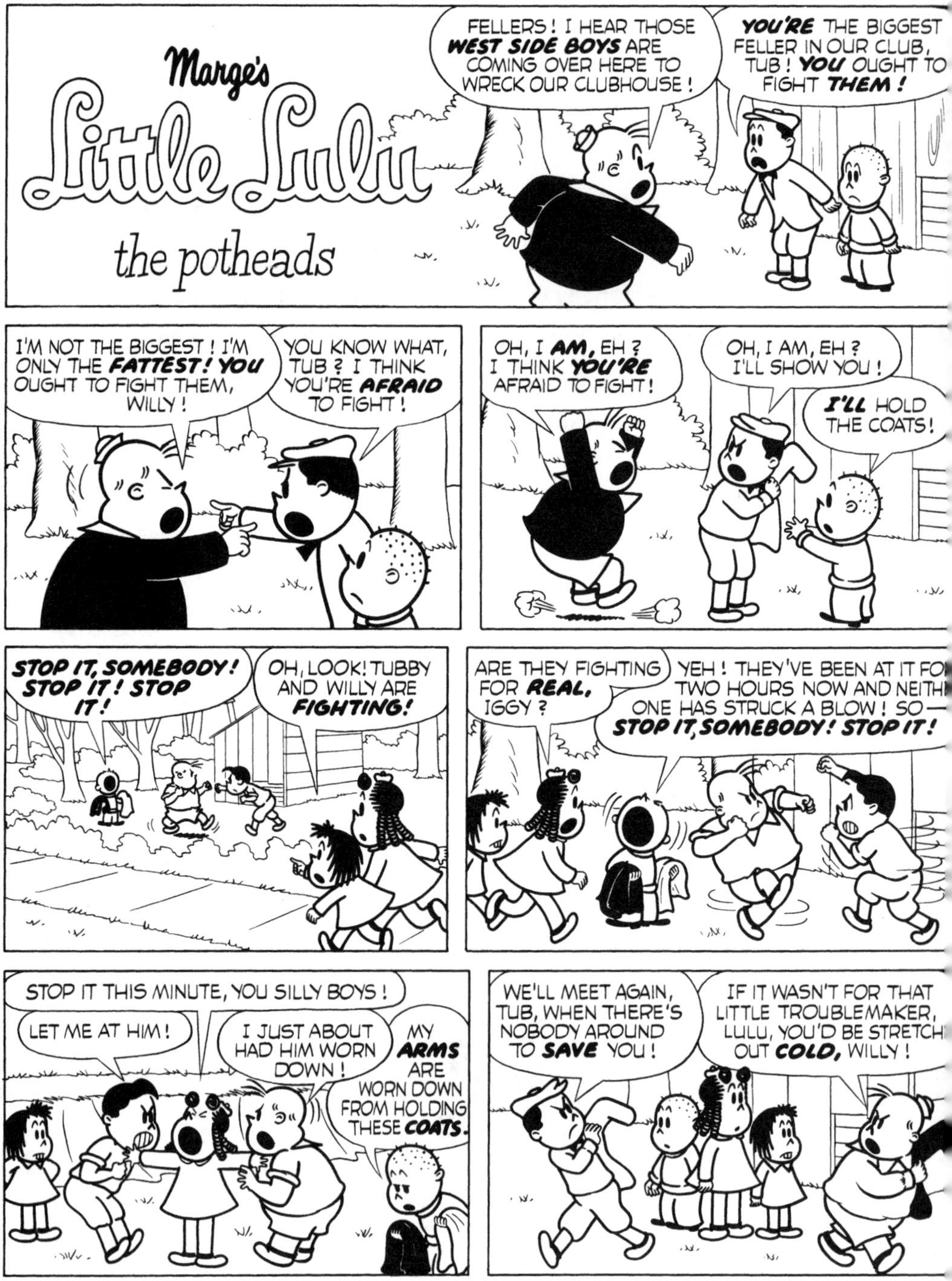
Marge's
Little Lulu
the potheads
FELLERS! I HEAR THOSE WEST SIDE BOYS ARE COMING OVER HERE TO WRECK OUR CLUBHOUSE!
YOU'RE THE BIGGEST FELLER IN OUR CLUB, TUB! YOU OUGHT TO FIGHT THEM!
I'M NOT THE BIGGEST! I'M ONLY THE FATTEST! YOU OUGHT TO FIGHT THEM, WILLY!
YOU KNOW WHAT, TUB? I THINK YOU'RE AFRAID TO FIGHT!
OH, I AM, EH? I THINK YOU'RE AFRAID TO FIGHT!
OH, I AM, EH? I'LL SHOW YOU!
I'LL HOLD THE COATS!
STOP IT, SOMEBODY! STOP IT! STOP IT!
OH, LOOK! TUBBY AND WILLY ARE FIGHTING!
ARE THEY FIGHTING FOR REAL, IGGY?
YEH! THEY'VE BEEN AT IT FO
TWO HOURS NOW AND NEITH
ONE HAS STRUCK A BLOW! SO—
STOP IT, SOMEBODY! STOP IT!
STOP IT THIS MINUTE, YOU SILLY BOYS!
LET ME AT HIM!
I JUST ABOUT HAD HIM WORN DOWN!
MY ARMS ARE WORN DOWN FROM HOLDING THESE COATS.
WE'LL MEET AGAIN, TUB, WHEN THERE'S NOBODY AROUND TO SAVE YOU!
IF IT WASN'T FOR THAT LITTLE TROUBLEMAKER, LULU, YOU'D BE STRETCH
OUT COLD, WILLY!

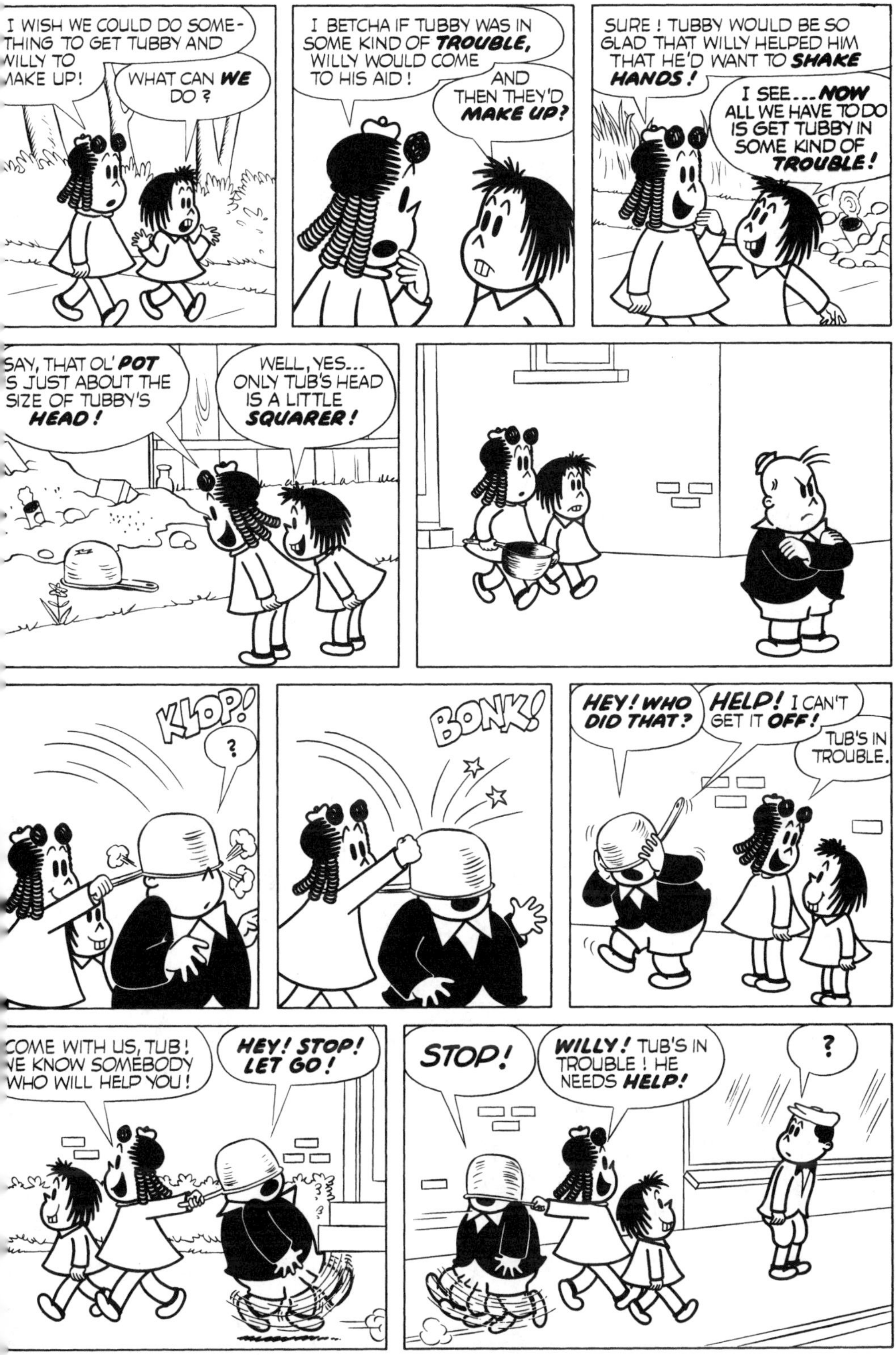
I WISH WE COULD DO SOMETHING TO GET TUBBY AND WILLY TO MAKE UP!
WHAT CAN WE DO ?
I BETCHA IF TUBBY WAS IN SOME KIND OF TROUBLE, WILLY WOULD COME TO HIS AID!
AND THEN THEY'D MAKE UP?
SURE! TUBBY WOULD BE SO GLAD THAT WILLY HELPED HIM THAT HE'D WANT TO SHAKE HANDS!
I SEE... NOW ALL WE HAVE TO DO IS GET TUBBY IN SOME KIND OF TROUBLE!
SAY, THAT OL' POT IS JUST ABOUT THE SIZE OF TUBBY'S HEAD!
WELL, YES... ONLY TUB'S HEAD IS A LITTLE SQUARER!
KLOP!
?
BONK!
HEY! WHO DID THAT?
HELP! I CAN'T GET IT OFF!
TUB'S IN TROUBLE.
COME WITH US, TUB! WE KNOW SOMEBODY WHO WILL HELP YOU!
HEY! STOP! LET GO!
STOP!
WILLY! TUB'S IN TROUBLE! HE NEEDS HELP!
?

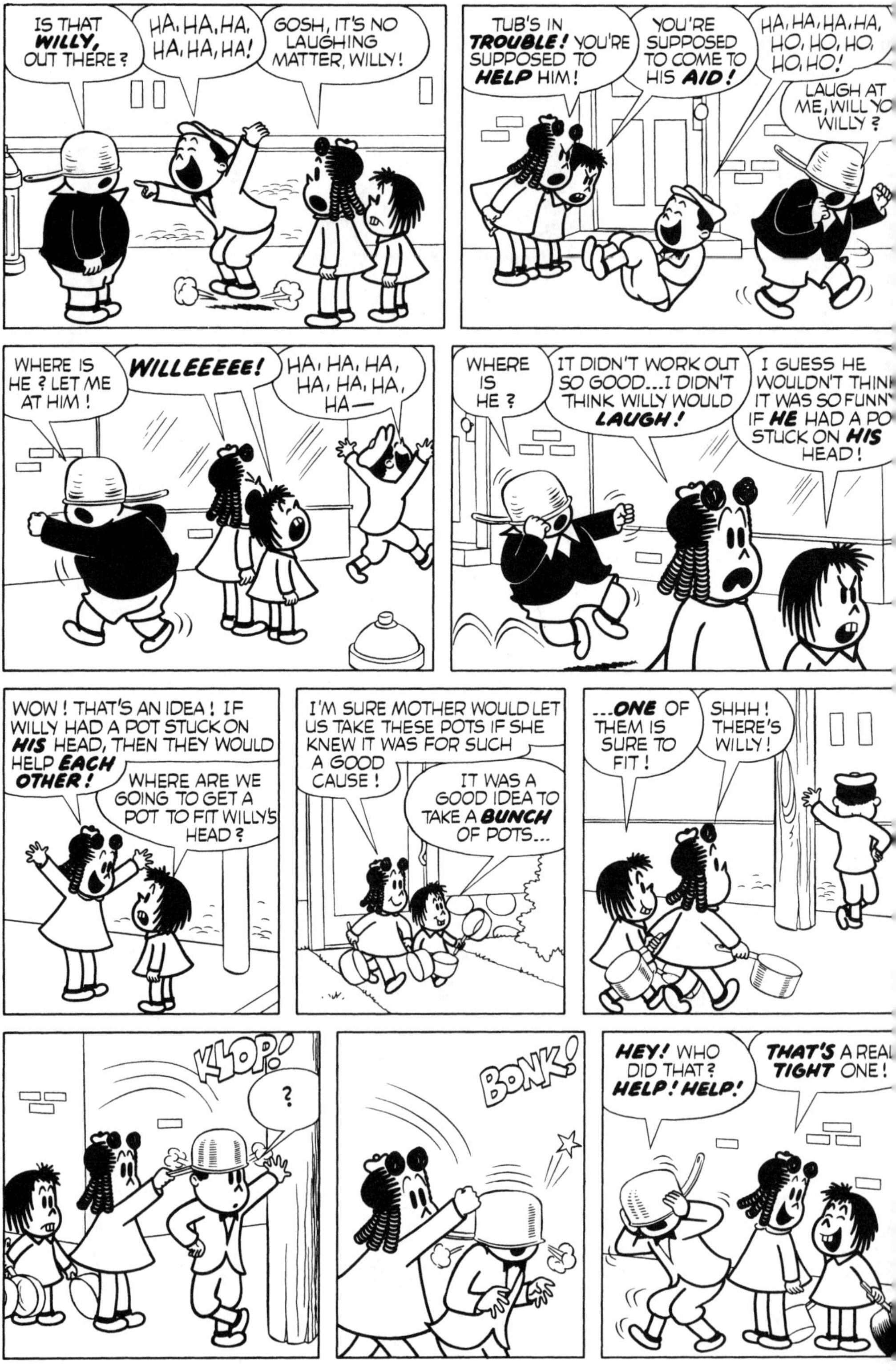

IS THAT **WILLY,** OUT THERE?
HA, HA, HA, HA, HA, HA!
GOSH, IT'S NO LAUGHING MATTER, WILLY!
TUB'S IN **TROUBLE!** YOU'RE SUPPOSED TO **HELP** HIM!
YOU'RE SUPPOSED TO COME TO HIS **AID!**
HA, HA, HA, HA, HO, HO, HO, HO, HO!
LAUGH AT ME, WILL YO WILLY?
WHERE IS HE? LET ME AT HIM!
WILLEEEEE!
HA, HA, HA, HA, HA, HA, HA—
WHERE IS HE?
IT DIDN'T WORK OUT SO GOOD...I DIDN'T THINK WILLY WOULD **LAUGH!**
I GUESS HE WOULDN'T THIN IT WAS SO FUNN IF **HE** HAD A PO STUCK ON **HIS** HEAD!
WOW! THAT'S AN IDEA! IF WILLY HAD A POT STUCK ON **HIS** HEAD, THEN THEY WOULD HELP **EACH OTHER!**
WHERE ARE WE GOING TO GET A POT TO FIT WILLY'S HEAD?
I'M SURE MOTHER WOULD LET US TAKE THESE POTS IF SHE KNEW IT WAS FOR SUCH A GOOD CAUSE!
IT WAS A GOOD IDEA TO TAKE A **BUNCH** OF POTS...
...**ONE** OF THEM IS SURE TO FIT!
SHHH! THERE'S WILLY!
KLOP!
?
BONK!
HEY! WHO DID THAT? **HELP! HELP!**
THAT'S A REA **TIGHT** ONE!

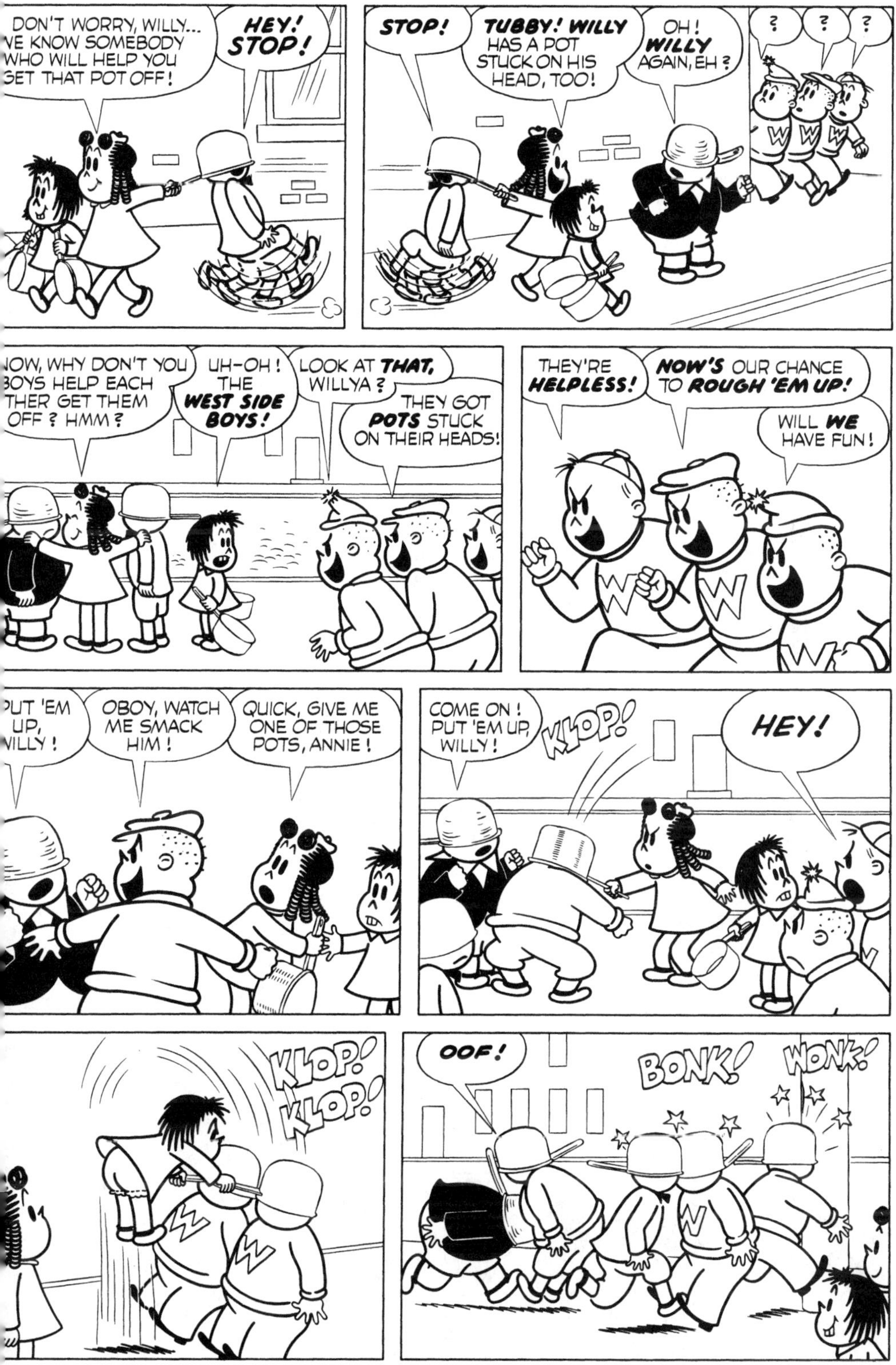

DON'T WORRY, WILLY... WE KNOW SOMEBODY WHO WILL HELP YOU GET THAT POT OFF!
HEY! STOP!
STOP!
TUBBY! WILLY HAS A POT STUCK ON HIS HEAD, TOO!
OH! WILLY AGAIN, EH?
?
?
?
NOW, WHY DON'T YOU BOYS HELP EACH OTHER GET THEM OFF? HMM?
UH-OH! THE WEST SIDE BOYS!
LOOK AT THAT, WILLYA?
THEY GOT POTS STUCK ON THEIR HEADS!
THEY'RE HELPLESS!
NOW'S OUR CHANCE TO ROUGH 'EM UP!
WILL WE HAVE FUN!
PUT 'EM UP, WILLY!
OBOY, WATCH ME SMACK HIM!
QUICK, GIVE ME ONE OF THOSE POTS, ANNIE!
COME ON! PUT 'EM UP, WILLY!
KLOP!
HEY!
KLOP!
KLOP!
OOF!
BONK!
WONK!

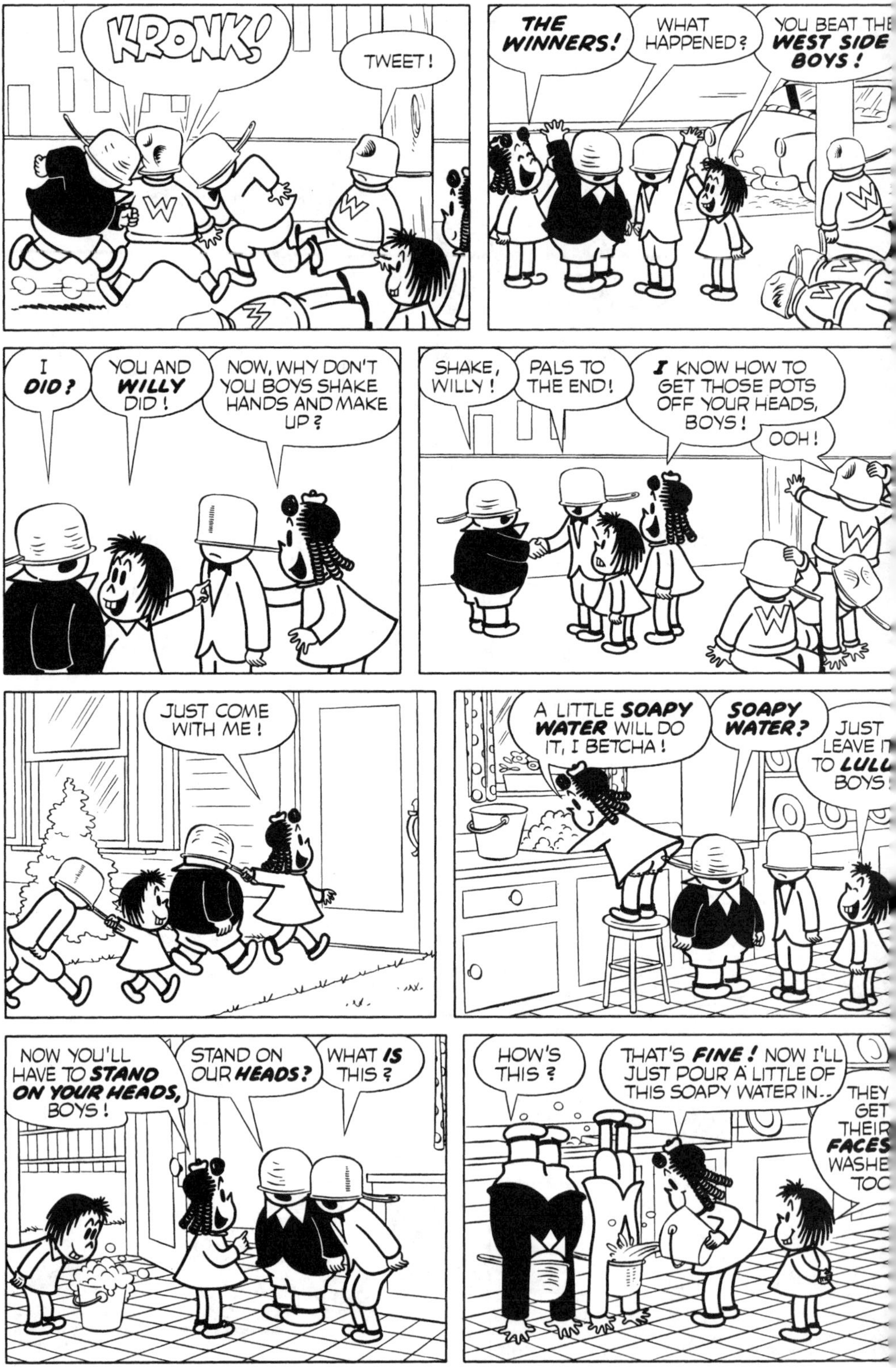
KRONK!
TWEET!
THE WINNERS!
WHAT HAPPENED?
YOU BEAT THE WEST SIDE BOYS!
I DID?
YOU AND WILLY DID!
NOW, WHY DON'T YOU BOYS SHAKE HANDS AND MAKE UP?
SHAKE, WILLY!
PALS TO THE END!
I KNOW HOW TO GET THOSE POTS OFF YOUR HEADS, BOYS!
OOH!
JUST COME WITH ME!
A LITTLE SOAPY WATER WILL DO IT, I BETCHA!
SOAPY WATER?
JUST LEAVE IT TO LULU BOYS!
NOW YOU'LL HAVE TO STAND ON YOUR HEADS, BOYS!
STAND ON OUR HEADS?
WHAT IS THIS?
HOW'S THIS?
THAT'S FINE! NOW I'LL JUST POUR A LITTLE OF THIS SOAPY WATER IN..
THEY GET THEIR FACES WASHE TOO

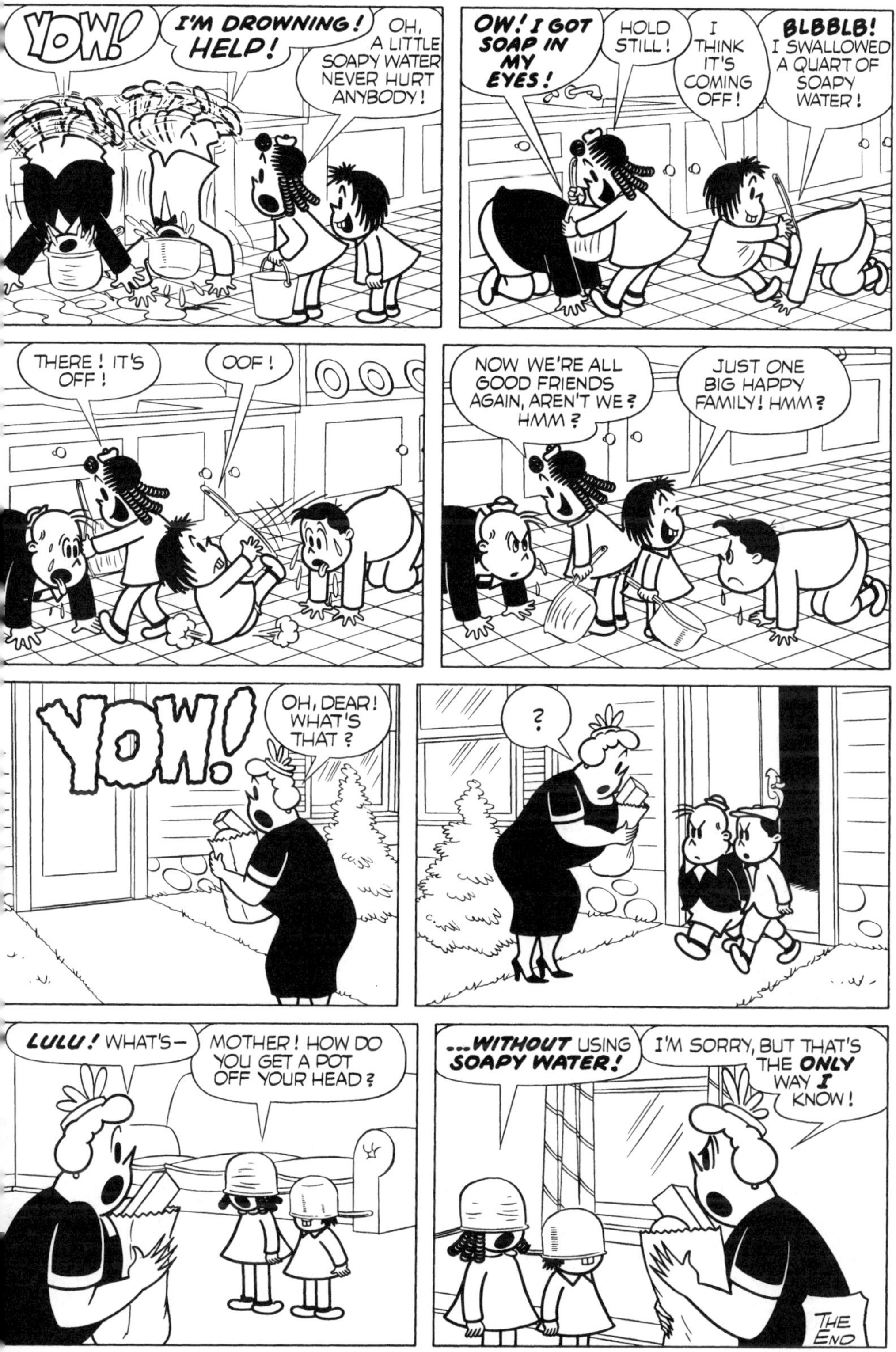
YOW!
I'M DROWNING! HELP!
OH, A LITTLE SOAPY WATER NEVER HURT ANYBODY!
OW! I GOT SOAP IN MY EYES!
HOLD STILL!
I THINK IT'S COMING OFF!
BLBBLB! I SWALLOWED A QUART OF SOAPY WATER!
THERE! IT'S OFF!
OOF!
NOW WE'RE ALL GOOD FRIENDS AGAIN, AREN'T WE? HMM?
JUST ONE BIG HAPPY FAMILY! HMM?
YOW!
OH, DEAR! WHAT'S THAT?
?
LULU! WHAT'S—
MOTHER! HOW DO YOU GET A POT OFF YOUR HEAD?
...WITHOUT USING SOAPY WATER!
I'M SORRY, BUT THAT'S THE ONLY WAY I KNOW!
THE END

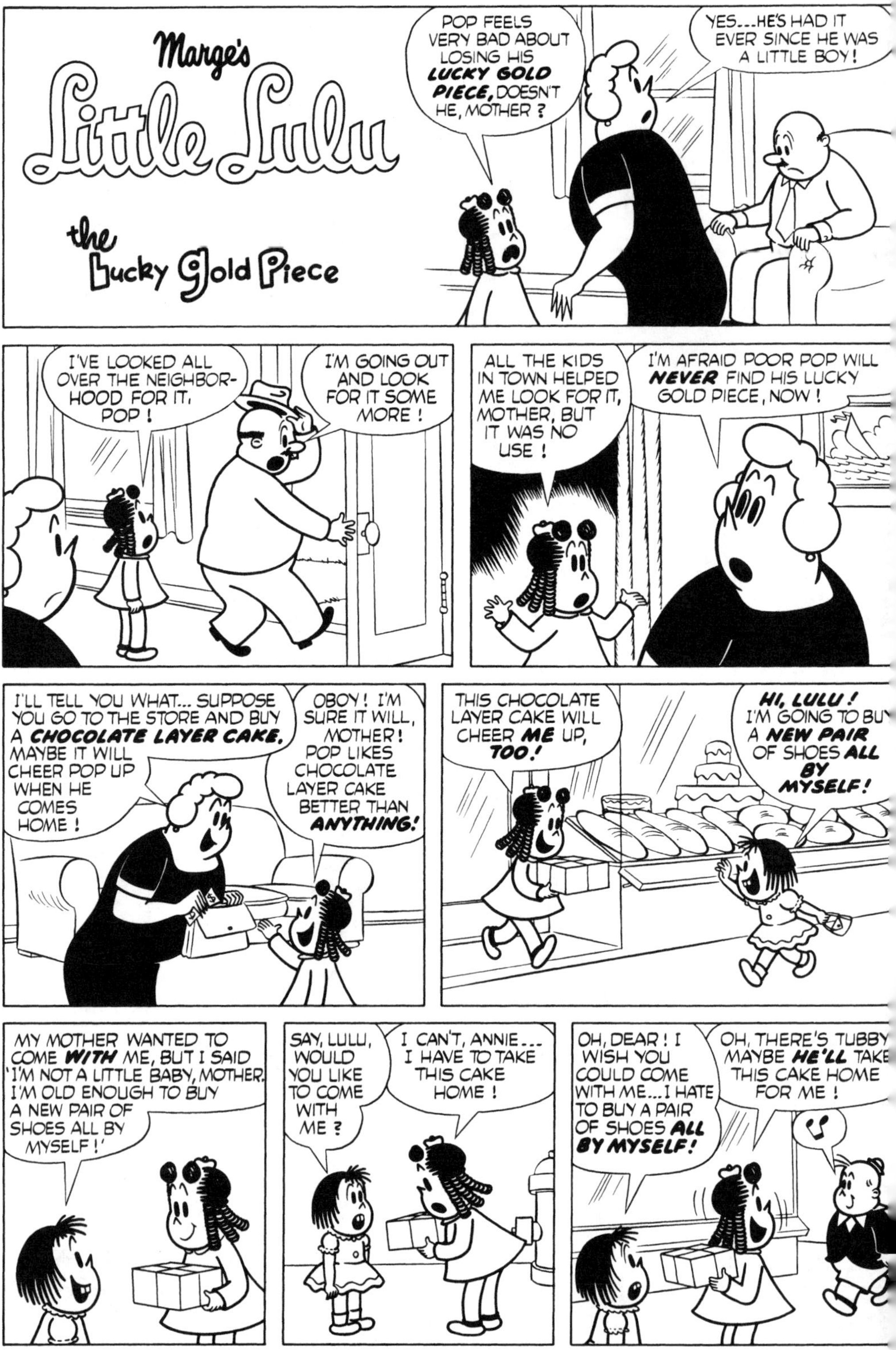
Marge's
Little Lulu
the Lucky Gold Piece
POP FEELS VERY BAD ABOUT LOSING HIS LUCKY GOLD PIECE, DOESN'T HE, MOTHER ?
YES...HE'S HAD IT EVER SINCE HE WAS A LITTLE BOY!
I'VE LOOKED ALL OVER THE NEIGHBOR-HOOD FOR IT, POP !
I'M GOING OUT AND LOOK FOR IT SOME MORE !
ALL THE KIDS IN TOWN HELPED ME LOOK FOR IT, MOTHER, BUT IT WAS NO USE !
I'M AFRAID POOR POP WILL NEVER FIND HIS LUCKY GOLD PIECE, NOW !
I'LL TELL YOU WHAT... SUPPOSE YOU GO TO THE STORE AND BUY A CHOCOLATE LAYER CAKE. MAYBE IT WILL CHEER POP UP WHEN HE COMES HOME !
OBOY ! I'M SURE IT WILL, MOTHER! POP LIKES CHOCOLATE LAYER CAKE BETTER THAN ANYTHING!
THIS CHOCOLATE LAYER CAKE WILL CHEER ME UP, TOO!
HI, LULU ! I'M GOING TO BUY A NEW PAIR OF SHOES ALL BY MYSELF!
MY MOTHER WANTED TO COME WITH ME, BUT I SAID 'I'M NOT A LITTLE BABY, MOTHER. I'M OLD ENOUGH TO BUY A NEW PAIR OF SHOES ALL BY MYSELF !'
SAY, LULU, WOULD YOU LIKE TO COME WITH ME ?
I CAN'T, ANNIE... I HAVE TO TAKE THIS CAKE HOME !
OH, DEAR ! I WISH YOU COULD COME WITH ME...I HATE TO BUY A PAIR OF SHOES ALL BY MYSELF!
OH, THERE'S TUBBY MAYBE HE'LL TAKE THIS CAKE HOME FOR ME !

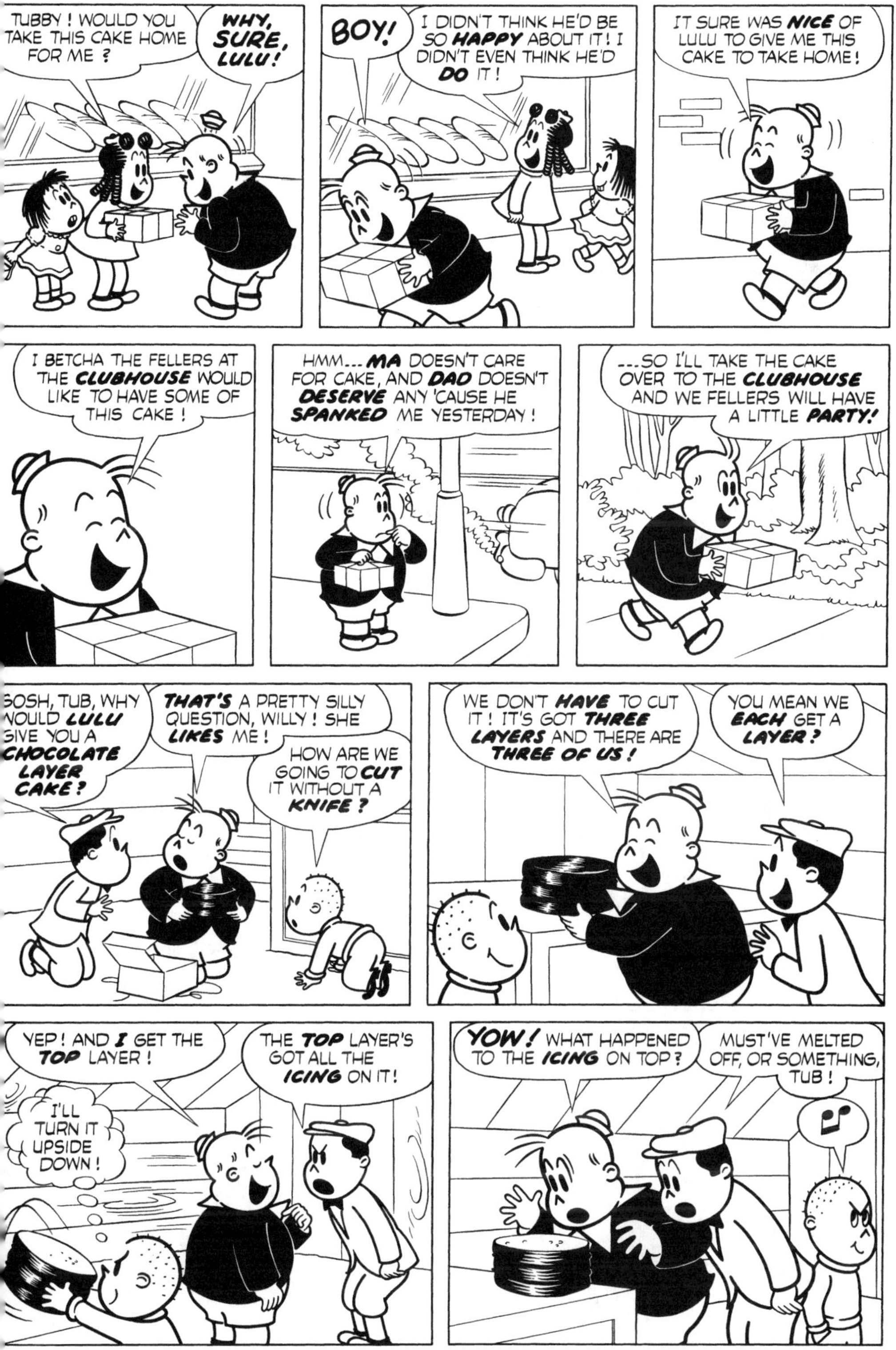
TUBBY! WOULD YOU TAKE THIS CAKE HOME FOR ME ?
WHY, SURE, LULU!
BOY!
I DIDN'T THINK HE'D BE SO HAPPY ABOUT IT! I DIDN'T EVEN THINK HE'D DO IT!
IT SURE WAS NICE OF LULU TO GIVE ME THIS CAKE TO TAKE HOME!
I BETCHA THE FELLERS AT THE CLUBHOUSE WOULD LIKE TO HAVE SOME OF THIS CAKE!
HMM... MA DOESN'T CARE FOR CAKE, AND DAD DOESN'T DESERVE ANY 'CAUSE HE SPANKED ME YESTERDAY!
...SO I'LL TAKE THE CAKE OVER TO THE CLUBHOUSE AND WE FELLERS WILL HAVE A LITTLE PARTY!
GOSH, TUB, WHY WOULD LULU GIVE YOU A CHOCOLATE LAYER CAKE?
THAT'S A PRETTY SILLY QUESTION, WILLY! SHE LIKES ME!
HOW ARE WE GOING TO CUT IT WITHOUT A KNIFE?
WE DON'T HAVE TO CUT IT! IT'S GOT THREE LAYERS AND THERE ARE THREE OF US!
YOU MEAN WE EACH GET A LAYER?
YEP! AND I GET THE TOP LAYER!
THE TOP LAYER'S GOT ALL THE ICING ON IT!
I'LL TURN IT UPSIDE DOWN!
YOW! WHAT HAPPENED TO THE ICING ON TOP?
MUST'VE MELTED OFF, OR SOMETHING, TUB!

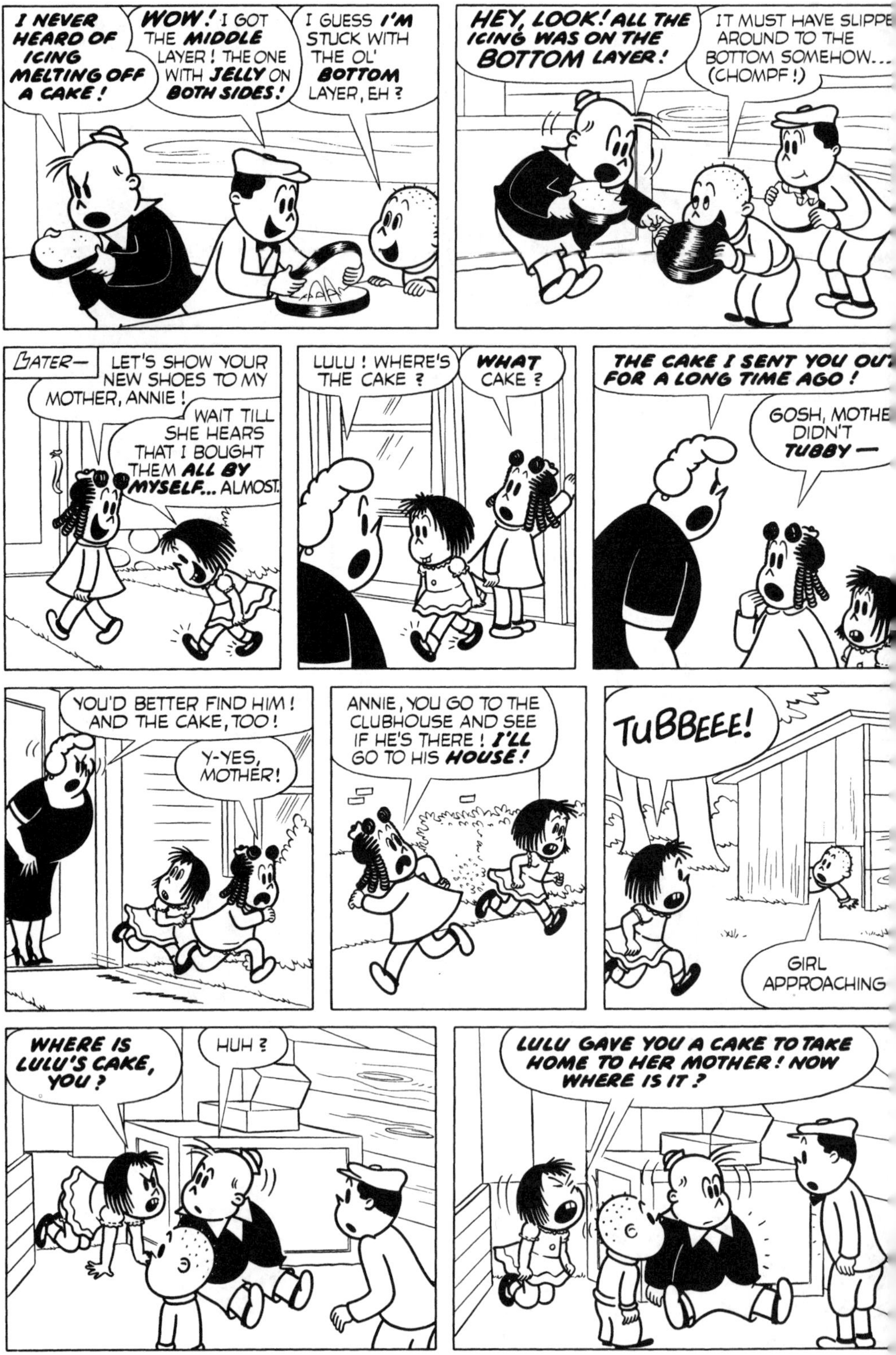
I NEVER HEARD OF ICING MELTING OFF A CAKE!
WOW! I GOT THE MIDDLE LAYER! THE ONE WITH JELLY ON BOTH SIDES!
I GUESS I'M STUCK WITH THE OL' BOTTOM LAYER, EH?
HEY, LOOK! ALL THE ICING WAS ON THE BOTTOM LAYER!
IT MUST HAVE SLIPPE AROUND TO THE BOTTOM SOMEHOW... (CHOMPF!)
LATER—
LET'S SHOW YOUR NEW SHOES TO MY MOTHER, ANNIE!
WAIT TILL SHE HEARS THAT I BOUGHT THEM ALL BY MYSELF... ALMOST.
LULU! WHERE'S THE CAKE?
WHAT CAKE?
THE CAKE I SENT YOU OU FOR A LONG TIME AGO!
GOSH, MOTHE DIDN'T TUBBY—
YOU'D BETTER FIND HIM! AND THE CAKE, TOO!
Y-YES, MOTHER!
ANNIE, YOU GO TO THE CLUBHOUSE AND SEE IF HE'S THERE! I'LL GO TO HIS HOUSE!
TUBBEEE!
GIRL APPROACHING
WHERE IS LULU'S CAKE, YOU?
HUH?
LULU GAVE YOU A CAKE TO TAKE HOME TO HER MOTHER! NOW WHERE IS IT?

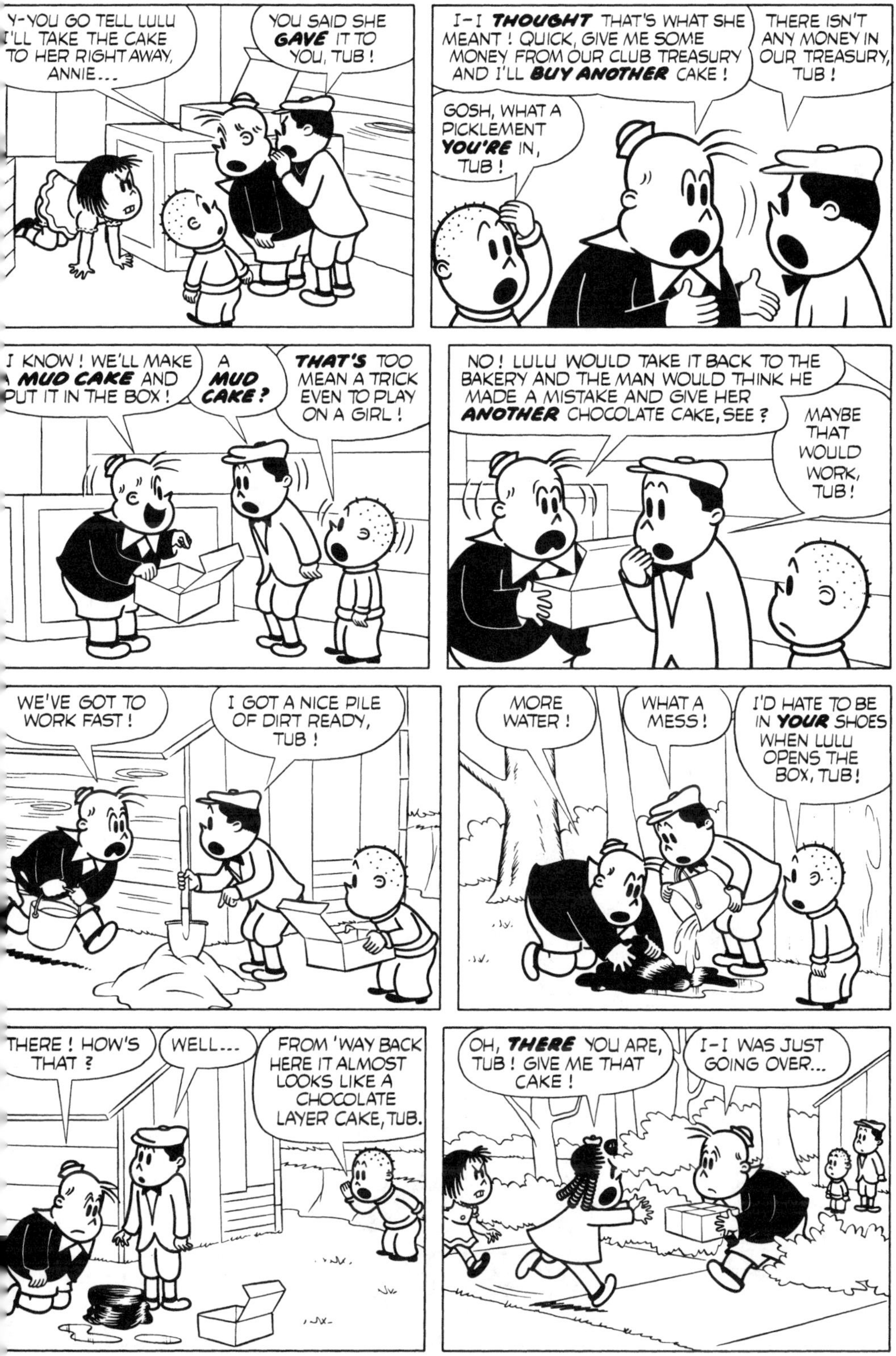
Y-YOU GO TELL LULU I'LL TAKE THE CAKE TO HER RIGHT AWAY, ANNIE...
YOU SAID SHE GAVE IT TO YOU, TUB!
I-I THOUGHT THAT'S WHAT SHE MEANT! QUICK, GIVE ME SOME MONEY FROM OUR CLUB TREASURY AND I'LL BUY ANOTHER CAKE!
THERE ISN'T ANY MONEY IN OUR TREASURY, TUB!
GOSH, WHAT A PICKLEMENT YOU'RE IN, TUB!
I KNOW! WE'LL MAKE A MUD CAKE AND PUT IT IN THE BOX!
A MUD CAKE?
THAT'S TOO MEAN A TRICK EVEN TO PLAY ON A GIRL!
NO! LULU WOULD TAKE IT BACK TO THE BAKERY AND THE MAN WOULD THINK HE MADE A MISTAKE AND GIVE HER ANOTHER CHOCOLATE CAKE, SEE?
MAYBE THAT WOULD WORK, TUB!
WE'VE GOT TO WORK FAST!
I GOT A NICE PILE OF DIRT READY, TUB!
MORE WATER!
WHAT A MESS!
I'D HATE TO BE IN YOUR SHOES WHEN LULU OPENS THE BOX, TUB!
THERE! HOW'S THAT?
WELL...
FROM 'WAY BACK HERE IT ALMOST LOOKS LIKE A CHOCOLATE LAYER CAKE, TUB.
OH, THERE YOU ARE, TUB! GIVE ME THAT CAKE!
I-I WAS JUST GOING OVER...

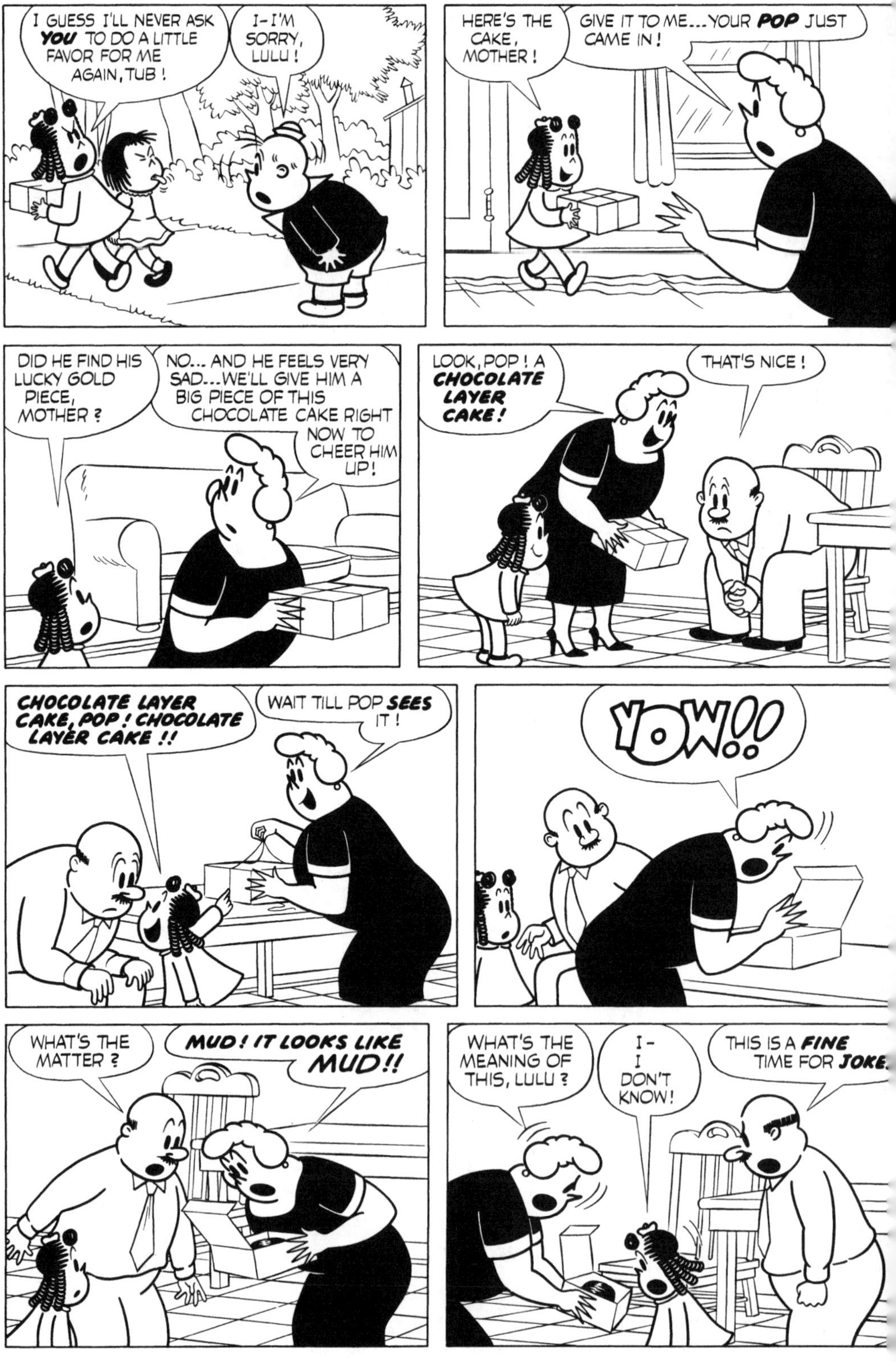
I GUESS I'LL NEVER ASK YOU TO DO A LITTLE FAVOR FOR ME AGAIN, TUB!
I-I'M SORRY, LULU!
HERE'S THE CAKE, MOTHER!
GIVE IT TO ME... YOUR POP JUST CAME IN!
DID HE FIND HIS LUCKY GOLD PIECE, MOTHER?
NO... AND HE FEELS VERY SAD... WE'LL GIVE HIM A BIG PIECE OF THIS CHOCOLATE CAKE RIGHT NOW TO CHEER HIM UP!
LOOK, POP! A CHOCOLATE LAYER CAKE!
THAT'S NICE!
CHOCOLATE LAYER CAKE, POP! CHOCOLATE LAYER CAKE!!
WAIT TILL POP SEES IT!
YOW!!
WHAT'S THE MATTER?
MUD! IT LOOKS LIKE MUD!!
WHAT'S THE MEANING OF THIS, LULU?
I- I DON'T KNOW!
THIS IS A FINE TIME FOR JOKE

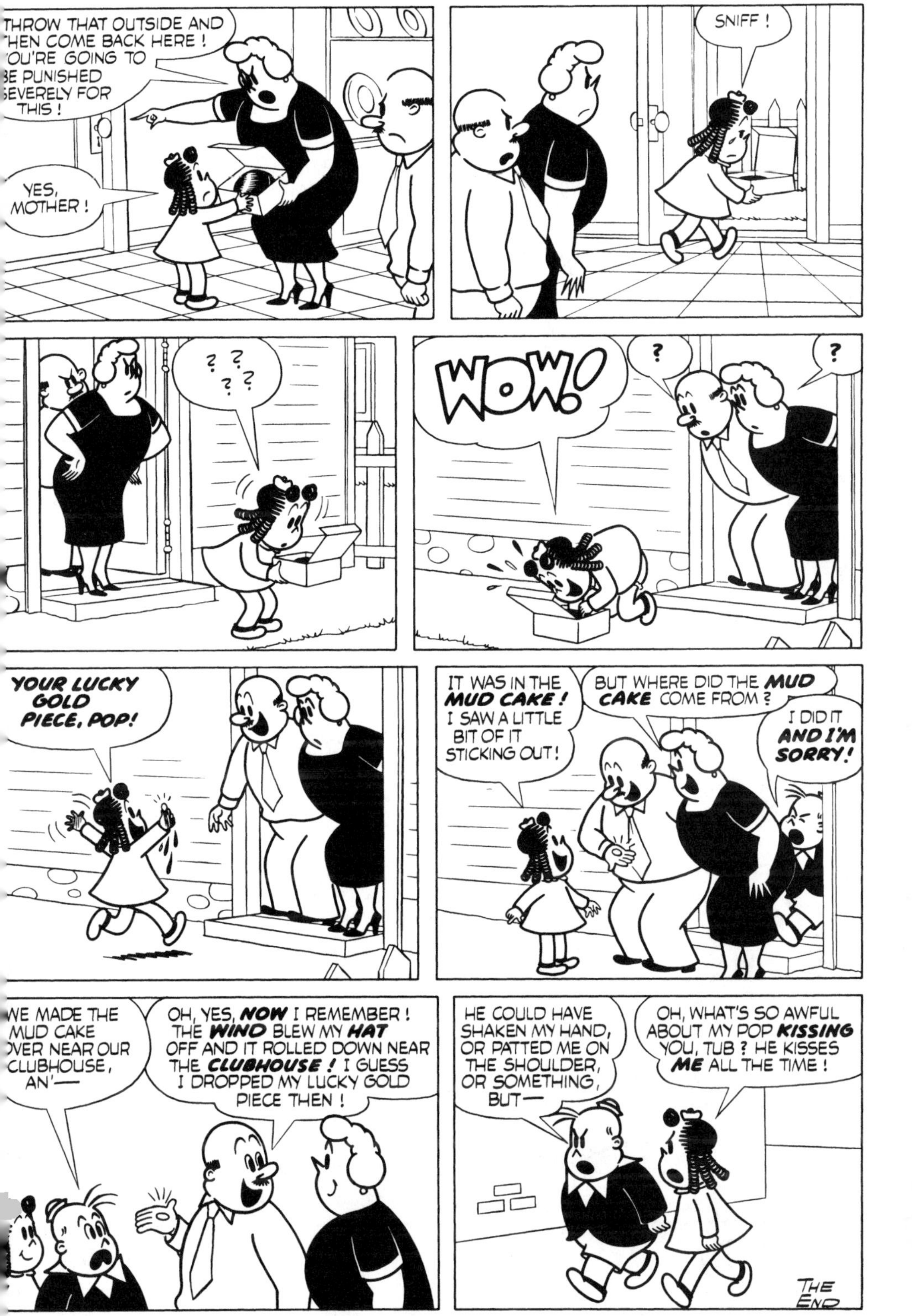

THROW THAT OUTSIDE AND THEN COME BACK HERE ! YOU'RE GOING TO BE PUNISHED SEVERELY FOR THIS !
YES, MOTHER !
SNIFF !
? ? ? ?
WOW!
?
?
YOUR LUCKY GOLD PIECE, POP!
IT WAS IN THE MUD CAKE ! I SAW A LITTLE BIT OF IT STICKING OUT !
BUT WHERE DID THE MUD CAKE COME FROM ?
I DID IT AND I'M SORRY!
WE MADE THE MUD CAKE OVER NEAR OUR CLUBHOUSE, AN'—
OH, YES, NOW I REMEMBER ! THE WIND BLEW MY HAT OFF AND IT ROLLED DOWN NEAR THE CLUBHOUSE ! I GUESS I DROPPED MY LUCKY GOLD PIECE THEN !
HE COULD HAVE SHAKEN MY HAND, OR PATTED ME ON THE SHOULDER, OR SOMETHING, BUT—
OH, WHAT'S SO AWFUL ABOUT MY POP KISSING YOU, TUB ? HE KISSES ME ALL THE TIME !
THE END

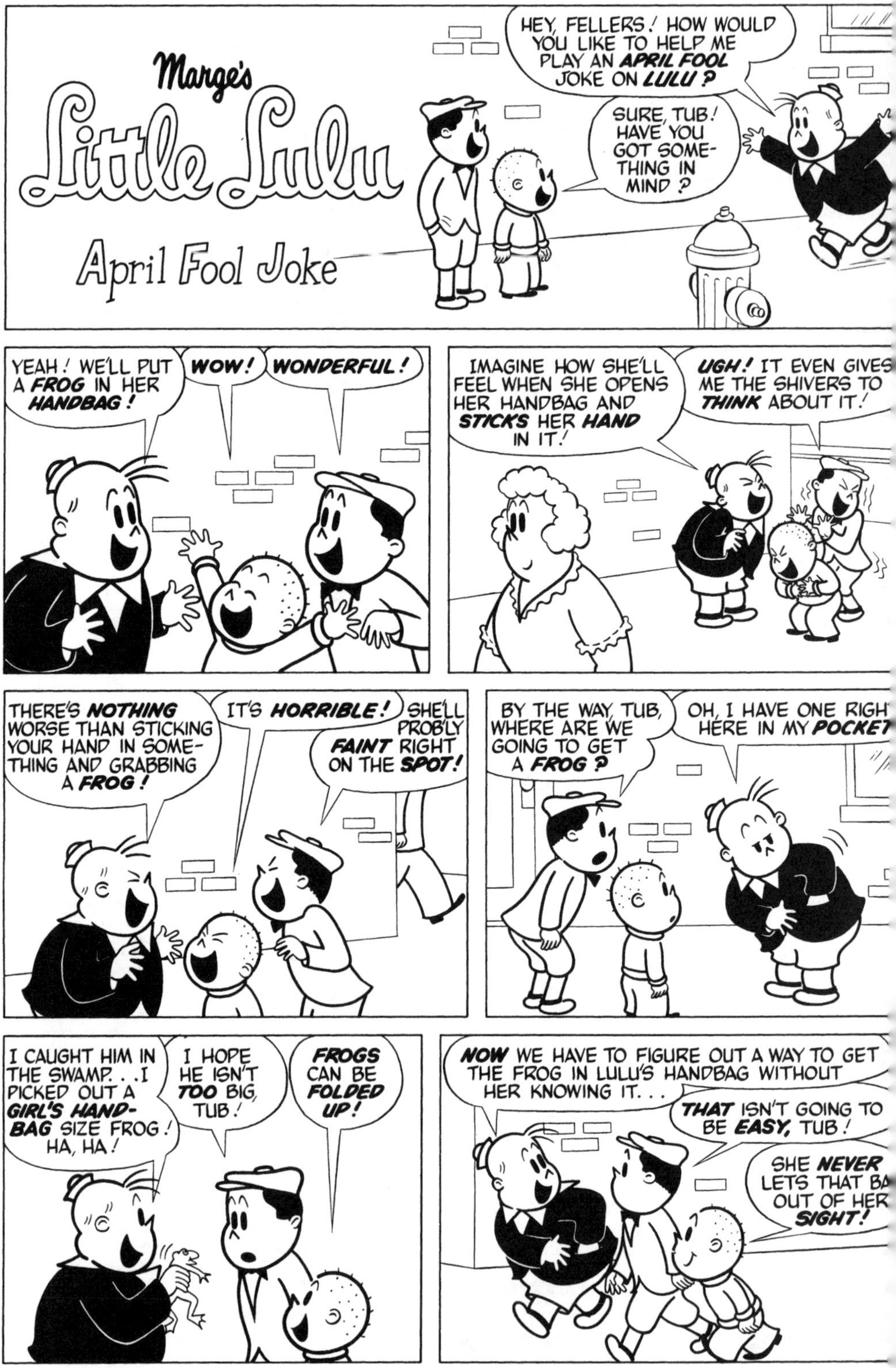
Marge's
Little Lulu
April Fool Joke
HEY, FELLERS! HOW WOULD YOU LIKE TO HELP ME PLAY AN APRIL FOOL JOKE ON LULU?
SURE, TUB! HAVE YOU GOT SOME-THING IN MIND?
YEAH! WE'LL PUT A FROG IN HER HANDBAG!
WOW!
WONDERFUL!
IMAGINE HOW SHE'LL FEEL WHEN SHE OPENS HER HANDBAG AND STICKS HER HAND IN IT!
UGH! IT EVEN GIVES ME THE SHIVERS TO THINK ABOUT IT!
THERE'S NOTHING WORSE THAN STICKING YOUR HAND IN SOME-THING AND GRABBING A FROG!
IT'S HORRIBLE!
SHE'LL PROB'LY FAINT RIGHT ON THE SPOT!
BY THE WAY, TUB, WHERE ARE WE GOING TO GET A FROG?
OH, I HAVE ONE RIGHT HERE IN MY POCKET
I CAUGHT HIM IN THE SWAMP. . . I PICKED OUT A GIRL'S HAND-BAG SIZE FROG! HA, HA!
I HOPE HE ISN'T TOO BIG, TUB!
FROGS CAN BE FOLDED UP!
NOW WE HAVE TO FIGURE OUT A WAY TO GET THE FROG IN LULU'S HANDBAG WITHOUT HER KNOWING IT. . .
THAT ISN'T GOING TO BE EASY, TUB!
SHE NEVER LETS THAT BA OUT OF HER SIGHT!

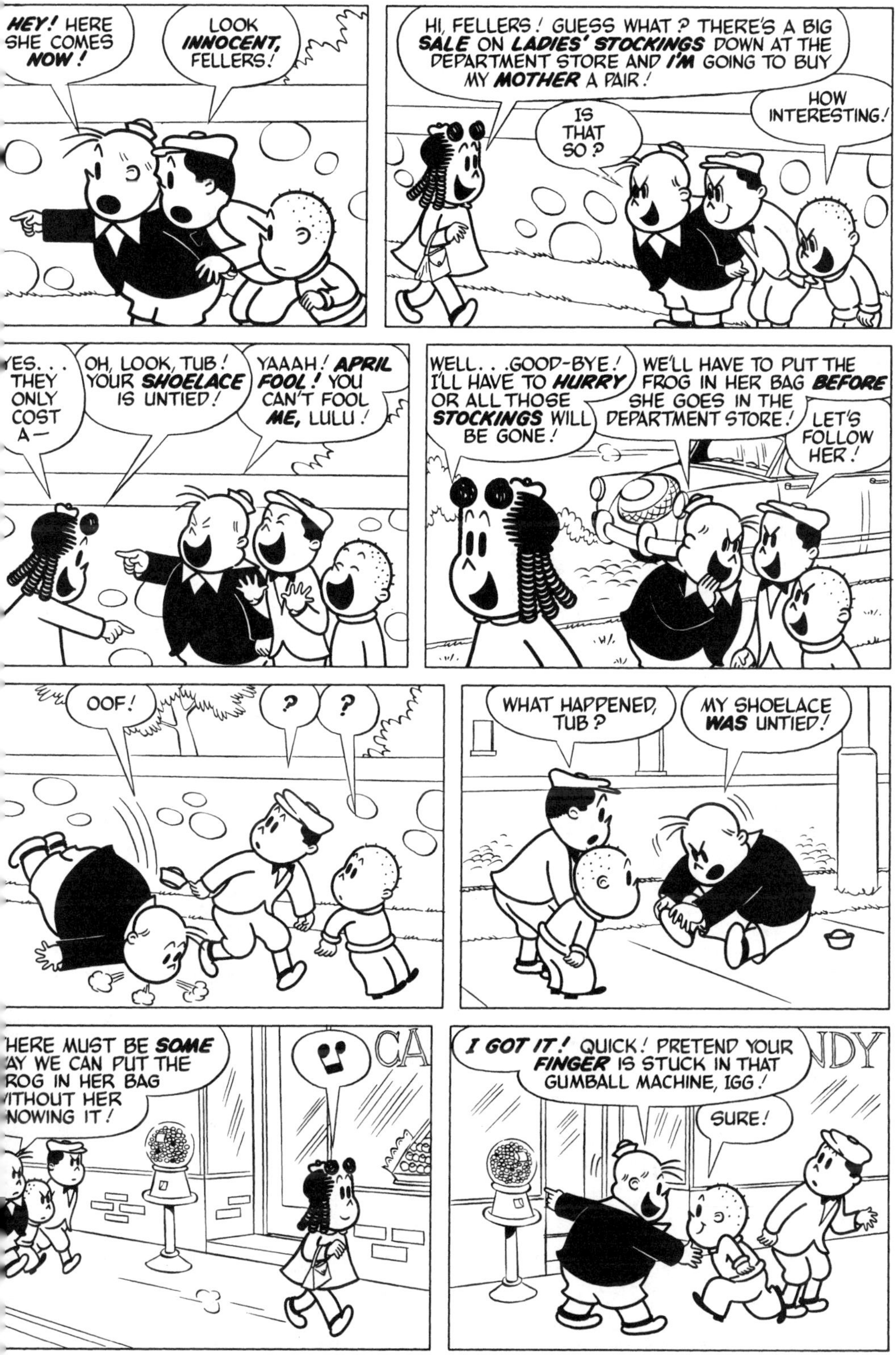
HEY! HERE SHE COMES NOW!
LOOK INNOCENT, FELLERS!
HI, FELLERS! GUESS WHAT? THERE'S A BIG SALE ON LADIES' STOCKINGS DOWN AT THE DEPARTMENT STORE AND I'M GOING TO BUY MY MOTHER A PAIR!
IS THAT SO?
HOW INTERESTING!
YES. . . THEY ONLY COST A—
OH, LOOK, TUB! YOUR SHOELACE IS UNTIED!
YAAAH! APRIL FOOL! YOU CAN'T FOOL ME, LULU!
WELL. . .GOOD-BYE! I'LL HAVE TO HURRY OR ALL THOSE STOCKINGS WILL BE GONE!
WE'LL HAVE TO PUT THE FROG IN HER BAG BEFORE SHE GOES IN THE DEPARTMENT STORE!
LET'S FOLLOW HER!
OOF!
?
?
WHAT HAPPENED, TUB?
MY SHOELACE WAS UNTIED!
HERE MUST BE SOME AY WE CAN PUT THE ROG IN HER BAG ITHOUT HER NOWING IT!
CA
I GOT IT! QUICK! PRETEND YOUR FINGER IS STUCK IN THAT GUMBALL MACHINE, IGG!
NDY
SURE!

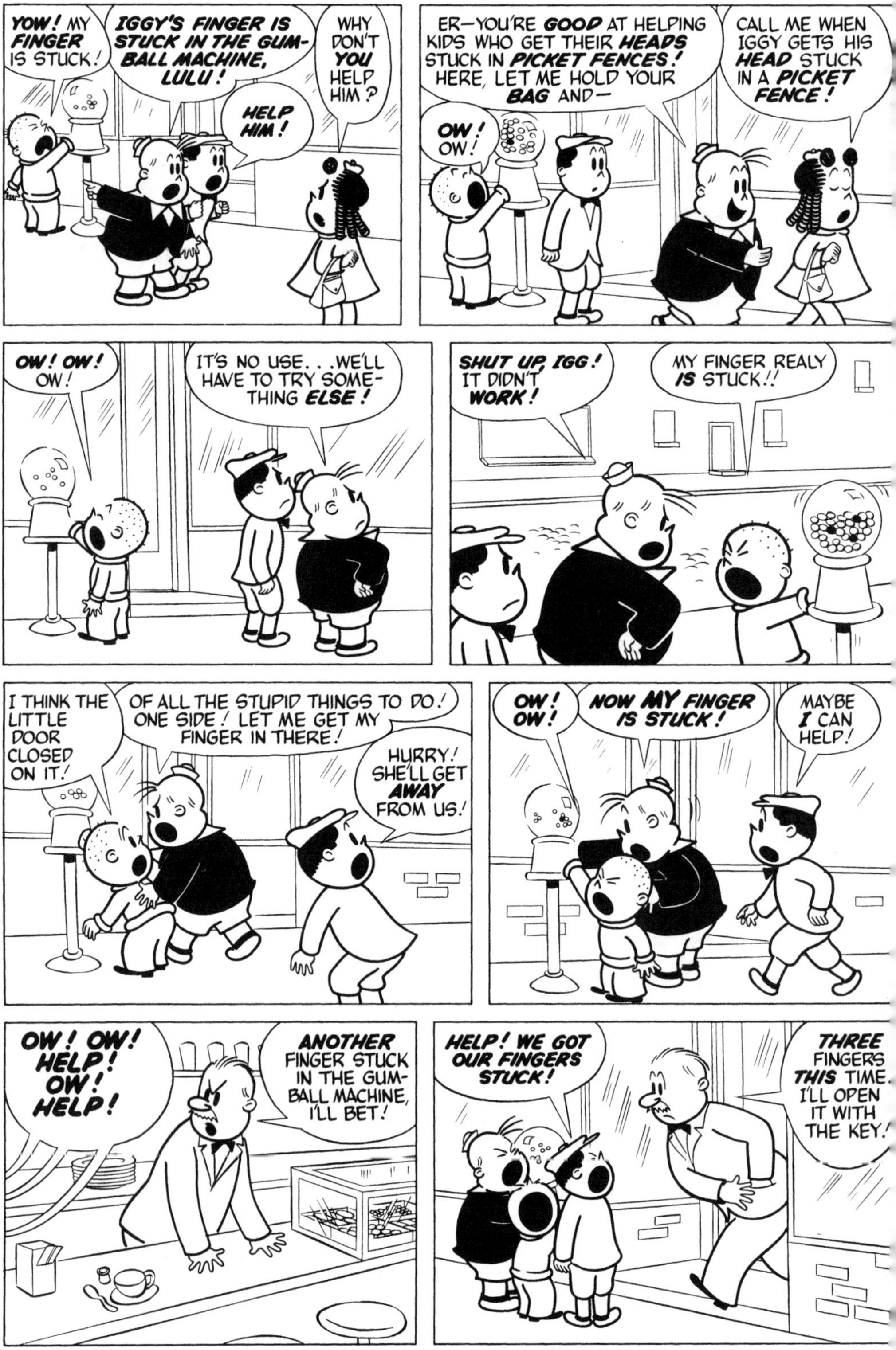
YOW! MY FINGER IS STUCK!
IGGY'S FINGER IS STUCK IN THE GUM-BALL MACHINE, LULU!
HELP HIM!
WHY DON'T YOU HELP HIM?
ER—YOU'RE GOOD AT HELPING KIDS WHO GET THEIR HEADS STUCK IN PICKET FENCES! HERE, LET ME HOLD YOUR BAG AND—
OW! OW!
CALL ME WHEN IGGY GETS HIS HEAD STUCK IN A PICKET FENCE!
OW! OW! OW!
IT'S NO USE. . .WE'LL HAVE TO TRY SOME-THING ELSE!
SHUT UP, IGG! IT DIDN'T WORK!
MY FINGER REALY IS STUCK!!
I THINK THE LITTLE DOOR CLOSED ON IT!
OF ALL THE STUPID THINGS TO DO! ONE SIDE! LET ME GET MY FINGER IN THERE!
HURRY! SHE'LL GET AWAY FROM US!
OW! OW!
NOW MY FINGER IS STUCK!
MAYBE I CAN HELP!
OW! OW! HELP! OW! HELP!
ANOTHER FINGER STUCK IN THE GUM-BALL MACHINE, I'LL BET!
HELP! WE GOT OUR FINGERS STUCK!
THREE FINGERS THIS TIME. I'LL OPEN IT WITH THE KEY.

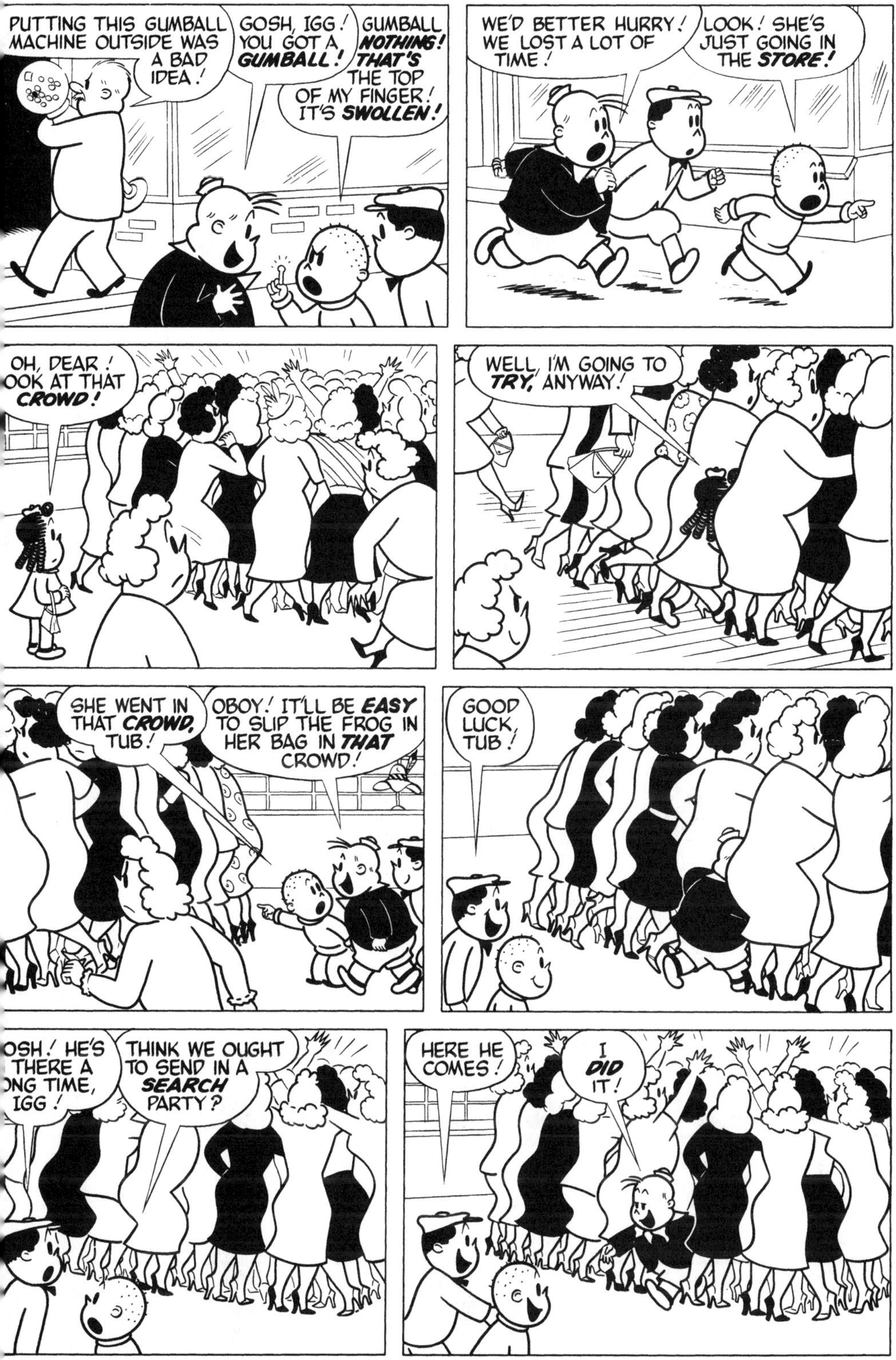
PUTTING THIS GUMBALL MACHINE OUTSIDE WAS A BAD IDEA!
GOSH, IGG! YOU GOT A GUMBALL!
GUMBALL NOTHING! THAT'S THE TOP OF MY FINGER! IT'S SWOLLEN!
WE'D BETTER HURRY! WE LOST A LOT OF TIME!
LOOK! SHE'S JUST GOING IN THE STORE!
OH, DEAR! OOK AT THAT CROWD!
WELL, I'M GOING TO TRY, ANYWAY!
SHE WENT IN THAT CROWD, TUB!
OBOY! IT'LL BE EASY TO SLIP THE FROG IN HER BAG IN THAT CROWD!
GOOD LUCK, TUB!
OSH! HE'S THERE A ONG TIME, IGG!
THINK WE OUGHT TO SEND IN A SEARCH PARTY?
HERE HE COMES!
I DID IT!

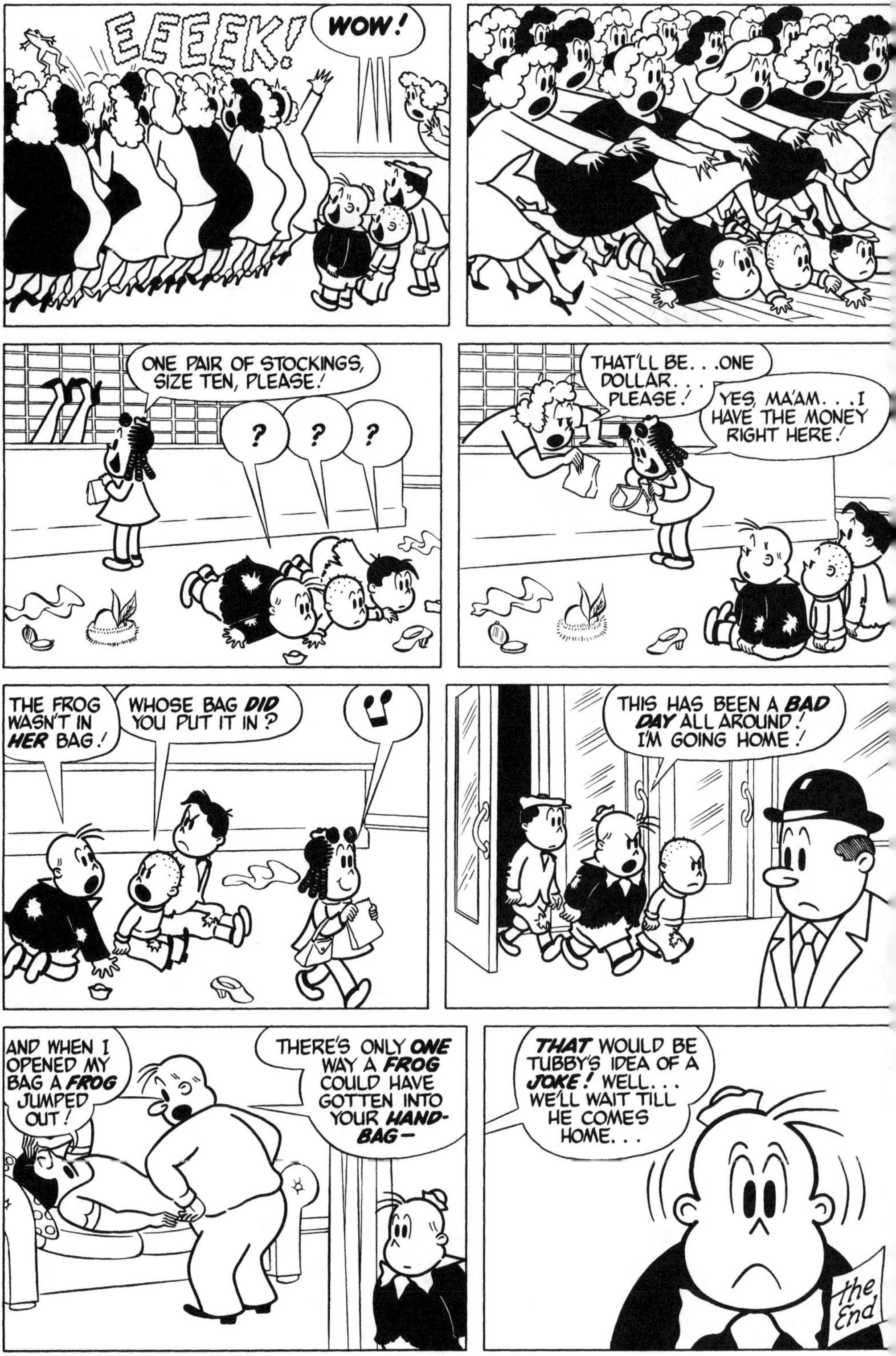
EEEEK!
WOW!
ONE PAIR OF STOCKINGS, SIZE TEN, PLEASE!
? ? ?
THAT'LL BE. . .ONE DOLLAR. . . PLEASE!
YES, MA'AM. . . I HAVE THE MONEY RIGHT HERE!
THE FROG WASN'T IN HER BAG!
WHOSE BAG DID YOU PUT IT IN?
THIS HAS BEEN A BAD DAY ALL AROUND! I'M GOING HOME!
AND WHEN I OPENED MY BAG A FROG JUMPED OUT!
THERE'S ONLY ONE WAY A FROG COULD HAVE GOTTEN INTO YOUR HAND-BAG—
THAT WOULD BE TUBBY'S IDEA OF A JOKE! WELL. . . WE'LL WAIT TILL HE COMES HOME. . .
the End

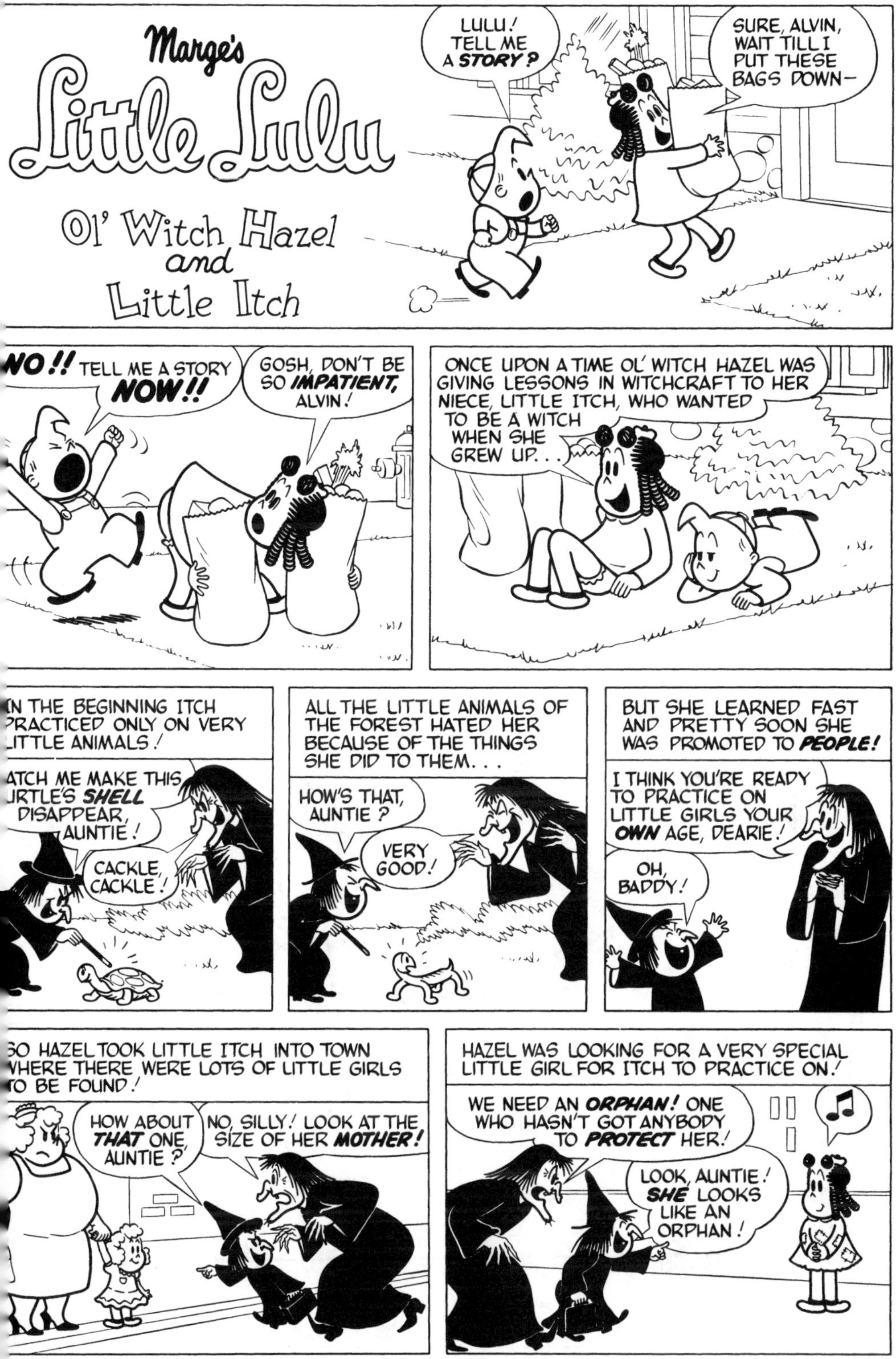

Marge's
Little Lulu
Ol' Witch Hazel and Little Itch
LULU! TELL ME A STORY?
SURE, ALVIN, WAIT TILL I PUT THESE BAGS DOWN—
NO!! TELL ME A STORY NOW!!
GOSH, DON'T BE SO IMPATIENT, ALVIN!
ONCE UPON A TIME OL' WITCH HAZEL WAS GIVING LESSONS IN WITCHCRAFT TO HER NIECE, LITTLE ITCH, WHO WANTED TO BE A WITCH WHEN SHE GREW UP...
IN THE BEGINNING ITCH PRACTICED ONLY ON VERY LITTLE ANIMALS!
ATCH ME MAKE THIS URTLE'S SHELL DISAPPEAR, AUNTIE!
CACKLE, CACKLE!
ALL THE LITTLE ANIMALS OF THE FOREST HATED HER BECAUSE OF THE THINGS SHE DID TO THEM...
HOW'S THAT, AUNTIE?
VERY GOOD!
BUT SHE LEARNED FAST AND PRETTY SOON SHE WAS PROMOTED TO PEOPLE!
I THINK YOU'RE READY TO PRACTICE ON LITTLE GIRLS YOUR OWN AGE, DEARIE!
OH, BADDY!
SO HAZEL TOOK LITTLE ITCH INTO TOWN WHERE THERE WERE LOTS OF LITTLE GIRLS TO BE FOUND!
HOW ABOUT THAT ONE, AUNTIE?
NO, SILLY! LOOK AT THE SIZE OF HER MOTHER!
HAZEL WAS LOOKING FOR A VERY SPECIAL LITTLE GIRL FOR ITCH TO PRACTICE ON!
WE NEED AN ORPHAN! ONE WHO HASN'T GOT ANYBODY TO PROTECT HER!
LOOK, AUNTIE! SHE LOOKS LIKE AN ORPHAN!

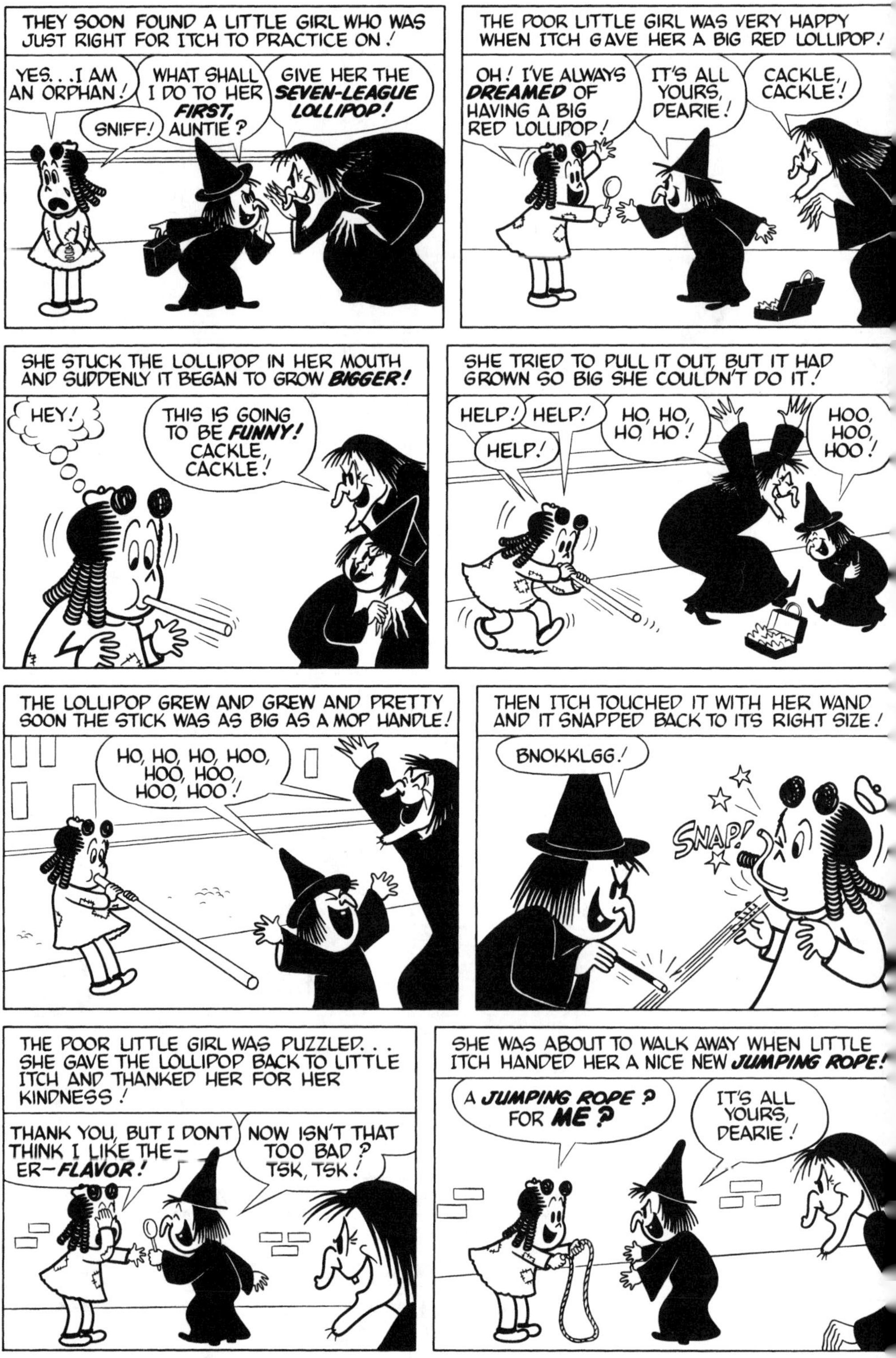
THEY SOON FOUND A LITTLE GIRL WHO WAS JUST RIGHT FOR ITCH TO PRACTICE ON!
YES. . .I AM AN ORPHAN!
SNIFF!
WHAT SHALL I DO TO HER FIRST, AUNTIE?
GIVE HER THE SEVEN-LEAGUE LOLLIPOP!
THE POOR LITTLE GIRL WAS VERY HAPPY WHEN ITCH GAVE HER A BIG RED LOLLIPOP!
OH! I'VE ALWAYS DREAMED OF HAVING A BIG RED LOLLIPOP!
IT'S ALL YOURS, DEARIE!
CACKLE, CACKLE!
SHE STUCK THE LOLLIPOP IN HER MOUTH AND SUDDENLY IT BEGAN TO GROW BIGGER!
HEY!
THIS IS GOING TO BE FUNNY! CACKLE, CACKLE!
SHE TRIED TO PULL IT OUT, BUT IT HAD GROWN SO BIG SHE COULDN'T DO IT!
HELP!
HELP!
HELP!
HO, HO, HO, HO!
HOO, HOO, HOO!
THE LOLLIPOP GREW AND GREW AND PRETTY SOON THE STICK WAS AS BIG AS A MOP HANDLE!
HO, HO, HO, HOO, HOO, HOO, HOO, HOO!
THEN ITCH TOUCHED IT WITH HER WAND AND IT SNAPPED BACK TO ITS RIGHT SIZE!
BNOKKLGG!
SNAP!
THE POOR LITTLE GIRL WAS PUZZLED. . . SHE GAVE THE LOLLIPOP BACK TO LITTLE ITCH AND THANKED HER FOR HER KINDNESS!
THANK YOU, BUT I DONT THINK I LIKE THE— ER—FLAVOR!
NOW ISN'T THAT TOO BAD? TSK, TSK!
SHE WAS ABOUT TO WALK AWAY WHEN LITTLE ITCH HANDED HER A NICE NEW JUMPING ROPE!
A JUMPING ROPE? FOR ME?
IT'S ALL YOURS, DEARIE!

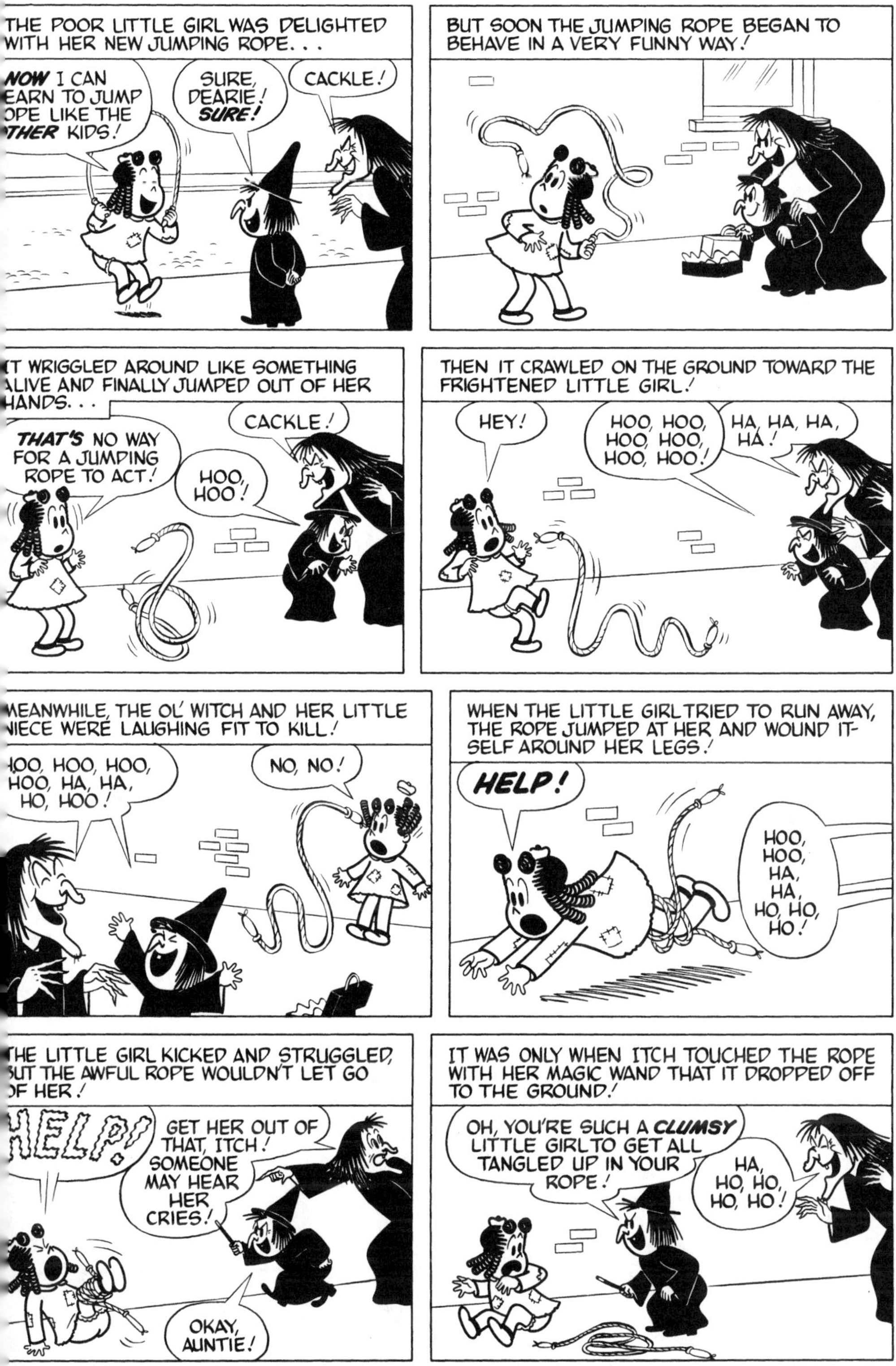
THE POOR LITTLE GIRL WAS DELIGHTED WITH HER NEW JUMPING ROPE. . .
NOW I CAN EARN TO JUMP OPE LIKE THE THER KIDS!
SURE, DEARIE! SURE!
CACKLE!
BUT SOON THE JUMPING ROPE BEGAN TO BEHAVE IN A VERY FUNNY WAY!
IT WRIGGLED AROUND LIKE SOMETHING ALIVE AND FINALLY JUMPED OUT OF HER HANDS. . .
THAT'S NO WAY FOR A JUMPING ROPE TO ACT!
CACKLE!
HOO, HOO!
THEN IT CRAWLED ON THE GROUND TOWARD THE FRIGHTENED LITTLE GIRL!
HEY!
HOO, HOO, HOO, HOO, HOO, HOO!
HA, HA, HA, HA!
MEANWHILE, THE OL' WITCH AND HER LITTLE NIECE WERE LAUGHING FIT TO KILL!
HOO, HOO, HOO, HOO, HA, HA, HO, HOO!
NO, NO!
WHEN THE LITTLE GIRL TRIED TO RUN AWAY, THE ROPE JUMPED AT HER AND WOUND ITSELF AROUND HER LEGS!
HELP!
HOO, HOO, HA, HA, HO, HO, HO!
THE LITTLE GIRL KICKED AND STRUGGLED, BUT THE AWFUL ROPE WOULDN'T LET GO OF HER!
HELP!
GET HER OUT OF THAT, ITCH! SOMEONE MAY HEAR HER CRIES!
OKAY, AUNTIE!
IT WAS ONLY WHEN ITCH TOUCHED THE ROPE WITH HER MAGIC WAND THAT IT DROPPED OFF TO THE GROUND!
OH, YOU'RE SUCH A CLUMSY LITTLE GIRL TO GET ALL TANGLED UP IN YOUR ROPE!
HA, HO, HO, HO, HO!

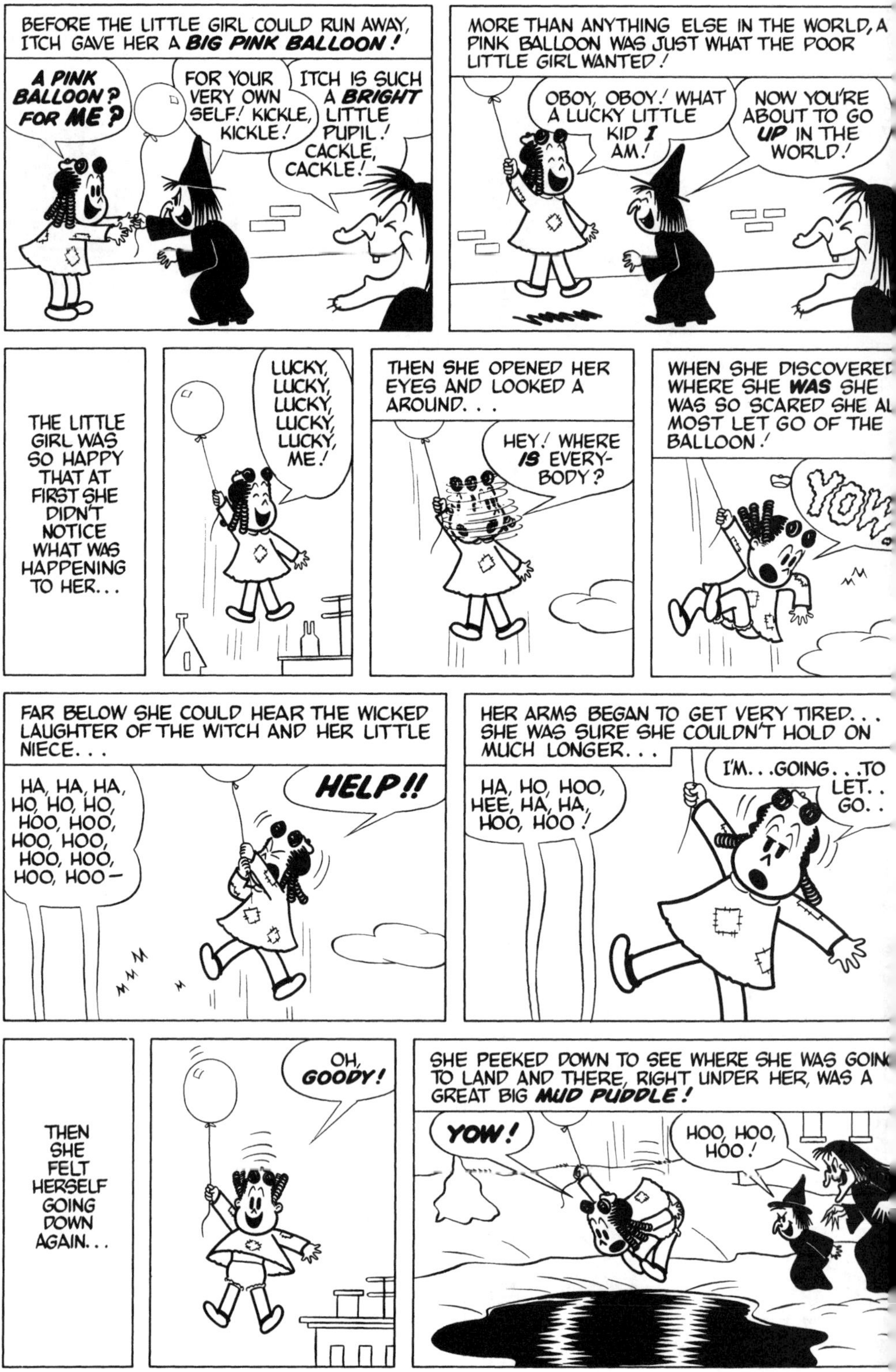

BEFORE THE LITTLE GIRL COULD RUN AWAY, ITCH GAVE HER A BIG PINK BALLOON!
A PINK BALLOON? FOR ME?
FOR YOUR VERY OWN SELF! KICKLE, KICKLE!
ITCH IS SUCH A BRIGHT LITTLE PUPIL! CACKLE, CACKLE!
MORE THAN ANYTHING ELSE IN THE WORLD, A PINK BALLOON WAS JUST WHAT THE POOR LITTLE GIRL WANTED!
OBOY, OBOY! WHAT A LUCKY LITTLE KID I AM!
NOW YOU'RE ABOUT TO GO UP IN THE WORLD!
THE LITTLE GIRL WAS SO HAPPY THAT AT FIRST SHE DIDN'T NOTICE WHAT WAS HAPPENING TO HER...
LUCKY, LUCKY, LUCKY, LUCKY, LUCKY, ME!
THEN SHE OPENED HER EYES AND LOOKED A AROUND...
HEY! WHERE IS EVERY-BODY?
WHEN SHE DISCOVERED WHERE SHE WAS SHE WAS SO SCARED SHE AL MOST LET GO OF THE BALLOON!
YOW!
FAR BELOW SHE COULD HEAR THE WICKED LAUGHTER OF THE WITCH AND HER LITTLE NIECE...
HA, HA, HA, HO, HO, HO, HOO, HOO, HOO, HOO, HOO, HOO, HOO, HOO—
HELP!!
HER ARMS BEGAN TO GET VERY TIRED... SHE WAS SURE SHE COULDN'T HOLD ON MUCH LONGER...
HA, HO, HOO, HEE, HA, HA, HOO, HOO!
I'M...GOING...TO LET.. GO..
THEN SHE FELT HERSELF GOING DOWN AGAIN...
OH, GOODY!
SHE PEEKED DOWN TO SEE WHERE SHE WAS GOING TO LAND AND THERE, RIGHT UNDER HER, WAS A GREAT BIG MUD PUDDLE!
YOW!
HOO, HOO, HOO!

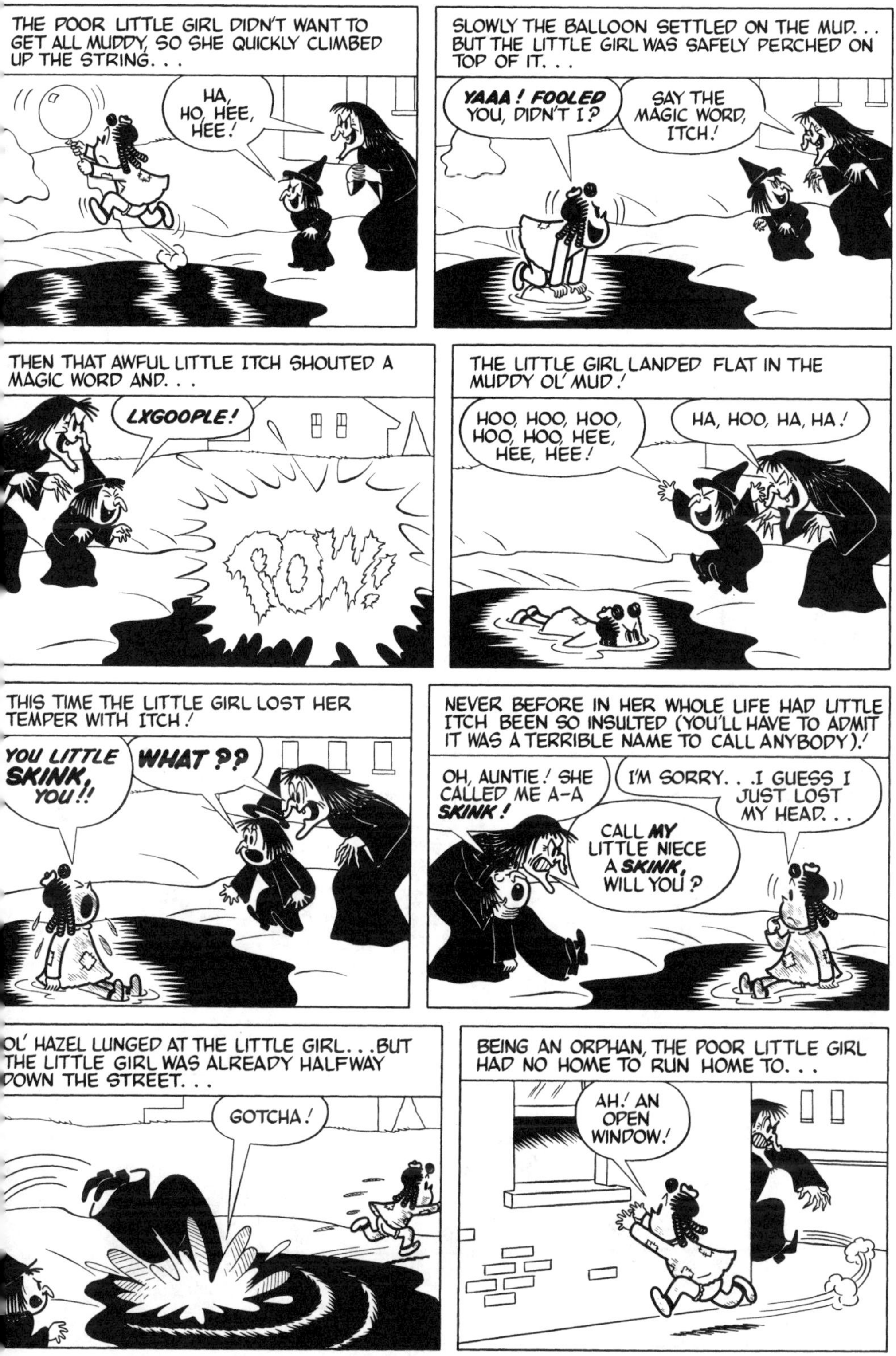
THE POOR LITTLE GIRL DIDN'T WANT TO GET ALL MUDDY, SO SHE QUICKLY CLIMBED UP THE STRING. . .
HA, HO, HEE, HEE!
SLOWLY THE BALLOON SETTLED ON THE MUD. . . BUT THE LITTLE GIRL WAS SAFELY PERCHED ON TOP OF IT. . .
YAAA! FOOLED YOU, DIDN'T I?
SAY THE MAGIC WORD, ITCH!
THEN THAT AWFUL LITTLE ITCH SHOUTED A MAGIC WORD AND. . .
LXGOOPLE!
POW!
THE LITTLE GIRL LANDED FLAT IN THE MUDDY OL' MUD!
HOO, HOO, HOO, HOO, HOO, HEE, HEE, HEE!
HA, HOO, HA, HA!
THIS TIME THE LITTLE GIRL LOST HER TEMPER WITH ITCH!
YOU LITTLE SKINK, YOU!!
WHAT??
NEVER BEFORE IN HER WHOLE LIFE HAD LITTLE ITCH BEEN SO INSULTED (YOU'LL HAVE TO ADMIT IT WAS A TERRIBLE NAME TO CALL ANYBODY)!
OH, AUNTIE! SHE CALLED ME A-A SKINK!
I'M SORRY. . .I GUESS I JUST LOST MY HEAD. . .
CALL MY LITTLE NIECE A SKINK, WILL YOU?
OL' HAZEL LUNGED AT THE LITTLE GIRL. . .BUT THE LITTLE GIRL WAS ALREADY HALFWAY DOWN THE STREET. . .
GOTCHA!
BEING AN ORPHAN, THE POOR LITTLE GIRL HAD NO HOME TO RUN HOME TO. . .
AH! AN OPEN WINDOW!

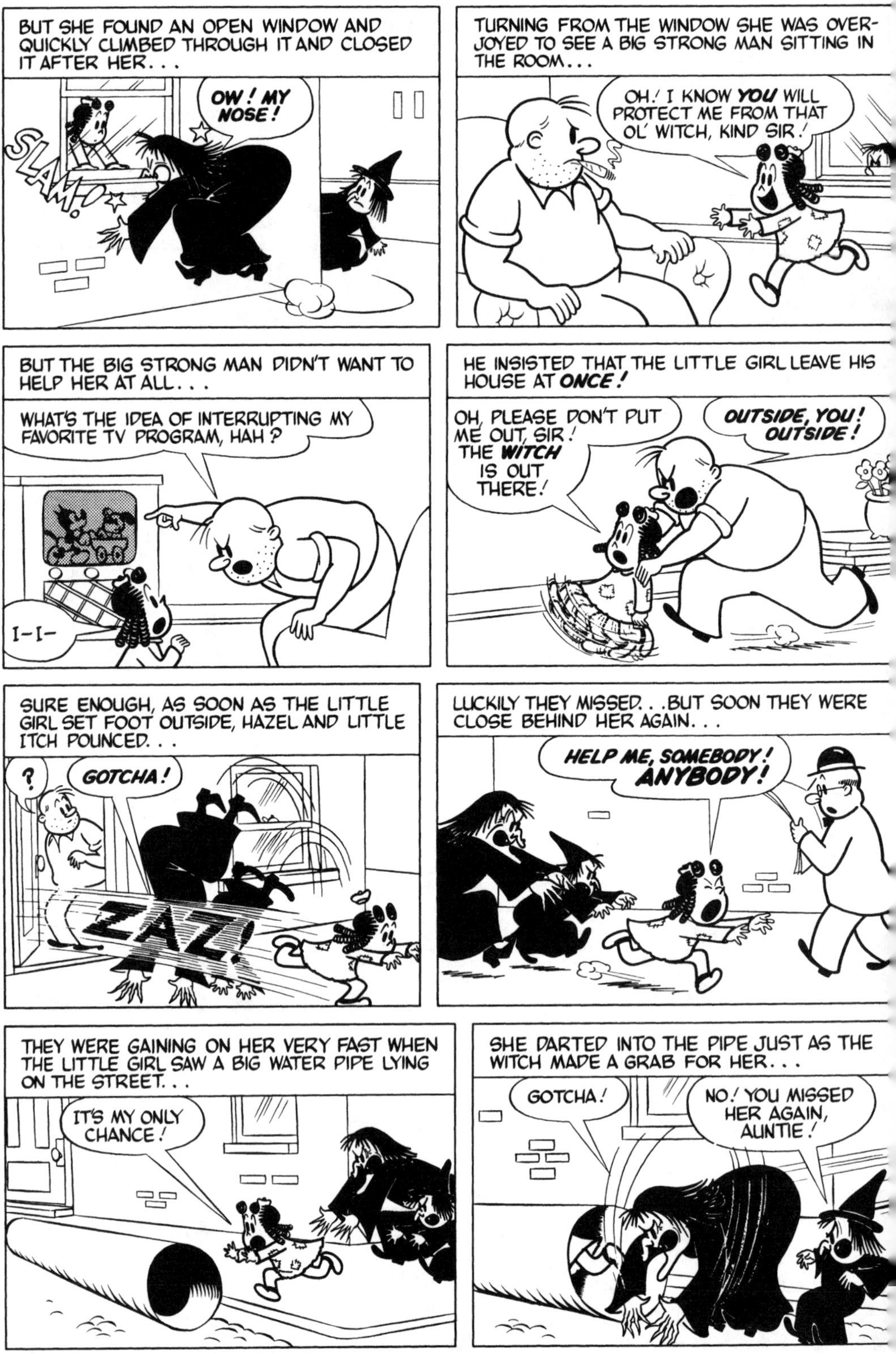

BUT SHE FOUND AN OPEN WINDOW AND QUICKLY CLIMBED THROUGH IT AND CLOSED IT AFTER HER. . .
OW! MY NOSE!
SLAM!
TURNING FROM THE WINDOW SHE WAS OVERJOYED TO SEE A BIG STRONG MAN SITTING IN THE ROOM. . .
OH! I KNOW YOU WILL PROTECT ME FROM THAT OL' WITCH, KIND SIR!
BUT THE BIG STRONG MAN DIDN'T WANT TO HELP HER AT ALL. . .
WHAT'S THE IDEA OF INTERRUPTING MY FAVORITE TV PROGRAM, HAH?
I-I-
HE INSISTED THAT THE LITTLE GIRL LEAVE HIS HOUSE AT ONCE!
OH, PLEASE DON'T PUT ME OUT, SIR! THE WITCH IS OUT THERE!
OUTSIDE, YOU! OUTSIDE!
SURE ENOUGH, AS SOON AS THE LITTLE GIRL SET FOOT OUTSIDE, HAZEL AND LITTLE ITCH POUNCED. . .
?
GOTCHA!
ZAZ!
LUCKILY THEY MISSED. . .BUT SOON THEY WERE CLOSE BEHIND HER AGAIN. . .
HELP ME, SOMEBODY! ANYBODY!
THEY WERE GAINING ON HER VERY FAST WHEN THE LITTLE GIRL SAW A BIG WATER PIPE LYING ON THE STREET. . .
IT'S MY ONLY CHANCE!
SHE DARTED INTO THE PIPE JUST AS THE WITCH MADE A GRAB FOR HER. . .
GOTCHA!
NO! YOU MISSED HER AGAIN, AUNTIE!

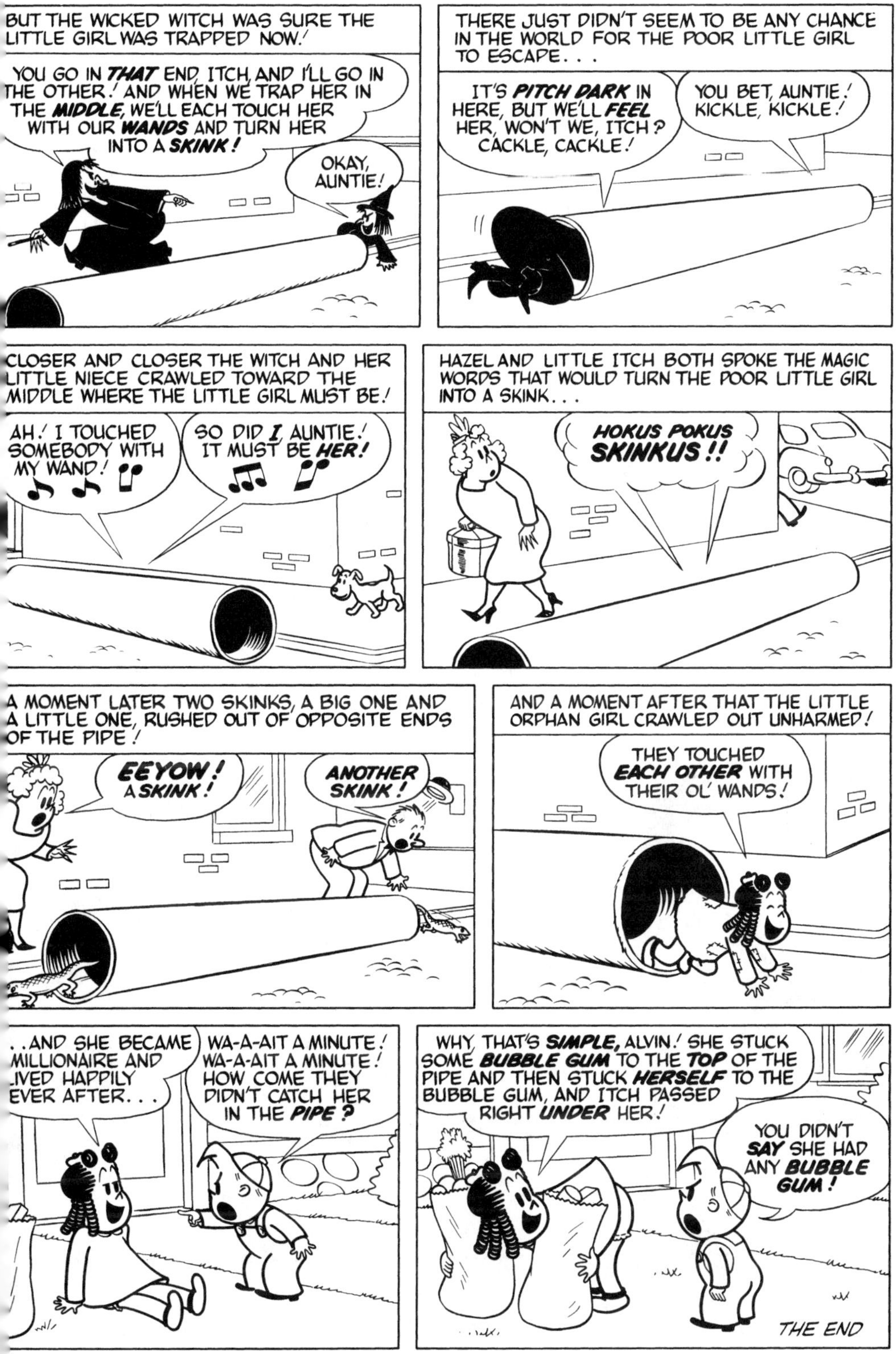
BUT THE WICKED WITCH WAS SURE THE LITTLE GIRL WAS TRAPPED NOW!
YOU GO IN THAT END, ITCH, AND I'LL GO IN THE OTHER! AND WHEN WE TRAP HER IN THE MIDDLE, WE'LL EACH TOUCH HER WITH OUR WANDS AND TURN HER INTO A SKINK!
OKAY, AUNTIE!
THERE JUST DIDN'T SEEM TO BE ANY CHANCE IN THE WORLD FOR THE POOR LITTLE GIRL TO ESCAPE . . .
IT'S PITCH DARK IN HERE, BUT WE'LL FEEL HER, WON'T WE, ITCH? CACKLE, CACKLE!
YOU BET, AUNTIE! KICKLE, KICKLE!
CLOSER AND CLOSER THE WITCH AND HER LITTLE NIECE CRAWLED TOWARD THE MIDDLE WHERE THE LITTLE GIRL MUST BE!
AH! I TOUCHED SOMEBODY WITH MY WAND!
SO DID I, AUNTIE! IT MUST BE HER!
HAZEL AND LITTLE ITCH BOTH SPOKE THE MAGIC WORDS THAT WOULD TURN THE POOR LITTLE GIRL INTO A SKINK . . .
HOKUS POKUS SKINKUS!!
A MOMENT LATER TWO SKINKS, A BIG ONE AND A LITTLE ONE, RUSHED OUT OF OPPOSITE ENDS OF THE PIPE!
EEYOW! A SKINK!
ANOTHER SKINK!
AND A MOMENT AFTER THAT THE LITTLE ORPHAN GIRL CRAWLED OUT UNHARMED!
THEY TOUCHED EACH OTHER WITH THEIR OL' WANDS!
. . AND SHE BECAME MILLIONAIRE AND LIVED HAPPILY EVER AFTER . . .
WA-A-AIT A MINUTE! WA-A-AIT A MINUTE! HOW COME THEY DIDN'T CATCH HER IN THE PIPE?
WHY, THAT'S SIMPLE, ALVIN! SHE STUCK SOME BUBBLE GUM TO THE TOP OF THE PIPE AND THEN STUCK HERSELF TO THE BUBBLE GUM, AND ITCH PASSED RIGHT UNDER HER!
YOU DIDN'T SAY SHE HAD ANY BUBBLE GUM!
THE END

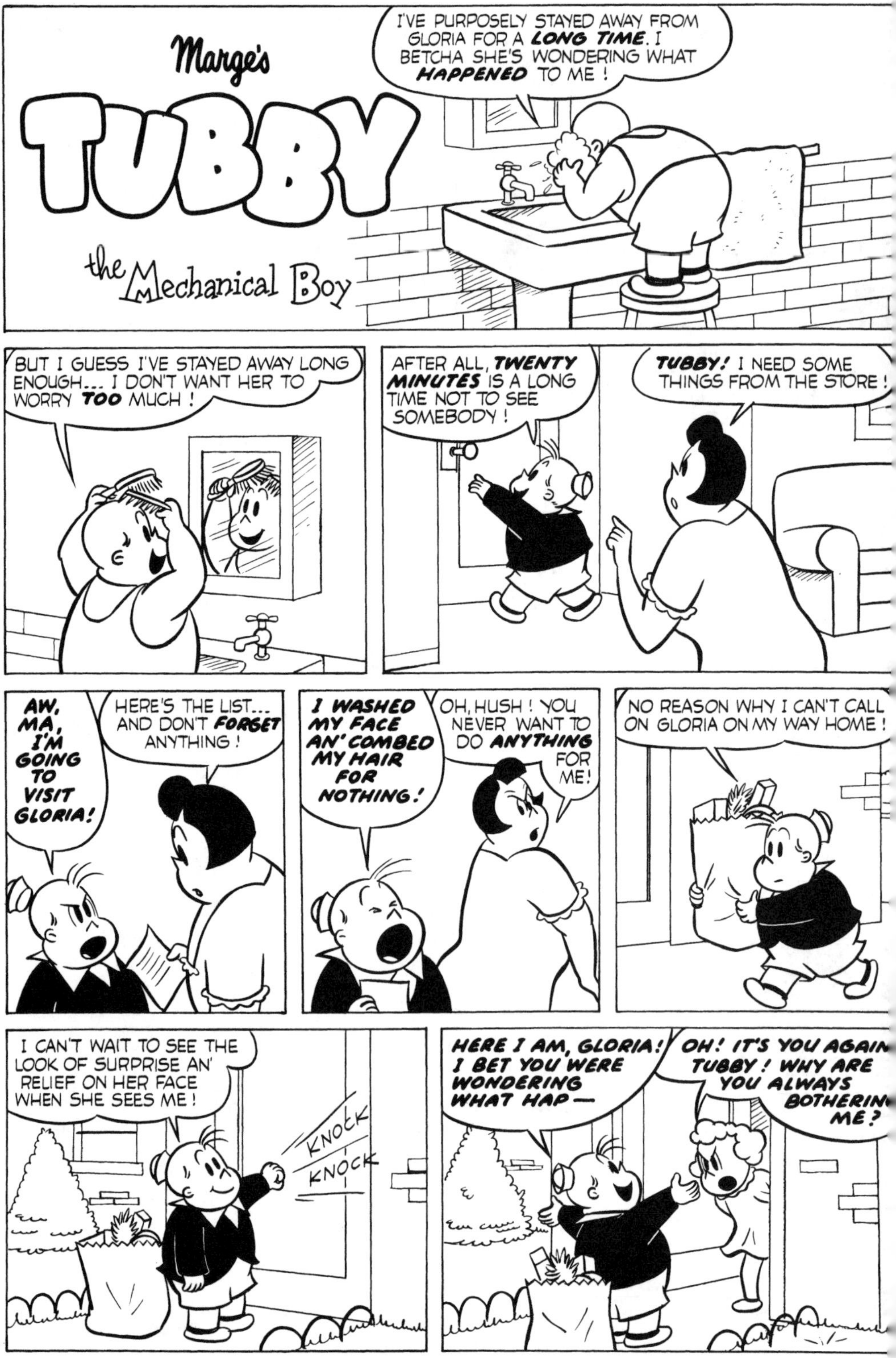
Marge's
TUBBY
the Mechanical Boy
I'VE PURPOSELY STAYED AWAY FROM GLORIA FOR A LONG TIME. I BETCHA SHE'S WONDERING WHAT HAPPENED TO ME!
BUT I GUESS I'VE STAYED AWAY LONG ENOUGH... I DON'T WANT HER TO WORRY TOO MUCH!
AFTER ALL, TWENTY MINUTES IS A LONG TIME NOT TO SEE SOMEBODY!
TUBBY! I NEED SOME THINGS FROM THE STORE!
AW, MA, I'M GOING TO VISIT GLORIA!
HERE'S THE LIST... AND DON'T FORGET ANYTHING!
I WASHED MY FACE AN' COMBED MY HAIR FOR NOTHING!
OH, HUSH! YOU NEVER WANT TO DO ANYTHING FOR ME!
NO REASON WHY I CAN'T CALL ON GLORIA ON MY WAY HOME!
I CAN'T WAIT TO SEE THE LOOK OF SURPRISE AN' RELIEF ON HER FACE WHEN SHE SEES ME!
KNOCK
KNOCK
HERE I AM, GLORIA! I BET YOU WERE WONDERING WHAT HAP—
OH! IT'S YOU AGAIN TUBBY! WHY ARE YOU ALWAYS BOTHERING ME?

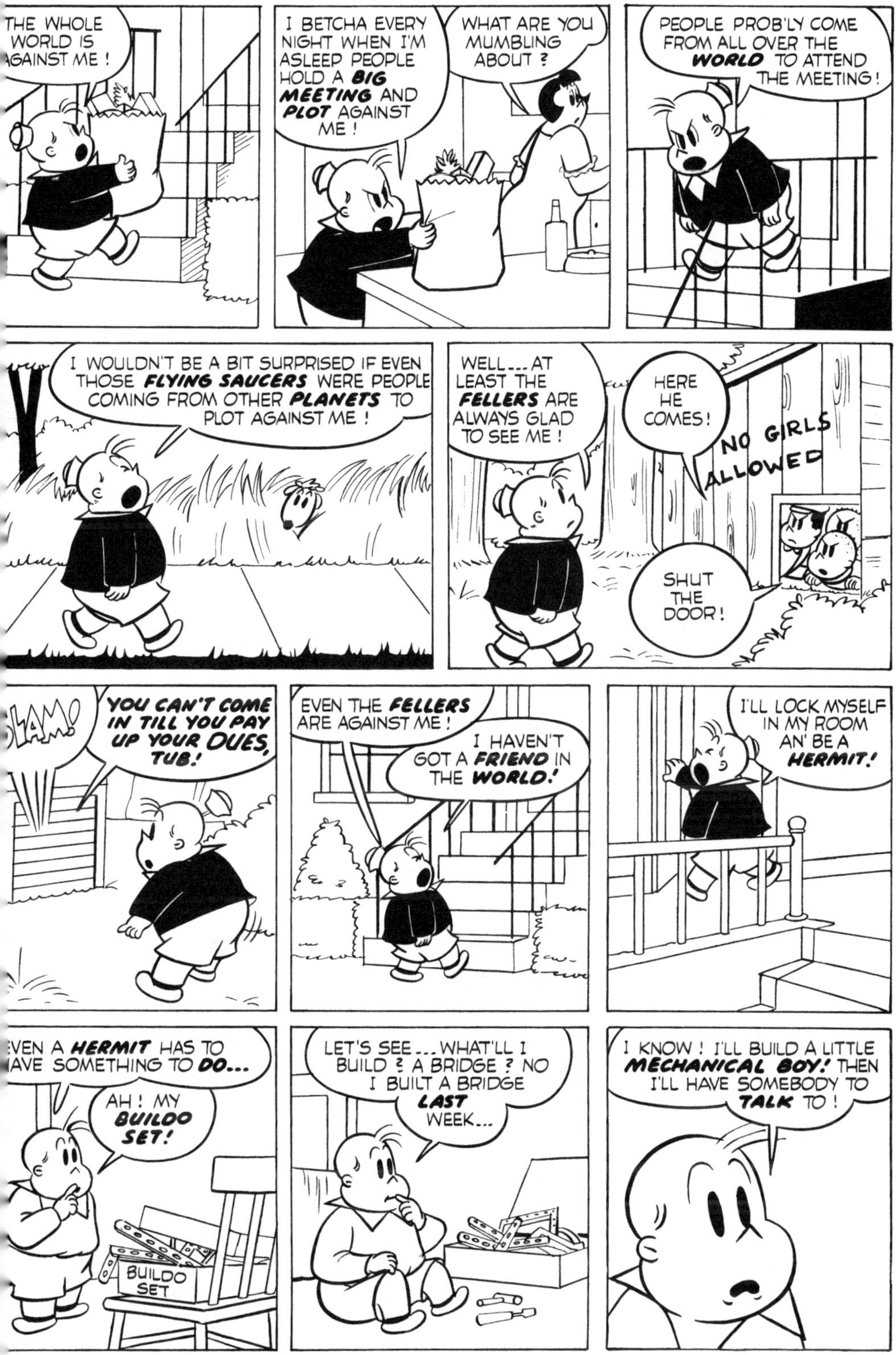

THE WHOLE WORLD IS AGAINST ME!
I BETCHA EVERY NIGHT WHEN I'M ASLEEP PEOPLE HOLD A BIG MEETING AND PLOT AGAINST ME!
WHAT ARE YOU MUMBLING ABOUT?
PEOPLE PROB'LY COME FROM ALL OVER THE WORLD TO ATTEND THE MEETING!
I WOULDN'T BE A BIT SURPRISED IF EVEN THOSE FLYING SAUCERS WERE PEOPLE COMING FROM OTHER PLANETS TO PLOT AGAINST ME!
WELL... AT LEAST THE FELLERS ARE ALWAYS GLAD TO SEE ME!
HERE HE COMES!
NO GIRLS ALLOWED
SHUT THE DOOR!
SLAM!
YOU CAN'T COME IN TILL YOU PAY UP YOUR DUES, TUB!
EVEN THE FELLERS ARE AGAINST ME!
I HAVEN'T GOT A FRIEND IN THE WORLD!
I'LL LOCK MYSELF IN MY ROOM AN' BE A HERMIT!
EVEN A HERMIT HAS TO HAVE SOMETHING TO DO...
AH! MY BUILDO SET!
BUILDO SET
LET'S SEE... WHAT'LL I BUILD? A BRIDGE? NO I BUILT A BRIDGE LAST WEEK...
I KNOW! I'LL BUILD A LITTLE MECHANICAL BOY! THEN I'LL HAVE SOMEBODY TO TALK TO!

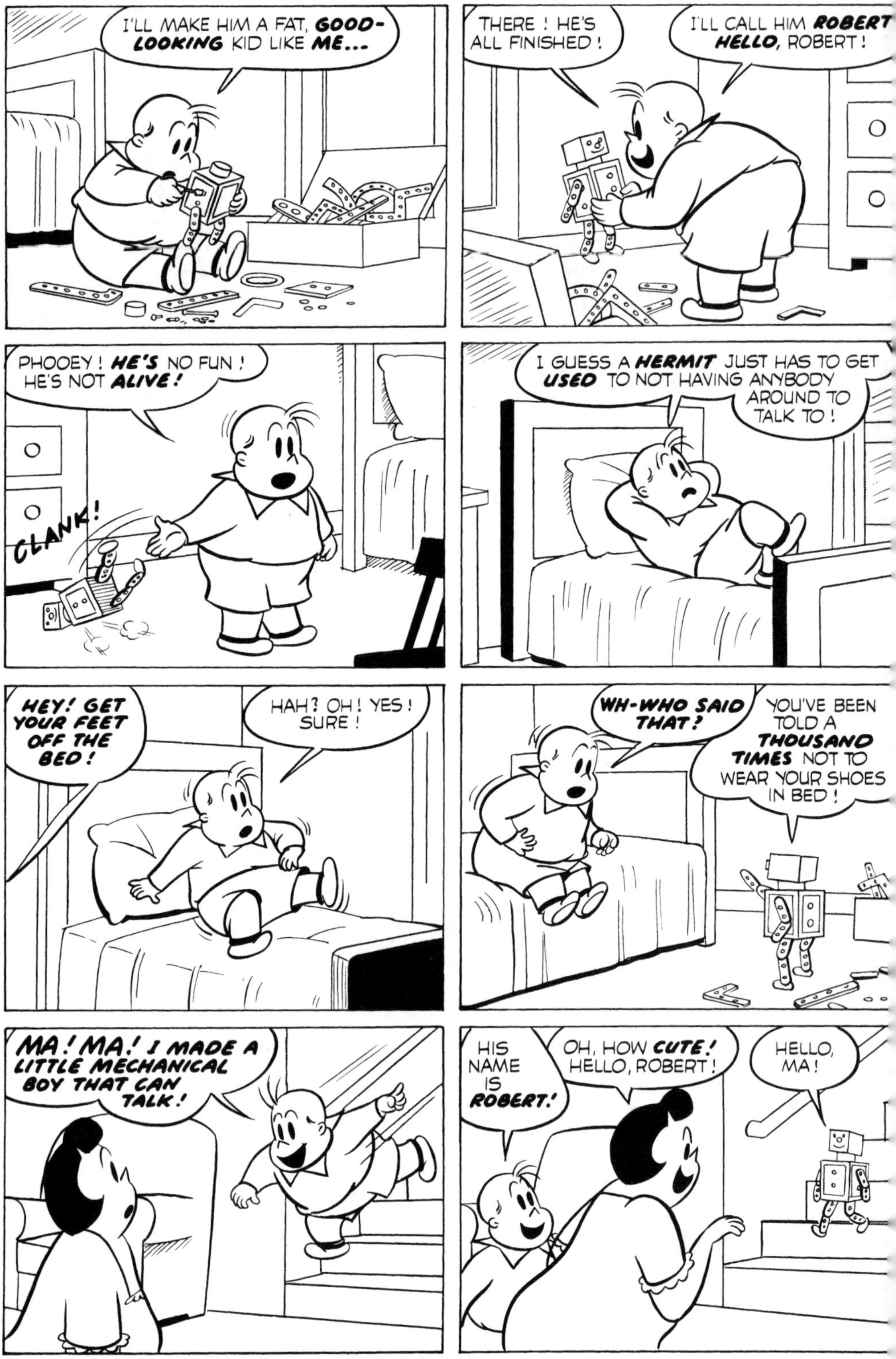
I'LL MAKE HIM A FAT, GOOD-LOOKING KID LIKE ME...
THERE ! HE'S ALL FINISHED !
I'LL CALL HIM ROBERT HELLO, ROBERT !
PHOOEY ! HE'S NO FUN ! HE'S NOT ALIVE !
CLANK!
I GUESS A HERMIT JUST HAS TO GET USED TO NOT HAVING ANYBODY AROUND TO TALK TO !
HEY! GET YOUR FEET OFF THE BED !
HAH? OH ! YES ! SURE !
WH-WHO SAID THAT?
YOU'VE BEEN TOLD A THOUSAND TIMES NOT TO WEAR YOUR SHOES IN BED !
MA! MA! I MADE A LITTLE MECHANICAL BOY THAT CAN TALK!
HIS NAME IS ROBERT!
OH, HOW CUTE! HELLO, ROBERT!
HELLO, MA!

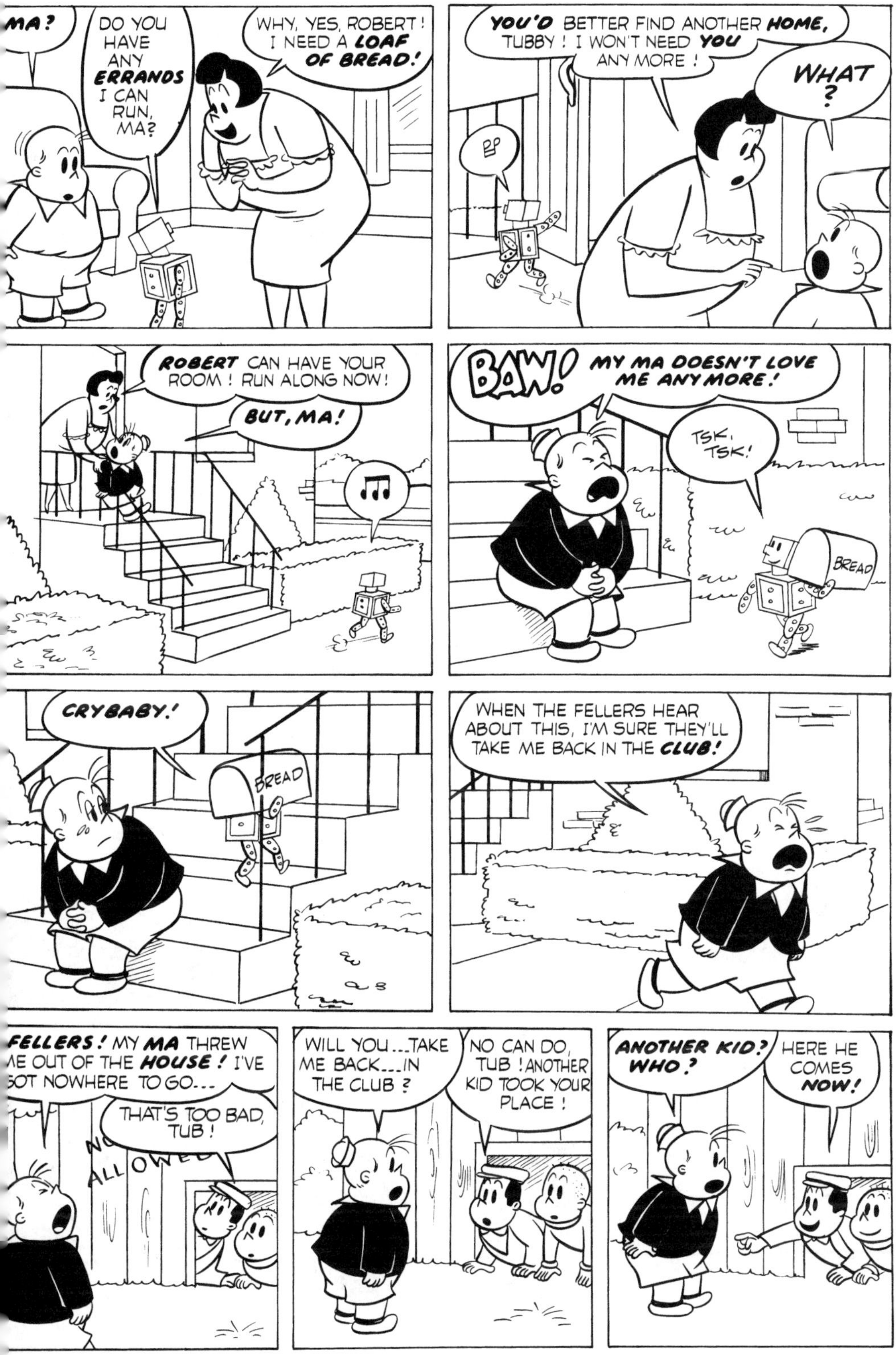
MA?
DO YOU HAVE ANY ERRANDS I CAN RUN, MA?
WHY, YES, ROBERT! I NEED A LOAF OF BREAD!
YOU'D BETTER FIND ANOTHER HOME, TUBBY! I WON'T NEED YOU ANY MORE!
WHAT?
ROBERT CAN HAVE YOUR ROOM! RUN ALONG NOW!
BUT, MA!
BAW!
MY MA DOESN'T LOVE ME ANYMORE!
TSK, TSK!
BREAD
CRYBABY!
BREAD
WHEN THE FELLERS HEAR ABOUT THIS, I'M SURE THEY'LL TAKE ME BACK IN THE CLUB!
FELLERS! MY MA THREW ME OUT OF THE HOUSE! I'VE GOT NOWHERE TO GO...
THAT'S TOO BAD, TUB!
WILL YOU...TAKE ME BACK...IN THE CLUB?
NO CAN DO, TUB! ANOTHER KID TOOK YOUR PLACE!
ANOTHER KID? WHO?
HERE HE COMES NOW!

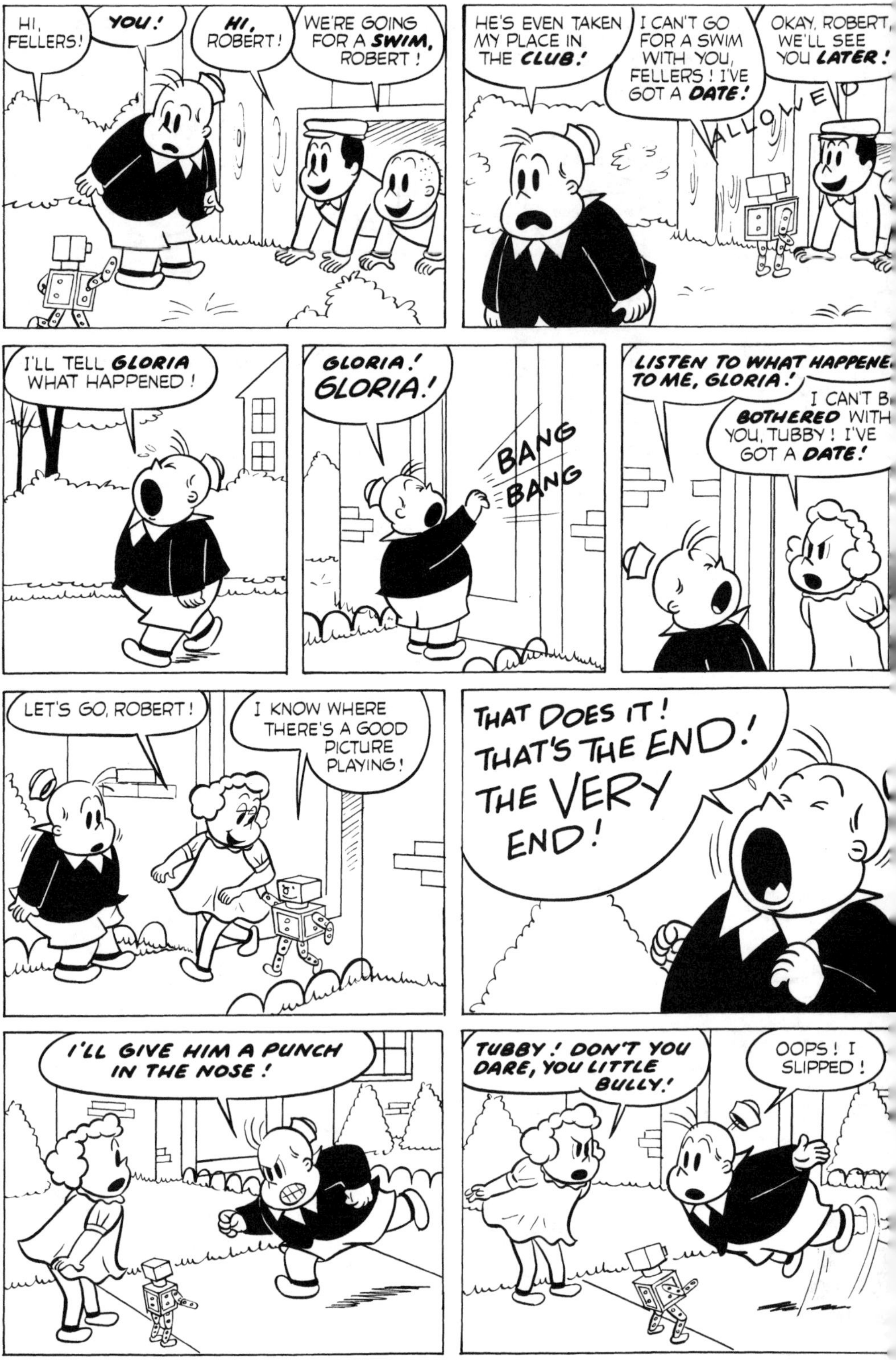
HI, FELLERS!
YOU!
HI, ROBERT!
WE'RE GOING FOR A SWIM, ROBERT!
HE'S EVEN TAKEN MY PLACE IN THE CLUB!
I CAN'T GO FOR A SWIM WITH YOU, FELLERS! I'VE GOT A DATE!
OKAY, ROBERT, WE'LL SEE YOU LATER!
I'LL TELL GLORIA WHAT HAPPENED!
GLORIA! GLORIA!
BANG
BANG
LISTEN TO WHAT HAPPENE
TO ME, GLORIA!
YOU, TUBBY! I'VE GOT A DATE!
LET'S GO, ROBERT!
I KNOW WHERE THERE'S A GOOD PICTURE PLAYING!
THAT DOES IT! THAT'S THE END! THE VERY END!
I'LL GIVE HIM A PUNCH IN THE NOSE!
TUBBY! DON'T YOU DARE, YOU LITTLE BULLY!
OOPS! I SLIPPED!

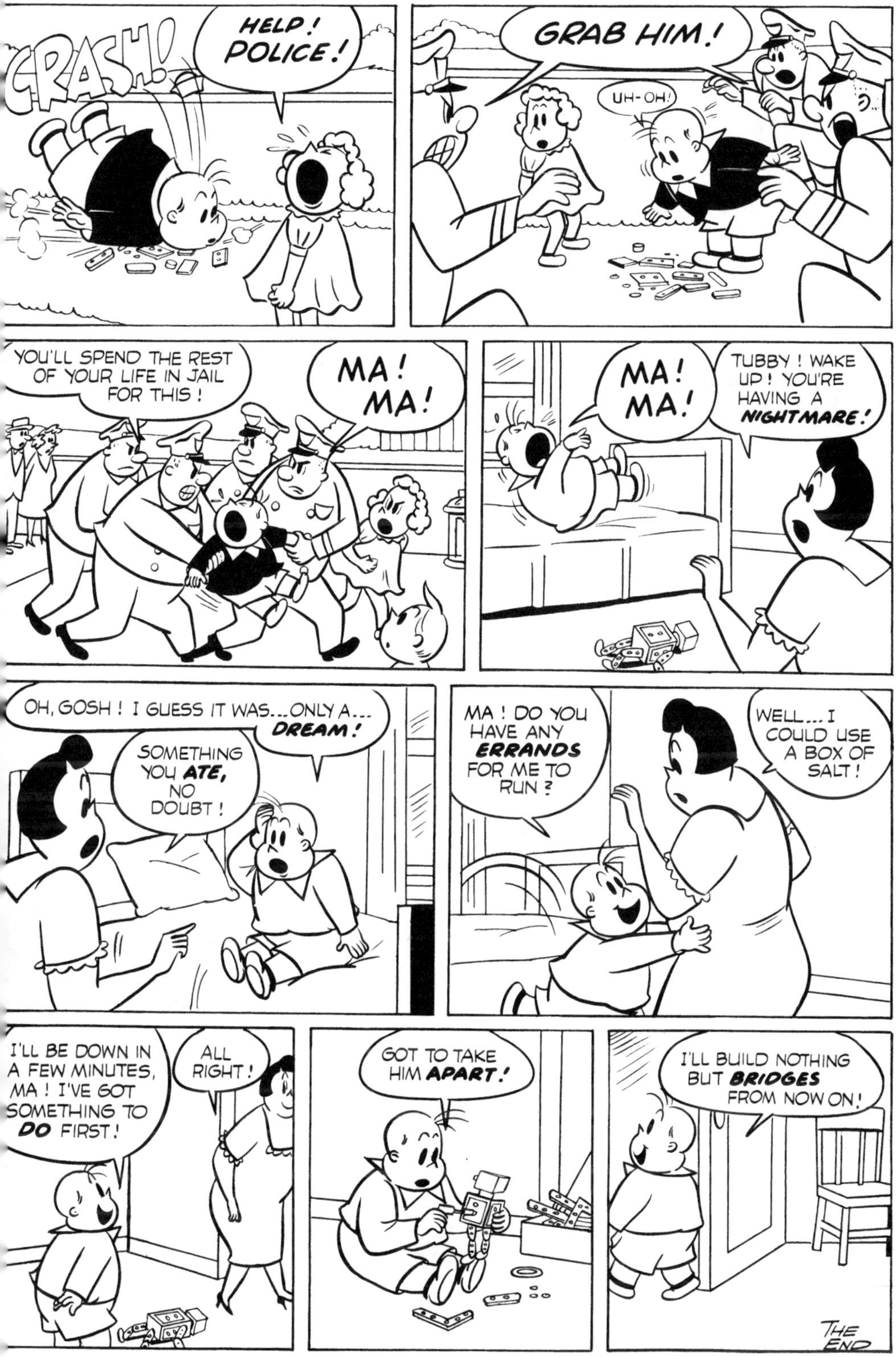
CRASH!
HELP! POLICE!
GRAB HIM!
UH-OH!
YOU'LL SPEND THE REST OF YOUR LIFE IN JAIL FOR THIS!
MA! MA!
MA! MA!
TUBBY! WAKE UP! YOU'RE HAVING A NIGHTMARE!
OH, GOSH! I GUESS IT WAS...ONLY A... DREAM!
SOMETHING YOU ATE, NO DOUBT!
MA! DO YOU HAVE ANY ERRANDS FOR ME TO RUN?
WELL... I COULD USE A BOX OF SALT!
I'LL BE DOWN IN A FEW MINUTES, MA! I'VE GOT SOMETHING TO DO FIRST!
ALL RIGHT!
GOT TO TAKE HIM APART!
I'LL BUILD NOTHING BUT BRIDGES FROM NOW ON!
THE END

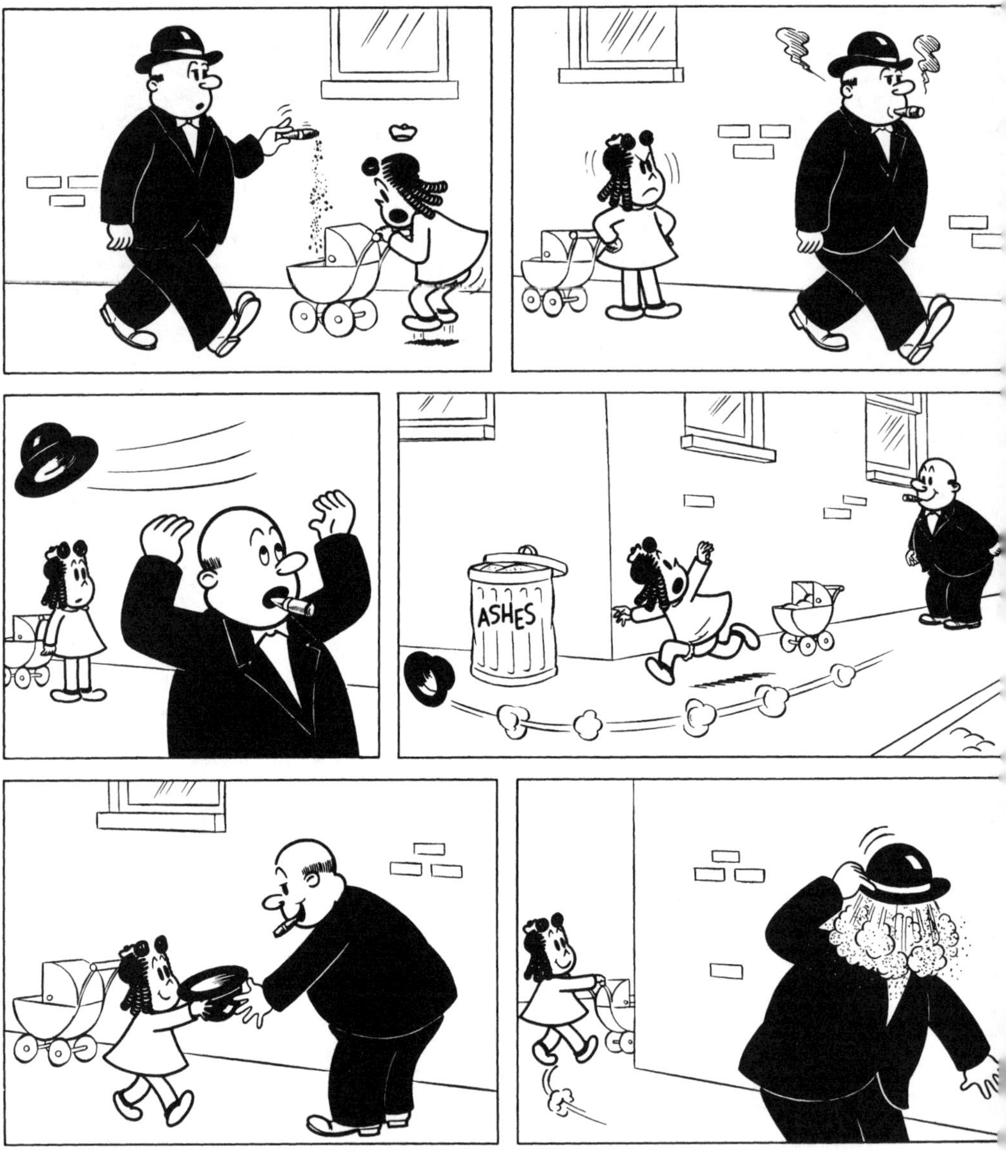
ASHES

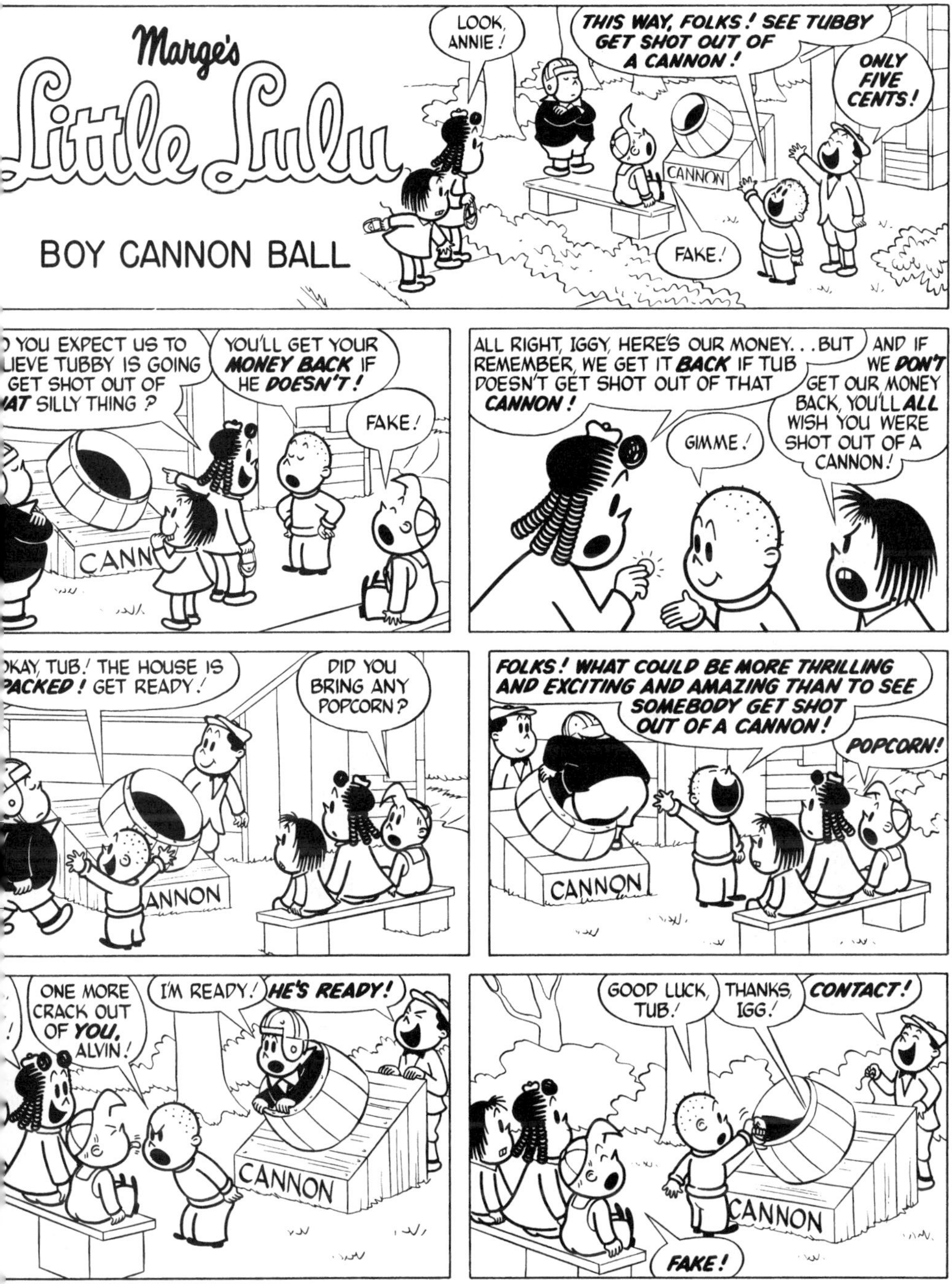
Marge's Little Lulu
BOY CANNON BALL
LOOK, ANNIE!
THIS WAY, FOLKS! SEE TUBBY GET SHOT OUT OF A CANNON!
ONLY FIVE CENTS!
CANNON
FAKE!
D YOU EXPECT US TO LIEVE TUBBY IS GOING GET SHOT OUT OF AT SILLY THING?
YOU'LL GET YOUR MONEY BACK IF HE DOESN'T!
FAKE!
CANN
ALL RIGHT, IGGY, HERE'S OUR MONEY. . . BUT REMEMBER, WE GET IT BACK IF TUB DOESN'T GET SHOT OUT OF THAT CANNON!
AND IF WE DON'T GET OUR MONEY BACK, YOU'LL ALL WISH YOU WERE SHOT OUT OF A CANNON!
GIMME!
KAY, TUB! THE HOUSE IS ACKED! GET READY!
DID YOU BRING ANY POPCORN?
ANNON
FOLKS! WHAT COULD BE MORE THRILLING AND EXCITING AND AMAZING THAN TO SEE SOMEBODY GET SHOT OUT OF A CANNON!
POPCORN!
CANNON
ONE MORE CRACK OUT OF YOU, ALVIN!
I'M READY!
HE'S READY!
CANNON
GOOD LUCK, TUB!
THANKS, IGG!
CONTACT!
CANNON
FAKE!

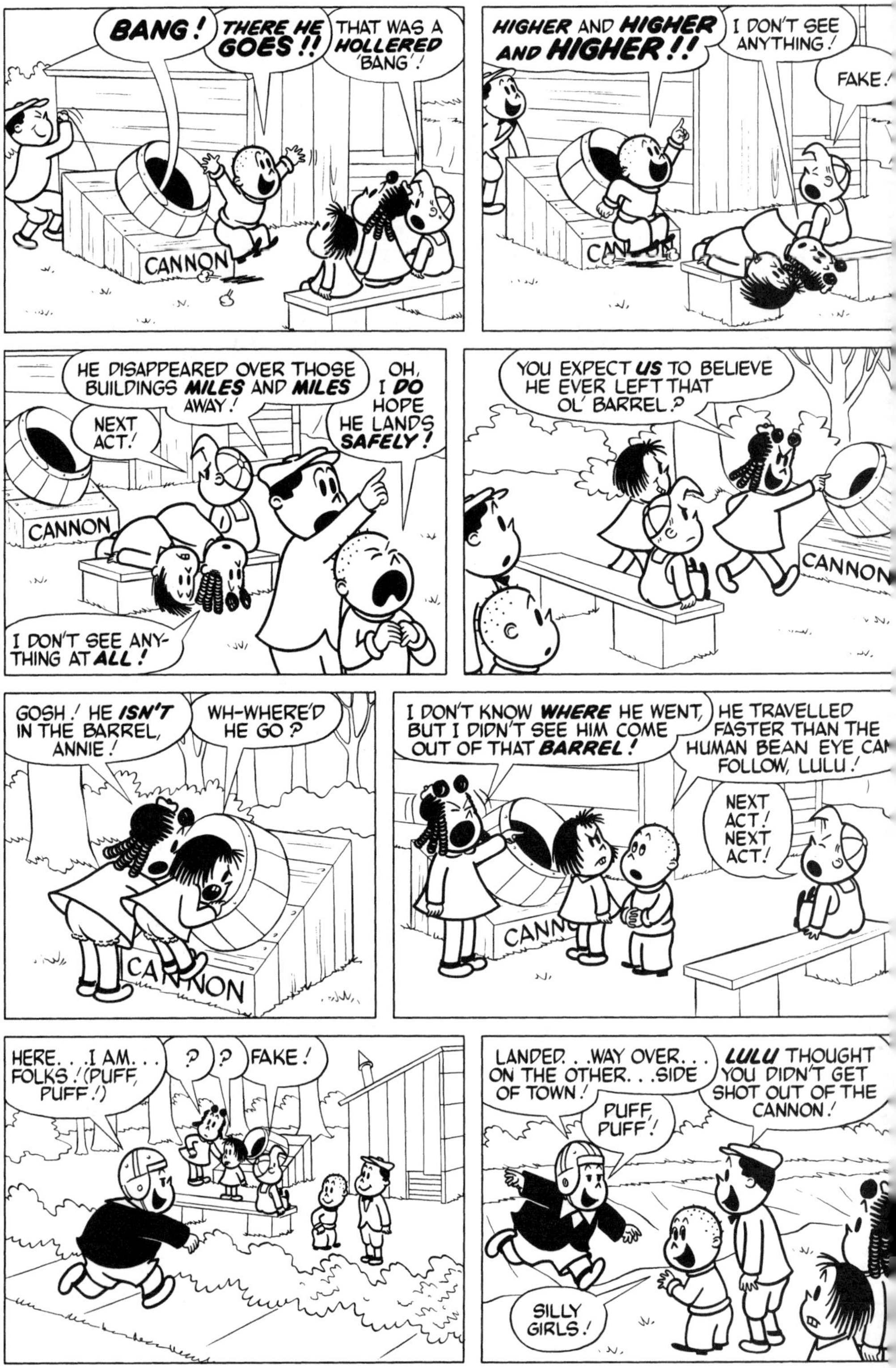
BANG!
THERE HE GOES!!
THAT WAS A HOLLERED 'BANG'!
HIGHER AND HIGHER AND HIGHER!!
I DON'T SEE ANYTHING!
FAKE!
CANNON
HE DISAPPEARED OVER THOSE BUILDINGS MILES AND MILES AWAY!
OH, I DO HOPE HE LANDS SAFELY!
NEXT ACT!
I DON'T SEE ANYTHING AT ALL!
YOU EXPECT US TO BELIEVE HE EVER LEFT THAT OL' BARREL?
GOSH! HE ISN'T IN THE BARREL, ANNIE!
WH-WHERE'D HE GO?
I DON'T KNOW WHERE HE WENT, BUT I DIDN'T SEE HIM COME OUT OF THAT BARREL!
HE TRAVELLED FASTER THAN THE HUMAN BEAN EYE CAN FOLLOW, LULU!
NEXT ACT! NEXT ACT!
HERE. . .I AM. . . FOLKS! (PUFF, PUFF!)
?
?
FAKE!
LANDED. . .WAY OVER. . . ON THE OTHER. . .SIDE OF TOWN!
PUFF, PUFF!
LULU THOUGHT YOU DIDN'T GET SHOT OUT OF THE CANNON!
SILLY GIRLS!

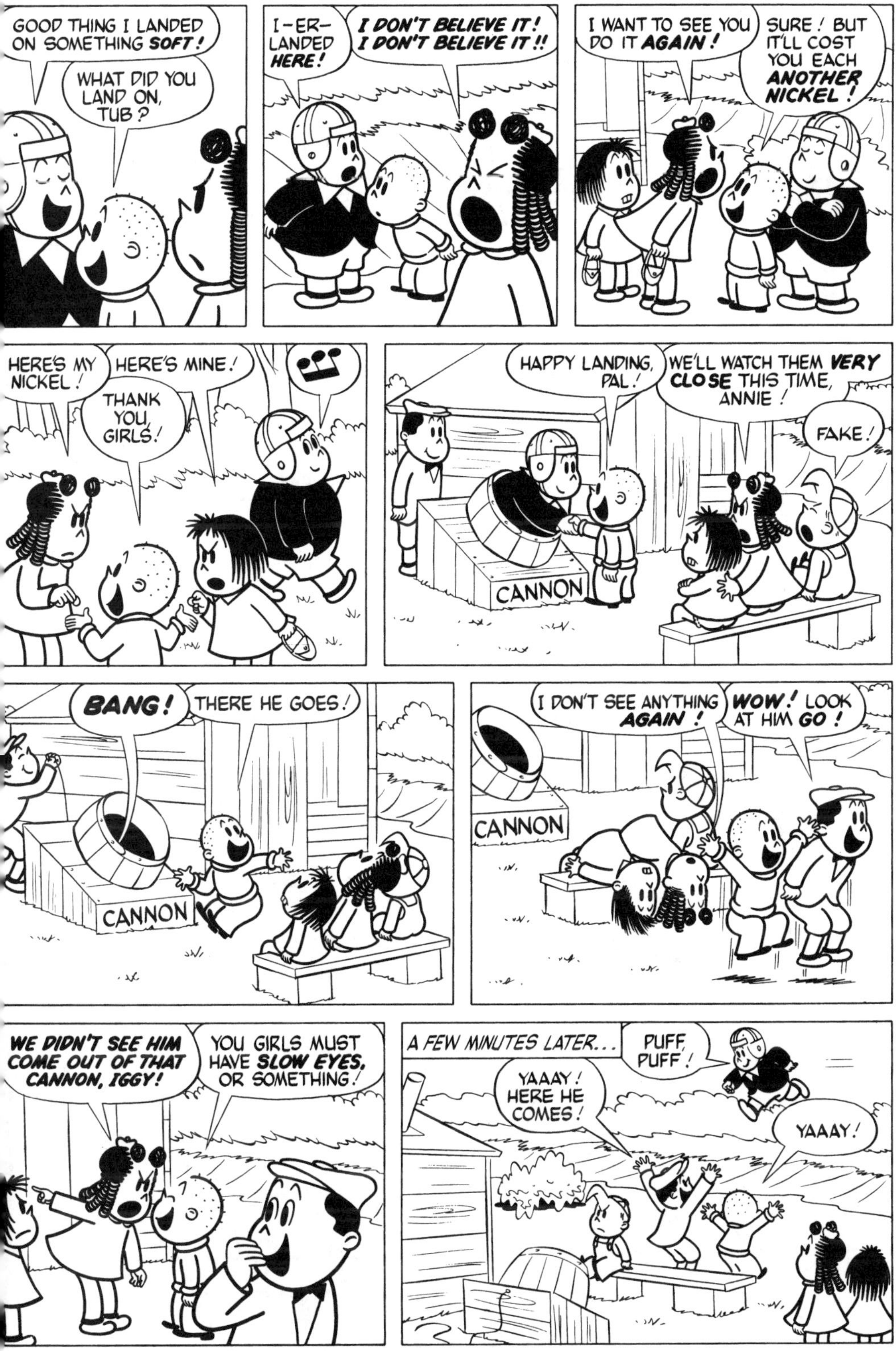
GOOD THING I LANDED ON SOMETHING SOFT!
WHAT DID YOU LAND ON, TUB?
I-ER-LANDED HERE!
I DON'T BELIEVE IT! I DON'T BELIEVE IT!!
I WANT TO SEE YOU DO IT AGAIN!
SURE! BUT IT'LL COST YOU EACH ANOTHER NICKEL!
HERE'S MY NICKEL!
HERE'S MINE!
THANK YOU, GIRLS!
HAPPY LANDING, PAL!
WE'LL WATCH THEM VERY CLOSE THIS TIME, ANNIE!
FAKE!
CANNON
BANG!
THERE HE GOES!
CANNON
I DON'T SEE ANYTHING AGAIN!
WOW! LOOK AT HIM GO!
CANNON
WE DIDN'T SEE HIM COME OUT OF THAT CANNON, IGGY!
YOU GIRLS MUST HAVE SLOW EYES, OR SOMETHING!
A FEW MINUTES LATER...
PUFF, PUFF!
YAAAY! HERE HE COMES!
YAAAY!

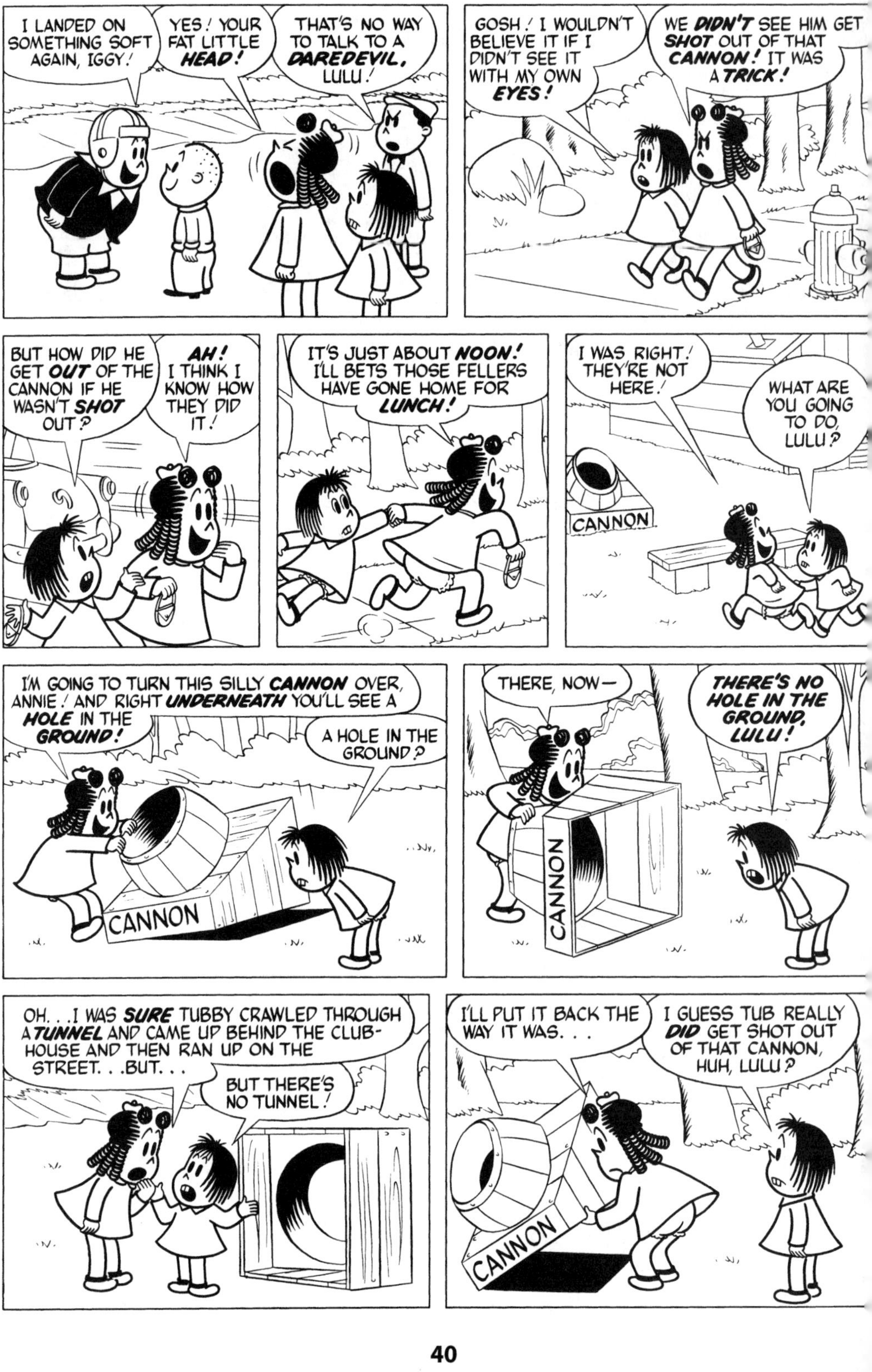
I LANDED ON SOMETHING SOFT AGAIN, IGGY!
YES! YOUR FAT LITTLE HEAD!
THAT'S NO WAY TO TALK TO A DAREDEVIL, LULU!
GOSH! I WOULDN'T BELIEVE IT IF I DIDN'T SEE IT WITH MY OWN EYES!
WE DIDN'T SEE HIM GET SHOT OUT OF THAT CANNON! IT WAS A TRICK!
BUT HOW DID HE GET OUT OF THE CANNON IF HE WASN'T SHOT OUT?
AH! I THINK I KNOW HOW THEY DID IT!
IT'S JUST ABOUT NOON! I'LL BETS THOSE FELLERS HAVE GONE HOME FOR LUNCH!
I WAS RIGHT! THEY'RE NOT HERE!
WHAT ARE YOU GOING TO DO, LULU?
CANNON
I'M GOING TO TURN THIS SILLY CANNON OVER, ANNIE! AND RIGHT UNDERNEATH YOU'LL SEE A HOLE IN THE GROUND!
A HOLE IN THE GROUND?
CANNON
THERE, NOW—
THERE'S NO HOLE IN THE GROUND, LULU!
CANNON
OH. . .I WAS SURE TUBBY CRAWLED THROUGH A TUNNEL AND CAME UP BEHIND THE CLUB-HOUSE AND THEN RAN UP ON THE STREET. . .BUT. . .
BUT THERE'S NO TUNNEL!
I'LL PUT IT BACK THE WAY IT WAS. . .
I GUESS TUB REALLY DID GET SHOT OUT OF THAT CANNON, HUH, LULU?
CANNON

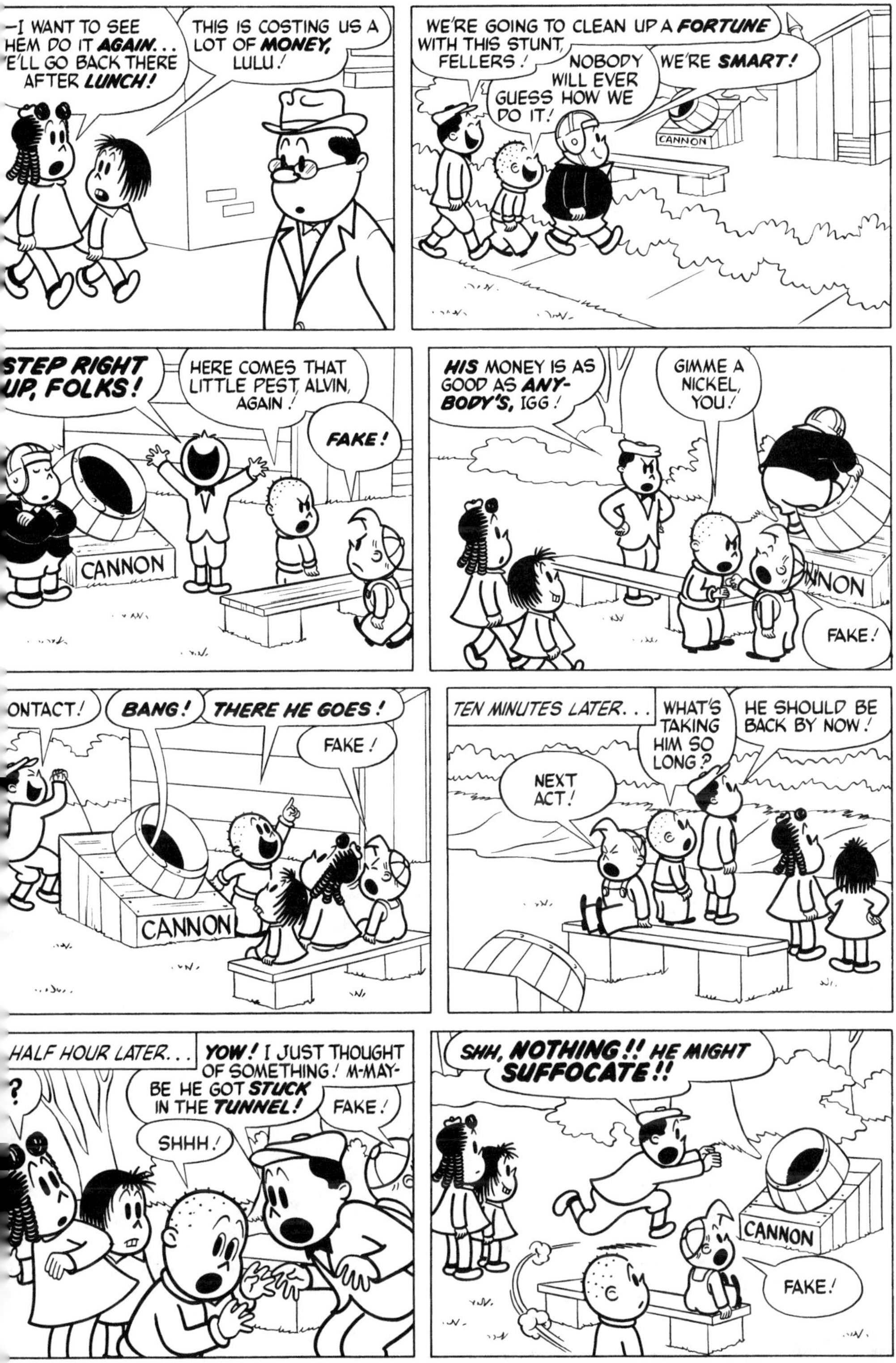
—I WANT TO SEE
HEM DO IT AGAIN...
'E'LL GO BACK THERE
AFTER LUNCH!
THIS IS COSTING US A LOT OF MONEY, LULU!
WE'RE GOING TO CLEAN UP A FORTUNE WITH THIS STUNT, FELLERS!
NOBODY WILL EVER GUESS HOW WE DO IT!
WE'RE SMART!
CANNON
STEP RIGHT
UP, FOLKS!
HERE COMES THAT LITTLE PEST, ALVIN, AGAIN!
FAKE!
CANNON
HIS MONEY IS AS GOOD AS ANY-BODY'S, IGG!
GIMME A NICKEL, YOU!
FAKE!
ONTACT!
BANG!
THERE HE GOES!
FAKE!
CANNON
TEN MINUTES LATER...
WHAT'S TAKING HIM SO LONG?
HE SHOULD BE BACK BY NOW!
NEXT ACT!
HALF HOUR LATER...
YOW! I JUST THOUGHT OF SOMETHING! M-MAY-BE HE GOT STUCK IN THE TUNNEL!
FAKE!
SHHH!
SHH, NOTHING!! HE MIGHT SUFFOCATE!!
CANNON
FAKE!

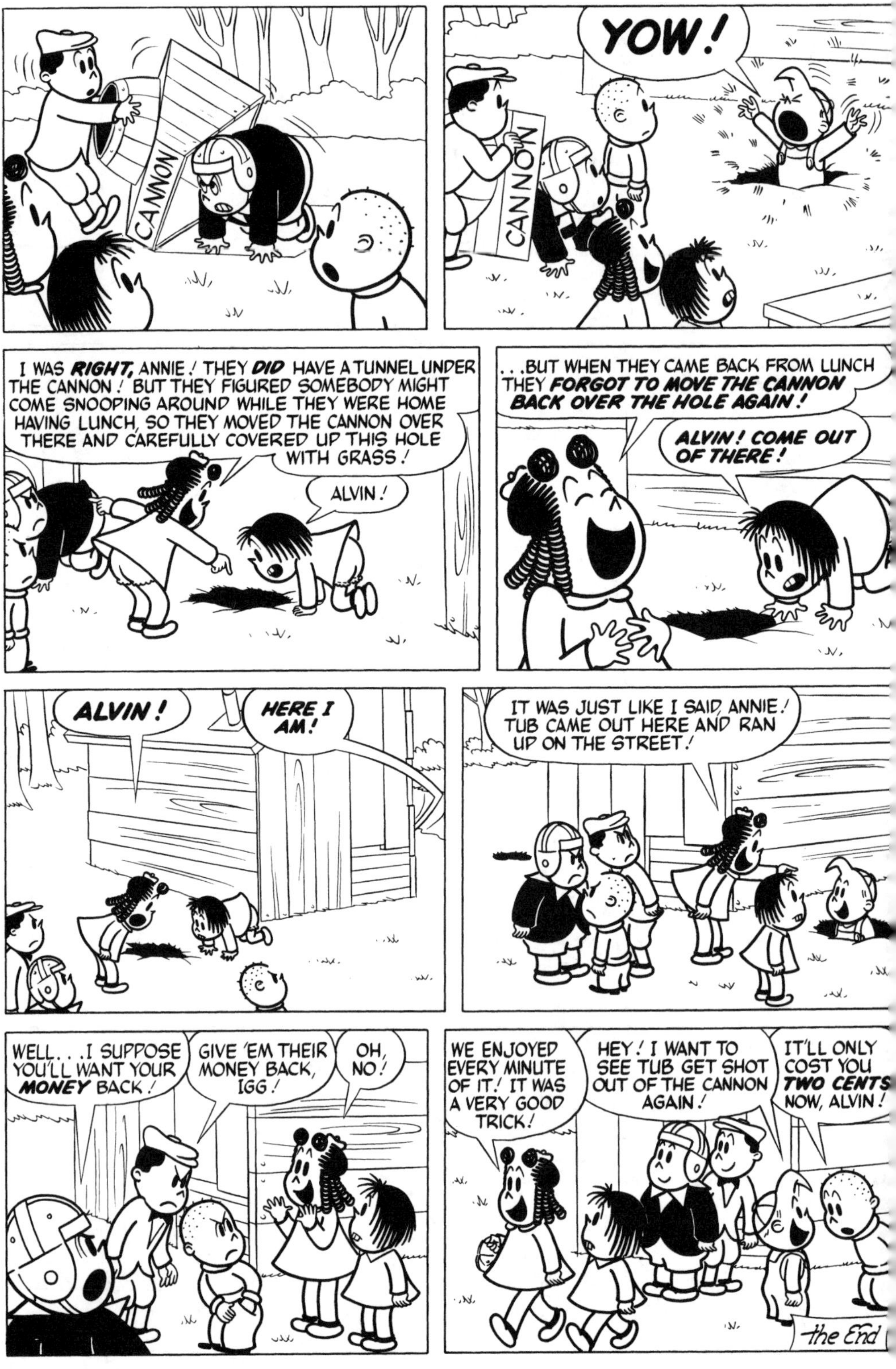
CANNON
YOW!
CANNON
I WAS RIGHT, ANNIE! THEY DID HAVE A TUNNEL UNDER THE CANNON! BUT THEY FIGURED SOMEBODY MIGHT COME SNOOPING AROUND WHILE THEY WERE HOME HAVING LUNCH, SO THEY MOVED THE CANNON OVER THERE AND CAREFULLY COVERED UP THIS HOLE WITH GRASS!
ALVIN!
...BUT WHEN THEY CAME BACK FROM LUNCH THEY FORGOT TO MOVE THE CANNON BACK OVER THE HOLE AGAIN!
ALVIN! COME OUT OF THERE!
ALVIN!
HERE I AM!
IT WAS JUST LIKE I SAID, ANNIE! TUB CAME OUT HERE AND RAN UP ON THE STREET!
WELL...I SUPPOSE YOU'LL WANT YOUR MONEY BACK!
GIVE 'EM THEIR MONEY BACK, IGG!
OH, NO!
WE ENJOYED EVERY MINUTE OF IT! IT WAS A VERY GOOD TRICK!
HEY! I WANT TO SEE TUB GET SHOT OUT OF THE CANNON AGAIN!
IT'LL ONLY COST YOU TWO CENTS NOW, ALVIN!
the End

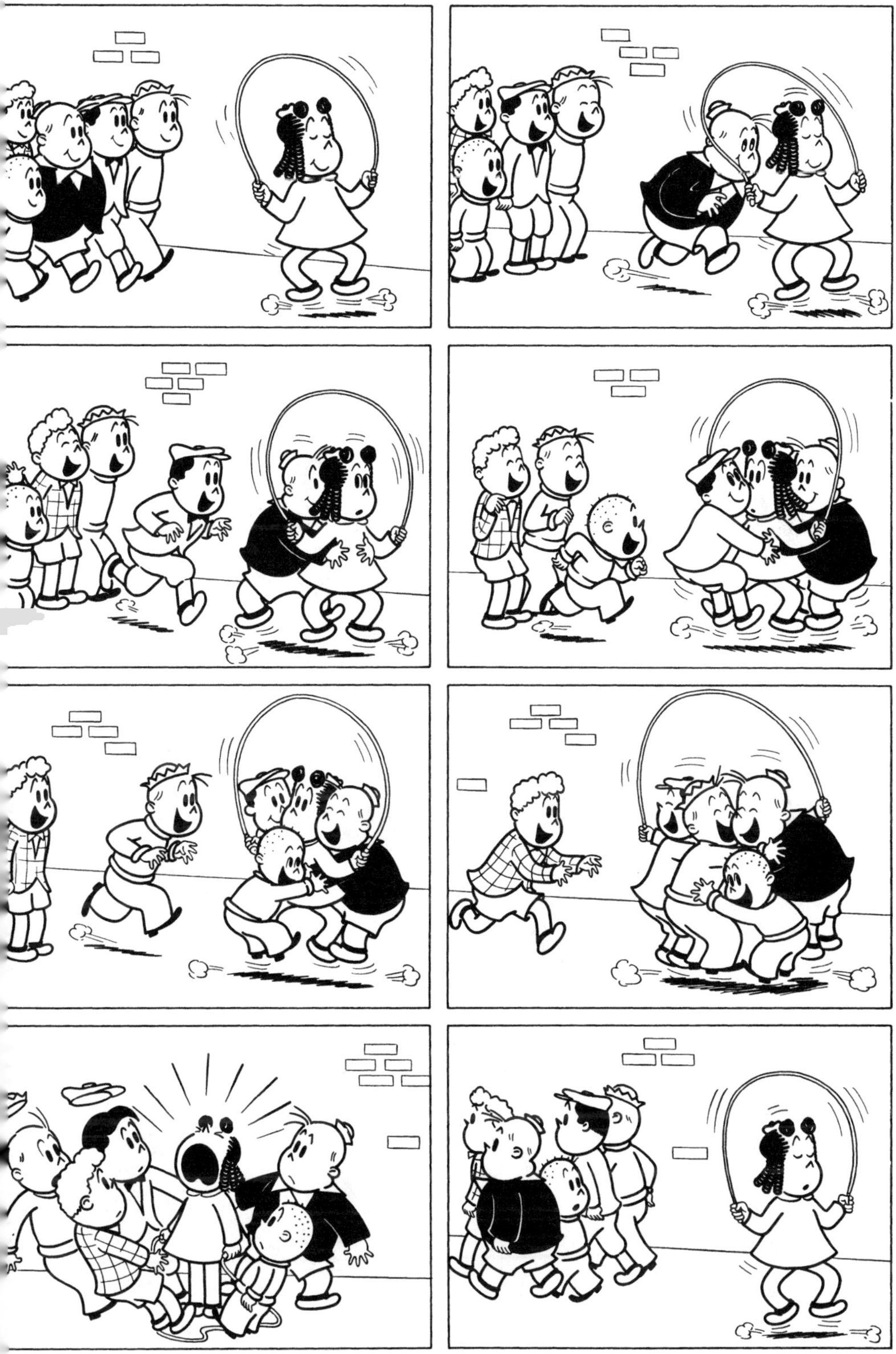

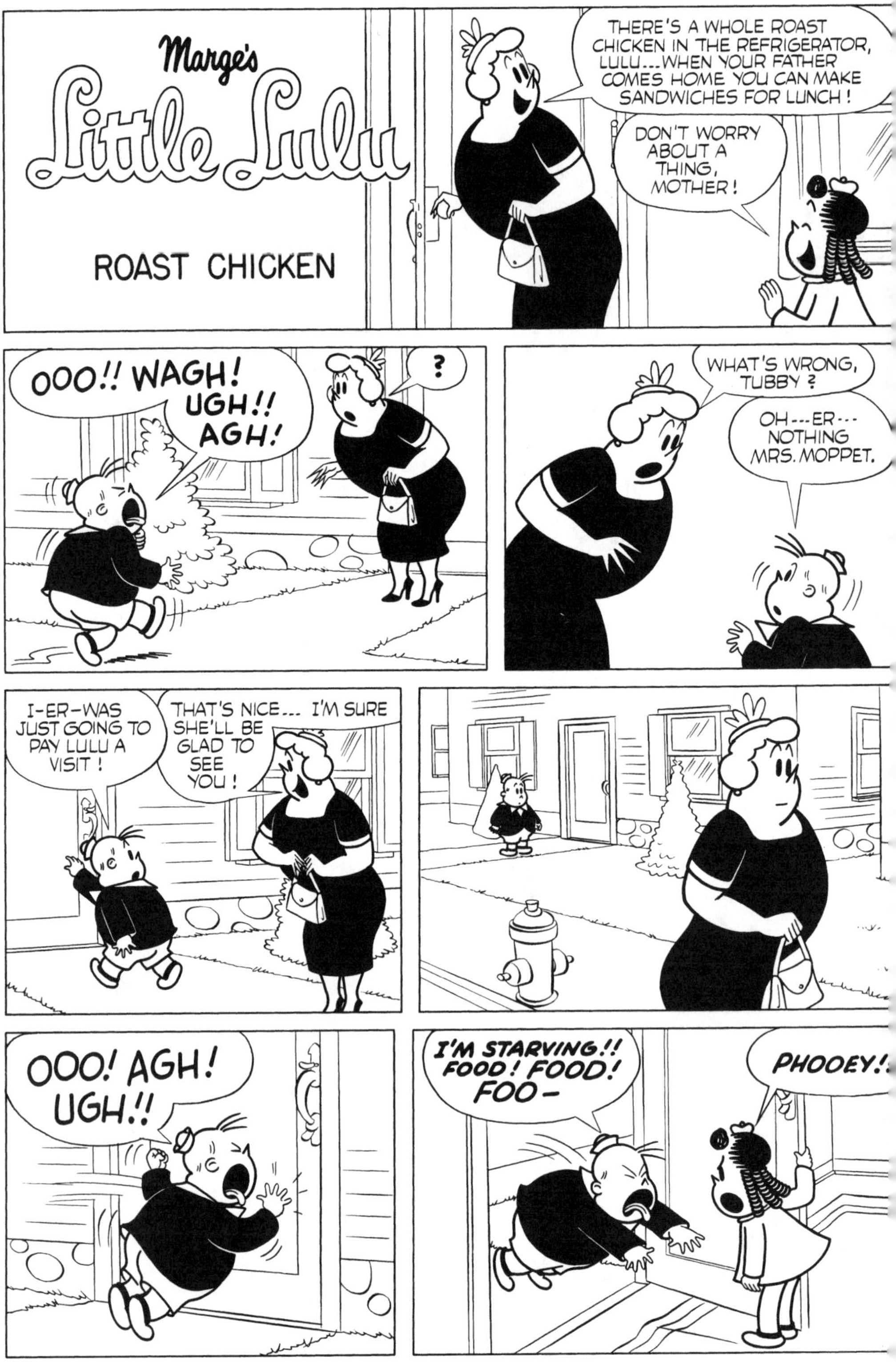
Marge's
Little Lulu
ROAST CHICKEN
THERE'S A WHOLE ROAST CHICKEN IN THE REFRIGERATOR, LULU...WHEN YOUR FATHER COMES HOME YOU CAN MAKE SANDWICHES FOR LUNCH!
DON'T WORRY ABOUT A THING, MOTHER!
OOO!! WAGH! UGH!! AGH!
?
WHAT'S WRONG, TUBBY?
OH---ER--- NOTHING MRS. MOPPET.
I-ER-WAS JUST GOING TO PAY LULU A VISIT!
THAT'S NICE... I'M SURE SHE'LL BE GLAD TO SEE YOU!
OOO! AGH! UGH!!
I'M STARVING!! FOOD! FOOD! FOO-
PHOOEY!!

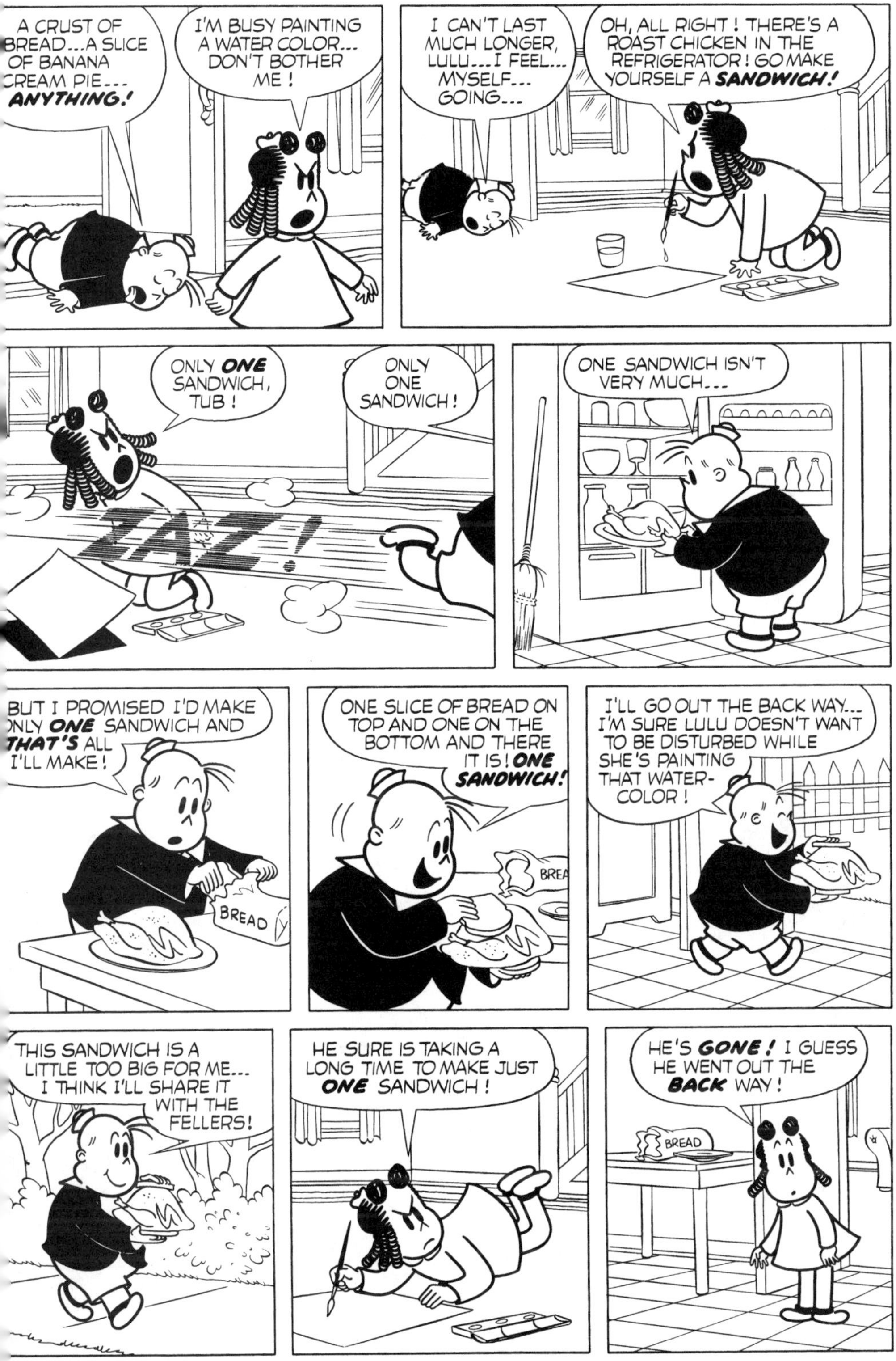
A CRUST OF BREAD...A SLICE OF BANANA CREAM PIE... ANYTHING!
I'M BUSY PAINTING A WATER COLOR... DON'T BOTHER ME!
I CAN'T LAST MUCH LONGER, LULU...I FEEL... MYSELF... GOING...
OH, ALL RIGHT! THERE'S A ROAST CHICKEN IN THE REFRIGERATOR! GO MAKE YOURSELF A SANDWICH!
ONLY ONE SANDWICH, TUB!
ONLY ONE SANDWICH!
ZAZ!
ONE SANDWICH ISN'T VERY MUCH...
BUT I PROMISED I'D MAKE ONLY ONE SANDWICH AND THAT'S ALL I'LL MAKE!
BREAD
ONE SLICE OF BREAD ON TOP AND ONE ON THE BOTTOM AND THERE IT IS! ONE SANDWICH!
I'LL GO OUT THE BACK WAY... I'M SURE LULU DOESN'T WANT TO BE DISTURBED WHILE SHE'S PAINTING THAT WATER-COLOR!
THIS SANDWICH IS A LITTLE TOO BIG FOR ME... I THINK I'LL SHARE IT WITH THE FELLERS!
HE SURE IS TAKING A LONG TIME TO MAKE JUST ONE SANDWICH!
HE'S GONE! I GUESS HE WENT OUT THE BACK WAY!
BREAD

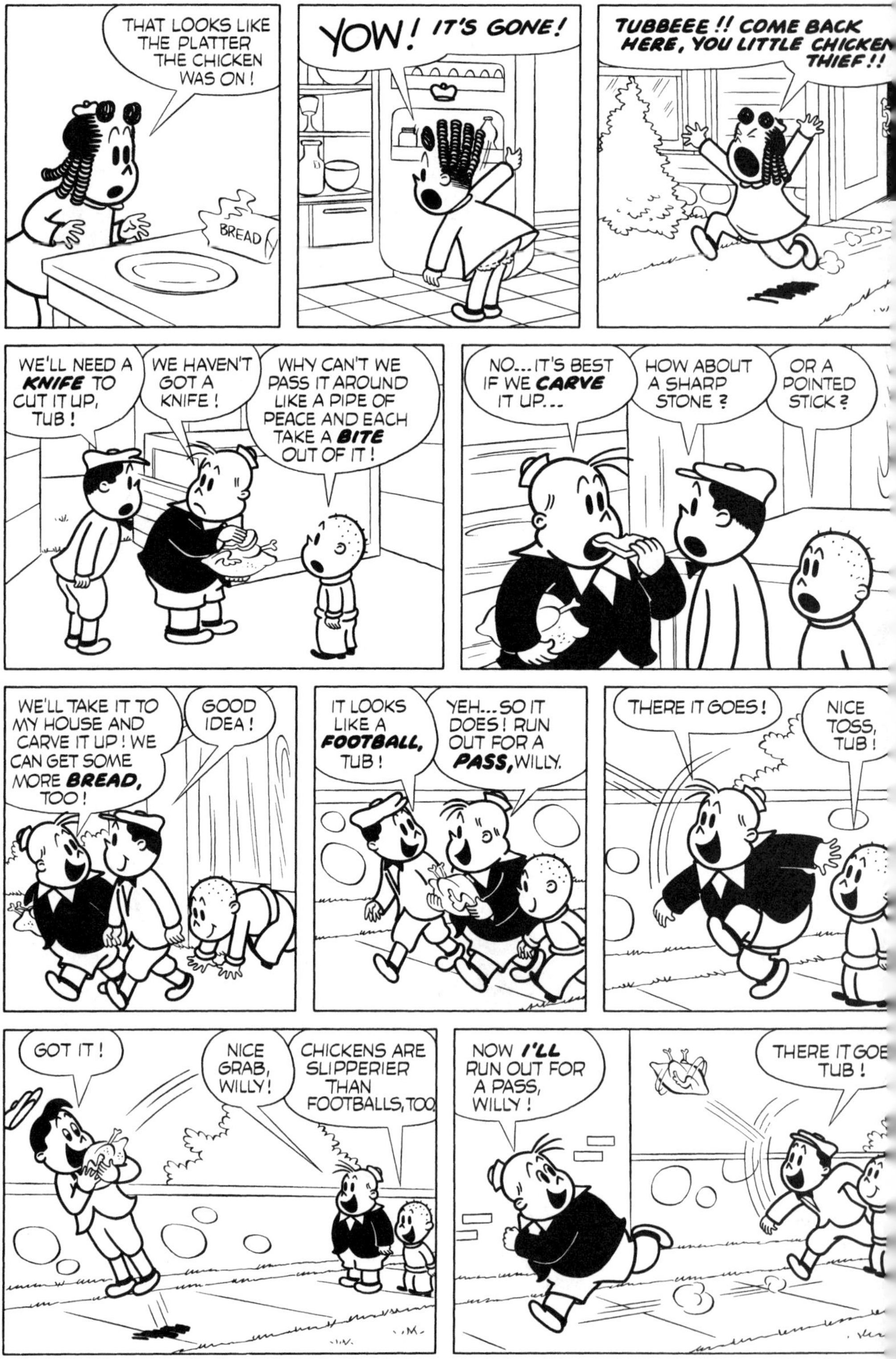
THAT LOOKS LIKE THE PLATTER THE CHICKEN WAS ON!
BREAD
YOW! IT'S GONE!
TUBBEEE!! COME BACK HERE, YOU LITTLE CHICKEN THIEF!!
WE'LL NEED A KNIFE TO CUT IT UP, TUB!
WE HAVEN'T GOT A KNIFE!
WHY CAN'T WE PASS IT AROUND LIKE A PIPE OF PEACE AND EACH TAKE A BITE OUT OF IT!
NO... IT'S BEST IF WE CARVE IT UP...
HOW ABOUT A SHARP STONE?
OR A POINTED STICK?
WE'LL TAKE IT TO MY HOUSE AND CARVE IT UP! WE CAN GET SOME MORE BREAD, TOO!
GOOD IDEA!
IT LOOKS LIKE A FOOTBALL, TUB!
YEH... SO IT DOES! RUN OUT FOR A PASS, WILLY.
THERE IT GOES!
NICE TOSS, TUB!
GOT IT!
NICE GRAB, WILLY!
CHICKENS ARE SLIPPERIER THAN FOOTBALLS, TOO
NOW I'LL RUN OUT FOR A PASS, WILLY!
THERE IT GOE TUB!

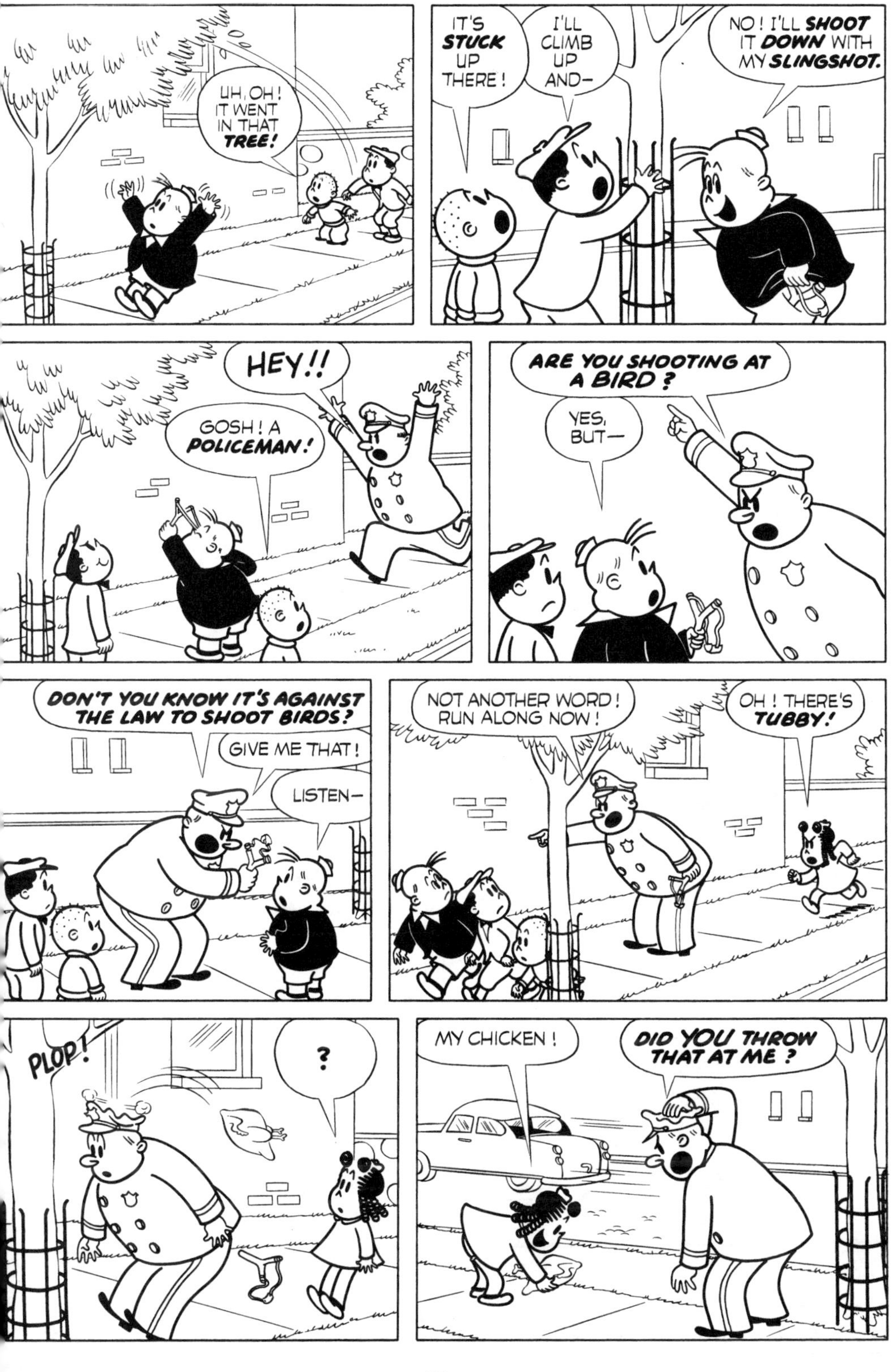
UH, OH! IT WENT IN THAT TREE!
IT'S STUCK UP THERE!
I'LL CLIMB UP AND—
NO! I'LL SHOOT IT DOWN WITH MY SLINGSHOT.
HEY!!
GOSH! A POLICEMAN!
ARE YOU SHOOTING AT A BIRD?
YES, BUT—
DON'T YOU KNOW IT'S AGAINST THE LAW TO SHOOT BIRDS?
GIVE ME THAT!
LISTEN—
NOT ANOTHER WORD! RUN ALONG NOW!
OH! THERE'S TUBBY!
PLOP!
?
MY CHICKEN!
DID YOU THROW THAT AT ME?

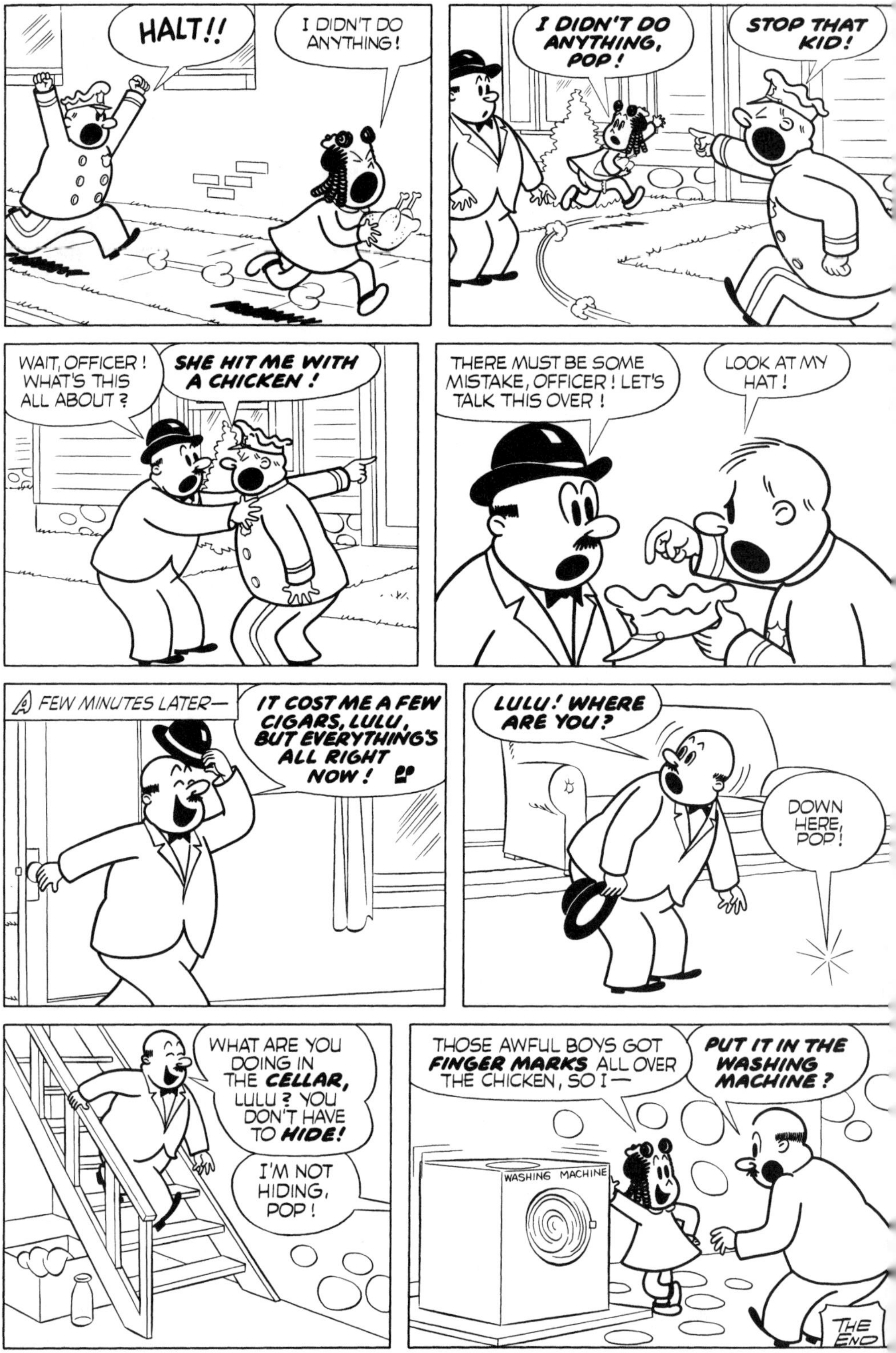

HALT!!
I DIDN'T DO ANYTHING!
I DIDN'T DO ANYTHING, POP!
STOP THAT KID!
WAIT, OFFICER! WHAT'S THIS ALL ABOUT?
SHE HIT ME WITH A CHICKEN!
THERE MUST BE SOME MISTAKE, OFFICER! LET'S TALK THIS OVER!
LOOK AT MY HAT!
A FEW MINUTES LATER—
IT COST ME A FEW CIGARS, LULU, BUT EVERYTHING'S ALL RIGHT NOW!
LULU! WHERE ARE YOU?
DOWN HERE, POP!
WHAT ARE YOU DOING IN THE CELLAR, LULU? YOU DON'T HAVE TO HIDE!
I'M NOT HIDING, POP!
THOSE AWFUL BOYS GOT FINGER MARKS ALL OVER THE CHICKEN, SO I—
PUT IT IN THE WASHING MACHINE?
WASHING MACHINE
THE END

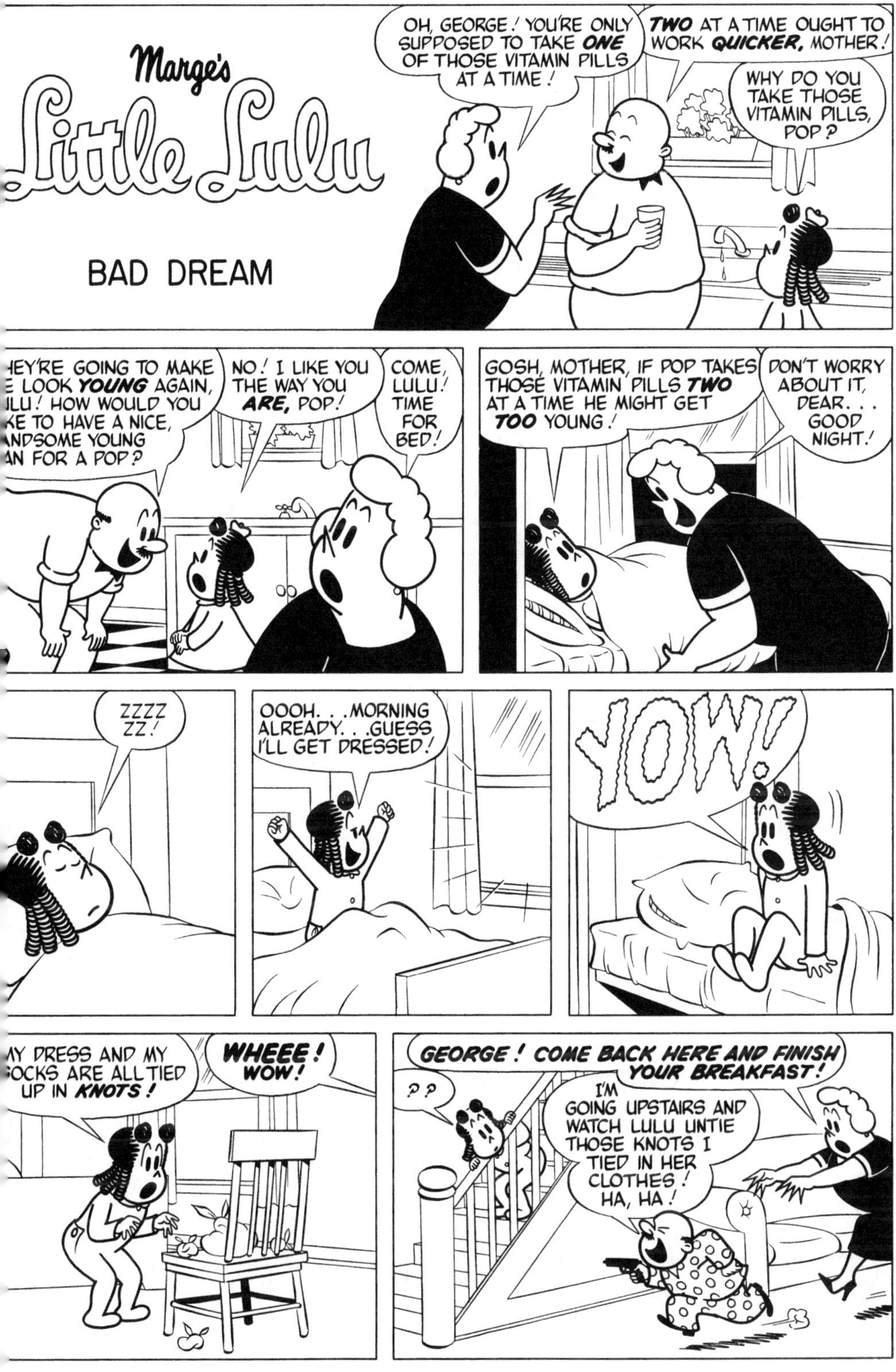
Marge's Little Lulu
BAD DREAM
OH, GEORGE! YOU'RE ONLY SUPPOSED TO TAKE ONE OF THOSE VITAMIN PILLS AT A TIME!
TWO AT A TIME OUGHT TO WORK QUICKER, MOTHER!
WHY DO YOU TAKE THOSE VITAMIN PILLS, POP?
HEY'RE GOING TO MAKE E LOOK YOUNG AGAIN, LULU! HOW WOULD YOU KE TO HAVE A NICE, ANDSOME YOUNG AN FOR A POP?
NO! I LIKE YOU THE WAY YOU ARE, POP!
COME, LULU! TIME FOR BED!
GOSH, MOTHER, IF POP TAKES THOSE VITAMIN PILLS TWO AT A TIME HE MIGHT GET TOO YOUNG!
DON'T WORRY ABOUT IT, DEAR. . . GOOD NIGHT!
ZZZZ ZZ!
OOOH. . .MORNING ALREADY. . .GUESS I'LL GET DRESSED!
YOW!
MY DRESS AND MY SOCKS ARE ALL TIED UP IN KNOTS!
WHEEE! WOW!
GEORGE! COME BACK HERE AND FINISH YOUR BREAKFAST!
? ?
I'M GOING UPSTAIRS AND WATCH LULU UNTIE THOSE KNOTS I TIED IN HER CLOTHES! HA, HA!

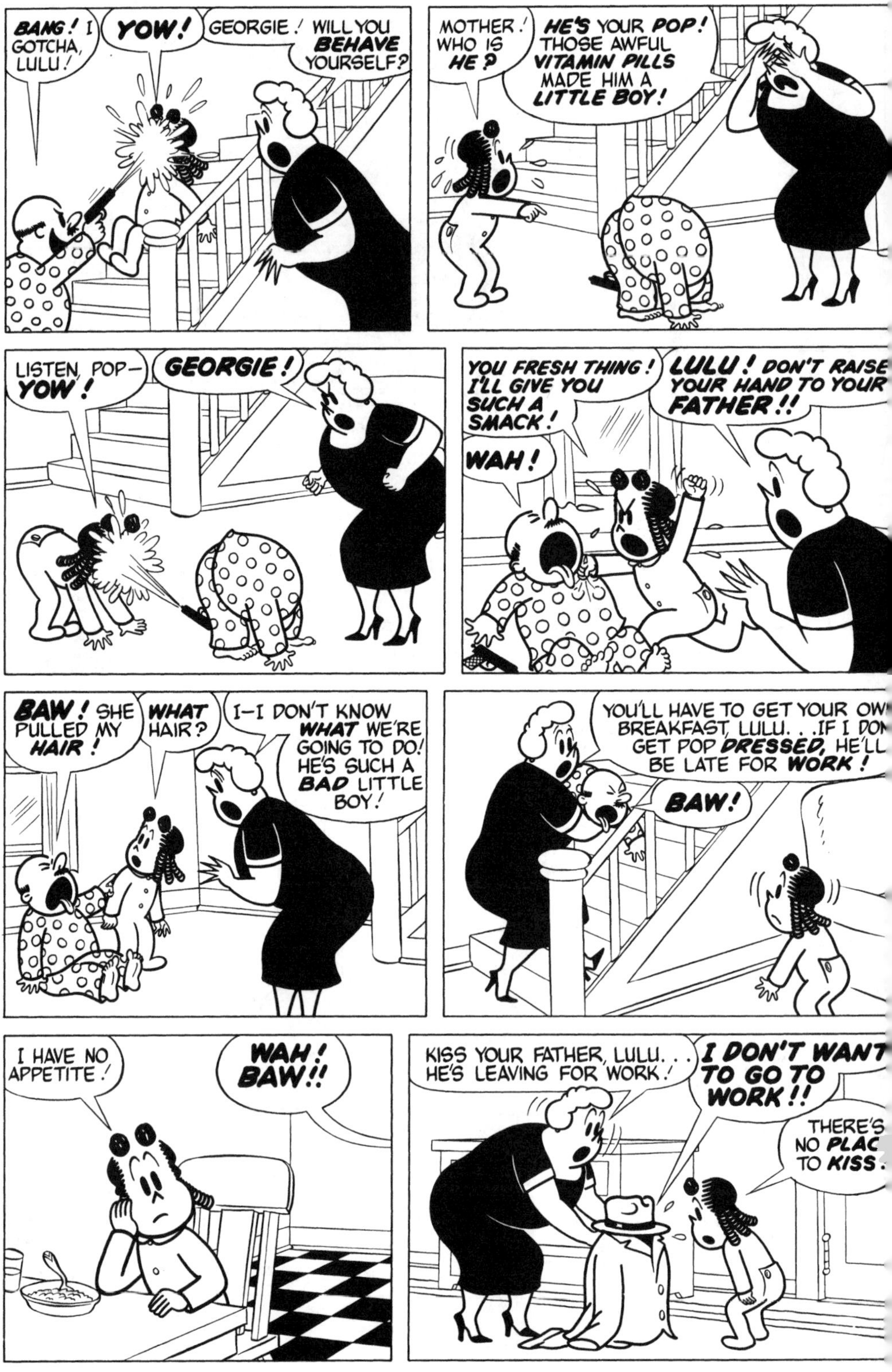
BANG! I GOTCHA, LULU!
YOW!
GEORGIE! WILL YOU BEHAVE YOURSELF?
MOTHER! WHO IS HE?
HE'S YOUR POP! THOSE AWFUL VITAMIN PILLS MADE HIM A LITTLE BOY!
LISTEN, POP— YOW!
GEORGIE!
YOU FRESH THING! I'LL GIVE YOU SUCH A SMACK!
WAH!
LULU! DON'T RAISE YOUR HAND TO YOUR FATHER!!
BAW! SHE PULLED MY HAIR!
WHAT HAIR?
I—I DON'T KNOW WHAT WE'RE GOING TO DO! HE'S SUCH A BAD LITTLE BOY!
YOU'LL HAVE TO GET YOUR OW BREAKFAST, LULU. . .IF I DON GET POP DRESSED, HE'LL BE LATE FOR WORK!
BAW!
I HAVE NO APPETITE!
WAH! BAW!!
KISS YOUR FATHER, LULU. . . HE'S LEAVING FOR WORK!
I DON'T WANT TO GO TO WORK!!
THERE'S NO PLAC TO KISS.

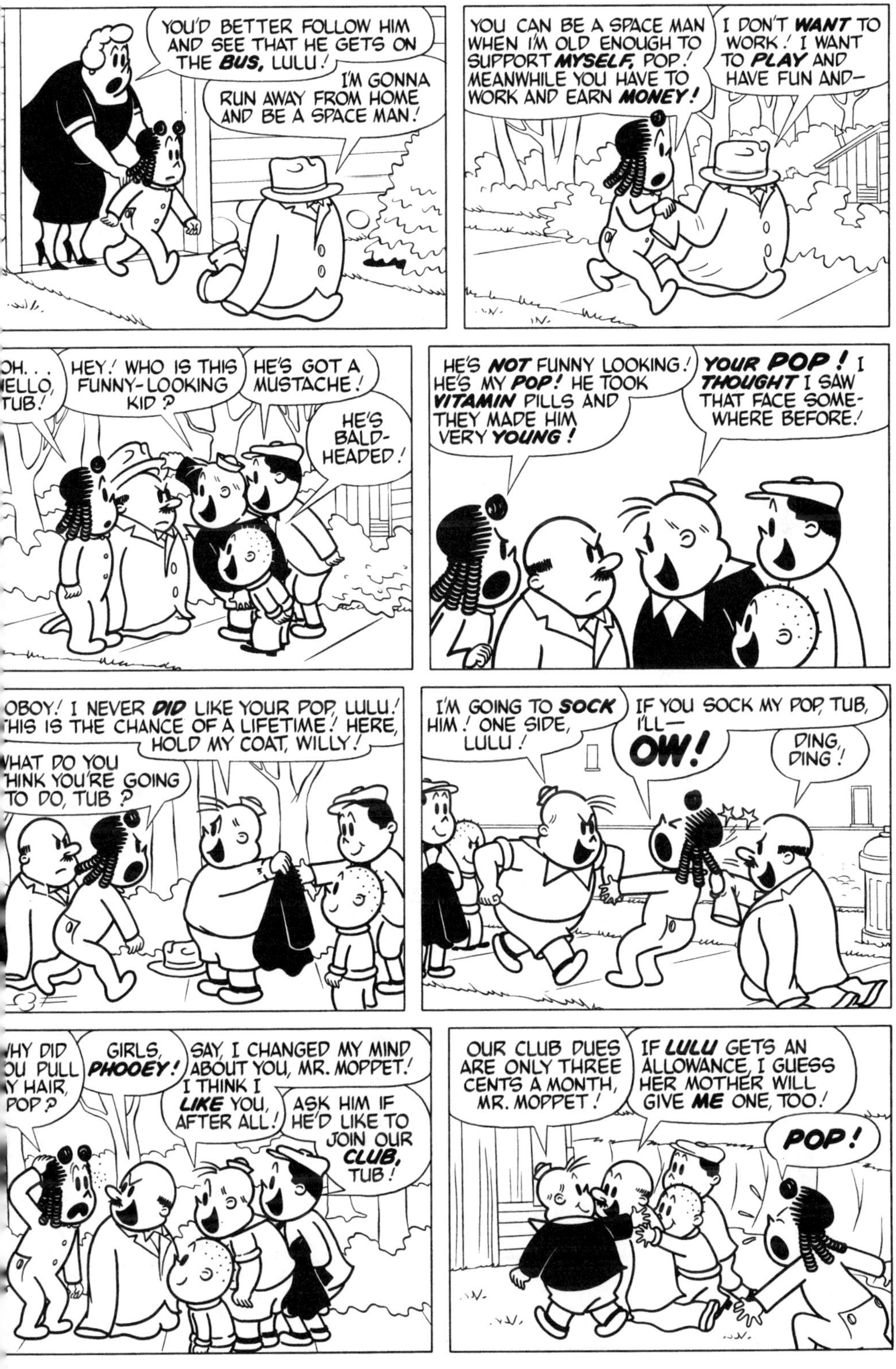
YOU'D BETTER FOLLOW HIM AND SEE THAT HE GETS ON THE BUS, LULU!
I'M GONNA RUN AWAY FROM HOME AND BE A SPACE MAN!
YOU CAN BE A SPACE MAN WHEN I'M OLD ENOUGH TO SUPPORT MYSELF, POP! MEANWHILE YOU HAVE TO WORK AND EARN MONEY!
I DON'T WANT TO WORK! I WANT TO PLAY AND HAVE FUN AND—
OH. . . ELLO, TUB!
HEY! WHO IS THIS FUNNY-LOOKING KID?
HE'S GOT A MUSTACHE!
HE'S BALD-HEADED!
HE'S NOT FUNNY LOOKING! HE'S MY POP! HE TOOK VITAMIN PILLS AND THEY MADE HIM VERY YOUNG!
YOUR POP! I THOUGHT I SAW THAT FACE SOME-WHERE BEFORE!
OBOY! I NEVER DID LIKE YOUR POP, LULU! THIS IS THE CHANCE OF A LIFETIME! HERE, HOLD MY COAT, WILLY!
HAT DO YOU HINK YOU'RE GOING TO DO, TUB?
I'M GOING TO SOCK HIM! ONE SIDE, LULU!
IF YOU SOCK MY POP, TUB, I'LL—
OW!
DING, DING!
HY DID OU PULL Y HAIR, POP?
GIRLS, PHOOEY!
SAY, I CHANGED MY MIND ABOUT YOU, MR. MOPPET! I THINK I LIKE YOU, AFTER ALL!
ASK HIM IF HE'D LIKE TO JOIN OUR CLUB, TUB!
OUR CLUB DUES ARE ONLY THREE CENTS A MONTH, MR. MOPPET!
IF LULU GETS AN ALLOWANCE, I GUESS HER MOTHER WILL GIVE ME ONE, TOO!
POP!

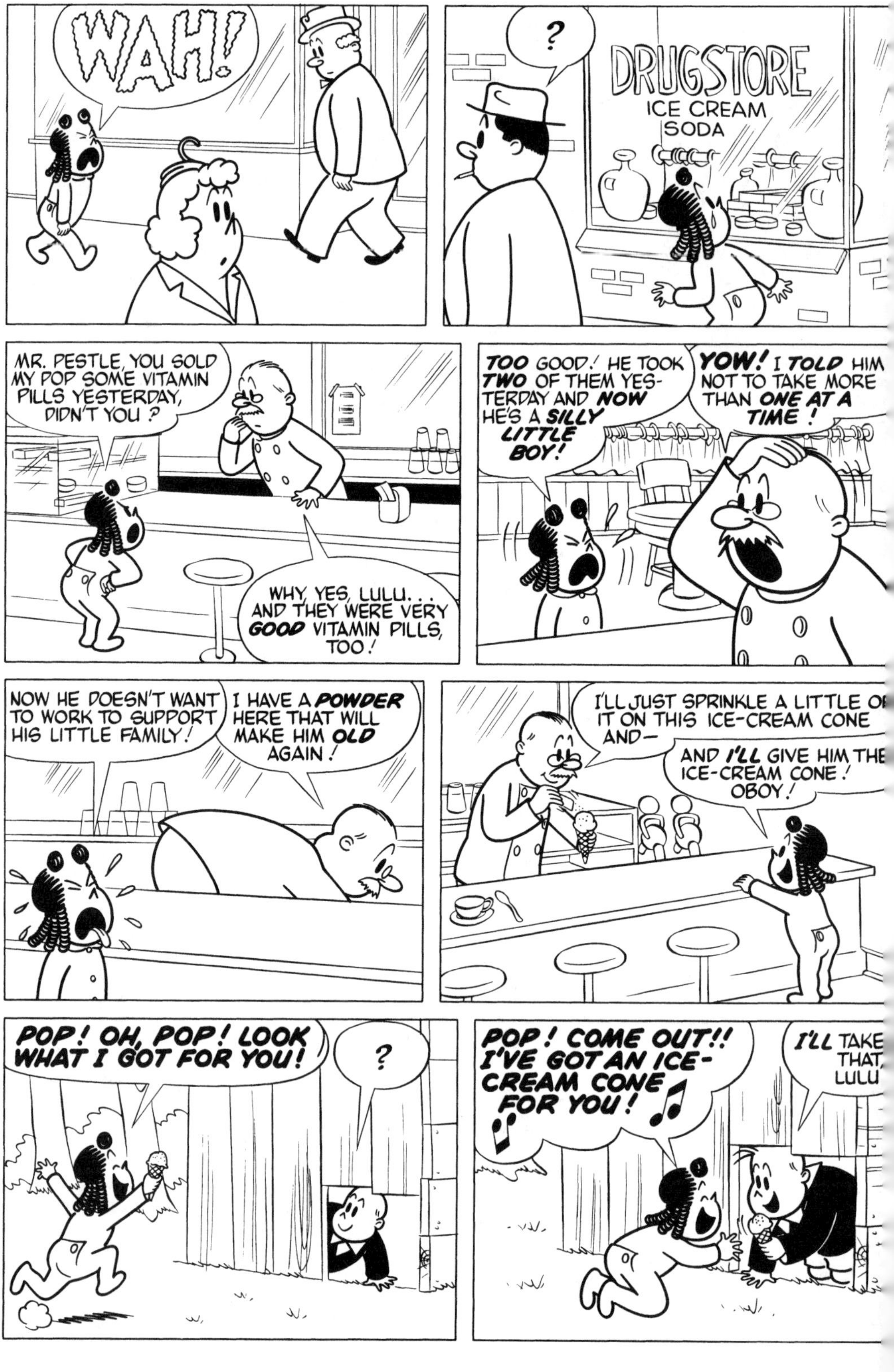
WAH!
?
DRUGSTORE
ICE CREAM
SODA
MR. PESTLE, YOU SOLD MY POP SOME VITAMIN PILLS YESTERDAY, DIDN'T YOU ?
WHY, YES, LULU... AND THEY WERE VERY GOOD VITAMIN PILLS, TOO !
TOO GOOD ! HE TOOK TWO OF THEM YESTERDAY AND NOW HE'S A SILLY LITTLE BOY!
YOW! I TOLD HIM NOT TO TAKE MORE THAN ONE AT A TIME !
NOW HE DOESN'T WANT TO WORK TO SUPPORT HIS LITTLE FAMILY !
I HAVE A POWDER HERE THAT WILL MAKE HIM OLD AGAIN !
I'LL JUST SPRINKLE A LITTLE OF IT ON THIS ICE-CREAM CONE AND—
AND I'LL GIVE HIM THE ICE-CREAM CONE ! OBOY !
POP ! OH, POP ! LOOK WHAT I GOT FOR YOU !
?
POP ! COME OUT !! I'VE GOT AN ICE-CREAM CONE FOR YOU !
I'LL TAKE THAT, LULU

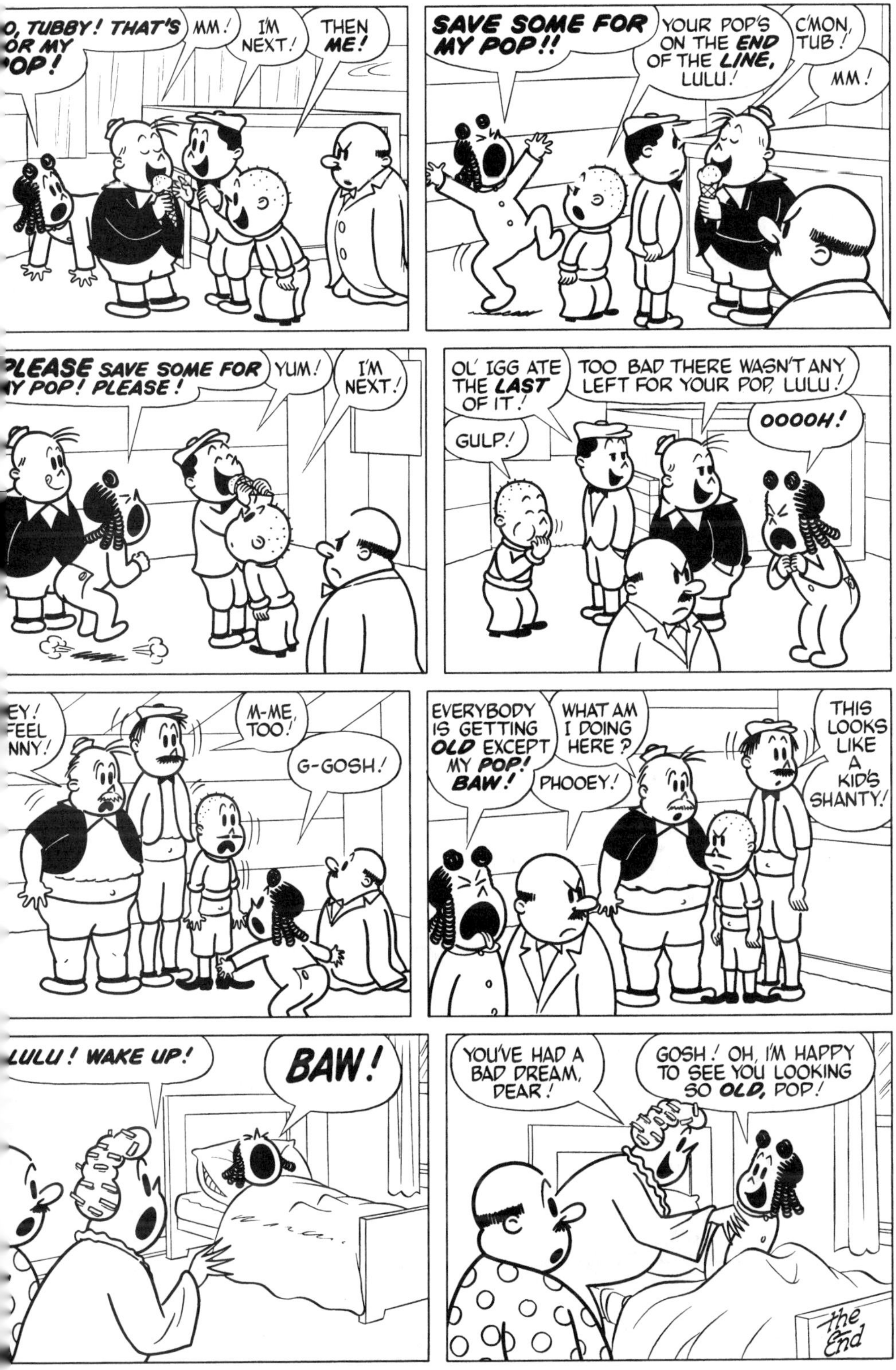
O, TUBBY! THAT'S OR MY OP!
MM!
I'M NEXT!
THEN ME!
SAVE SOME FOR MY POP!!
YOUR POP'S ON THE END OF THE LINE, LULU!
C'MON, TUB!
MM!
PLEASE SAVE SOME FOR Y POP! PLEASE!
YUM!
I'M NEXT!
OL' IGG ATE THE LAST OF IT!
TOO BAD THERE WASN'T ANY LEFT FOR YOUR POP, LULU!
GULP!
OOOOH!
EY! FEEL NNY!
M-ME, TOO!
G-GOSH!
EVERYBODY IS GETTING OLD EXCEPT MY POP! BAW!
WHAT AM I DOING HERE?
PHOOEY!
THIS LOOKS LIKE A KID'S SHANTY!
LULU! WAKE UP!
BAW!
YOU'VE HAD A BAD DREAM, DEAR!
GOSH! OH, I'M HAPPY TO SEE YOU LOOKING SO OLD, POP!
the End

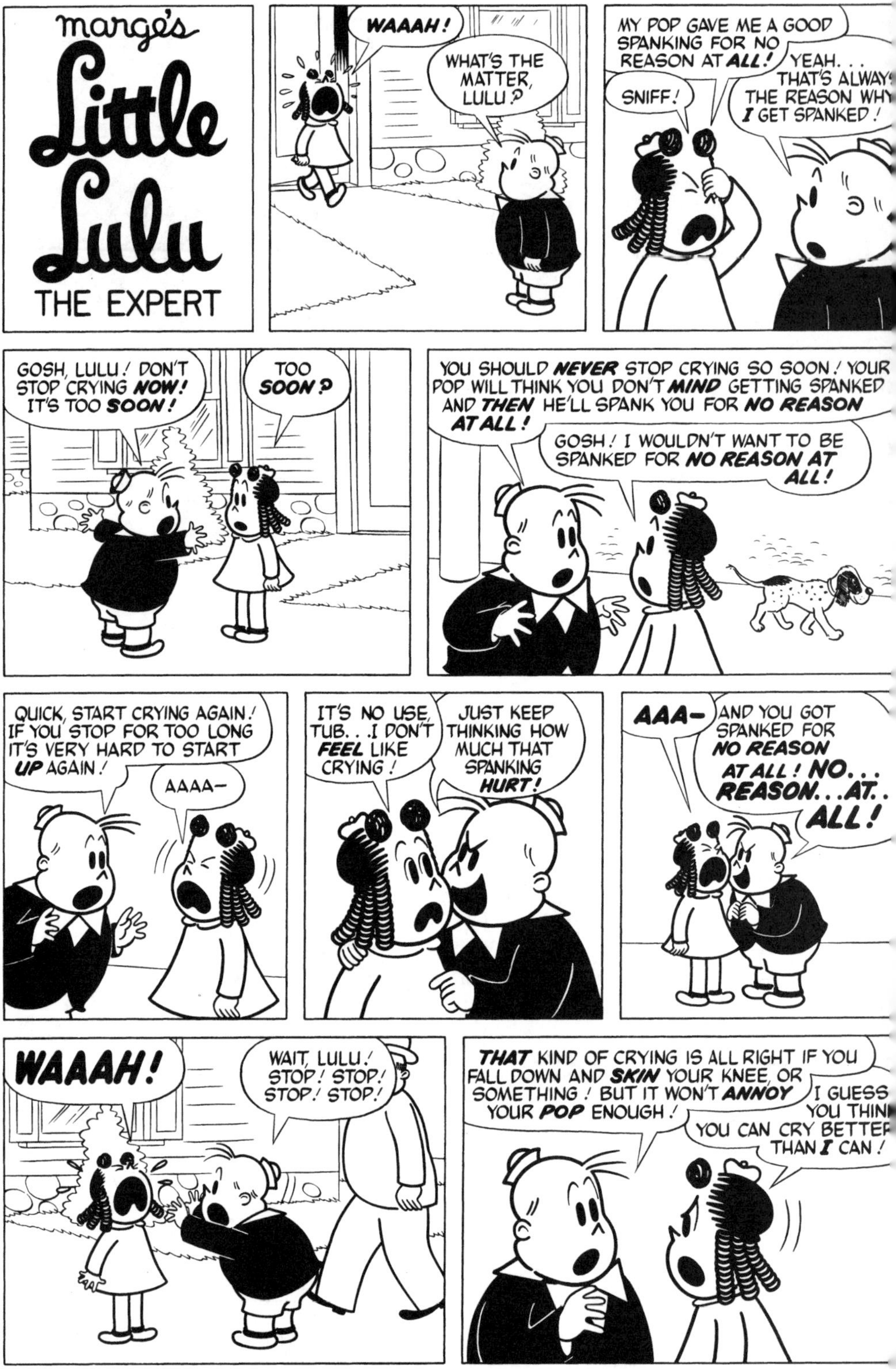
marge's
Little Lulu
THE EXPERT
WAAAH!
WHAT'S THE MATTER, LULU?
MY POP GAVE ME A GOOD SPANKING FOR NO REASON AT ALL!
SNIFF!
YEAH. . . THAT'S ALWAYS THE REASON WHY I GET SPANKED!
GOSH, LULU! DON'T STOP CRYING NOW! IT'S TOO SOON!
TOO SOON?
YOU SHOULD NEVER STOP CRYING SO SOON! YOUR POP WILL THINK YOU DON'T MIND GETTING SPANKED AND THEN HE'LL SPANK YOU FOR NO REASON AT ALL!
GOSH! I WOULDN'T WANT TO BE SPANKED FOR NO REASON AT ALL!
QUICK, START CRYING AGAIN! IF YOU STOP FOR TOO LONG IT'S VERY HARD TO START UP AGAIN!
AAAA—
IT'S NO USE, TUB. . . I DON'T FEEL LIKE CRYING!
JUST KEEP THINKING HOW MUCH THAT SPANKING HURT!
AAA—
AND YOU GOT SPANKED FOR NO REASON AT ALL! NO. . . REASON. . . AT. . . ALL!
WAAAH!
WAIT, LULU! STOP! STOP! STOP! STOP!
THAT KIND OF CRYING IS ALL RIGHT IF YOU FALL DOWN AND SKIN YOUR KNEE, OR SOMETHING! BUT IT WON'T ANNOY YOUR POP ENOUGH!
I GUESS YOU THINK YOU CAN CRY BETTER THAN I CAN!

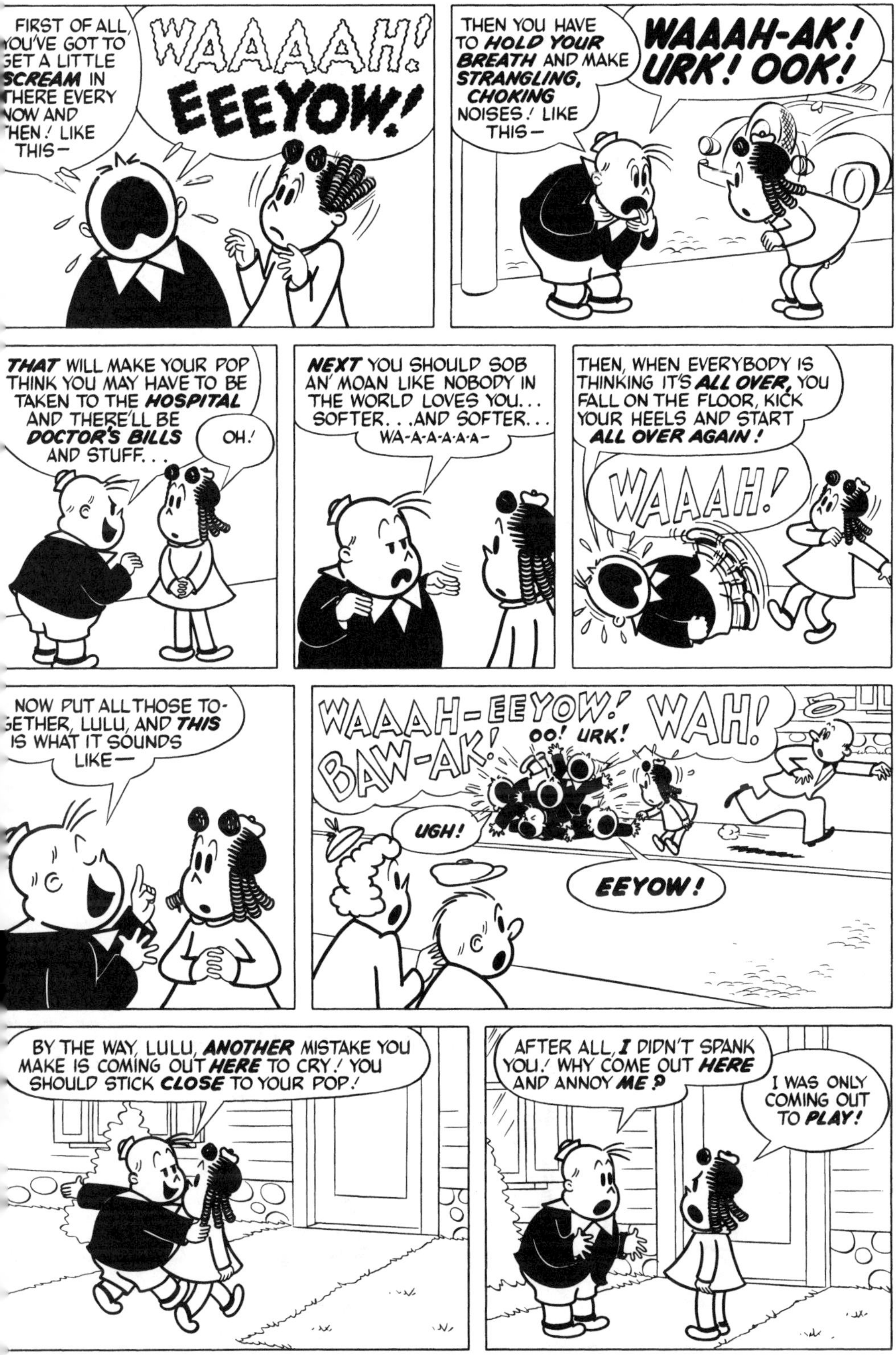

FIRST OF ALL, YOU'VE GOT TO GET A LITTLE SCREAM IN THERE EVERY NOW AND THEN! LIKE THIS—
WAAAAAH! EEEYOW!
THEN YOU HAVE TO HOLD YOUR BREATH AND MAKE STRANGLING, CHOKING NOISES! LIKE THIS—
WAAAH-AK! URK! OOK!
THAT WILL MAKE YOUR POP THINK YOU MAY HAVE TO BE TAKEN TO THE HOSPITAL AND THERE'LL BE DOCTOR'S BILLS AND STUFF. . .
OH!
NEXT YOU SHOULD SOB AN' MOAN LIKE NOBODY IN THE WORLD LOVES YOU. . . SOFTER. . .AND SOFTER. . .
WA-A-A-A-A-A—
THEN, WHEN EVERYBODY IS THINKING IT'S ALL OVER, YOU FALL ON THE FLOOR, KICK YOUR HEELS AND START ALL OVER AGAIN!
WAAAH!
NOW PUT ALL THOSE TOGETHER, LULU, AND THIS IS WHAT IT SOUNDS LIKE—
WAAAH-EEYOW! WAH!
BAW-AK!
OO! URK!
UGH!
EEYOW!
BY THE WAY, LULU, ANOTHER MISTAKE YOU MAKE IS COMING OUT HERE TO CRY! YOU SHOULD STICK CLOSE TO YOUR POP!
AFTER ALL, I DIDN'T SPANK YOU! WHY COME OUT HERE AND ANNOY ME?
I WAS ONLY COMING OUT TO PLAY!

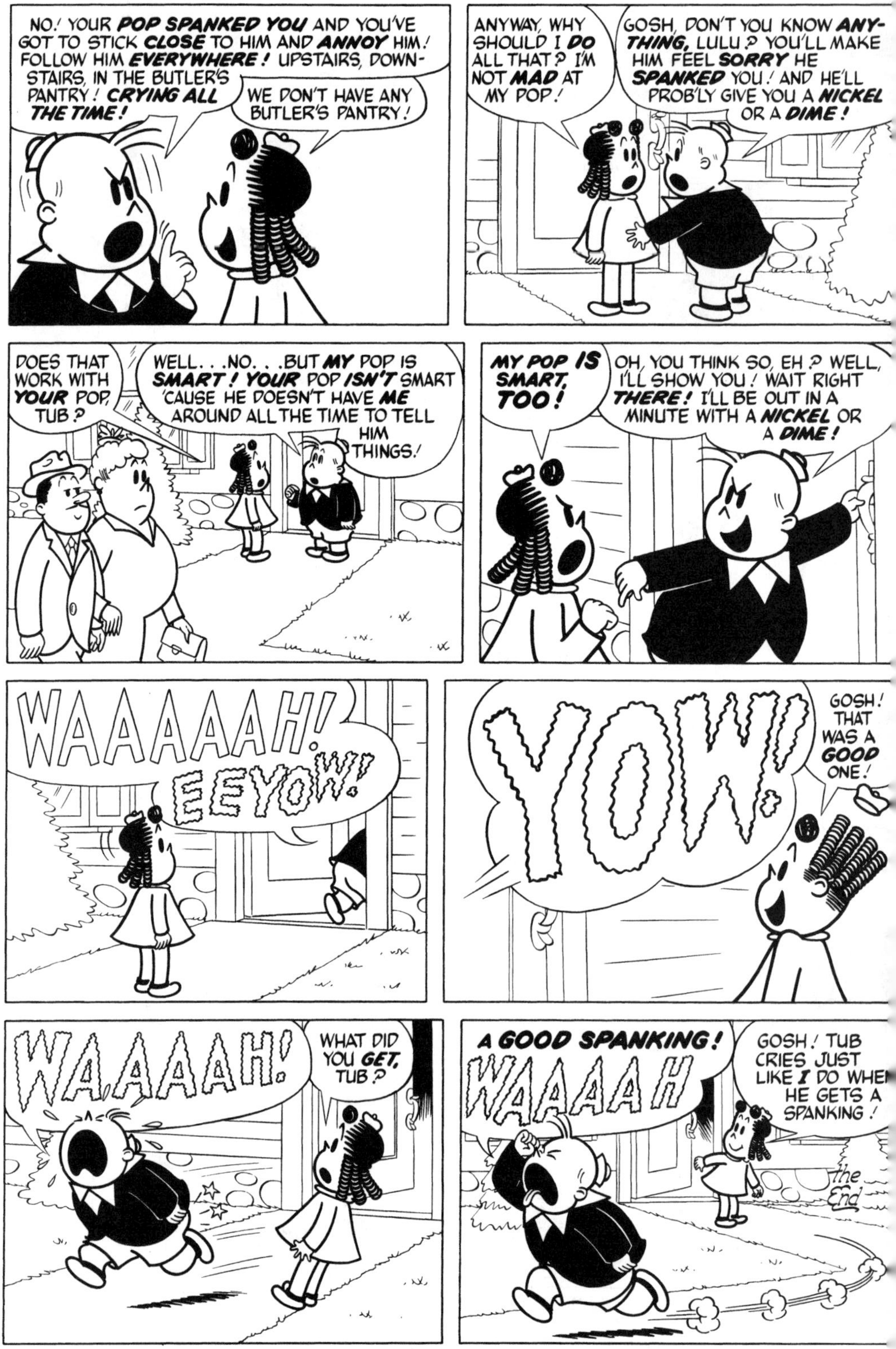
NO! YOUR POP SPANKED YOU AND YOU'VE GOT TO STICK CLOSE TO HIM AND ANNOY HIM! FOLLOW HIM EVERYWHERE! UPSTAIRS, DOWN-STAIRS, IN THE BUTLER'S PANTRY! CRYING ALL THE TIME!
WE DON'T HAVE ANY BUTLER'S PANTRY!
ANYWAY, WHY SHOULD I DO ALL THAT? I'M NOT MAD AT MY POP!
GOSH, DON'T YOU KNOW ANY-THING, LULU? YOU'LL MAKE HIM FEEL SORRY HE SPANKED YOU! AND HE'LL PROB'LY GIVE YOU A NICKEL OR A DIME!
DOES THAT WORK WITH YOUR POP, TUB?
WELL. . .NO. . .BUT MY POP IS SMART! YOUR POP ISN'T SMART 'CAUSE HE DOESN'T HAVE ME AROUND ALL THE TIME TO TELL HIM THINGS!
MY POP IS SMART, TOO!
OH, YOU THINK SO, EH? WELL, I'LL SHOW YOU! WAIT RIGHT THERE! I'LL BE OUT IN A MINUTE WITH A NICKEL OR A DIME!
WAAAAAH!
EEYOW!
YOW!
GOSH! THAT WAS A GOOD ONE!
WAAAAH!
WHAT DID YOU GET, TUB?
A GOOD SPANKING!
WAAAAH
GOSH! TUB CRIES JUST LIKE I DO WHEN HE GETS A SPANKING!
The End

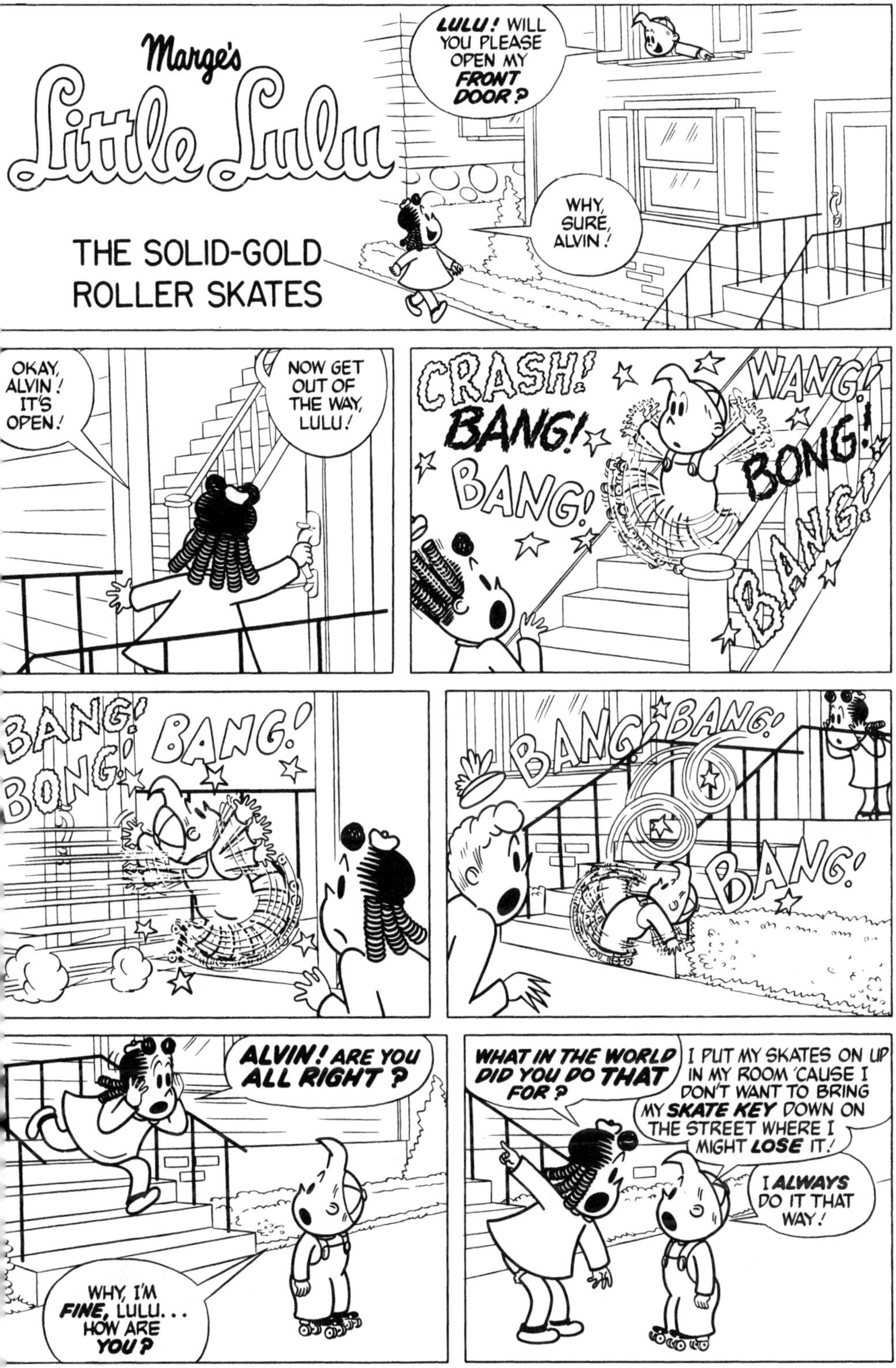

Marge's Little Lulu
THE SOLID-GOLD ROLLER SKATES
LULU! WILL YOU PLEASE OPEN MY FRONT DOOR?
WHY, SURE, ALVIN!
OKAY, ALVIN! IT'S OPEN!
NOW GET OUT OF THE WAY, LULU!
CRASH! BANG! BANG! WANG! BONG! BANG!
BANG! BONG! BANG!
BANG! BANG! BANG!
ALVIN! ARE YOU ALL RIGHT?
WHY, I'M FINE, LULU... HOW ARE YOU?
WHAT IN THE WORLD DID YOU DO THAT FOR?
I PUT MY SKATES ON UP IN MY ROOM 'CAUSE I DON'T WANT TO BRING MY SKATE KEY DOWN ON THE STREET WHERE I MIGHT LOSE IT!
I ALWAYS DO IT THAT WAY!

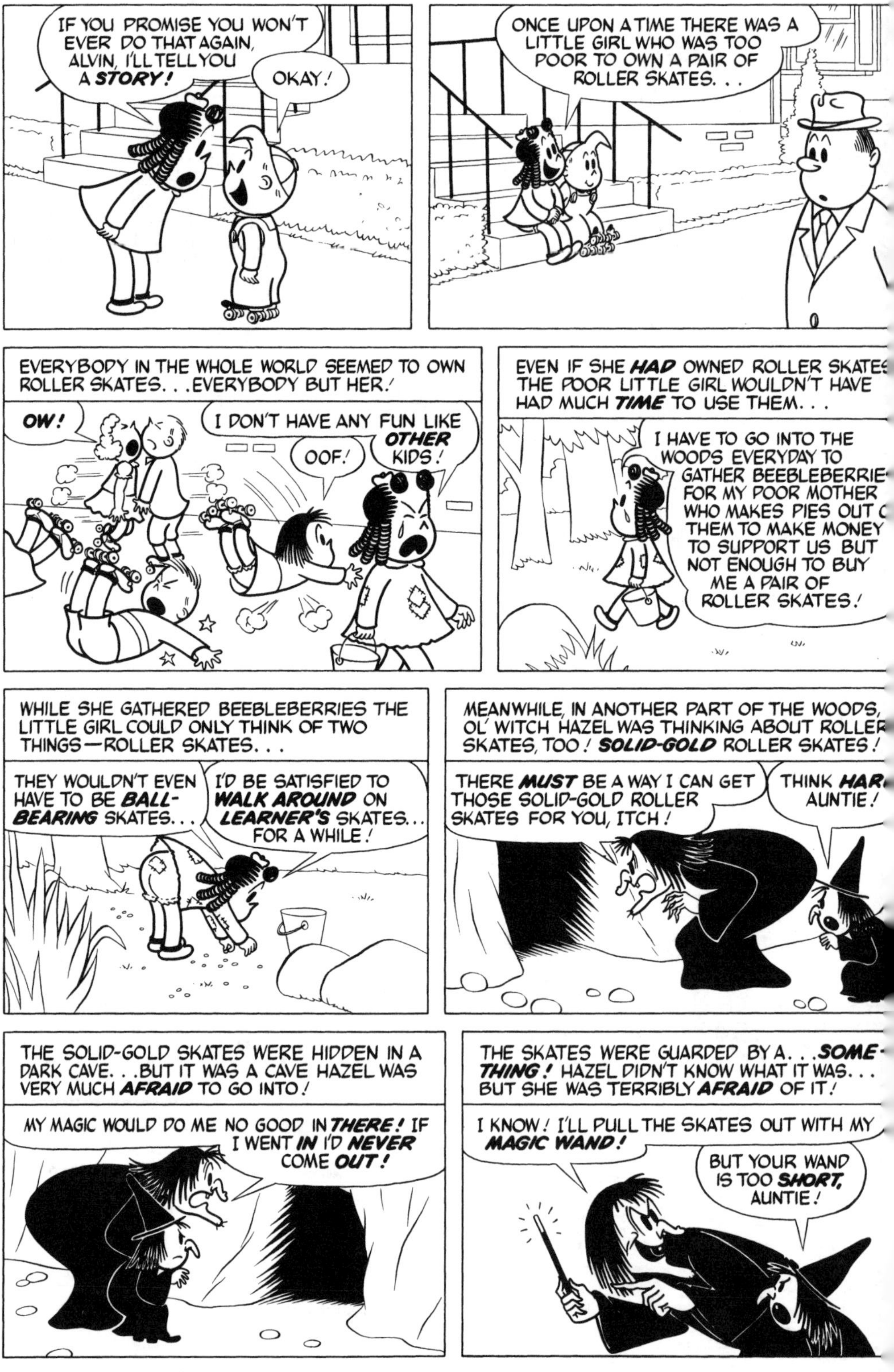
IF YOU PROMISE YOU WON'T EVER DO THAT AGAIN, ALVIN, I'LL TELL YOU A STORY!
OKAY!
ONCE UPON A TIME THERE WAS A LITTLE GIRL WHO WAS TOO POOR TO OWN A PAIR OF ROLLER SKATES. . .
EVERYBODY IN THE WHOLE WORLD SEEMED TO OWN ROLLER SKATES. . .EVERYBODY BUT HER!
OW!
I DON'T HAVE ANY FUN LIKE OTHER KIDS!
OOF!
EVEN IF SHE HAD OWNED ROLLER SKATES THE POOR LITTLE GIRL WOULDN'T HAVE HAD MUCH TIME TO USE THEM. . .
I HAVE TO GO INTO THE WOODS EVERYDAY TO GATHER BEEBLEBERRIES FOR MY POOR MOTHER WHO MAKES PIES OUT OF THEM TO MAKE MONEY TO SUPPORT US BUT NOT ENOUGH TO BUY ME A PAIR OF ROLLER SKATES!
WHILE SHE GATHERED BEEBLEBERRIES THE LITTLE GIRL COULD ONLY THINK OF TWO THINGS—ROLLER SKATES. . .
THEY WOULDN'T EVEN HAVE TO BE BALL-BEARING SKATES. . .
I'D BE SATISFIED TO WALK AROUND ON LEARNER'S SKATES. . . FOR A WHILE!
MEANWHILE, IN ANOTHER PART OF THE WOODS, OL' WITCH HAZEL WAS THINKING ABOUT ROLLER SKATES, TOO! SOLID-GOLD ROLLER SKATES!
THERE MUST BE A WAY I CAN GET THOSE SOLID-GOLD ROLLER SKATES FOR YOU, ITCH!
AUNTIE!
THE SOLID-GOLD SKATES WERE HIDDEN IN A DARK CAVE. . .BUT IT WAS A CAVE HAZEL WAS VERY MUCH AFRAID TO GO INTO!
MY MAGIC WOULD DO ME NO GOOD IN THERE! IF I WENT IN I'D NEVER COME OUT!
THE SKATES WERE GUARDED BY A. . .SOME-THING! HAZEL DIDN'T KNOW WHAT IT WAS. . . BUT SHE WAS TERRIBLY AFRAID OF IT!
I KNOW! I'LL PULL THE SKATES OUT WITH MY MAGIC WAND!
BUT YOUR WAND IS TOO SHORT, AUNTIE!

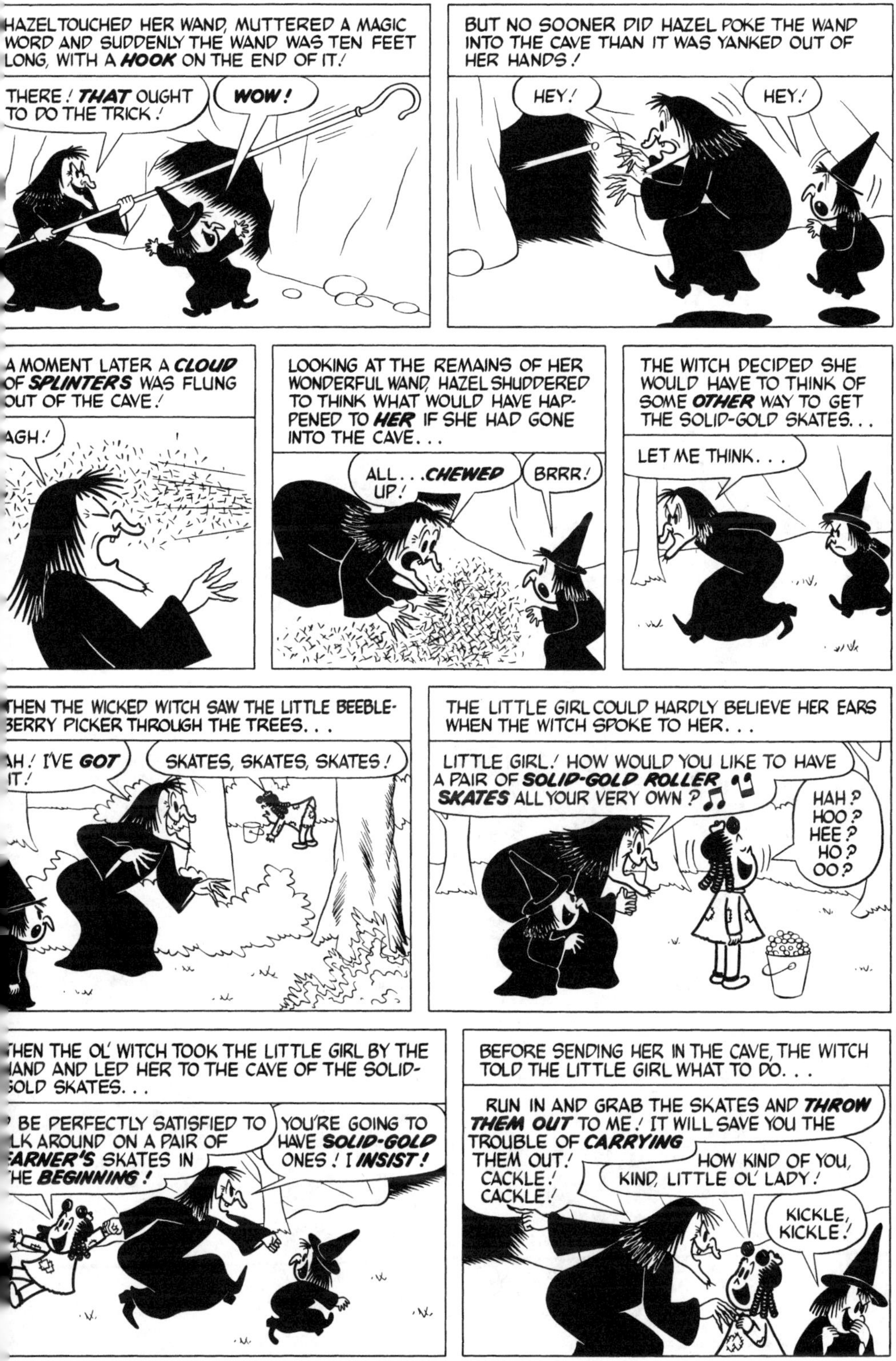
HAZEL TOUCHED HER WAND, MUTTERED A MAGIC WORD AND SUDDENLY THE WAND WAS TEN FEET LONG, WITH A HOOK ON THE END OF IT!
THERE! THAT OUGHT TO DO THE TRICK!
WOW!
BUT NO SOONER DID HAZEL POKE THE WAND INTO THE CAVE THAN IT WAS YANKED OUT OF HER HANDS!
HEY!
HEY!
A MOMENT LATER A CLOUD OF SPLINTERS WAS FLUNG OUT OF THE CAVE!
AGH!
LOOKING AT THE REMAINS OF HER WONDERFUL WAND, HAZEL SHUDDERED TO THINK WHAT WOULD HAVE HAPPENED TO HER IF SHE HAD GONE INTO THE CAVE...
ALL...CHEWED UP!
BRRR!
THE WITCH DECIDED SHE WOULD HAVE TO THINK OF SOME OTHER WAY TO GET THE SOLID-GOLD SKATES...
LET ME THINK...
THEN THE WICKED WITCH SAW THE LITTLE BEEBLEBERRY PICKER THROUGH THE TREES...
AH! I'VE GOT IT!
SKATES, SKATES, SKATES!
THE LITTLE GIRL COULD HARDLY BELIEVE HER EARS WHEN THE WITCH SPOKE TO HER...
LITTLE GIRL! HOW WOULD YOU LIKE TO HAVE A PAIR OF SOLID-GOLD ROLLER SKATES ALL YOUR VERY OWN?
HAH? HOO? HEE? HO? OO?
THEN THE OL' WITCH TOOK THE LITTLE GIRL BY THE HAND AND LED HER TO THE CAVE OF THE SOLID-GOLD SKATES...
BE PERFECTLY SATISFIED TO LK AROUND ON A PAIR OF ARNER'S SKATES IN HE BEGINNING!
YOU'RE GOING TO HAVE SOLID-GOLD ONES! I INSIST!
BEFORE SENDING HER IN THE CAVE, THE WITCH TOLD THE LITTLE GIRL WHAT TO DO...
RUN IN AND GRAB THE SKATES AND THROW THEM OUT TO ME! IT WILL SAVE YOU THE TROUBLE OF CARRYING THEM OUT! CACKLE! CACKLE!
HOW KIND OF YOU, KIND, LITTLE OL' LADY!
KICKLE, KICKLE!

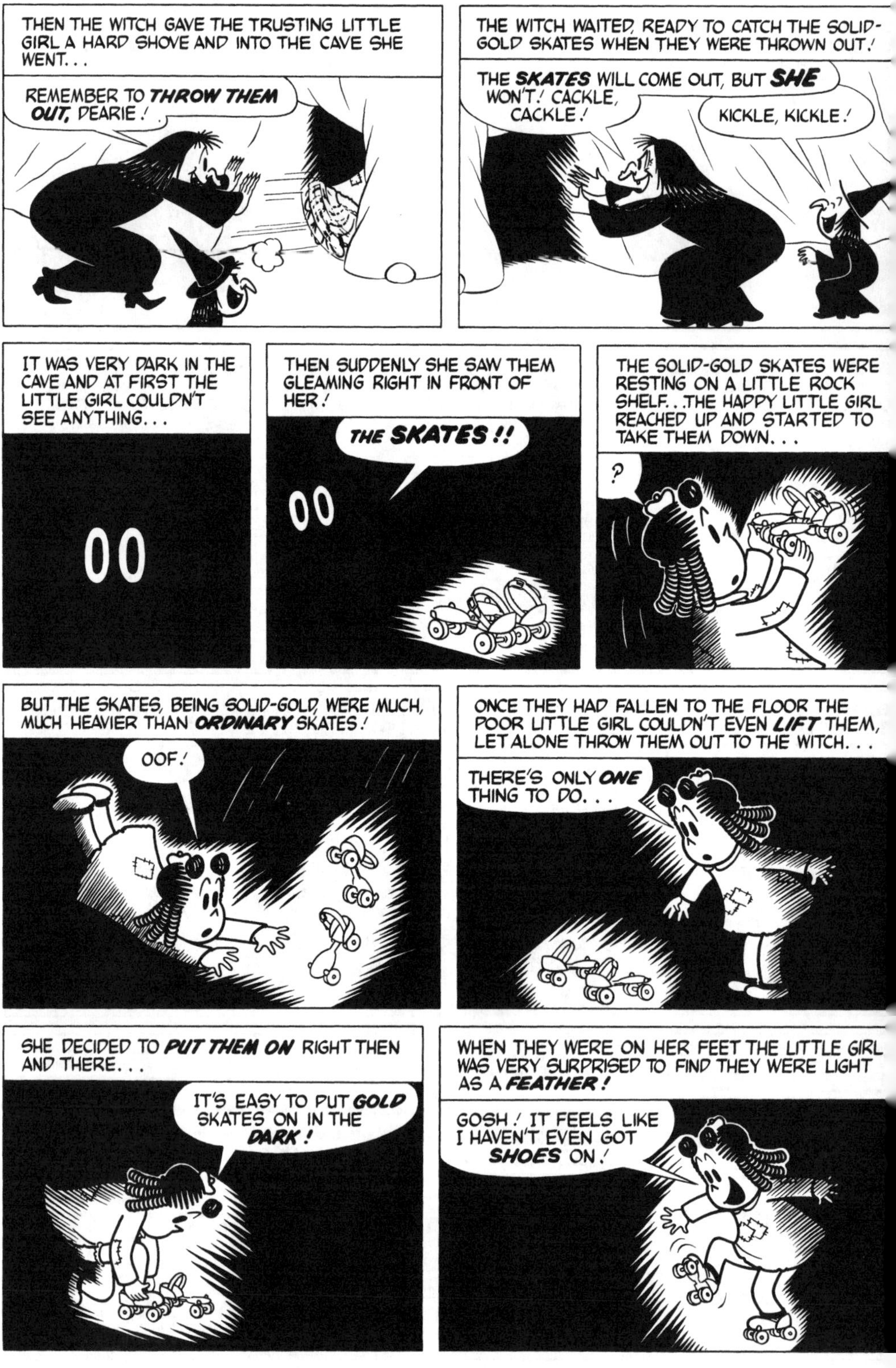
THEN THE WITCH GAVE THE TRUSTING LITTLE GIRL A HARD SHOVE AND INTO THE CAVE SHE WENT. . .
REMEMBER TO THROW THEM OUT, DEARIE!
THE WITCH WAITED, READY TO CATCH THE SOLID-GOLD SKATES WHEN THEY WERE THROWN OUT!
THE SKATES WILL COME OUT, BUT SHE WON'T! CACKLE, CACKLE!
KICKLE, KICKLE!
IT WAS VERY DARK IN THE CAVE AND AT FIRST THE LITTLE GIRL COULDN'T SEE ANYTHING. . .
THEN SUDDENLY SHE SAW THEM GLEAMING RIGHT IN FRONT OF HER!
THE SKATES!!
THE SOLID-GOLD SKATES WERE RESTING ON A LITTLE ROCK SHELF. . .THE HAPPY LITTLE GIRL REACHED UP AND STARTED TO TAKE THEM DOWN. . .
?
BUT THE SKATES, BEING SOLID-GOLD, WERE MUCH, MUCH HEAVIER THAN ORDINARY SKATES!
OOF!
ONCE THEY HAD FALLEN TO THE FLOOR THE POOR LITTLE GIRL COULDN'T EVEN LIFT THEM, LET ALONE THROW THEM OUT TO THE WITCH. . .
THERE'S ONLY ONE THING TO DO. . .
SHE DECIDED TO PUT THEM ON RIGHT THEN AND THERE. . .
IT'S EASY TO PUT GOLD SKATES ON IN THE DARK!
WHEN THEY WERE ON HER FEET THE LITTLE GIRL WAS VERY SURPRISED TO FIND THEY WERE LIGHT AS A FEATHER!
GOSH! IT FEELS LIKE I HAVEN'T EVEN GOT SHOES ON!

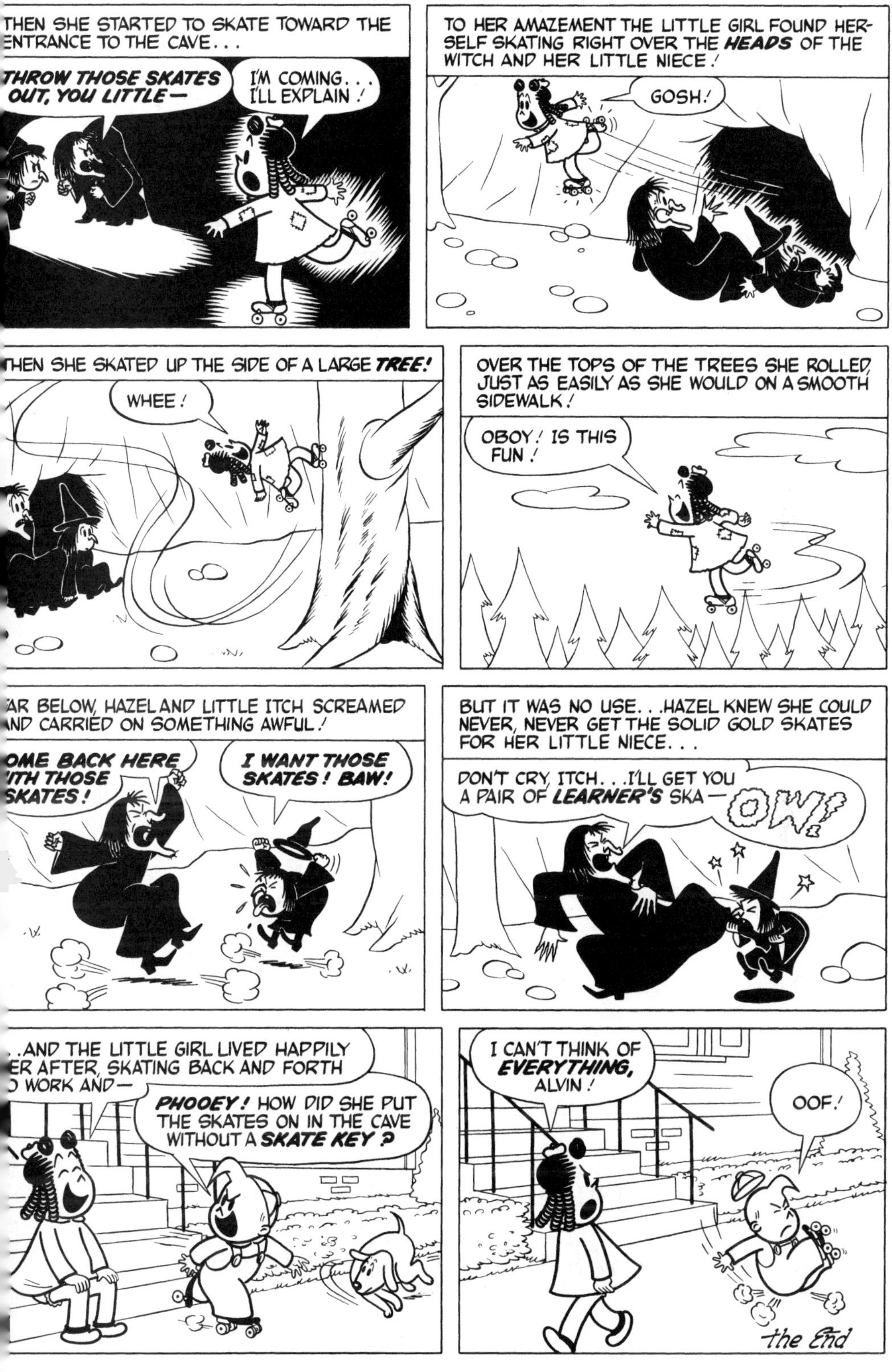
THEN SHE STARTED TO SKATE TOWARD THE ENTRANCE TO THE CAVE...
THROW THOSE SKATES OUT, YOU LITTLE—
I'M COMING... I'LL EXPLAIN!
TO HER AMAZEMENT THE LITTLE GIRL FOUND HERSELF SKATING RIGHT OVER THE HEADS OF THE WITCH AND HER LITTLE NIECE!
GOSH!
THEN SHE SKATED UP THE SIDE OF A LARGE TREE!
WHEE!
OVER THE TOPS OF THE TREES SHE ROLLED, JUST AS EASILY AS SHE WOULD ON A SMOOTH SIDEWALK!
OBOY! IS THIS FUN!
AR BELOW, HAZEL AND LITTLE ITCH SCREAMED ND CARRIED ON SOMETHING AWFUL!
OME BACK HERE ITH THOSE SKATES!
I WANT THOSE SKATES! BAW!
BUT IT WAS NO USE...HAZEL KNEW SHE COULD NEVER, NEVER GET THE SOLID GOLD SKATES FOR HER LITTLE NIECE...
DON'T CRY, ITCH...I'LL GET YOU A PAIR OF LEARNER'S SKA—
OW!
..AND THE LITTLE GIRL LIVED HAPPILY ER AFTER, SKATING BACK AND FORTH O WORK AND—
PHOOEY! HOW DID SHE PUT THE SKATES ON IN THE CAVE WITHOUT A SKATE KEY?
I CAN'T THINK OF EVERYTHING, ALVIN!
OOF!
the End

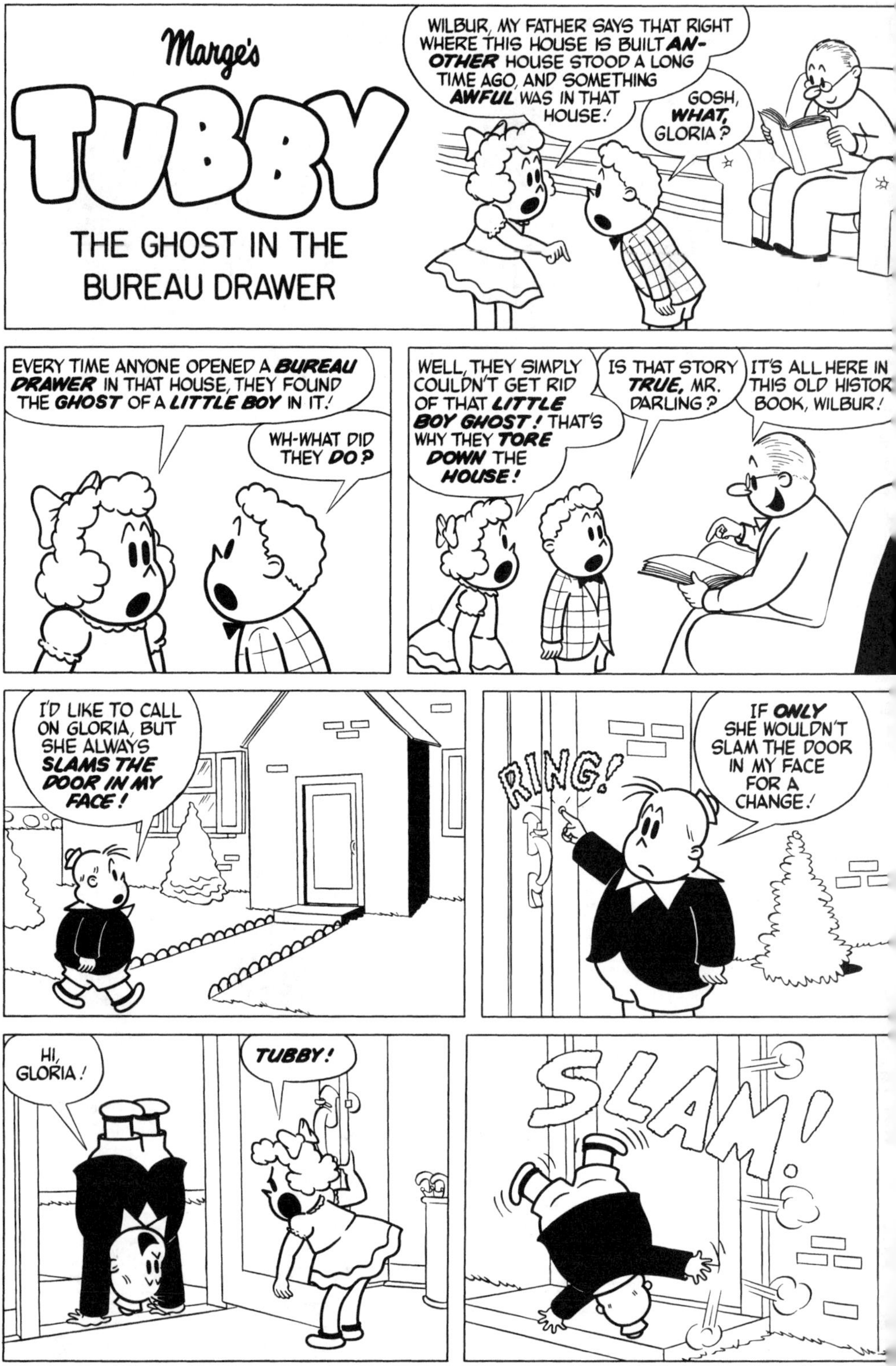
Marge's
TUBBY
THE GHOST IN THE BUREAU DRAWER
WILBUR, MY FATHER SAYS THAT RIGHT WHERE THIS HOUSE IS BUILT ANOTHER HOUSE STOOD A LONG TIME AGO, AND SOMETHING AWFUL WAS IN THAT HOUSE!
GOSH, WHAT, GLORIA?
EVERY TIME ANYONE OPENED A BUREAU DRAWER IN THAT HOUSE, THEY FOUND THE GHOST OF A LITTLE BOY IN IT!
WH-WHAT DID THEY DO?
WELL, THEY SIMPLY COULDN'T GET RID OF THAT LITTLE BOY GHOST! THAT'S WHY THEY TORE DOWN THE HOUSE!
IS THAT STORY TRUE, MR. DARLING?
IT'S ALL HERE IN THIS OLD HISTOR BOOK, WILBUR!
I'D LIKE TO CALL ON GLORIA, BUT SHE ALWAYS SLAMS THE DOOR IN MY FACE!
RING!
IF ONLY SHE WOULDN'T SLAM THE DOOR IN MY FACE FOR A CHANGE!
HI, GLORIA!
TUBBY!
SLAM!

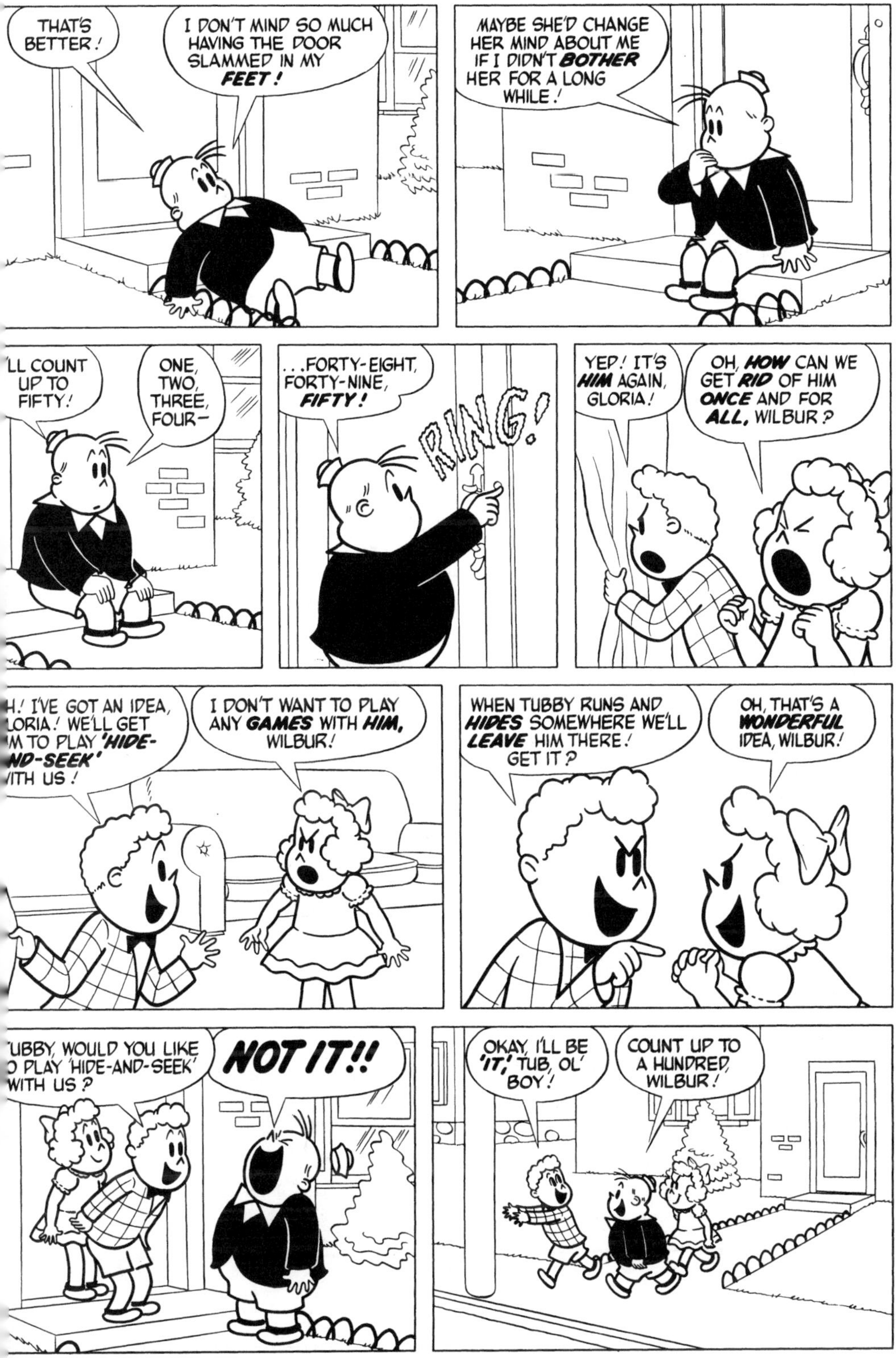
THAT'S BETTER!
I DON'T MIND SO MUCH HAVING THE DOOR SLAMMED IN MY FEET!
MAYBE SHE'D CHANGE HER MIND ABOUT ME IF I DIDN'T BOTHER HER FOR A LONG WHILE!
'LL COUNT UP TO FIFTY!
ONE, TWO, THREE, FOUR—
...FORTY-EIGHT, FORTY-NINE, FIFTY!
RING!
YEP! IT'S HIM AGAIN, GLORIA!
OH, HOW CAN WE GET RID OF HIM ONCE AND FOR ALL, WILBUR?
H! I'VE GOT AN IDEA, LORIA! WE'LL GET M TO PLAY 'HIDE- ND-SEEK' VITH US!
I DON'T WANT TO PLAY ANY GAMES WITH HIM, WILBUR!
WHEN TUBBY RUNS AND HIDES SOMEWHERE WE'LL LEAVE HIM THERE! GET IT?
OH, THAT'S A WONDERFUL IDEA, WILBUR!
UBBY, WOULD YOU LIKE O PLAY 'HIDE-AND-SEEK' WITH US?
NOT IT!!
OKAY, I'LL BE 'IT,' TUB, OL' BOY!
COUNT UP TO A HUNDRED, WILBUR!

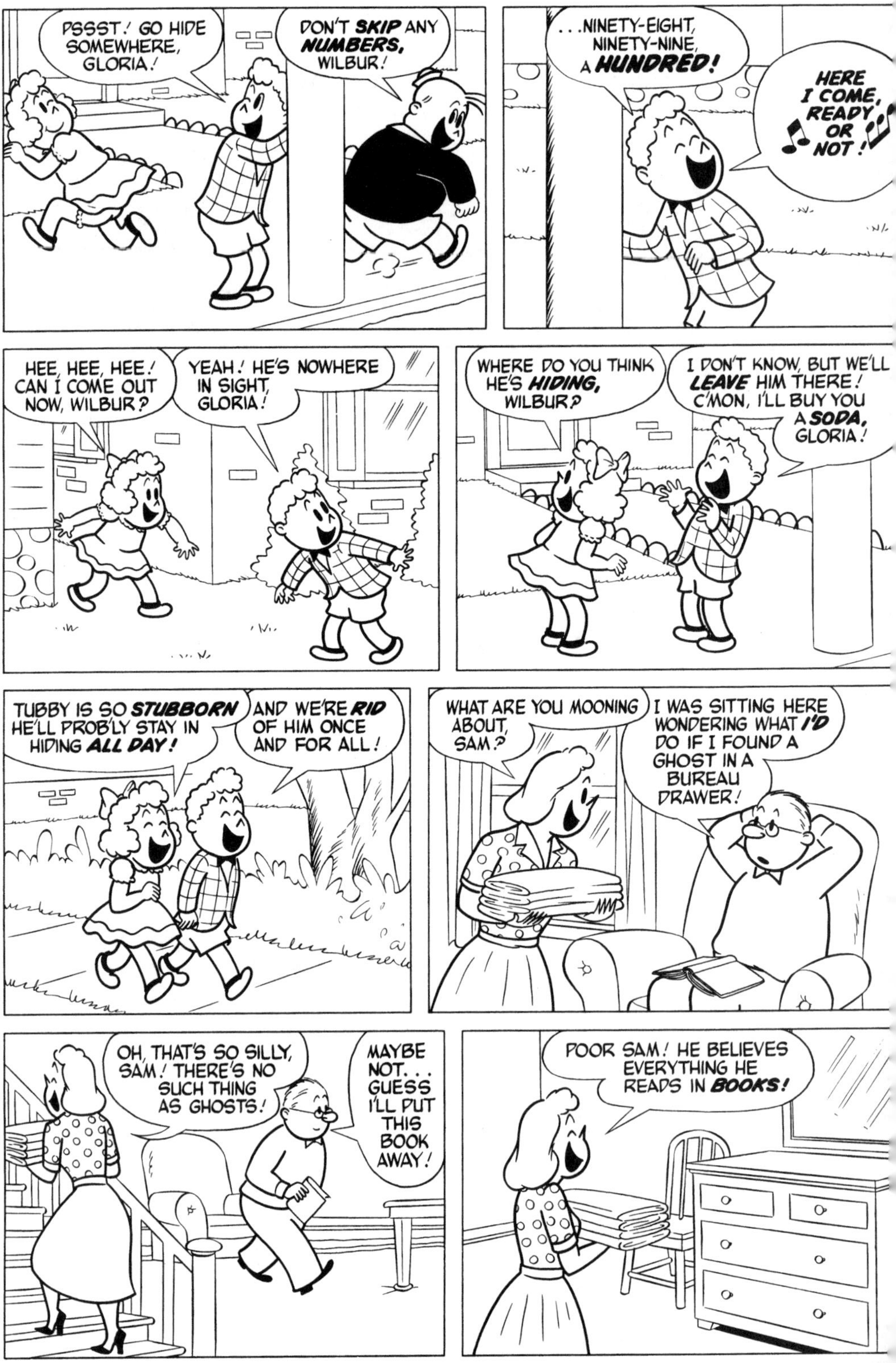
PSSST! GO HIDE SOMEWHERE, GLORIA!
DON'T SKIP ANY NUMBERS, WILBUR!
...NINETY-EIGHT, NINETY-NINE, A HUNDRED!
HERE I COME, READY OR NOT!
HEE, HEE, HEE! CAN I COME OUT NOW, WILBUR?
YEAH! HE'S NOWHERE IN SIGHT, GLORIA!
WHERE DO YOU THINK HE'S HIDING, WILBUR?
I DON'T KNOW, BUT WE'LL LEAVE HIM THERE! C'MON, I'LL BUY YOU A SODA, GLORIA!
TUBBY IS SO STUBBORN HE'LL PROB'LY STAY IN HIDING ALL DAY!
AND WE'RE RID OF HIM ONCE AND FOR ALL!
WHAT ARE YOU MOONING ABOUT, SAM?
I WAS SITTING HERE WONDERING WHAT I'D DO IF I FOUND A GHOST IN A BUREAU DRAWER!
OH, THAT'S SO SILLY, SAM! THERE'S NO SUCH THING AS GHOSTS!
MAYBE NOT... GUESS I'LL PUT THIS BOOK AWAY!
POOR SAM! HE BELIEVES EVERYTHING HE READS IN BOOKS!

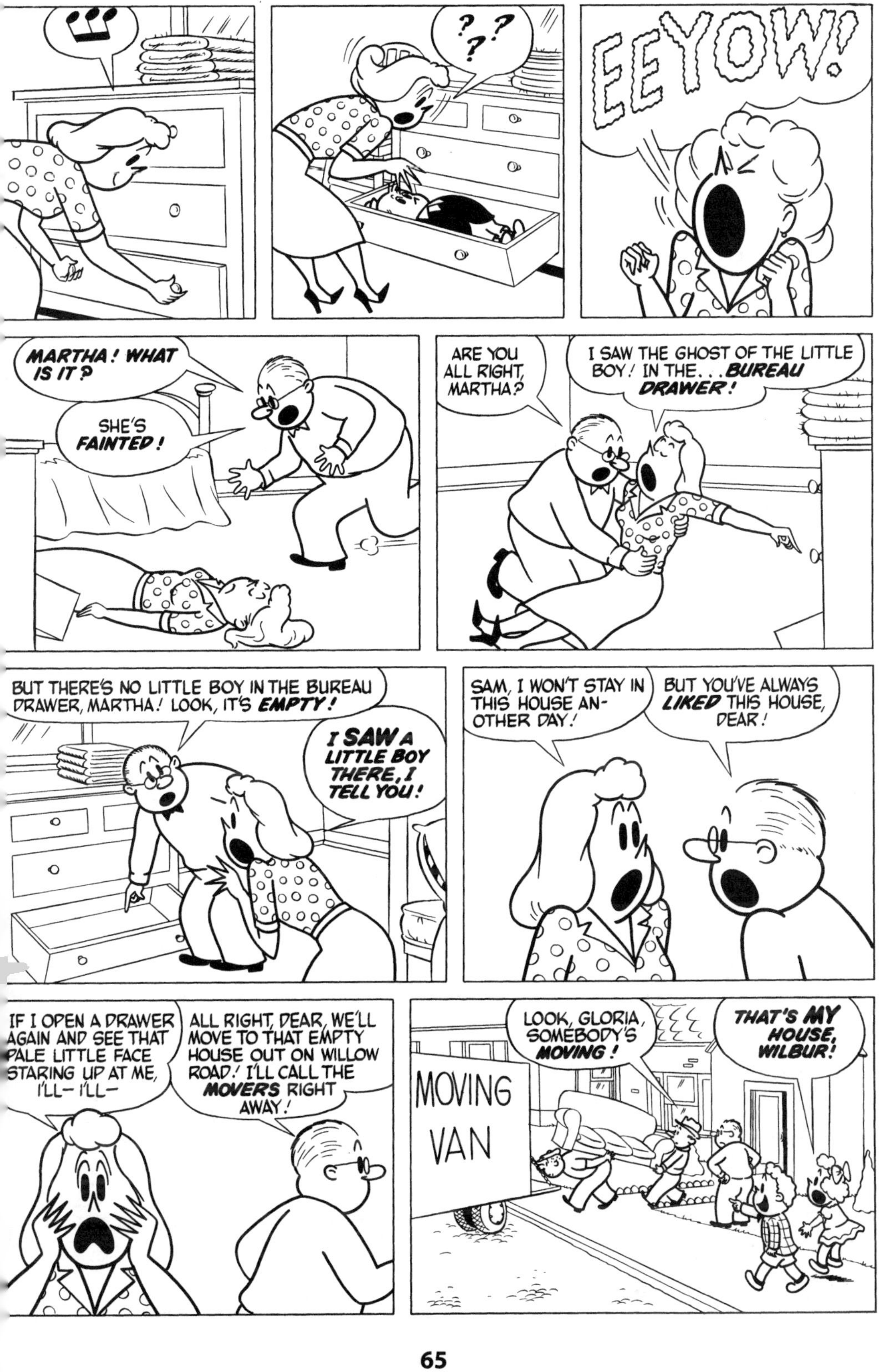

?? ?
EEYOW!
MARTHA! WHAT IS IT?
SHE'S FAINTED!
ARE YOU ALL RIGHT, MARTHA?
I SAW THE GHOST OF THE LITTLE BOY! IN THE. . .BUREAU DRAWER!
BUT THERE'S NO LITTLE BOY IN THE BUREAU DRAWER, MARTHA! LOOK, IT'S EMPTY!
I SAW A LITTLE BOY THERE, I TELL YOU!
SAM, I WON'T STAY IN THIS HOUSE ANOTHER DAY!
BUT YOU'VE ALWAYS LIKED THIS HOUSE, DEAR!
IF I OPEN A DRAWER AGAIN AND SEE THAT PALE LITTLE FACE STARING UP AT ME, I'LL– I'LL–
ALL RIGHT, DEAR, WE'LL MOVE TO THAT EMPTY HOUSE OUT ON WILLOW ROAD! I'LL CALL THE MOVERS RIGHT AWAY!
MOVING VAN
LOOK, GLORIA, SOMEBODY'S MOVING!
THAT'S MY HOUSE, WILBUR!

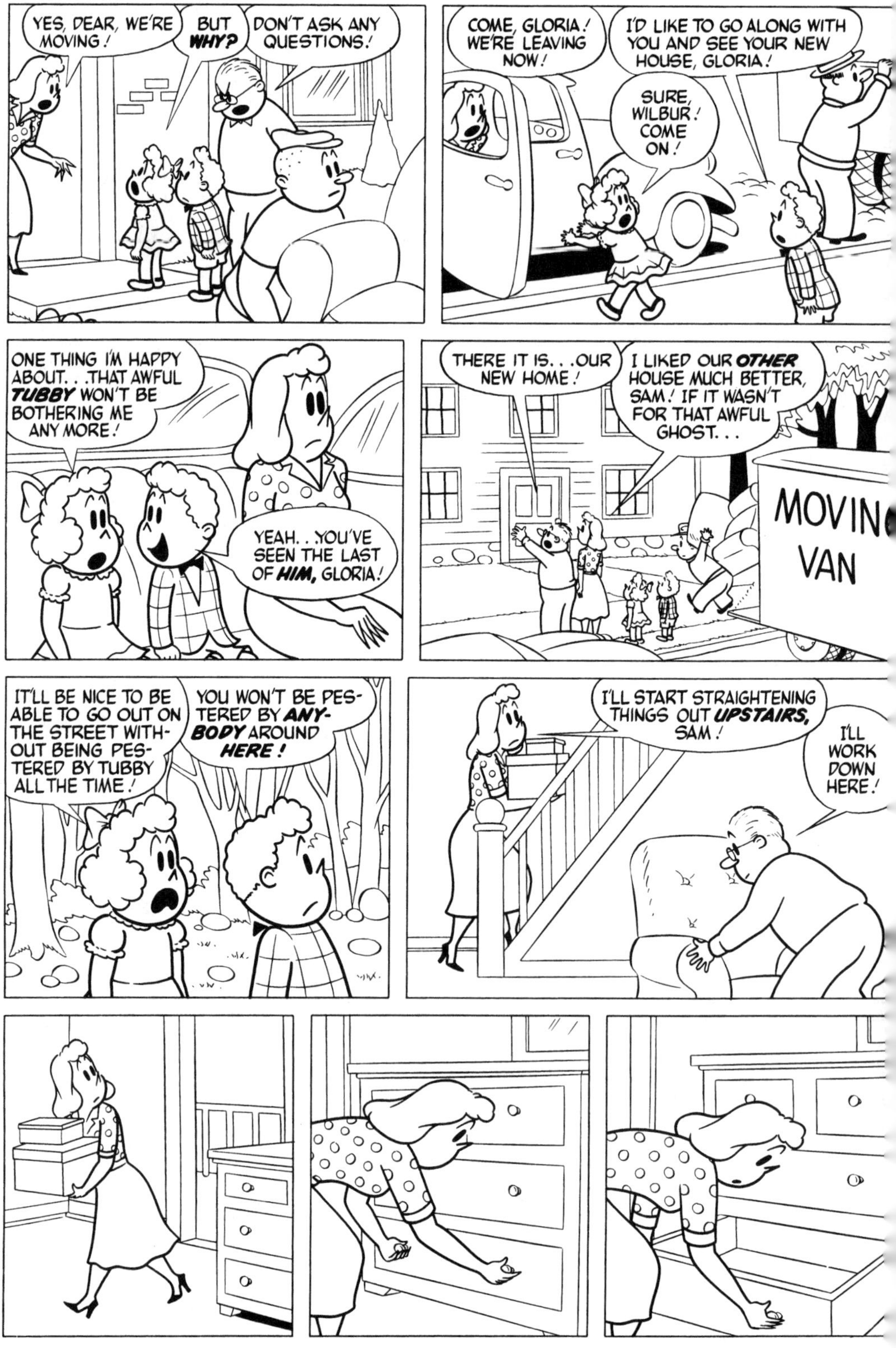
YES, DEAR, WE'RE MOVING!
BUT WHY?
DON'T ASK ANY QUESTIONS!
COME, GLORIA! WE'RE LEAVING NOW!
I'D LIKE TO GO ALONG WITH YOU AND SEE YOUR NEW HOUSE, GLORIA!
SURE, WILBUR! COME ON!
ONE THING I'M HAPPY ABOUT. . .THAT AWFUL TUBBY WON'T BE BOTHERING ME ANY MORE!
YEAH. . .YOU'VE SEEN THE LAST OF HIM, GLORIA!
THERE IT IS. . .OUR NEW HOME!
I LIKED OUR OTHER HOUSE MUCH BETTER, SAM! IF IT WASN'T FOR THAT AWFUL GHOST. . .
MOVING VAN
IT'LL BE NICE TO BE ABLE TO GO OUT ON THE STREET WITHOUT BEING PESTERED BY TUBBY ALL THE TIME!
YOU WON'T BE PESTERED BY ANYBODY AROUND HERE!
I'LL START STRAIGHTENING THINGS OUT UPSTAIRS, SAM!
I'LL WORK DOWN HERE!

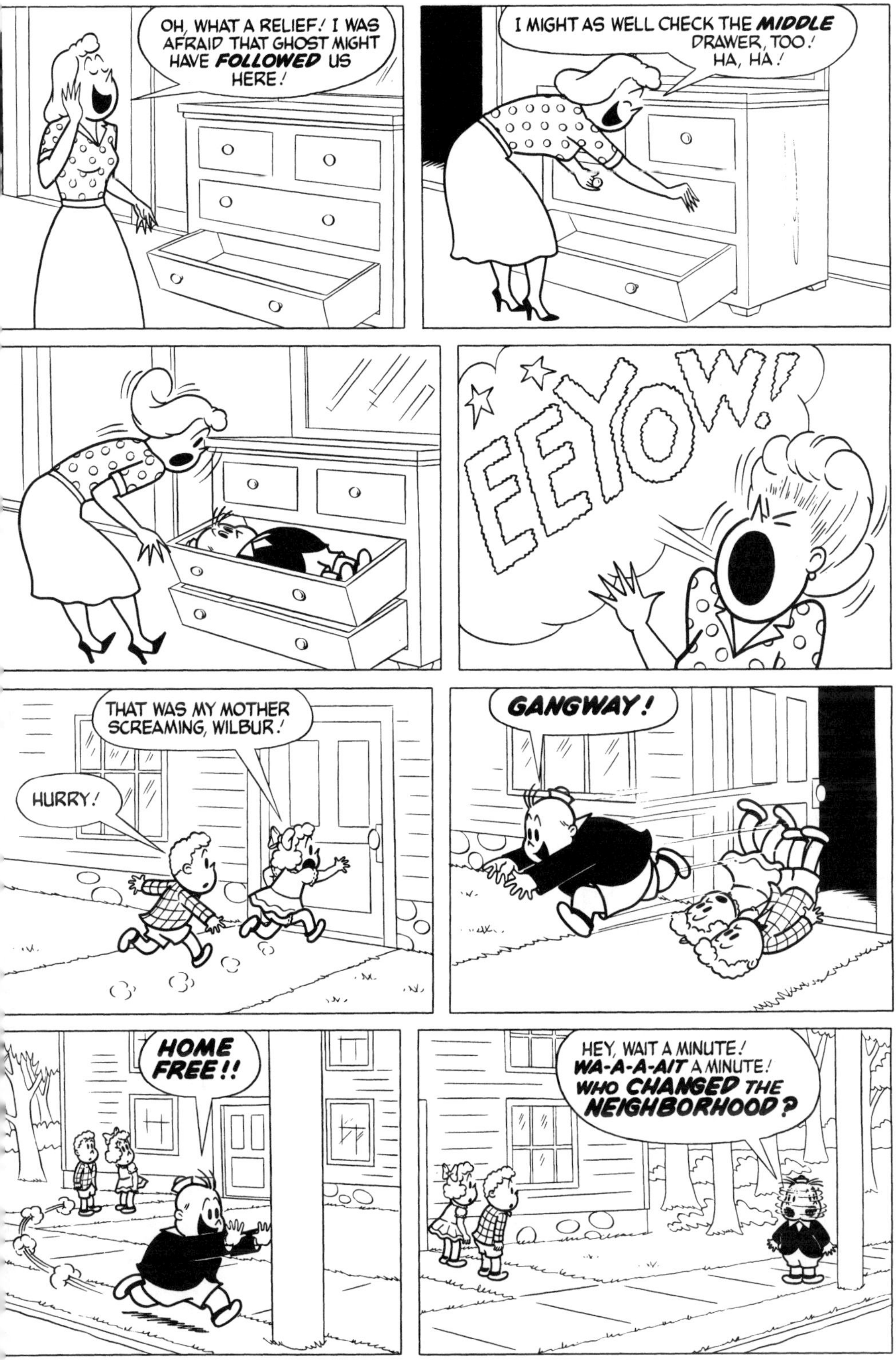
OH, WHAT A RELIEF! I WAS AFRAID THAT GHOST MIGHT HAVE FOLLOWED US HERE!
I MIGHT AS WELL CHECK THE MIDDLE DRAWER, TOO! HA, HA!
EEYOW!
THAT WAS MY MOTHER SCREAMING, WILBUR!
HURRY!
GANGWAY!
HOME FREE!!
HEY, WAIT A MINUTE! WA-A-A-AIT A MINUTE! WHO CHANGED THE NEIGHBORHOOD?

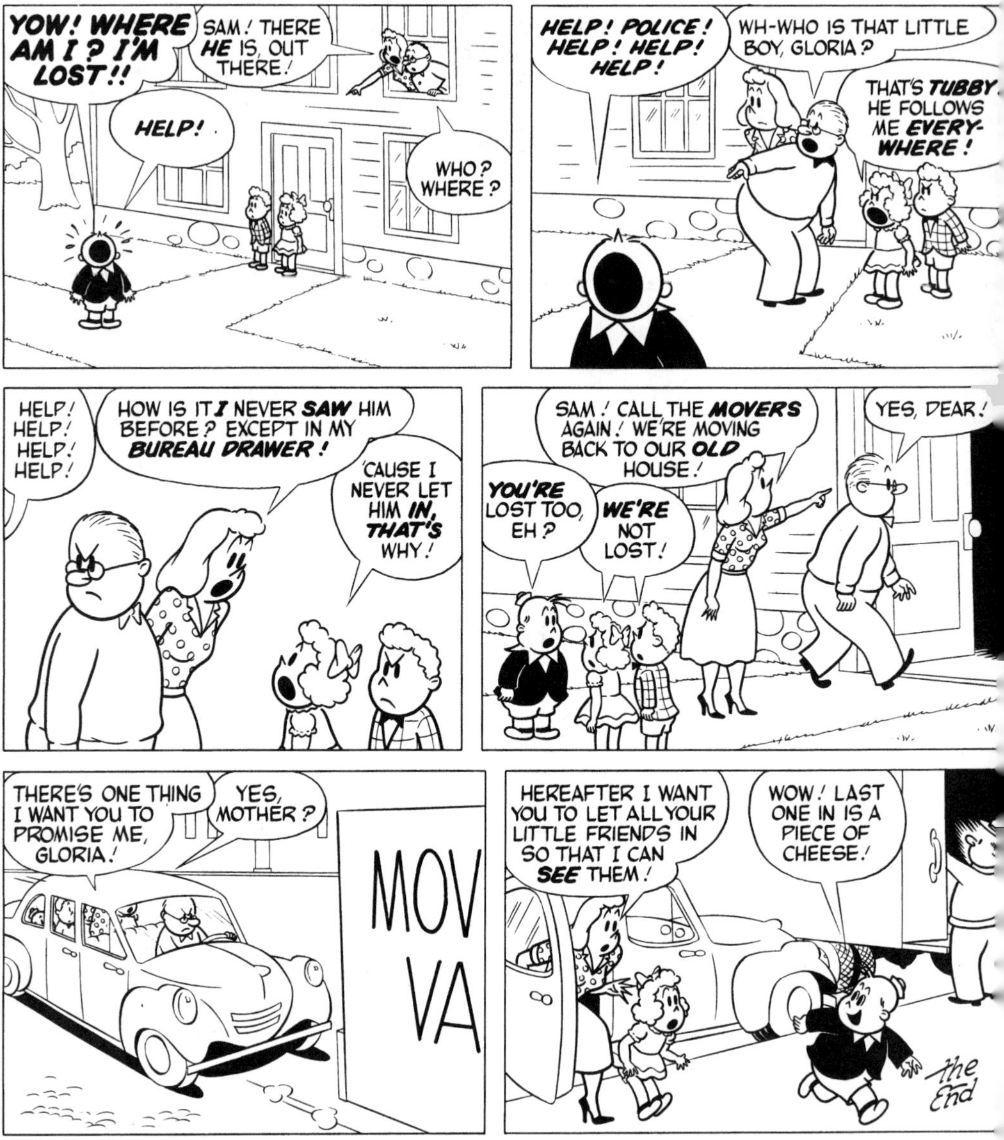
YOW! WHERE AM I ? I'M LOST!!
SAM! THERE HE IS, OUT THERE!
HELP!
WHO? WHERE?
HELP! POLICE! HELP! HELP! HELP!
WH-WHO IS THAT LITTLE BOY, GLORIA?
THAT'S TUBBY. HE FOLLOWS ME EVERY-WHERE!
HELP! HELP! HELP! HELP!
HOW IS IT I NEVER SAW HIM BEFORE? EXCEPT IN MY BUREAU DRAWER!
'CAUSE I NEVER LET HIM IN, THAT'S WHY!
SAM! CALL THE MOVERS AGAIN! WE'RE MOVING BACK TO OUR OLD HOUSE!
YES, DEAR!
YOU'RE LOST TOO, EH?
WE'RE NOT LOST!
THERE'S ONE THING I WANT YOU TO PROMISE ME, GLORIA!
YES, MOTHER?
MOV
VA
HEREAFTER I WANT YOU TO LET ALL YOUR LITTLE FRIENDS IN SO THAT I CAN SEE THEM!
WOW! LAST ONE IN IS A PIECE OF CHEESE!
the End

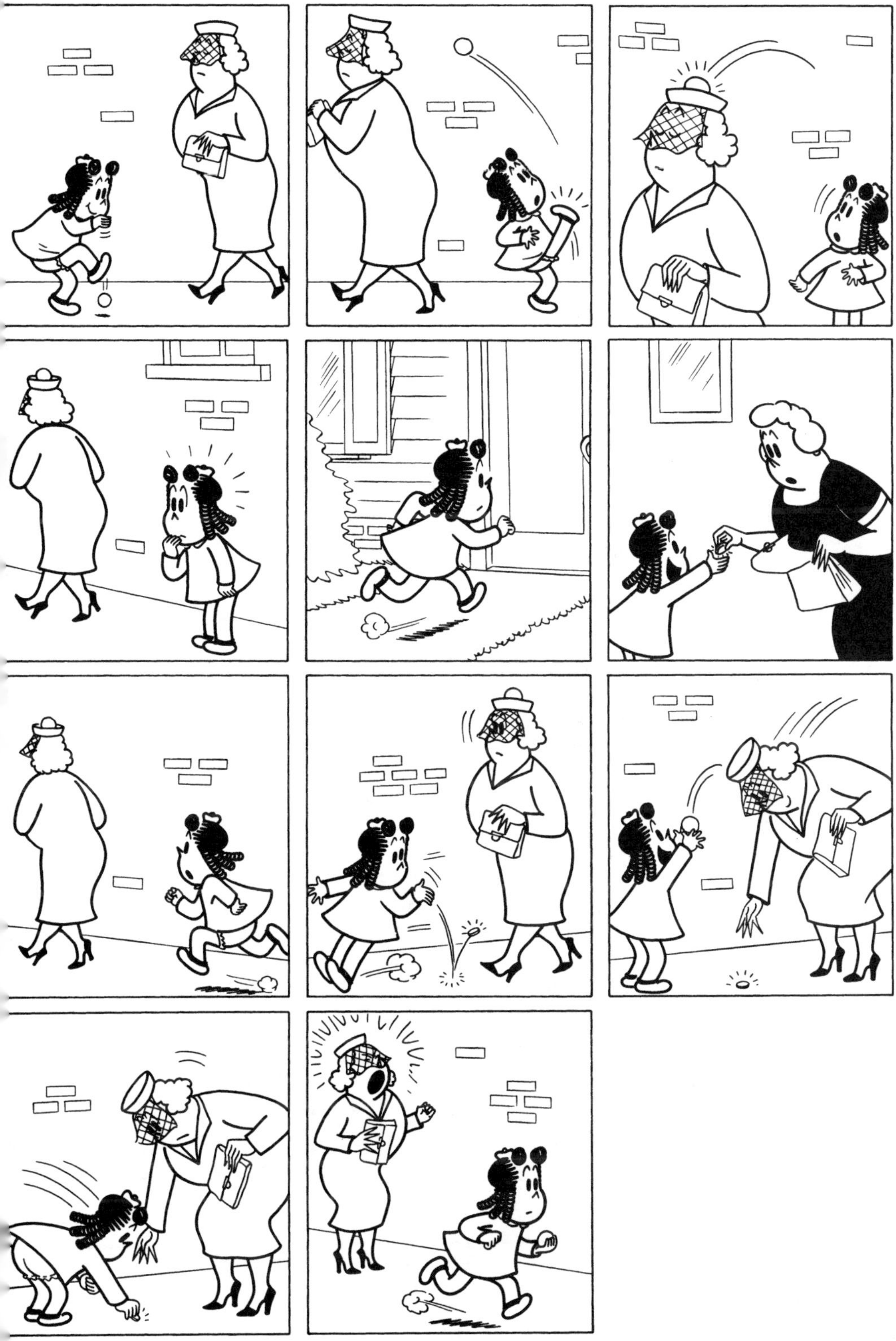

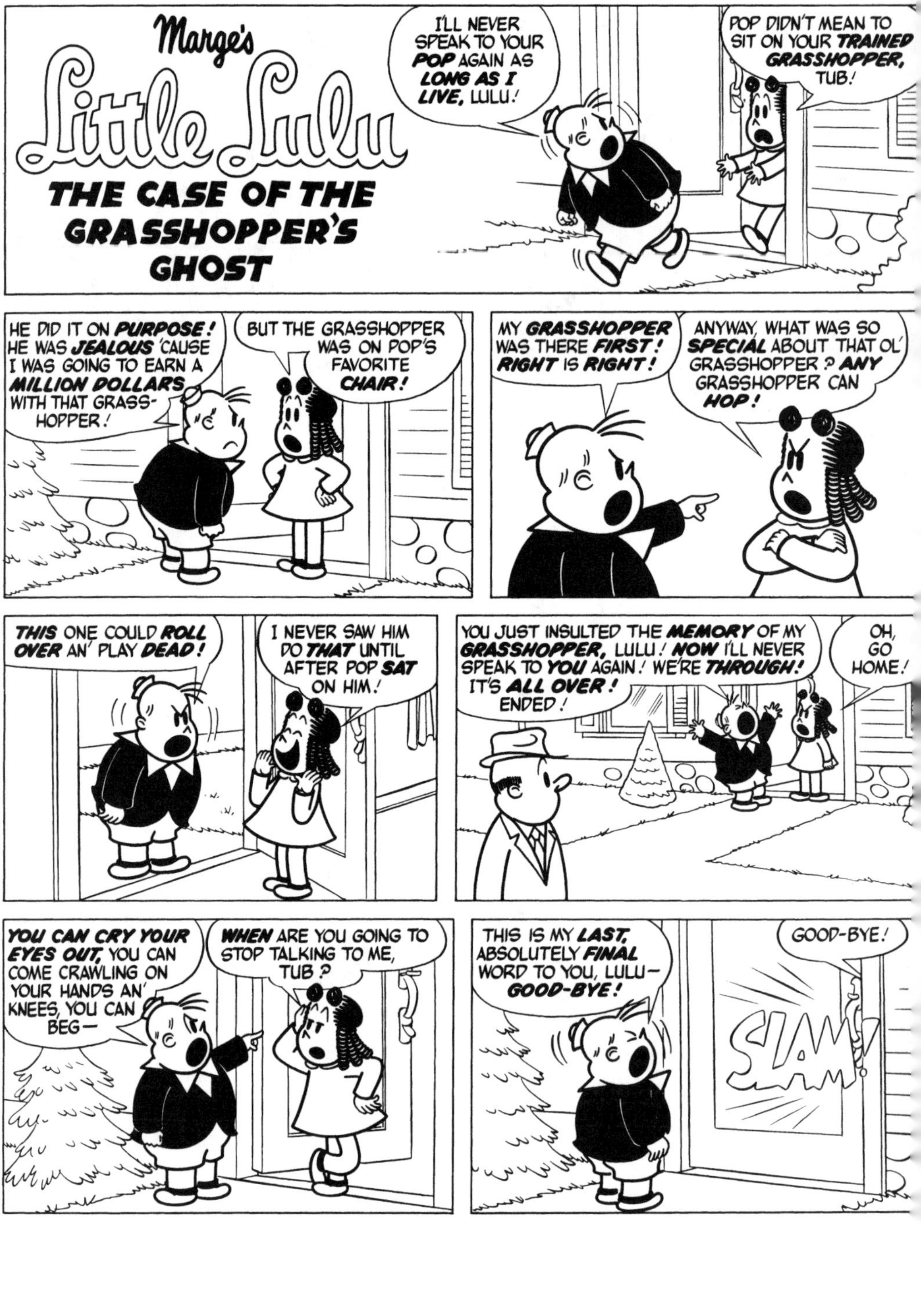
Marge's
Little Lulu
THE CASE OF THE GRASSHOPPER'S GHOST
I'LL NEVER SPEAK TO YOUR POP AGAIN AS LONG AS I LIVE, LULU!
POP DIDN'T MEAN TO SIT ON YOUR TRAINED GRASSHOPPER, TUB!
HE DID IT ON PURPOSE! HE WAS JEALOUS 'CAUSE I WAS GOING TO EARN A MILLION DOLLARS WITH THAT GRASS-HOPPER!
BUT THE GRASSHOPPER WAS ON POP'S FAVORITE CHAIR!
MY GRASSHOPPER WAS THERE FIRST! RIGHT IS RIGHT!
ANYWAY, WHAT WAS SO SPECIAL ABOUT THAT OL' GRASSHOPPER? ANY GRASSHOPPER CAN HOP!
THIS ONE COULD ROLL OVER AN' PLAY DEAD!
I NEVER SAW HIM DO THAT UNTIL AFTER POP SAT ON HIM!
YOU JUST INSULTED THE MEMORY OF MY GRASSHOPPER, LULU! NOW I'LL NEVER SPEAK TO YOU AGAIN! WE'RE THROUGH! IT'S ALL OVER! ENDED!
OH, GO HOME!
YOU CAN CRY YOUR EYES OUT, YOU CAN COME CRAWLING ON YOUR HANDS AN' KNEES, YOU CAN BEG—
WHEN ARE YOU GOING TO STOP TALKING TO ME, TUB?
THIS IS MY LAST, ABSOLUTELY FINAL WORD TO YOU, LULU— GOOD-BYE!
GOOD-BYE!
SLAM!

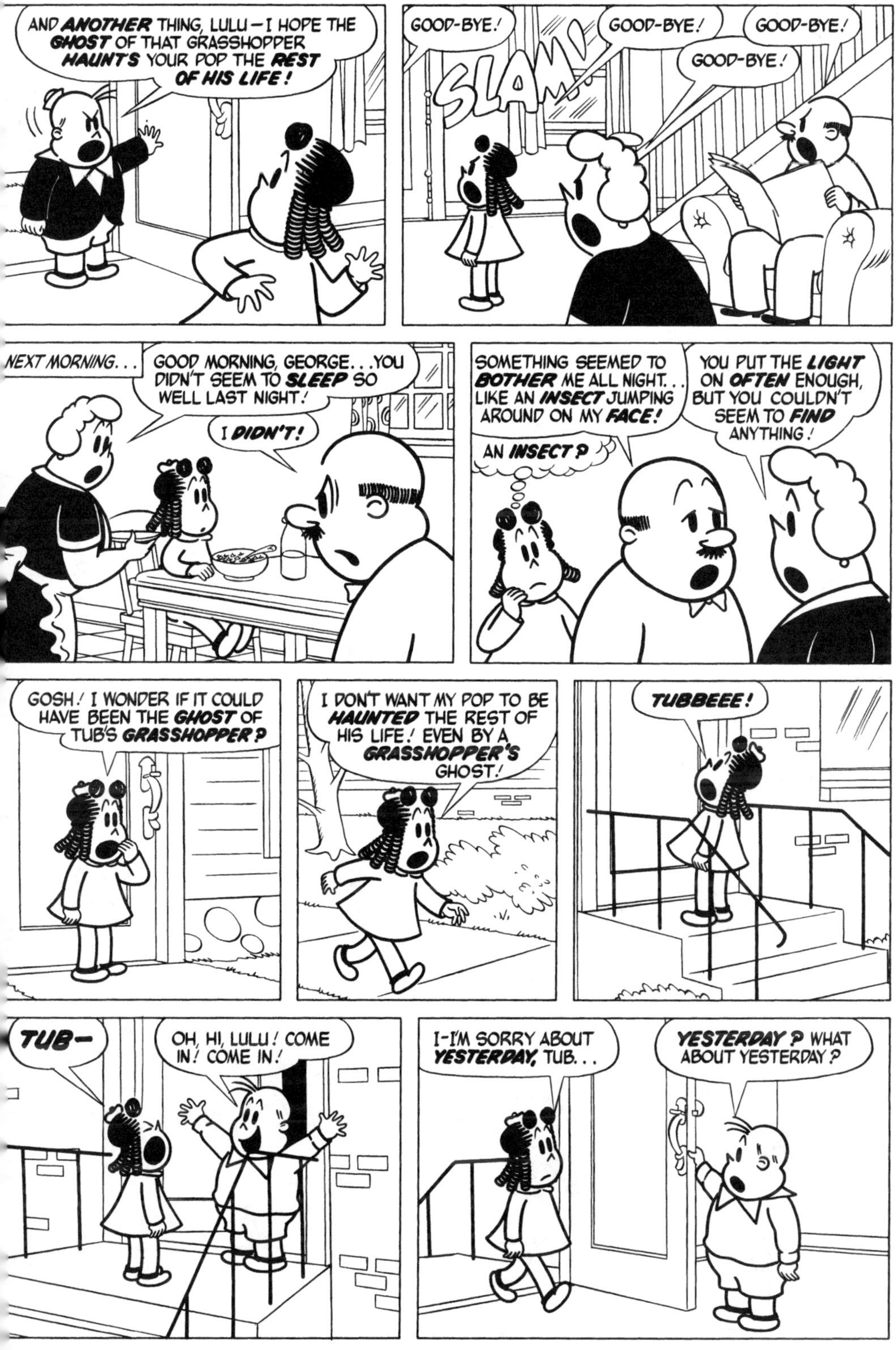
AND ANOTHER THING, LULU — I HOPE THE GHOST OF THAT GRASSHOPPER HAUNTS YOUR POP THE REST OF HIS LIFE!
GOOD-BYE!
SLAM!
GOOD-BYE!
GOOD-BYE!
GOOD-BYE!
NEXT MORNING...
GOOD MORNING, GEORGE...YOU DIDN'T SEEM TO SLEEP SO WELL LAST NIGHT!
I DIDN'T!
SOMETHING SEEMED TO BOTHER ME ALL NIGHT... LIKE AN INSECT JUMPING AROUND ON MY FACE!
YOU PUT THE LIGHT ON OFTEN ENOUGH, BUT YOU COULDN'T SEEM TO FIND ANYTHING!
AN INSECT?
GOSH! I WONDER IF IT COULD HAVE BEEN THE GHOST OF TUB'S GRASSHOPPER?
I DON'T WANT MY POP TO BE HAUNTED THE REST OF HIS LIFE! EVEN BY A GRASSHOPPER'S GHOST!
TUBBEEE!
TUB—
OH, HI, LULU! COME IN! COME IN!
I-I'M SORRY ABOUT YESTERDAY, TUB...
YESTERDAY? WHAT ABOUT YESTERDAY?

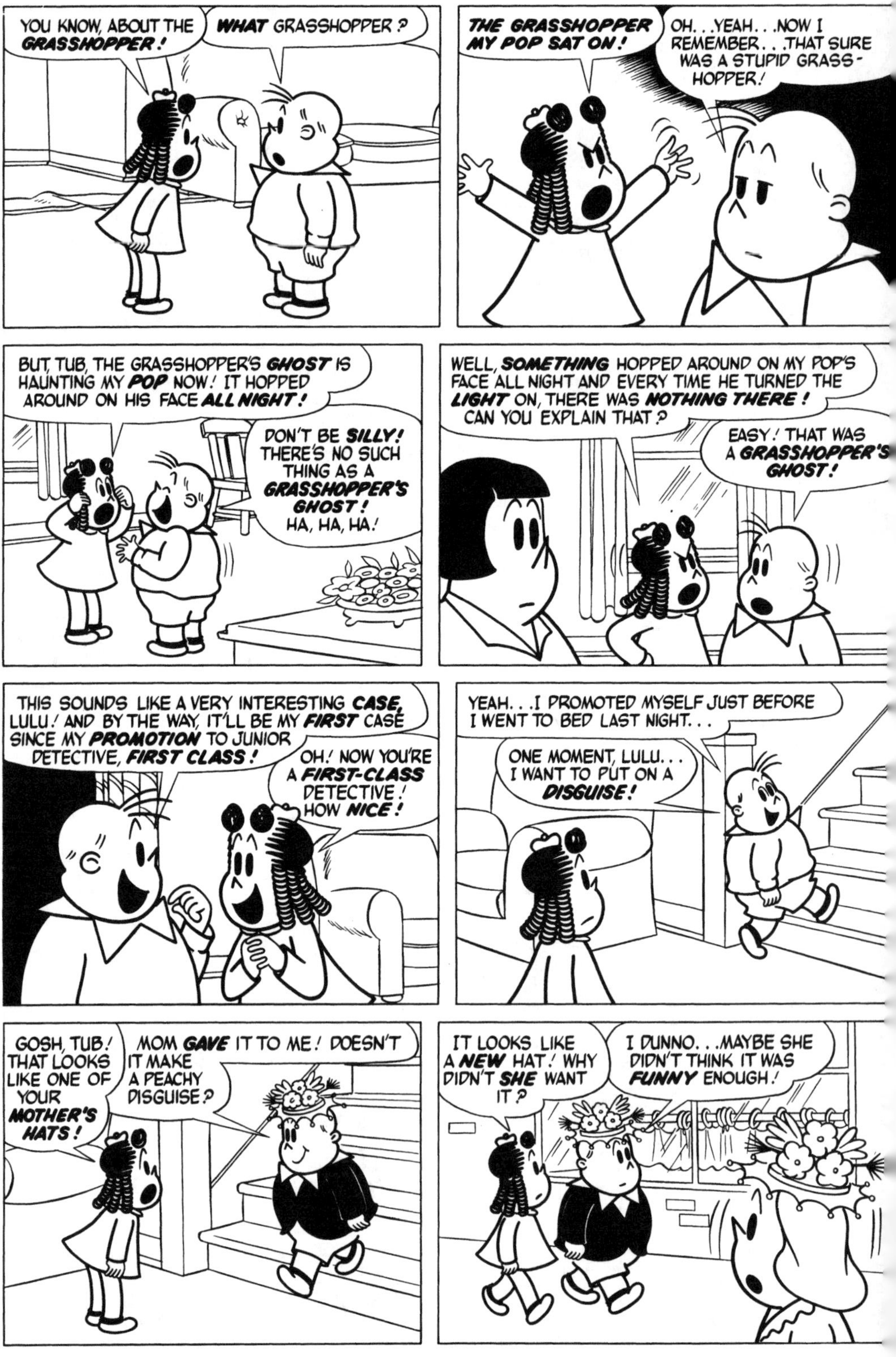

YOU KNOW, ABOUT THE **GRASSHOPPER!**
WHAT GRASSHOPPER?
THE GRASSHOPPER MY POP SAT ON!
OH. . .YEAH. . .NOW I REMEMBER. . .THAT SURE WAS A STUPID GRASS-HOPPER!
BUT, TUB, THE GRASSHOPPER'S **GHOST** IS HAUNTING MY **POP** NOW! IT HOPPED AROUND ON HIS FACE **ALL NIGHT!**
DON'T BE **SILLY!** THERE'S NO SUCH THING AS A **GRASSHOPPER'S GHOST!** HA, HA, HA!
WELL, **SOMETHING** HOPPED AROUND ON MY POP'S FACE ALL NIGHT AND EVERY TIME HE TURNED THE **LIGHT** ON, THERE WAS **NOTHING THERE!** CAN YOU EXPLAIN THAT?
EASY! THAT WAS A **GRASSHOPPER'S GHOST!**
THIS SOUNDS LIKE A VERY INTERESTING **CASE,** LULU! AND BY THE WAY, IT'LL BE MY **FIRST** CASE SINCE MY **PROMOTION** TO JUNIOR DETECTIVE, **FIRST CLASS!**
OH! NOW YOU'RE A **FIRST-CLASS** DETECTIVE! HOW **NICE!**
YEAH. . .I PROMOTED MYSELF JUST BEFORE I WENT TO BED LAST NIGHT. . .
ONE MOMENT, LULU. . . I WANT TO PUT ON A **DISGUISE!**
GOSH, TUB! THAT LOOKS LIKE ONE OF YOUR **MOTHER'S HATS!**
MOM **GAVE** IT TO ME! DOESN'T IT MAKE A PEACHY DISGUISE?
IT LOOKS LIKE A **NEW** HAT! WHY DIDN'T **SHE** WANT IT?
I DUNNO. . .MAYBE SHE DIDN'T THINK IT WAS **FUNNY** ENOUGH!

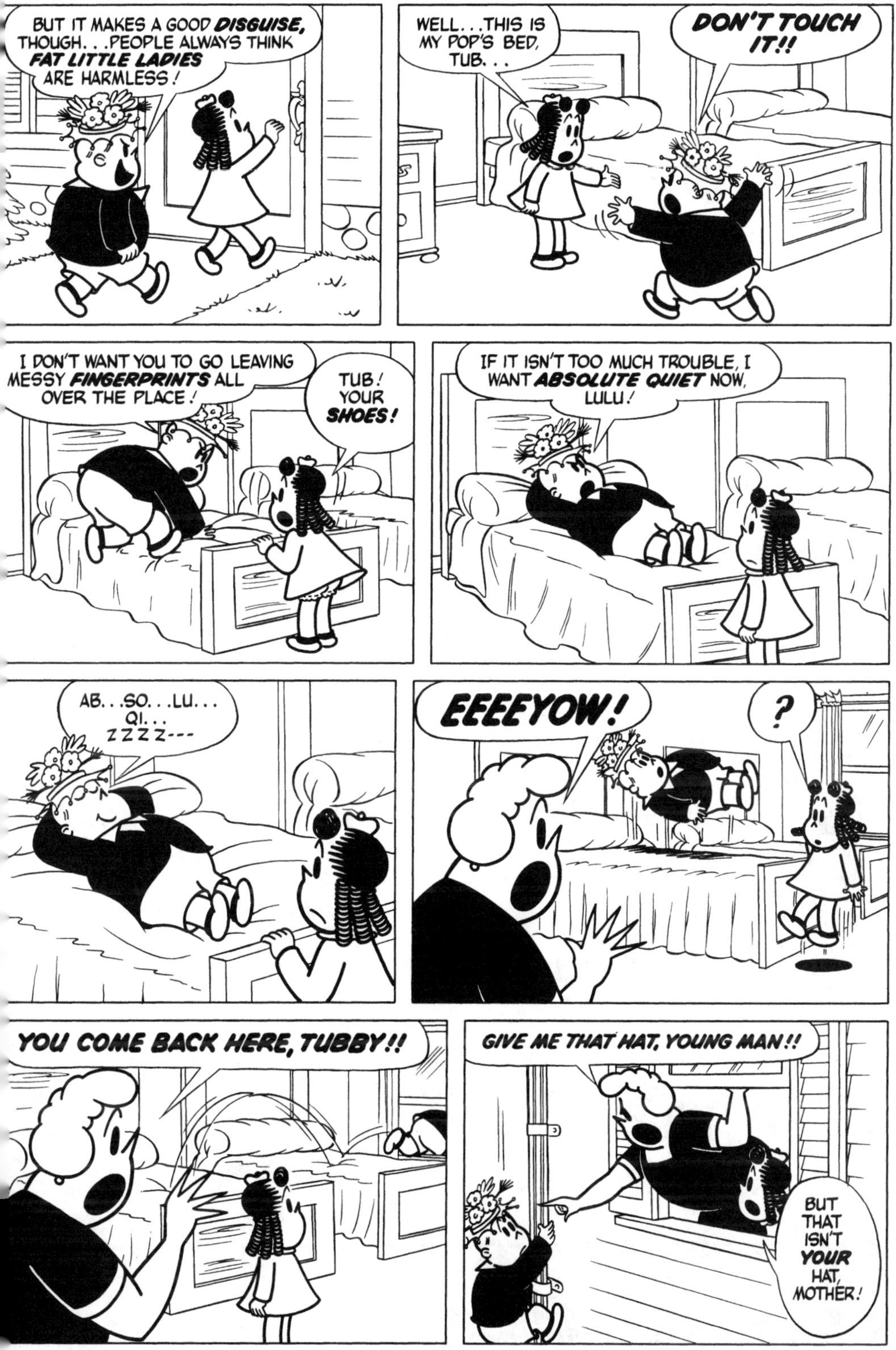

BUT IT MAKES A GOOD DISGUISE, THOUGH. . .PEOPLE ALWAYS THINK FAT LITTLE LADIES ARE HARMLESS!
WELL. . .THIS IS MY POP'S BED, TUB. . .
DON'T TOUCH IT!!
I DON'T WANT YOU TO GO LEAVING MESSY FINGERPRINTS ALL OVER THE PLACE!
TUB! YOUR SHOES!
IF IT ISN'T TOO MUCH TROUBLE, I WANT ABSOLUTE QUIET NOW, LULU!
AB. . .SO. . .LU. . . QI. . . ZZZZ---
EEEEYOW!
?
YOU COME BACK HERE, TUBBY!!
GIVE ME THAT HAT, YOUNG MAN!!
BUT THAT ISN'T YOUR HAT, MOTHER!

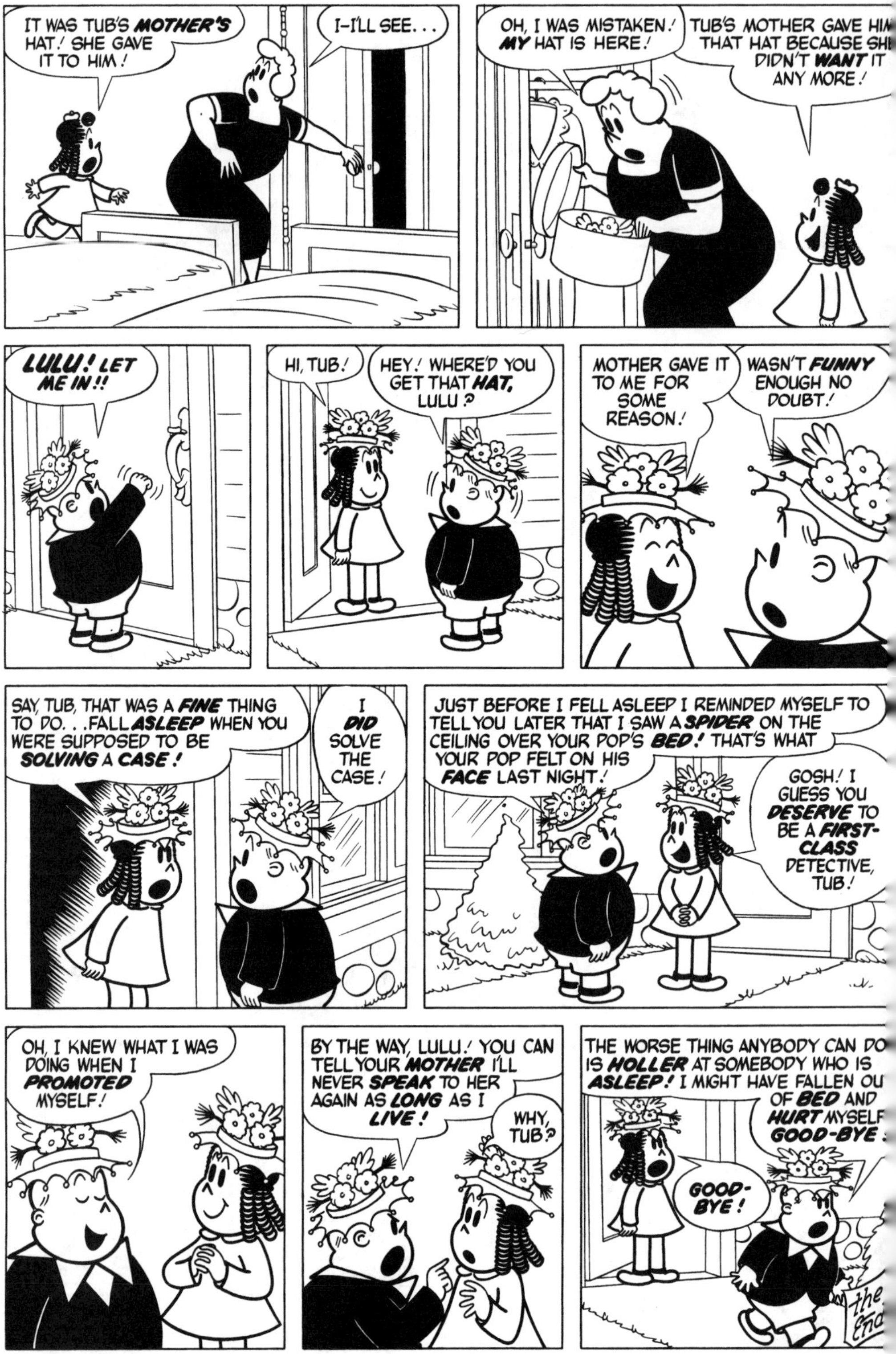
IT WAS TUB'S MOTHER'S HAT! SHE GAVE IT TO HIM!
I-I'LL SEE...
OH, I WAS MISTAKEN! MY HAT IS HERE!
TUB'S MOTHER GAVE HIM THAT HAT BECAUSE SHE DIDN'T WANT IT ANY MORE!
LULU! LET ME IN!!
HI, TUB!
HEY! WHERE'D YOU GET THAT HAT, LULU?
MOTHER GAVE IT TO ME FOR SOME REASON!
WASN'T FUNNY ENOUGH NO DOUBT!
SAY, TUB, THAT WAS A FINE THING TO DO...FALL ASLEEP WHEN YOU WERE SUPPOSED TO BE SOLVING A CASE!
I DID SOLVE THE CASE!
JUST BEFORE I FELL ASLEEP I REMINDED MYSELF TO TELL YOU LATER THAT I SAW A SPIDER ON THE CEILING OVER YOUR POP'S BED! THAT'S WHAT YOUR POP FELT ON HIS FACE LAST NIGHT!
GOSH! I GUESS YOU DESERVE TO BE A FIRST-CLASS DETECTIVE, TUB!
OH, I KNEW WHAT I WAS DOING WHEN I PROMOTED MYSELF!
BY THE WAY, LULU! YOU CAN TELL YOUR MOTHER I'LL NEVER SPEAK TO HER AGAIN AS LONG AS I LIVE!
WHY, TUB?
THE WORSE THING ANYBODY CAN DO IS HOLLER AT SOMEBODY WHO IS ASLEEP! I MIGHT HAVE FALLEN OUT OF BED AND HURT MYSELF! GOOD-BYE!
GOOD-BYE!
the end

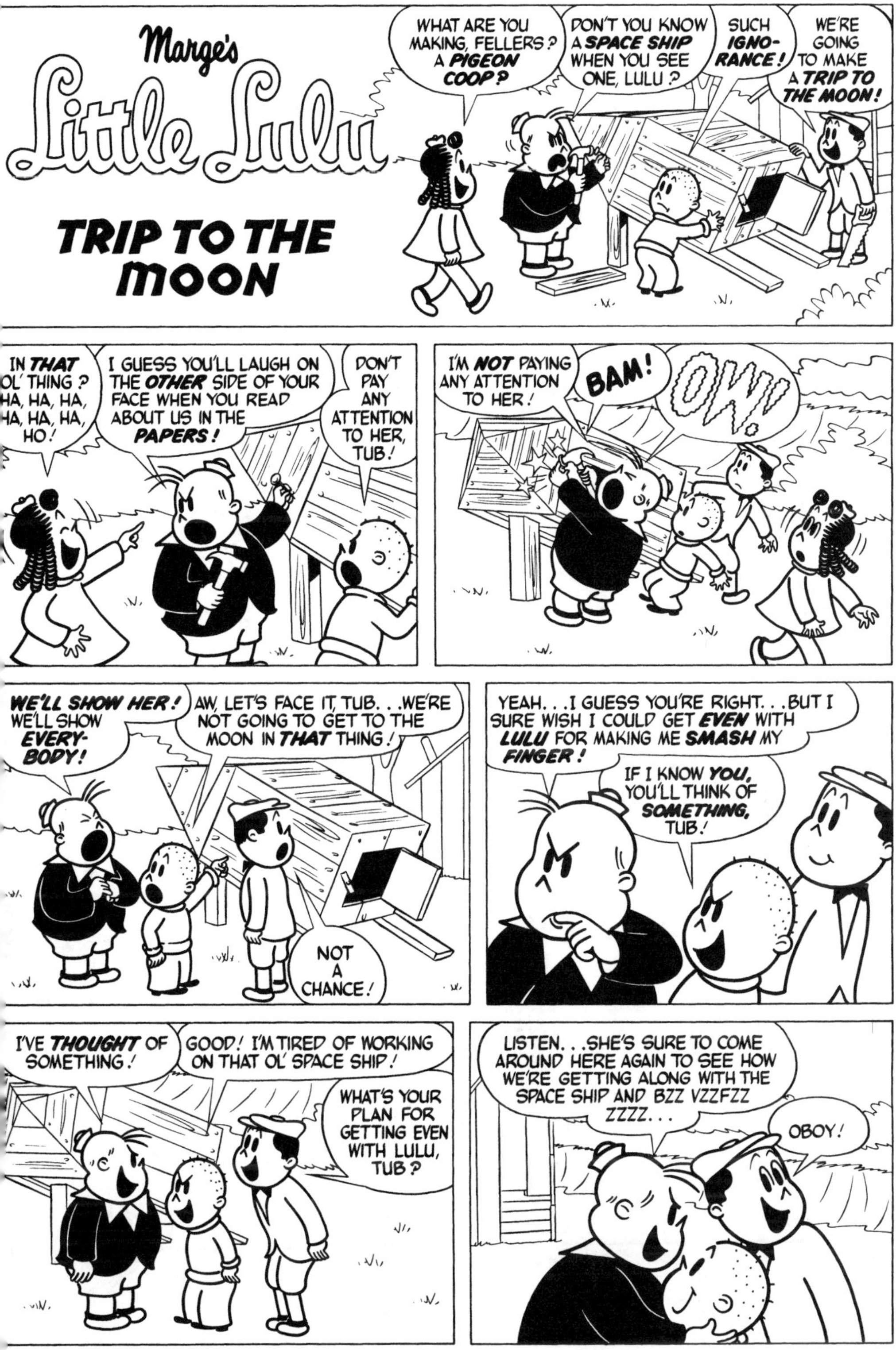
Marge's Little Lulu
TRIP TO THE MOON
WHAT ARE YOU MAKING, FELLERS? A PIGEON COOP?
DON'T YOU KNOW A SPACE SHIP WHEN YOU SEE ONE, LULU?
SUCH IGNO-RANCE!
WE'RE GOING TO MAKE A TRIP TO THE MOON!
IN THAT OL' THING? HA, HA, HA, HA, HA, HA, HO!
I GUESS YOU'LL LAUGH ON THE OTHER SIDE OF YOUR FACE WHEN YOU READ ABOUT US IN THE PAPERS!
DON'T PAY ANY ATTENTION TO HER, TUB!
I'M NOT PAYING ANY ATTENTION TO HER!
BAM!
OW!
WE'LL SHOW HER! WE'LL SHOW EVERY-BODY!
AW, LET'S FACE IT, TUB. . .WE'RE NOT GOING TO GET TO THE MOON IN THAT THING!
NOT A CHANCE!
YEAH. . .I GUESS YOU'RE RIGHT. . .BUT I SURE WISH I COULD GET EVEN WITH LULU FOR MAKING ME SMASH MY FINGER!
IF I KNOW YOU, YOU'LL THINK OF SOMETHING, TUB!
I'VE THOUGHT OF SOMETHING!
GOOD! I'M TIRED OF WORKING ON THAT OL' SPACE SHIP!
WHAT'S YOUR PLAN FOR GETTING EVEN WITH LULU, TUB?
LISTEN. . .SHE'S SURE TO COME AROUND HERE AGAIN TO SEE HOW WE'RE GETTING ALONG WITH THE SPACE SHIP AND BZZ VZZFZZ ZZZZ. . .
OBOY!

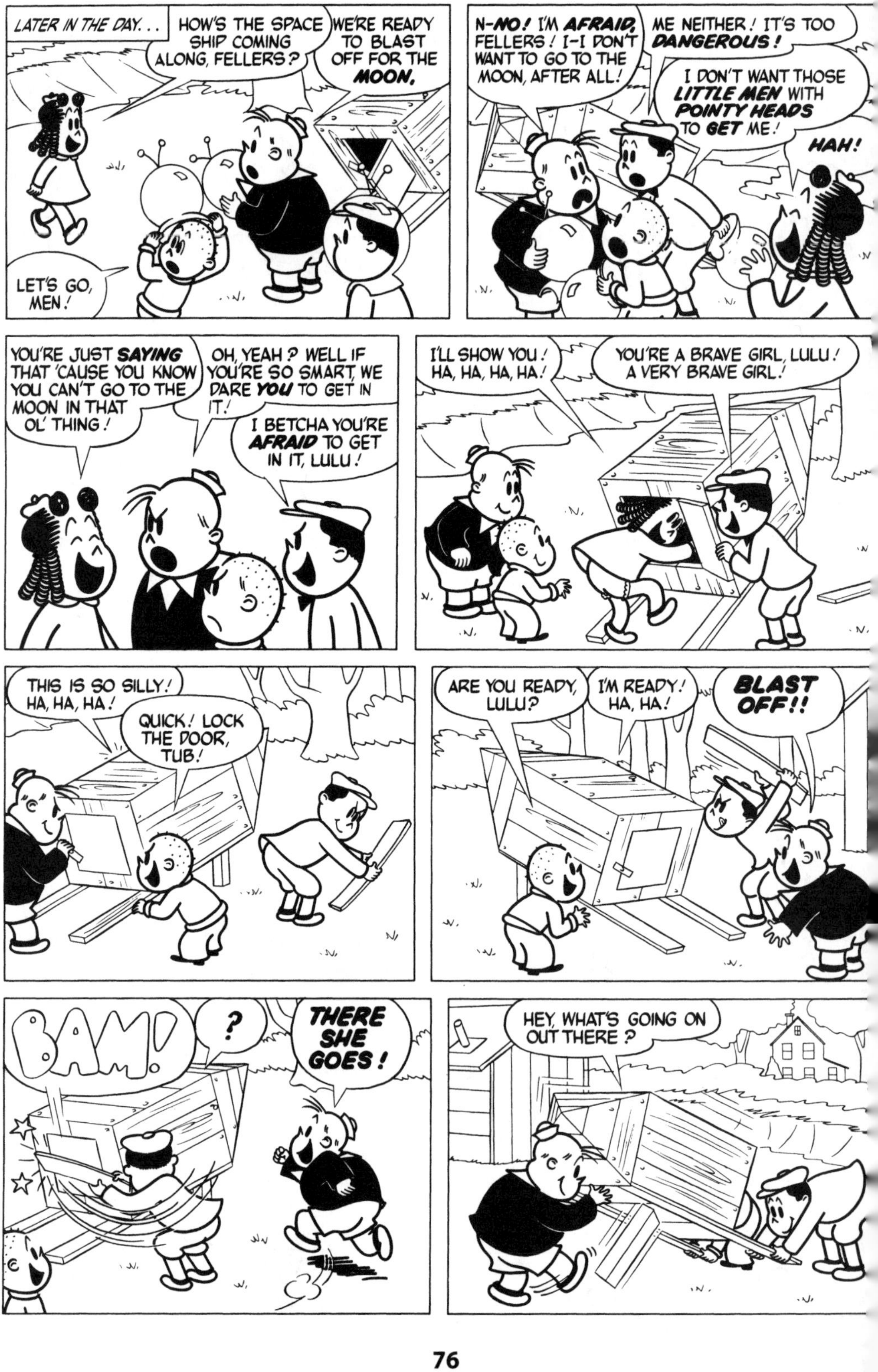
LATER IN THE DAY...
HOW'S THE SPACE SHIP COMING ALONG, FELLERS?
WE'RE READY TO BLAST OFF FOR THE MOON.
LET'S GO, MEN!
N-NO! I'M AFRAID, FELLERS! I-I DON'T WANT TO GO TO THE MOON, AFTER ALL!
ME NEITHER! IT'S TOO DANGEROUS!
I DON'T WANT THOSE LITTLE MEN WITH POINTY HEADS TO GET ME!
HAH!
YOU'RE JUST SAYING THAT 'CAUSE YOU KNOW YOU CAN'T GO TO THE MOON IN THAT OL' THING!
OH, YEAH? WELL IF YOU'RE SO SMART, WE DARE YOU TO GET IN IT!
I BETCHA YOU'RE AFRAID TO GET IN IT, LULU!
I'LL SHOW YOU! HA, HA, HA, HA!
YOU'RE A BRAVE GIRL, LULU! A VERY BRAVE GIRL!
THIS IS SO SILLY! HA, HA, HA!
QUICK! LOCK THE DOOR, TUB!
ARE YOU READY, LULU?
I'M READY! HA, HA!
BLAST OFF!!
BAM!
?
THERE SHE GOES!
HEY, WHAT'S GOING ON OUT THERE?

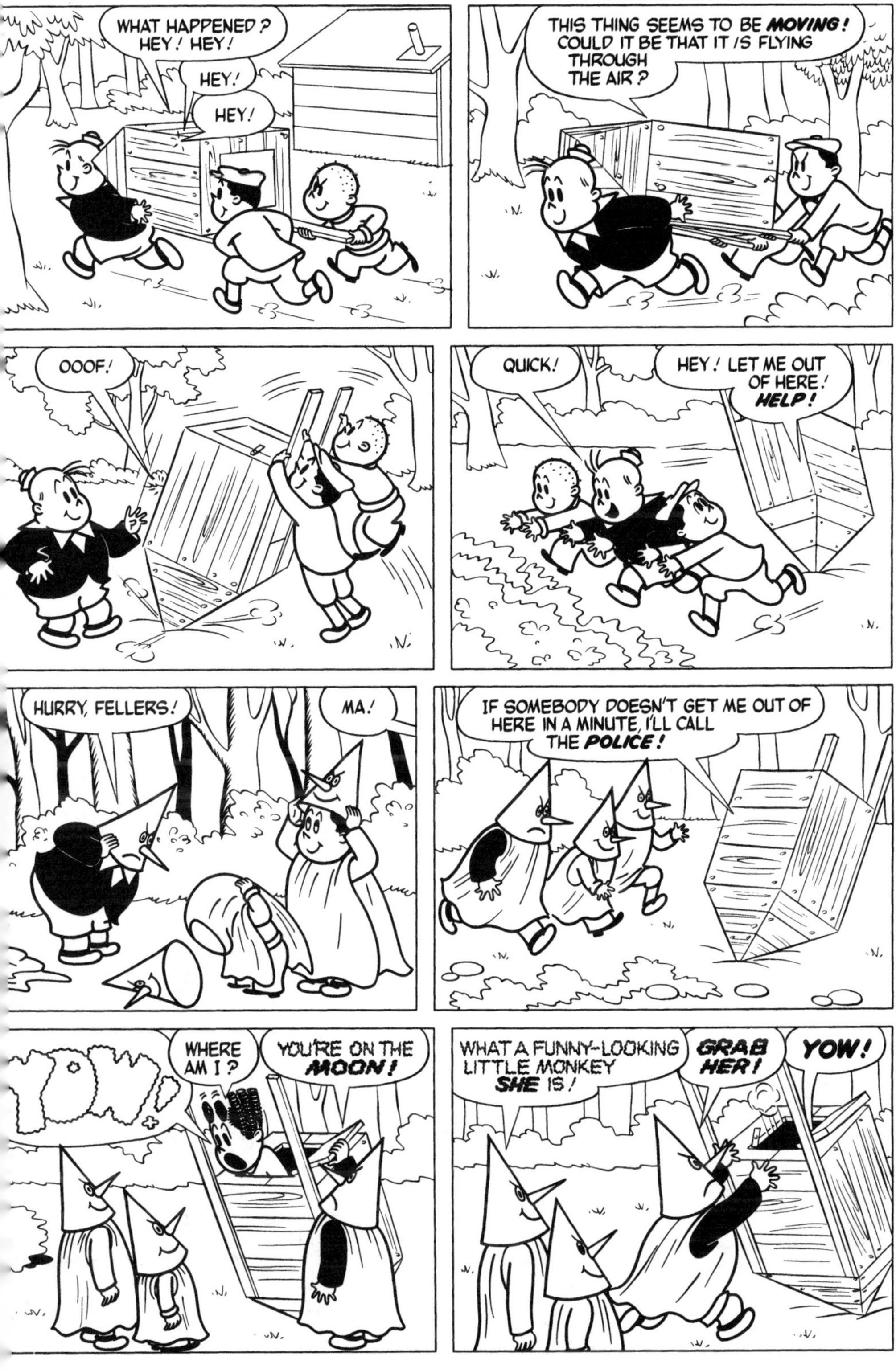
WHAT HAPPENED? HEY! HEY!
HEY!
HEY!
THIS THING SEEMS TO BE MOVING! COULD IT BE THAT IT IS FLYING THROUGH THE AIR?
OOOF!
QUICK!
HEY! LET ME OUT OF HERE! HELP!
HURRY, FELLERS!
MA!
IF SOMEBODY DOESN'T GET ME OUT OF HERE IN A MINUTE, I'LL CALL THE POLICE!
YOW!
WHERE AM I?
YOU'RE ON THE MOON!
WHAT A FUNNY-LOOKING LITTLE MONKEY SHE IS!
GRAB HER!
YOW!

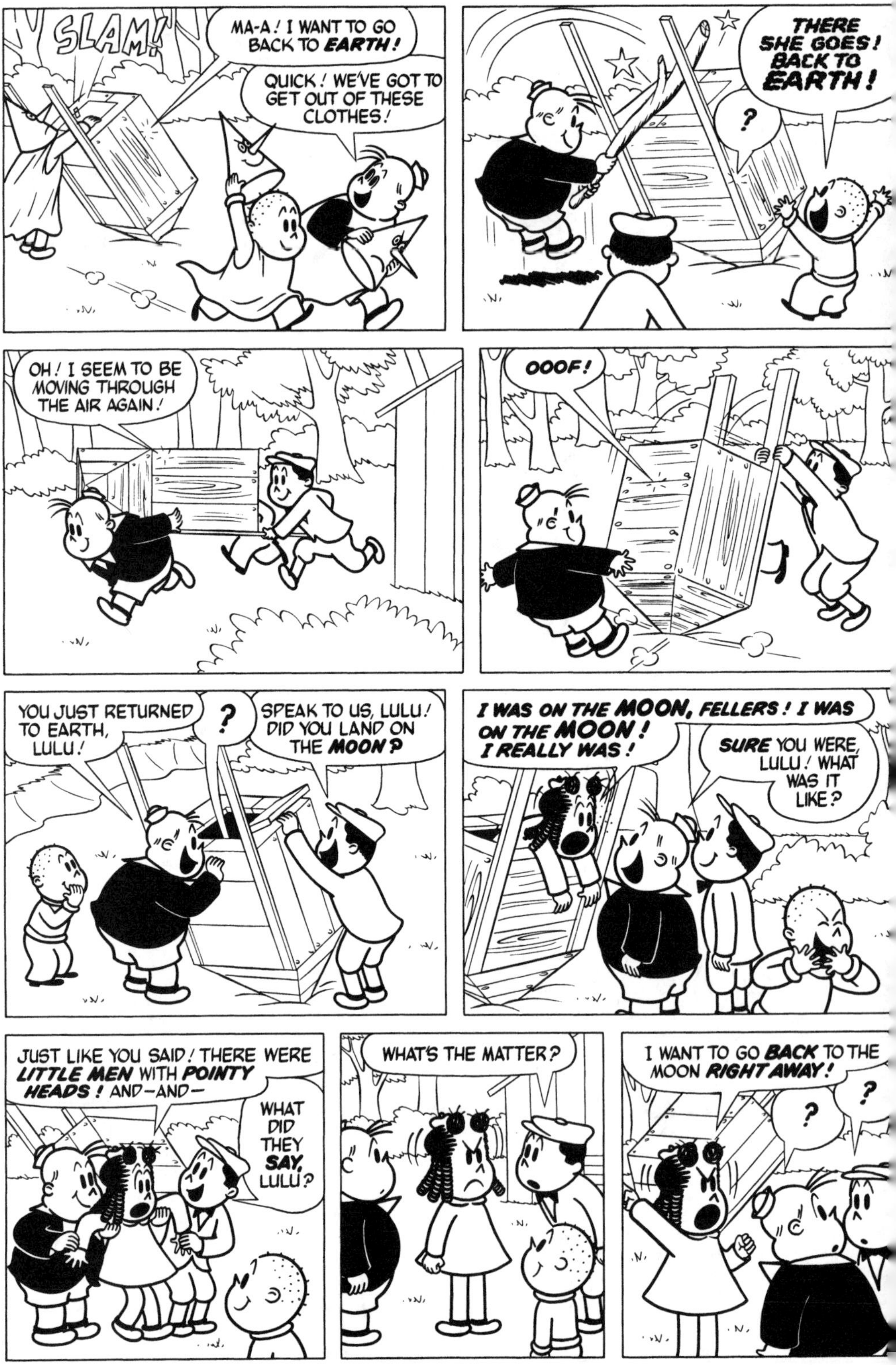
SLAM!
MA-A! I WANT TO GO BACK TO EARTH!
QUICK! WE'VE GOT TO GET OUT OF THESE CLOTHES!
THERE SHE GOES! BACK TO EARTH!
?
OH! I SEEM TO BE MOVING THROUGH THE AIR AGAIN!
OOOF!
YOU JUST RETURNED TO EARTH, LULU!
?
SPEAK TO US, LULU! DID YOU LAND ON THE MOON?
I WAS ON THE MOON, FELLERS! I WAS ON THE MOON! I REALLY WAS!
SURE YOU WERE, LULU! WHAT WAS IT LIKE?
JUST LIKE YOU SAID! THERE WERE LITTLE MEN WITH POINTY HEADS! AND—AND—
WHAT DID THEY SAY, LULU?
WHAT'S THE MATTER?
I WANT TO GO BACK TO THE MOON RIGHT AWAY!
?
?

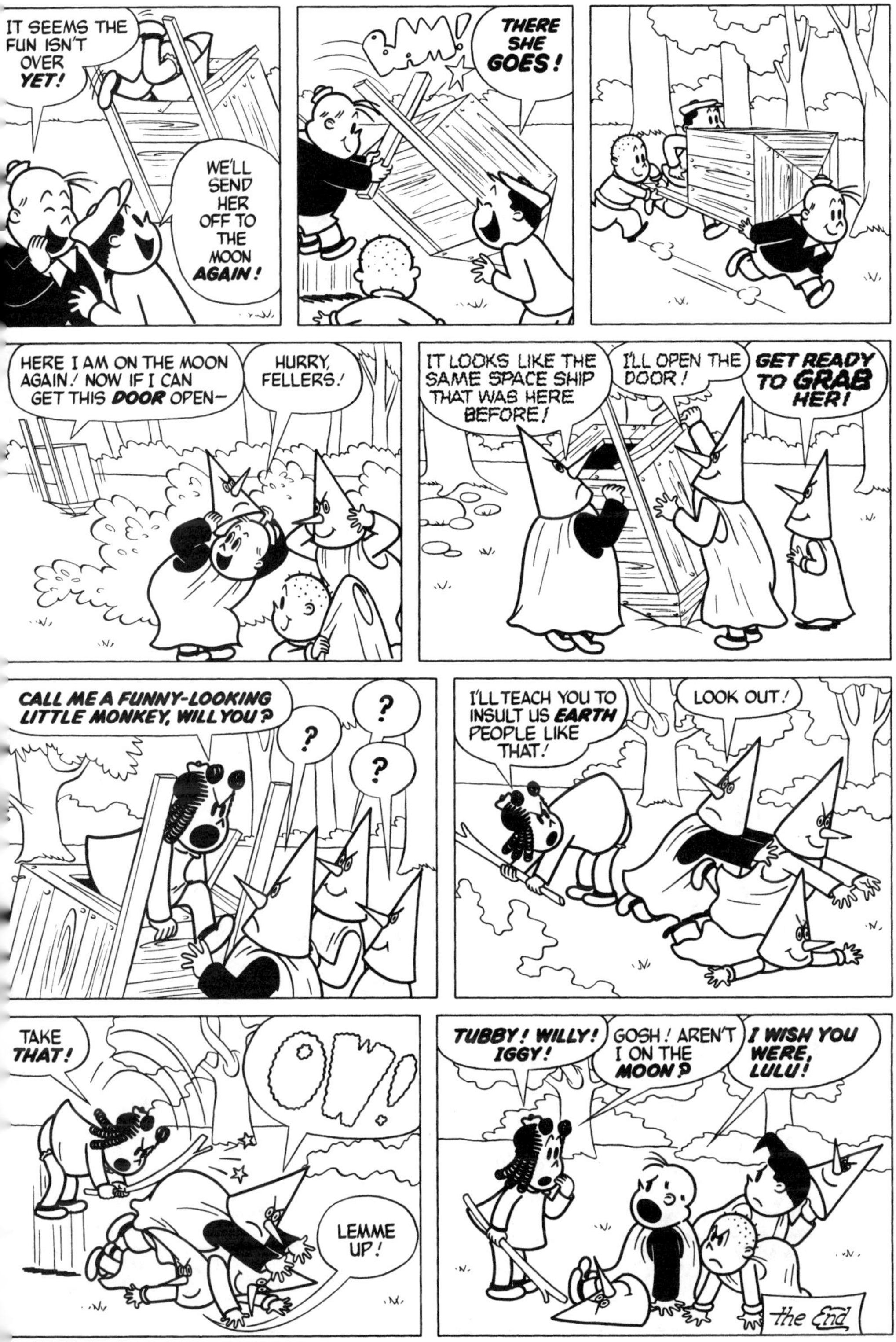
IT SEEMS THE FUN ISN'T OVER YET!
WE'LL SEND HER OFF TO THE MOON AGAIN!
BAM!
THERE SHE GOES!
HERE I AM ON THE MOON AGAIN! NOW IF I CAN GET THIS DOOR OPEN—
HURRY, FELLERS!
IT LOOKS LIKE THE SAME SPACE SHIP THAT WAS HERE BEFORE!
I'LL OPEN THE DOOR!
GET READY TO GRAB HER!
CALL ME A FUNNY-LOOKING LITTLE MONKEY, WILL YOU?
?
?
?
I'LL TEACH YOU TO INSULT US EARTH PEOPLE LIKE THAT!
LOOK OUT!
TAKE THAT!
OW!
LEMME UP!
TUBBY! WILLY! IGGY!
GOSH! AREN'T I ON THE MOON?
I WISH YOU WERE, LULU!
the End

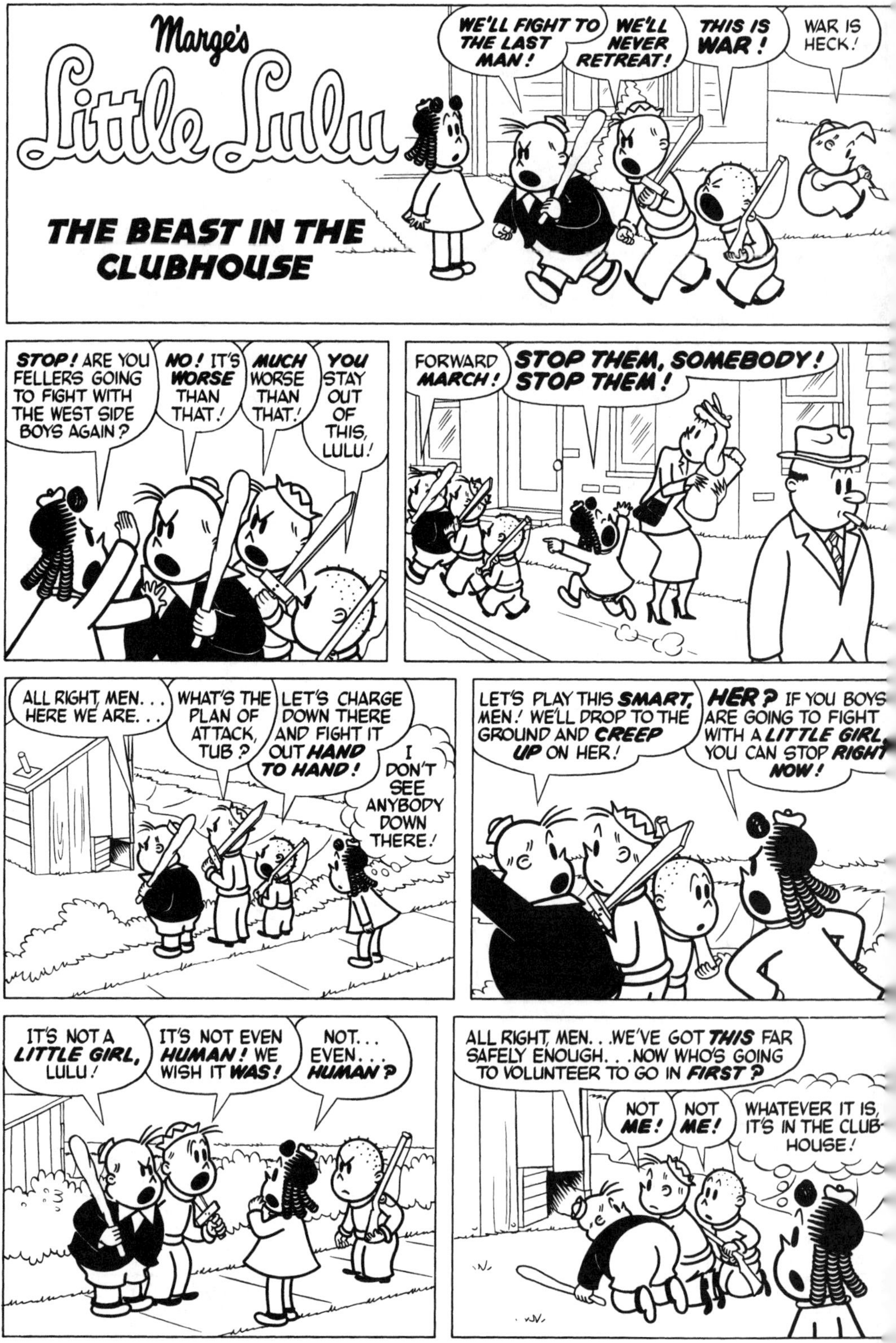
Marge's Little Lulu
THE BEAST IN THE CLUBHOUSE
WE'LL FIGHT TO THE LAST MAN!
WE'LL NEVER RETREAT!
THIS IS WAR!
WAR IS HECK!
STOP! ARE YOU FELLERS GOING TO FIGHT WITH THE WEST SIDE BOYS AGAIN?
NO! IT'S WORSE THAN THAT!
MUCH WORSE THAN THAT!
YOU STAY OUT OF THIS, LULU!
FORWARD MARCH!
STOP THEM, SOMEBODY! STOP THEM!
ALL RIGHT, MEN... HERE WE ARE...
WHAT'S THE PLAN OF ATTACK, TUB?
LET'S CHARGE DOWN THERE AND FIGHT IT OUT HAND TO HAND!
I DON'T SEE ANYBODY DOWN THERE!
LET'S PLAY THIS SMART, MEN! WE'LL DROP TO THE GROUND AND CREEP UP ON HER!
HER? IF YOU BOYS ARE GOING TO FIGHT WITH A LITTLE GIRL, YOU CAN STOP RIGHT NOW!
IT'S NOT A LITTLE GIRL, LULU!
IT'S NOT EVEN HUMAN! WE WISH IT WAS!
NOT... EVEN... HUMAN?
ALL RIGHT, MEN...WE'VE GOT THIS FAR SAFELY ENOUGH...NOW WHO'S GOING TO VOLUNTEER TO GO IN FIRST?
NOT ME!
NOT ME!
WHATEVER IT IS, IT'S IN THE CLUB-HOUSE!

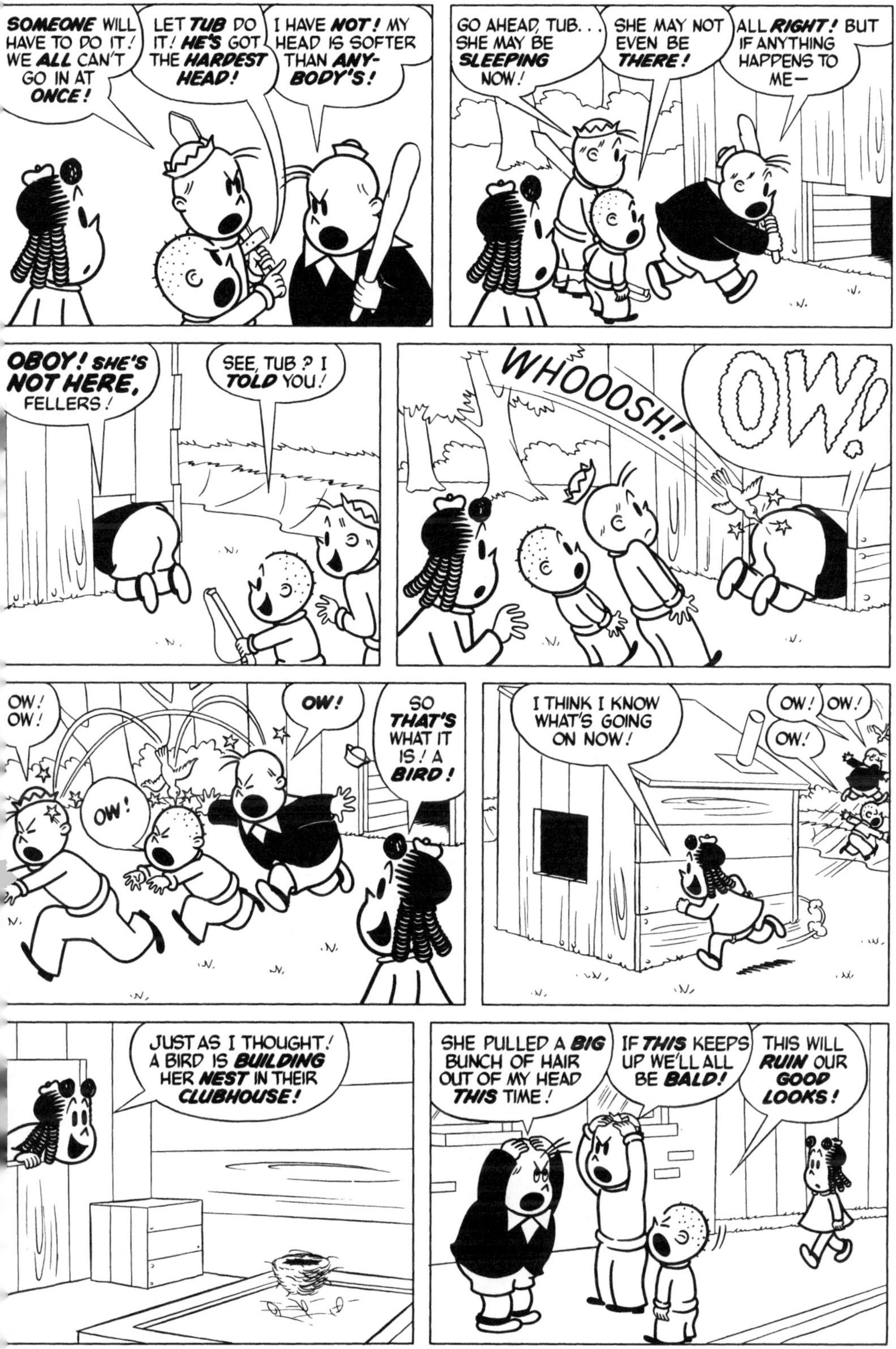

SOMEONE WILL HAVE TO DO IT! WE ALL CAN'T GO IN AT ONCE!
LET TUB DO IT! HE'S GOT THE HARDEST HEAD!
I HAVE NOT! MY HEAD IS SOFTER THAN ANYBODY'S!
GO AHEAD, TUB. . . SHE MAY BE SLEEPING NOW!
SHE MAY NOT EVEN BE THERE!
ALL RIGHT! BUT IF ANYTHING HAPPENS TO ME—
OBOY! SHE'S NOT HERE, FELLERS!
SEE, TUB? I TOLD YOU!
WHOOOSH!
OW!
OW! OW!
OW!
OW!
SO THAT'S WHAT IT IS! A BIRD!
I THINK I KNOW WHAT'S GOING ON NOW!
OW! OW!
OW!
JUST AS I THOUGHT! A BIRD IS BUILDING HER NEST IN THEIR CLUBHOUSE!
SHE PULLED A BIG BUNCH OF HAIR OUT OF MY HEAD THIS TIME!
IF THIS KEEPS UP WE'LL ALL BE BALD!
THIS WILL RUIN OUR GOOD LOOKS!

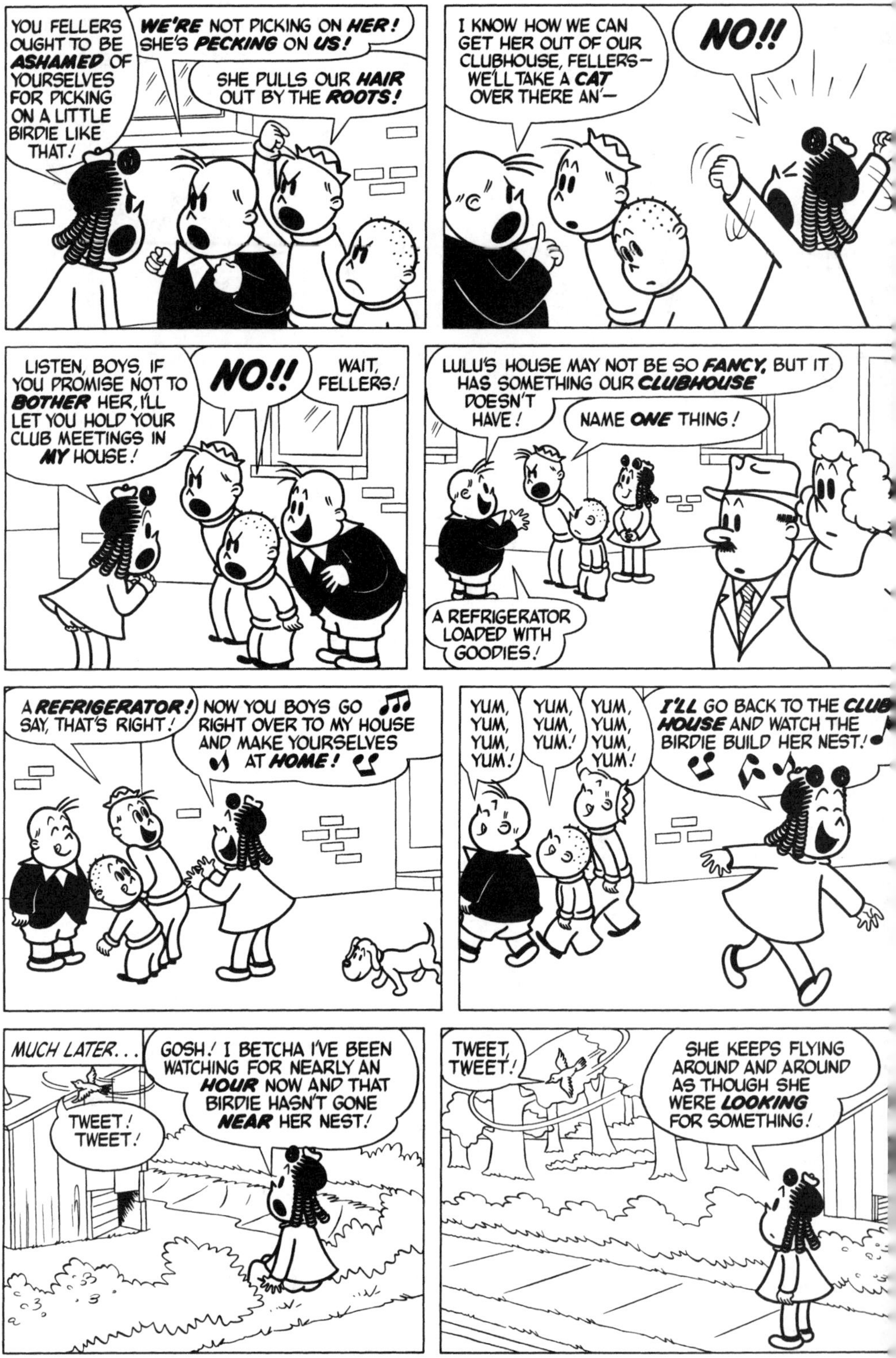

YOU FELLERS OUGHT TO BE ASHAMED OF YOURSELVES FOR PICKING ON A LITTLE BIRDIE LIKE THAT!
WE'RE NOT PICKING ON HER! SHE'S PECKING ON US!
SHE PULLS OUR HAIR OUT BY THE ROOTS!
I KNOW HOW WE CAN GET HER OUT OF OUR CLUBHOUSE, FELLERS— WE'LL TAKE A CAT OVER THERE AN'—
NO!!
LISTEN, BOYS, IF YOU PROMISE NOT TO BOTHER HER, I'LL LET YOU HOLD YOUR CLUB MEETINGS IN MY HOUSE!
NO!!
WAIT, FELLERS!
LULU'S HOUSE MAY NOT BE SO FANCY, BUT IT HAS SOMETHING OUR CLUBHOUSE DOESN'T HAVE!
NAME ONE THING!
A REFRIGERATOR LOADED WITH GOODIES!
A REFRIGERATOR! SAY, THAT'S RIGHT!
NOW YOU BOYS GO RIGHT OVER TO MY HOUSE AND MAKE YOURSELVES AT HOME!
YUM, YUM, YUM, YUM!
YUM, YUM, YUM!
YUM, YUM, YUM, YUM!
I'LL GO BACK TO THE CLUB HOUSE AND WATCH THE BIRDIE BUILD HER NEST!
MUCH LATER...
GOSH! I BETCHA I'VE BEEN WATCHING FOR NEARLY AN HOUR NOW AND THAT BIRDIE HASN'T GONE NEAR HER NEST!
TWEET! TWEET!
TWEET, TWEET!
SHE KEEPS FLYING AROUND AND AROUND AS THOUGH SHE WERE LOOKING FOR SOMETHING!

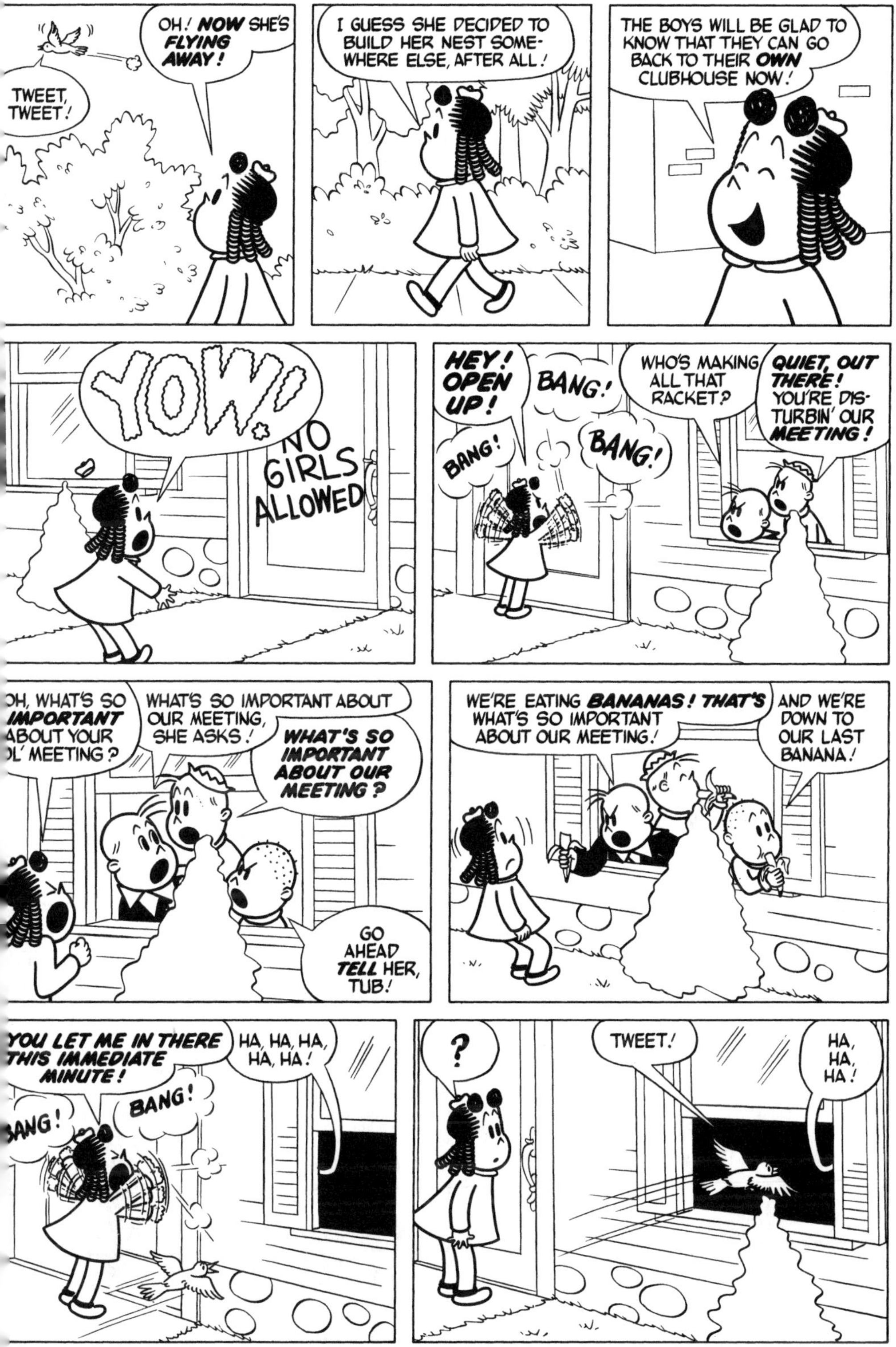
TWEET, TWEET!
OH! **NOW** SHE'S **FLYING AWAY!**
I GUESS SHE DECIDED TO BUILD HER NEST SOME-WHERE ELSE, AFTER ALL!
THE BOYS WILL BE GLAD TO KNOW THAT THEY CAN GO BACK TO THEIR **OWN** CLUBHOUSE NOW!
YOW!
NO GIRLS ALLOWED
HEY! OPEN UP!
BANG!
BANG!
BANG!
WHO'S MAKING ALL THAT RACKET?
QUIET, OUT THERE! YOU'RE DIS-TURBIN' OUR **MEETING!**
OH, WHAT'S SO **IMPORTANT** ABOUT YOUR OL' MEETING?
WHAT'S SO IMPORTANT ABOUT OUR MEETING, SHE ASKS!
WHAT'S SO IMPORTANT ABOUT OUR MEETING?
GO AHEAD **TELL** HER, TUB!
WE'RE EATING **BANANAS! THAT'S** WHAT'S SO IMPORTANT ABOUT OUR MEETING!
AND WE'RE DOWN TO OUR LAST BANANA!
YOU LET ME IN THERE THIS IMMEDIATE MINUTE!
BANG!
BANG!
HA, HA, HA, HA, HA!
?
TWEET!
HA, HA, HA!

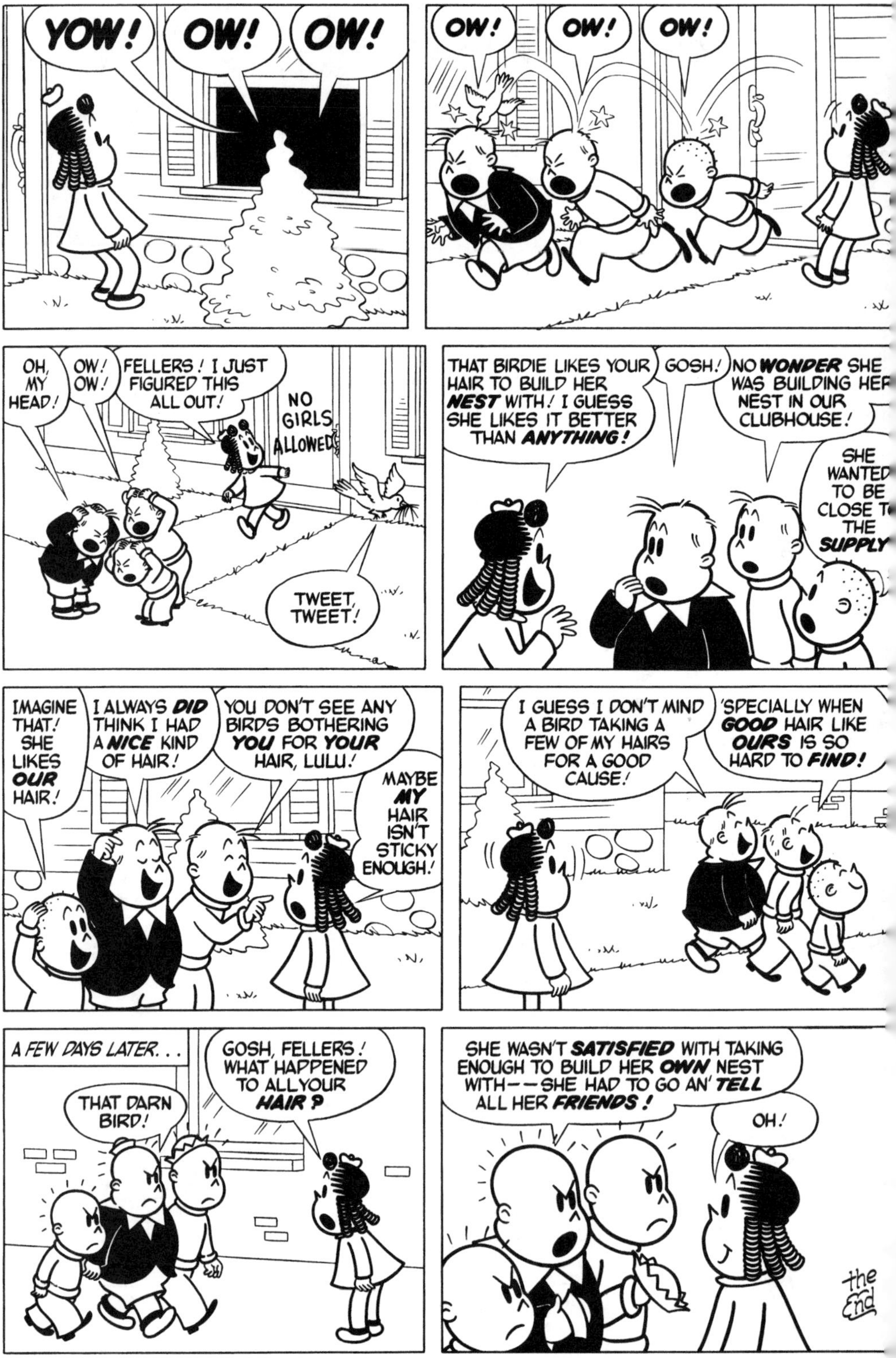
YOW!
OW!
OW!
OW!
OW!
OW!
OH, MY HEAD!
OW! OW!
FELLERS! I JUST FIGURED THIS ALL OUT!
NO GIRLS ALLOWED
TWEET, TWEET!
THAT BIRDIE LIKES YOUR HAIR TO BUILD HER NEST WITH! I GUESS SHE LIKES IT BETTER THAN ANYTHING!
GOSH!
NO WONDER SHE WAS BUILDING HER NEST IN OUR CLUBHOUSE!
SHE WANTED TO BE CLOSE T THE SUPPLY
IMAGINE THAT! SHE LIKES OUR HAIR!
I ALWAYS DID THINK I HAD A NICE KIND OF HAIR!
YOU DON'T SEE ANY BIRDS BOTHERING YOU FOR YOUR HAIR, LULU!
MAYBE MY HAIR ISN'T STICKY ENOUGH!
I GUESS I DON'T MIND A BIRD TAKING A FEW OF MY HAIRS FOR A GOOD CAUSE!
'SPECIALLY WHEN GOOD HAIR LIKE OURS IS SO HARD TO FIND!
A FEW DAYS LATER...
GOSH, FELLERS! WHAT HAPPENED TO ALL YOUR HAIR?
THAT DARN BIRD!
SHE WASN'T SATISFIED WITH TAKING ENOUGH TO BUILD HER OWN NEST WITH--SHE HAD TO GO AN' TELL ALL HER FRIENDS!
OH!
the End

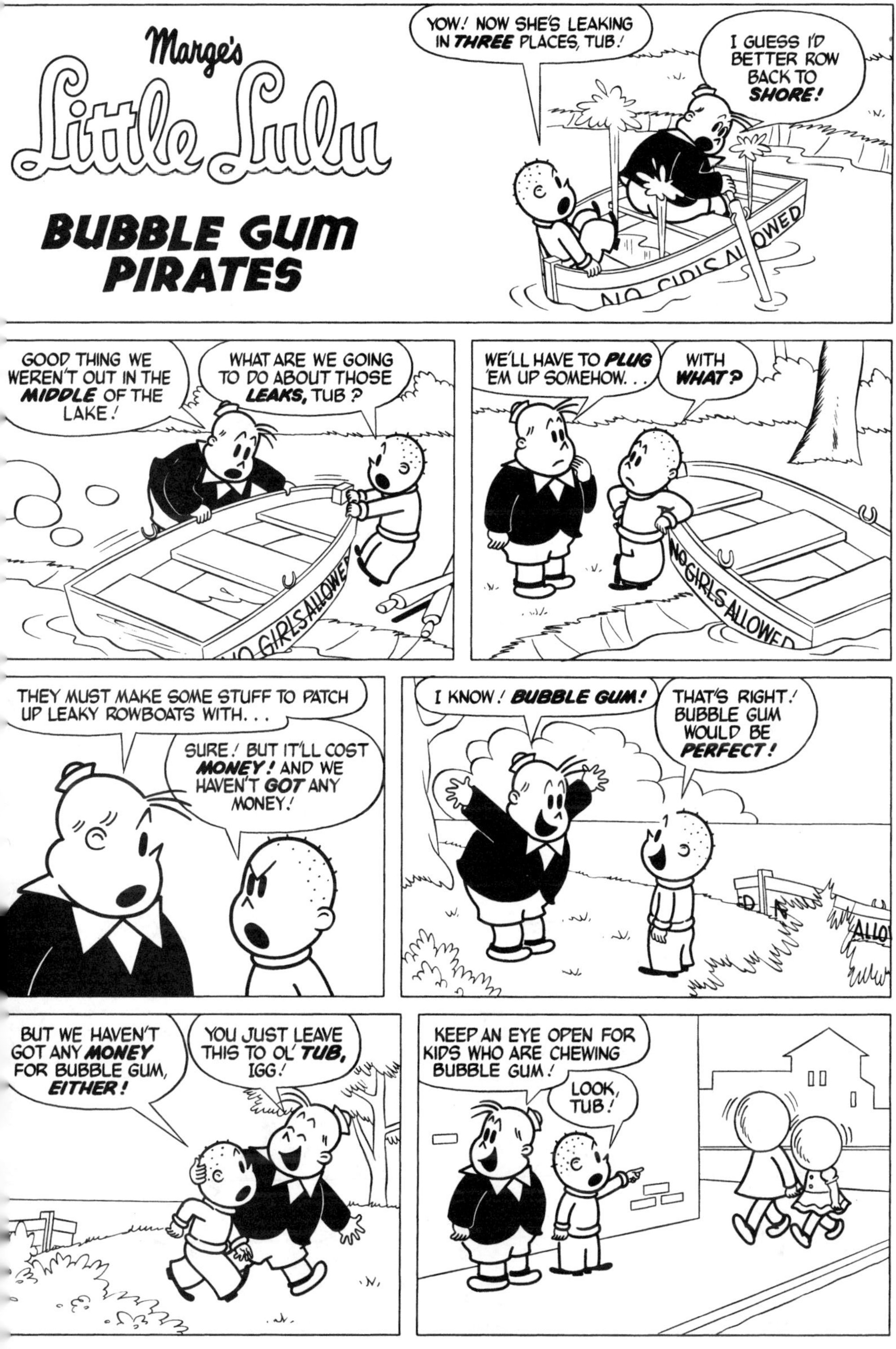
Marge's Little Lulu
BUBBLE GUM PIRATES
YOW! NOW SHE'S LEAKING IN THREE PLACES, TUB!
I GUESS I'D BETTER ROW BACK TO SHORE!
GOOD THING WE WEREN'T OUT IN THE MIDDLE OF THE LAKE!
WHAT ARE WE GOING TO DO ABOUT THOSE LEAKS, TUB?
WE'LL HAVE TO PLUG 'EM UP SOMEHOW. . .
WITH WHAT?
NO GIRLS ALLOWED
THEY MUST MAKE SOME STUFF TO PATCH UP LEAKY ROWBOATS WITH. . .
SURE! BUT IT'LL COST MONEY! AND WE HAVEN'T GOT ANY MONEY!
I KNOW! BUBBLE GUM!
THAT'S RIGHT! BUBBLE GUM WOULD BE PERFECT!
BUT WE HAVEN'T GOT ANY MONEY FOR BUBBLE GUM, EITHER!
YOU JUST LEAVE THIS TO OL' TUB, IGG!
KEEP AN EYE OPEN FOR KIDS WHO ARE CHEWING BUBBLE GUM!
LOOK, TUB!

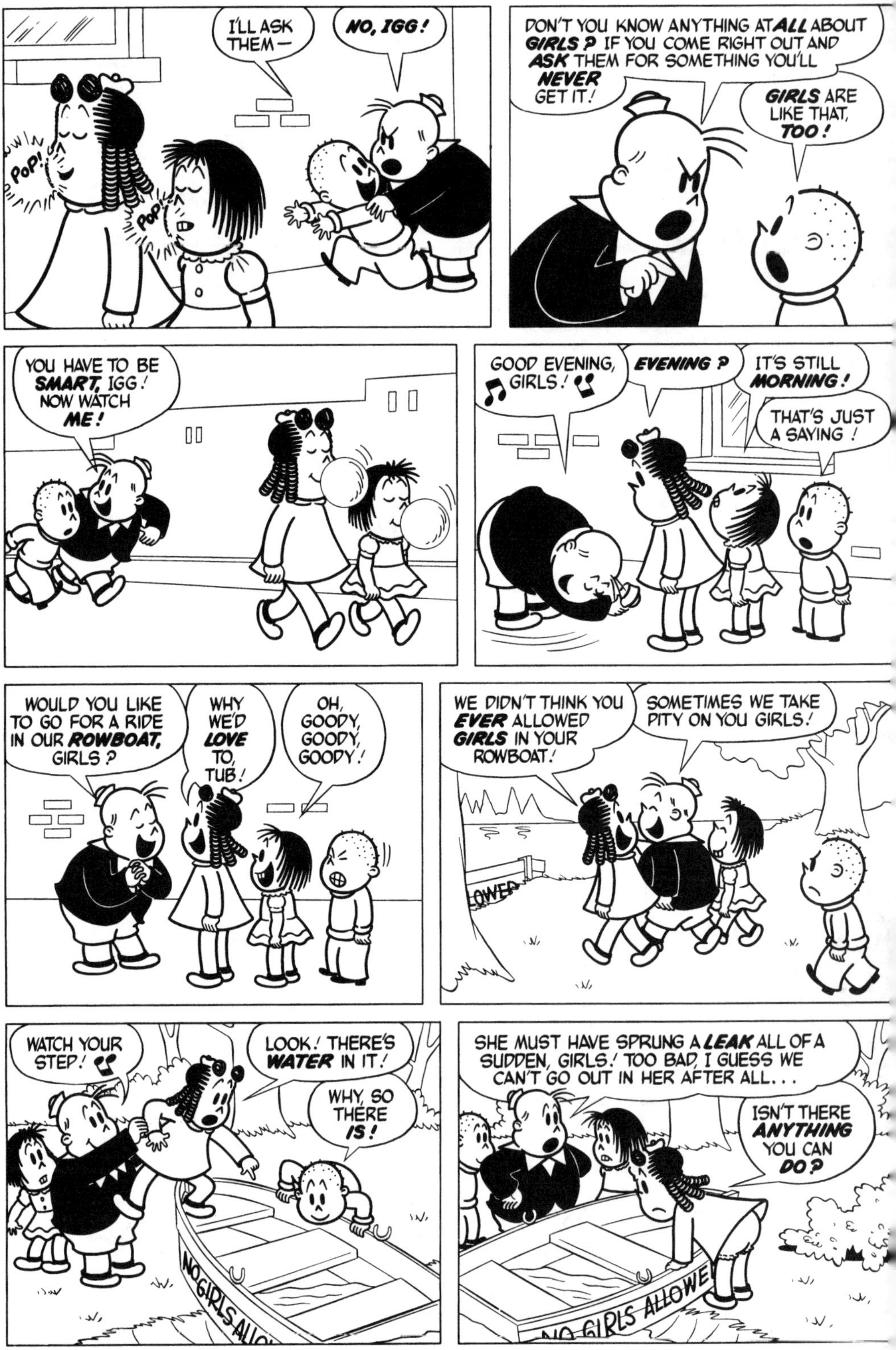
POP!
POP!
I'LL ASK THEM —
NO, IGG!
DON'T YOU KNOW ANYTHING AT ALL ABOUT GIRLS? IF YOU COME RIGHT OUT AND ASK THEM FOR SOMETHING YOU'LL NEVER GET IT!
GIRLS ARE LIKE THAT, TOO!
YOU HAVE TO BE SMART, IGG! NOW WATCH ME!
GOOD EVENING, GIRLS!
EVENING?
IT'S STILL MORNING!
THAT'S JUST A SAYING!
WOULD YOU LIKE TO GO FOR A RIDE IN OUR ROWBOAT, GIRLS?
WHY WE'D LOVE TO, TUB!
OH, GOODY, GOODY, GOODY!
WE DIDN'T THINK YOU EVER ALLOWED GIRLS IN YOUR ROWBOAT!
SOMETIMES WE TAKE PITY ON YOU GIRLS!
WATCH YOUR STEP!
LOOK! THERE'S WATER IN IT!
WHY, SO THERE IS!
SHE MUST HAVE SPRUNG A LEAK ALL OF A SUDDEN, GIRLS! TOO BAD, I GUESS WE CAN'T GO OUT IN HER AFTER ALL...
ISN'T THERE ANYTHING YOU CAN DO?

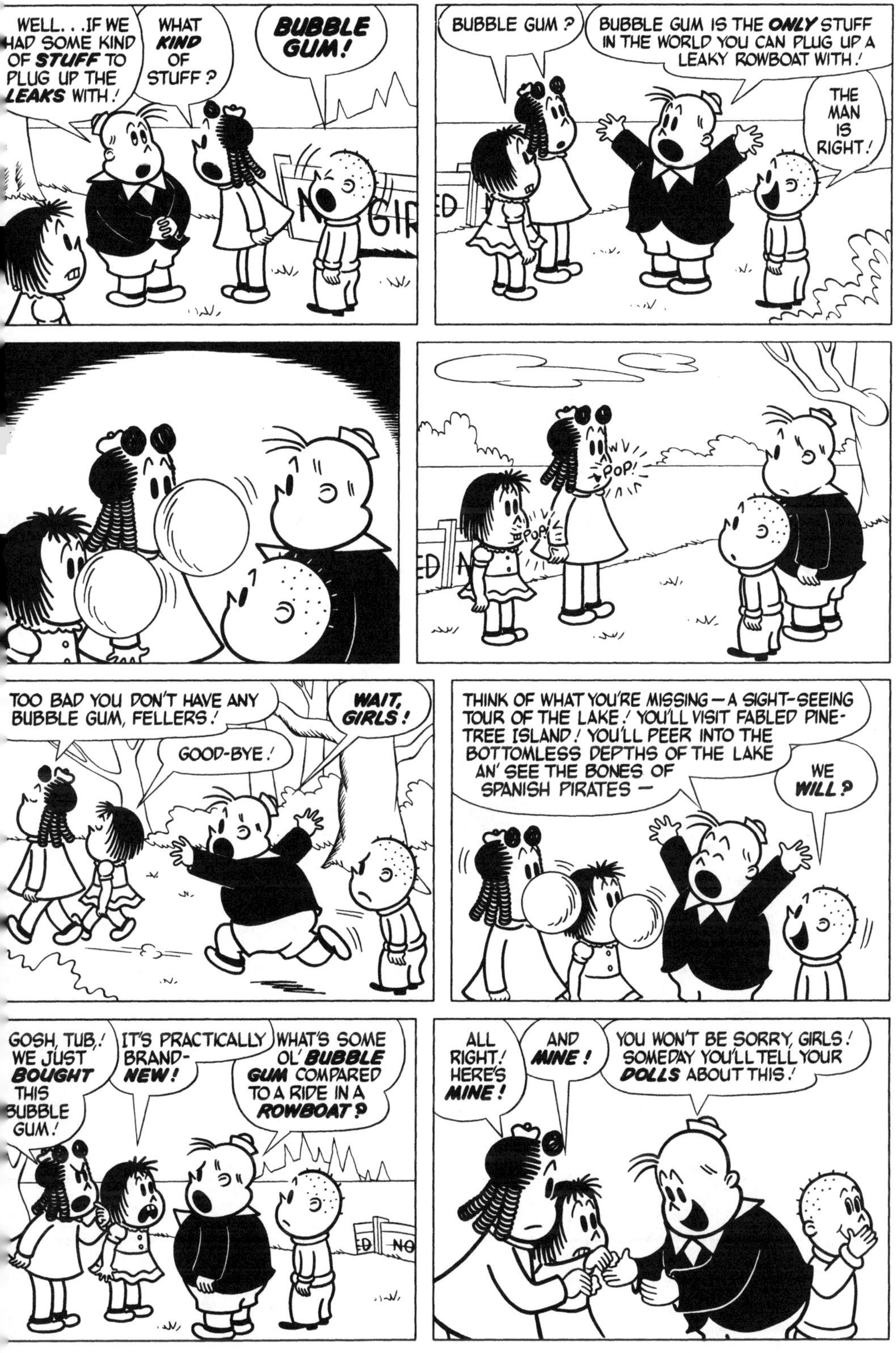

WELL. . .IF WE HAD SOME KIND OF STUFF TO PLUG UP THE LEAKS WITH!
WHAT KIND OF STUFF?
BUBBLE GUM!
NO GIR
BUBBLE GUM?
BUBBLE GUM IS THE ONLY STUFF IN THE WORLD YOU CAN PLUG UP A LEAKY ROWBOAT WITH!
THE MAN IS RIGHT!
ED
POP!
POP!
ED
TOO BAD YOU DON'T HAVE ANY BUBBLE GUM, FELLERS!
GOOD-BYE!
WAIT, GIRLS!
THINK OF WHAT YOU'RE MISSING — A SIGHT-SEEING TOUR OF THE LAKE! YOU'LL VISIT FABLED PINE-TREE ISLAND! YOU'LL PEER INTO THE BOTTOMLESS DEPTHS OF THE LAKE AN' SEE THE BONES OF SPANISH PIRATES —
WE WILL?
GOSH, TUB! WE JUST BOUGHT THIS BUBBLE GUM!
IT'S PRACTICALLY BRAND-NEW!
WHAT'S SOME OL' BUBBLE GUM COMPARED TO A RIDE IN A ROWBOAT?
ED NO
ALL RIGHT! HERE'S MINE!
AND MINE!
YOU WON'T BE SORRY, GIRLS! SOMEDAY YOU'LL TELL YOUR DOLLS ABOUT THIS!

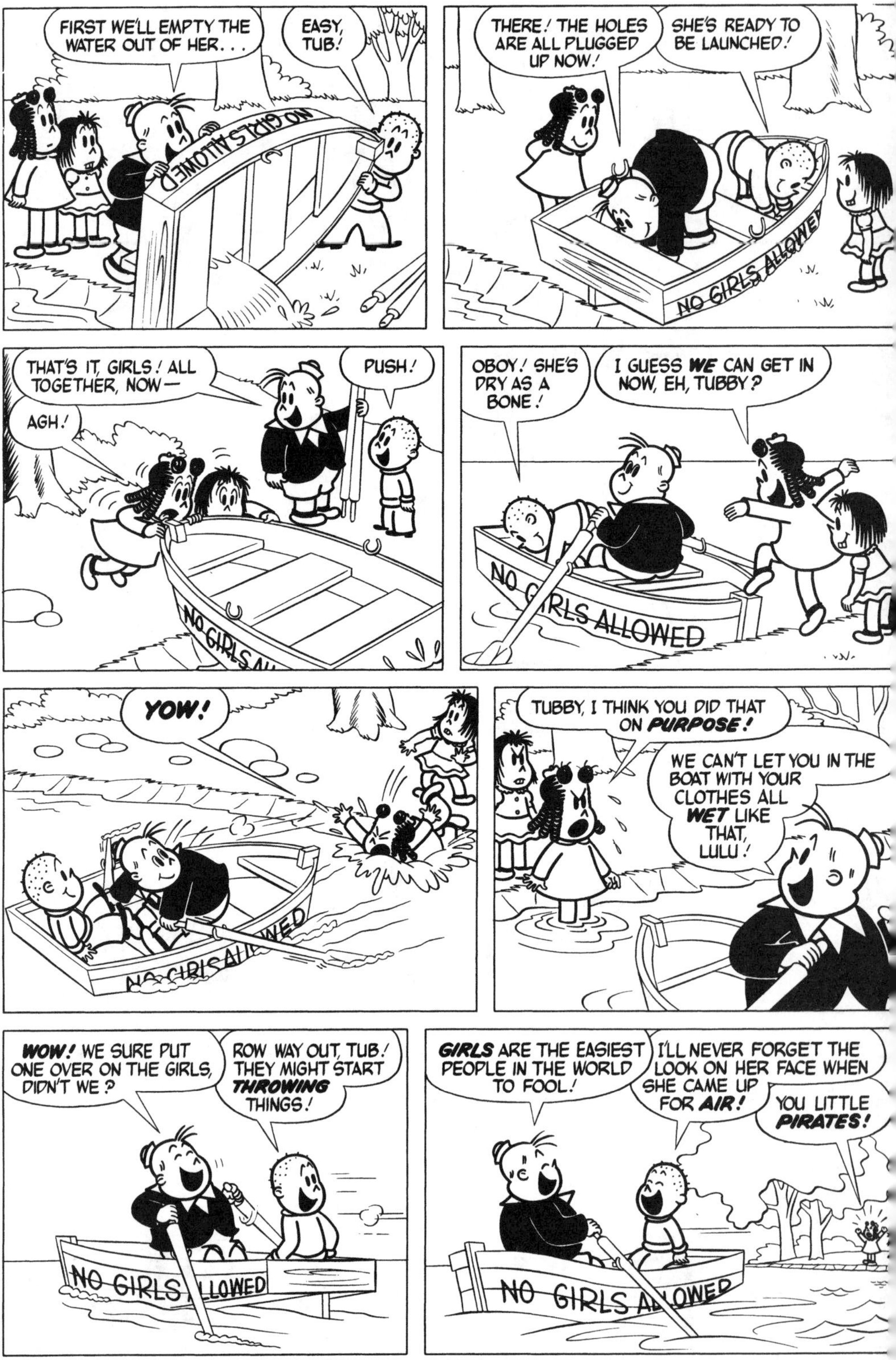

FIRST WE'LL EMPTY THE WATER OUT OF HER. . .
EASY, TUB!
THERE! THE HOLES ARE ALL PLUGGED UP NOW!
SHE'S READY TO BE LAUNCHED!
THAT'S IT, GIRLS! ALL TOGETHER, NOW—
PUSH!
AGH!
OBOY! SHE'S DRY AS A BONE!
I GUESS WE CAN GET IN NOW, EH, TUBBY?
YOW!
TUBBY, I THINK YOU DID THAT ON PURPOSE!
WE CAN'T LET YOU IN THE BOAT WITH YOUR CLOTHES ALL WET LIKE THAT, LULU!
WOW! WE SURE PUT ONE OVER ON THE GIRLS, DIDN'T WE?
ROW WAY OUT, TUB! THEY MIGHT START THROWING THINGS!
NO GIRLS ALLOWED
GIRLS ARE THE EASIEST PEOPLE IN THE WORLD TO FOOL!
I'LL NEVER FORGET THE LOOK ON HER FACE WHEN SHE CAME UP FOR AIR!
YOU LITTLE PIRATES!

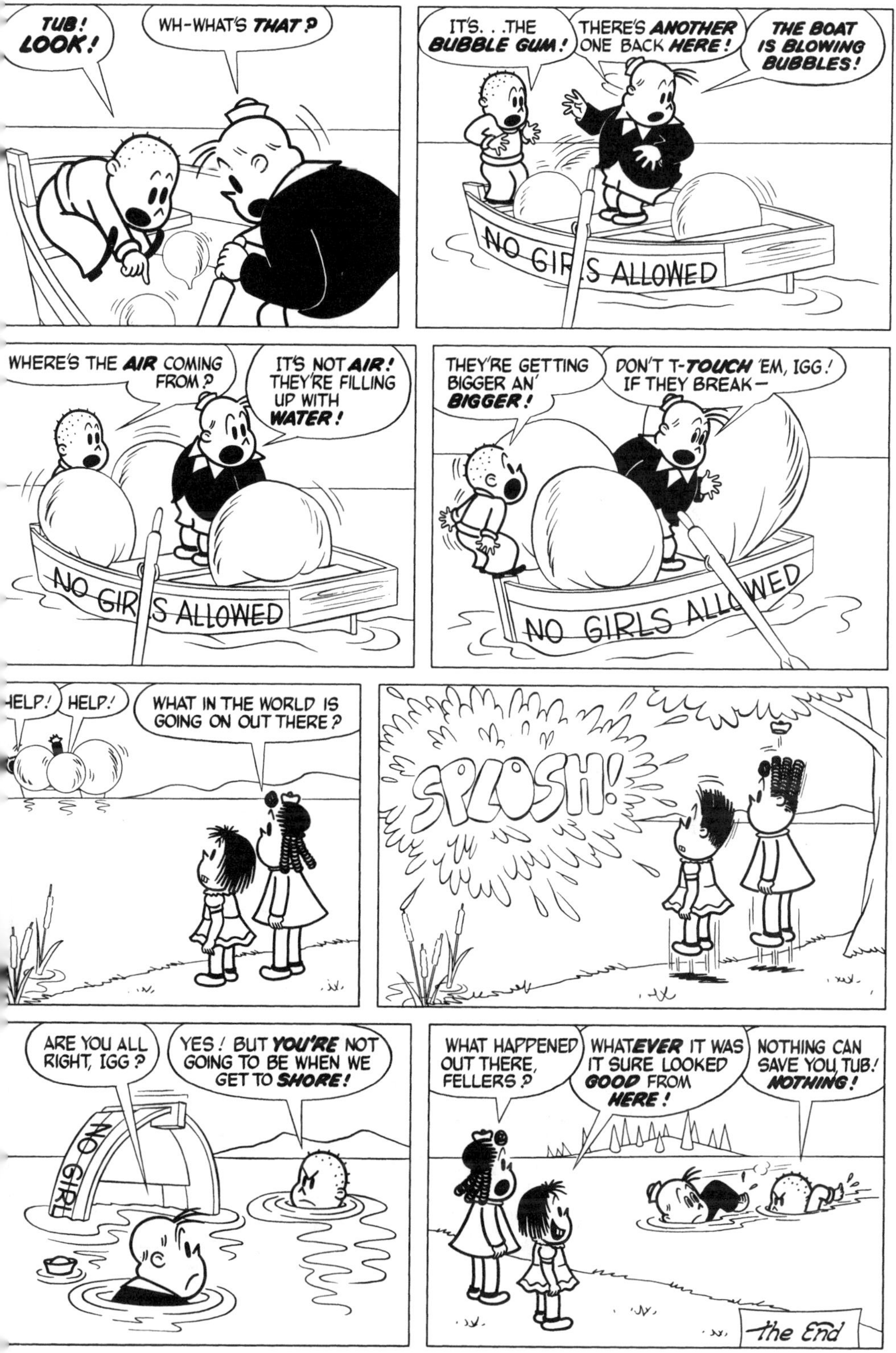
TUB! LOOK!
WH-WHAT'S THAT?
IT'S. . .THE BUBBLE GUM!
THERE'S ANOTHER ONE BACK HERE!
THE BOAT IS BLOWING BUBBLES!
NO GIRLS ALLOWED
WHERE'S THE AIR COMING FROM?
IT'S NOT AIR! THEY'RE FILLING UP WITH WATER!
NO GIRLS ALLOWED
THEY'RE GETTING BIGGER AN' BIGGER!
DON'T T-TOUCH 'EM, IGG! IF THEY BREAK—
NO GIRLS ALLOWED
HELP!
HELP!
WHAT IN THE WORLD IS GOING ON OUT THERE?
SPLOSH!
ARE YOU ALL RIGHT, IGG?
YES! BUT YOU'RE NOT GOING TO BE WHEN WE GET TO SHORE!
NO GIRL
WHAT HAPPENED OUT THERE, FELLERS?
WHATEVER IT WAS IT SURE LOOKED GOOD FROM HERE!
NOTHING CAN SAVE YOU, TUB! NOTHING!
The End

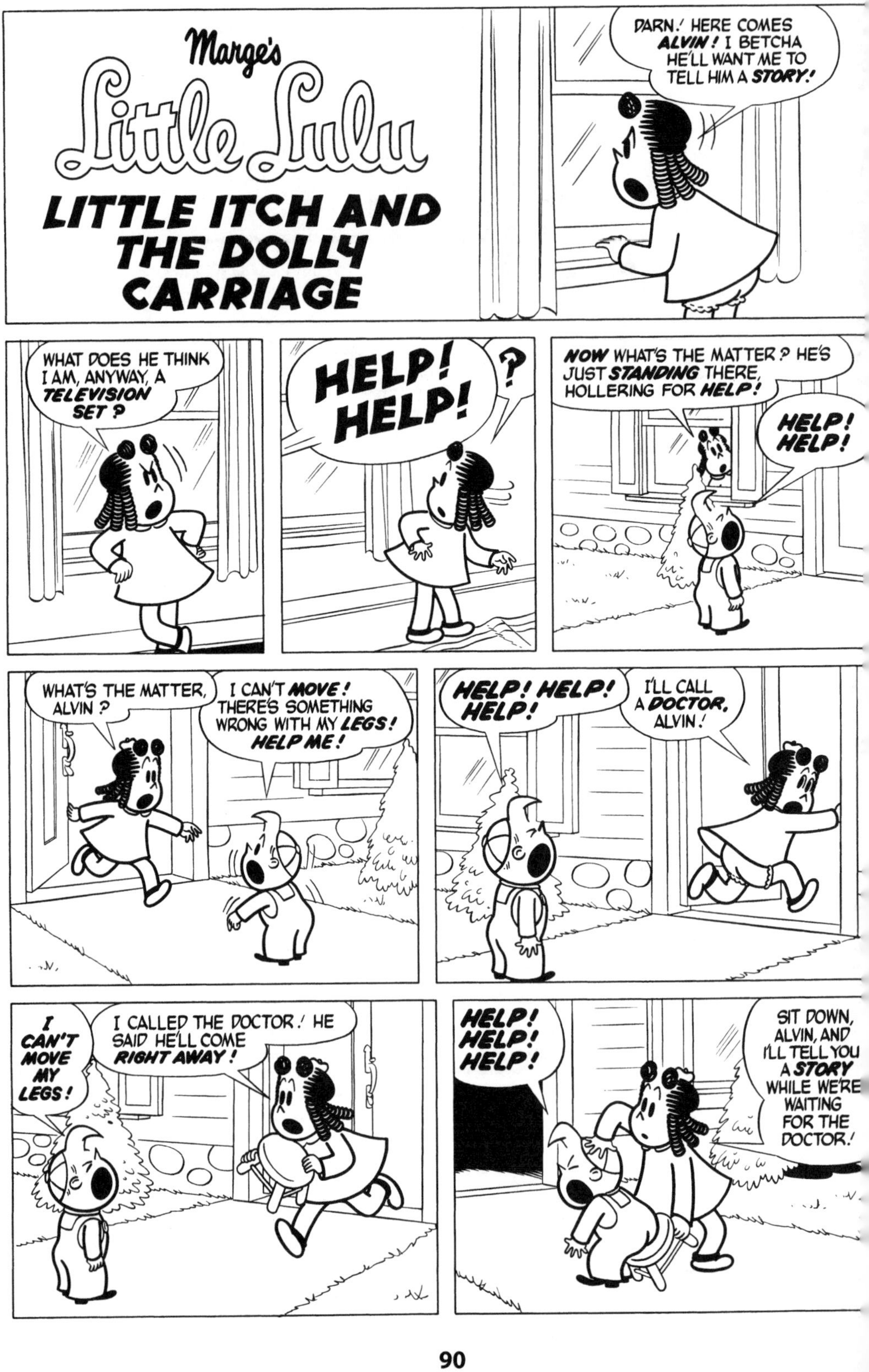
Marge's
Little Lulu
LITTLE ITCH AND THE DOLLY CARRIAGE
DARN.' HERE COMES ALVIN! I BETCHA HE'LL WANT ME TO TELL HIM A STORY!
WHAT DOES HE THINK I AM, ANYWAY, A TELEVISION SET?
HELP! HELP!
?
NOW WHAT'S THE MATTER? HE'S JUST STANDING THERE, HOLLERING FOR HELP!
HELP! HELP!
WHAT'S THE MATTER, ALVIN?
I CAN'T MOVE! THERE'S SOMETHING WRONG WITH MY LEGS! HELP ME!
HELP! HELP! HELP!
I'LL CALL A DOCTOR, ALVIN.'
I CAN'T MOVE MY LEGS!
I CALLED THE DOCTOR.' HE SAID HE'LL COME RIGHT AWAY!
HELP! HELP! HELP!
SIT DOWN, ALVIN, AND I'LL TELL YOU A STORY WHILE WE'RE WAITING FOR THE DOCTOR.'

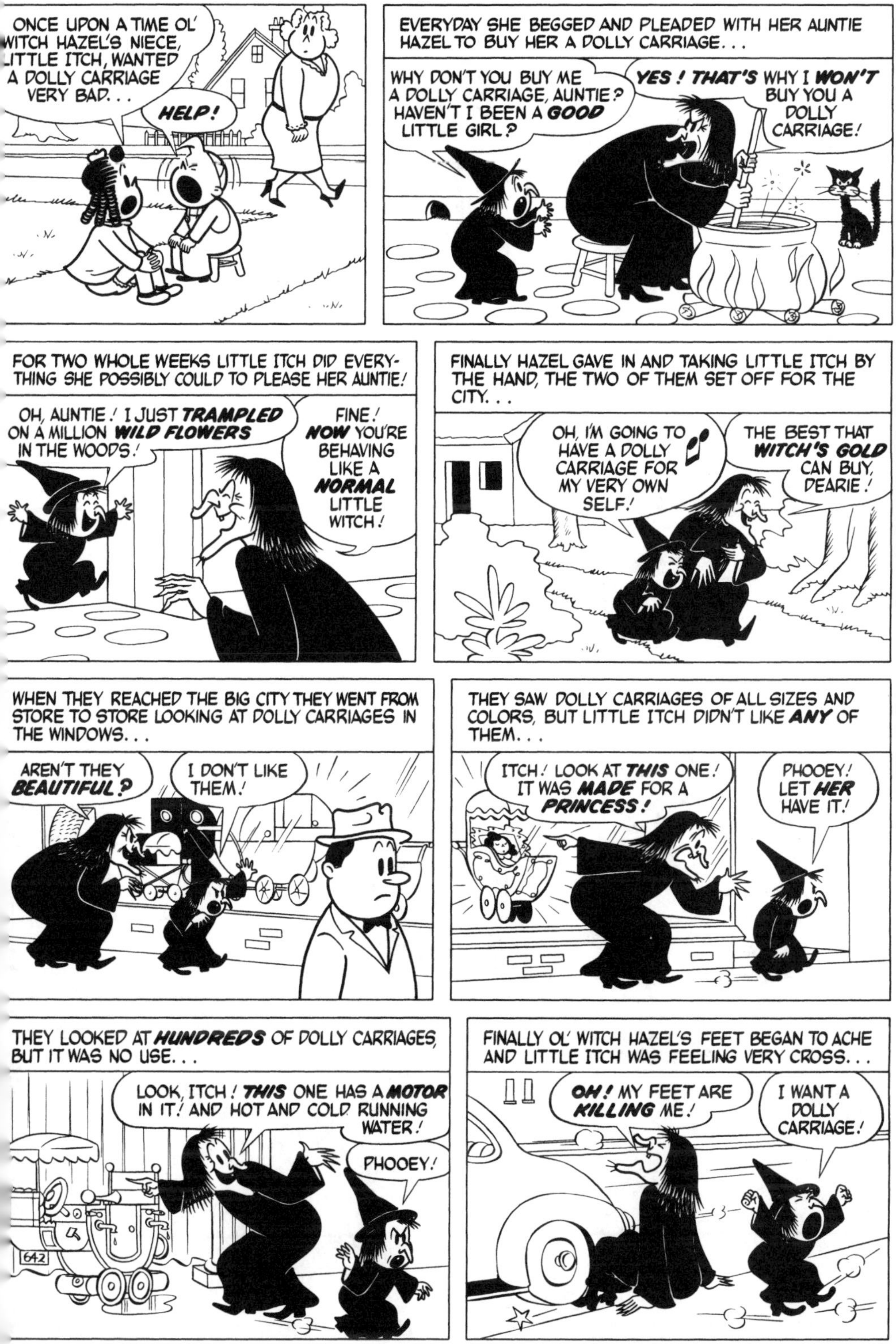

ONCE UPON A TIME OL' WITCH HAZEL'S NIECE, LITTLE ITCH, WANTED A DOLLY CARRIAGE VERY BAD...
HELP!
EVERYDAY SHE BEGGED AND PLEADED WITH HER AUNTIE HAZEL TO BUY HER A DOLLY CARRIAGE...
WHY DON'T YOU BUY ME A DOLLY CARRIAGE, AUNTIE? HAVEN'T I BEEN A GOOD LITTLE GIRL?
YES! THAT'S WHY I WON'T BUY YOU A DOLLY CARRIAGE!
FOR TWO WHOLE WEEKS LITTLE ITCH DID EVERYTHING SHE POSSIBLY COULD TO PLEASE HER AUNTIE!
OH, AUNTIE! I JUST TRAMPLED ON A MILLION WILD FLOWERS IN THE WOODS!
FINE! NOW YOU'RE BEHAVING LIKE A NORMAL LITTLE WITCH!
FINALLY HAZEL GAVE IN AND TAKING LITTLE ITCH BY THE HAND, THE TWO OF THEM SET OFF FOR THE CITY...
OH, I'M GOING TO HAVE A DOLLY CARRIAGE FOR MY VERY OWN SELF!
THE BEST THAT WITCH'S GOLD CAN BUY, DEARIE!
WHEN THEY REACHED THE BIG CITY THEY WENT FROM STORE TO STORE LOOKING AT DOLLY CARRIAGES IN THE WINDOWS...
AREN'T THEY BEAUTIFUL?
I DON'T LIKE THEM!
THEY SAW DOLLY CARRIAGES OF ALL SIZES AND COLORS, BUT LITTLE ITCH DIDN'T LIKE ANY OF THEM...
ITCH! LOOK AT THIS ONE! IT WAS MADE FOR A PRINCESS!
PHOOEY! LET HER HAVE IT!
THEY LOOKED AT HUNDREDS OF DOLLY CARRIAGES, BUT IT WAS NO USE...
LOOK, ITCH! THIS ONE HAS A MOTOR IN IT! AND HOT AND COLD RUNNING WATER!
PHOOEY!
642
FINALLY OL' WITCH HAZEL'S FEET BEGAN TO ACHE AND LITTLE ITCH WAS FEELING VERY CROSS...
OH! MY FEET ARE KILLING ME!
I WANT A DOLLY CARRIAGE!

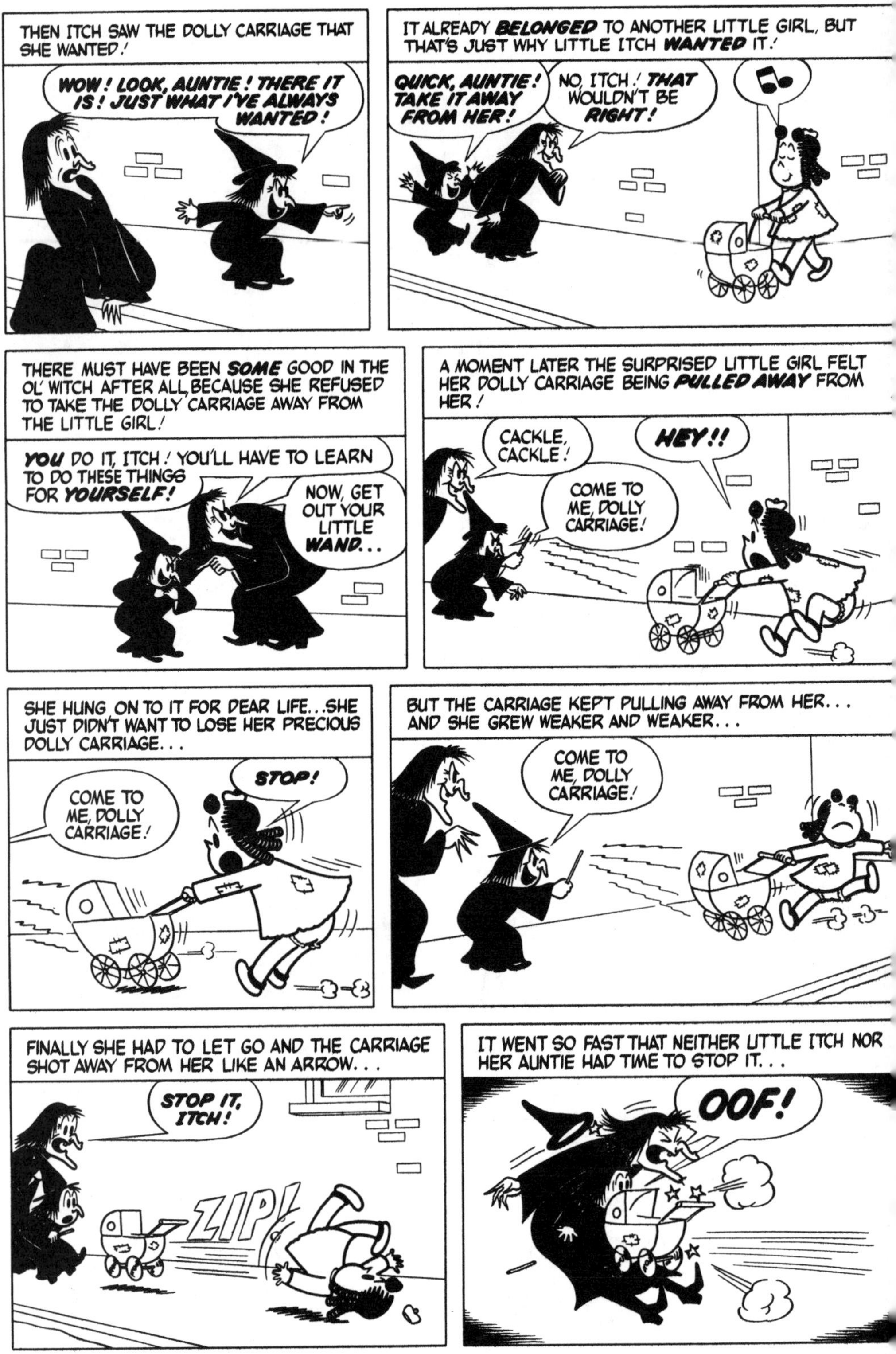

THEN ITCH SAW THE DOLLY CARRIAGE THAT SHE WANTED!
WOW! LOOK, AUNTIE! THERE IT IS! JUST WHAT I'VE ALWAYS WANTED!
IT ALREADY BELONGED TO ANOTHER LITTLE GIRL, BUT THAT'S JUST WHY LITTLE ITCH WANTED IT!
QUICK, AUNTIE! TAKE IT AWAY FROM HER!
NO, ITCH! THAT WOULDN'T BE RIGHT!
THERE MUST HAVE BEEN SOME GOOD IN THE OL' WITCH AFTER ALL, BECAUSE SHE REFUSED TO TAKE THE DOLLY CARRIAGE AWAY FROM THE LITTLE GIRL!
YOU DO IT, ITCH! YOU'LL HAVE TO LEARN TO DO THESE THINGS FOR YOURSELF!
NOW, GET OUT YOUR LITTLE WAND...
A MOMENT LATER THE SURPRISED LITTLE GIRL FELT HER DOLLY CARRIAGE BEING PULLED AWAY FROM HER!
CACKLE, CACKLE!
HEY!!
COME TO ME, DOLLY CARRIAGE!
SHE HUNG ON TO IT FOR DEAR LIFE...SHE JUST DIDN'T WANT TO LOSE HER PRECIOUS DOLLY CARRIAGE...
COME TO ME, DOLLY CARRIAGE!
STOP!
BUT THE CARRIAGE KEPT PULLING AWAY FROM HER... AND SHE GREW WEAKER AND WEAKER...
COME TO ME, DOLLY CARRIAGE!
FINALLY SHE HAD TO LET GO AND THE CARRIAGE SHOT AWAY FROM HER LIKE AN ARROW...
STOP IT, ITCH!
ZIP!
IT WENT SO FAST THAT NEITHER LITTLE ITCH NOR HER AUNTIE HAD TIME TO STOP IT...
OOF!

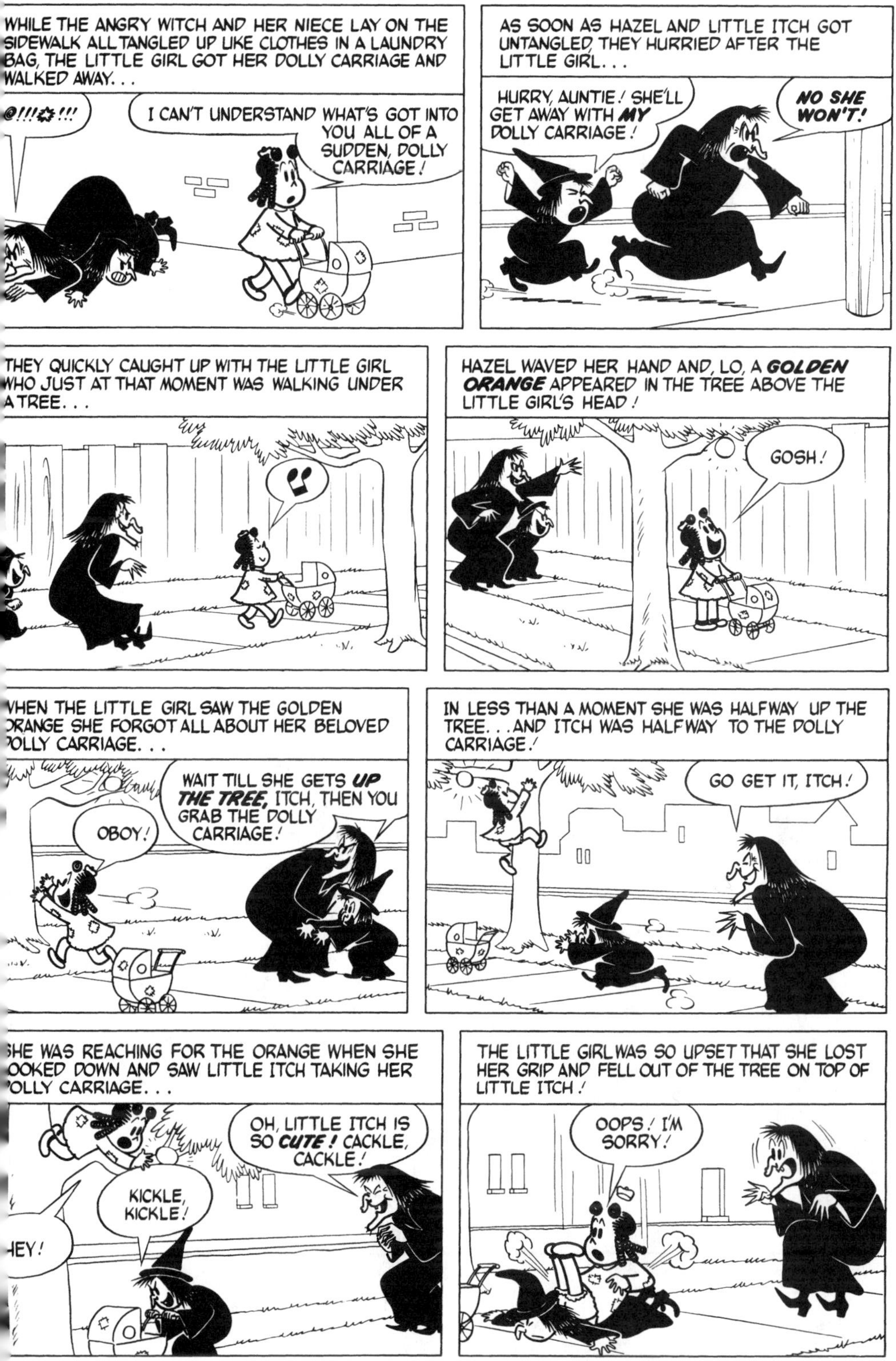
WHILE THE ANGRY WITCH AND HER NIECE LAY ON THE SIDEWALK ALL TANGLED UP LIKE CLOTHES IN A LAUNDRY BAG, THE LITTLE GIRL GOT HER DOLLY CARRIAGE AND WALKED AWAY. . .
@!!!✪!!!
I CAN'T UNDERSTAND WHAT'S GOT INTO YOU ALL OF A SUDDEN, DOLLY CARRIAGE!
AS SOON AS HAZEL AND LITTLE ITCH GOT UNTANGLED, THEY HURRIED AFTER THE LITTLE GIRL. . .
HURRY, AUNTIE! SHE'LL GET AWAY WITH MY DOLLY CARRIAGE!
NO SHE WON'T!
THEY QUICKLY CAUGHT UP WITH THE LITTLE GIRL WHO JUST AT THAT MOMENT WAS WALKING UNDER A TREE. . .
HAZEL WAVED HER HAND AND, LO, A GOLDEN ORANGE APPEARED IN THE TREE ABOVE THE LITTLE GIRL'S HEAD!
GOSH!
VHEN THE LITTLE GIRL SAW THE GOLDEN RANGE SHE FORGOT ALL ABOUT HER BELOVED OLLY CARRIAGE. . .
OBOY!
WAIT TILL SHE GETS UP THE TREE, ITCH, THEN YOU GRAB THE DOLLY CARRIAGE!
IN LESS THAN A MOMENT SHE WAS HALFWAY UP THE TREE. . . AND ITCH WAS HALFWAY TO THE DOLLY CARRIAGE!
GO GET IT, ITCH!
HE WAS REACHING FOR THE ORANGE WHEN SHE OOKED DOWN AND SAW LITTLE ITCH TAKING HER OLLY CARRIAGE. . .
HEY!
KICKLE, KICKLE!
OH, LITTLE ITCH IS SO CUTE! CACKLE, CACKLE!
THE LITTLE GIRL WAS SO UPSET THAT SHE LOST HER GRIP AND FELL OUT OF THE TREE ON TOP OF LITTLE ITCH!
OOPS! I'M SORRY!

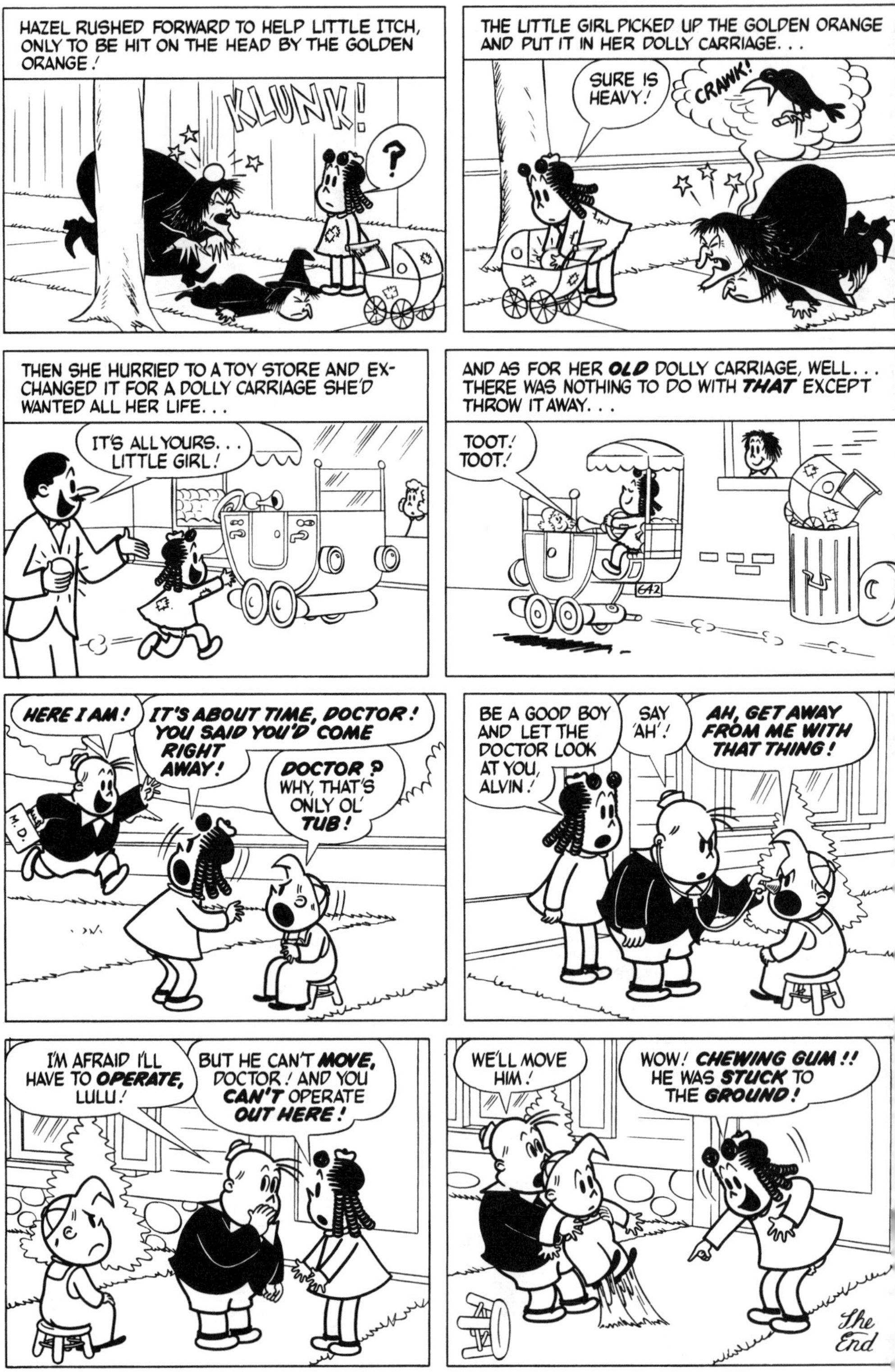
HAZEL RUSHED FORWARD TO HELP LITTLE ITCH, ONLY TO BE HIT ON THE HEAD BY THE GOLDEN ORANGE!
KLUNK!
?
THE LITTLE GIRL PICKED UP THE GOLDEN ORANGE AND PUT IT IN HER DOLLY CARRIAGE...
SURE IS HEAVY!
CRAWK!
THEN SHE HURRIED TO A TOY STORE AND EXCHANGED IT FOR A DOLLY CARRIAGE SHE'D WANTED ALL HER LIFE...
IT'S ALL YOURS... LITTLE GIRL!
AND AS FOR HER OLD DOLLY CARRIAGE, WELL... THERE WAS NOTHING TO DO WITH THAT EXCEPT THROW IT AWAY...
TOOT! TOOT!
642
HERE I AM!
IT'S ABOUT TIME, DOCTOR! YOU SAID YOU'D COME RIGHT AWAY!
M.D.
DOCTOR? WHY, THAT'S ONLY OL' TUB!
BE A GOOD BOY AND LET THE DOCTOR LOOK AT YOU, ALVIN!
SAY 'AH'!
AH, GET AWAY FROM ME WITH THAT THING!
I'M AFRAID I'LL HAVE TO OPERATE, LULU!
BUT HE CAN'T MOVE, DOCTOR! AND YOU CAN'T OPERATE OUT HERE!
WE'LL MOVE HIM!
WOW! CHEWING GUM!! HE WAS STUCK TO THE GROUND!
The End

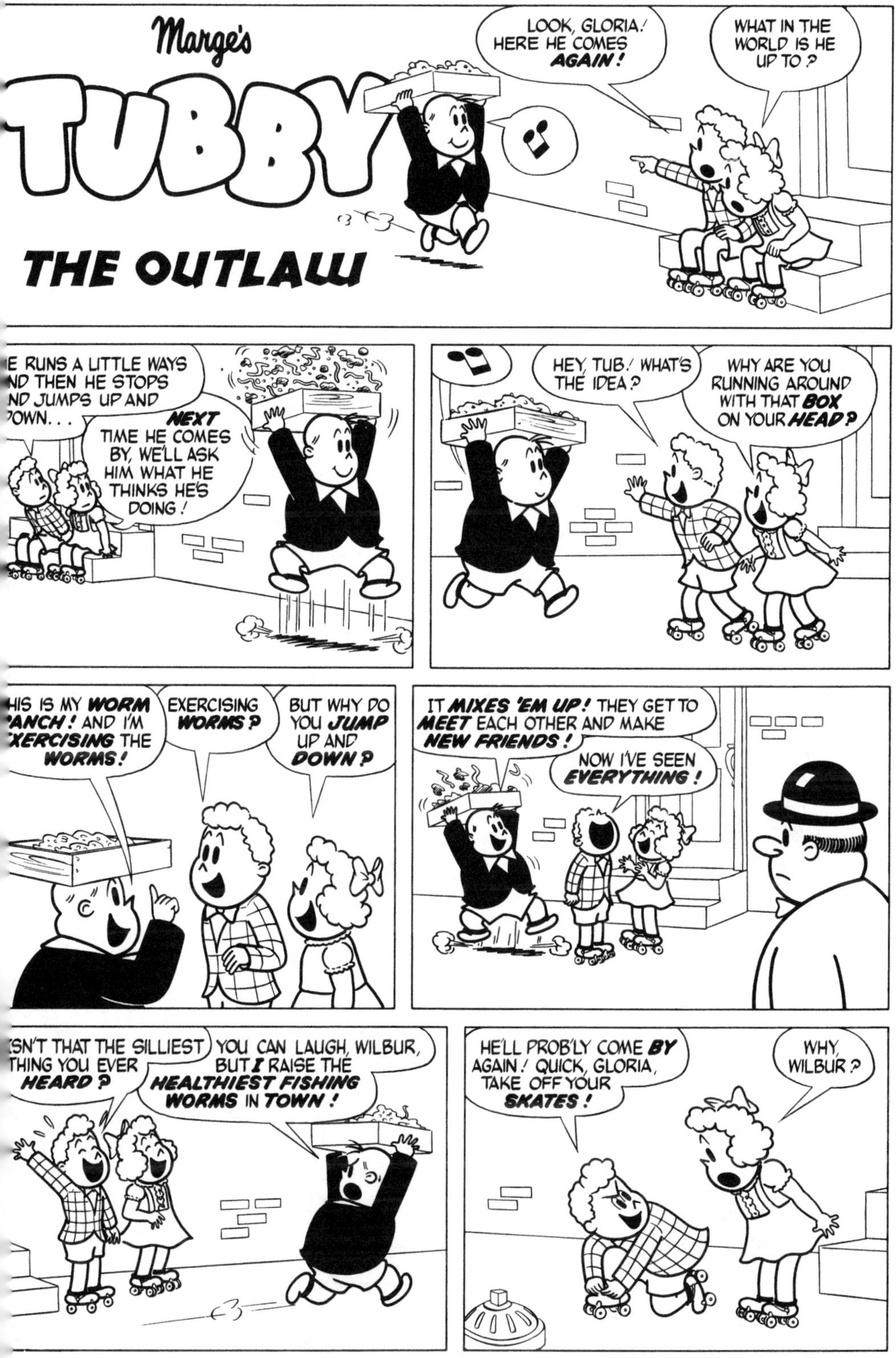

Marge's
TUBBY
THE OUTLAW
LOOK, GLORIA! HERE HE COMES AGAIN!
WHAT IN THE WORLD IS HE UP TO?
E RUNS A LITTLE WAYS ND THEN HE STOPS ND JUMPS UP AND OWN...
NEXT TIME HE COMES BY, WE'LL ASK HIM WHAT HE THINKS HE'S DOING!
HEY, TUB! WHAT'S THE IDEA?
WHY ARE YOU RUNNING AROUND WITH THAT BOX ON YOUR HEAD?
HIS IS MY WORM ANCH! AND I'M XERCISING THE WORMS!
EXERCISING WORMS?
BUT WHY DO YOU JUMP UP AND DOWN?
IT MIXES 'EM UP! THEY GET TO MEET EACH OTHER AND MAKE NEW FRIENDS!
NOW I'VE SEEN EVERYTHING!
SN'T THAT THE SILLIEST THING YOU EVER HEARD?
YOU CAN LAUGH, WILBUR, BUT I RAISE THE HEALTHIEST FISHING WORMS IN TOWN!
HE'LL PROB'LY COME BY AGAIN! QUICK, GLORIA, TAKE OFF YOUR SKATES!
WHY, WILBUR?

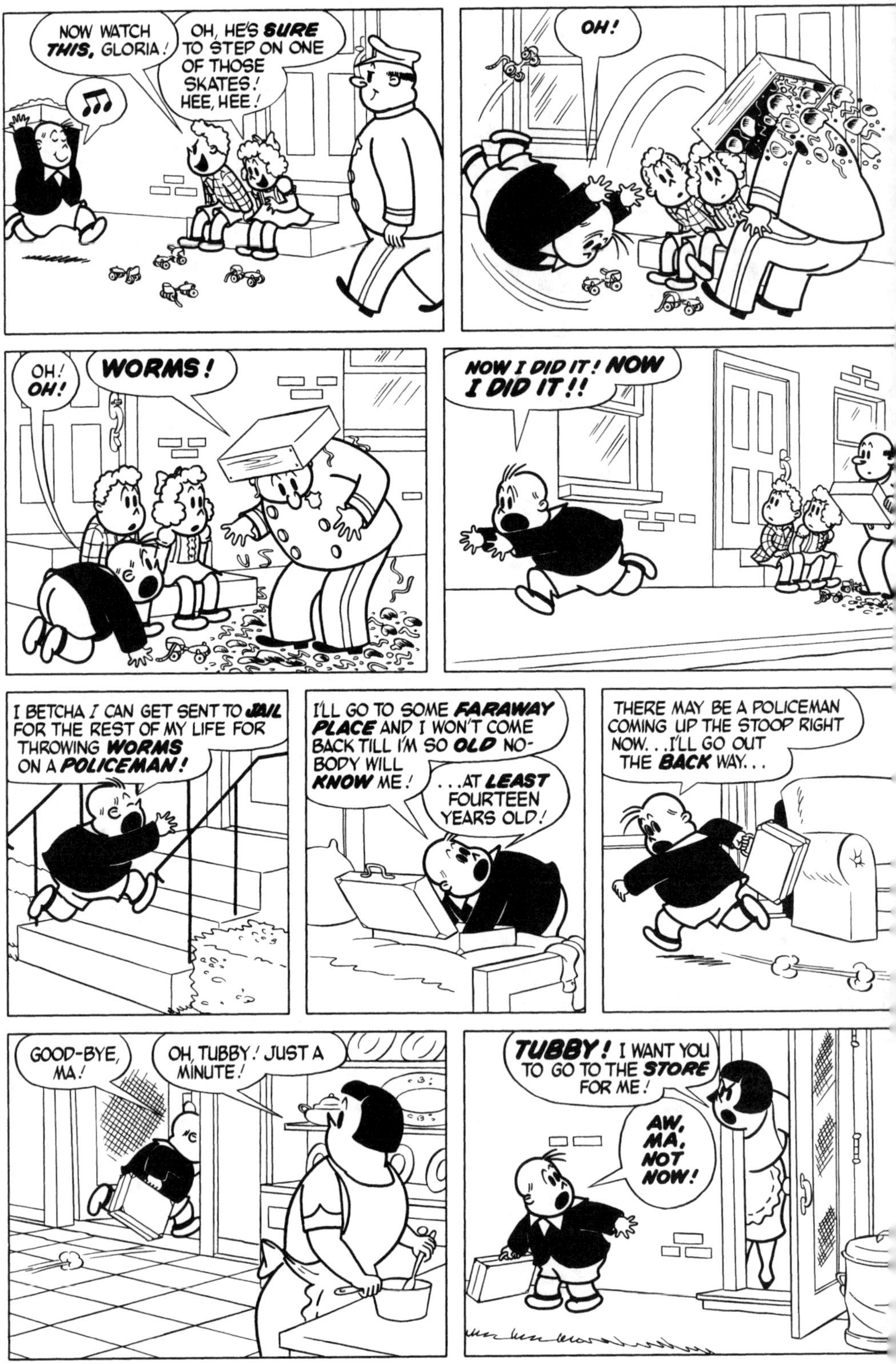
NOW WATCH THIS, GLORIA!
OH, HE'S SURE TO STEP ON ONE OF THOSE SKATES! HEE, HEE!
OH!
OH! OH!
WORMS!
NOW I DID IT! NOW I DID IT!!
I BETCHA I CAN GET SENT TO JAIL FOR THE REST OF MY LIFE FOR THROWING WORMS ON A POLICEMAN!
I'LL GO TO SOME FARAWAY PLACE AND I WON'T COME BACK TILL I'M SO OLD NO-BODY WILL KNOW ME!
...AT LEAST FOURTEEN YEARS OLD!
THERE MAY BE A POLICEMAN COMING UP THE STOOP RIGHT NOW...I'LL GO OUT THE BACK WAY...
GOOD-BYE, MA!
OH, TUBBY! JUST A MINUTE!
TUBBY! I WANT YOU TO GO TO THE STORE FOR ME!
AW, MA, NOT NOW!

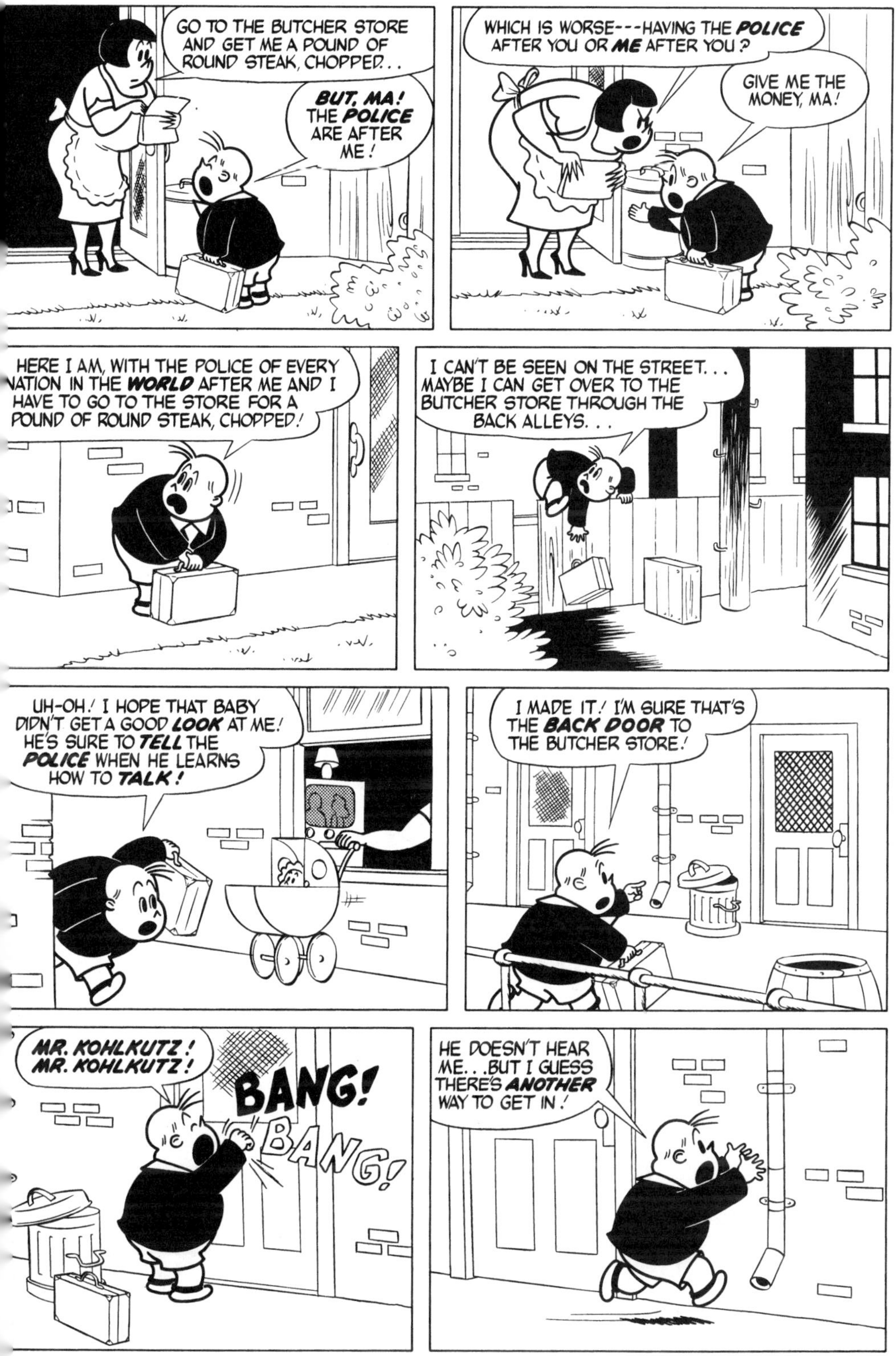
GO TO THE BUTCHER STORE AND GET ME A POUND OF ROUND STEAK, CHOPPED. . .
BUT, MA! THE POLICE ARE AFTER ME!
WHICH IS WORSE---HAVING THE POLICE AFTER YOU OR ME AFTER YOU?
GIVE ME THE MONEY, MA!
HERE I AM, WITH THE POLICE OF EVERY NATION IN THE WORLD AFTER ME AND I HAVE TO GO TO THE STORE FOR A POUND OF ROUND STEAK, CHOPPED!
I CAN'T BE SEEN ON THE STREET. . . MAYBE I CAN GET OVER TO THE BUTCHER STORE THROUGH THE BACK ALLEYS. . .
UH-OH! I HOPE THAT BABY DIDN'T GET A GOOD LOOK AT ME! HE'S SURE TO TELL THE POLICE WHEN HE LEARNS HOW TO TALK!
I MADE IT! I'M SURE THAT'S THE BACK DOOR TO THE BUTCHER STORE!
MR. KOHLKUTZ! MR. KOHLKUTZ!
BANG!
BANG!
HE DOESN'T HEAR ME. . .BUT I GUESS THERE'S ANOTHER WAY TO GET IN!

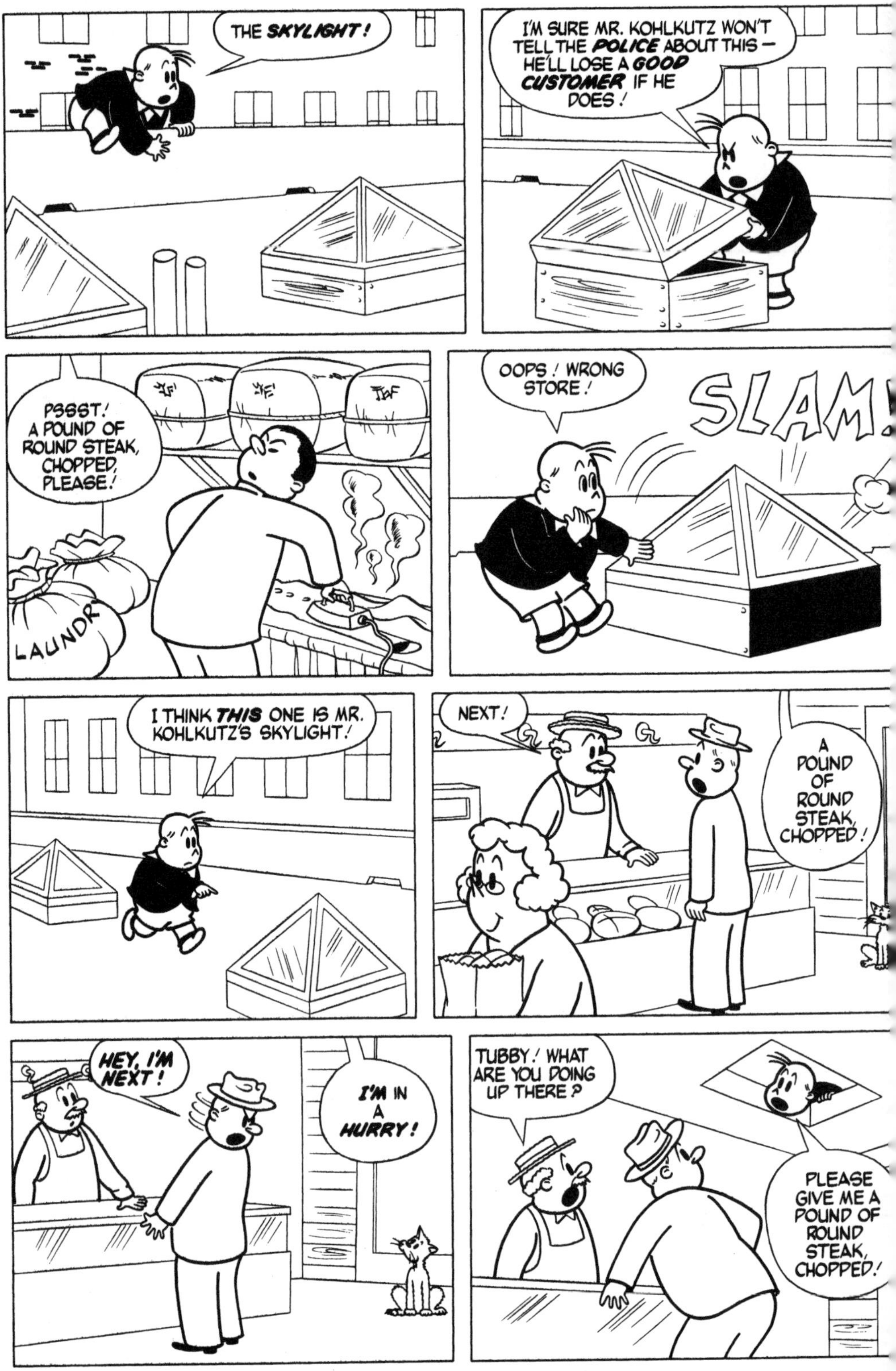
THE SKYLIGHT!
I'M SURE MR. KOHLKUTZ WON'T TELL THE POLICE ABOUT THIS— HE'LL LOSE A GOOD CUSTOMER IF HE DOES!
PSSST! A POUND OF ROUND STEAK, CHOPPED, PLEASE!
LAUNDR
OOPS! WRONG STORE!
SLAM!
I THINK THIS ONE IS MR. KOHLKUTZ'S SKYLIGHT!
NEXT!
A POUND OF ROUND STEAK, CHOPPED!
HEY, I'M NEXT!
I'M IN A HURRY!
TUBBY! WHAT ARE YOU DOING UP THERE?
PLEASE GIVE ME A POUND OF ROUND STEAK, CHOPPED!

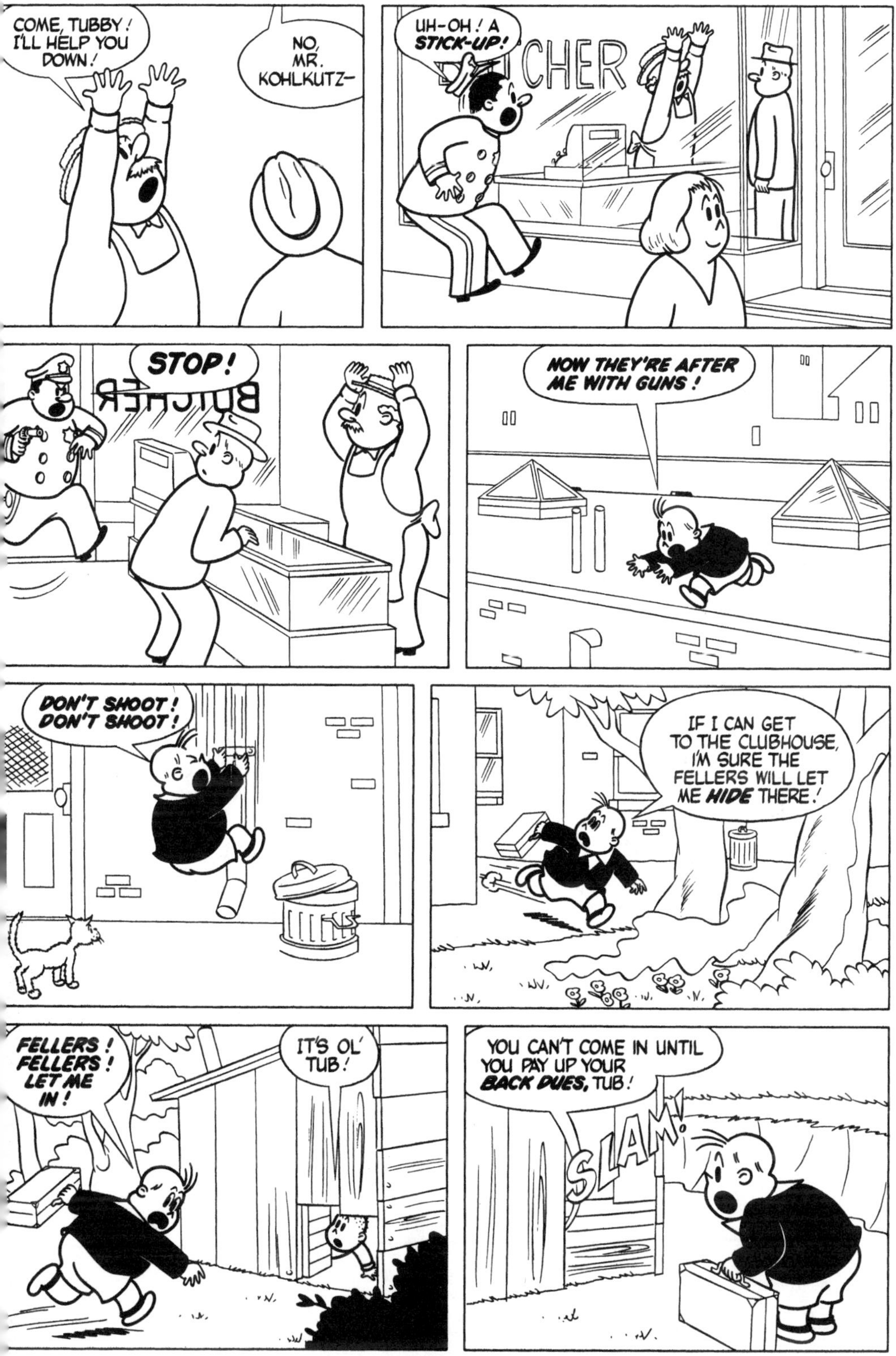

COME, TUBBY! I'LL HELP YOU DOWN!
NO, MR. KOHLKUTZ—
UH-OH! A STICK-UP!
BUTCHER
STOP!
BUTCHER
NOW THEY'RE AFTER ME WITH GUNS!
DON'T SHOOT! DON'T SHOOT!
IF I CAN GET TO THE CLUBHOUSE, I'M SURE THE FELLERS WILL LET ME HIDE THERE!
FELLERS! FELLERS! LET ME IN!
IT'S OL' TUB!
YOU CAN'T COME IN UNTIL YOU PAY UP YOUR BACK DUES, TUB!
SLAM!

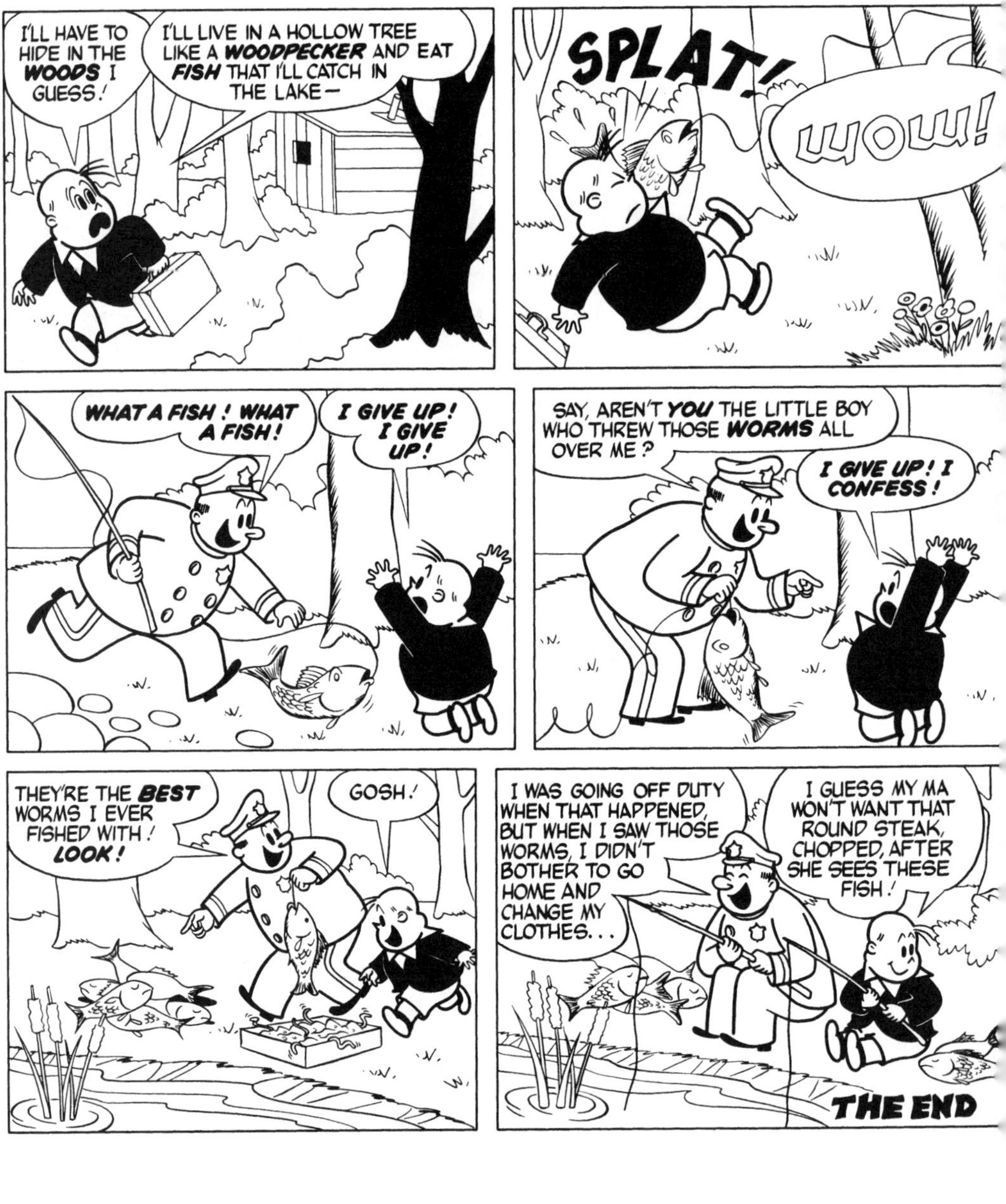
I'LL HAVE TO HIDE IN THE WOODS I GUESS.!
I'LL LIVE IN A HOLLOW TREE LIKE A WOODPECKER AND EAT FISH THAT I'LL CATCH IN THE LAKE—
SPLAT!
WOW!
WHAT A FISH! WHAT A FISH!
I GIVE UP! I GIVE UP!
SAY, AREN'T YOU THE LITTLE BOY WHO THREW THOSE WORMS ALL OVER ME?
I GIVE UP! I CONFESS!
THEY'RE THE BEST WORMS I EVER FISHED WITH! LOOK!
GOSH!
I WAS GOING OFF DUTY WHEN THAT HAPPENED, BUT WHEN I SAW THOSE WORMS, I DIDN'T BOTHER TO GO HOME AND CHANGE MY CLOTHES...
I GUESS MY MA WON'T WANT THAT ROUND STEAK, CHOPPED, AFTER SHE SEES THESE FISH!
THE END

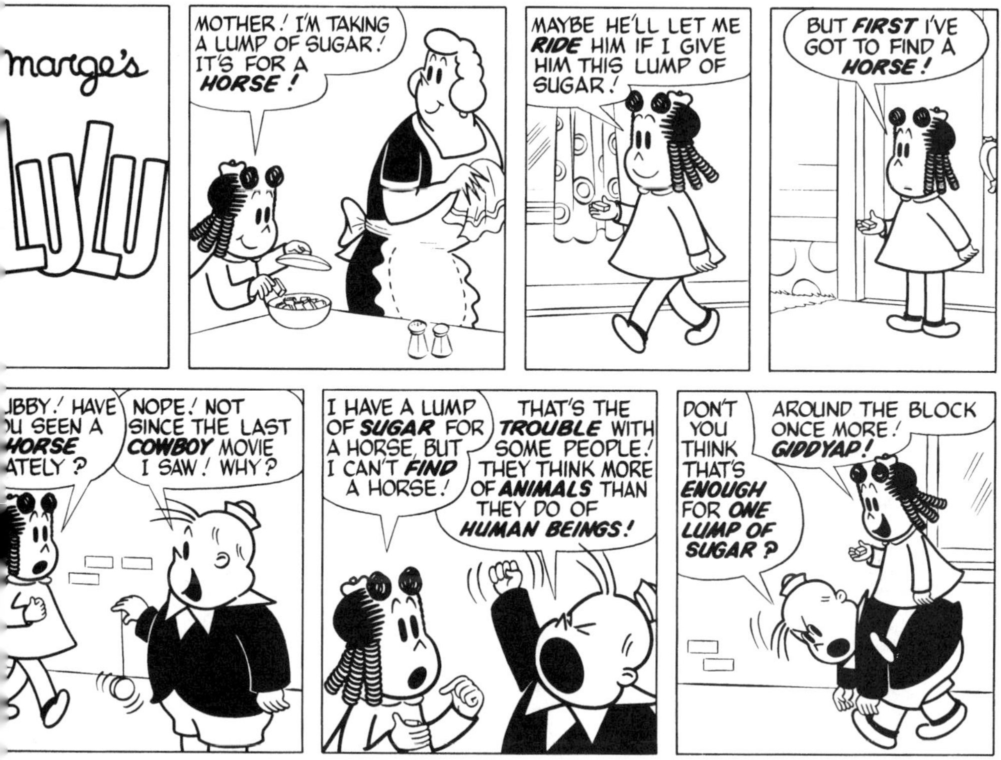
marge's
LULU
MOTHER! I'M TAKING A LUMP OF SUGAR! IT'S FOR A **HORSE**!
MAYBE HE'LL LET ME **RIDE** HIM IF I GIVE HIM THIS LUMP OF SUGAR!
BUT **FIRST** I'VE GOT TO FIND A **HORSE**!
BBY! HAVE U SEEN A **HORSE** ATELY?
NOPE! NOT SINCE THE LAST **COWBOY** MOVIE I SAW! WHY?
I HAVE A LUMP OF **SUGAR** FOR A HORSE, BUT I CAN'T **FIND** A HORSE!
THAT'S THE **TROUBLE** WITH SOME PEOPLE! THEY THINK MORE OF **ANIMALS** THAN THEY DO OF **HUMAN BEINGS**!
DON'T YOU THINK THAT'S **ENOUGH** FOR **ONE LUMP OF SUGAR**?
AROUND THE BLOCK ONCE MORE! **GIDDYAP!**

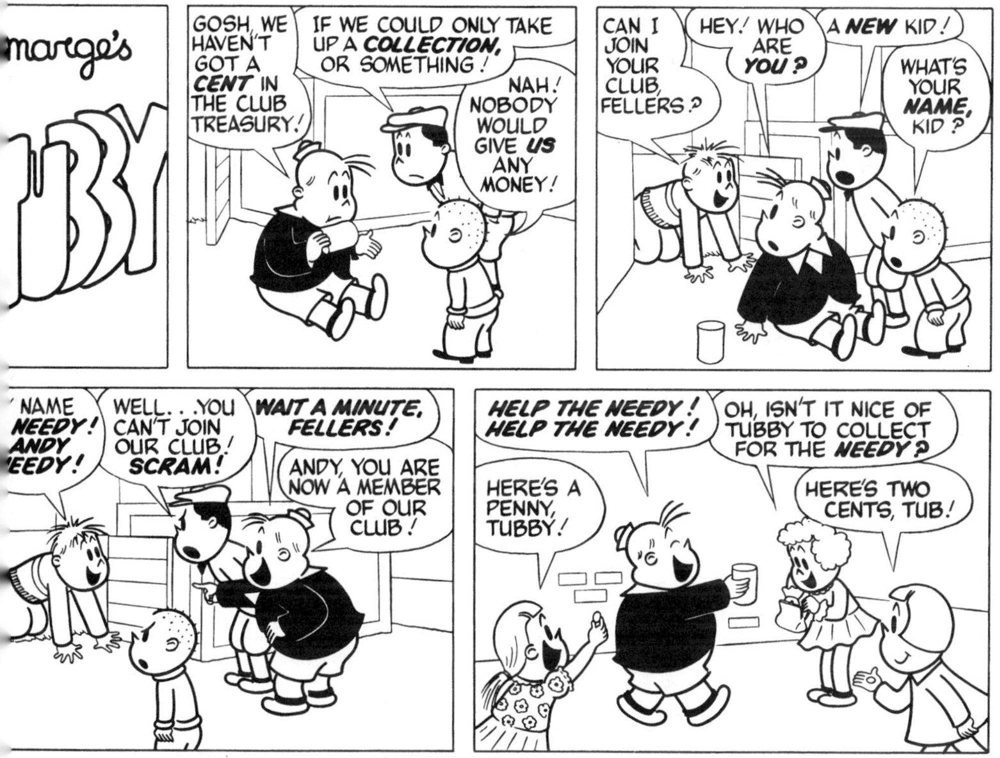
marge's
GOSH, WE HAVEN'T GOT A **CENT** IN THE CLUB TREASURY!
IF WE COULD ONLY TAKE UP A **COLLECTION**, OR SOMETHING!
NAH! NOBODY WOULD GIVE **US** ANY MONEY!
CAN I JOIN YOUR CLUB, FELLERS?
HEY! WHO ARE **YOU**?
A **NEW** KID!
WHAT'S YOUR **NAME**, KID?
NAME **NEEDY**! **ANDY EEDY**!
WELL. . .YOU CAN'T JOIN OUR CLUB! **SCRAM!**
WAIT A MINUTE, FELLERS!
ANDY, YOU ARE NOW A MEMBER OF OUR CLUB!
HELP THE NEEDY! HELP THE NEEDY!
OH, ISN'T IT NICE OF TUBBY TO COLLECT FOR THE **NEEDY**?
HERE'S A PENNY, TUBBY!
HERE'S TWO CENTS, TUB!

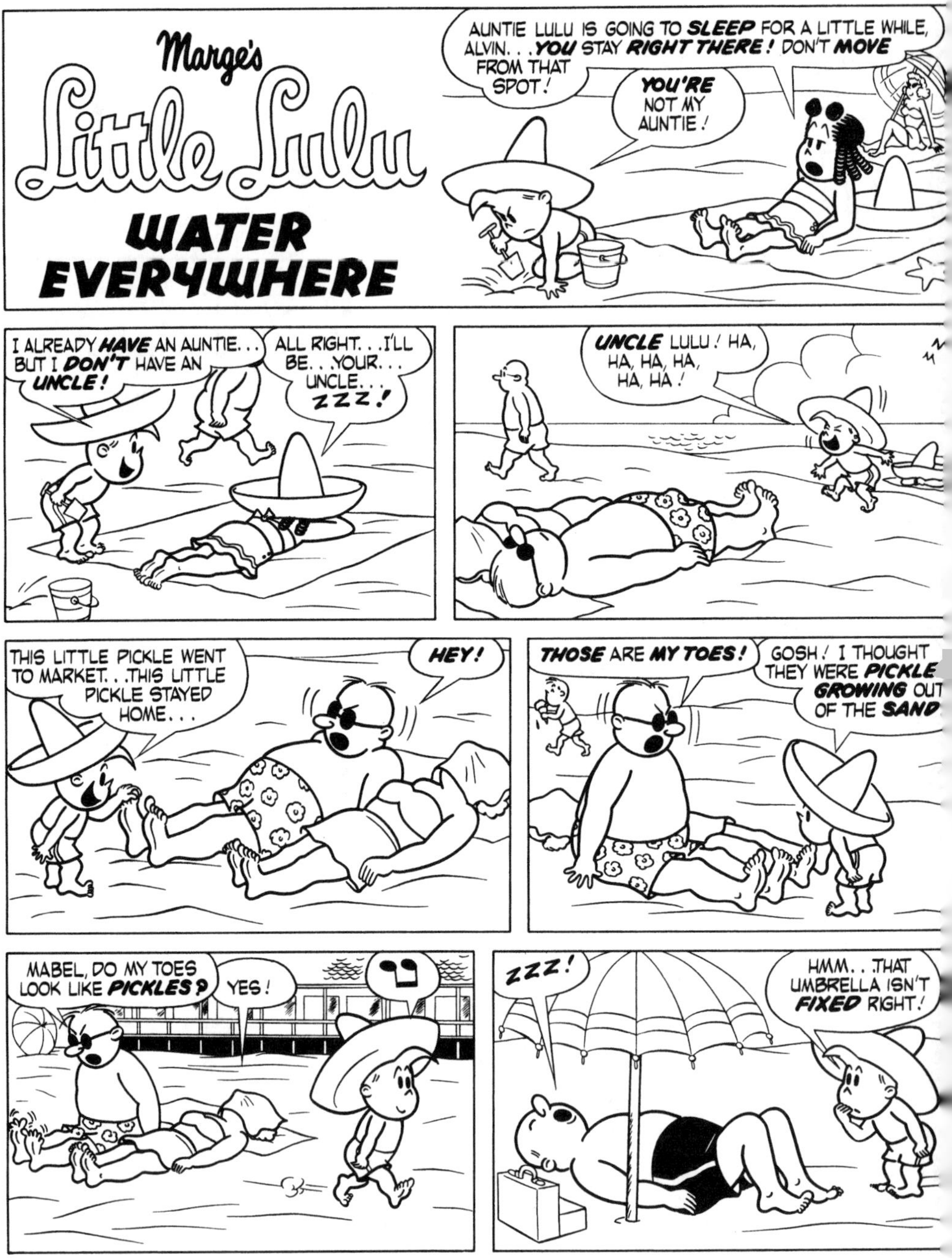
Marge's
Little Lulu
WATER EVERYWHERE
AUNTIE LULU IS GOING TO SLEEP FOR A LITTLE WHILE, ALVIN. . .YOU STAY RIGHT THERE! DON'T MOVE FROM THAT SPOT!
YOU'RE NOT MY AUNTIE!
I ALREADY HAVE AN AUNTIE. . . BUT I DON'T HAVE AN UNCLE!
ALL RIGHT. . .I'LL BE. . .YOUR. . . UNCLE. . . ZZZ!
UNCLE LULU! HA, HA, HA, HA, HA, HA!
THIS LITTLE PICKLE WENT TO MARKET. . .THIS LITTLE PICKLE STAYED HOME. . .
HEY!
THOSE ARE MY TOES!
GOSH! I THOUGHT THEY WERE PICKLE GROWING OUT OF THE SAND
MABEL, DO MY TOES LOOK LIKE PICKLES?
YES!
ZZZ!
HMM. . .THAT UMBRELLA ISN'T FIXED RIGHT!

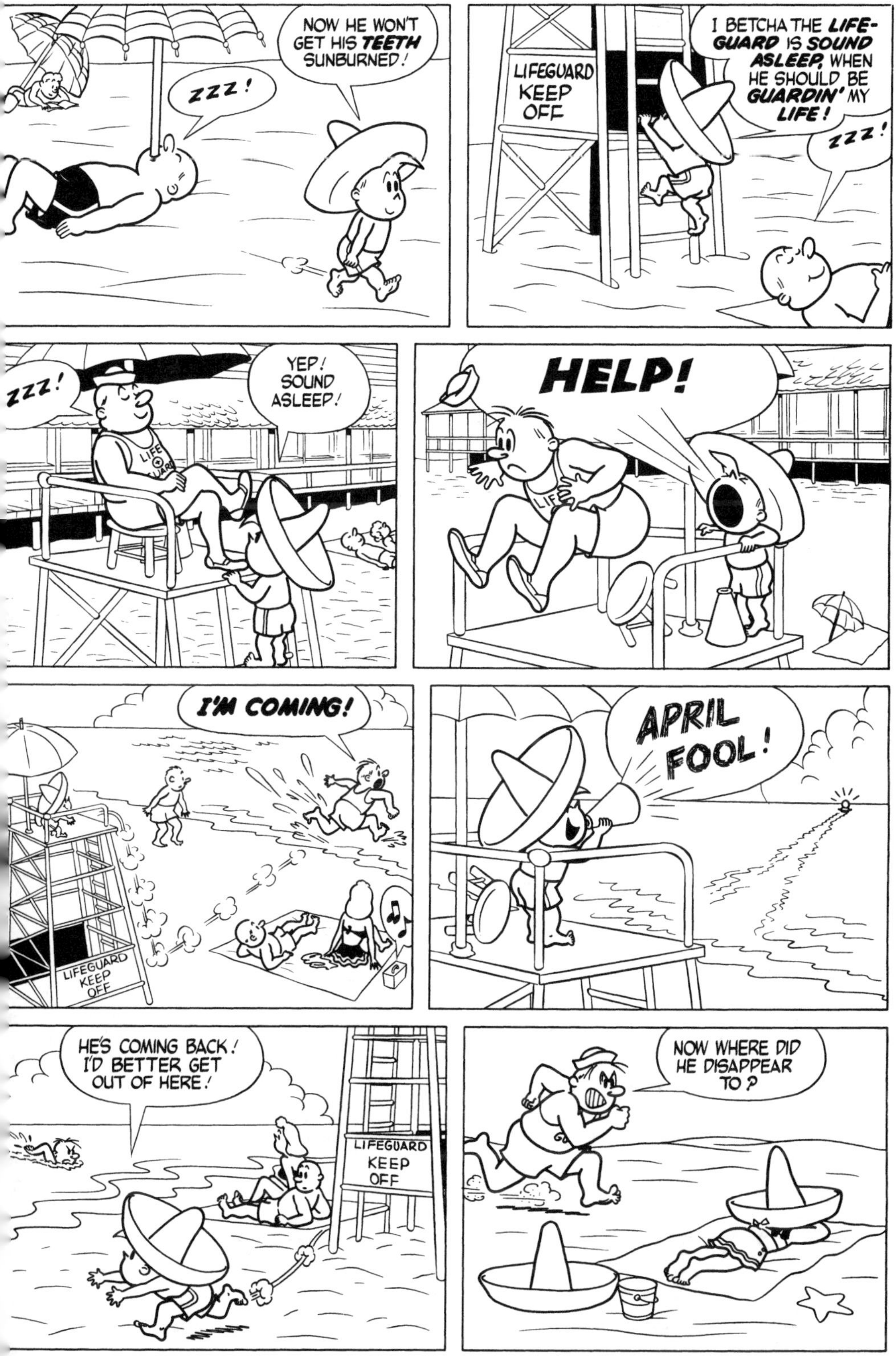
ZZZ!
NOW HE WON'T GET HIS TEETH SUNBURNED!
LIFEGUARD KEEP OFF
I BETCHA THE LIFE-GUARD IS SOUND ASLEEP, WHEN HE SHOULD BE GUARDIN' MY LIFE!
ZZZ!
ZZZ!
YEP! SOUND ASLEEP!
HELP!
I'M COMING!
LIFEGUARD KEEP OFF
APRIL FOOL!
HE'S COMING BACK! I'D BETTER GET OUT OF HERE!
LIFEGUARD KEEP OFF
NOW WHERE DID HE DISAPPEAR TO?

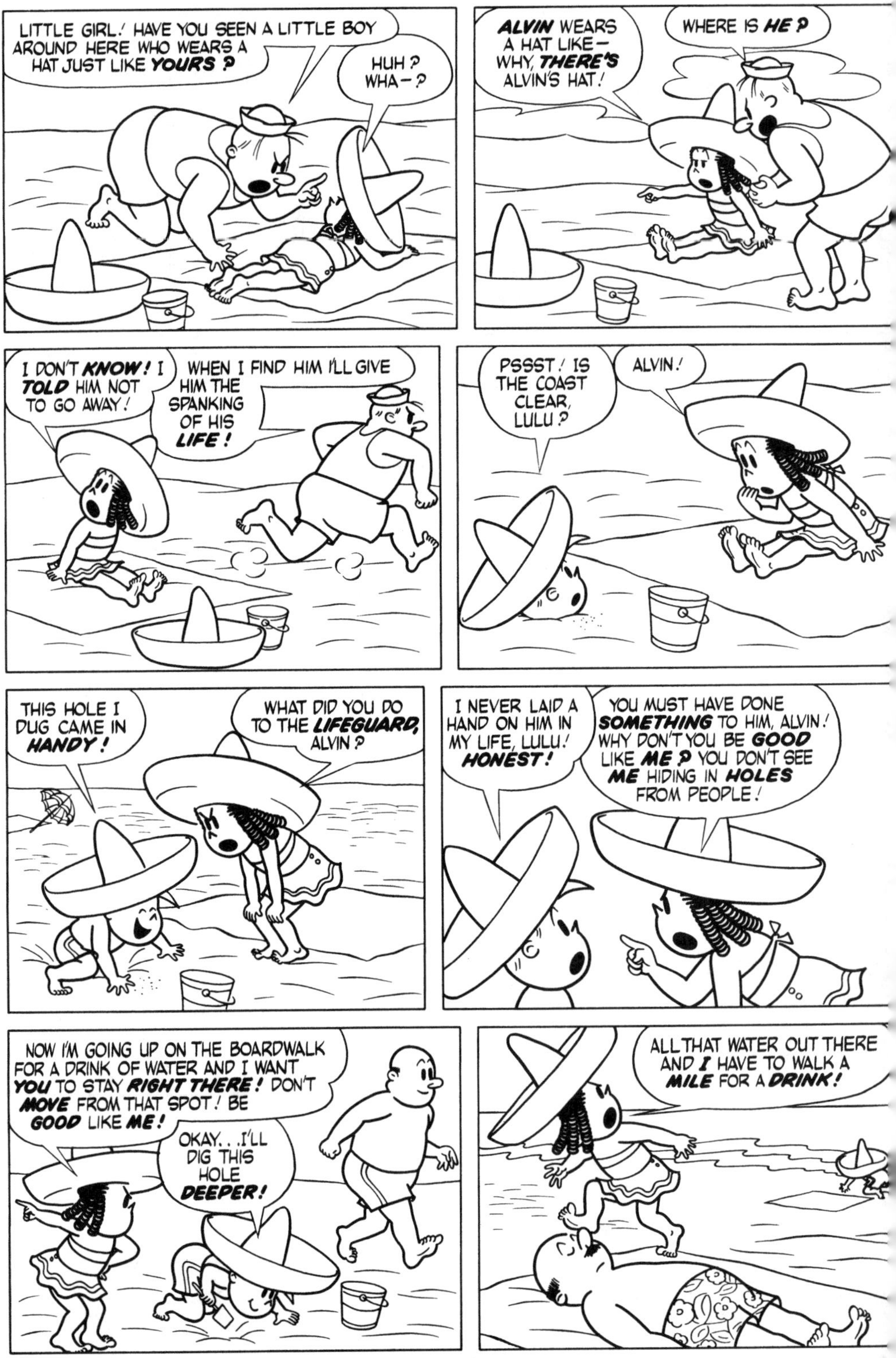
LITTLE GIRL! HAVE YOU SEEN A LITTLE BOY AROUND HERE WHO WEARS A HAT JUST LIKE **YOURS**?
HUH? WHA-?
ALVIN WEARS A HAT LIKE— WHY, **THERE'S** ALVIN'S HAT!
WHERE IS **HE**?
I DON'T **KNOW**! I **TOLD** HIM NOT TO GO AWAY!
WHEN I FIND HIM I'LL GIVE HIM THE SPANKING OF HIS **LIFE**!
PSSST! IS THE COAST CLEAR, LULU?
ALVIN!
THIS HOLE I DUG CAME IN **HANDY**!
WHAT DID YOU DO TO THE **LIFEGUARD**, ALVIN?
I NEVER LAID A HAND ON HIM IN MY LIFE, LULU! **HONEST**!
YOU MUST HAVE DONE **SOMETHING** TO HIM, ALVIN! WHY DON'T YOU BE **GOOD** LIKE **ME**? YOU DON'T SEE **ME** HIDING IN **HOLES** FROM PEOPLE!
NOW I'M GOING UP ON THE BOARDWALK FOR A DRINK OF WATER AND I WANT **YOU** TO STAY **RIGHT THERE**! DON'T **MOVE** FROM THAT SPOT! BE **GOOD** LIKE **ME**!
OKAY. . .I'LL DIG THIS HOLE **DEEPER**!
ALL THAT WATER OUT THERE AND **I** HAVE TO WALK A **MILE** FOR A **DRINK**!

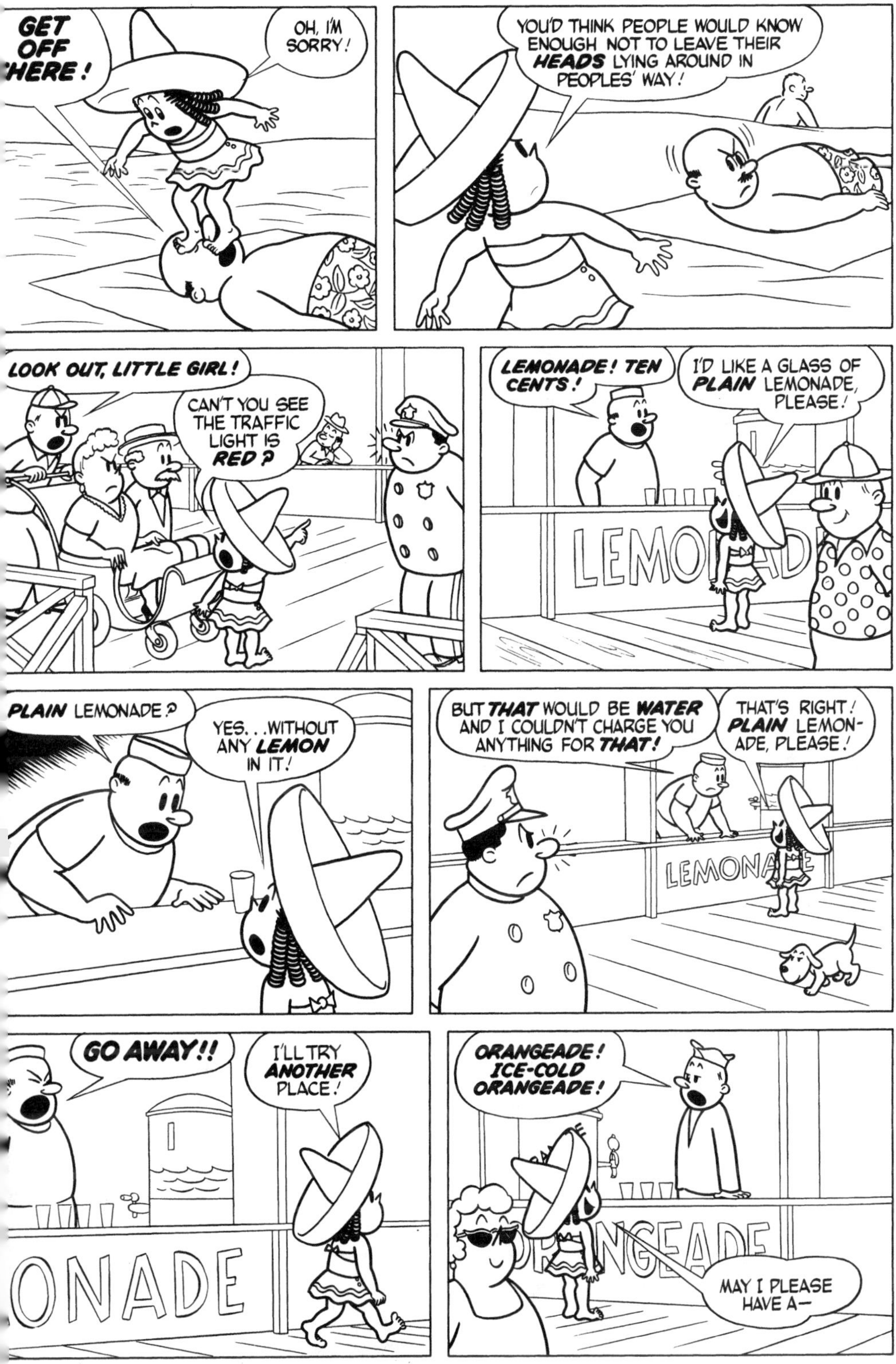
GET OFF HERE!
OH, I'M SORRY!
YOU'D THINK PEOPLE WOULD KNOW ENOUGH NOT TO LEAVE THEIR HEADS LYING AROUND IN PEOPLES' WAY!
LOOK OUT, LITTLE GIRL!
CAN'T YOU SEE THE TRAFFIC LIGHT IS RED?
LEMONADE! TEN CENTS!
I'D LIKE A GLASS OF PLAIN LEMONADE, PLEASE!
LEMONADE
PLAIN LEMONADE?
YES...WITHOUT ANY LEMON IN IT!
BUT THAT WOULD BE WATER AND I COULDN'T CHARGE YOU ANYTHING FOR THAT!
THAT'S RIGHT! PLAIN LEMON-ADE, PLEASE!
GO AWAY!!
I'LL TRY ANOTHER PLACE!
ONADE
ORANGEADE! ICE-COLD ORANGEADE!
MAY I PLEASE HAVE A—

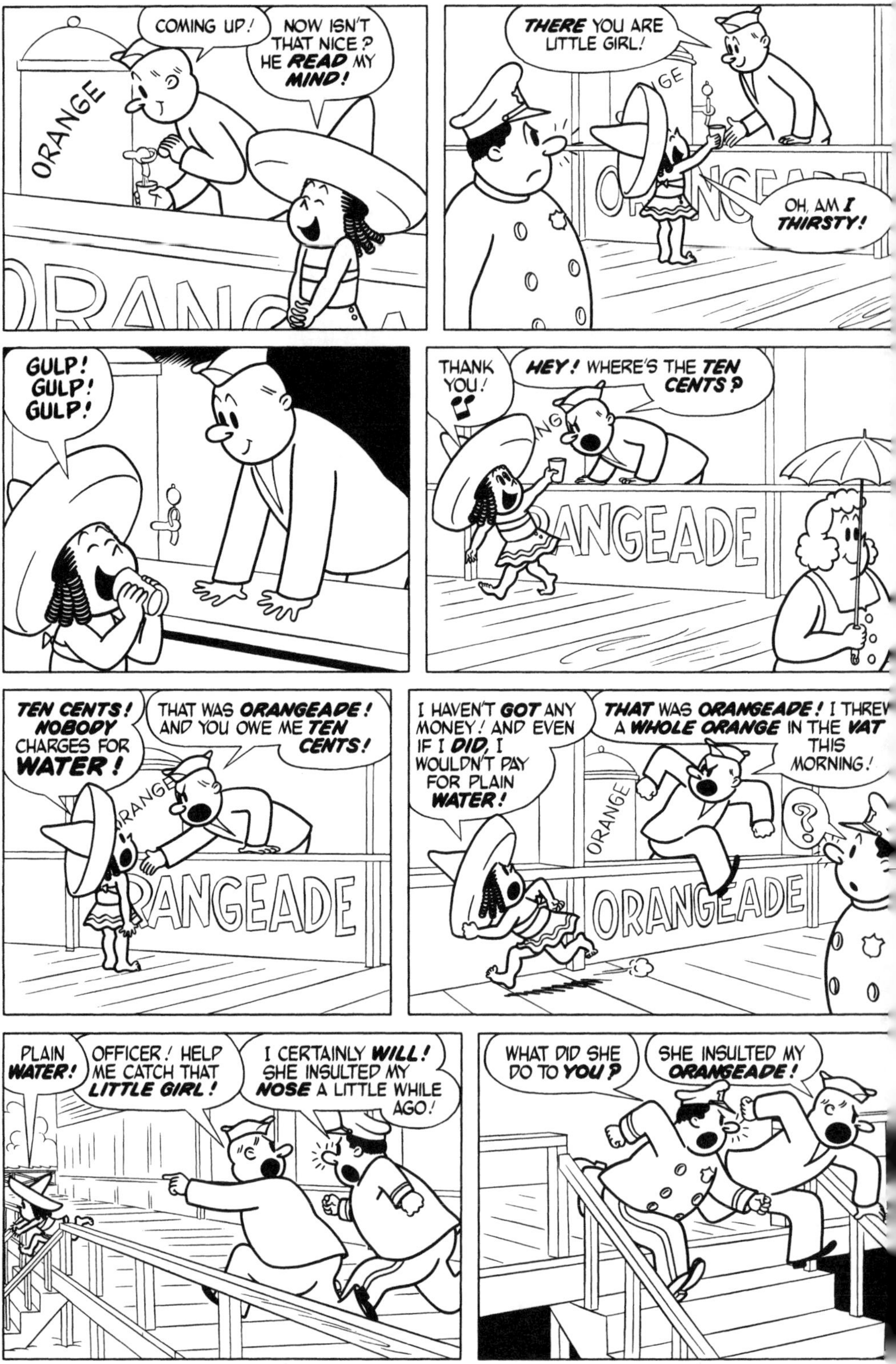

ORANGE
COMING UP!
NOW ISN'T THAT NICE? HE **READ** MY **MIND!**
THERE YOU ARE LITTLE GIRL!
OH, AM **I THIRSTY!**
GULP! GULP! GULP!
THANK YOU!
HEY! WHERE'S THE **TEN CENTS?**
TEN CENTS! NOBODY CHARGES FOR **WATER!**
THAT WAS **ORANGEADE!** AND YOU OWE ME **TEN CENTS!**
I HAVEN'T **GOT** ANY MONEY! AND EVEN IF I **DID**, I WOULDN'T PAY FOR PLAIN **WATER!**
THAT WAS **ORANGEADE!** I THREW A **WHOLE ORANGE** IN THE **VAT** THIS MORNING!
ORANGE
ORANGEADE
?
PLAIN **WATER!**
OFFICER! HELP ME CATCH THAT **LITTLE GIRL!**
I CERTAINLY **WILL!** SHE INSULTED MY **NOSE** A LITTLE WHILE AGO!
WHAT DID SHE DO TO **YOU?**
SHE INSULTED MY **ORANGEADE!**

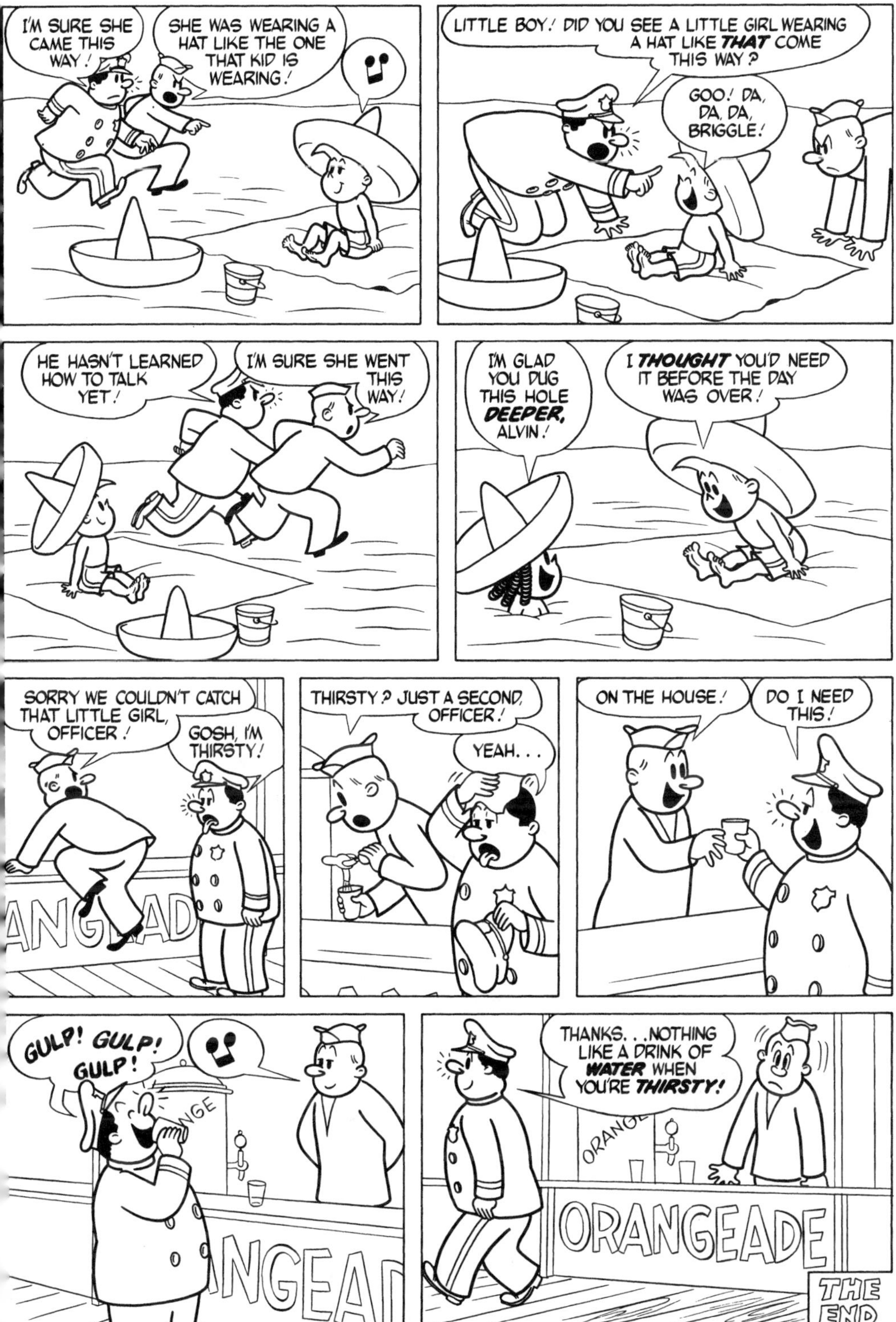
I'M SURE SHE CAME THIS WAY!
SHE WAS WEARING A HAT LIKE THE ONE THAT KID IS WEARING!
LITTLE BOY! DID YOU SEE A LITTLE GIRL WEARING A HAT LIKE THAT COME THIS WAY?
GOO! DA, DA, DA, BRIGGLE!
HE HASN'T LEARNED HOW TO TALK YET!
I'M SURE SHE WENT THIS WAY!
I'M GLAD YOU DUG THIS HOLE DEEPER, ALVIN!
I THOUGHT YOU'D NEED IT BEFORE THE DAY WAS OVER!
SORRY WE COULDN'T CATCH THAT LITTLE GIRL, OFFICER!
GOSH, I'M THIRSTY!
ANGEAD
THIRSTY? JUST A SECOND, OFFICER!
YEAH. . .
ON THE HOUSE!
DO I NEED THIS!
GULP! GULP! GULP!
NGE
NGEAD
THANKS. . .NOTHING LIKE A DRINK OF WATER WHEN YOU'RE THIRSTY!
ORANGE
ORANGEADE
THE END

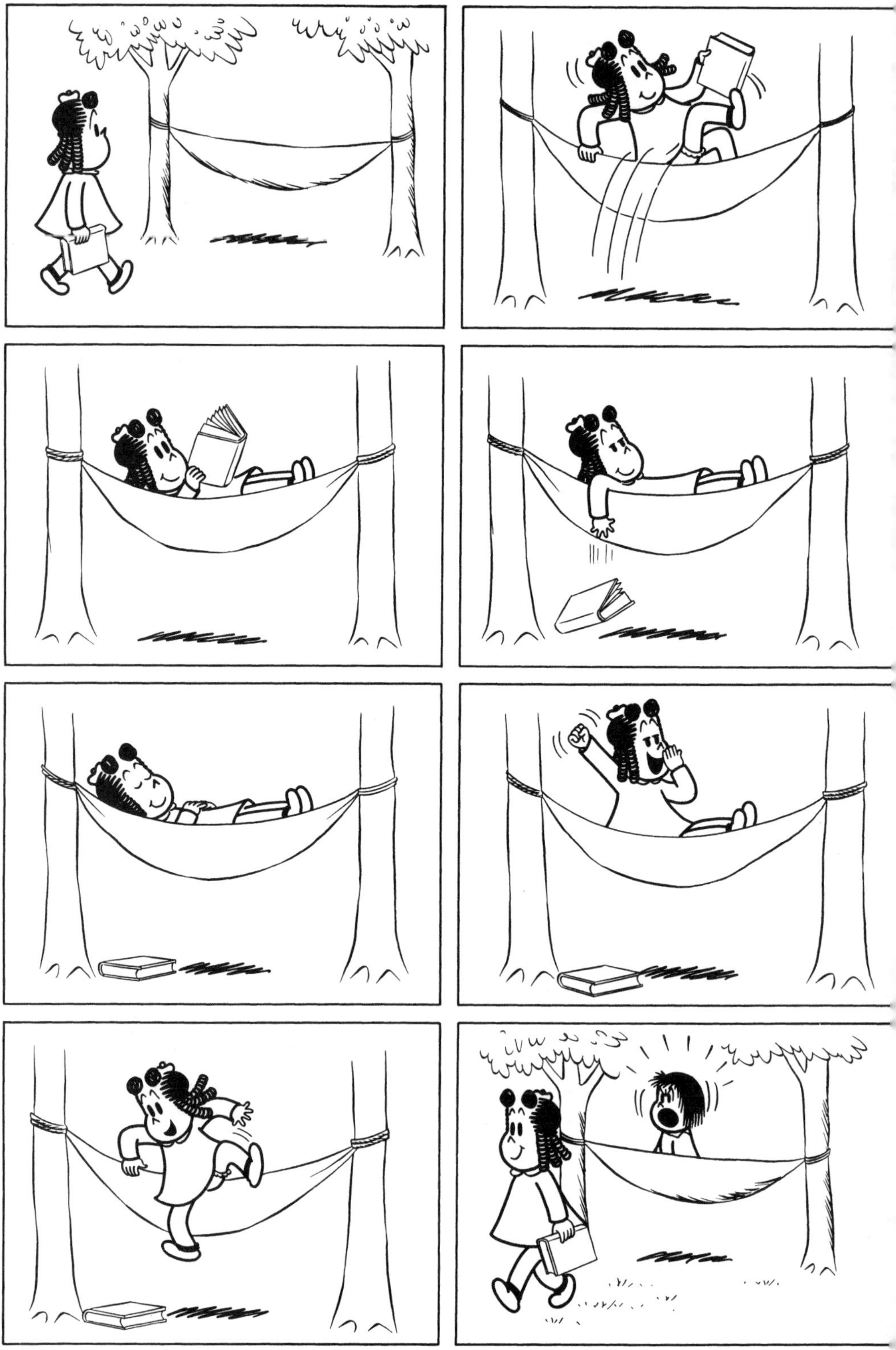

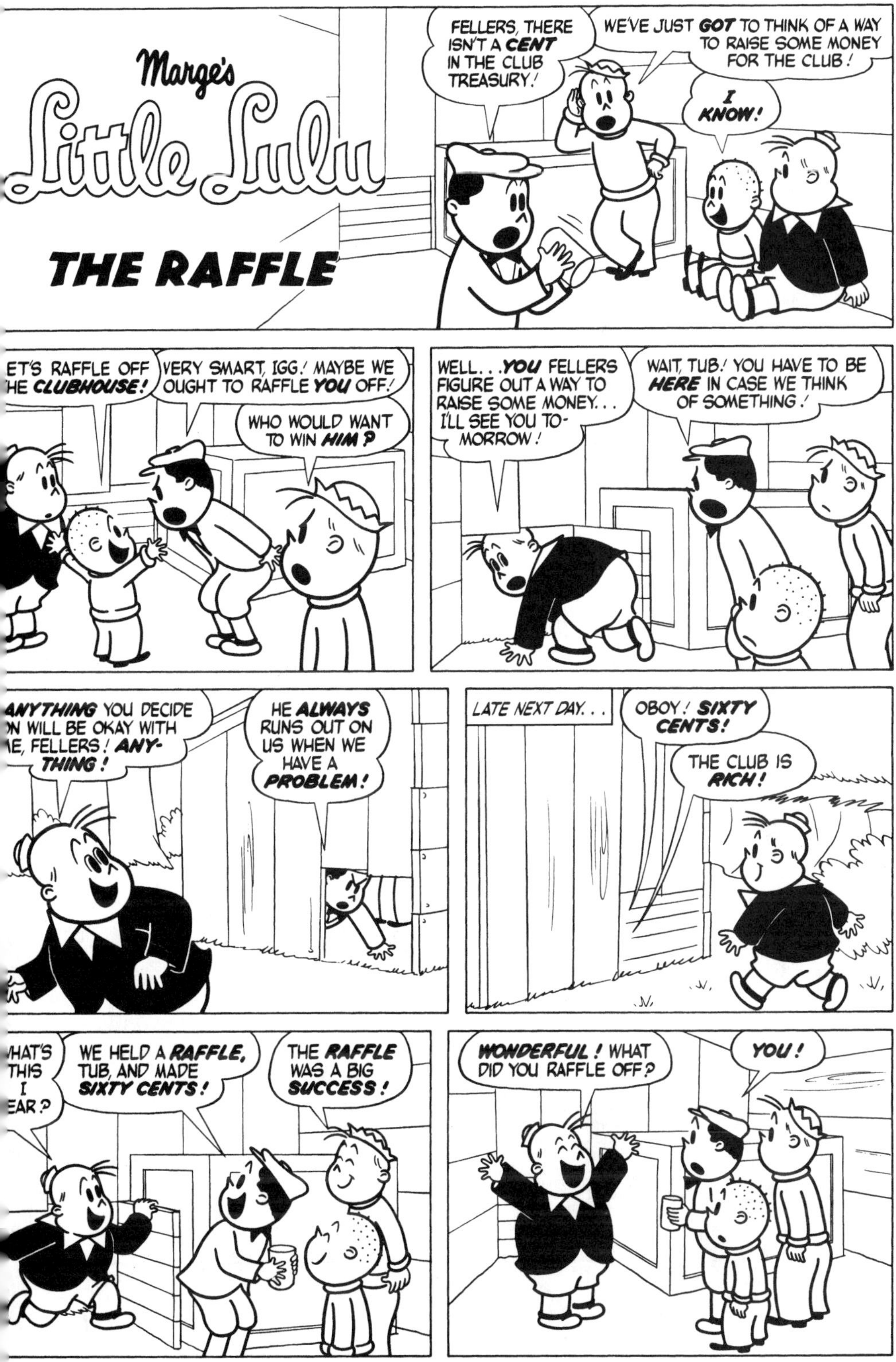
Marge's Little Lulu
THE RAFFLE
FELLERS, THERE ISN'T A CENT IN THE CLUB TREASURY!
WE'VE JUST GOT TO THINK OF A WAY TO RAISE SOME MONEY FOR THE CLUB!
I KNOW!
ET'S RAFFLE OFF HE CLUBHOUSE!
VERY SMART, IGG! MAYBE WE OUGHT TO RAFFLE YOU OFF!
WHO WOULD WANT TO WIN HIM?
WELL...YOU FELLERS FIGURE OUT A WAY TO RAISE SOME MONEY... I'LL SEE YOU TO-MORROW!
WAIT, TUB! YOU HAVE TO BE HERE IN CASE WE THINK OF SOMETHING!
ANYTHING YOU DECIDE N WILL BE OKAY WITH IE, FELLERS! ANY-THING!
HE ALWAYS RUNS OUT ON US WHEN WE HAVE A PROBLEM!
LATE NEXT DAY...
OBOY! SIXTY CENTS!
THE CLUB IS RICH!
HAT'S THIS I EAR?
WE HELD A RAFFLE, TUB, AND MADE SIXTY CENTS!
THE RAFFLE WAS A BIG SUCCESS!
WONDERFUL! WHAT DID YOU RAFFLE OFF?
YOU!

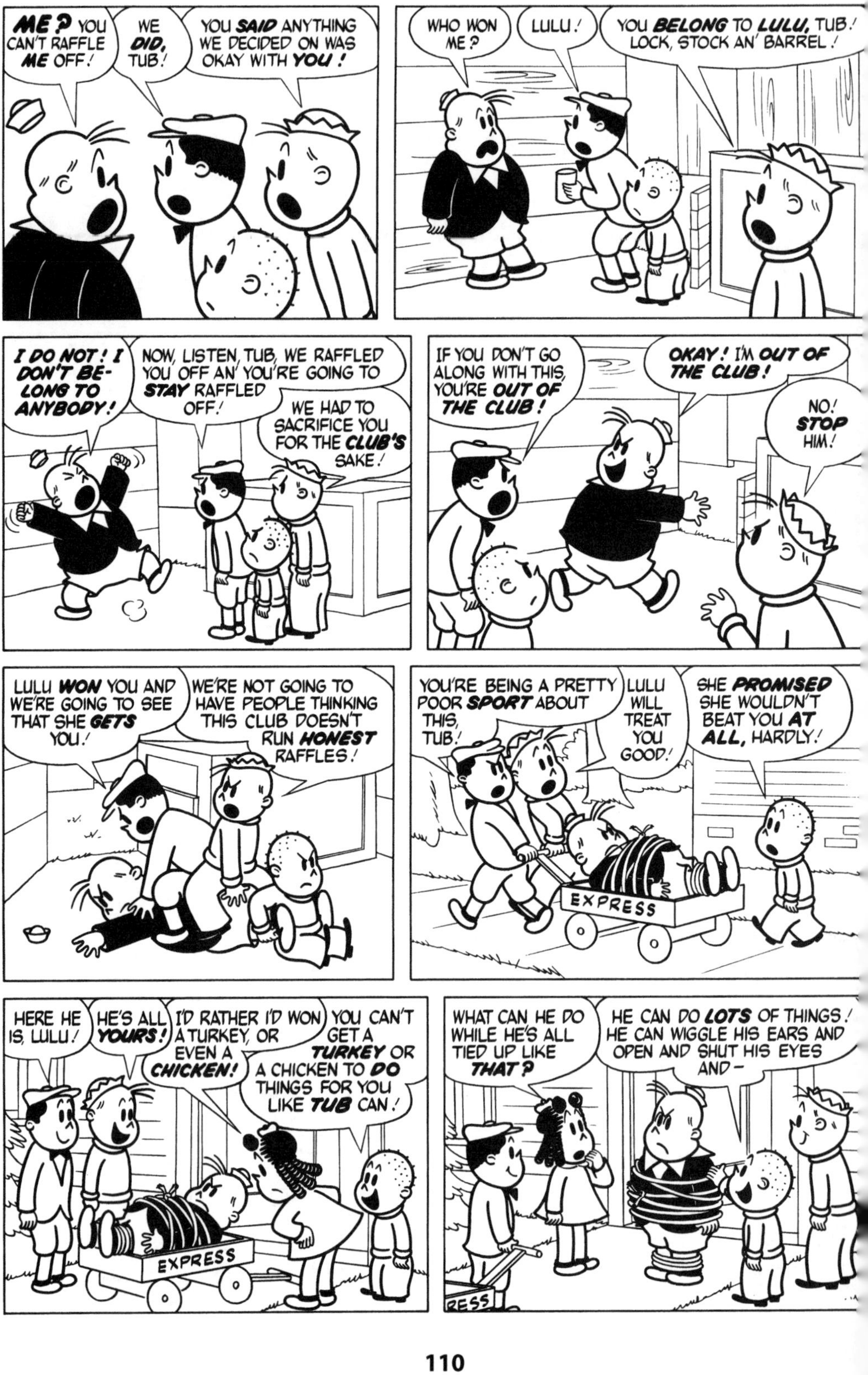
ME? YOU CAN'T RAFFLE ME OFF!
WE DID, TUB!
YOU SAID ANYTHING WE DECIDED ON WAS OKAY WITH YOU!
WHO WON ME?
LULU!
YOU BELONG TO LULU, TUB! LOCK, STOCK AN' BARREL!
I DO NOT! I DON'T BE-LONG TO ANYBODY!
NOW, LISTEN, TUB, WE RAFFLED YOU OFF AN' YOU'RE GOING TO STAY RAFFLED OFF!
WE HAD TO SACRIFICE YOU FOR THE CLUB'S SAKE!
IF YOU DON'T GO ALONG WITH THIS, YOU'RE OUT OF THE CLUB!
OKAY! I'M OUT OF THE CLUB!
NO! STOP HIM!
LULU WON YOU AND WE'RE GOING TO SEE THAT SHE GETS YOU!
WE'RE NOT GOING TO HAVE PEOPLE THINKING THIS CLUB DOESN'T RUN HONEST RAFFLES!
YOU'RE BEING A PRETTY POOR SPORT ABOUT THIS, TUB!
LULU WILL TREAT YOU GOOD!
SHE PROMISED SHE WOULDN'T BEAT YOU AT ALL, HARDLY!
EXPRESS
HERE HE IS, LULU!
HE'S ALL YOURS!
I'D RATHER I'D WON A TURKEY, OR EVEN A CHICKEN!
YOU CAN'T GET A TURKEY OR A CHICKEN TO DO THINGS FOR YOU LIKE TUB CAN!
EXPRESS
WHAT CAN HE DO WHILE HE'S ALL TIED UP LIKE THAT?
HE CAN DO LOTS OF THINGS! HE CAN WIGGLE HIS EARS AND OPEN AND SHUT HIS EYES AND—
RESS

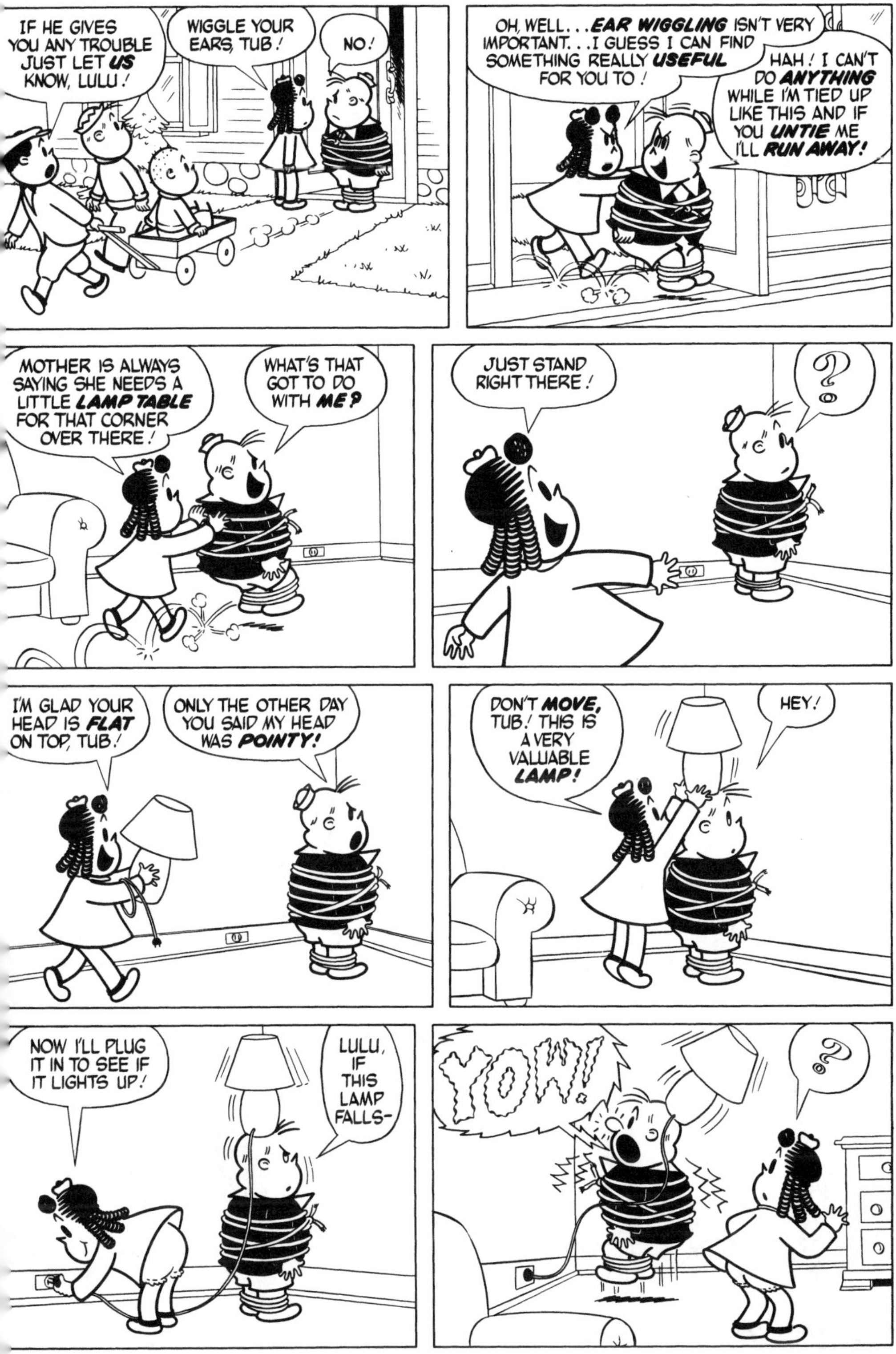
IF HE GIVES YOU ANY TROUBLE JUST LET US KNOW, LULU!
WIGGLE YOUR EARS, TUB!
NO!
OH, WELL... EAR WIGGLING ISN'T VERY IMPORTANT... I GUESS I CAN FIND SOMETHING REALLY USEFUL FOR YOU TO!
HAH! I CAN'T DO ANYTHING WHILE I'M TIED UP LIKE THIS AND IF YOU UNTIE ME I'LL RUN AWAY!
MOTHER IS ALWAYS SAYING SHE NEEDS A LITTLE LAMP TABLE FOR THAT CORNER OVER THERE!
WHAT'S THAT GOT TO DO WITH ME?
JUST STAND RIGHT THERE!
?
I'M GLAD YOUR HEAD IS FLAT ON TOP, TUB!
ONLY THE OTHER DAY YOU SAID MY HEAD WAS POINTY!
DON'T MOVE, TUB! THIS IS A VERY VALUABLE LAMP!
HEY!
NOW I'LL PLUG IT IN TO SEE IF IT LIGHTS UP!
LULU, IF THIS LAMP FALLS-
YOW!
?

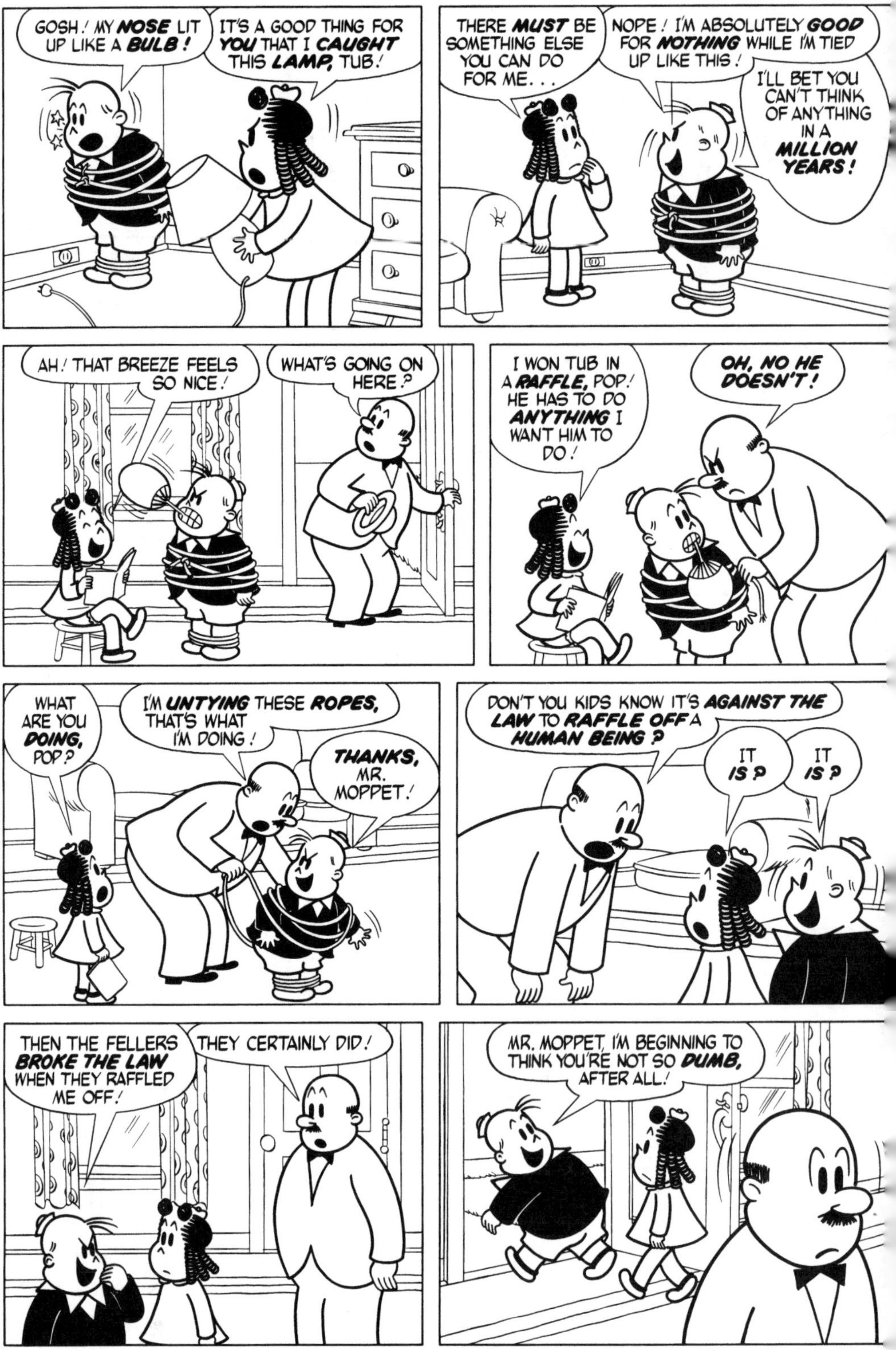
GOSH! MY NOSE LIT UP LIKE A BULB!
IT'S A GOOD THING FOR YOU THAT I CAUGHT THIS LAMP, TUB!
THERE MUST BE SOMETHING ELSE YOU CAN DO FOR ME...
NOPE! I'M ABSOLUTELY GOOD FOR NOTHING WHILE I'M TIED UP LIKE THIS!
I'LL BET YOU CAN'T THINK OF ANYTHING IN A MILLION YEARS!
AH! THAT BREEZE FEELS SO NICE!
WHAT'S GOING ON HERE?
I WON TUB IN A RAFFLE, POP! HE HAS TO DO ANYTHING I WANT HIM TO DO!
OH, NO HE DOESN'T!
WHAT ARE YOU DOING, POP?
I'M UNTYING THESE ROPES, THAT'S WHAT I'M DOING!
THANKS, MR. MOPPET!
DON'T YOU KIDS KNOW IT'S AGAINST THE LAW TO RAFFLE OFF A HUMAN BEING?
IT IS?
IT IS?
THEN THE FELLERS BROKE THE LAW WHEN THEY RAFFLED ME OFF!
THEY CERTAINLY DID!
MR. MOPPET, I'M BEGINNING TO THINK YOU'RE NOT SO DUMB, AFTER ALL!

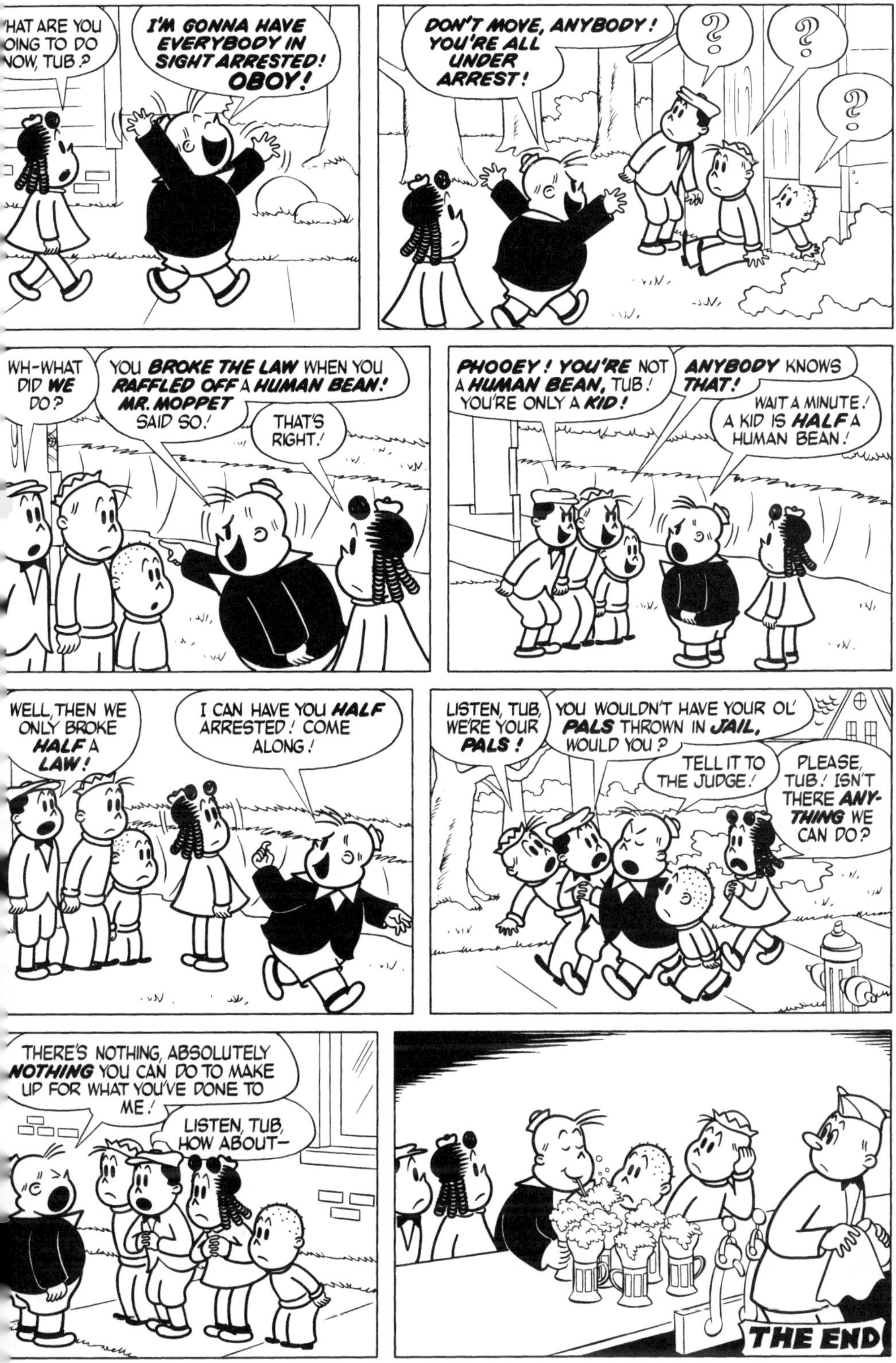
HAT ARE YOU OING TO DO NOW, TUB?
I'M GONNA HAVE EVERYBODY IN SIGHT ARRESTED! OBOY!
DON'T MOVE, ANYBODY! YOU'RE ALL UNDER ARREST!
?
?
?
WH-WHAT DID WE DO?
YOU BROKE THE LAW WHEN YOU RAFFLED OFF A HUMAN BEAN! MR. MOPPET SAID SO!
THAT'S RIGHT!
PHOOEY! YOU'RE NOT A HUMAN BEAN, TUB! YOU'RE ONLY A KID!
ANYBODY KNOWS THAT!
WAIT A MINUTE! A KID IS HALF A HUMAN BEAN!
WELL, THEN WE ONLY BROKE HALF A LAW!
I CAN HAVE YOU HALF ARRESTED! COME ALONG!
LISTEN, TUB, WE'RE YOUR PALS!
YOU WOULDN'T HAVE YOUR OL' PALS THROWN IN JAIL, WOULD YOU?
TELL IT TO THE JUDGE!
PLEASE, TUB! ISN'T THERE ANYTHING WE CAN DO?
THERE'S NOTHING, ABSOLUTELY NOTHING YOU CAN DO TO MAKE UP FOR WHAT YOU'VE DONE TO ME!
LISTEN, TUB, HOW ABOUT—
THE END

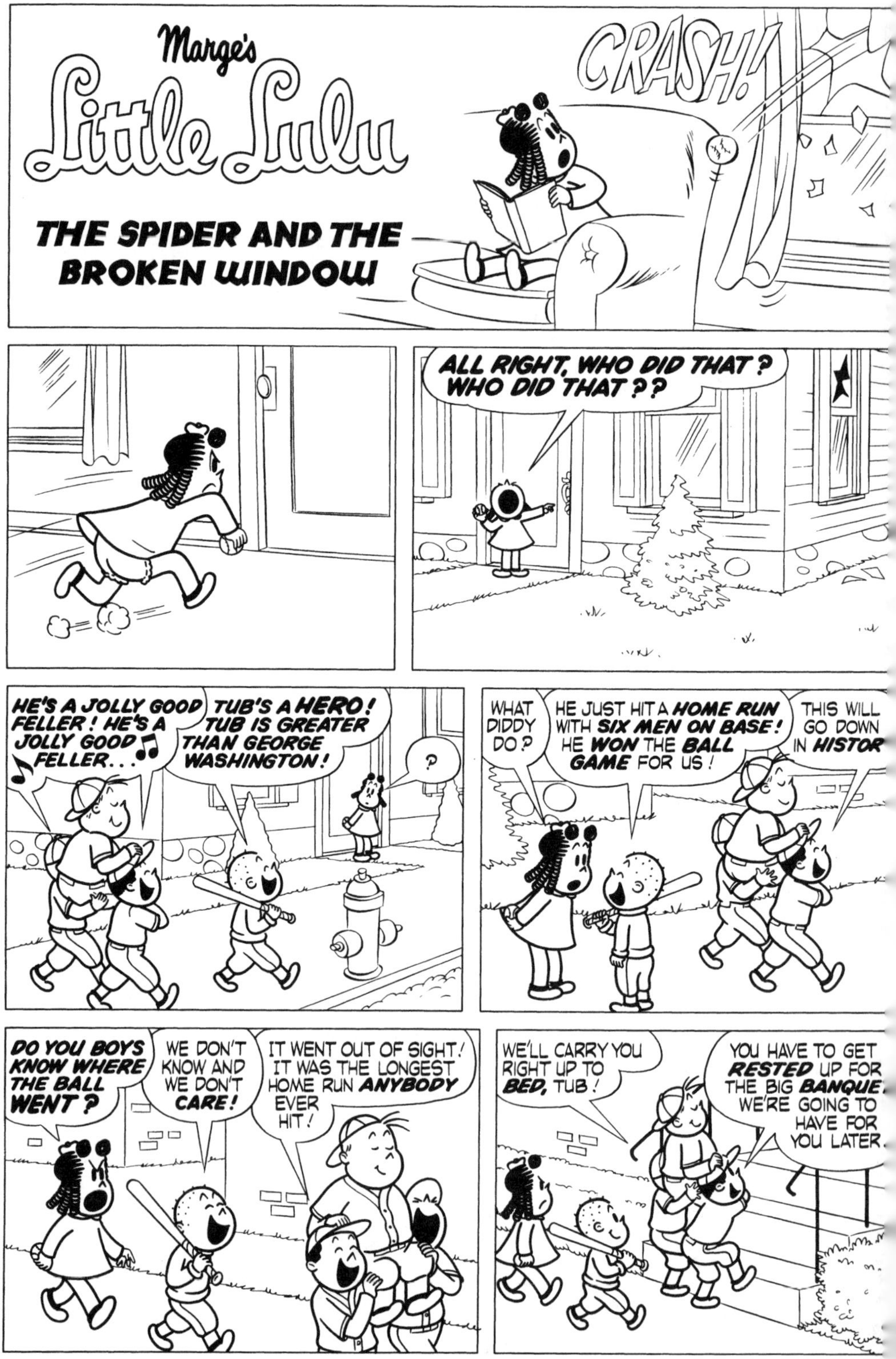
Marge's
Little Lulu
THE SPIDER AND THE BROKEN WINDOW
CRASH!!
ALL RIGHT, WHO DID THAT? WHO DID THAT??
HE'S A JOLLY GOOD FELLER! HE'S A JOLLY GOOD FELLER...
TUB'S A HERO! TUB IS GREATER THAN GEORGE WASHINGTON!
?
WHAT DIDDY DO?
HE JUST HIT A HOME RUN WITH SIX MEN ON BASE! HE WON THE BALL GAME FOR US!
THIS WILL GO DOWN IN HISTOR
DO YOU BOYS KNOW WHERE THE BALL WENT?
WE DON'T KNOW AND WE DON'T CARE!
IT WENT OUT OF SIGHT! IT WAS THE LONGEST HOME RUN ANYBODY EVER HIT!
WE'LL CARRY YOU RIGHT UP TO BED, TUB!
YOU HAVE TO GET RESTED UP FOR THE BIG BANQUE WE'RE GOING TO HAVE FOR YOU LATER.

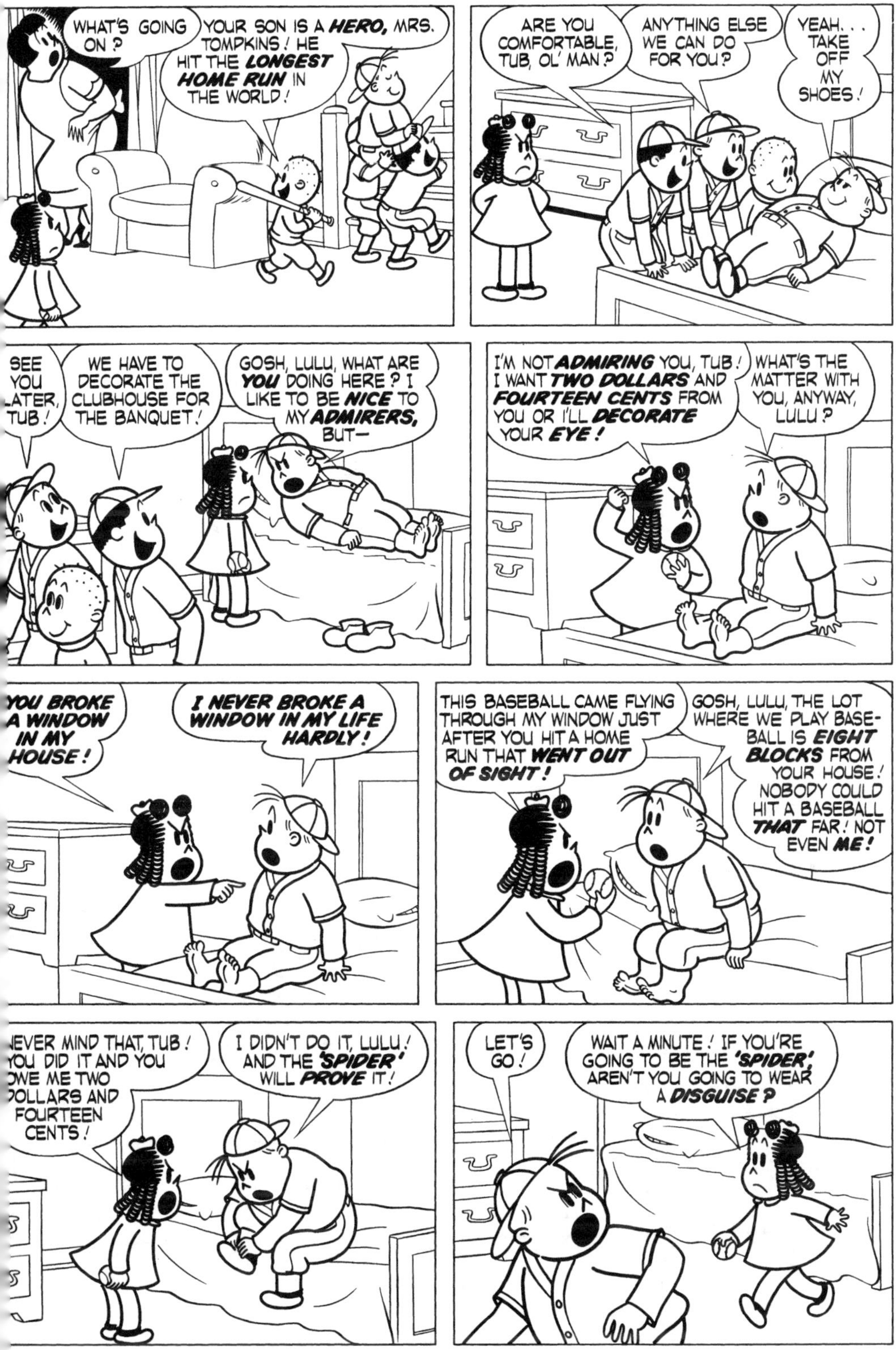
WHAT'S GOING ON ?
YOUR SON IS A HERO, MRS. TOMPKINS! HE HIT THE LONGEST HOME RUN IN THE WORLD!
ARE YOU COMFORTABLE, TUB, OL' MAN ?
ANYTHING ELSE WE CAN DO FOR YOU ?
YEAH. . . TAKE OFF MY SHOES!
SEE YOU LATER, TUB!
WE HAVE TO DECORATE THE CLUBHOUSE FOR THE BANQUET!
GOSH, LULU, WHAT ARE YOU DOING HERE ? I LIKE TO BE NICE TO MY ADMIRERS, BUT—
I'M NOT ADMIRING YOU, TUB! I WANT TWO DOLLARS AND FOURTEEN CENTS FROM YOU OR I'LL DECORATE YOUR EYE!
WHAT'S THE MATTER WITH YOU, ANYWAY, LULU ?
YOU BROKE A WINDOW IN MY HOUSE!
I NEVER BROKE A WINDOW IN MY LIFE HARDLY!
THIS BASEBALL CAME FLYING THROUGH MY WINDOW JUST AFTER YOU HIT A HOME RUN THAT WENT OUT OF SIGHT!
GOSH, LULU, THE LOT WHERE WE PLAY BASE-BALL IS EIGHT BLOCKS FROM YOUR HOUSE! NOBODY COULD HIT A BASEBALL THAT FAR! NOT EVEN ME!
NEVER MIND THAT, TUB! YOU DID IT AND YOU OWE ME TWO DOLLARS AND FOURTEEN CENTS!
I DIDN'T DO IT, LULU! AND THE 'SPIDER' WILL PROVE IT!
LET'S GO!
WAIT A MINUTE! IF YOU'RE GOING TO BE THE 'SPIDER', AREN'T YOU GOING TO WEAR A DISGUISE ?

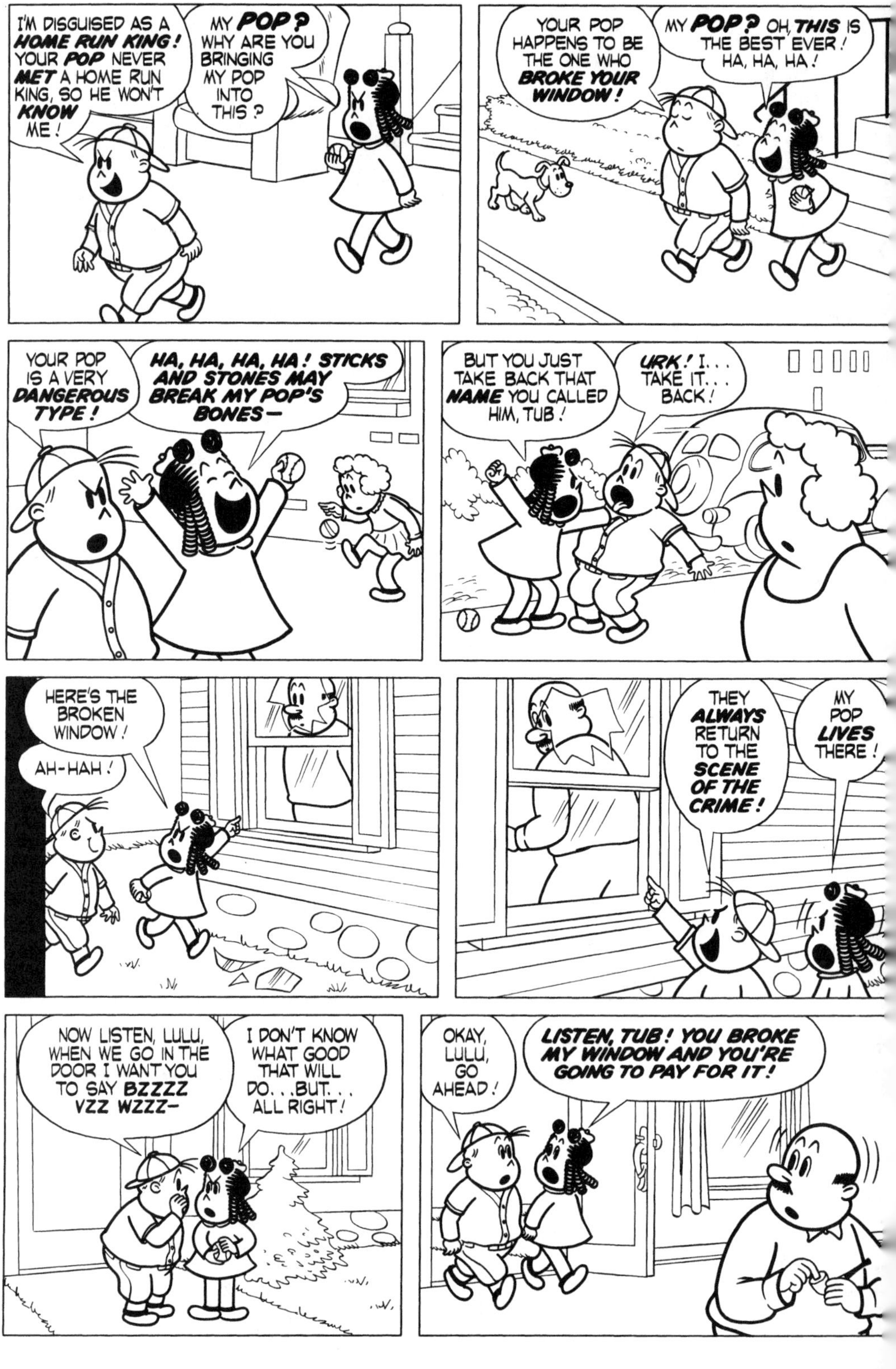
I'M DISGUISED AS A HOME RUN KING! YOUR POP NEVER MET A HOME RUN KING, SO HE WON'T KNOW ME!
MY POP? WHY ARE YOU BRINGING MY POP INTO THIS?
YOUR POP HAPPENS TO BE THE ONE WHO BROKE YOUR WINDOW!
MY POP? OH, THIS IS THE BEST EVER! HA, HA, HA!
YOUR POP IS A VERY DANGEROUS TYPE!
HA, HA, HA, HA! STICKS AND STONES MAY BREAK MY POP'S BONES—
BUT YOU JUST TAKE BACK THAT NAME YOU CALLED HIM, TUB!
URK! I... TAKE IT... BACK!
HERE'S THE BROKEN WINDOW!
AH-HAH!
THEY ALWAYS RETURN TO THE SCENE OF THE CRIME!
MY POP LIVES THERE!
NOW LISTEN, LULU, WHEN WE GO IN THE DOOR I WANT YOU TO SAY BZZZZ VZZ WZZZ—
I DON'T KNOW WHAT GOOD THAT WILL DO...BUT... ALL RIGHT!
OKAY, LULU, GO AHEAD!
LISTEN, TUB! YOU BROKE MY WINDOW AND YOU'RE GOING TO PAY FOR IT!

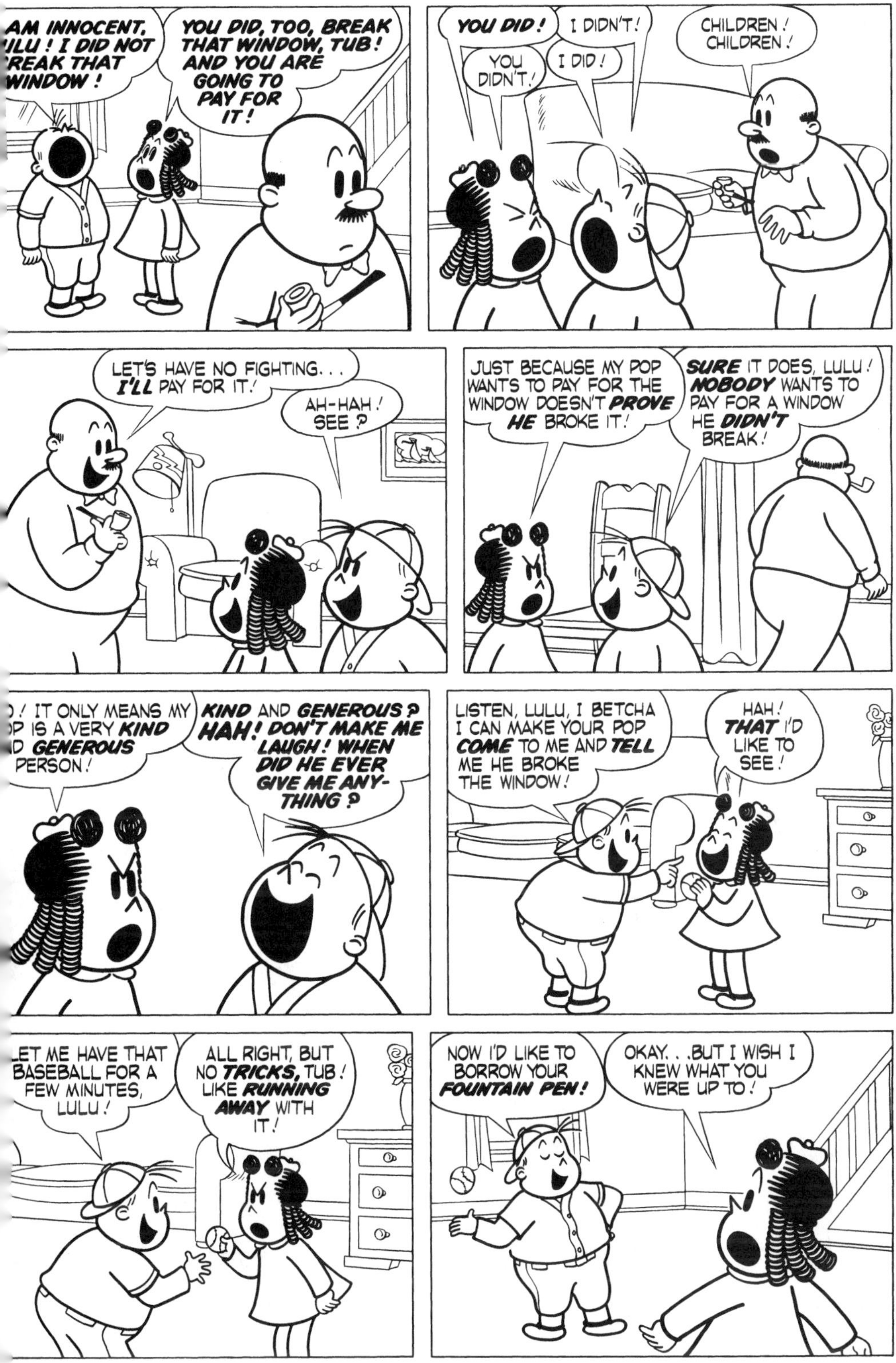
AM INNOCENT, LU! I DID NOT REAK THAT WINDOW!
YOU DID, TOO, BREAK THAT WINDOW, TUB! AND YOU ARE GOING TO PAY FOR IT!
YOU DID!
YOU DIDN'T!
I DIDN'T!
I DID!
CHILDREN! CHILDREN!
LET'S HAVE NO FIGHTING... I'LL PAY FOR IT!
AH-HAH! SEE?
JUST BECAUSE MY POP WANTS TO PAY FOR THE WINDOW DOESN'T PROVE HE BROKE IT!
SURE IT DOES, LULU! NOBODY WANTS TO PAY FOR A WINDOW HE DIDN'T BREAK!
! IT ONLY MEANS MY P IS A VERY KIND D GENEROUS PERSON!
KIND AND GENEROUS? HAH! DON'T MAKE ME LAUGH! WHEN DID HE EVER GIVE ME ANY-THING?
LISTEN, LULU, I BETCHA I CAN MAKE YOUR POP COME TO ME AND TELL ME HE BROKE THE WINDOW!
HAH! THAT I'D LIKE TO SEE!
LET ME HAVE THAT BASEBALL FOR A FEW MINUTES, LULU!
ALL RIGHT, BUT NO TRICKS, TUB! LIKE RUNNING AWAY WITH IT!
NOW I'D LIKE TO BORROW YOUR FOUNTAIN PEN!
OKAY...BUT I WISH I KNEW WHAT YOU WERE UP TO!

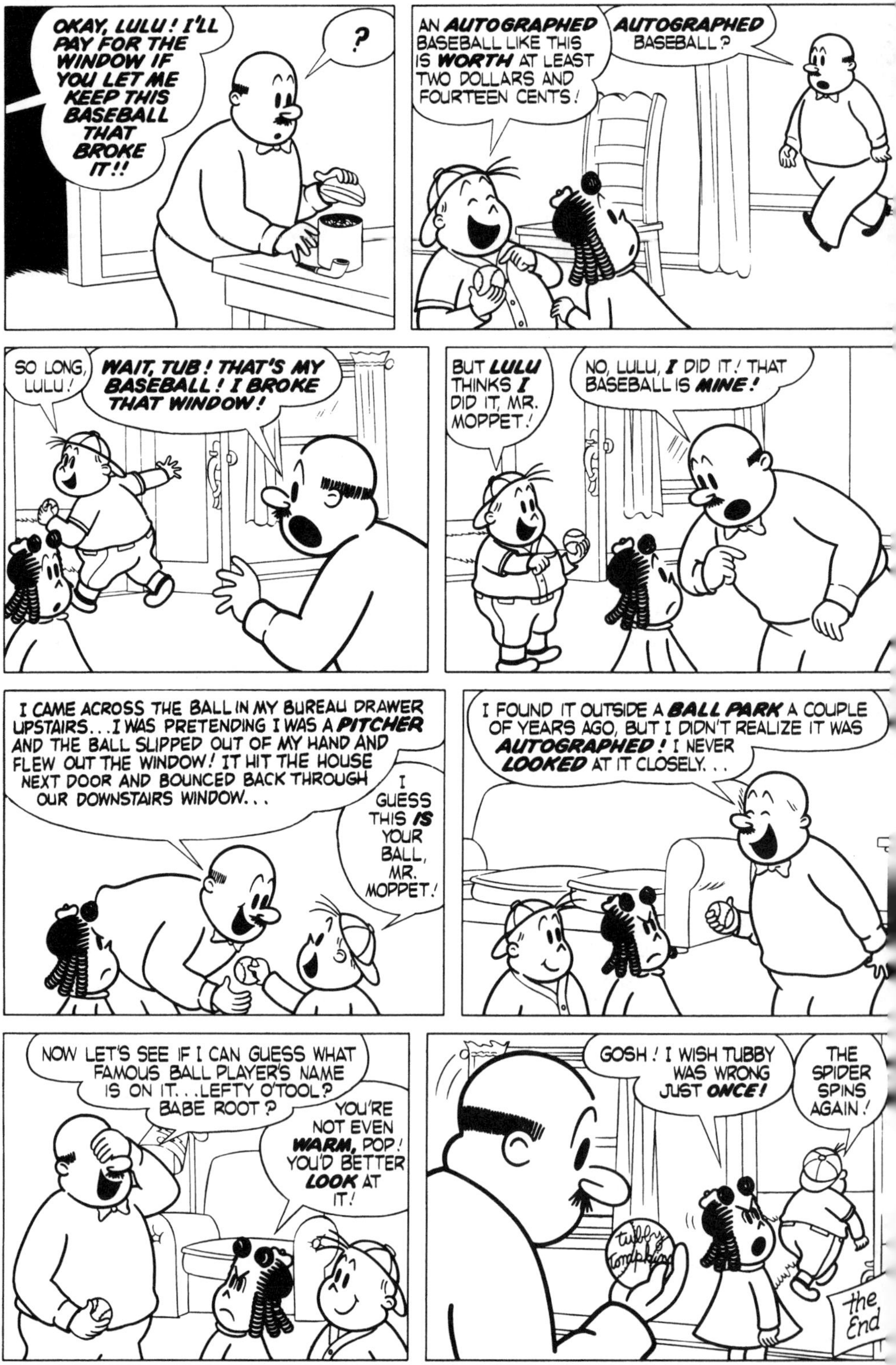
OKAY, LULU! I'LL PAY FOR THE WINDOW IF YOU LET ME KEEP THIS BASEBALL THAT BROKE IT!!
?
AN AUTOGRAPHED BASEBALL LIKE THIS IS WORTH AT LEAST TWO DOLLARS AND FOURTEEN CENTS!
AUTOGRAPHED BASEBALL?
SO LONG, LULU!
WAIT, TUB! THAT'S MY BASEBALL! I BROKE THAT WINDOW!
BUT LULU THINKS I DID IT, MR. MOPPET!
NO, LULU, I DID IT! THAT BASEBALL IS MINE!
I CAME ACROSS THE BALL IN MY BUREAU DRAWER UPSTAIRS...I WAS PRETENDING I WAS A PITCHER AND THE BALL SLIPPED OUT OF MY HAND AND FLEW OUT THE WINDOW! IT HIT THE HOUSE NEXT DOOR AND BOUNCED BACK THROUGH OUR DOWNSTAIRS WINDOW...
I GUESS THIS IS YOUR BALL, MR. MOPPET!
I FOUND IT OUTSIDE A BALL PARK A COUPLE OF YEARS AGO, BUT I DIDN'T REALIZE IT WAS AUTOGRAPHED! I NEVER LOOKED AT IT CLOSELY...
NOW LET'S SEE IF I CAN GUESS WHAT FAMOUS BALL PLAYER'S NAME IS ON IT...LEFTY O'TOOL? BABE ROOT?
YOU'RE NOT EVEN WARM, POP! YOU'D BETTER LOOK AT IT!
GOSH! I WISH TUBBY WAS WRONG JUST ONCE!
THE SPIDER SPINS AGAIN!
tubby tompkins
the End

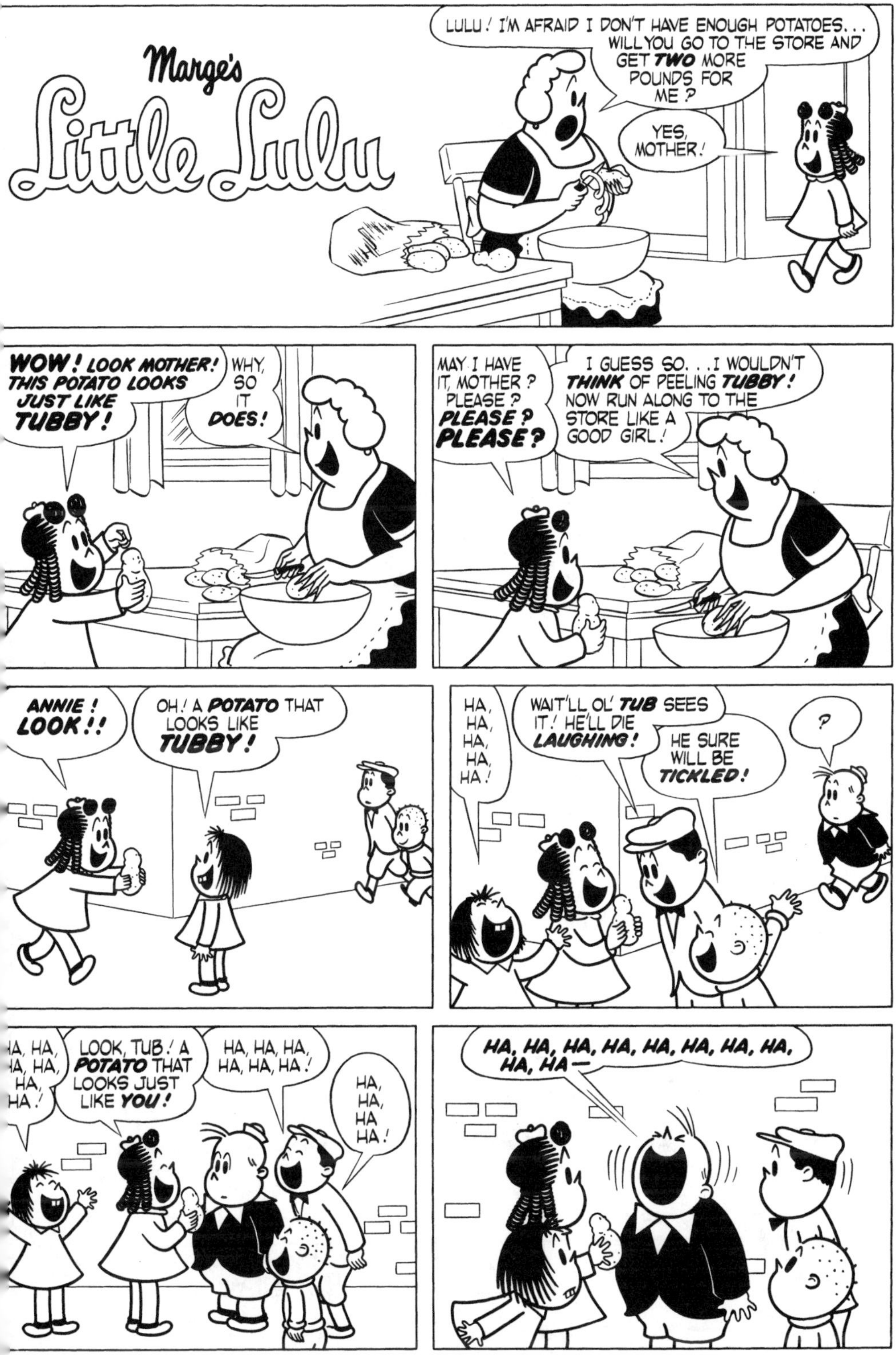

Marge's Little Lulu
LULU! I'M AFRAID I DON'T HAVE ENOUGH POTATOES... WILL YOU GO TO THE STORE AND GET TWO MORE POUNDS FOR ME?
YES, MOTHER!
WOW! LOOK MOTHER! THIS POTATO LOOKS JUST LIKE TUBBY!
WHY, SO IT DOES!
MAY I HAVE IT, MOTHER? PLEASE? PLEASE? PLEASE?
I GUESS SO... I WOULDN'T THINK OF PEELING TUBBY! NOW RUN ALONG TO THE STORE LIKE A GOOD GIRL!
ANNIE! LOOK!!
OH! A POTATO THAT LOOKS LIKE TUBBY!
HA, HA, HA, HA, HA!
WAIT'LL OL' TUB SEES IT! HE'LL DIE LAUGHING!
HE SURE WILL BE TICKLED!
?
HA, HA, HA, HA, HA, HA!
LOOK, TUB! A POTATO THAT LOOKS JUST LIKE YOU!
HA, HA, HA, HA, HA, HA!
HA, HA, HA HA!
HA, HA, HA, HA, HA, HA, HA, HA, HA, HA—

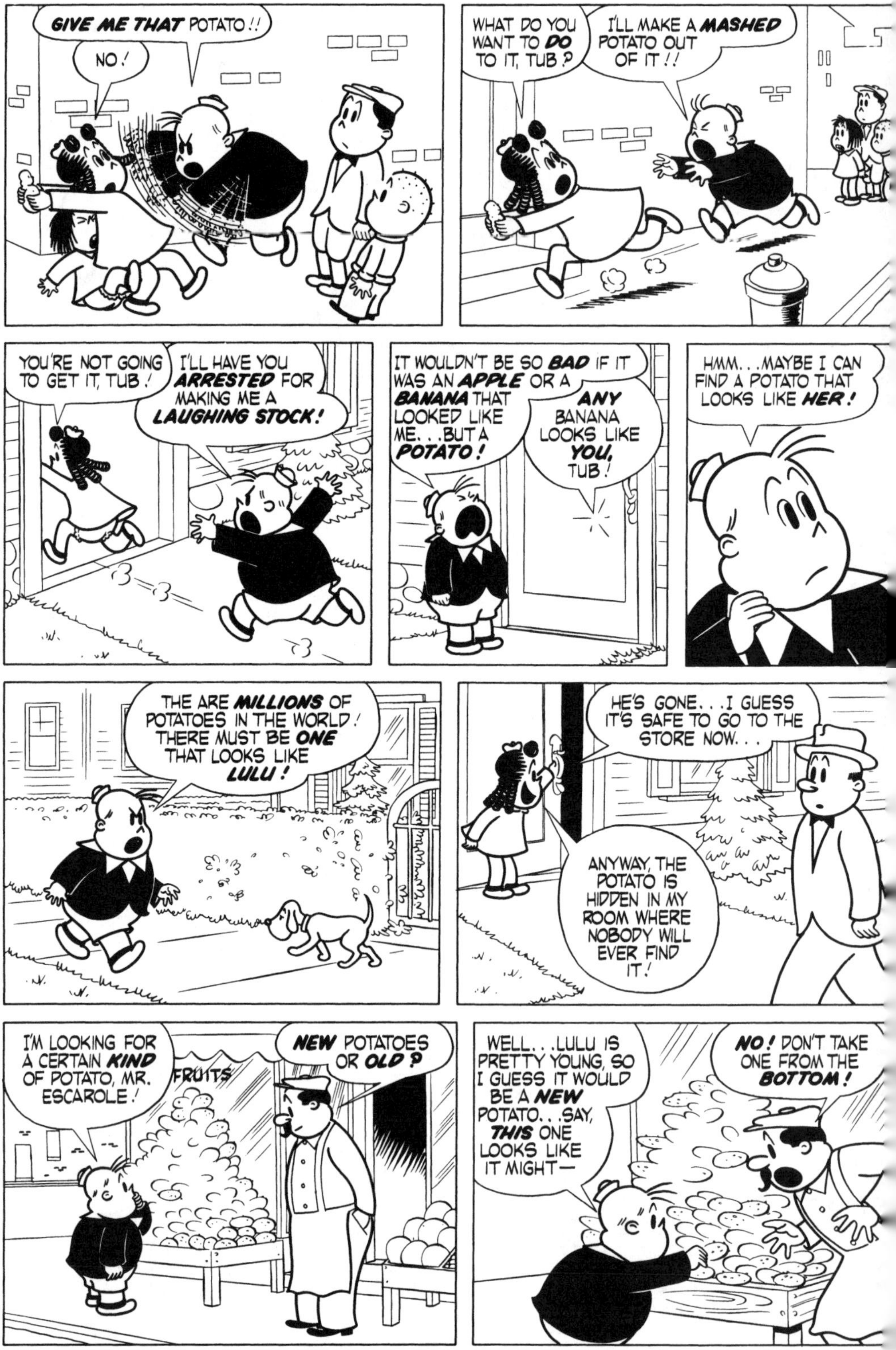
GIVE ME THAT POTATO!!
NO!
WHAT DO YOU WANT TO DO TO IT, TUB?
I'LL MAKE A MASHED POTATO OUT OF IT!!
YOU'RE NOT GOING TO GET IT, TUB!
I'LL HAVE YOU ARRESTED FOR MAKING ME A LAUGHING STOCK!
IT WOULDN'T BE SO BAD IF IT WAS AN APPLE OR A BANANA THAT LOOKED LIKE ME...BUT A POTATO!
ANY BANANA LOOKS LIKE YOU, TUB!
HMM...MAYBE I CAN FIND A POTATO THAT LOOKS LIKE HER!
THE ARE MILLIONS OF POTATOES IN THE WORLD! THERE MUST BE ONE THAT LOOKS LIKE LULU!
HE'S GONE...I GUESS IT'S SAFE TO GO TO THE STORE NOW...
ANYWAY, THE POTATO IS HIDDEN IN MY ROOM WHERE NOBODY WILL EVER FIND IT!
I'M LOOKING FOR A CERTAIN KIND OF POTATO, MR. ESCAROLE!
NEW POTATOES OR OLD?
FRUITS
WELL...LULU IS PRETTY YOUNG, SO I GUESS IT WOULD BE A NEW POTATO...SAY, THIS ONE LOOKS LIKE IT MIGHT—
NO! DON'T TAKE ONE FROM THE BOTTOM!

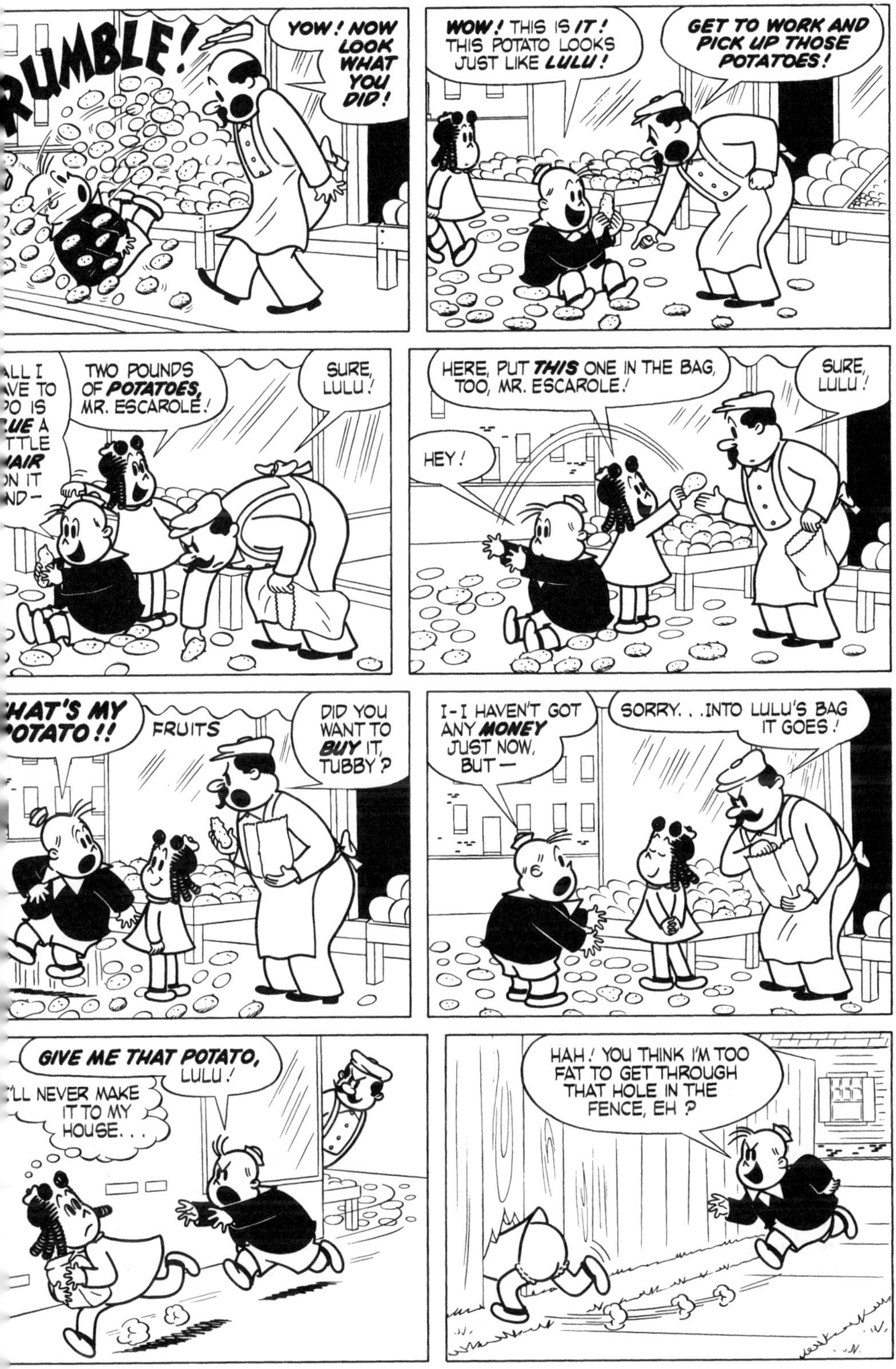
RUMBLE!
YOW! NOW LOOK WHAT YOU DID!
WOW! THIS IS IT! THIS POTATO LOOKS JUST LIKE LULU!
GET TO WORK AND PICK UP THOSE POTATOES!
ALL I AVE TO DO IS UE A TTLE AIR N IT ND—
TWO POUNDS OF POTATOES, MR. ESCAROLE!
SURE, LULU!
HERE, PUT THIS ONE IN THE BAG, TOO, MR. ESCAROLE!
SURE, LULU!
HEY!
HAT'S MY OTATO!!
FRUITS
DID YOU WANT TO BUY IT, TUBBY?
I-I HAVEN'T GOT ANY MONEY JUST NOW, BUT—
SORRY. . .INTO LULU'S BAG IT GOES!
GIVE ME THAT POTATO, LULU!
'LL NEVER MAKE IT TO MY HOUSE. . .
HAH! YOU THINK I'M TOO FAT TO GET THROUGH THAT HOLE IN THE FENCE, EH?

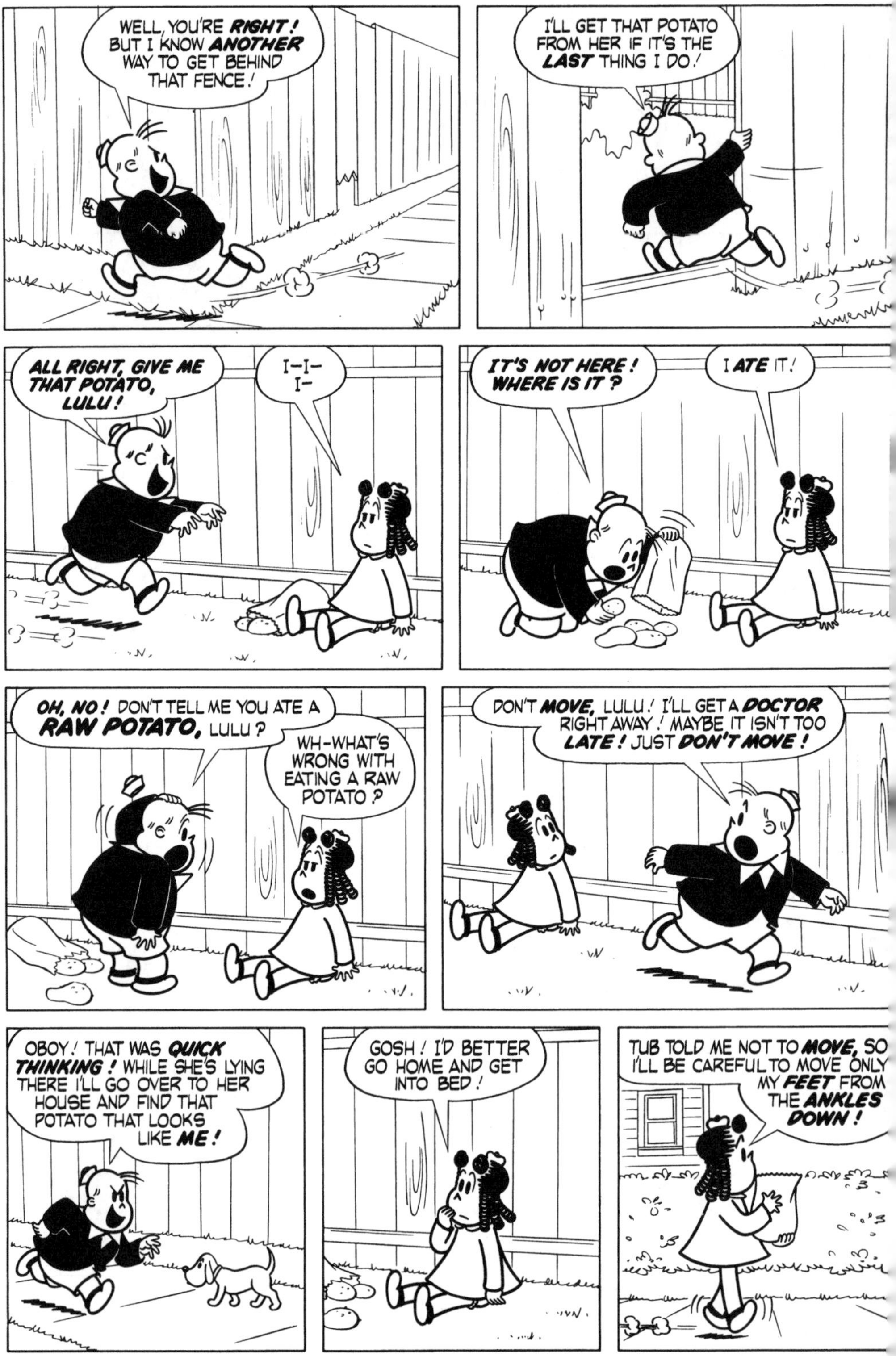

WELL, YOU'RE RIGHT! BUT I KNOW ANOTHER WAY TO GET BEHIND THAT FENCE!
I'LL GET THAT POTATO FROM HER IF IT'S THE LAST THING I DO!
ALL RIGHT, GIVE ME THAT POTATO, LULU!
I—I— I—
IT'S NOT HERE! WHERE IS IT?
I ATE IT!
OH, NO! DON'T TELL ME YOU ATE A RAW POTATO, LULU?
WH-WHAT'S WRONG WITH EATING A RAW POTATO?
DON'T MOVE, LULU! I'LL GET A DOCTOR RIGHT AWAY! MAYBE IT ISN'T TOO LATE! JUST DON'T MOVE!
OBOY! THAT WAS QUICK THINKING! WHILE SHE'S LYING THERE I'LL GO OVER TO HER HOUSE AND FIND THAT POTATO THAT LOOKS LIKE ME!
GOSH! I'D BETTER GO HOME AND GET INTO BED!
TUB TOLD ME NOT TO MOVE, SO I'LL BE CAREFUL TO MOVE ONLY MY FEET FROM THE ANKLES DOWN!

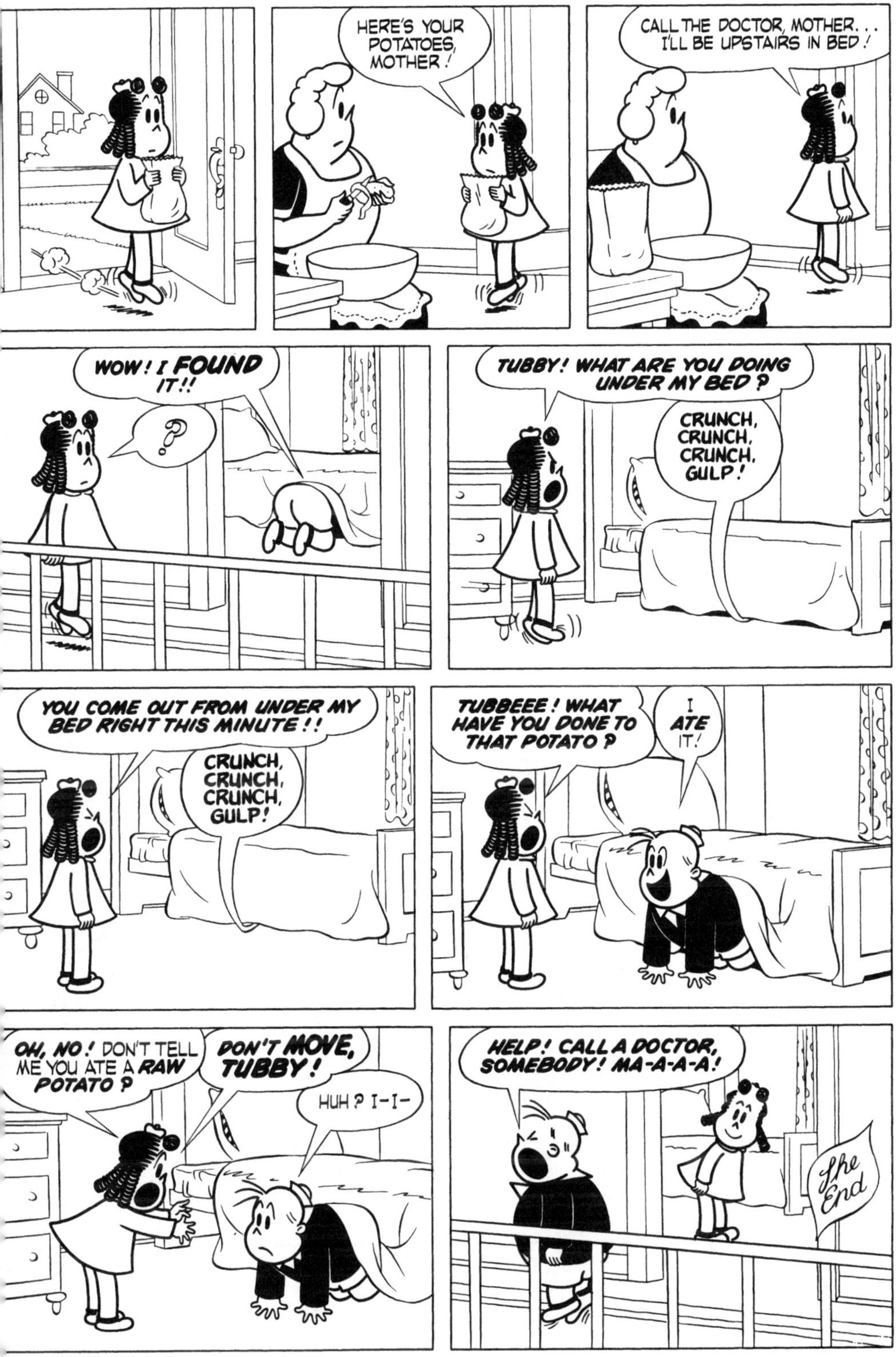
HERE'S YOUR POTATOES, MOTHER!
CALL THE DOCTOR, MOTHER... I'LL BE UPSTAIRS IN BED!
WOW! I FOUND IT!!
?
TUBBY! WHAT ARE YOU DOING UNDER MY BED?
CRUNCH, CRUNCH, CRUNCH, GULP!
YOU COME OUT FROM UNDER MY BED RIGHT THIS MINUTE!!
CRUNCH, CRUNCH, CRUNCH, GULP!
TUBBEEE! WHAT HAVE YOU DONE TO THAT POTATO?
I ATE IT!
OH, NO! DON'T TELL ME YOU ATE A RAW POTATO?
DON'T MOVE, TUBBY!
HUH? I-I-
HELP! CALL A DOCTOR, SOMEBODY! MA-A-A-A!
The End

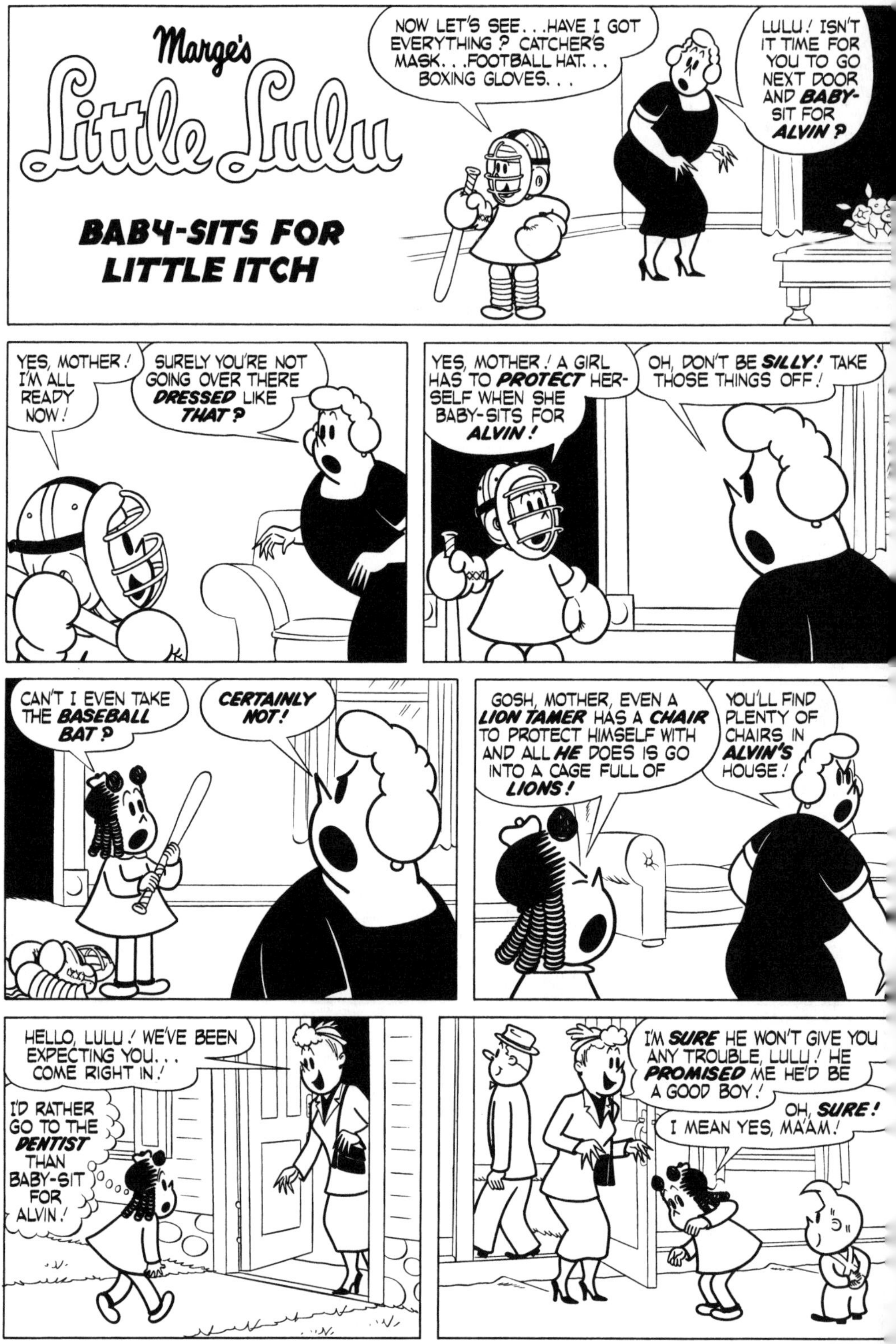
Marge's Little Lulu
BABY-SITS FOR LITTLE ITCH
NOW LET'S SEE. . .HAVE I GOT EVERYTHING? CATCHER'S MASK. . .FOOTBALL HAT. . . BOXING GLOVES. . .
LULU! ISN'T IT TIME FOR YOU TO GO NEXT DOOR AND BABY-SIT FOR ALVIN?
YES, MOTHER! I'M ALL READY NOW!
SURELY YOU'RE NOT GOING OVER THERE DRESSED LIKE THAT?
YES, MOTHER! A GIRL HAS TO PROTECT HER-SELF WHEN SHE BABY-SITS FOR ALVIN!
OH, DON'T BE SILLY! TAKE THOSE THINGS OFF!
CAN'T I EVEN TAKE THE BASEBALL BAT?
CERTAINLY NOT!
GOSH, MOTHER, EVEN A LION TAMER HAS A CHAIR TO PROTECT HIMSELF WITH AND ALL HE DOES IS GO INTO A CAGE FULL OF LIONS!
YOU'LL FIND PLENTY OF CHAIRS IN ALVIN'S HOUSE!
HELLO, LULU! WE'VE BEEN EXPECTING YOU. . . COME RIGHT IN!
I'D RATHER GO TO THE DENTIST THAN BABY-SIT FOR ALVIN!
I'M SURE HE WON'T GIVE YOU ANY TROUBLE, LULU! HE PROMISED ME HE'D BE A GOOD BOY!
OH, SURE! I MEAN YES, MA'AM!

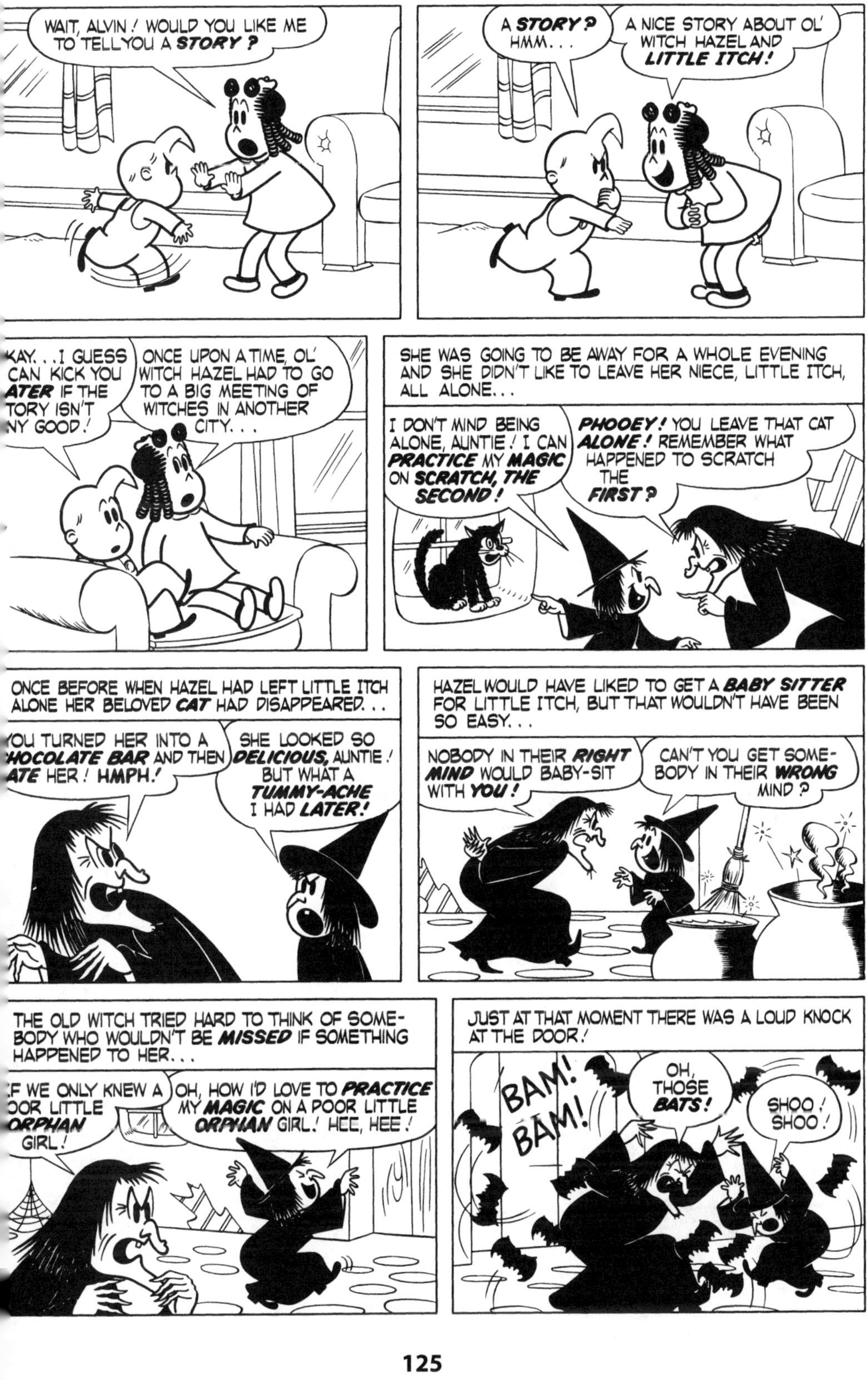
WAIT, ALVIN! WOULD YOU LIKE ME TO TELL YOU A STORY?
A STORY? HMM...
A NICE STORY ABOUT OL' WITCH HAZEL AND LITTLE ITCH!
KAY...I GUESS CAN KICK YOU ATER IF THE TORY ISN'T NY GOOD!
ONCE UPON A TIME, OL' WITCH HAZEL HAD TO GO TO A BIG MEETING OF WITCHES IN ANOTHER CITY...
SHE WAS GOING TO BE AWAY FOR A WHOLE EVENING AND SHE DIDN'T LIKE TO LEAVE HER NIECE, LITTLE ITCH, ALL ALONE...
I DON'T MIND BEING ALONE, AUNTIE! I CAN PRACTICE MY MAGIC ON SCRATCH, THE SECOND!
PHOOEY! YOU LEAVE THAT CAT ALONE! REMEMBER WHAT HAPPENED TO SCRATCH THE FIRST?
ONCE BEFORE WHEN HAZEL HAD LEFT LITTLE ITCH ALONE HER BELOVED CAT HAD DISAPPEARED...
OU TURNED HER INTO A HOCOLATE BAR AND THEN ATE HER! HMPH!
SHE LOOKED SO DELICIOUS, AUNTIE! BUT WHAT A TUMMY-ACHE I HAD LATER!
HAZEL WOULD HAVE LIKED TO GET A BABY SITTER FOR LITTLE ITCH, BUT THAT WOULDN'T HAVE BEEN SO EASY...
NOBODY IN THEIR RIGHT MIND WOULD BABY-SIT WITH YOU!
CAN'T YOU GET SOME-BODY IN THEIR WRONG MIND?
THE OLD WITCH TRIED HARD TO THINK OF SOME-BODY WHO WOULDN'T BE MISSED IF SOMETHING HAPPENED TO HER...
F WE ONLY KNEW A OOR LITTLE ORPHAN GIRL!
OH, HOW I'D LOVE TO PRACTICE MY MAGIC ON A POOR LITTLE ORPHAN GIRL! HEE, HEE!
JUST AT THAT MOMENT THERE WAS A LOUD KNOCK AT THE DOOR!
BAM! BAM!
OH, THOSE BATS!
SHOO! SHOO!

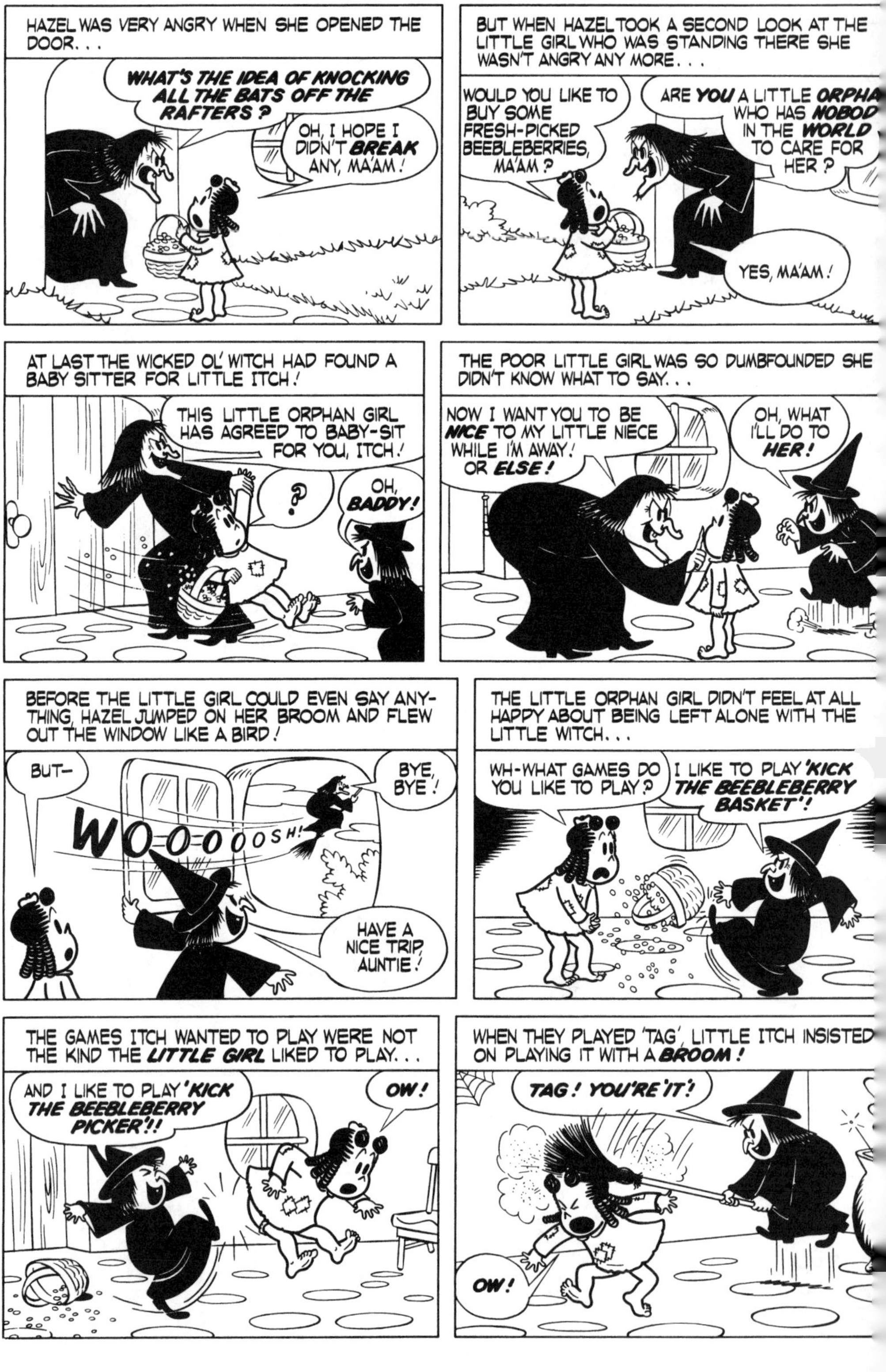
HAZEL WAS VERY ANGRY WHEN SHE OPENED THE DOOR. . .
WHAT'S THE IDEA OF KNOCKING ALL THE BATS OFF THE RAFTERS?
OH, I HOPE I DIDN'T BREAK ANY, MA'AM!
BUT WHEN HAZEL TOOK A SECOND LOOK AT THE LITTLE GIRL WHO WAS STANDING THERE SHE WASN'T ANGRY ANY MORE. . .
WOULD YOU LIKE TO BUY SOME FRESH-PICKED BEEBLEBERRIES, MA'AM?
ARE YOU A LITTLE ORPHA WHO HAS NOBOD IN THE WORLD TO CARE FOR HER?
YES, MA'AM!
AT LAST THE WICKED OL' WITCH HAD FOUND A BABY SITTER FOR LITTLE ITCH!
THIS LITTLE ORPHAN GIRL HAS AGREED TO BABY-SIT FOR YOU, ITCH!
?
OH, BADDY!
THE POOR LITTLE GIRL WAS SO DUMBFOUNDED SHE DIDN'T KNOW WHAT TO SAY. . .
NOW I WANT YOU TO BE NICE TO MY LITTLE NIECE WHILE I'M AWAY! OR ELSE!
OH, WHAT I'LL DO TO HER!
BEFORE THE LITTLE GIRL COULD EVEN SAY ANYTHING, HAZEL JUMPED ON HER BROOM AND FLEW OUT THE WINDOW LIKE A BIRD!
BUT—
BYE, BYE!
WOOOOOOSH!
HAVE A NICE TRIP, AUNTIE!
THE LITTLE ORPHAN GIRL DIDN'T FEEL AT ALL HAPPY ABOUT BEING LEFT ALONE WITH THE LITTLE WITCH. . .
WH-WHAT GAMES DO YOU LIKE TO PLAY?
I LIKE TO PLAY 'KICK THE BEEBLEBERRY BASKET'!
THE GAMES ITCH WANTED TO PLAY WERE NOT THE KIND THE LITTLE GIRL LIKED TO PLAY. . .
AND I LIKE TO PLAY 'KICK THE BEEBLEBERRY PICKER'!!
OW!
WHEN THEY PLAYED 'TAG', LITTLE ITCH INSISTED ON PLAYING IT WITH A BROOM!
TAG! YOU'RE 'IT'!
OW!

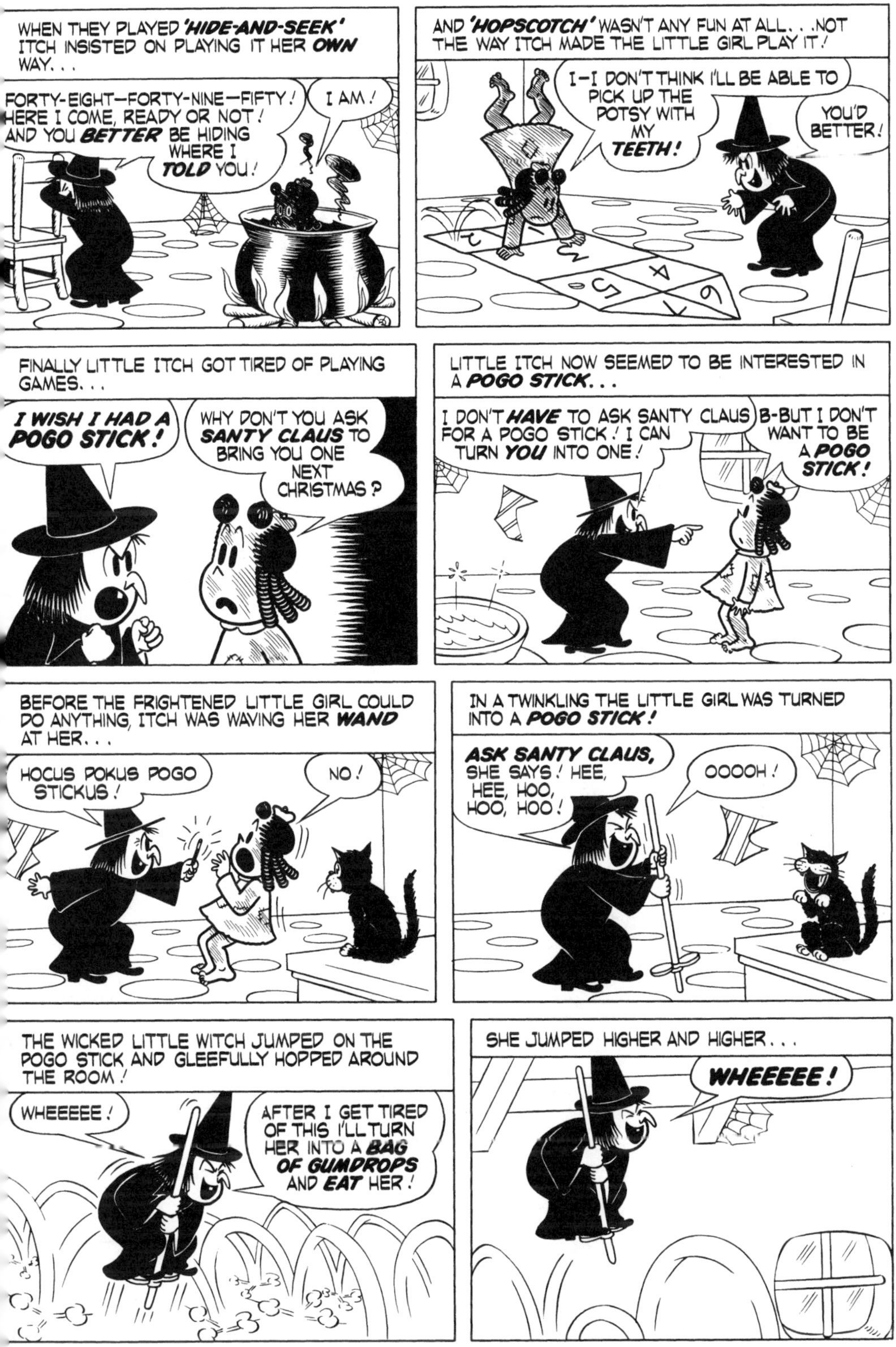

WHEN THEY PLAYED 'HIDE-AND-SEEK' ITCH INSISTED ON PLAYING IT HER OWN WAY. . .
FORTY-EIGHT—FORTY-NINE—FIFTY! HERE I COME, READY OR NOT! AND YOU BETTER BE HIDING WHERE I TOLD YOU!
I AM!
AND 'HOPSCOTCH' WASN'T ANY FUN AT ALL. . .NOT THE WAY ITCH MADE THE LITTLE GIRL PLAY IT!
I-I DON'T THINK I'LL BE ABLE TO PICK UP THE POTSY WITH MY TEETH!
YOU'D BETTER!
FINALLY LITTLE ITCH GOT TIRED OF PLAYING GAMES. . .
I WISH I HAD A POGO STICK!
WHY DON'T YOU ASK SANTY CLAUS TO BRING YOU ONE NEXT CHRISTMAS?
LITTLE ITCH NOW SEEMED TO BE INTERESTED IN A POGO STICK. . .
I DON'T HAVE TO ASK SANTY CLAUS FOR A POGO STICK! I CAN TURN YOU INTO ONE!
B-BUT I DON'T WANT TO BE A POGO STICK!
BEFORE THE FRIGHTENED LITTLE GIRL COULD DO ANYTHING, ITCH WAS WAVING HER WAND AT HER. . .
HOCUS POKUS POGO STICKUS!
NO!
IN A TWINKLING THE LITTLE GIRL WAS TURNED INTO A POGO STICK!
ASK SANTY CLAUS, SHE SAYS! HEE, HEE, HOO, HOO, HOO!
OOOOH!
THE WICKED LITTLE WITCH JUMPED ON THE POGO STICK AND GLEEFULLY HOPPED AROUND THE ROOM!
WHEEEEE!
AFTER I GET TIRED OF THIS I'LL TURN HER INTO A BAG OF GUMDROPS AND EAT HER!
SHE JUMPED HIGHER AND HIGHER. . .
WHEEEEE!

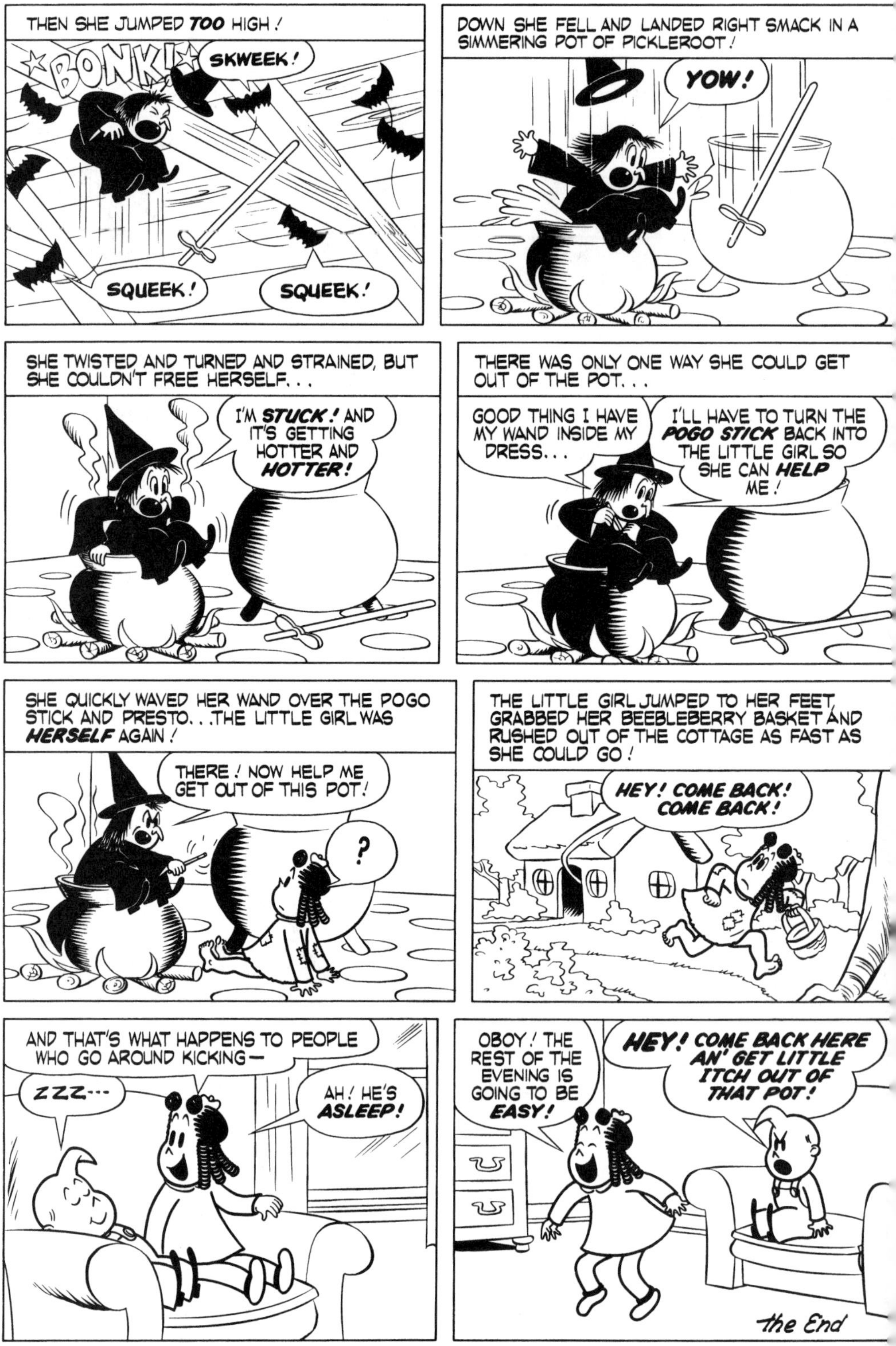
THEN SHE JUMPED TOO HIGH!
BONK!
SKWEEK!
SQUEEK!
SQUEEK!
DOWN SHE FELL AND LANDED RIGHT SMACK IN A SIMMERING POT OF PICKLEROOT!
YOW!
SHE TWISTED AND TURNED AND STRAINED, BUT SHE COULDN'T FREE HERSELF...
I'M STUCK! AND IT'S GETTING HOTTER AND HOTTER!
THERE WAS ONLY ONE WAY SHE COULD GET OUT OF THE POT...
GOOD THING I HAVE MY WAND INSIDE MY DRESS...
I'LL HAVE TO TURN THE POGO STICK BACK INTO THE LITTLE GIRL SO SHE CAN HELP ME!
SHE QUICKLY WAVED HER WAND OVER THE POGO STICK AND PRESTO...THE LITTLE GIRL WAS HERSELF AGAIN!
THERE! NOW HELP ME GET OUT OF THIS POT!
?
THE LITTLE GIRL JUMPED TO HER FEET, GRABBED HER BEEBLEBERRY BASKET AND RUSHED OUT OF THE COTTAGE AS FAST AS SHE COULD GO!
HEY! COME BACK! COME BACK!
AND THAT'S WHAT HAPPENS TO PEOPLE WHO GO AROUND KICKING—
ZZZ---
AH! HE'S ASLEEP!
OBOY! THE REST OF THE EVENING IS GOING TO BE EASY!
HEY! COME BACK HERE AN' GET LITTLE ITCH OUT OF THAT POT!
the End

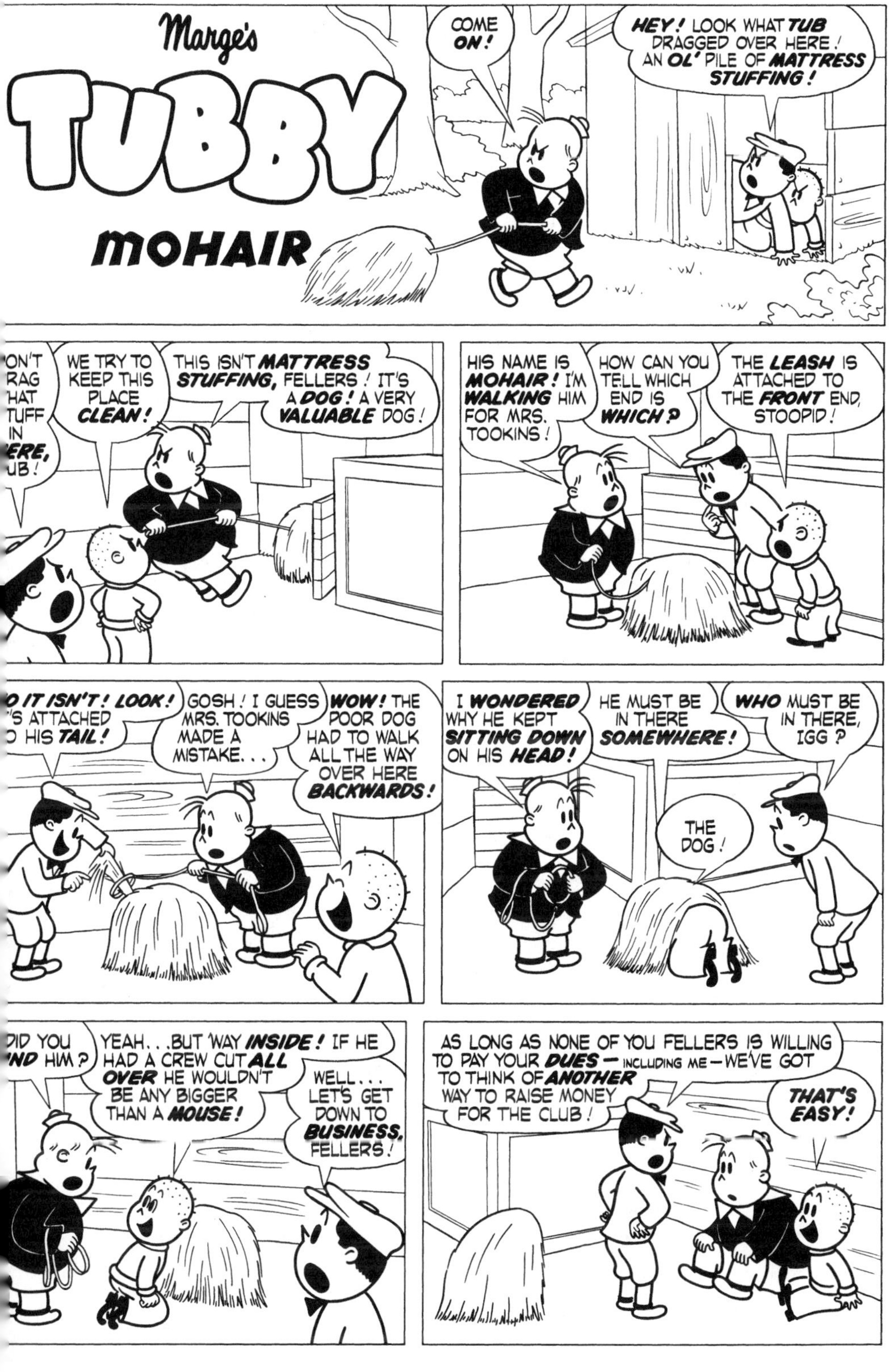
Marge's
TUBBY
MOHAIR
COME ON!
HEY! LOOK WHAT TUB DRAGGED OVER HERE! AN OL' PILE OF MATTRESS STUFFING!
ON'T RAG HAT TUFF IN ERE, UB!
WE TRY TO KEEP THIS PLACE CLEAN!
THIS ISN'T MATTRESS STUFFING, FELLERS! IT'S A DOG! A VERY VALUABLE DOG!
HIS NAME IS MOHAIR! I'M WALKING HIM FOR MRS. TOOKINS!
HOW CAN YOU TELL WHICH END IS WHICH?
THE LEASH IS ATTACHED TO THE FRONT END, STOOPID!
O IT ISN'T! LOOK! 'S ATTACHED O HIS TAIL!
GOSH! I GUESS MRS. TOOKINS MADE A MISTAKE...
WOW! THE POOR DOG HAD TO WALK ALL THE WAY OVER HERE BACKWARDS!
I WONDERED WHY HE KEPT SITTING DOWN ON HIS HEAD!
HE MUST BE IN THERE SOMEWHERE!
WHO MUST BE IN THERE, IGG?
THE DOG!
DID YOU ND HIM?
YEAH...BUT 'WAY INSIDE! IF HE HAD A CREW CUT ALL OVER HE WOULDN'T BE ANY BIGGER THAN A MOUSE!
WELL... LET'S GET DOWN TO BUSINESS, FELLERS!
AS LONG AS NONE OF YOU FELLERS IS WILLING TO PAY YOUR DUES— INCLUDING ME —WE'VE GOT TO THINK OF ANOTHER WAY TO RAISE MONEY FOR THE CLUB!
THAT'S EASY!

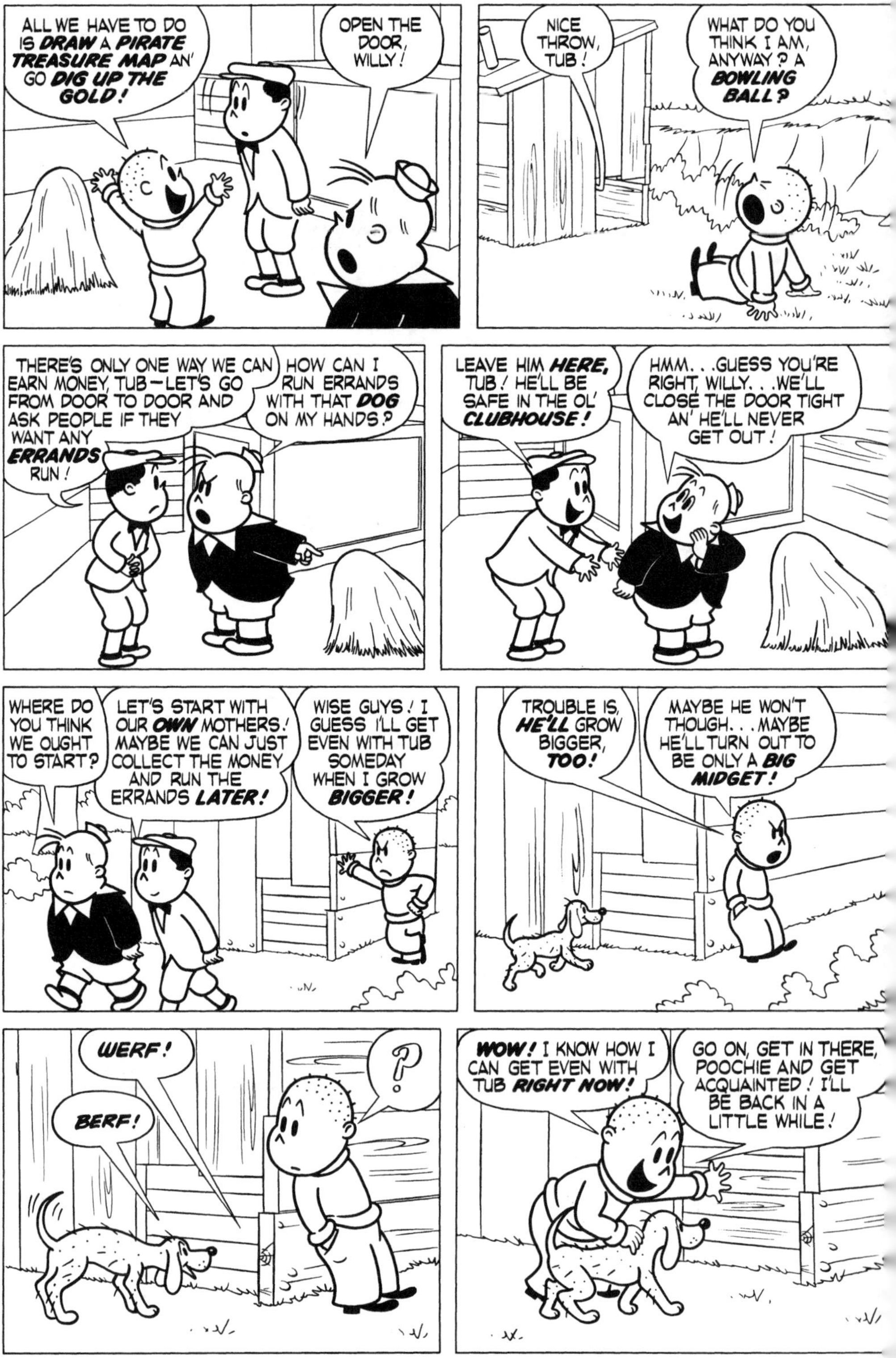
ALL WE HAVE TO DO IS DRAW A PIRATE TREASURE MAP AN' GO DIG UP THE GOLD!
OPEN THE DOOR, WILLY!
NICE THROW, TUB!
WHAT DO YOU THINK I AM, ANYWAY? A BOWLING BALL?
THERE'S ONLY ONE WAY WE CAN EARN MONEY, TUB—LET'S GO FROM DOOR TO DOOR AND ASK PEOPLE IF THEY WANT ANY ERRANDS RUN!
HOW CAN I RUN ERRANDS WITH THAT DOG ON MY HANDS?
LEAVE HIM HERE, TUB! HE'LL BE SAFE IN THE OL' CLUBHOUSE!
HMM. . .GUESS YOU'RE RIGHT, WILLY. . .WE'LL CLOSE THE DOOR TIGHT AN' HE'LL NEVER GET OUT!
WHERE DO YOU THINK WE OUGHT TO START?
LET'S START WITH OUR OWN MOTHERS! MAYBE WE CAN JUST COLLECT THE MONEY AND RUN THE ERRANDS LATER!
WISE GUYS! I GUESS I'LL GET EVEN WITH TUB SOMEDAY WHEN I GROW BIGGER!
TROUBLE IS, HE'LL GROW BIGGER, TOO!
MAYBE HE WON'T THOUGH. . . MAYBE HE'LL TURN OUT TO BE ONLY A BIG MIDGET!
WERF!
BERF!
?
WOW! I KNOW HOW I CAN GET EVEN WITH TUB RIGHT NOW!
GO ON, GET IN THERE, POOCHIE AND GET ACQUAINTED! I'LL BE BACK IN A LITTLE WHILE!

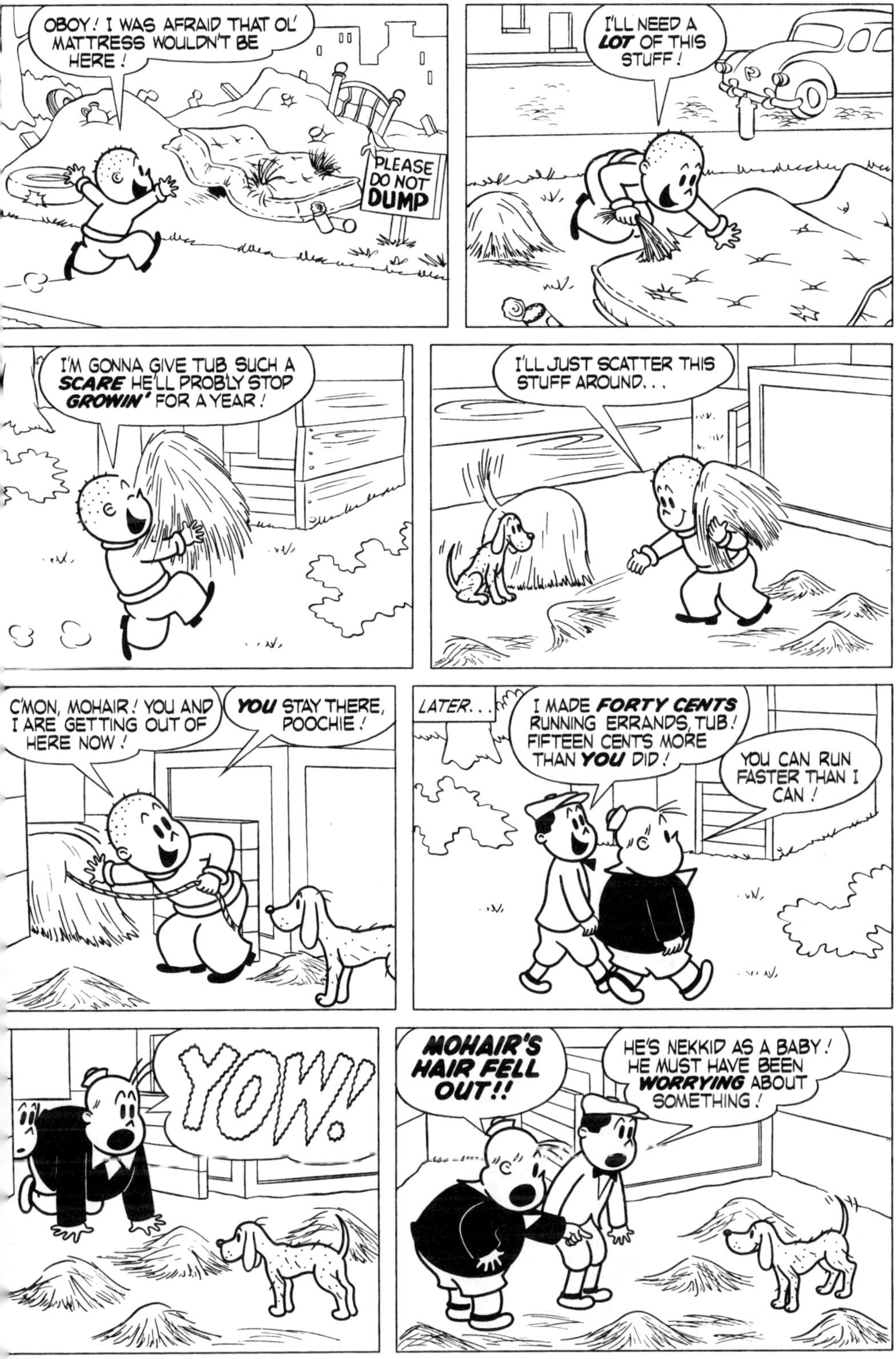
OBOY! I WAS AFRAID THAT OL' MATTRESS WOULDN'T BE HERE!
PLEASE DO NOT DUMP
I'LL NEED A LOT OF THIS STUFF!
I'M GONNA GIVE TUB SUCH A SCARE HE'LL PROB'LY STOP GROWIN' FOR A YEAR!
I'LL JUST SCATTER THIS STUFF AROUND...
C'MON, MOHAIR! YOU AND I ARE GETTING OUT OF HERE NOW!
YOU STAY THERE, POOCHIE!
LATER...
I MADE FORTY CENTS RUNNING ERRANDS, TUB! FIFTEEN CENTS MORE THAN YOU DID!
YOU CAN RUN FASTER THAN I CAN!
YOW!
MOHAIR'S HAIR FELL OUT!!
HE'S NEKKID AS A BABY! HE MUST HAVE BEEN WORRYING ABOUT SOMETHING!

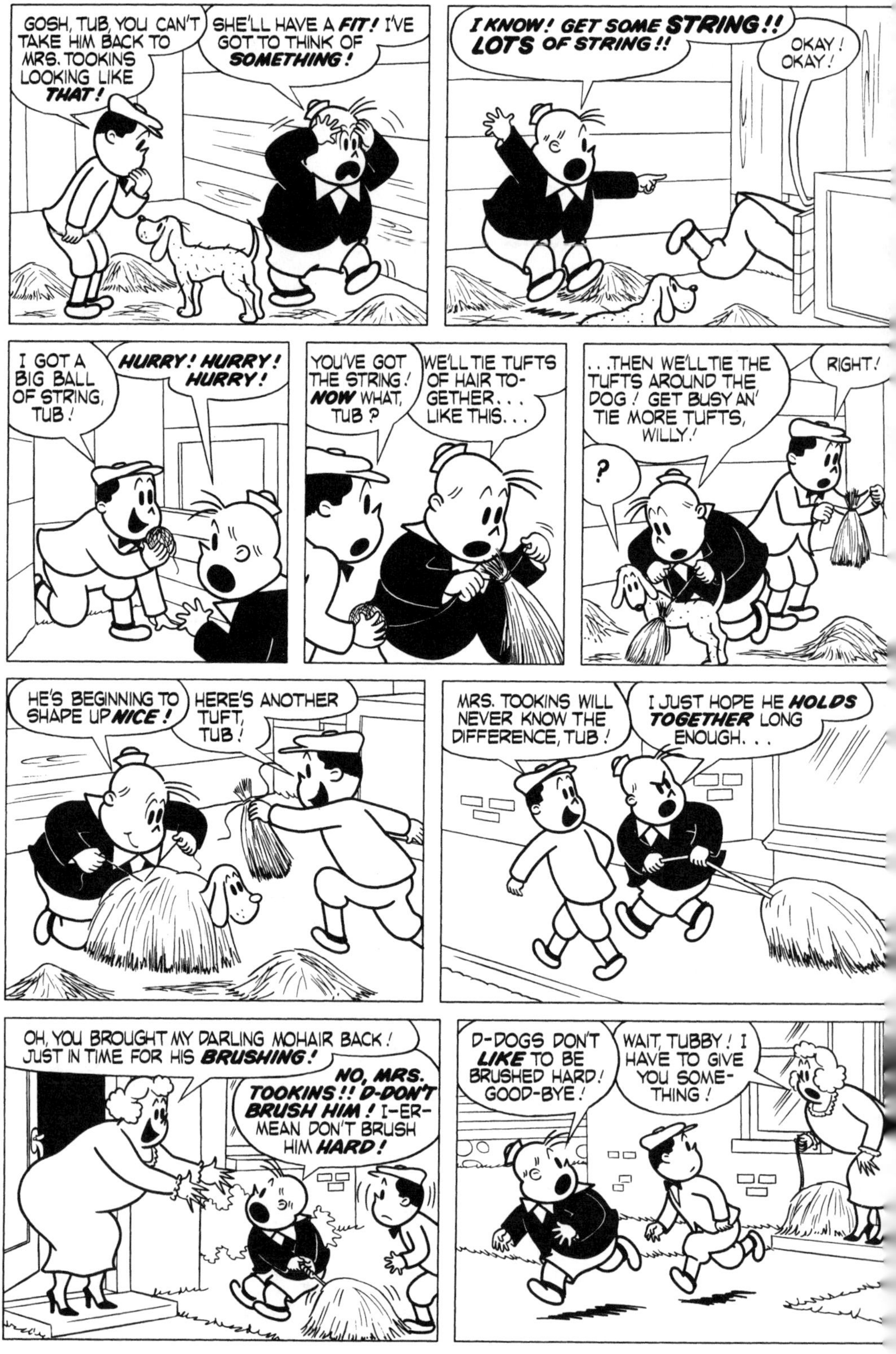
GOSH, TUB, YOU CAN'T TAKE HIM BACK TO MRS. TOOKINS LOOKING LIKE THAT!
SHE'LL HAVE A FIT! I'VE GOT TO THINK OF SOMETHING!
I KNOW! GET SOME STRING!! LOTS OF STRING!!
OKAY! OKAY!
I GOT A BIG BALL OF STRING, TUB!
HURRY! HURRY! HURRY!
YOU'VE GOT THE STRING! NOW WHAT, TUB?
WE'LL TIE TUFTS OF HAIR TO-GETHER... LIKE THIS...
...THEN WE'LL TIE THE TUFTS AROUND THE DOG! GET BUSY AN' TIE MORE TUFTS, WILLY!
RIGHT!
?
HE'S BEGINNING TO SHAPE UP NICE!
HERE'S ANOTHER TUFT, TUB!
MRS. TOOKINS WILL NEVER KNOW THE DIFFERENCE, TUB!
I JUST HOPE HE HOLDS TOGETHER LONG ENOUGH...
OH, YOU BROUGHT MY DARLING MOHAIR BACK! JUST IN TIME FOR HIS BRUSHING!
NO, MRS. TOOKINS!! D-DON'T BRUSH HIM! I-ER-MEAN DON'T BRUSH HIM HARD!
D-DOGS DON'T LIKE TO BE BRUSHED HARD! GOOD-BYE!
WAIT, TUBBY! I HAVE TO GIVE YOU SOME-THING!

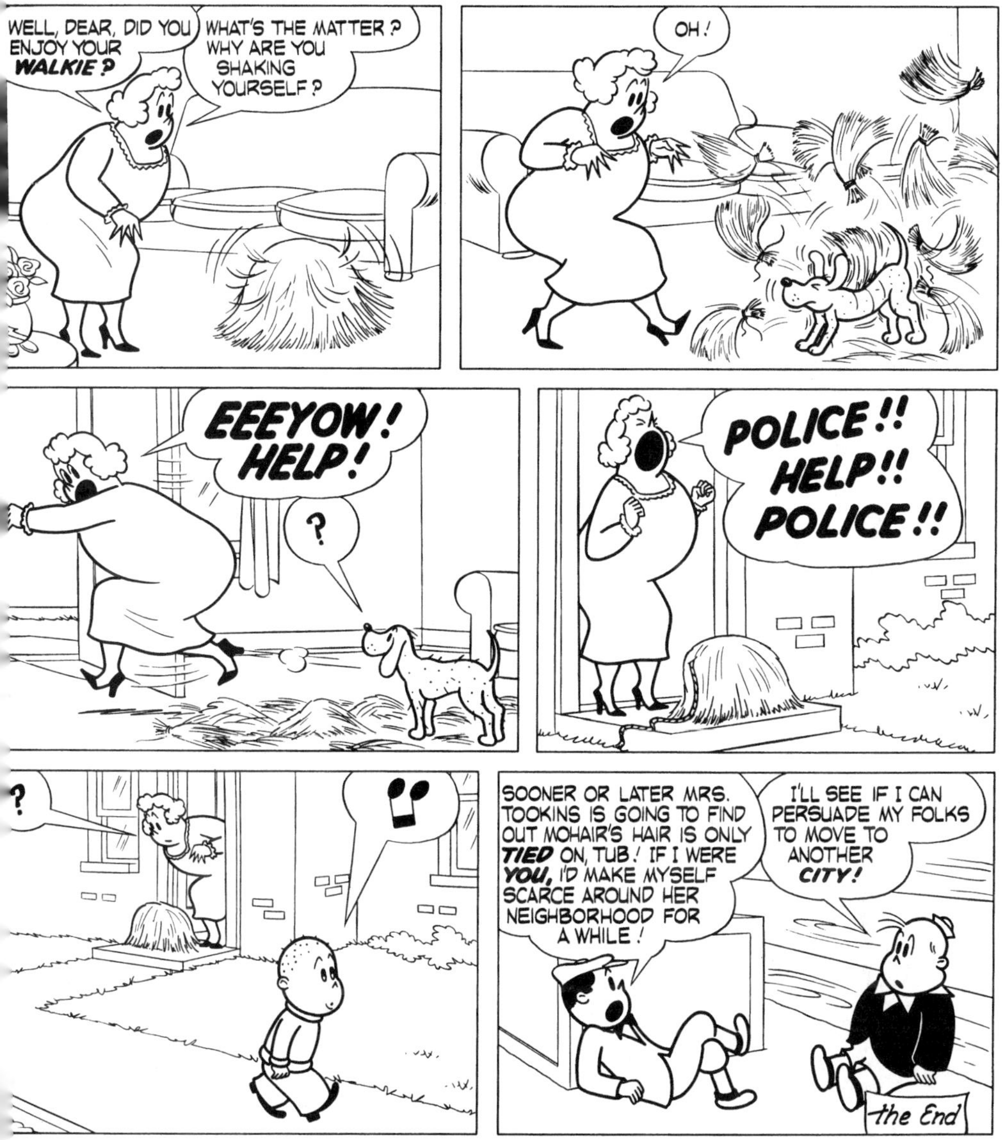
WELL, DEAR, DID YOU ENJOY YOUR WALKIE ?
WHAT'S THE MATTER ? WHY ARE YOU SHAKING YOURSELF ?
OH !
EEEYOW ! HELP !
?
POLICE !! HELP !! POLICE !!
?
SOONER OR LATER MRS. TOOKINS IS GOING TO FIND OUT MOHAIR'S HAIR IS ONLY TIED ON, TUB ! IF I WERE YOU, I'D MAKE MYSELF SCARCE AROUND HER NEIGHBORHOOD FOR A WHILE !
I'LL SEE IF I CAN PERSUADE MY FOLKS TO MOVE TO ANOTHER CITY !
the End

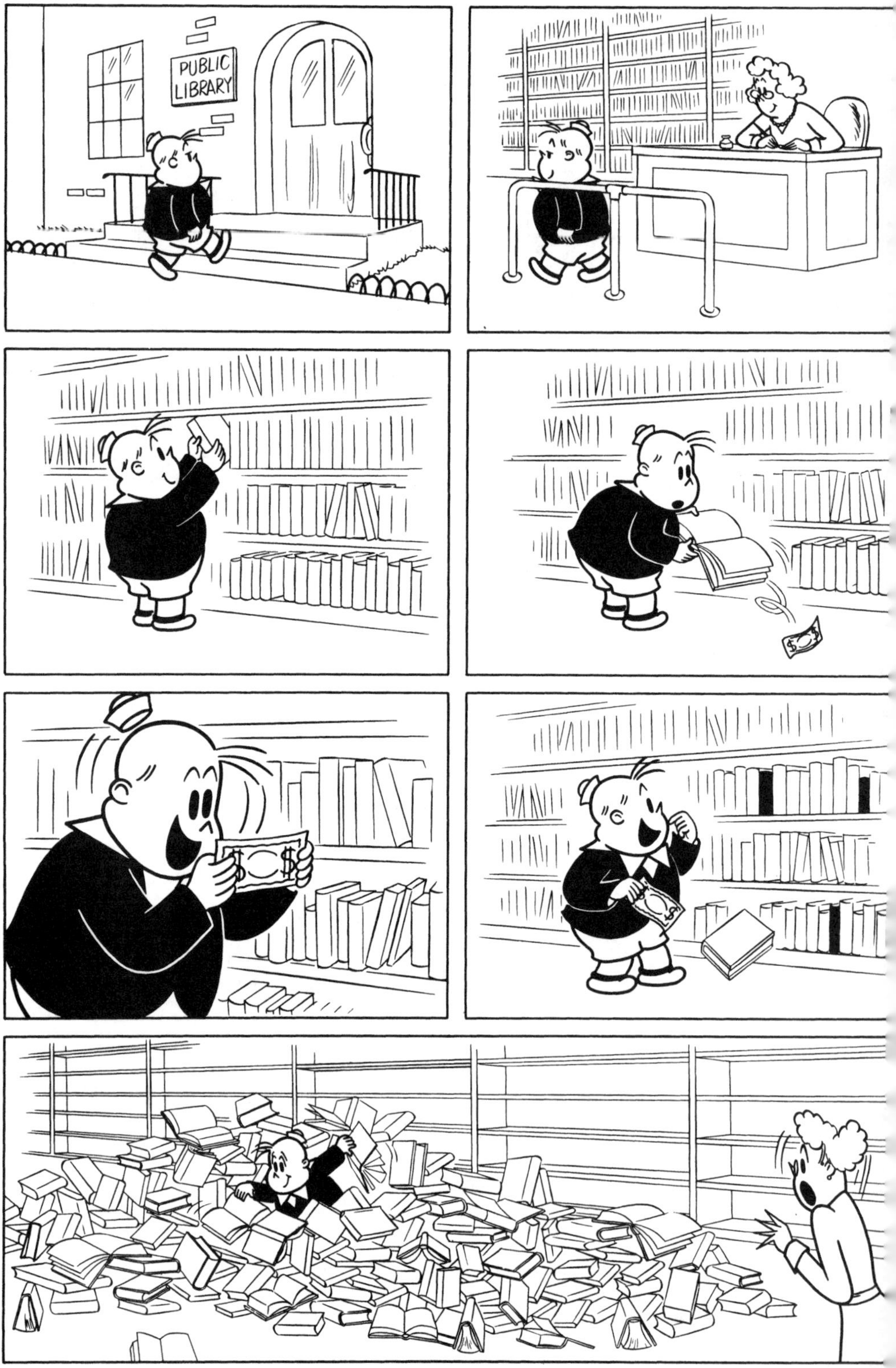
PUBLIC LIBRARY

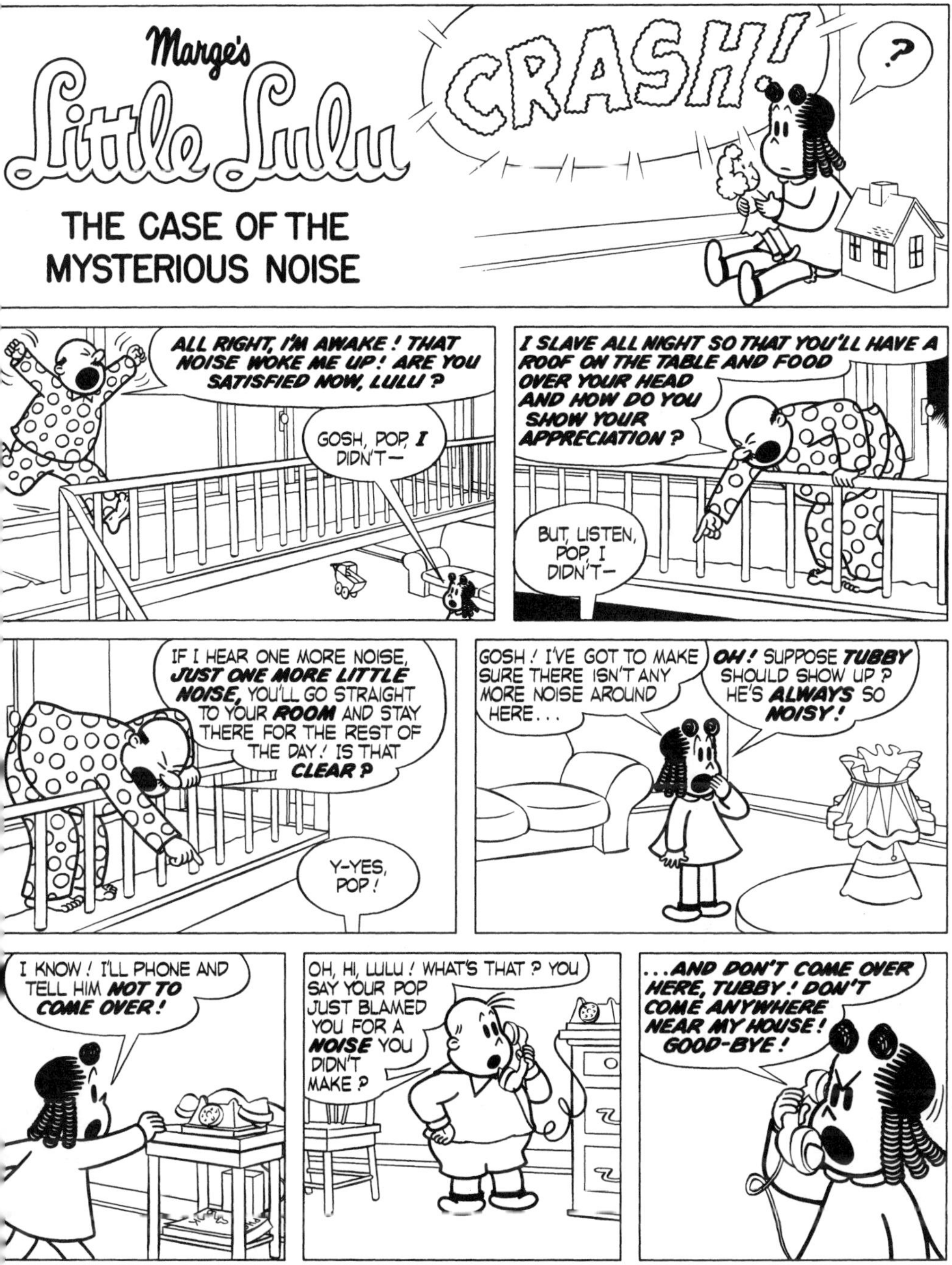

Marge's Little Lulu
THE CASE OF THE MYSTERIOUS NOISE
CRASH!
?
ALL RIGHT, I'M AWAKE! THAT NOISE WOKE ME UP! ARE YOU SATISFIED NOW, LULU?
GOSH, POP, I DIDN'T—
I SLAVE ALL NIGHT SO THAT YOU'LL HAVE A ROOF ON THE TABLE AND FOOD OVER YOUR HEAD AND HOW DO YOU SHOW YOUR APPRECIATION?
BUT, LISTEN, POP, I DIDN'T—
IF I HEAR ONE MORE NOISE, JUST ONE MORE LITTLE NOISE, YOU'LL GO STRAIGHT TO YOUR ROOM AND STAY THERE FOR THE REST OF THE DAY! IS THAT CLEAR?
Y-YES, POP!
GOSH! I'VE GOT TO MAKE SURE THERE ISN'T ANY MORE NOISE AROUND HERE...
OH! SUPPOSE TUBBY SHOULD SHOW UP? HE'S ALWAYS SO NOISY!
I KNOW! I'LL PHONE AND TELL HIM NOT TO COME OVER!
OH, HI, LULU! WHAT'S THAT? YOU SAY YOUR POP JUST BLAMED YOU FOR A NOISE YOU DIDN'T MAKE?
...AND DON'T COME OVER HERE, TUBBY! DON'T COME ANYWHERE NEAR MY HOUSE! GOOD-BYE!

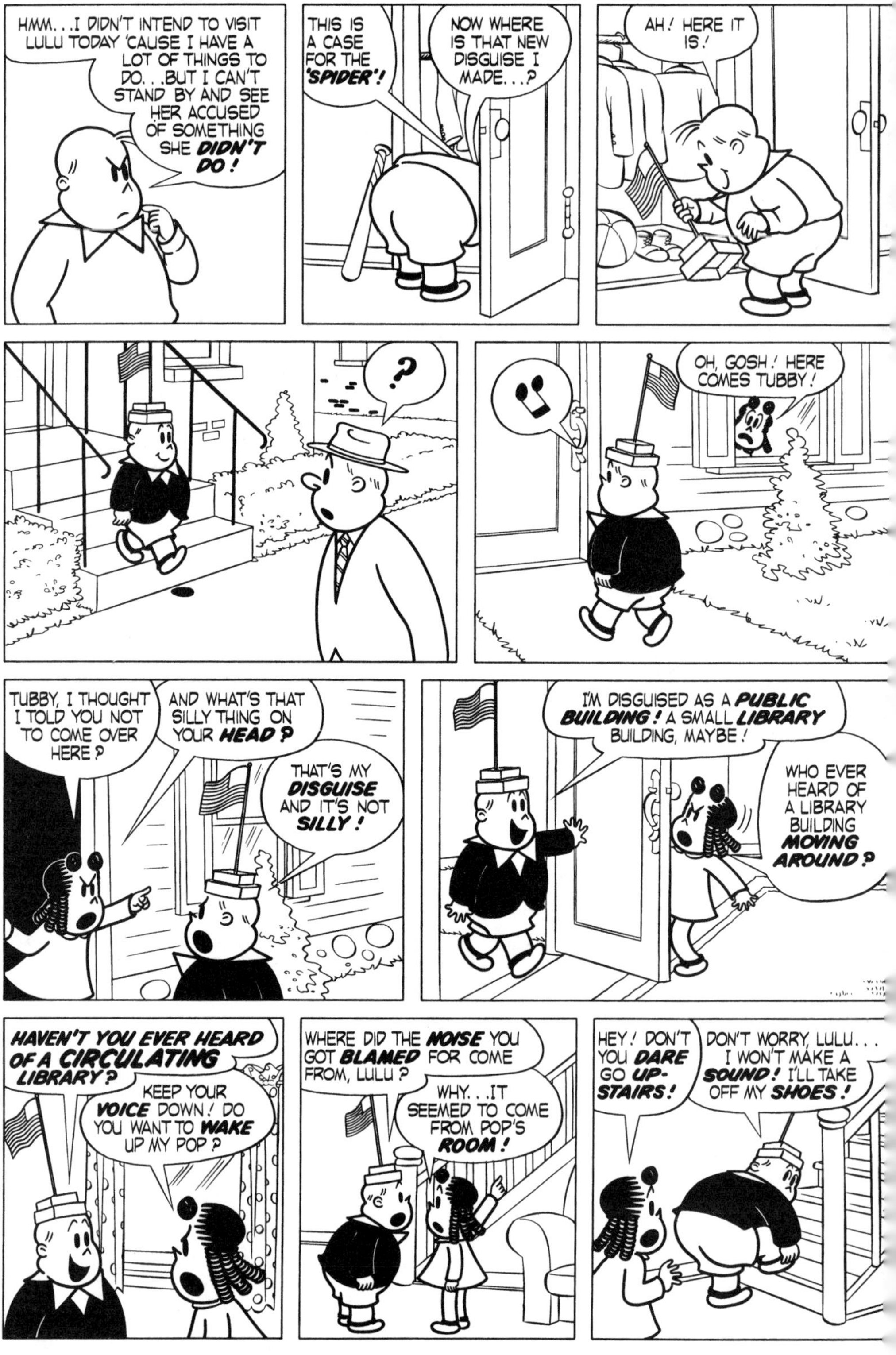
HMM...I DIDN'T INTEND TO VISIT LULU TODAY 'CAUSE I HAVE A LOT OF THINGS TO DO...BUT I CAN'T STAND BY AND SEE HER ACCUSED OF SOMETHING SHE DIDN'T DO!
THIS IS A CASE FOR THE 'SPIDER'!
NOW WHERE IS THAT NEW DISGUISE I MADE...?
AH! HERE IT IS!
?
OH, GOSH! HERE COMES TUBBY!
TUBBY, I THOUGHT I TOLD YOU NOT TO COME OVER HERE?
AND WHAT'S THAT SILLY THING ON YOUR HEAD?
THAT'S MY DISGUISE AND IT'S NOT SILLY!
I'M DISGUISED AS A PUBLIC BUILDING! A SMALL LIBRARY BUILDING, MAYBE!
WHO EVER HEARD OF A LIBRARY BUILDING MOVING AROUND?
HAVEN'T YOU EVER HEARD OF A CIRCULATING LIBRARY?
KEEP YOUR VOICE DOWN! DO YOU WANT TO WAKE UP MY POP?
WHERE DID THE NOISE YOU GOT BLAMED FOR COME FROM, LULU?
WHY...IT SEEMED TO COME FROM POP'S ROOM!
HEY! DON'T YOU DARE GO UP-STAIRS!
DON'T WORRY, LULU... I WON'T MAKE A SOUND! I'LL TAKE OFF MY SHOES!

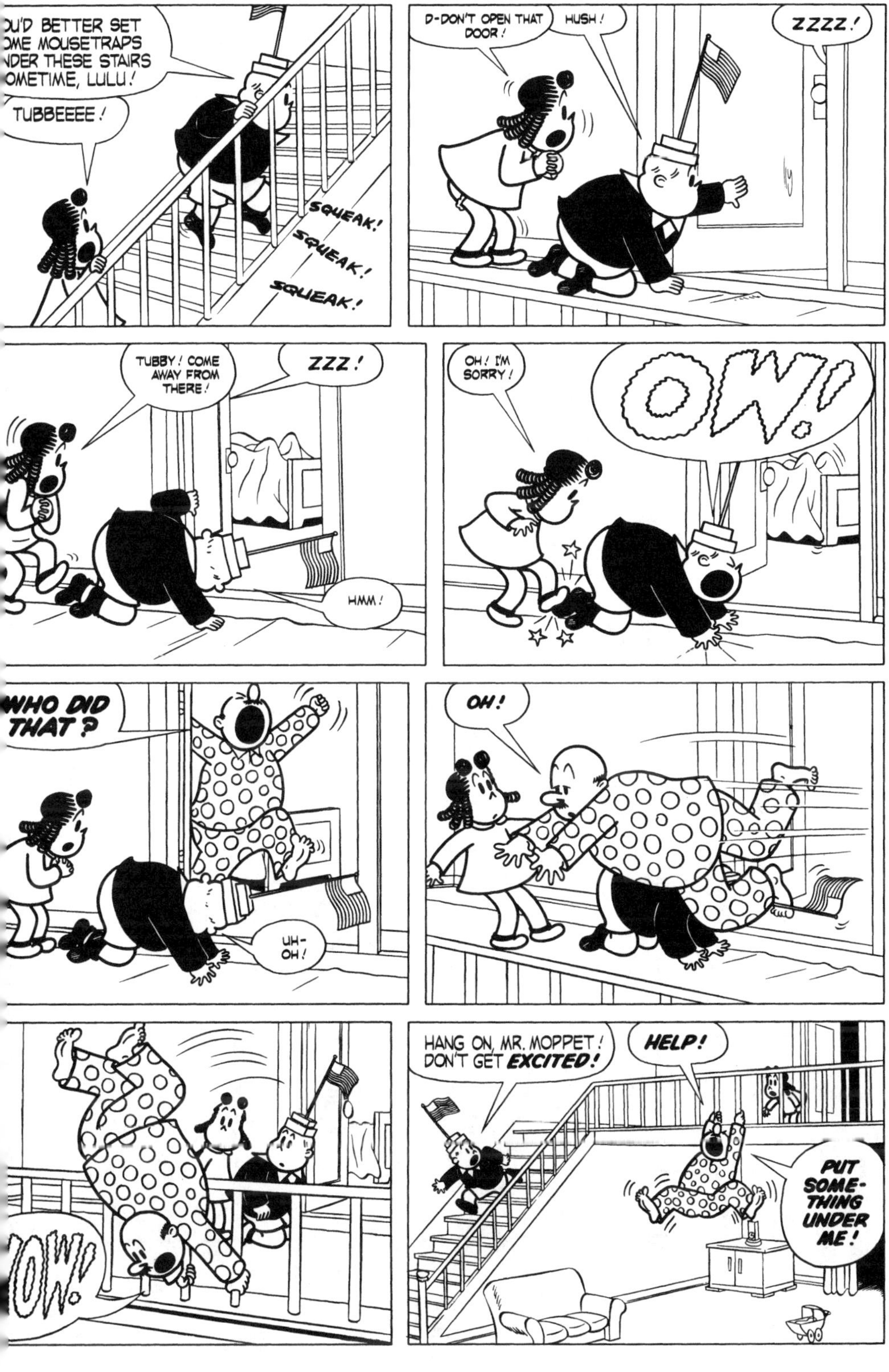
OU'D BETTER SET
OME MOUSETRAPS
NDER THESE STAIRS
OMETIME, LULU!
TUBBEEEE!
SQUEAK!
SQUEAK!
SQUEAK!
D-DON'T OPEN THAT DOOR!
HUSH!
ZZZZ!
TUBBY! COME AWAY FROM THERE!
ZZZ!
HMM!
OH! I'M SORRY!
OW!
WHO DID THAT?
UH-OH!
OH!
OW!
HANG ON, MR. MOPPET! DON'T GET EXCITED!
HELP!
PUT SOME-THING UNDER ME!

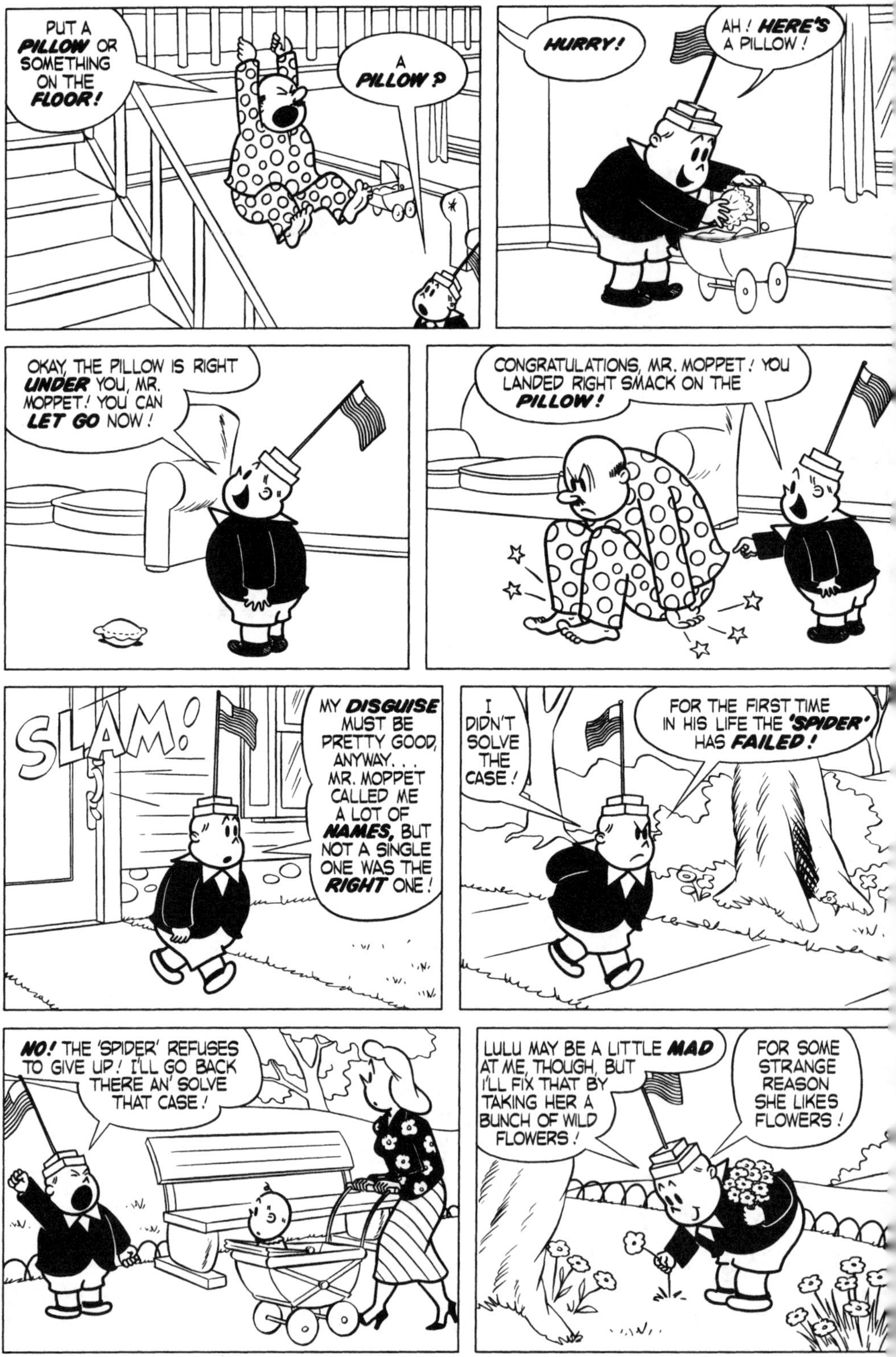

PUT A PILLOW OR SOMETHING ON THE FLOOR!
A PILLOW?
HURRY!
AH! HERE'S A PILLOW!
OKAY, THE PILLOW IS RIGHT UNDER YOU, MR. MOPPET! YOU CAN LET GO NOW!
CONGRATULATIONS, MR. MOPPET! YOU LANDED RIGHT SMACK ON THE PILLOW!
SLAM!
MY DISGUISE MUST BE PRETTY GOOD, ANYWAY. . . MR. MOPPET CALLED ME A LOT OF NAMES, BUT NOT A SINGLE ONE WAS THE RIGHT ONE!
I DIDN'T SOLVE THE CASE!
FOR THE FIRST TIME IN HIS LIFE THE 'SPIDER' HAS FAILED!
NO! THE 'SPIDER' REFUSES TO GIVE UP! I'LL GO BACK THERE AN' SOLVE THAT CASE!
LULU MAY BE A LITTLE MAD AT ME, THOUGH, BUT I'LL FIX THAT BY TAKING HER A BUNCH OF WILD FLOWERS!
FOR SOME STRANGE REASON SHE LIKES FLOWERS!

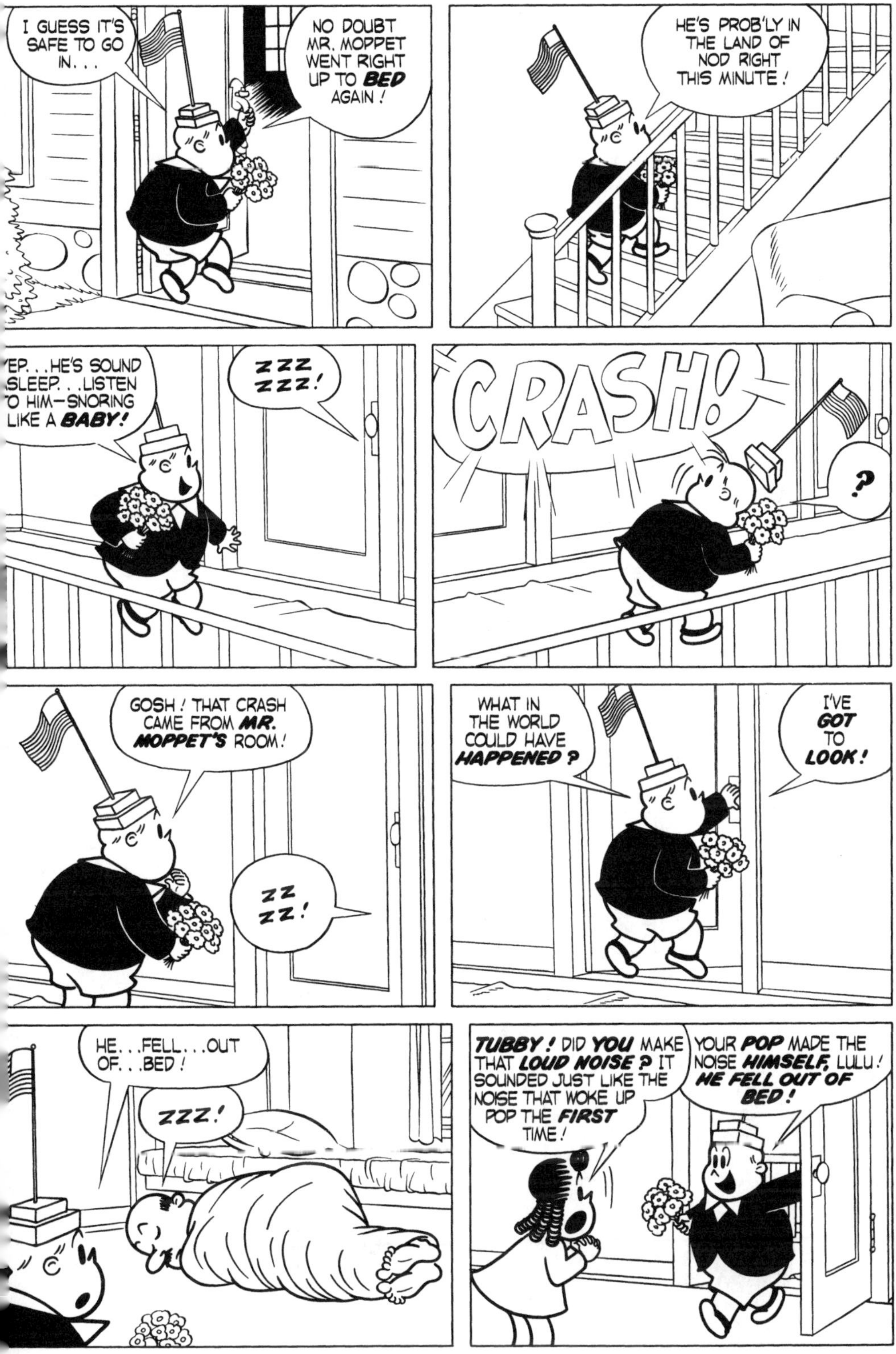
I GUESS IT'S SAFE TO GO IN. . .
NO DOUBT MR. MOPPET WENT RIGHT UP TO BED AGAIN!
HE'S PROB'LY IN THE LAND OF NOD RIGHT THIS MINUTE!
EP. . .HE'S SOUND SLEEP. . .LISTEN O HIM—SNORING LIKE A BABY!
ZZZ ZZZ!
CRASH!
?
GOSH! THAT CRASH CAME FROM MR. MOPPET'S ROOM!
ZZ ZZ!
WHAT IN THE WORLD COULD HAVE HAPPENED?
I'VE GOT TO LOOK!
HE. . .FELL. . .OUT OF. . .BED!
ZZZ!
TUBBY! DID YOU MAKE THAT LOUD NOISE? IT SOUNDED JUST LIKE THE NOISE THAT WOKE UP POP THE FIRST TIME!
YOUR POP MADE THE NOISE HIMSELF, LULU! HE FELL OUT OF BED!

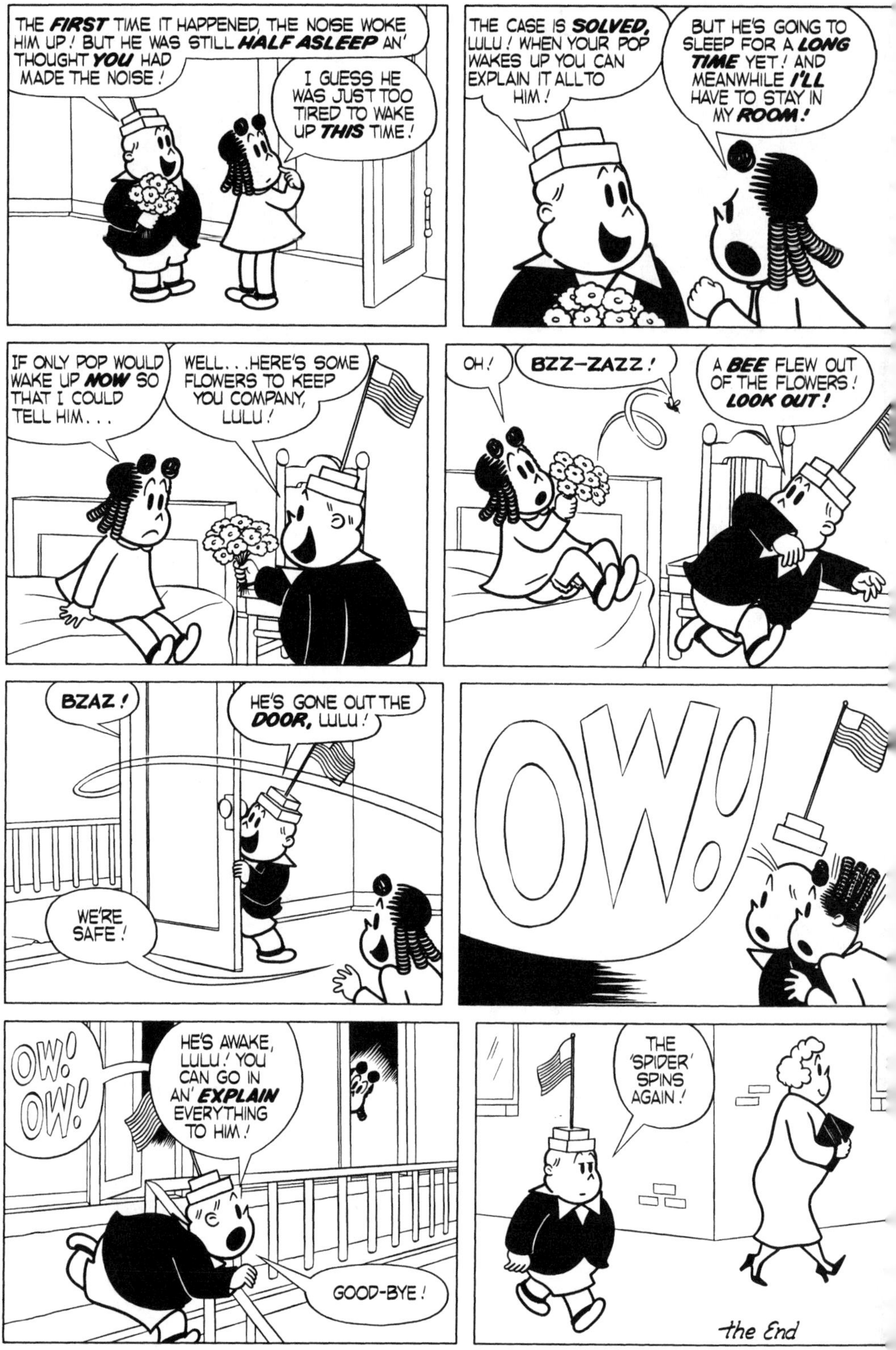
THE FIRST TIME IT HAPPENED, THE NOISE WOKE HIM UP! BUT HE WAS STILL HALF ASLEEP AN' THOUGHT YOU HAD MADE THE NOISE!
I GUESS HE WAS JUST TOO TIRED TO WAKE UP THIS TIME!
THE CASE IS SOLVED, LULU! WHEN YOUR POP WAKES UP YOU CAN EXPLAIN IT ALL TO HIM!
BUT HE'S GOING TO SLEEP FOR A LONG TIME YET! AND MEANWHILE I'LL HAVE TO STAY IN MY ROOM!
IF ONLY POP WOULD WAKE UP NOW SO THAT I COULD TELL HIM...
WELL...HERE'S SOME FLOWERS TO KEEP YOU COMPANY, LULU!
OH!
BZZ-ZAZZ!
A BEE FLEW OUT OF THE FLOWERS! LOOK OUT!
BZAZ!
HE'S GONE OUT THE DOOR, LULU!
WE'RE SAFE!
OW!
OW! OW!
HE'S AWAKE, LULU! YOU CAN GO IN AN' EXPLAIN EVERYTHING TO HIM!
GOOD-BYE!
THE 'SPIDER' SPINS AGAIN!
the End

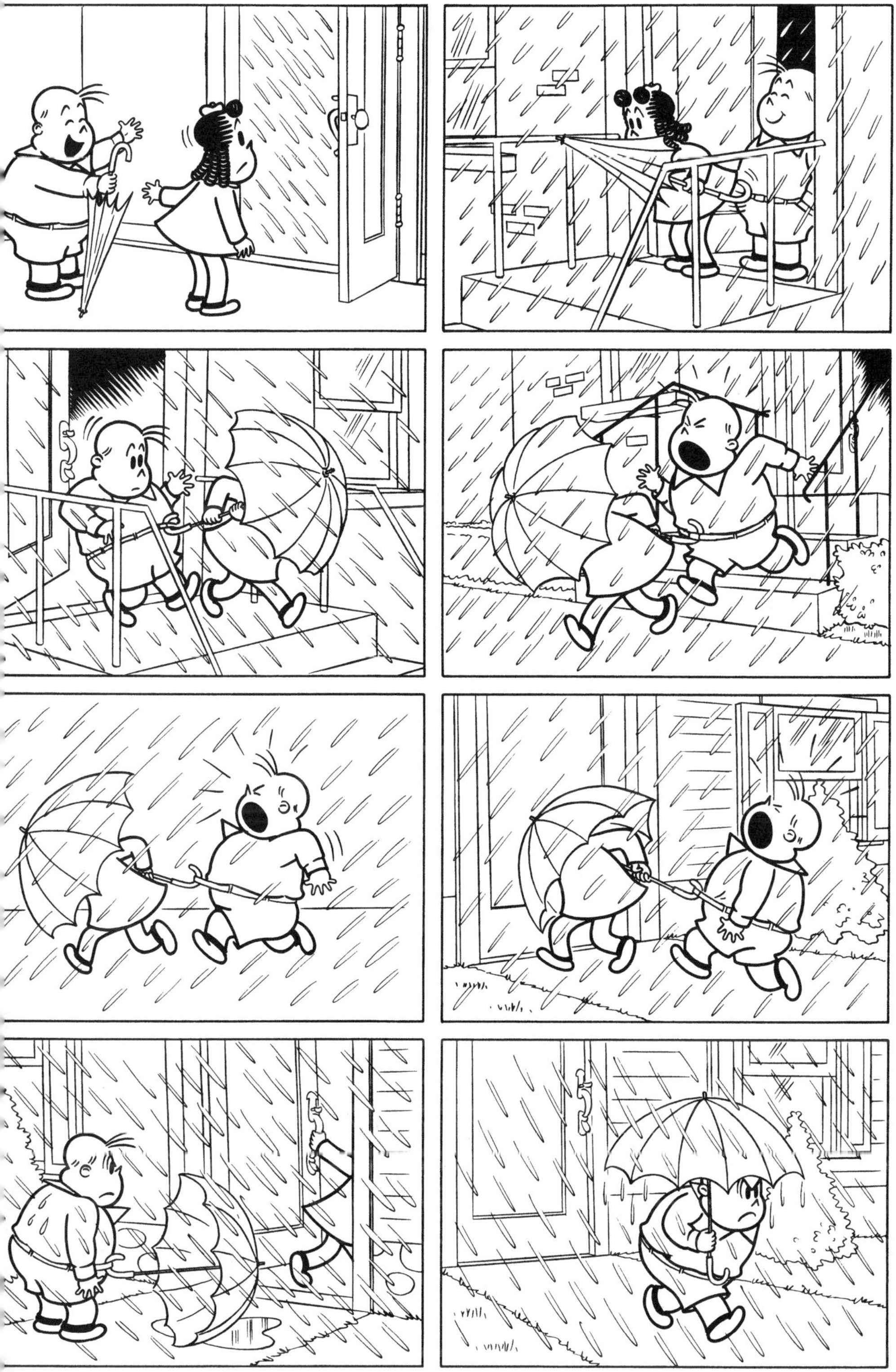

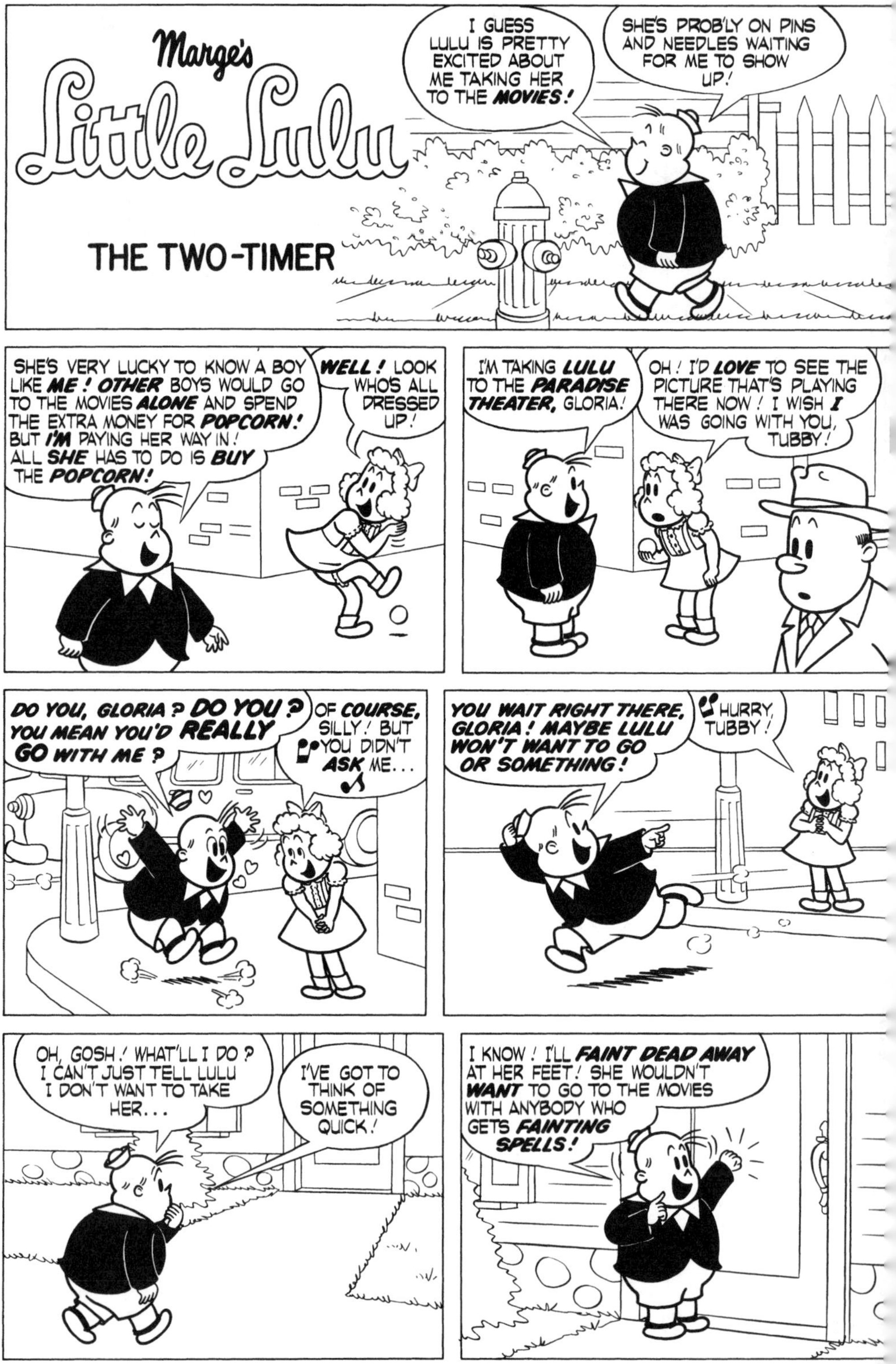

Marge's Little Lulu
THE TWO-TIMER
I GUESS LULU IS PRETTY EXCITED ABOUT ME TAKING HER TO THE MOVIES!
SHE'S PROB'LY ON PINS AND NEEDLES WAITING FOR ME TO SHOW UP!
SHE'S VERY LUCKY TO KNOW A BOY LIKE ME! OTHER BOYS WOULD GO TO THE MOVIES ALONE AND SPEND THE EXTRA MONEY FOR POPCORN! BUT I'M PAYING HER WAY IN! ALL SHE HAS TO DO IS BUY THE POPCORN!
WELL! LOOK WHO'S ALL DRESSED UP!
I'M TAKING LULU TO THE PARADISE THEATER, GLORIA!
OH! I'D LOVE TO SEE THE PICTURE THAT'S PLAYING THERE NOW! I WISH I WAS GOING WITH YOU, TUBBY!
DO YOU, GLORIA? DO YOU? YOU MEAN YOU'D REALLY GO WITH ME?
OF COURSE, SILLY! BUT YOU DIDN'T ASK ME...
YOU WAIT RIGHT THERE, GLORIA! MAYBE LULU WON'T WANT TO GO OR SOMETHING!
HURRY, TUBBY!
OH, GOSH! WHAT'LL I DO? I CAN'T JUST TELL LULU I DON'T WANT TO TAKE HER...
I'VE GOT TO THINK OF SOMETHING QUICK!
I KNOW! I'LL FAINT DEAD AWAY AT HER FEET! SHE WOULDN'T WANT TO GO TO THE MOVIES WITH ANYBODY WHO GETS FAINTING SPELLS!

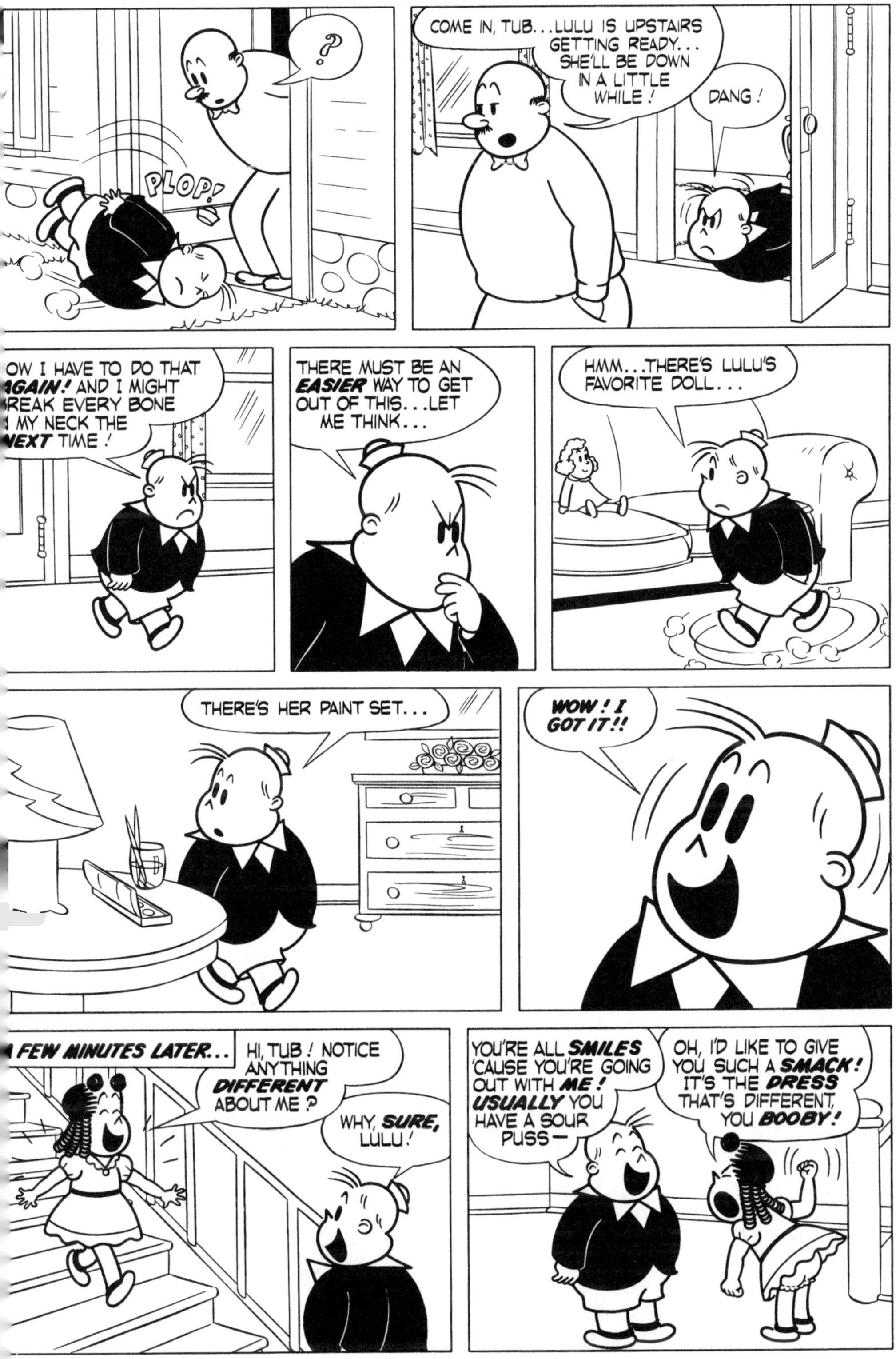
?
PLOP!
COME IN, TUB... LULU IS UPSTAIRS GETTING READY... SHE'LL BE DOWN IN A LITTLE WHILE!
DANG!
OW I HAVE TO DO THAT AGAIN! AND I MIGHT REAK EVERY BONE MY NECK THE NEXT TIME!
THERE MUST BE AN EASIER WAY TO GET OUT OF THIS... LET ME THINK...
HMM... THERE'S LULU'S FAVORITE DOLL...
THERE'S HER PAINT SET...
WOW! I GOT IT!!
FEW MINUTES LATER...
HI, TUB! NOTICE ANYTHING DIFFERENT ABOUT ME?
WHY, SURE, LULU!
YOU'RE ALL SMILES 'CAUSE YOU'RE GOING OUT WITH ME! USUALLY YOU HAVE A SOUR PUSS—
OH, I'D LIKE TO GIVE YOU SUCH A SMACK! IT'S THE DRESS THAT'S DIFFERENT, YOU BOOBY!

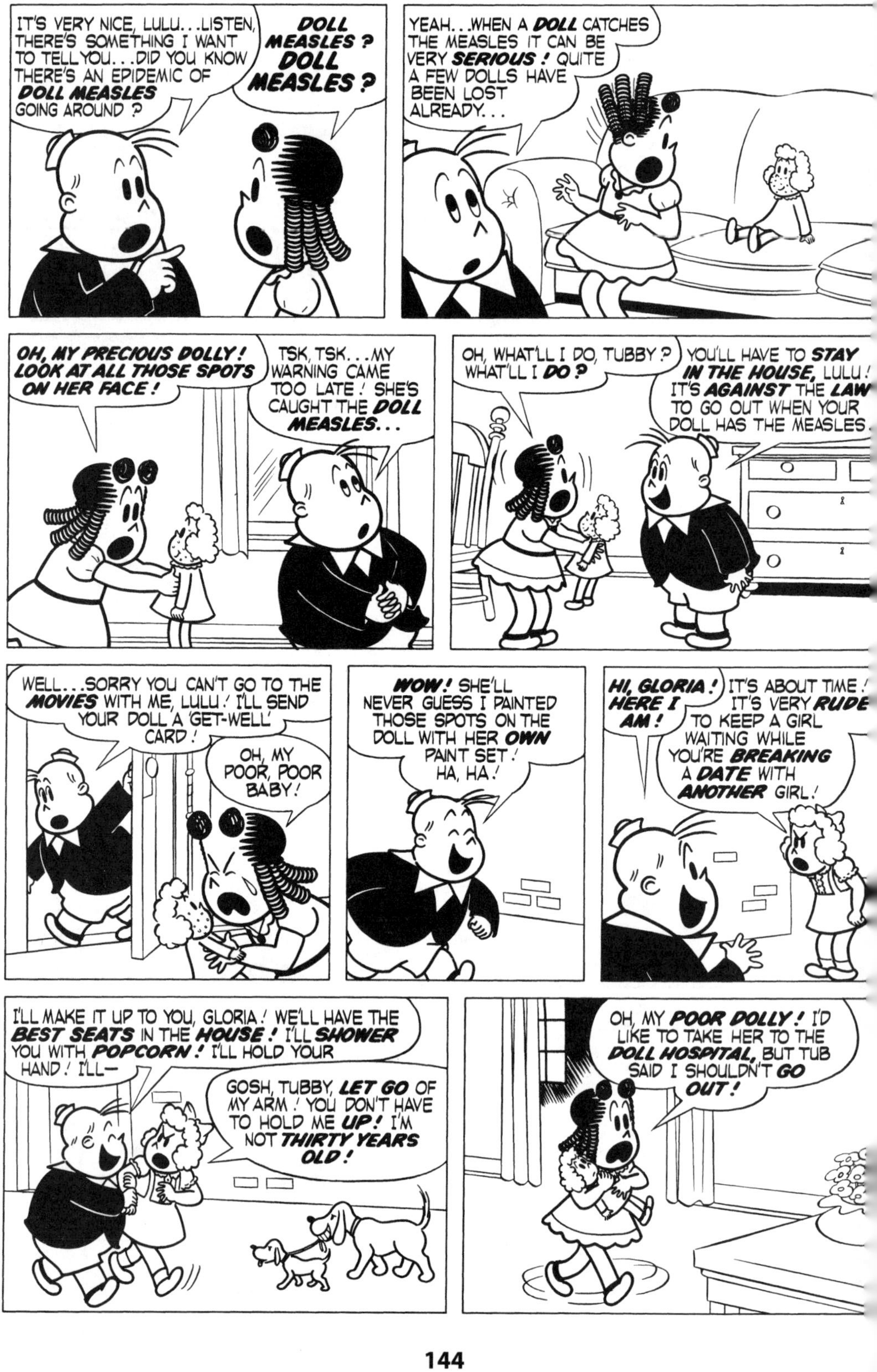

IT'S VERY NICE, LULU...LISTEN, THERE'S SOMETHING I WANT TO TELL YOU...DID YOU KNOW THERE'S AN EPIDEMIC OF DOLL MEASLES GOING AROUND ?
DOLL MEASLES ? DOLL MEASLES ?
YEAH...WHEN A DOLL CATCHES THE MEASLES IT CAN BE VERY SERIOUS ! QUITE A FEW DOLLS HAVE BEEN LOST ALREADY...
OH, MY PRECIOUS DOLLY ! LOOK AT ALL THOSE SPOTS ON HER FACE !
TSK, TSK...MY WARNING CAME TOO LATE ! SHE'S CAUGHT THE DOLL MEASLES...
OH, WHAT'LL I DO, TUBBY ? WHAT'LL I DO ?
YOU'LL HAVE TO STAY IN THE HOUSE, LULU ! IT'S AGAINST THE LAW TO GO OUT WHEN YOUR DOLL HAS THE MEASLES.
WELL...SORRY YOU CAN'T GO TO THE MOVIES WITH ME, LULU ! I'LL SEND YOUR DOLL A 'GET-WELL' CARD !
OH, MY POOR, POOR BABY !
WOW ! SHE'LL NEVER GUESS I PAINTED THOSE SPOTS ON THE DOLL WITH HER OWN PAINT SET ! HA, HA !
HI, GLORIA ! HERE I AM !
IT'S ABOUT TIME ! IT'S VERY RUDE TO KEEP A GIRL WAITING WHILE YOU'RE BREAKING A DATE WITH ANOTHER GIRL !
I'LL MAKE IT UP TO YOU, GLORIA ! WE'LL HAVE THE BEST SEATS IN THE HOUSE ! I'LL SHOWER YOU WITH POPCORN ! I'LL HOLD YOUR HAND ! I'LL—
GOSH, TUBBY, LET GO OF MY ARM ! YOU DON'T HAVE TO HOLD ME UP ! I'M NOT THIRTY YEARS OLD !
OH, MY POOR DOLLY ! I'D LIKE TO TAKE HER TO THE DOLL HOSPITAL, BUT TUB SAID I SHOULDN'T GO OUT !

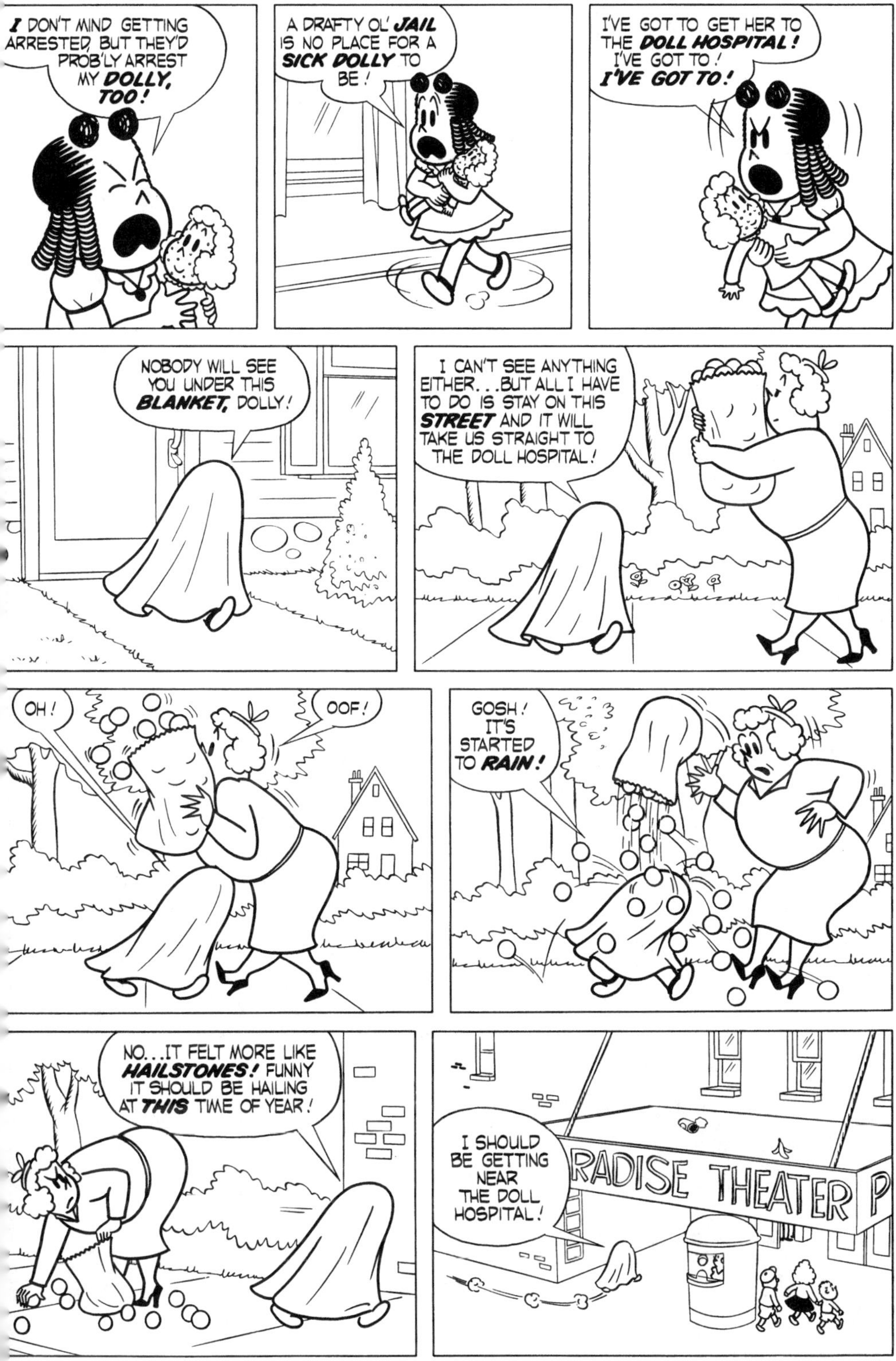
I DON'T MIND GETTING ARRESTED BUT THEY'D PROB'LY ARREST MY DOLLY, TOO!
A DRAFTY OL' JAIL IS NO PLACE FOR A SICK DOLLY TO BE!
I'VE GOT TO GET HER TO THE DOLL HOSPITAL! I'VE GOT TO! I'VE GOT TO!
NOBODY WILL SEE YOU UNDER THIS BLANKET, DOLLY!
I CAN'T SEE ANYTHING EITHER. . .BUT ALL I HAVE TO DO IS STAY ON THIS STREET AND IT WILL TAKE US STRAIGHT TO THE DOLL HOSPITAL!
OH!
OOF!
GOSH! IT'S STARTED TO RAIN!
NO...IT FELT MORE LIKE HAILSTONES! FUNNY IT SHOULD BE HAILING AT THIS TIME OF YEAR!
I SHOULD BE GETTING NEAR THE DOLL HOSPITAL!
RADISE THEATER P

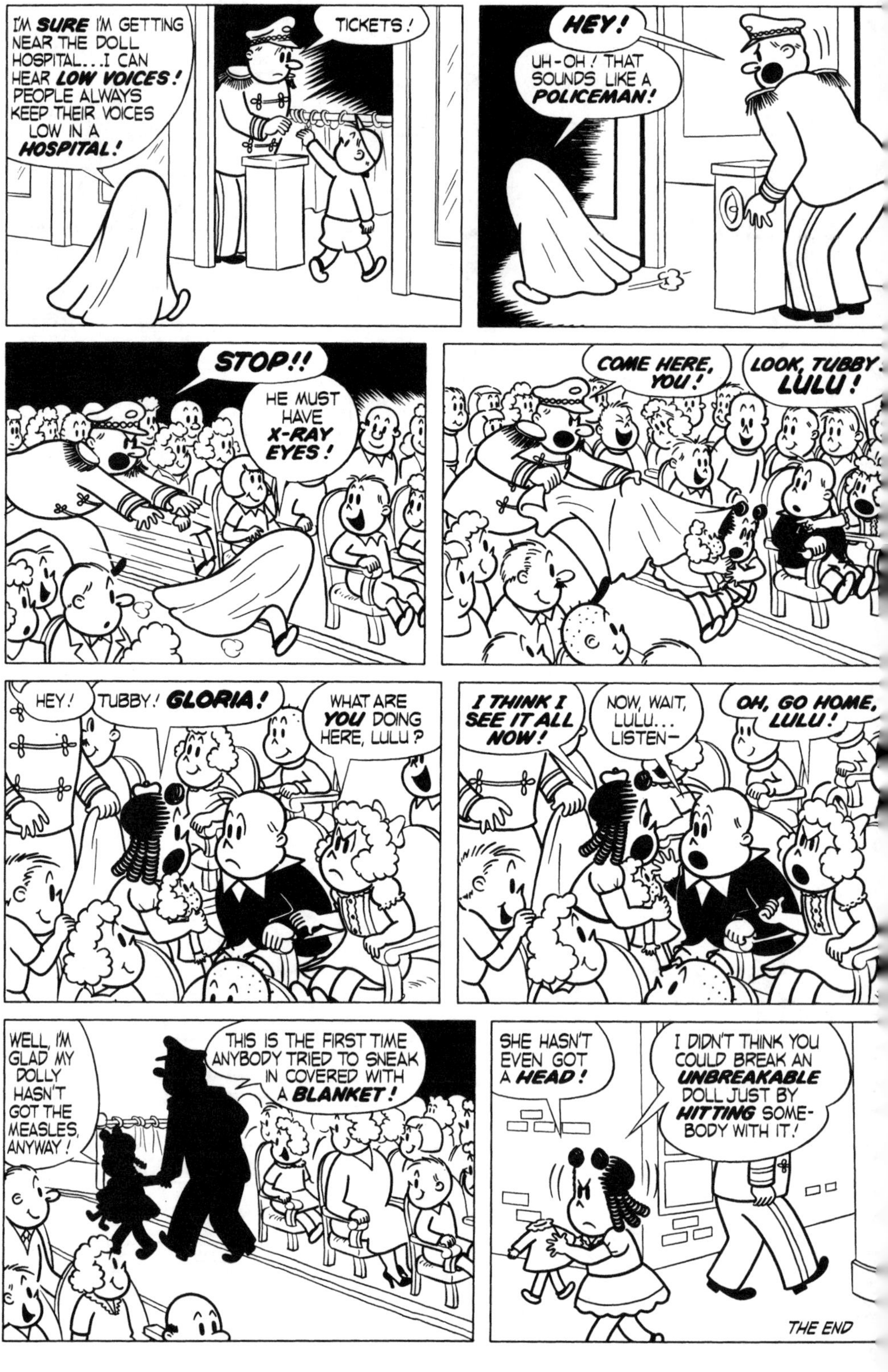

I'M SURE I'M GETTING NEAR THE DOLL HOSPITAL...I CAN HEAR LOW VOICES! PEOPLE ALWAYS KEEP THEIR VOICES LOW IN A HOSPITAL!
TICKETS!
HEY!
UH-OH! THAT SOUNDS LIKE A POLICEMAN!
STOP!!
HE MUST HAVE X-RAY EYES!
COME HERE, YOU!
LOOK, TUBBY... LULU!
HEY!
TUBBY! GLORIA!
WHAT ARE YOU DOING HERE, LULU?
I THINK I SEE IT ALL NOW!
NOW, WAIT, LULU... LISTEN—
OH, GO HOME, LULU!
WELL, I'M GLAD MY DOLLY HASN'T GOT THE MEASLES, ANYWAY!
THIS IS THE FIRST TIME ANYBODY TRIED TO SNEAK IN COVERED WITH A BLANKET!
SHE HASN'T EVEN GOT A HEAD!
I DIDN'T THINK YOU COULD BREAK AN UNBREAKABLE DOLL JUST BY HITTING SOMEBODY WITH IT!
THE END

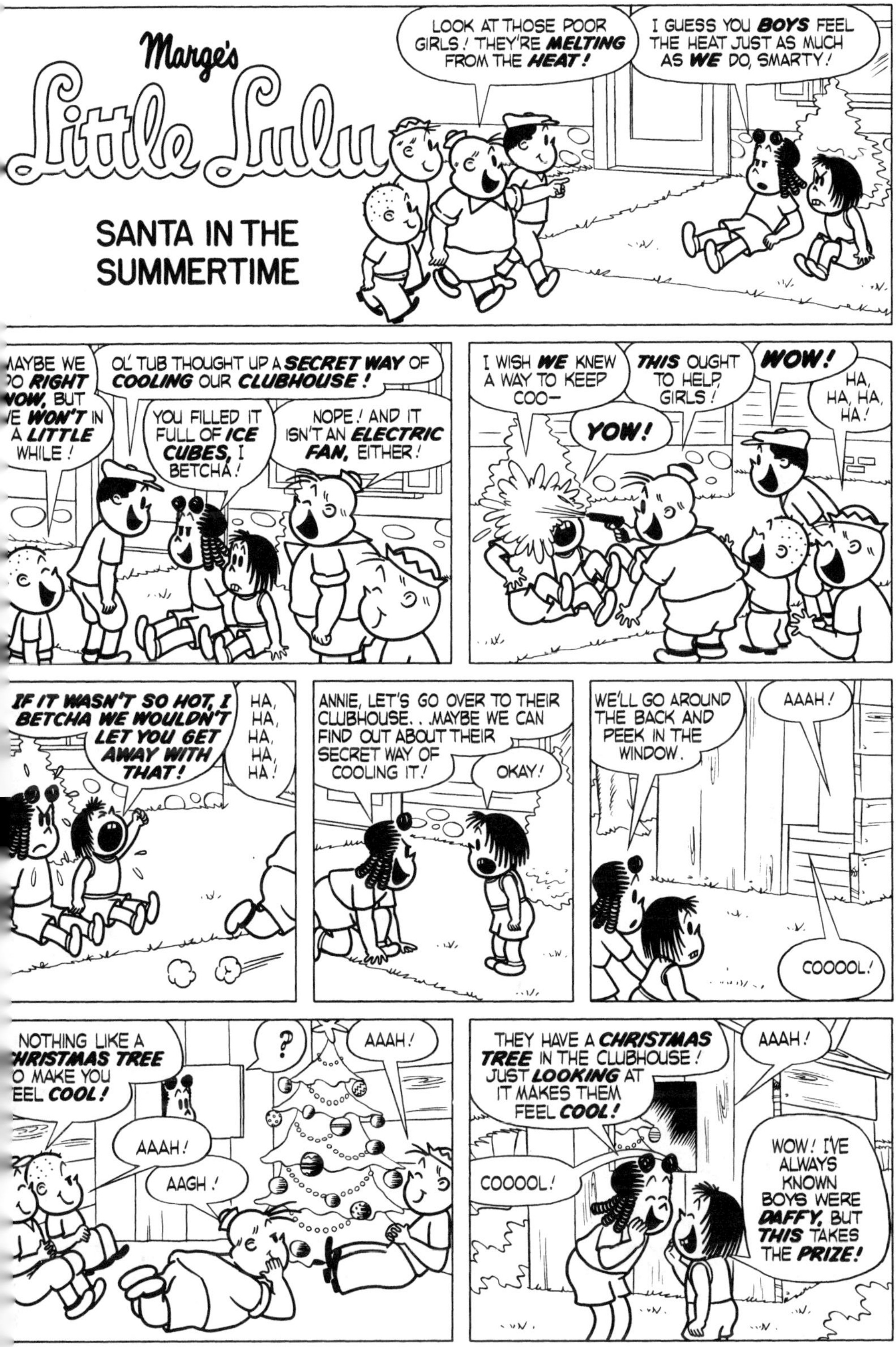
Marge's
Little Lulu
SANTA IN THE SUMMERTIME
LOOK AT THOSE POOR GIRLS! THEY'RE MELTING FROM THE HEAT!
I GUESS YOU BOYS FEEL THE HEAT JUST AS MUCH AS WE DO, SMARTY!
AYBE WE O RIGHT NOW, BUT E WON'T IN A LITTLE WHILE!
OL' TUB THOUGHT UP A SECRET WAY OF COOLING OUR CLUBHOUSE!
YOU FILLED IT FULL OF ICE CUBES, I BETCHA!
NOPE! AND IT ISN'T AN ELECTRIC FAN, EITHER!
I WISH WE KNEW A WAY TO KEEP COO—
THIS OUGHT TO HELP, GIRLS!
YOW!
WOW!
HA, HA, HA, HA!
IF IT WASN'T SO HOT, I BETCHA WE WOULDN'T LET YOU GET AWAY WITH THAT!
HA, HA, HA, HA, HA!
ANNIE, LET'S GO OVER TO THEIR CLUBHOUSE. . .MAYBE WE CAN FIND OUT ABOUT THEIR SECRET WAY OF COOLING IT!
OKAY!
WE'LL GO AROUND THE BACK AND PEEK IN THE WINDOW.
AAAH!
COOOOL!
NOTHING LIKE A HRISTMAS TREE O MAKE YOU EEL COOL!
?
AAAH!
AAAH!
AAGH!
THEY HAVE A CHRISTMAS TREE IN THE CLUBHOUSE! JUST LOOKING AT IT MAKES THEM FEEL COOL!
AAAH!
COOOOL!
WOW! I'VE ALWAYS KNOWN BOYS WERE DAFFY, BUT THIS TAKES THE PRIZE!

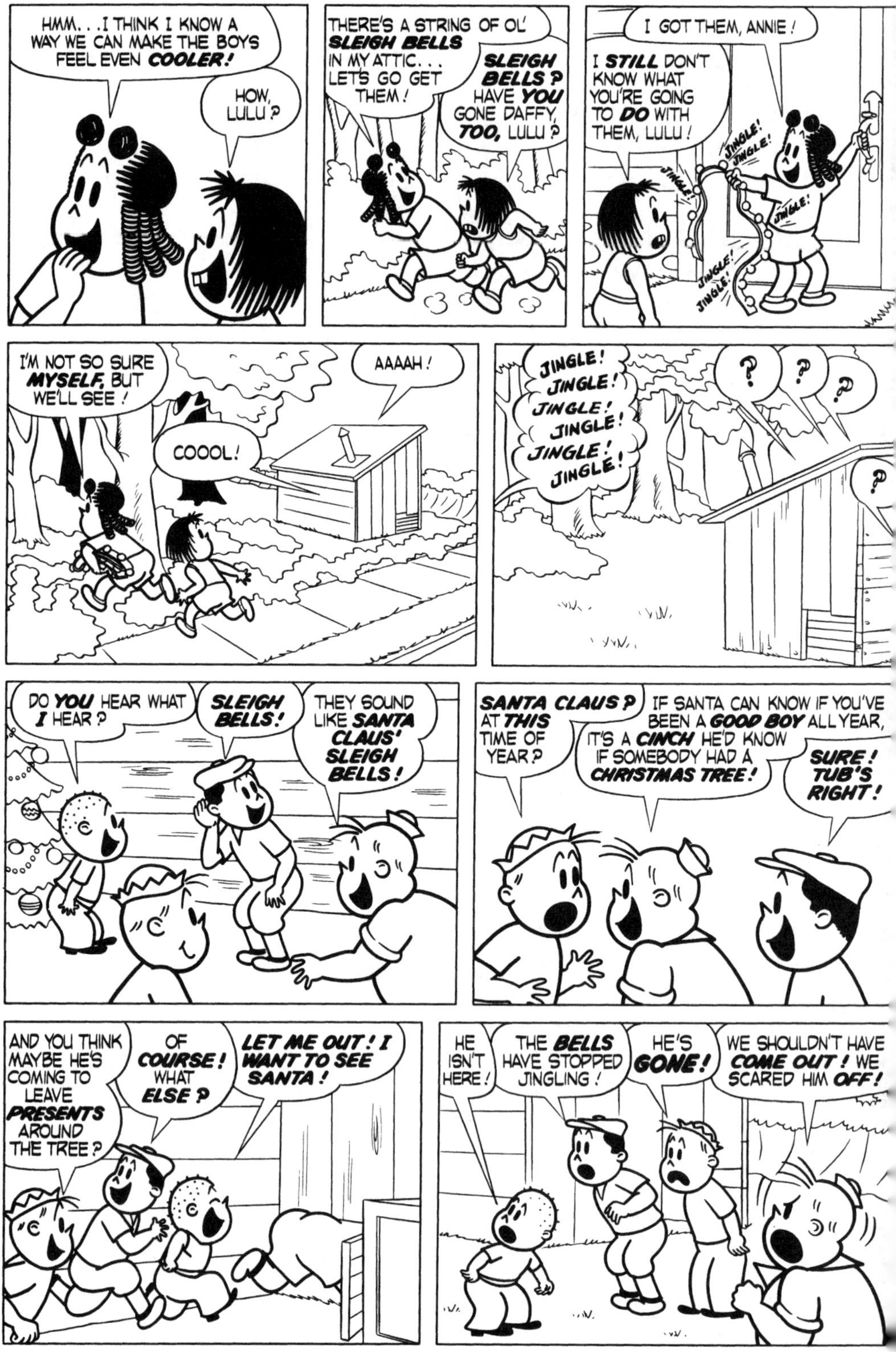
HMM. . . I THINK I KNOW A WAY WE CAN MAKE THE BOYS FEEL EVEN COOLER!
HOW, LULU?
THERE'S A STRING OF OL' SLEIGH BELLS IN MY ATTIC. . . LET'S GO GET THEM!
SLEIGH BELLS? HAVE YOU GONE DAFFY, TOO, LULU?
I GOT THEM, ANNIE!
I STILL DON'T KNOW WHAT YOU'RE GOING TO DO WITH THEM, LULU!
JINGLE! JINGLE! JINGLE! JINGLE! JINGLE! JINGLE!
I'M NOT SO SURE MYSELF, BUT WE'LL SEE!
AAAAH!
COOOL!
JINGLE! JINGLE! JINGLE! JINGLE! JINGLE! JINGLE!
?
?
?
?
DO YOU HEAR WHAT I HEAR?
SLEIGH BELLS!
THEY SOUND LIKE SANTA CLAUS' SLEIGH BELLS!
SANTA CLAUS? AT THIS TIME OF YEAR?
IF SANTA CAN KNOW IF YOU'VE BEEN A GOOD BOY ALL YEAR, IT'S A CINCH HE'D KNOW IF SOMEBODY HAD A CHRISTMAS TREE!
SURE! TUB'S RIGHT!
AND YOU THINK MAYBE HE'S COMING TO LEAVE PRESENTS AROUND THE TREE?
OF COURSE! WHAT ELSE?
LET ME OUT! I WANT TO SEE SANTA!
HE ISN'T HERE!
THE BELLS HAVE STOPPED JINGLING!
HE'S GONE!
WE SHOULDN'T HAVE COME OUT! WE SCARED HIM OFF!

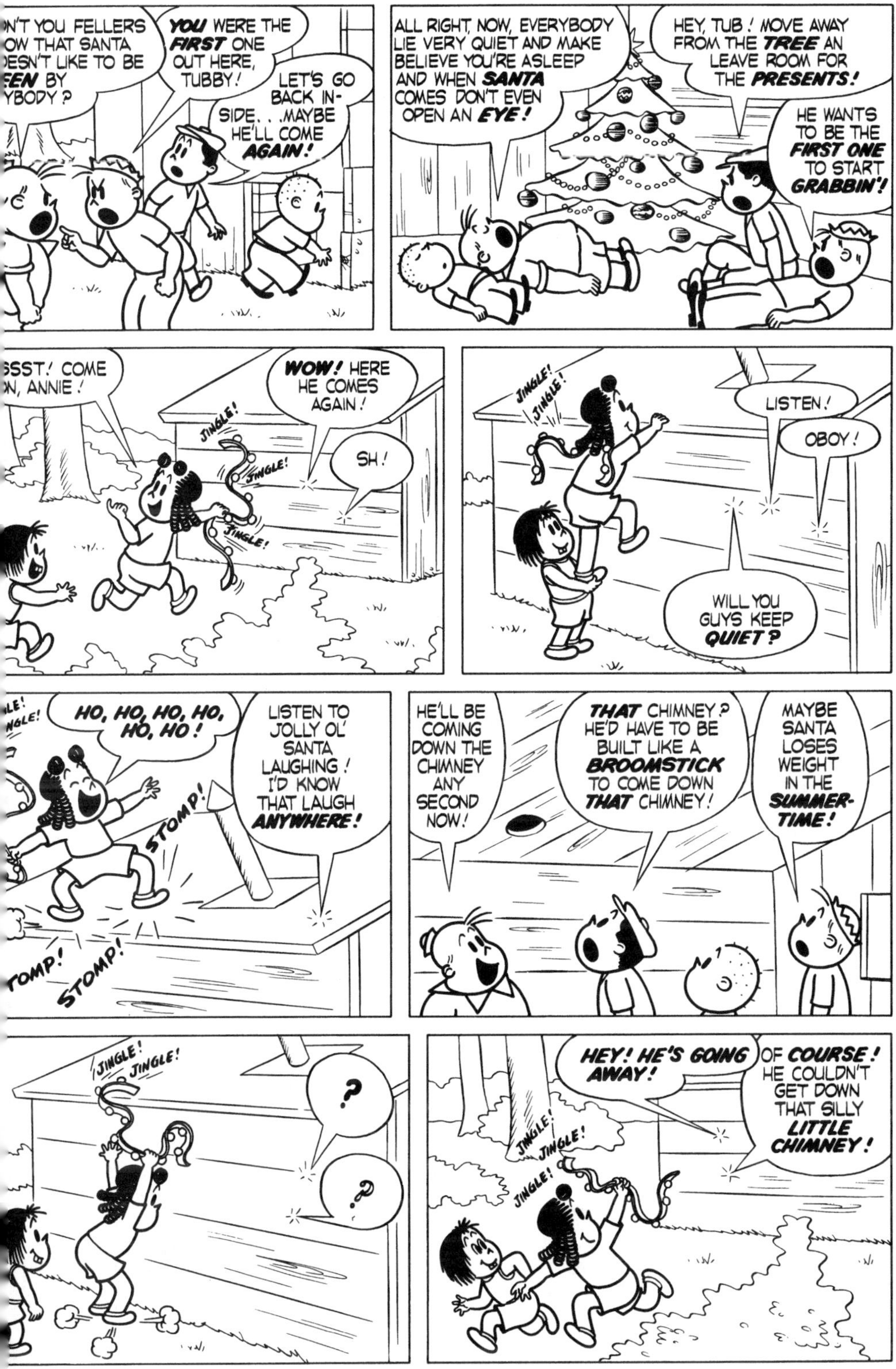
N'T YOU FELLERS OW THAT SANTA ESN'T LIKE TO BE EEN BY YBODY ?
YOU WERE THE FIRST ONE OUT HERE, TUBBY!
LET'S GO BACK IN-SIDE. . .MAYBE HE'LL COME AGAIN!
ALL RIGHT, NOW, EVERYBODY LIE VERY QUIET AND MAKE BELIEVE YOU'RE ASLEEP AND WHEN SANTA COMES DON'T EVEN OPEN AN EYE!
HEY, TUB! MOVE AWAY FROM THE TREE AN LEAVE ROOM FOR THE PRESENTS!
HE WANTS TO BE THE FIRST ONE TO START GRABBIN'!
SSST! COME N, ANNIE!
WOW! HERE HE COMES AGAIN!
JINGLE!
JINGLE!
JINGLE!
SH!
JINGLE!
JINGLE!
LISTEN!
OBOY!
WILL YOU GUYS KEEP QUIET?
HO, HO, HO, HO, HO, HO!
LISTEN TO JOLLY OL' SANTA LAUGHING! I'D KNOW THAT LAUGH ANYWHERE!
STOMP!
TOMP!
STOMP!
HE'LL BE COMING DOWN THE CHIMNEY ANY SECOND NOW!
THAT CHIMNEY? HE'D HAVE TO BE BUILT LIKE A BROOMSTICK TO COME DOWN THAT CHIMNEY!
MAYBE SANTA LOSES WEIGHT IN THE SUMMER-TIME!
JINGLE!
JINGLE!
?
?
HEY! HE'S GOING AWAY!
OF COURSE! HE COULDN'T GET DOWN THAT SILLY LITTLE CHIMNEY!
JINGLE!
JINGLE!
JINGLE!

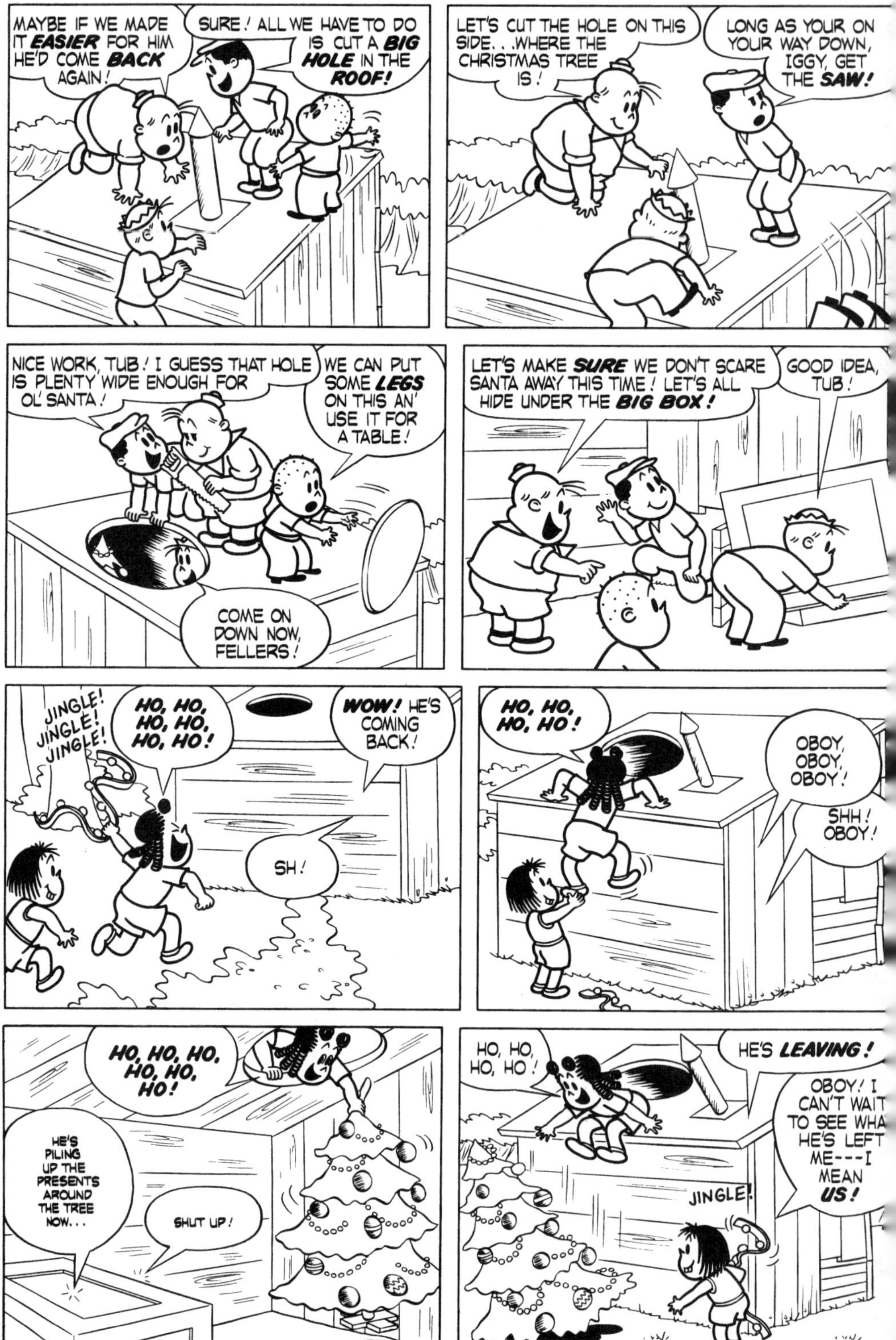
MAYBE IF WE MADE IT EASIER FOR HIM HE'D COME BACK AGAIN!
SURE! ALL WE HAVE TO DO IS CUT A BIG HOLE IN THE ROOF!
LET'S CUT THE HOLE ON THIS SIDE. . .WHERE THE CHRISTMAS TREE IS!
LONG AS YOUR ON YOUR WAY DOWN, IGGY, GET THE SAW!
NICE WORK, TUB! I GUESS THAT HOLE IS PLENTY WIDE ENOUGH FOR OL' SANTA!
WE CAN PUT SOME LEGS ON THIS AN' USE IT FOR A TABLE!
COME ON DOWN NOW, FELLERS!
LET'S MAKE SURE WE DON'T SCARE SANTA AWAY THIS TIME! LET'S ALL HIDE UNDER THE BIG BOX!
GOOD IDEA, TUB!
JINGLE! JINGLE! JINGLE!
HO, HO, HO, HO, HO, HO!
WOW! HE'S COMING BACK!
SH!
HO, HO, HO, HO!
OBOY, OBOY, OBOY!
SHH! OBOY!
HO, HO, HO, HO, HO, HO!
HE'S PILING UP THE PRESENTS AROUND THE TREE NOW. . .
SHUT UP!
HO, HO, HO, HO!
HE'S LEAVING!
OBOY! I CAN'T WAIT TO SEE WHAT HE'S LEFT ME---I MEAN US!
JINGLE!

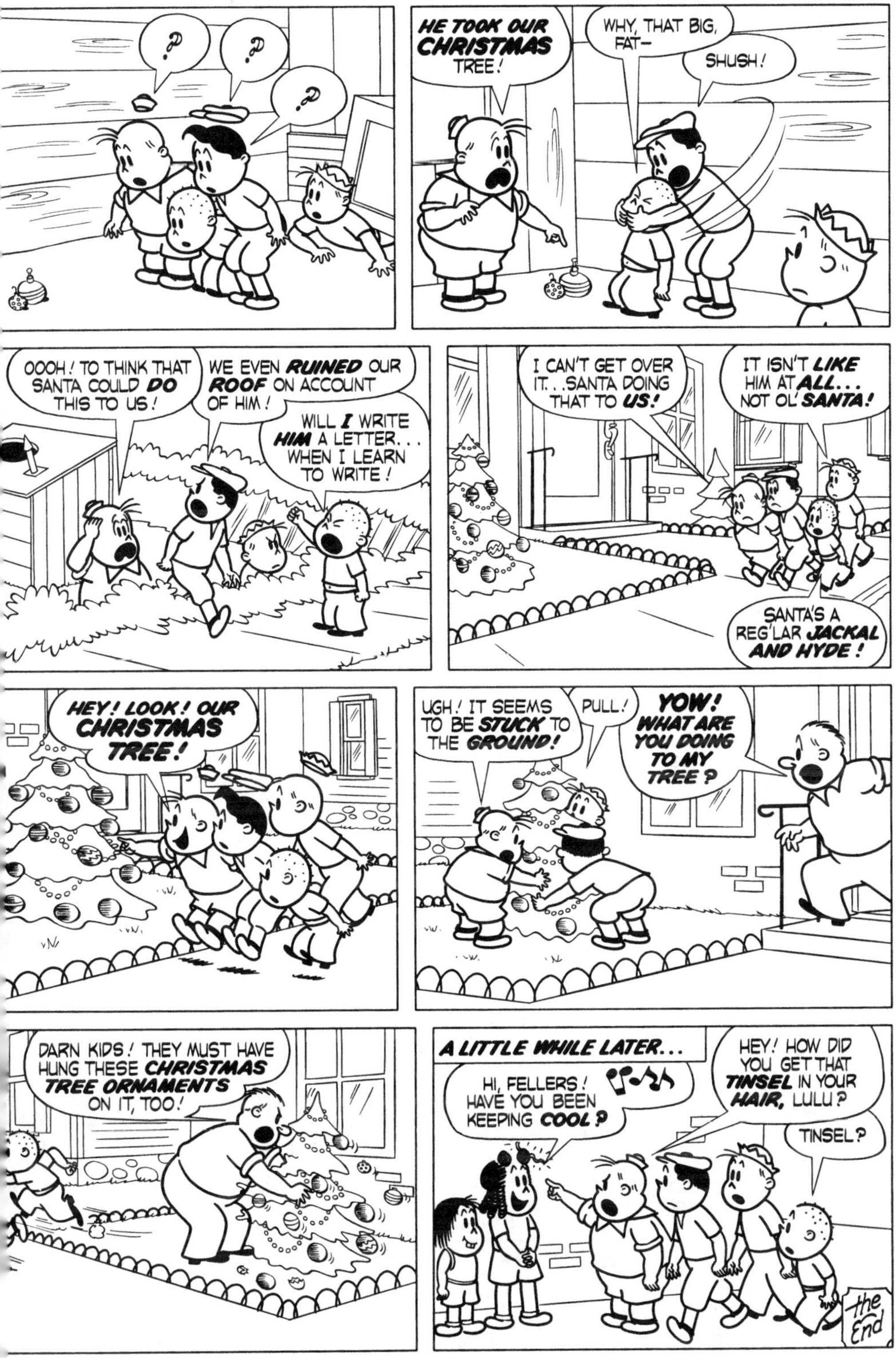

?
?
?
HE TOOK OUR CHRISTMAS TREE!
WHY, THAT BIG, FAT—
SHUSH!
OOOH! TO THINK THAT SANTA COULD DO THIS TO US!
WE EVEN RUINED OUR ROOF ON ACCOUNT OF HIM!
WILL I WRITE HIM A LETTER... WHEN I LEARN TO WRITE!
I CAN'T GET OVER IT. . SANTA DOING THAT TO US!
IT ISN'T LIKE HIM AT ALL... NOT OL' SANTA!
SANTA'S A REG'LAR JACKAL AND HYDE!
HEY! LOOK! OUR CHRISTMAS TREE!
UGH! IT SEEMS TO BE STUCK TO THE GROUND!
PULL!
YOW! WHAT ARE YOU DOING TO MY TREE?
DARN KIDS! THEY MUST HAVE HUNG THESE CHRISTMAS TREE ORNAMENTS ON IT, TOO!
A LITTLE WHILE LATER...
HI, FELLERS! HAVE YOU BEEN KEEPING COOL?
HEY! HOW DID YOU GET THAT TINSEL IN YOUR HAIR, LULU?
TINSEL?
the End

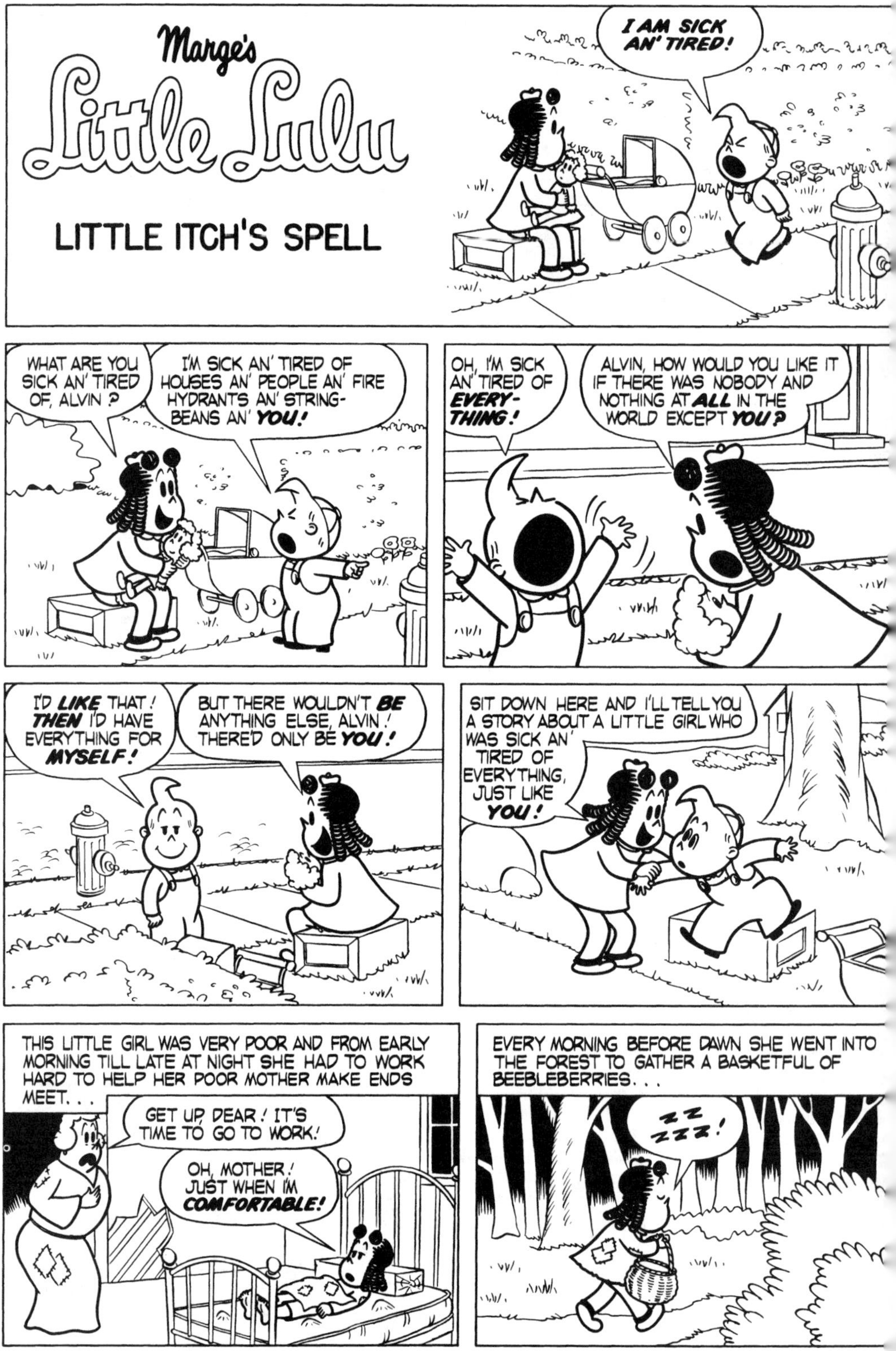
Marge's
Little Lulu
LITTLE ITCH'S SPELL
I AM SICK AN' TIRED!
WHAT ARE YOU SICK AN' TIRED OF, ALVIN ?
I'M SICK AN' TIRED OF HOUSES AN' PEOPLE AN' FIRE HYDRANTS AN' STRING-BEANS AN' YOU!
OH, I'M SICK AN' TIRED OF EVERY-THING!
ALVIN, HOW WOULD YOU LIKE IT IF THERE WAS NOBODY AND NOTHING AT ALL IN THE WORLD EXCEPT YOU?
I'D LIKE THAT! THEN I'D HAVE EVERYTHING FOR MYSELF!
BUT THERE WOULDN'T BE ANYTHING ELSE, ALVIN! THERE'D ONLY BE YOU!
SIT DOWN HERE AND I'LL TELL YOU A STORY ABOUT A LITTLE GIRL WHO WAS SICK AN' TIRED OF EVERYTHING, JUST LIKE YOU!
THIS LITTLE GIRL WAS VERY POOR AND FROM EARLY MORNING TILL LATE AT NIGHT SHE HAD TO WORK HARD TO HELP HER POOR MOTHER MAKE ENDS MEET. . .
GET UP, DEAR! IT'S TIME TO GO TO WORK!
OH, MOTHER! JUST WHEN I'M COMFORTABLE!
EVERY MORNING BEFORE DAWN SHE WENT INTO THE FOREST TO GATHER A BASKETFUL OF BEEBLEBERRIES. . .
Z Z Z Z Z!

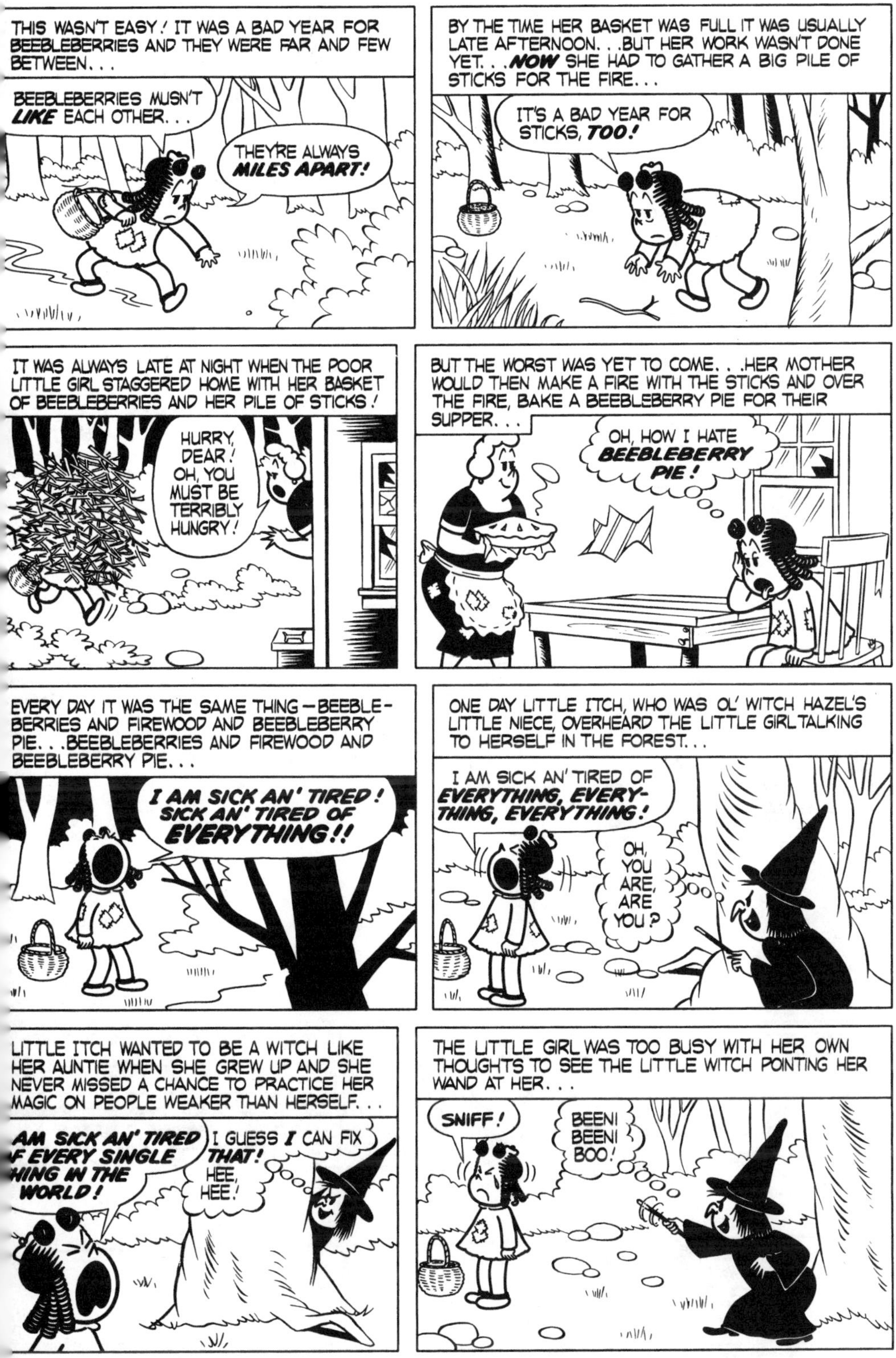

THIS WASN'T EASY! IT WAS A BAD YEAR FOR BEEBLEBERRIES AND THEY WERE FAR AND FEW BETWEEN. . .
BEEBLEBERRIES MUSN'T LIKE EACH OTHER. . .
THEY'RE ALWAYS MILES APART!
BY THE TIME HER BASKET WAS FULL IT WAS USUALLY LATE AFTERNOON. . .BUT HER WORK WASN'T DONE YET. . .NOW SHE HAD TO GATHER A BIG PILE OF STICKS FOR THE FIRE. . .
IT'S A BAD YEAR FOR STICKS, TOO!
IT WAS ALWAYS LATE AT NIGHT WHEN THE POOR LITTLE GIRL STAGGERED HOME WITH HER BASKET OF BEEBLEBERRIES AND HER PILE OF STICKS!
HURRY, DEAR! OH, YOU MUST BE TERRIBLY HUNGRY!
BUT THE WORST WAS YET TO COME. . .HER MOTHER WOULD THEN MAKE A FIRE WITH THE STICKS AND OVER THE FIRE, BAKE A BEEBLEBERRY PIE FOR THEIR SUPPER. . .
OH, HOW I HATE BEEBLEBERRY PIE!
EVERY DAY IT WAS THE SAME THING—BEEBLE-BERRIES AND FIREWOOD AND BEEBLEBERRY PIE. . .BEEBLEBERRIES AND FIREWOOD AND BEEBLEBERRY PIE. . .
I AM SICK AN' TIRED! SICK AN' TIRED OF EVERYTHING!!
ONE DAY LITTLE ITCH, WHO WAS OL' WITCH HAZEL'S LITTLE NIECE, OVERHEARD THE LITTLE GIRL TALKING TO HERSELF IN THE FOREST. . .
I AM SICK AN' TIRED OF EVERYTHING, EVERY-THING, EVERYTHING!
OH, YOU ARE, ARE YOU?
LITTLE ITCH WANTED TO BE A WITCH LIKE HER AUNTIE WHEN SHE GREW UP AND SHE NEVER MISSED A CHANCE TO PRACTICE HER MAGIC ON PEOPLE WEAKER THAN HERSELF. . .
AM SICK AN' TIRED F EVERY SINGLE HING IN THE WORLD!
I GUESS I CAN FIX THAT! HEE, HEE!
THE LITTLE GIRL WAS TOO BUSY WITH HER OWN THOUGHTS TO SEE THE LITTLE WITCH POINTING HER WAND AT HER. . .
SNIFF!
BEENI BEENI BOO!

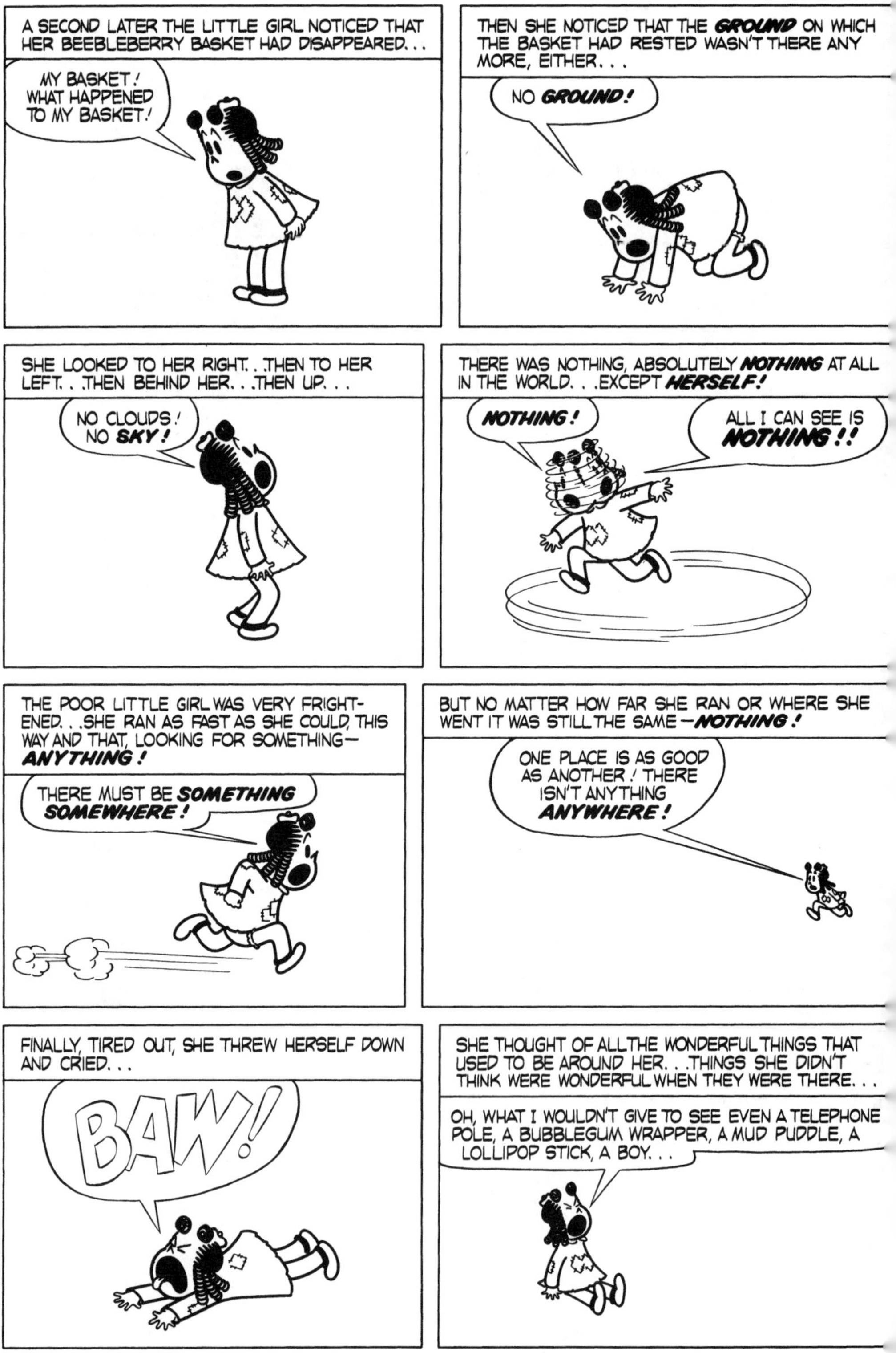
A SECOND LATER THE LITTLE GIRL NOTICED THAT HER BEEBLEBERRY BASKET HAD DISAPPEARED. . .
MY BASKET! WHAT HAPPENED TO MY BASKET!
THEN SHE NOTICED THAT THE **GROUND** ON WHICH THE BASKET HAD RESTED WASN'T THERE ANY MORE, EITHER. . .
NO **GROUND!**
SHE LOOKED TO HER RIGHT. . .THEN TO HER LEFT. . .THEN BEHIND HER. . .THEN UP. . .
NO CLOUDS! NO **SKY!**
THERE WAS NOTHING, ABSOLUTELY **NOTHING** AT ALL IN THE WORLD. . .EXCEPT **HERSELF!**
NOTHING!
ALL I CAN SEE IS **NOTHING!!**
THE POOR LITTLE GIRL WAS VERY FRIGHTENED. . .SHE RAN AS FAST AS SHE COULD, THIS WAY AND THAT, LOOKING FOR SOMETHING— **ANYTHING!**
THERE MUST BE **SOMETHING SOMEWHERE!**
BUT NO MATTER HOW FAR SHE RAN OR WHERE SHE WENT IT WAS STILL THE SAME—**NOTHING!**
ONE PLACE IS AS GOOD AS ANOTHER! THERE ISN'T ANYTHING **ANYWHERE!**
FINALLY, TIRED OUT, SHE THREW HERSELF DOWN AND CRIED. . .
BAW!
SHE THOUGHT OF ALL THE WONDERFUL THINGS THAT USED TO BE AROUND HER. . .THINGS SHE DIDN'T THINK WERE WONDERFUL WHEN THEY WERE THERE. . .
OH, WHAT I WOULDN'T GIVE TO SEE EVEN A TELEPHONE POLE, A BUBBLEGUM WRAPPER, A MUD PUDDLE, A LOLLIPOP STICK, A BOY. . .

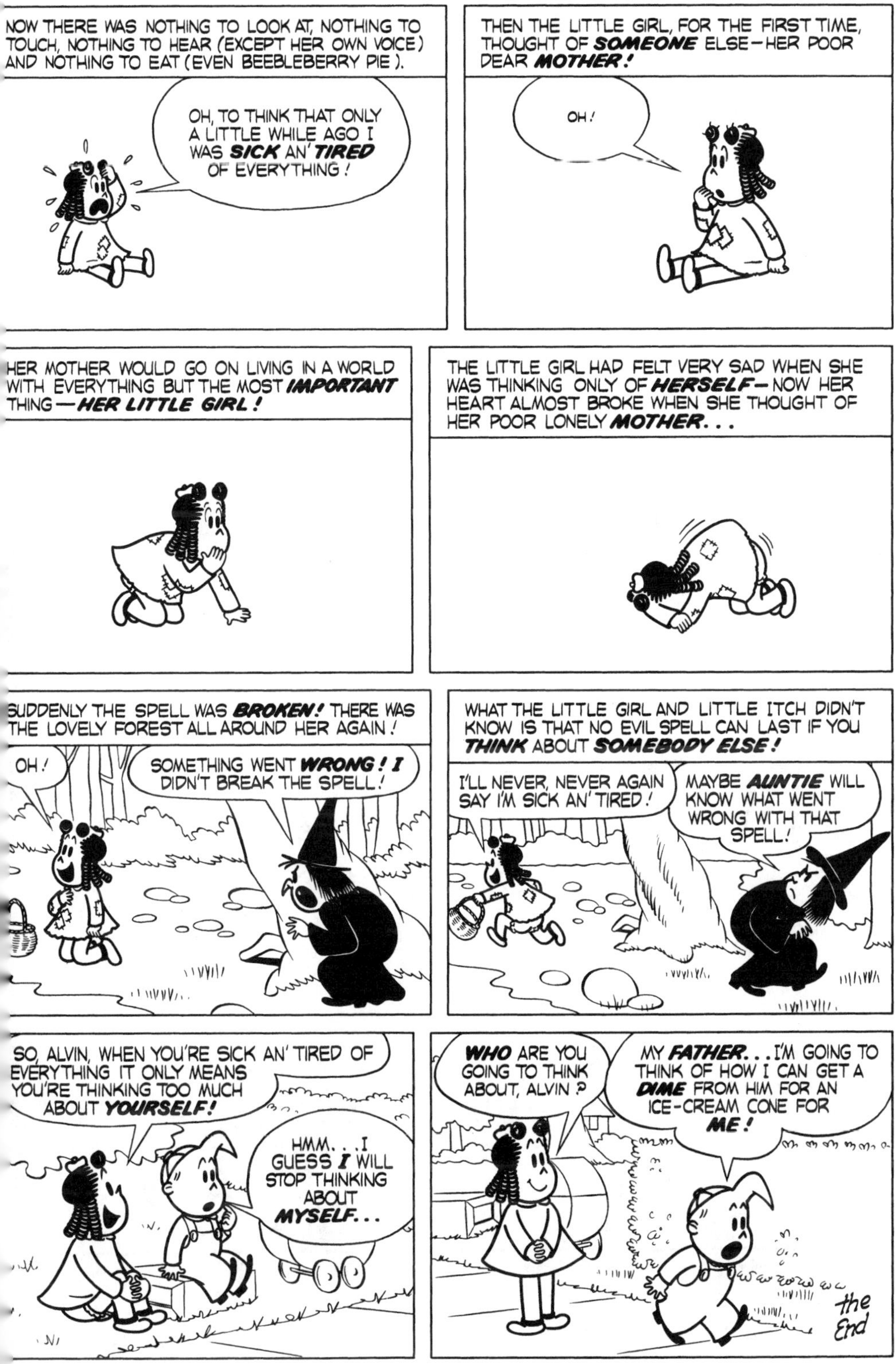
NOW THERE WAS NOTHING TO LOOK AT, NOTHING TO TOUCH, NOTHING TO HEAR (EXCEPT HER OWN VOICE) AND NOTHING TO EAT (EVEN BEEBLEBERRY PIE).
OH, TO THINK THAT ONLY A LITTLE WHILE AGO I WAS SICK AN' TIRED OF EVERYTHING!
THEN THE LITTLE GIRL, FOR THE FIRST TIME, THOUGHT OF SOMEONE ELSE—HER POOR DEAR MOTHER!
OH!
HER MOTHER WOULD GO ON LIVING IN A WORLD WITH EVERYTHING BUT THE MOST IMPORTANT THING—HER LITTLE GIRL!
THE LITTLE GIRL HAD FELT VERY SAD WHEN SHE WAS THINKING ONLY OF HERSELF—NOW HER HEART ALMOST BROKE WHEN SHE THOUGHT OF HER POOR LONELY MOTHER...
SUDDENLY THE SPELL WAS BROKEN! THERE WAS THE LOVELY FOREST ALL AROUND HER AGAIN!
OH!
SOMETHING WENT WRONG! I DIDN'T BREAK THE SPELL!
WHAT THE LITTLE GIRL AND LITTLE ITCH DIDN'T KNOW IS THAT NO EVIL SPELL CAN LAST IF YOU THINK ABOUT SOMEBODY ELSE!
I'LL NEVER, NEVER AGAIN SAY I'M SICK AN' TIRED!
MAYBE AUNTIE WILL KNOW WHAT WENT WRONG WITH THAT SPELL!
SO, ALVIN, WHEN YOU'RE SICK AN' TIRED OF EVERYTHING IT ONLY MEANS YOU'RE THINKING TOO MUCH ABOUT YOURSELF!
HMM...I GUESS I WILL STOP THINKING ABOUT MYSELF...
WHO ARE YOU GOING TO THINK ABOUT, ALVIN?
MY FATHER...I'M GOING TO THINK OF HOW I CAN GET A DIME FROM HIM FOR AN ICE-CREAM CONE FOR ME!
the End

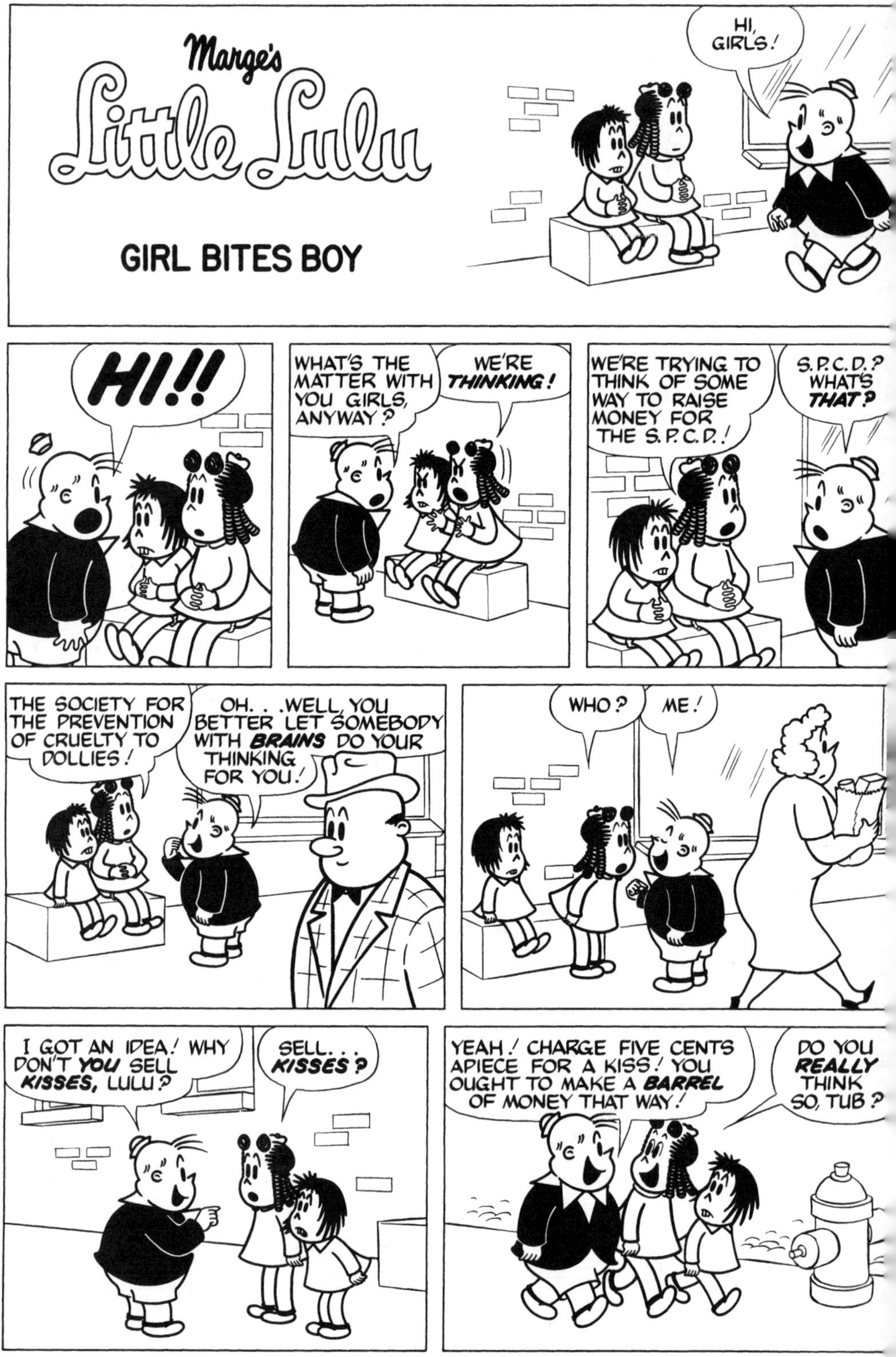
Marge's
Little Lulu
GIRL BITES BOY
HI, GIRLS!
HI!!
WHAT'S THE MATTER WITH YOU GIRLS, ANYWAY?
WE'RE THINKING!
WE'RE TRYING TO THINK OF SOME WAY TO RAISE MONEY FOR THE S.P.C.D.!
S.P.C.D.? WHAT'S THAT?
THE SOCIETY FOR THE PREVENTION OF CRUELTY TO DOLLIES!
OH. . .WELL, YOU BETTER LET SOMEBODY WITH BRAINS DO YOUR THINKING FOR YOU!
WHO?
ME!
I GOT AN IDEA! WHY DON'T YOU SELL KISSES, LULU?
SELL. . . KISSES?
YEAH! CHARGE FIVE CENTS APIECE FOR A KISS! YOU OUGHT TO MAKE A BARREL OF MONEY THAT WAY!
DO YOU REALLY THINK SO, TUB?

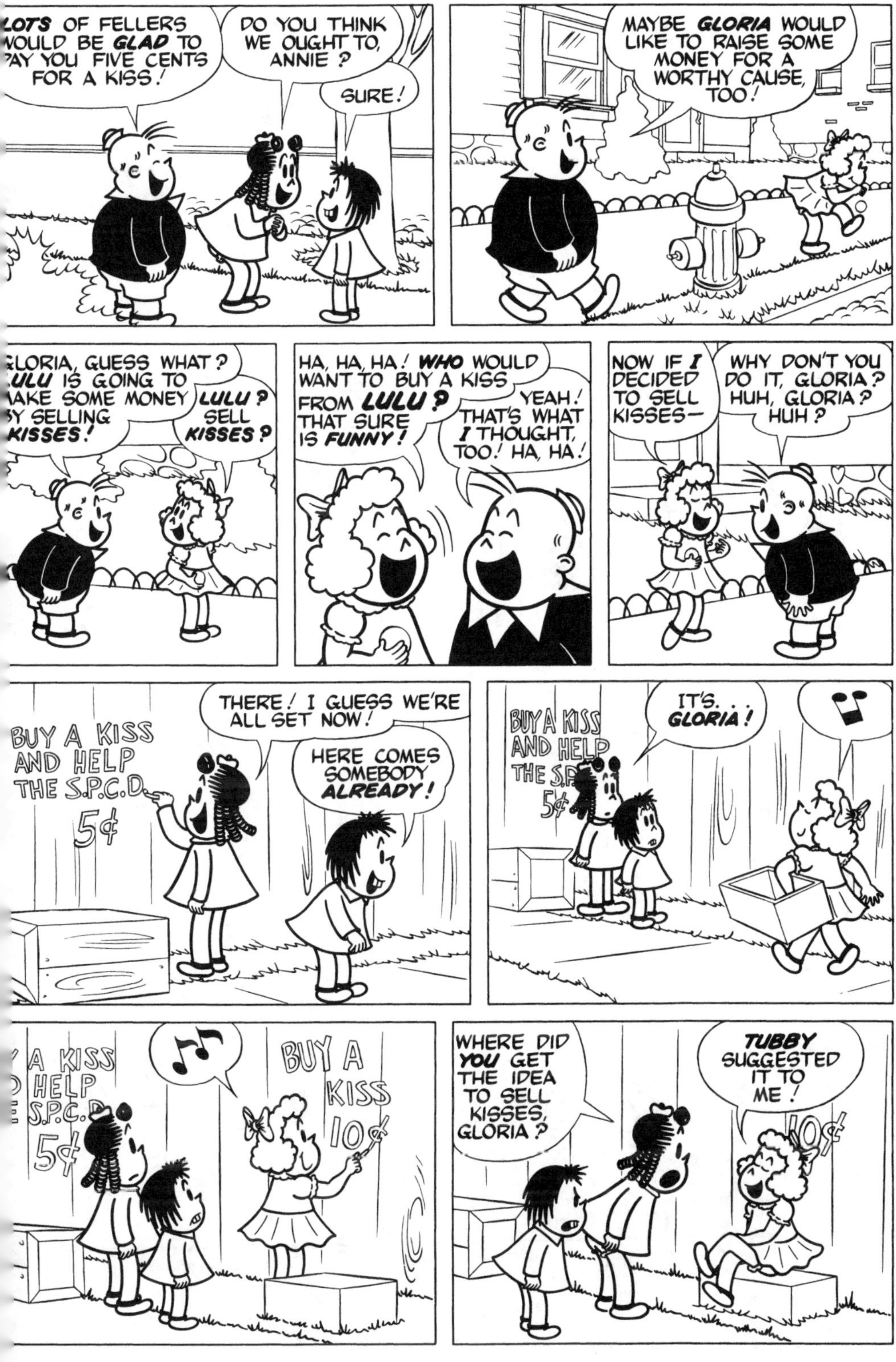
LOTS OF FELLERS WOULD BE GLAD TO PAY YOU FIVE CENTS FOR A KISS!
DO YOU THINK WE OUGHT TO, ANNIE?
SURE!
MAYBE GLORIA WOULD LIKE TO RAISE SOME MONEY FOR A WORTHY CAUSE, TOO!
GLORIA, GUESS WHAT? LULU IS GOING TO MAKE SOME MONEY BY SELLING KISSES!
LULU? SELL KISSES?
HA, HA, HA! WHO WOULD WANT TO BUY A KISS FROM LULU? THAT SURE IS FUNNY!
YEAH! THAT'S WHAT I THOUGHT, TOO! HA, HA!
NOW IF I DECIDED TO SELL KISSES—
WHY DON'T YOU DO IT, GLORIA? HUH, GLORIA? HUH?
BUY A KISS AND HELP THE S.P.C.D. 5¢
THERE! I GUESS WE'RE ALL SET NOW!
HERE COMES SOMEBODY ALREADY!
IT'S... GLORIA!
BUY A KISS 10¢
WHERE DID YOU GET THE IDEA TO SELL KISSES, GLORIA?
TUBBY SUGGESTED IT TO ME!

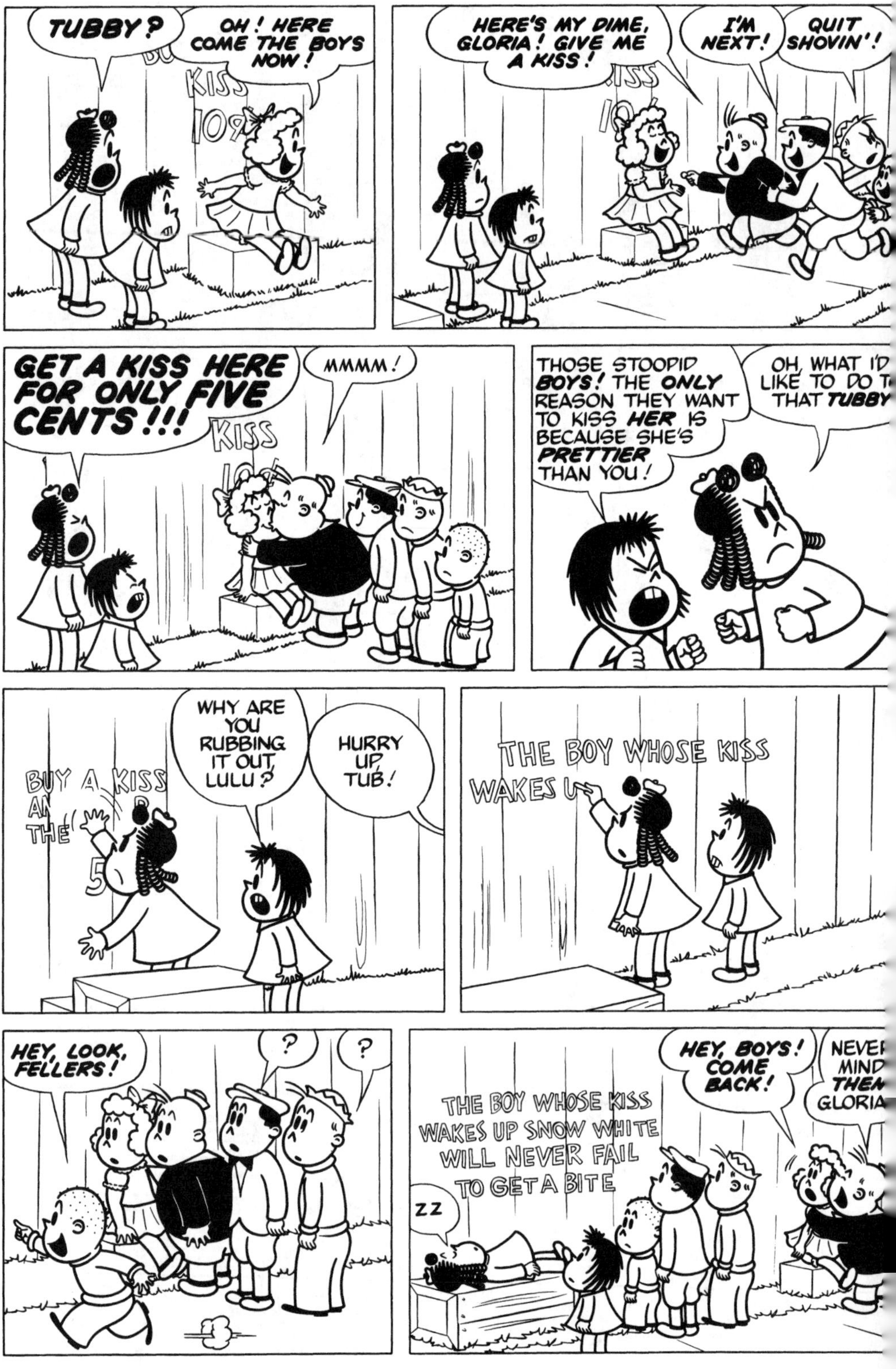
TUBBY?
OH! HERE COME THE BOYS NOW!
KISS 10¢
HERE'S MY DIME, GLORIA! GIVE ME A KISS!
I'M NEXT!
QUIT SHOVIN'!
GET A KISS HERE FOR ONLY FIVE CENTS!!!
MMMM!
KISS
THOSE STOOPID BOYS! THE ONLY REASON THEY WANT TO KISS HER IS BECAUSE SHE'S PRETTIER THAN YOU!
OH, WHAT I'D LIKE TO DO T THAT TUBBY
BUY A KISS
WHY ARE YOU RUBBING IT OUT, LULU?
HURRY UP, TUB!
THE BOY WHOSE KISS
WAKES U
HEY, LOOK, FELLERS!
?
?
THE BOY WHOSE KISS WAKES UP SNOW WHITE WILL NEVER FAIL TO GET A BITE
ZZ
HEY, BOYS! COME BACK!
NEVEF MIND THEM GLORIA

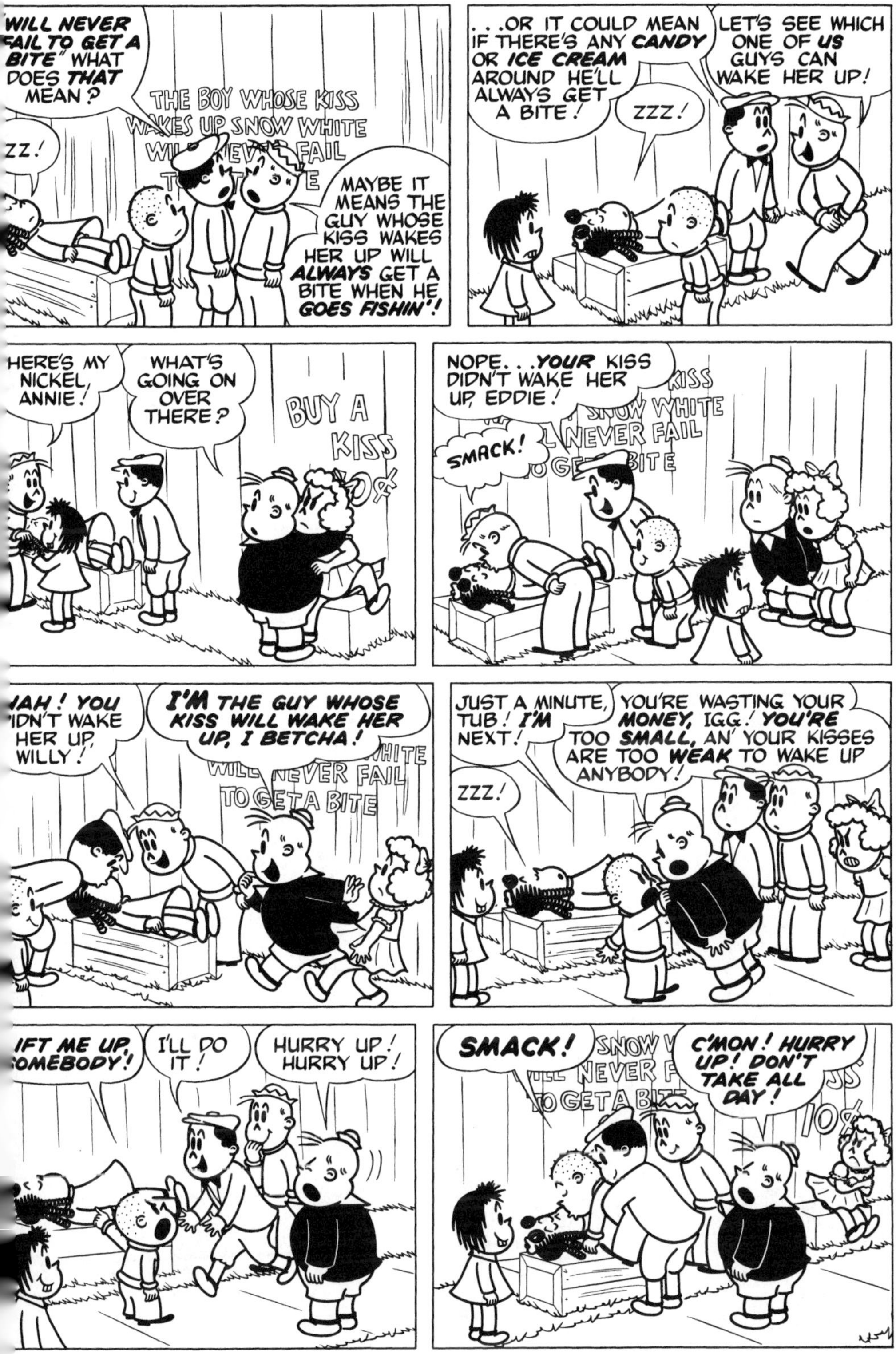
WILL NEVER FAIL TO GET A BITE" WHAT DOES THAT MEAN?
THE BOY WHOSE KISS WAKES UP SNOW WHITE WILL NEVER FAIL TO GET A BITE
ZZ!
MAYBE IT MEANS THE GUY WHOSE KISS WAKES HER UP WILL ALWAYS GET A BITE WHEN HE GOES FISHIN'!
. . .OR IT COULD MEAN IF THERE'S ANY CANDY OR ICE CREAM AROUND HE'LL ALWAYS GET A BITE!
LET'S SEE WHICH ONE OF US GUYS CAN WAKE HER UP!
ZZZ!
HERE'S MY NICKEL, ANNIE!
WHAT'S GOING ON OVER THERE?
BUY A KISS 10¢
NOPE. . .YOUR KISS DIDN'T WAKE HER UP, EDDIE!
SMACK!
NEVER FAIL
AH! YOU DIDN'T WAKE HER UP, WILLY!
I'M THE GUY WHOSE KISS WILL WAKE HER UP, I BETCHA!
WILL NEVER FAIL TO GET A BITE
JUST A MINUTE, TUB! I'M NEXT!
YOU'RE WASTING YOUR MONEY, IGG! YOU'RE TOO SMALL, AN' YOUR KISSES ARE TOO WEAK TO WAKE UP ANYBODY!
ZZZ!
IFT ME UP, OMEBODY!
I'LL DO IT!
HURRY UP! HURRY UP!
SMACK!
C'MON! HURRY UP! DON'T TAKE ALL DAY!
NEVER F
TO GET A BIT
10¢

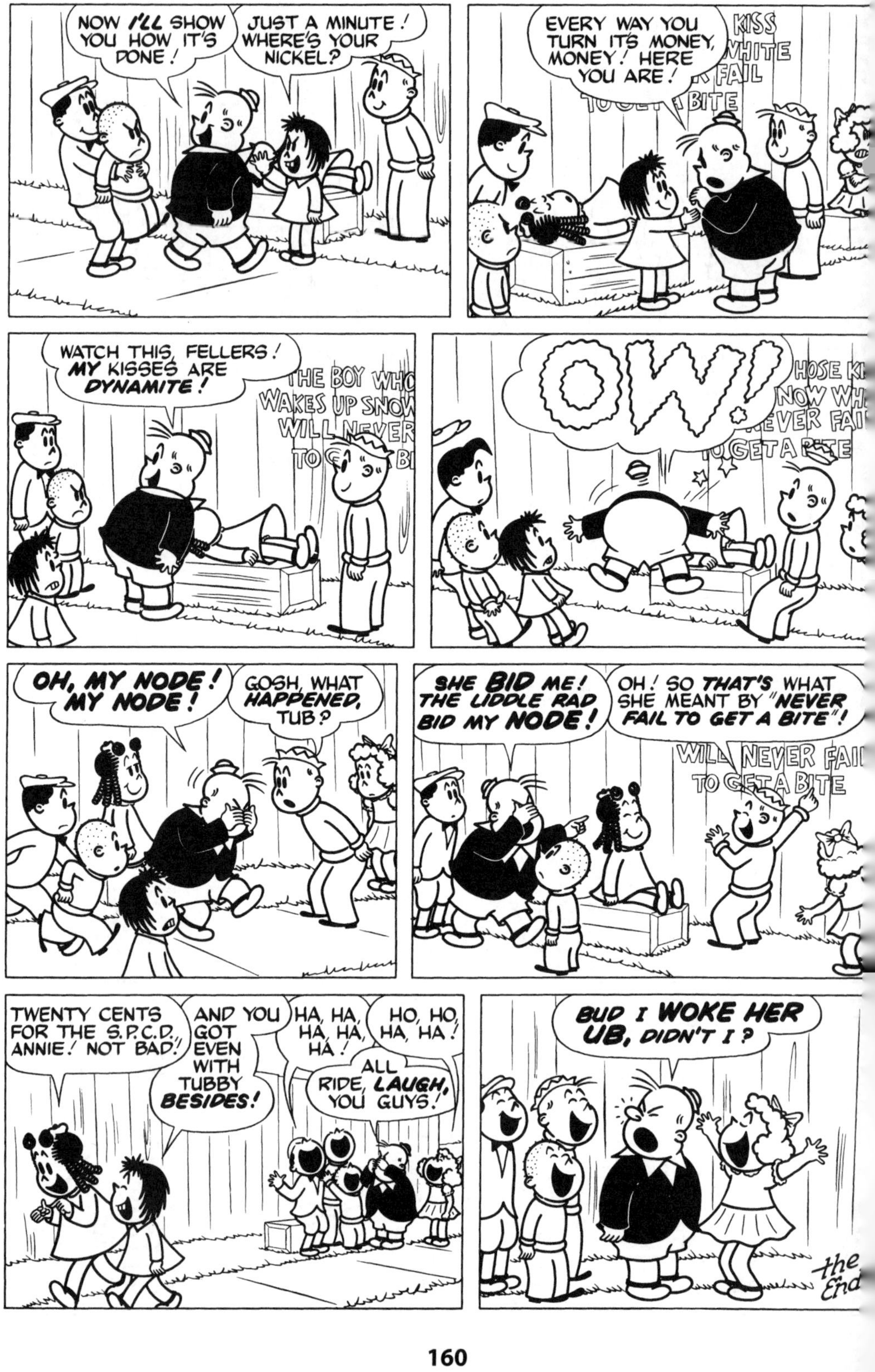
NOW I'LL SHOW YOU HOW IT'S DONE!
JUST A MINUTE! WHERE'S YOUR NICKEL?
EVERY WAY YOU TURN IT'S MONEY, MONEY! HERE YOU ARE!
WATCH THIS, FELLERS! MY KISSES ARE DYNAMITE!
OW!
OH, MY NODE! MY NODE!
GOSH, WHAT HAPPENED, TUB?
SHE BID ME! THE LIDDLE RAD BID MY NODE!
OH! SO THAT'S WHAT SHE MEANT BY "NEVER FAIL TO GET A BITE"!
TWENTY CENTS FOR THE S.P.C.D., ANNIE! NOT BAD!
AND YOU GOT EVEN WITH TUBBY BESIDES!
HA, HA, HA, HA, HA!
HO, HO, HA, HA!
ALL RIDE, LAUGH, YOU GUYS!
BUD I WOKE HER UB, DIDN'T I?
the End

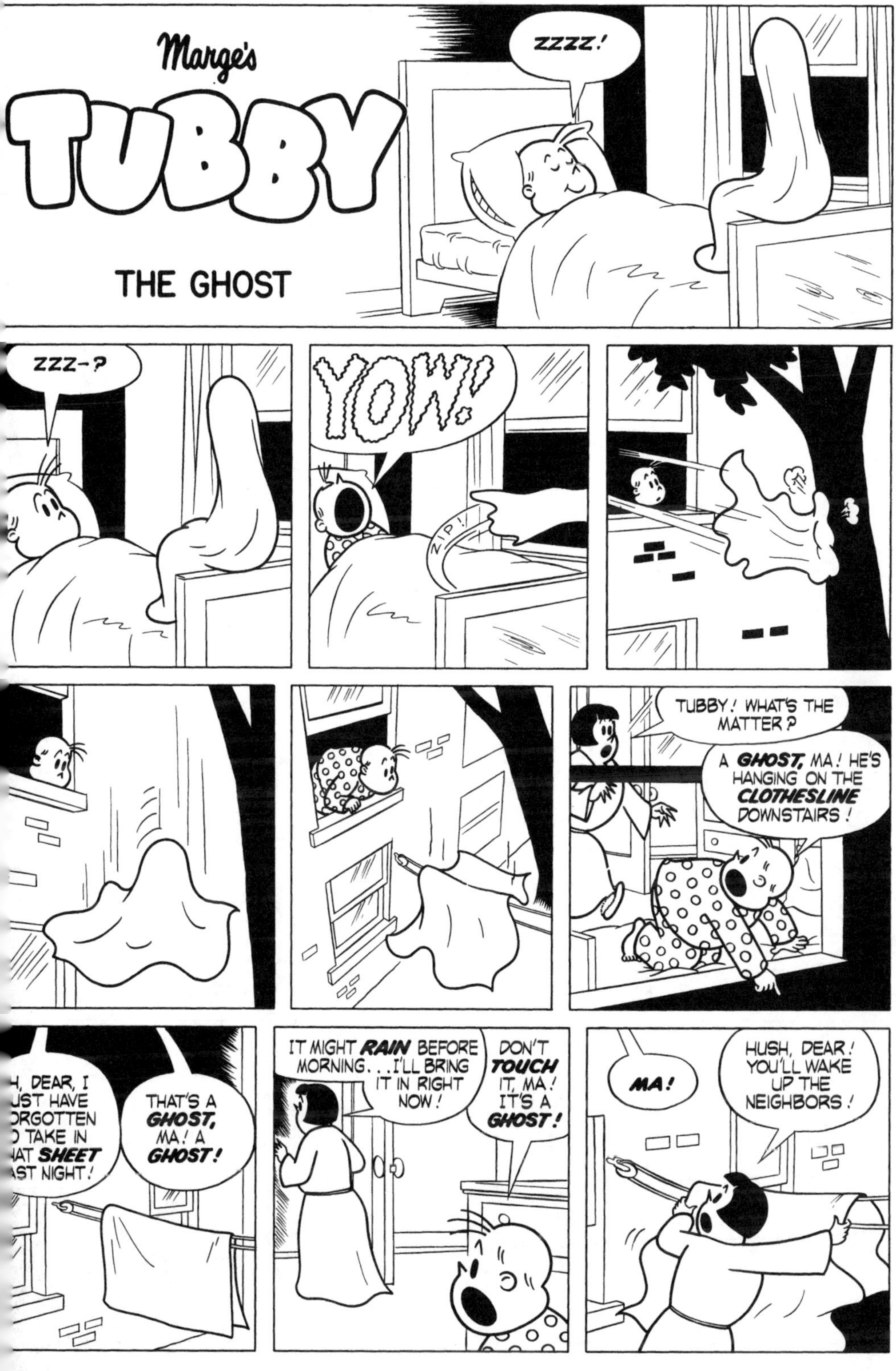
Marge's
TUBBY
THE GHOST
ZZZZ!
ZZZ-?
YOW!
ZIP!
TUBBY! WHAT'S THE MATTER?
A GHOST, MA! HE'S HANGING ON THE CLOTHESLINE DOWNSTAIRS!
H, DEAR, I UST HAVE ORGOTTEN O TAKE IN HAT SHEET AST NIGHT!
THAT'S A GHOST, MA! A GHOST!
IT MIGHT RAIN BEFORE MORNING...I'LL BRING IT IN RIGHT NOW!
DON'T TOUCH IT, MA! IT'S A GHOST!
MA!
HUSH, DEAR! YOU'LL WAKE UP THE NEIGHBORS!

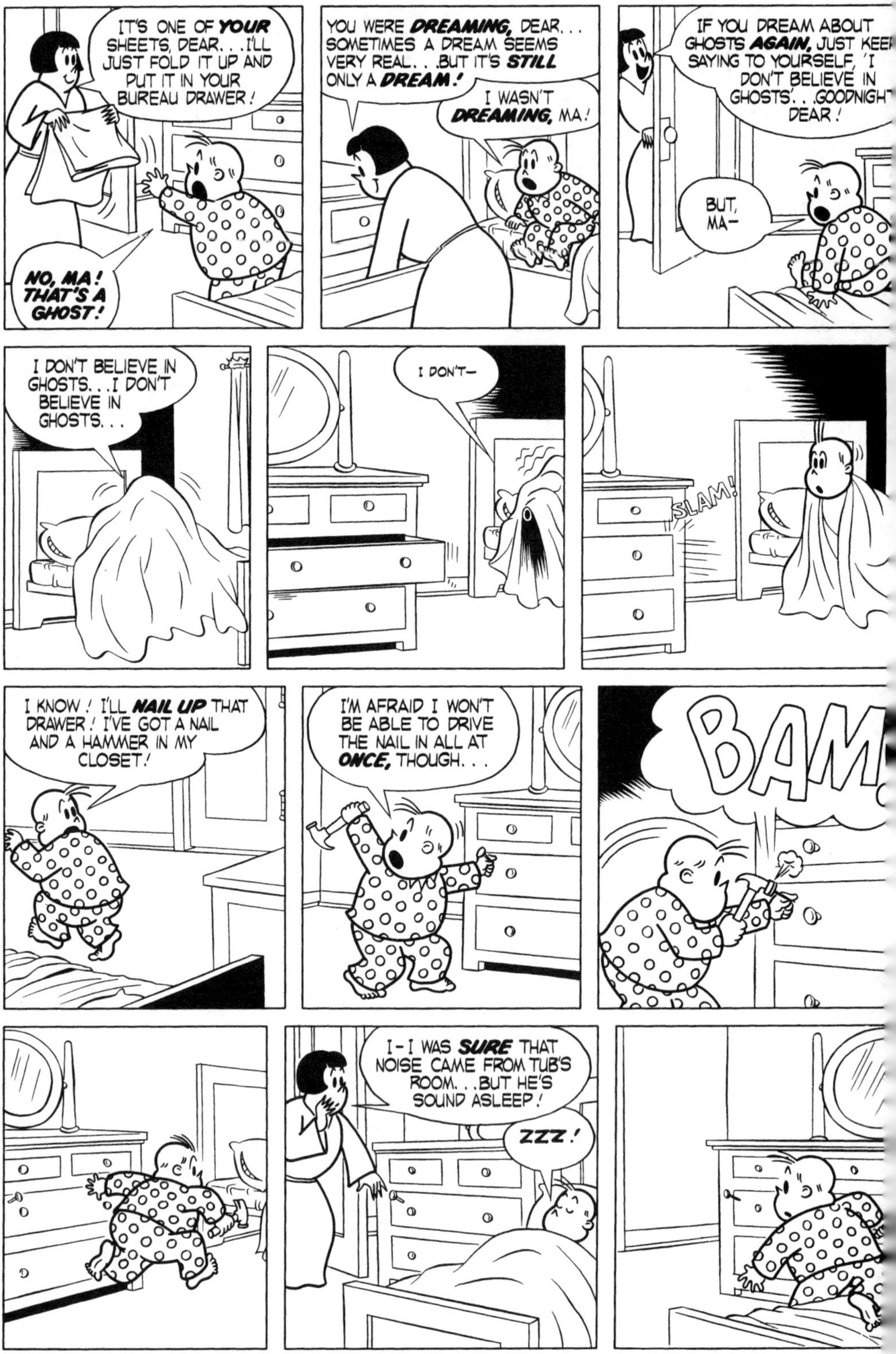
IT'S ONE OF YOUR SHEETS, DEAR. . . I'LL JUST FOLD IT UP AND PUT IT IN YOUR BUREAU DRAWER!
NO, MA! THAT'S A GHOST!
YOU WERE DREAMING, DEAR. . . SOMETIMES A DREAM SEEMS VERY REAL. . .BUT IT'S STILL ONLY A DREAM!
I WASN'T DREAMING, MA!
IF YOU DREAM ABOUT GHOSTS AGAIN, JUST KEEP SAYING TO YOURSELF, 'I DON'T BELIEVE IN GHOSTS'. . .GOODNIGHT DEAR!
BUT, MA–
I DON'T BELIEVE IN GHOSTS. . . I DON'T BELIEVE IN GHOSTS. . .
I DON'T–
SLAM!
I KNOW! I'LL NAIL UP THAT DRAWER! I'VE GOT A NAIL AND A HAMMER IN MY CLOSET!
I'M AFRAID I WON'T BE ABLE TO DRIVE THE NAIL IN ALL AT ONCE, THOUGH. . .
BAM
I-I WAS SURE THAT NOISE CAME FROM TUB'S ROOM. . .BUT HE'S SOUND ASLEEP!
ZZZ!

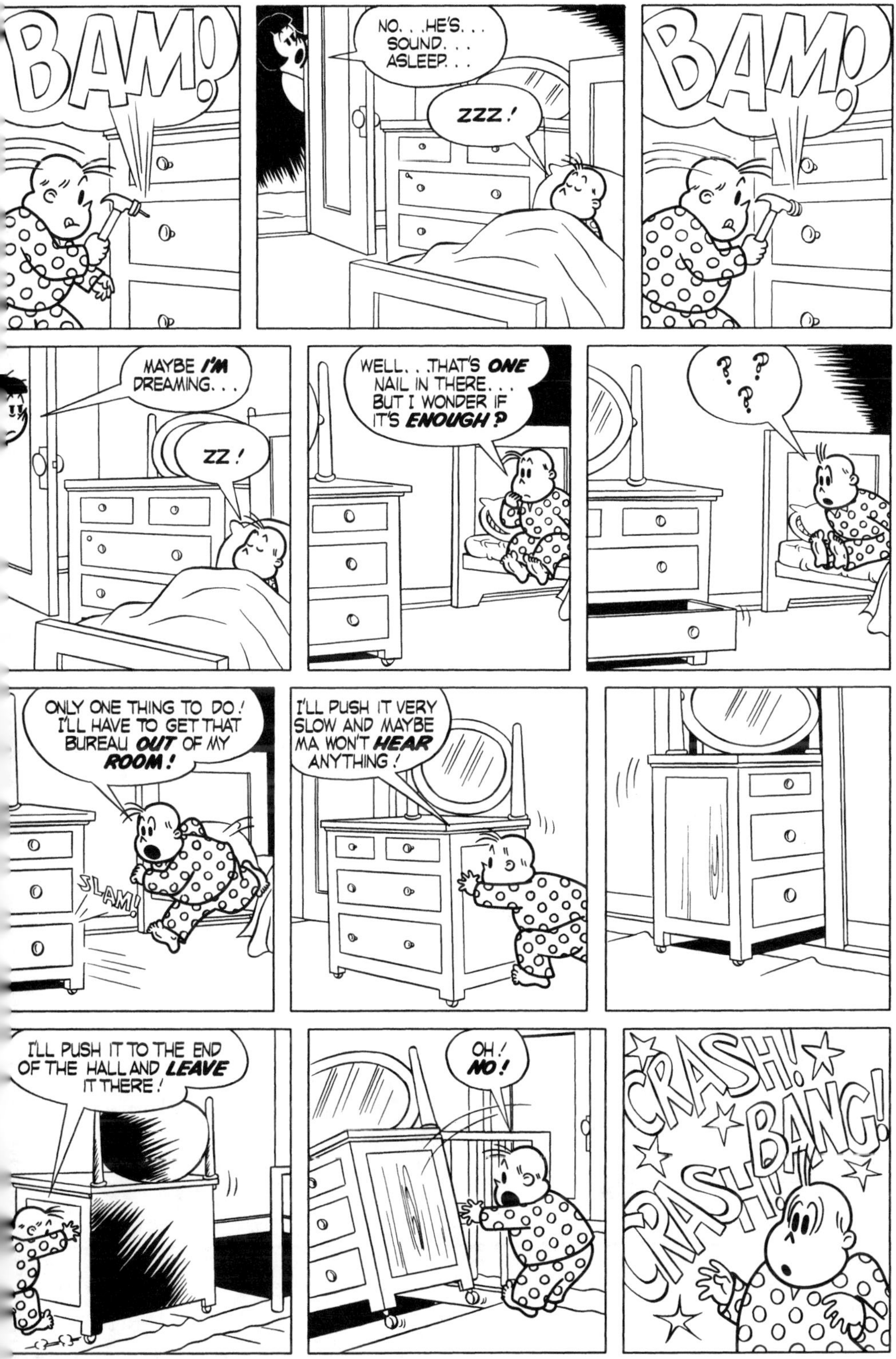
BAM!
NO. . .HE'S. . . SOUND. . . ASLEEP. . .
ZZZ!
BAM!
MAYBE I'M DREAMING. . .
ZZ!
WELL. . .THAT'S ONE NAIL IN THERE. . . BUT I WONDER IF IT'S ENOUGH?
? ? ?
ONLY ONE THING TO DO! I'LL HAVE TO GET THAT BUREAU OUT OF MY ROOM!
SLAM!
I'LL PUSH IT VERY SLOW AND MAYBE MA WON'T HEAR ANYTHING!
I'LL PUSH IT TO THE END OF THE HALL AND LEAVE IT THERE!
OH! NO!
CRASH! CRASH! BANG!

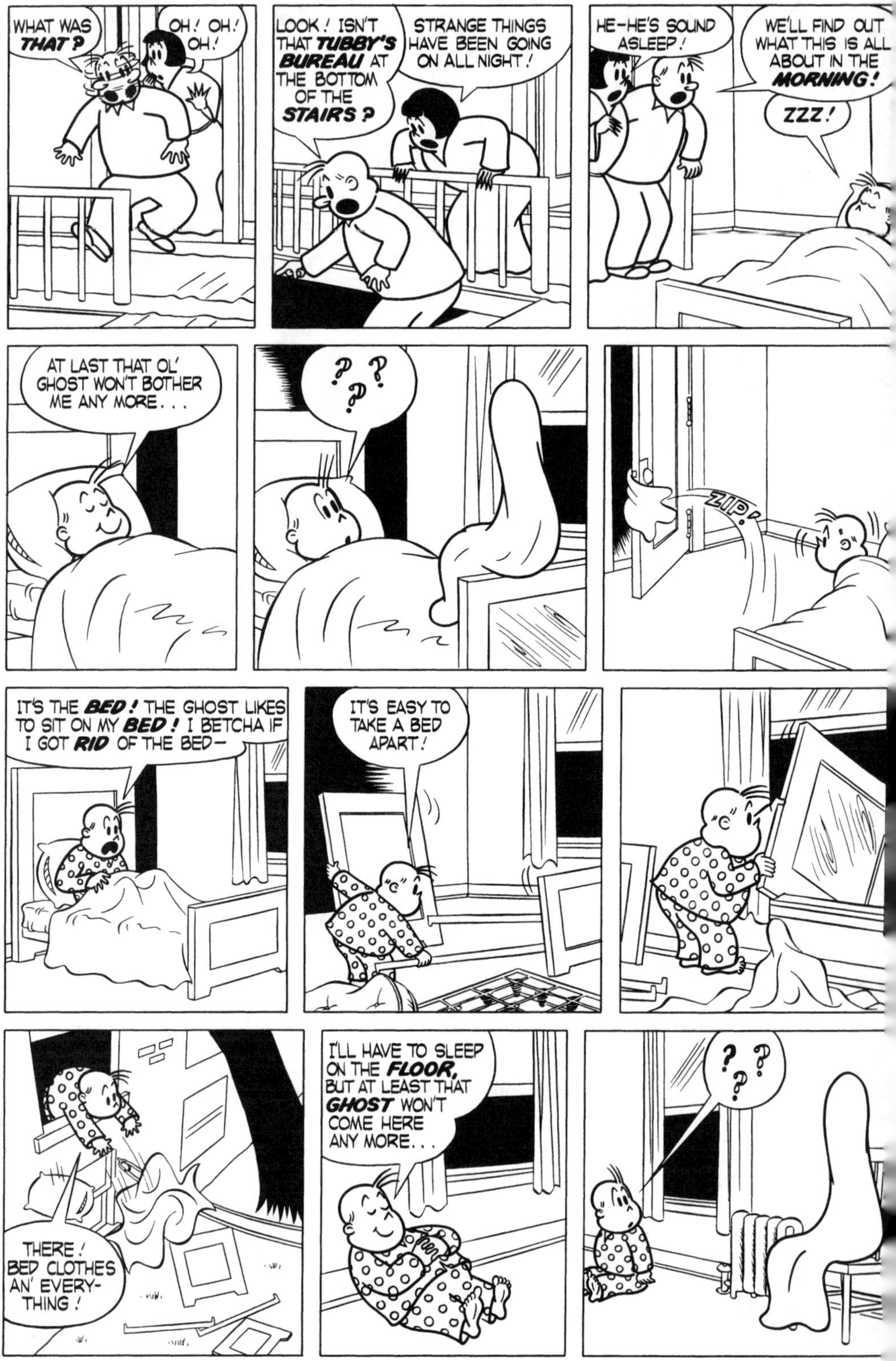
WHAT WAS THAT?
OH! OH! OH!
LOOK! ISN'T THAT TUBBY'S BUREAU AT THE BOTTOM OF THE STAIRS?
STRANGE THINGS HAVE BEEN GOING ON ALL NIGHT!
HE-HE'S SOUND ASLEEP!
WE'LL FIND OUT WHAT THIS IS ALL ABOUT IN THE MORNING!
ZZZ!
AT LAST THAT OL' GHOST WON'T BOTHER ME ANY MORE...
???
ZIP!
IT'S THE BED! THE GHOST LIKES TO SIT ON MY BED! I BETCHA IF I GOT RID OF THE BED—
IT'S EASY TO TAKE A BED APART!
THERE! BED CLOTHES AN' EVERY-THING!
I'LL HAVE TO SLEEP ON THE FLOOR, BUT AT LEAST THAT GHOST WON'T COME HERE ANY MORE...
???

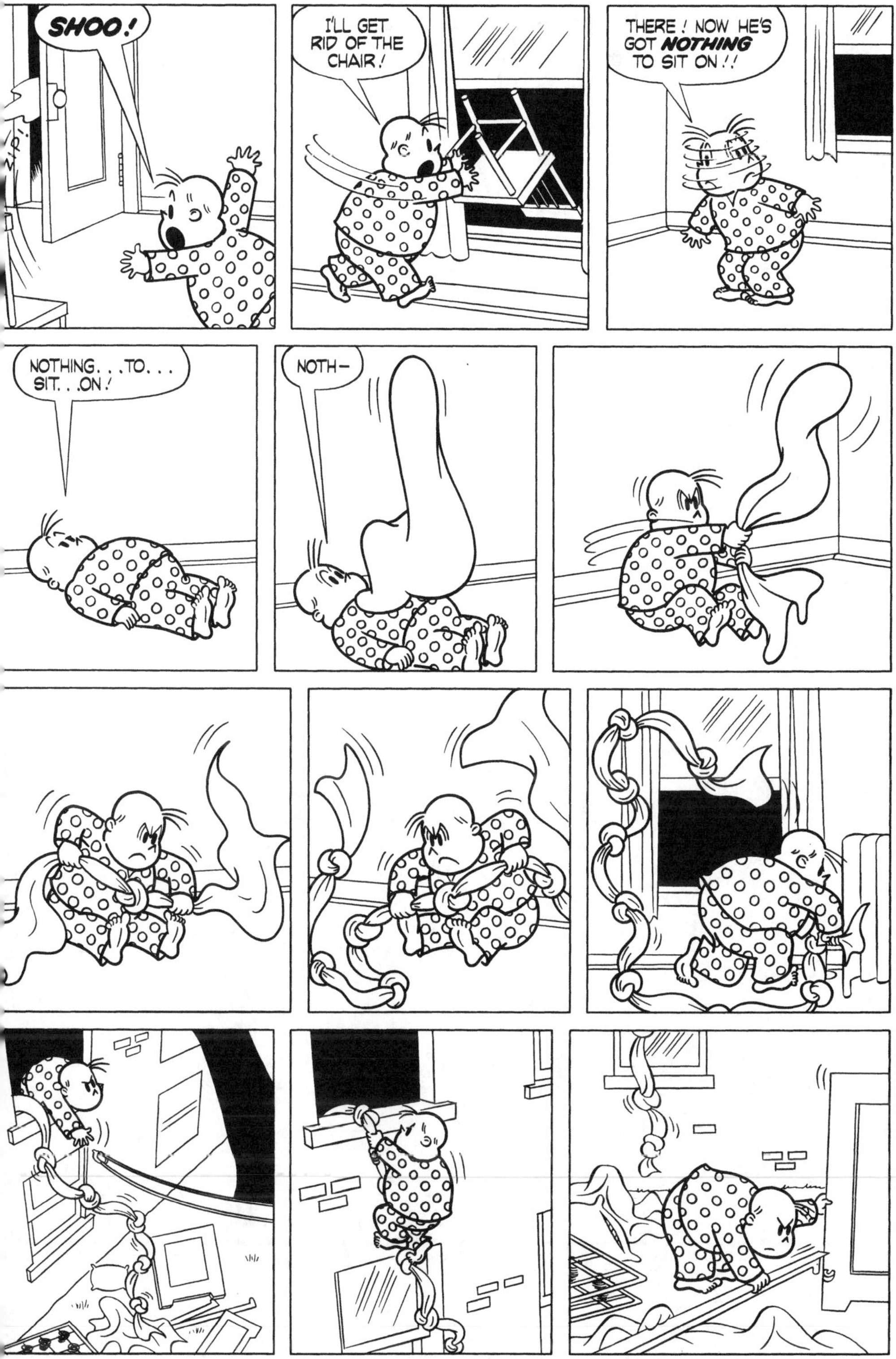
SHOO!
ZIP!
I'LL GET RID OF THE CHAIR!
THERE! NOW HE'S GOT NOTHING TO SIT ON!!
NOTHING. . .TO. . . SIT. . .ON!
NOTH–

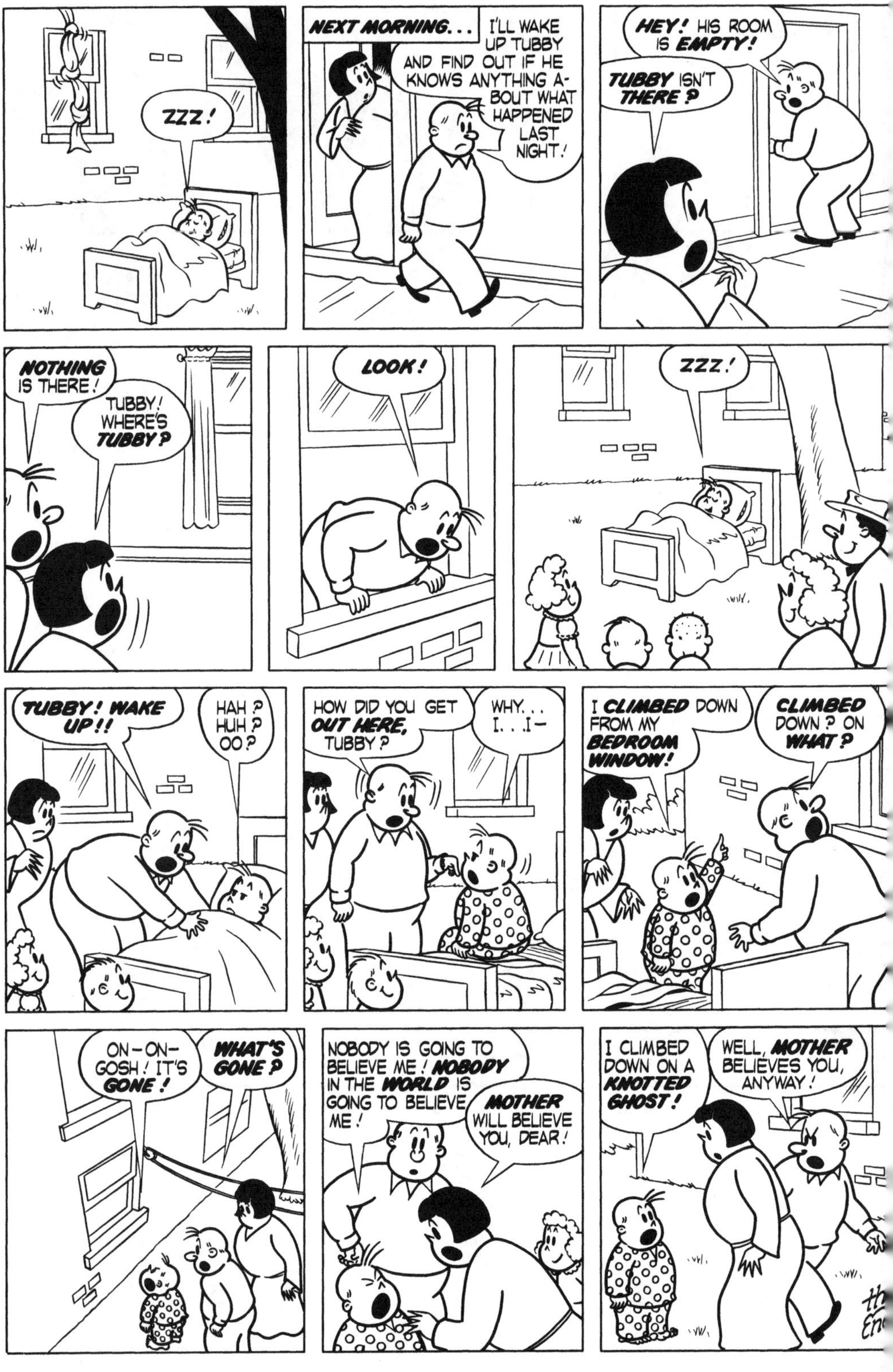
ZZZ!
NEXT MORNING...
I'LL WAKE UP TUBBY AND FIND OUT IF HE KNOWS ANYTHING A-BOUT WHAT HAPPENED LAST NIGHT!
HEY! HIS ROOM IS EMPTY!
TUBBY ISN'T THERE?
NOTHING IS THERE!
TUBBY! WHERE'S TUBBY?
LOOK!
ZZZ!
TUBBY! WAKE UP!!
HAH? HUH? OO?
HOW DID YOU GET OUT HERE, TUBBY?
WHY... I...I—
I CLIMBED DOWN FROM MY BEDROOM WINDOW!
CLIMBED DOWN? ON WHAT?
ON-ON-GOSH! IT'S GONE!
WHAT'S GONE?
NOBODY IS GOING TO BELIEVE ME! NOBODY IN THE WORLD IS GOING TO BELIEVE ME!
MOTHER WILL BELIEVE YOU, DEAR!
I CLIMBED DOWN ON A KNOTTED GHOST!
WELL, MOTHER BELIEVES YOU, ANYWAY!

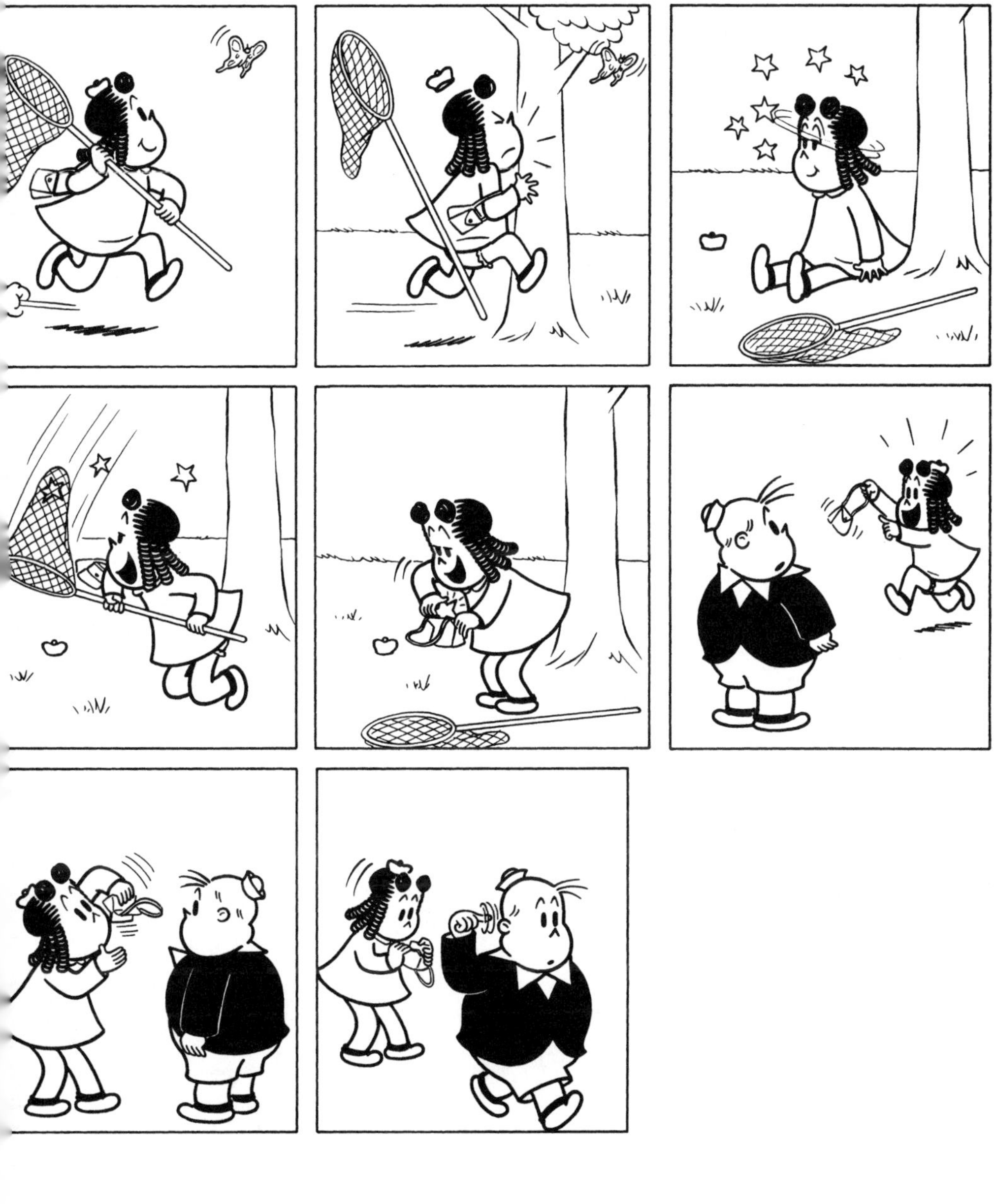

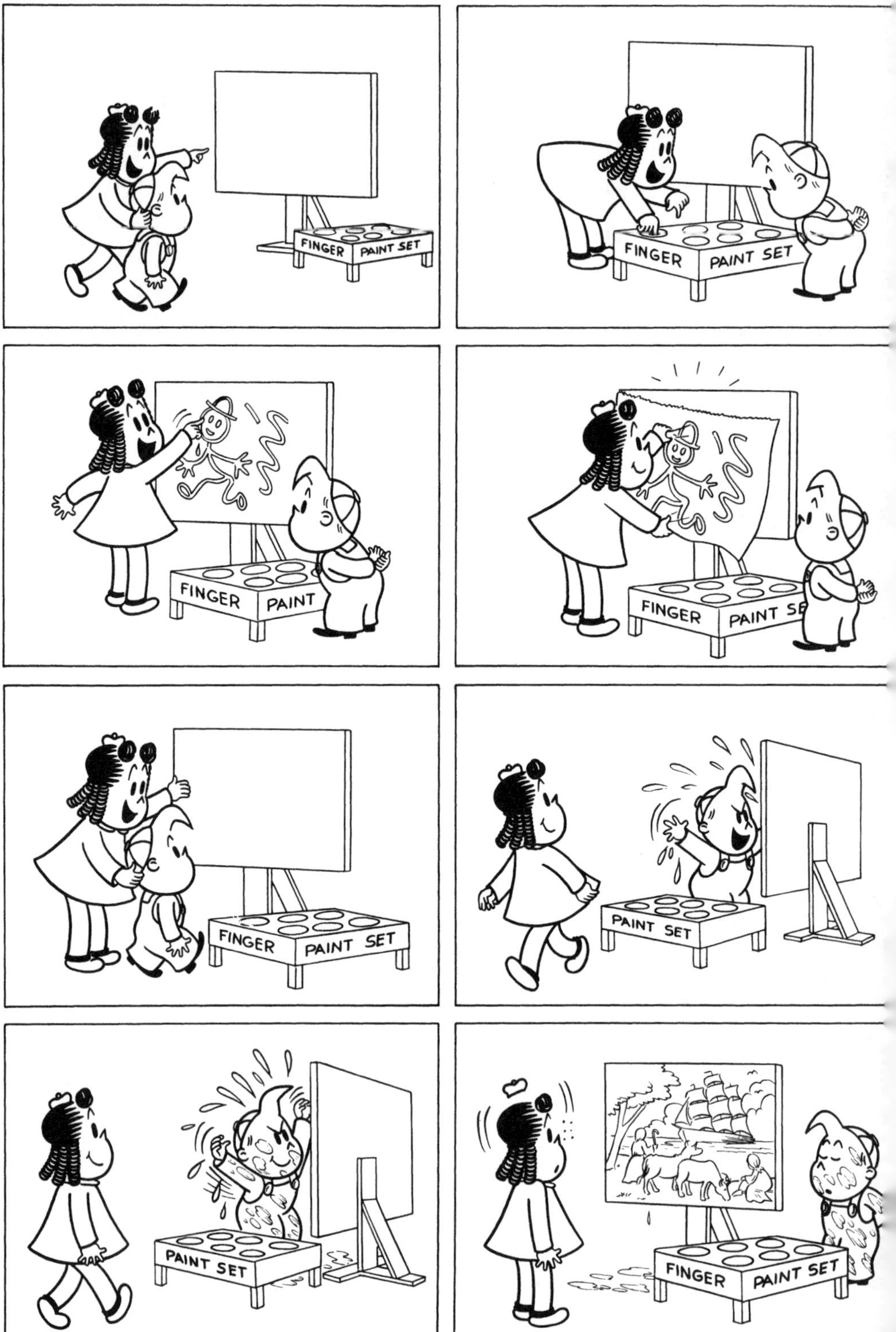
FINGER PAINT SET
FINGER PAINT SET
FINGER PAINT
FINGER PAINT SE
FINGER PAINT SET
PAINT SET
PAINT SET
FINGER PAINT SET

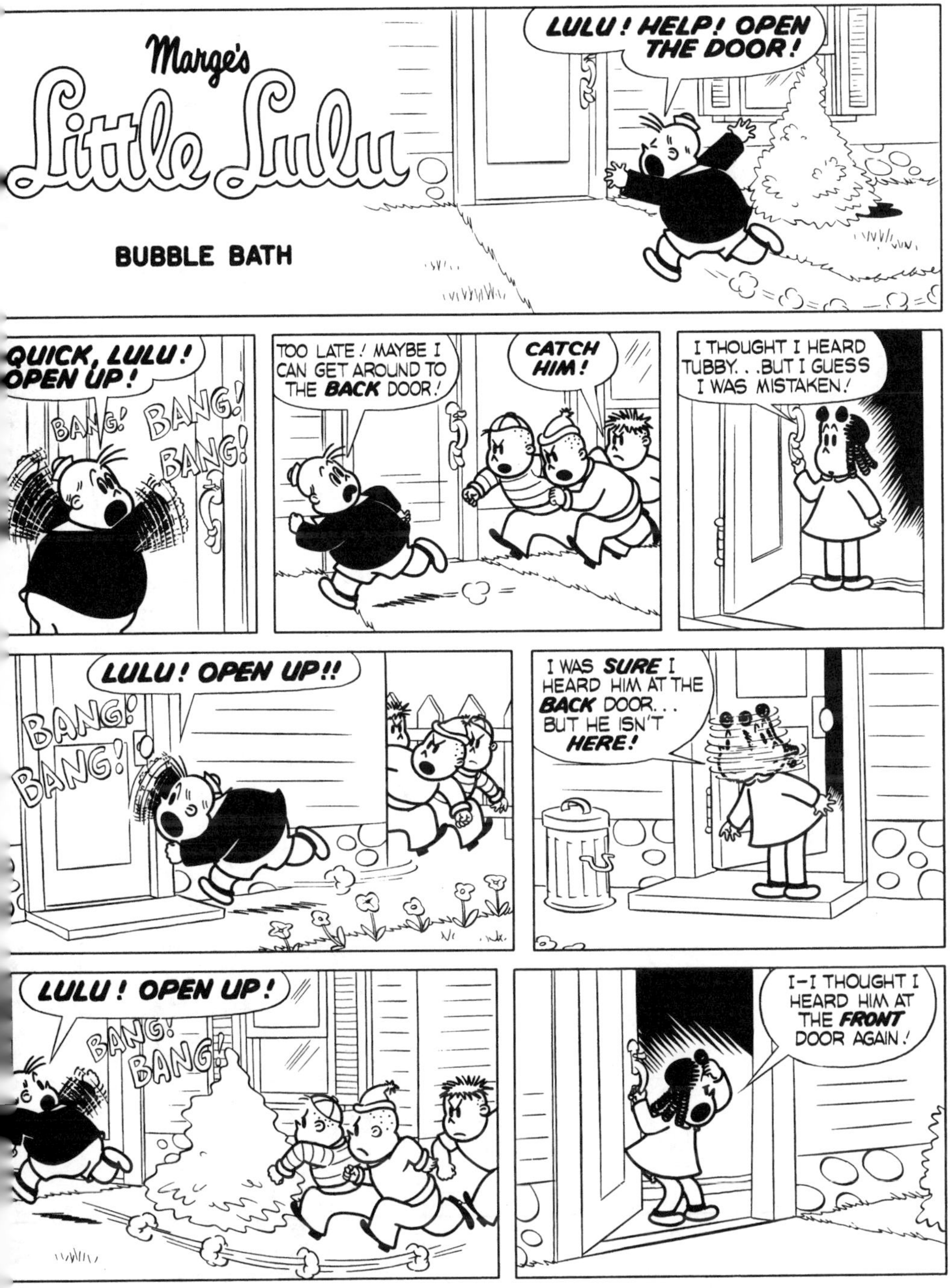
Marge's
Little Lulu
BUBBLE BATH
LULU! HELP! OPEN THE DOOR!
QUICK, LULU! OPEN UP!
BANG! BANG! BANG!
TOO LATE! MAYBE I CAN GET AROUND TO THE BACK DOOR!
CATCH HIM!
I THOUGHT I HEARD TUBBY. . .BUT I GUESS I WAS MISTAKEN!
LULU! OPEN UP!!
BANG! BANG!
I WAS SURE I HEARD HIM AT THE BACK DOOR. . . BUT HE ISN'T HERE!
LULU! OPEN UP!
BANG! BANG!
I-I THOUGHT I HEARD HIM AT THE FRONT DOOR AGAIN!

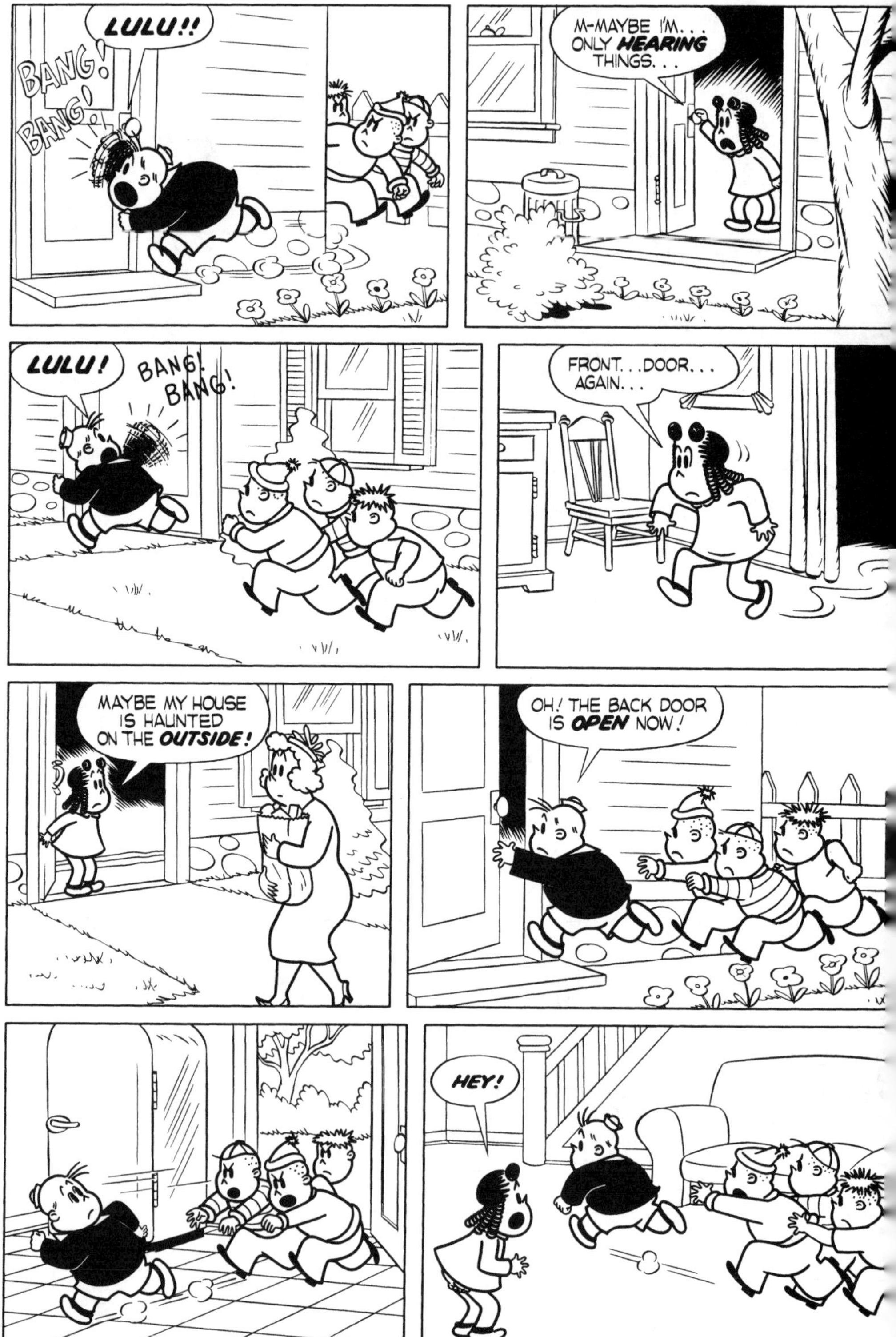
LULU!!
BANG! BANG!
M-MAYBE I'M... ONLY HEARING THINGS...
LULU!
BANG! BANG!
FRONT...DOOR... AGAIN...
MAYBE MY HOUSE IS HAUNTED ON THE OUTSIDE!
OH! THE BACK DOOR IS OPEN NOW!
HEY!

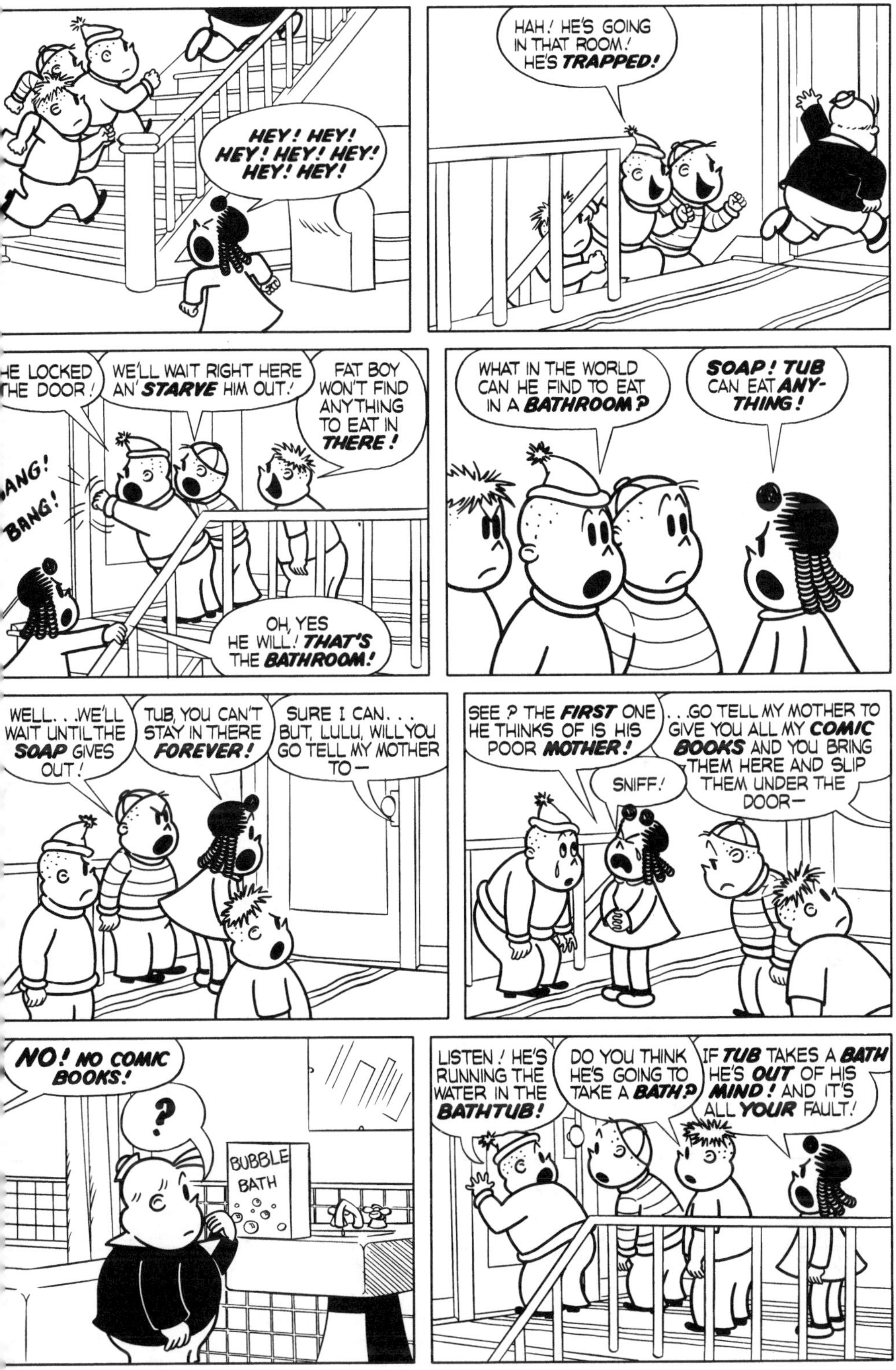
HEY! HEY!
HEY! HEY! HEY!
HEY! HEY!
HAH! HE'S GOING
IN THAT ROOM!
HE'S TRAPPED!
HE LOCKED
THE DOOR!
WE'LL WAIT RIGHT HERE
AN' STARVE HIM OUT!
FAT BOY
WON'T FIND
ANYTHING
TO EAT IN
THERE!
BANG!
BANG!
OH, YES
HE WILL! THAT'S
THE BATHROOM!
WHAT IN THE WORLD
CAN HE FIND TO EAT
IN A BATHROOM?
SOAP! TUB
CAN EAT ANY-
THING!
WELL...WE'LL
WAIT UNTIL THE
SOAP GIVES
OUT!
TUB, YOU CAN'T
STAY IN THERE
FOREVER!
SURE I CAN...
BUT, LULU, WILL YOU
GO TELL MY MOTHER
TO—
SEE? THE FIRST ONE
HE THINKS OF IS HIS
POOR MOTHER!
SNIFF!
...GO TELL MY MOTHER TO
GIVE YOU ALL MY COMIC
BOOKS AND YOU BRING
THEM HERE AND SLIP
THEM UNDER THE
DOOR—
NO! NO COMIC
BOOKS!
?
BUBBLE
BATH
LISTEN! HE'S
RUNNING THE
WATER IN THE
BATHTUB!
DO YOU THINK
HE'S GOING TO
TAKE A BATH?
IF TUB TAKES A BATH
HE'S OUT OF HIS
MIND! AND IT'S
ALL YOUR FAULT!

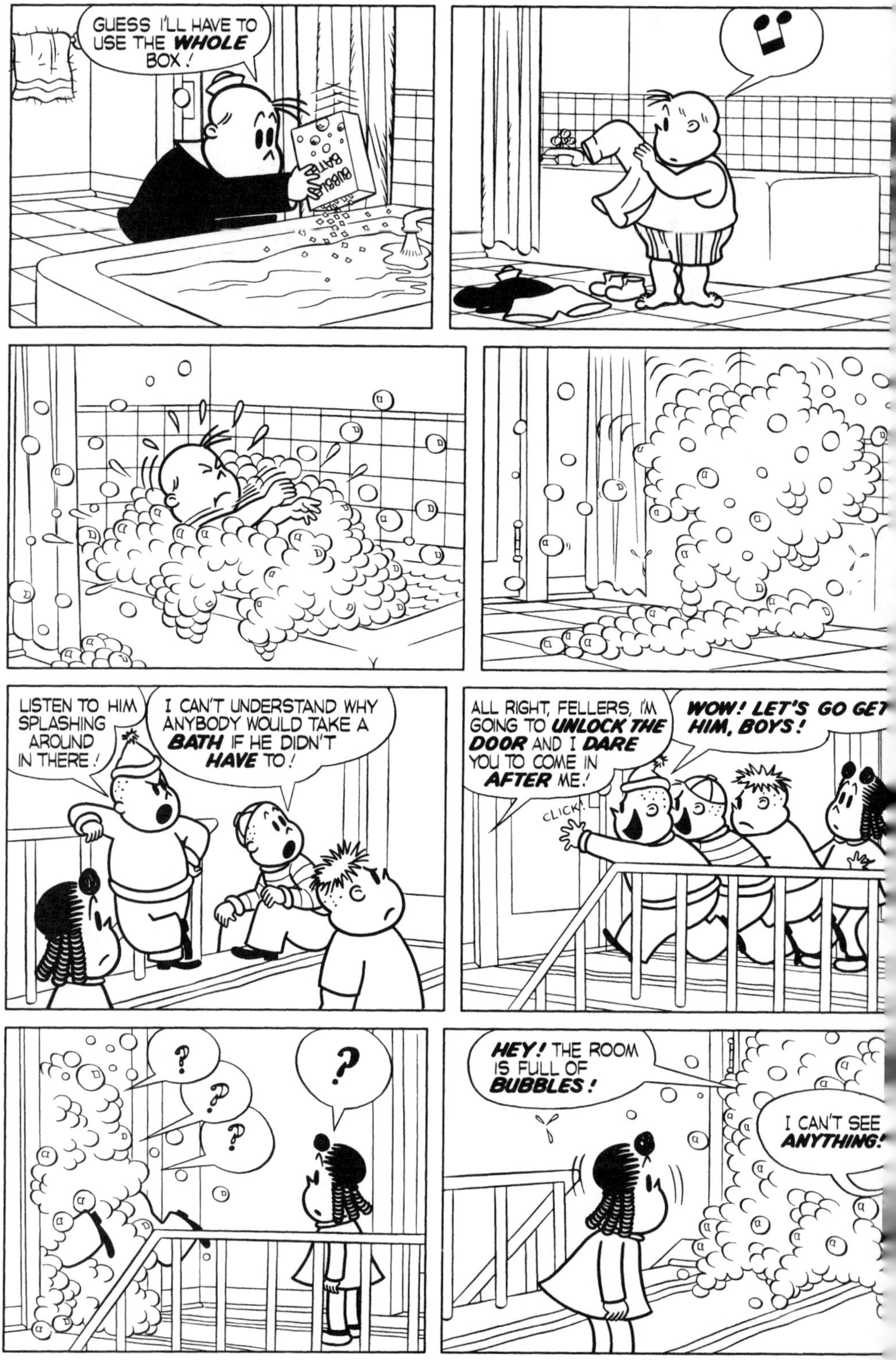
GUESS I'LL HAVE TO USE THE WHOLE BOX!
BUBBLE BATH
LISTEN TO HIM SPLASHING AROUND IN THERE!
I CAN'T UNDERSTAND WHY ANYBODY WOULD TAKE A BATH IF HE DIDN'T HAVE TO!
ALL RIGHT, FELLERS, I'M GOING TO UNLOCK THE DOOR AND I DARE YOU TO COME IN AFTER ME!
CLICK!
WOW! LET'S GO GET HIM, BOYS!
?
?
?
?
HEY! THE ROOM IS FULL OF BUBBLES!
I CAN'T SEE ANYTHING!

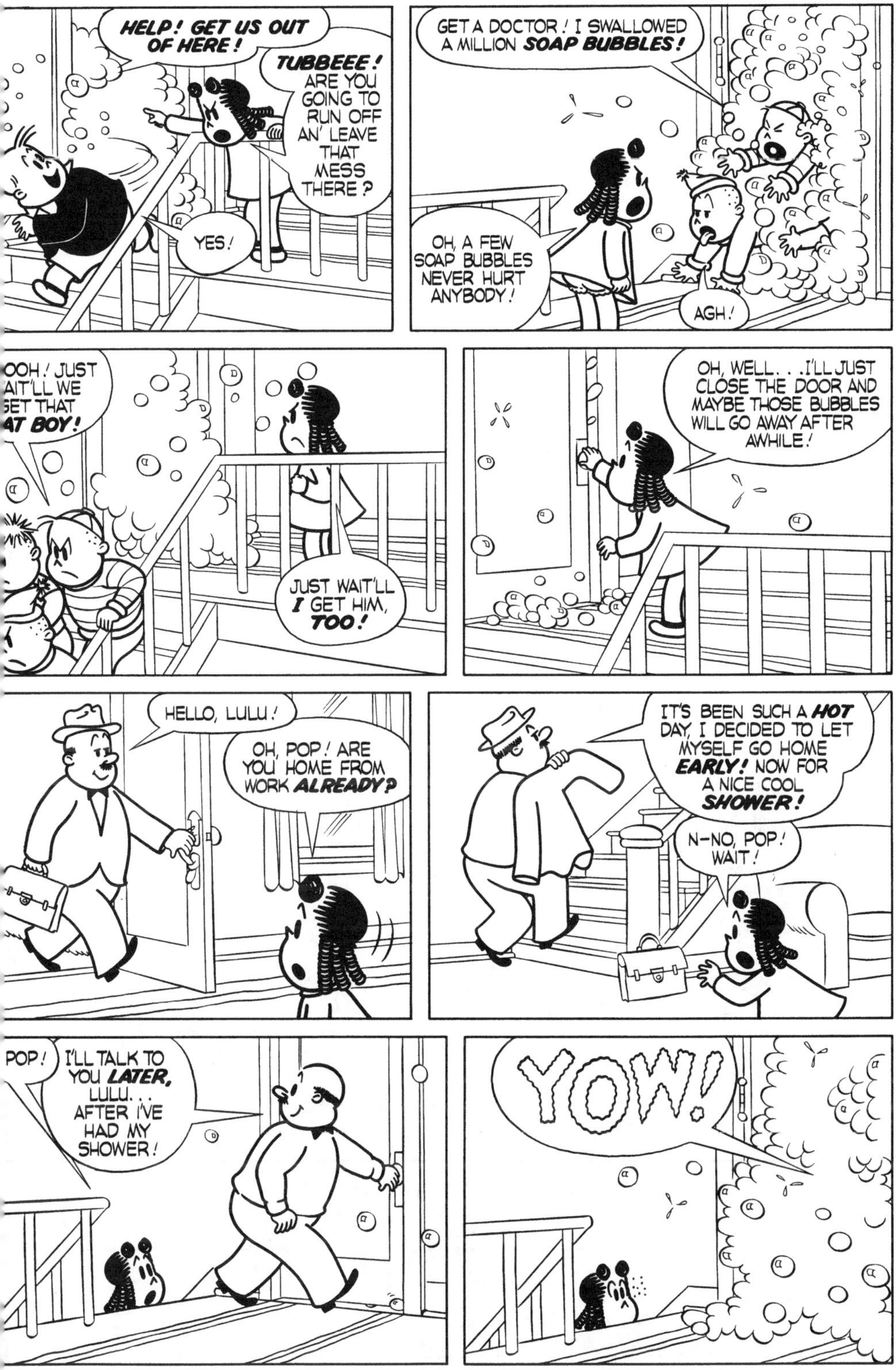
HELP! GET US OUT OF HERE!
TUBBEEE! ARE YOU GOING TO RUN OFF AN' LEAVE THAT MESS THERE?
YES!
GET A DOCTOR! I SWALLOWED A MILLION SOAP BUBBLES!
OH, A FEW SOAP BUBBLES NEVER HURT ANYBODY!
AGH!
OOH! JUST AIT'LL WE GET THAT AT BOY!
JUST WAIT'LL I GET HIM, TOO!
OH, WELL. . .I'LL JUST CLOSE THE DOOR AND MAYBE THOSE BUBBLES WILL GO AWAY AFTER AWHILE!
HELLO, LULU!
OH, POP! ARE YOU HOME FROM WORK ALREADY?
IT'S BEEN SUCH A HOT DAY, I DECIDED TO LET MYSELF GO HOME EARLY! NOW FOR A NICE COOL SHOWER!
N-NO, POP! WAIT!
POP!
I'LL TALK TO YOU LATER, LULU... AFTER I'VE HAD MY SHOWER!
YOW!

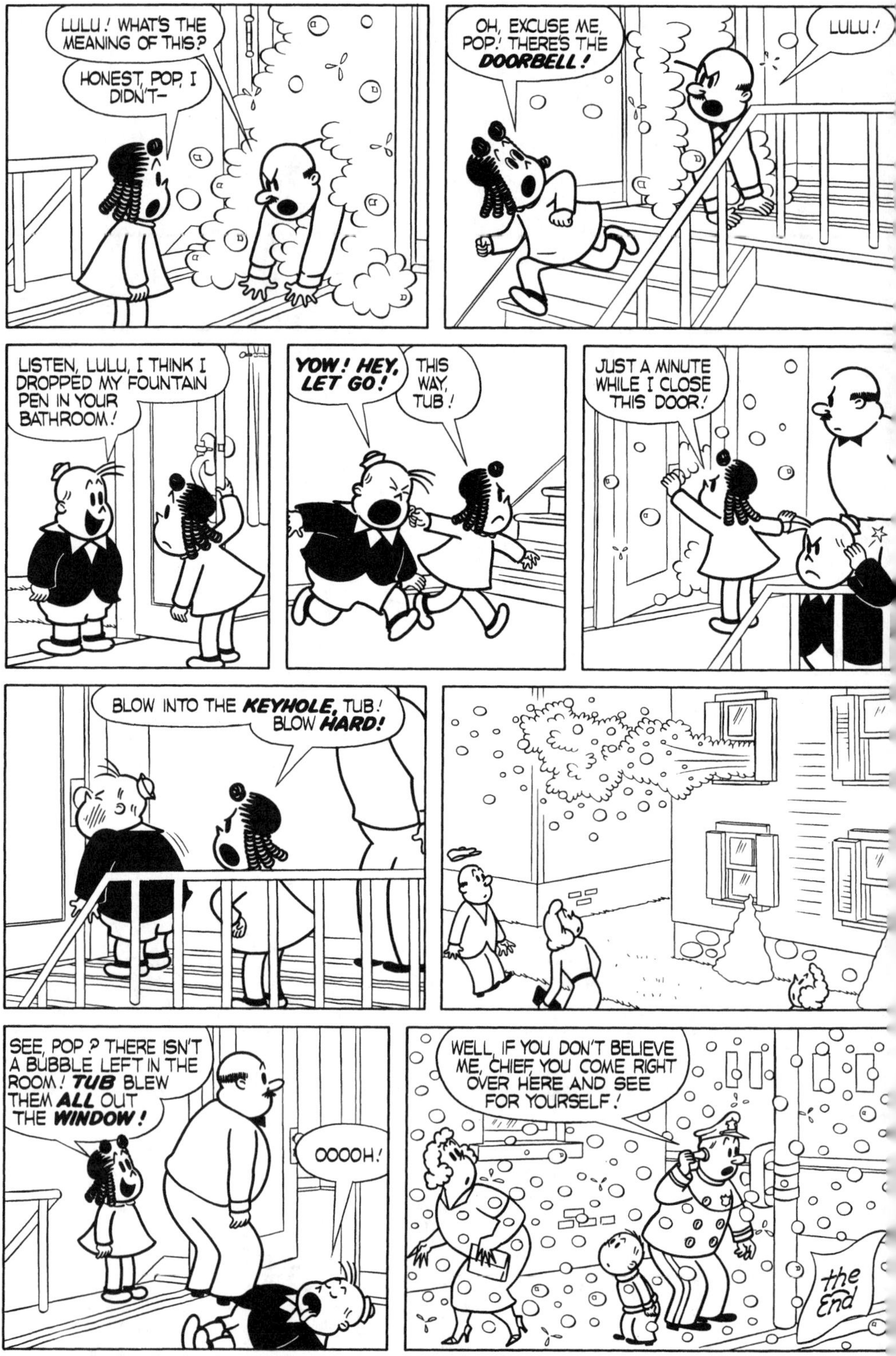
LULU! WHAT'S THE MEANING OF THIS?
HONEST, POP, I DIDN'T—
OH, EXCUSE ME, POP! THERE'S THE DOORBELL!
LULU!
LISTEN, LULU, I THINK I DROPPED MY FOUNTAIN PEN IN YOUR BATHROOM!
YOW! HEY, LET GO!
THIS WAY, TUB!
JUST A MINUTE WHILE I CLOSE THIS DOOR!
BLOW INTO THE KEYHOLE, TUB! BLOW HARD!
SEE, POP? THERE ISN'T A BUBBLE LEFT IN THE ROOM! TUB BLEW THEM ALL OUT THE WINDOW!
OOOOH!
WELL, IF YOU DON'T BELIEVE ME, CHIEF, YOU COME RIGHT OVER HERE AND SEE FOR YOURSELF!
the End

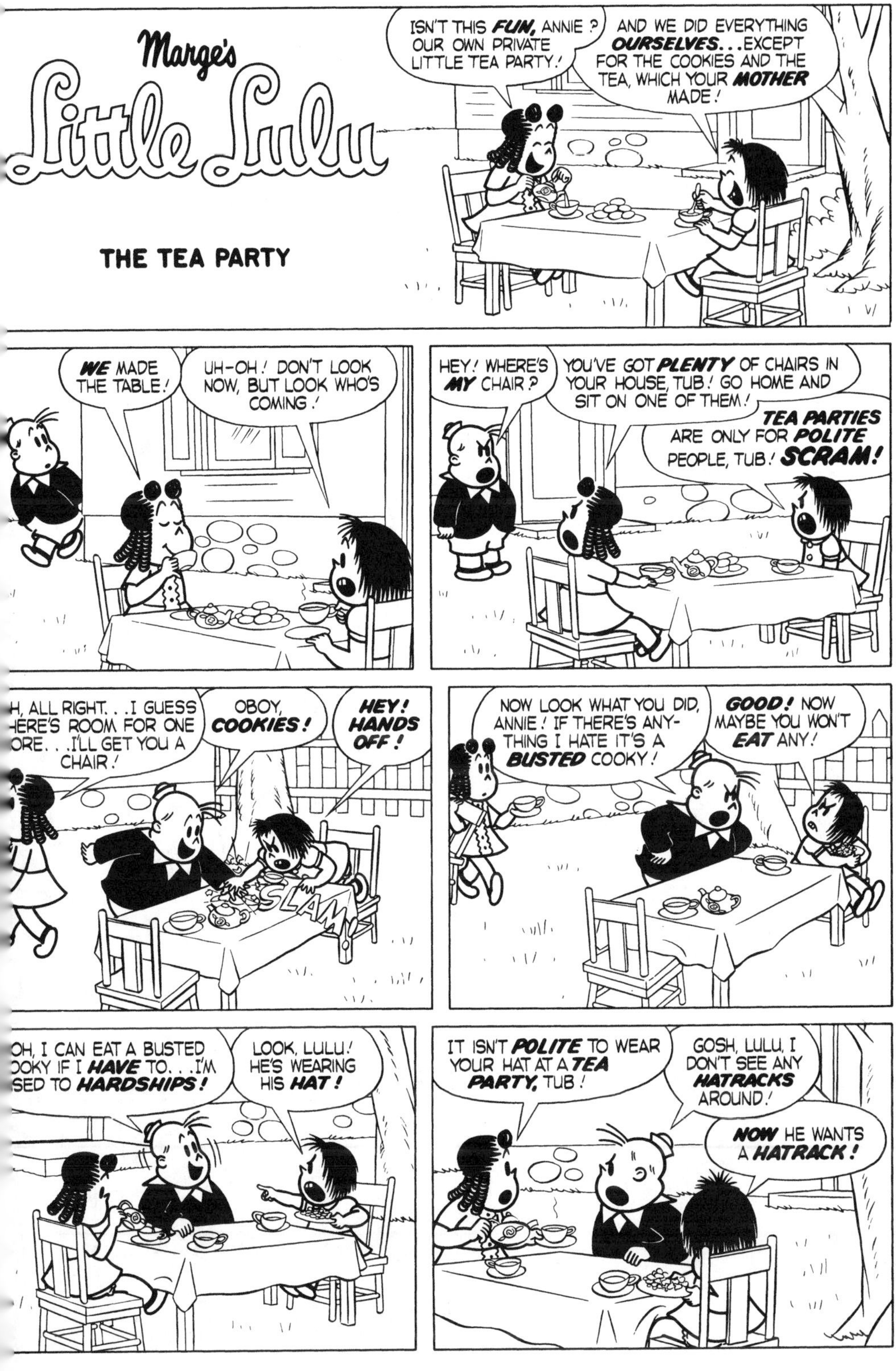
Marge's Little Lulu
THE TEA PARTY
ISN'T THIS FUN, ANNIE ? OUR OWN PRIVATE LITTLE TEA PARTY !
AND WE DID EVERYTHING OURSELVES. . .EXCEPT FOR THE COOKIES AND THE TEA, WHICH YOUR MOTHER MADE !
WE MADE THE TABLE !
UH-OH ! DON'T LOOK NOW, BUT LOOK WHO'S COMING !
HEY ! WHERE'S MY CHAIR ?
YOU'VE GOT PLENTY OF CHAIRS IN YOUR HOUSE, TUB ! GO HOME AND SIT ON ONE OF THEM !
TEA PARTIES ARE ONLY FOR POLITE PEOPLE, TUB ! SCRAM !
H, ALL RIGHT. . .I GUESS HERE'S ROOM FOR ONE ORE. . .I'LL GET YOU A CHAIR !
OBOY, COOKIES !
HEY ! HANDS OFF !
SLAM
NOW LOOK WHAT YOU DID, ANNIE ! IF THERE'S ANY-THING I HATE IT'S A BUSTED COOKY !
GOOD ! NOW MAYBE YOU WON'T EAT ANY !
OH, I CAN EAT A BUSTED OOKY IF I HAVE TO. . .I'M SED TO HARDSHIPS !
LOOK, LULU ! HE'S WEARING HIS HAT !
IT ISN'T POLITE TO WEAR YOUR HAT AT A TEA PARTY, TUB !
GOSH, LULU, I DON'T SEE ANY HATRACKS AROUND !
NOW HE WANTS A HATRACK !

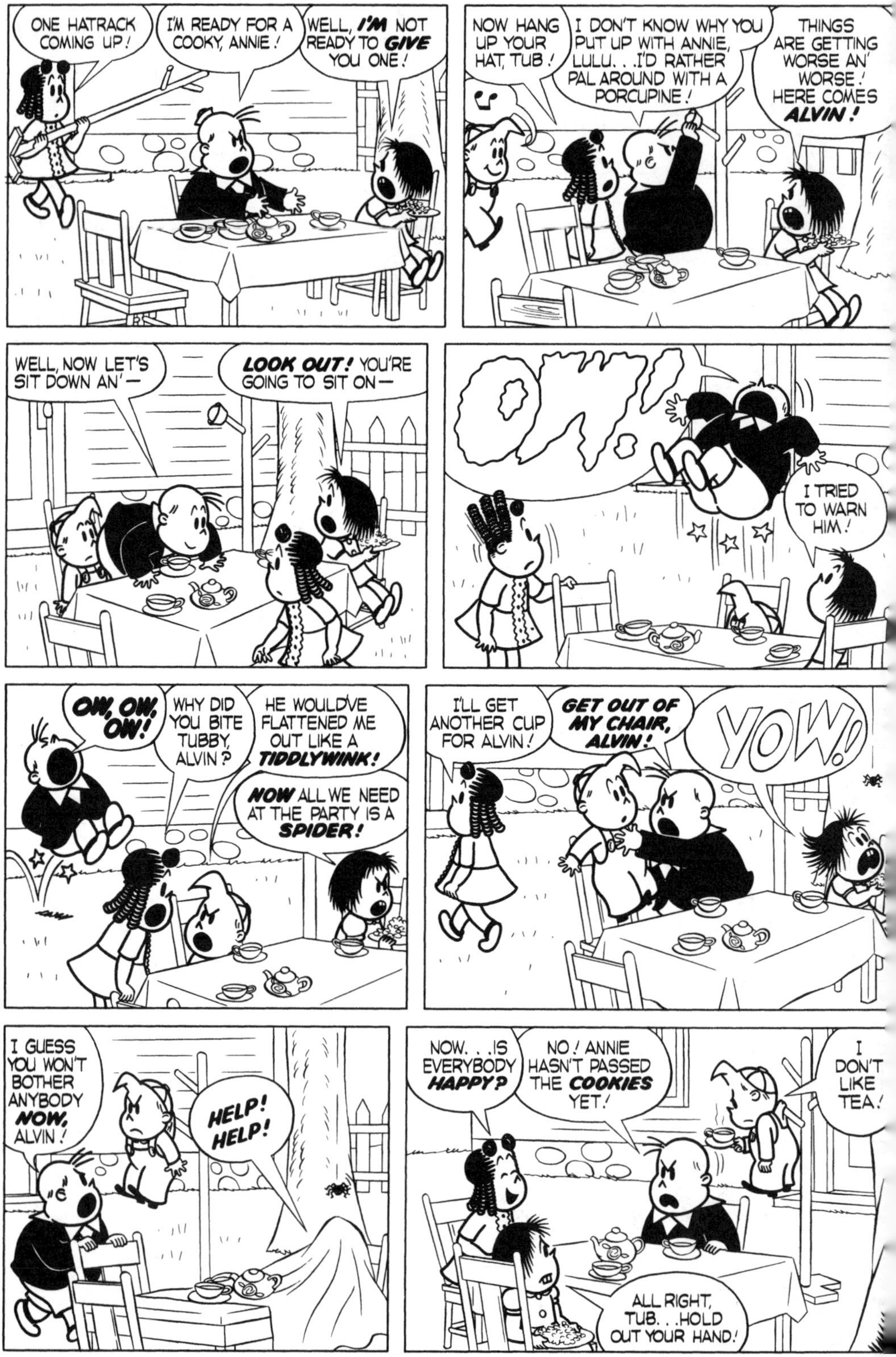

ONE HATRACK COMING UP!
I'M READY FOR A COOKY, ANNIE!
WELL, I'M NOT READY TO GIVE YOU ONE!
NOW HANG UP YOUR HAT, TUB!
I DON'T KNOW WHY YOU PUT UP WITH ANNIE, LULU. . .I'D RATHER PAL AROUND WITH A PORCUPINE!
THINGS ARE GETTING WORSE AN' WORSE! HERE COMES ALVIN!
WELL, NOW LET'S SIT DOWN AN'—
LOOK OUT! YOU'RE GOING TO SIT ON—
OW!
I TRIED TO WARN HIM!
OW, OW, OW!
WHY DID YOU BITE TUBBY, ALVIN?
HE WOULD'VE FLATTENED ME OUT LIKE A TIDDLYWINK!
NOW ALL WE NEED AT THE PARTY IS A SPIDER!
I'LL GET ANOTHER CUP FOR ALVIN!
GET OUT OF MY CHAIR, ALVIN!
YOW!
I GUESS YOU WON'T BOTHER ANYBODY NOW, ALVIN!
HELP! HELP!
NOW. . .IS EVERYBODY HAPPY?
NO! ANNIE HASN'T PASSED THE COOKIES YET!
I DON'T LIKE TEA!
ALL RIGHT, TUB. . .HOLD OUT YOUR HAND!

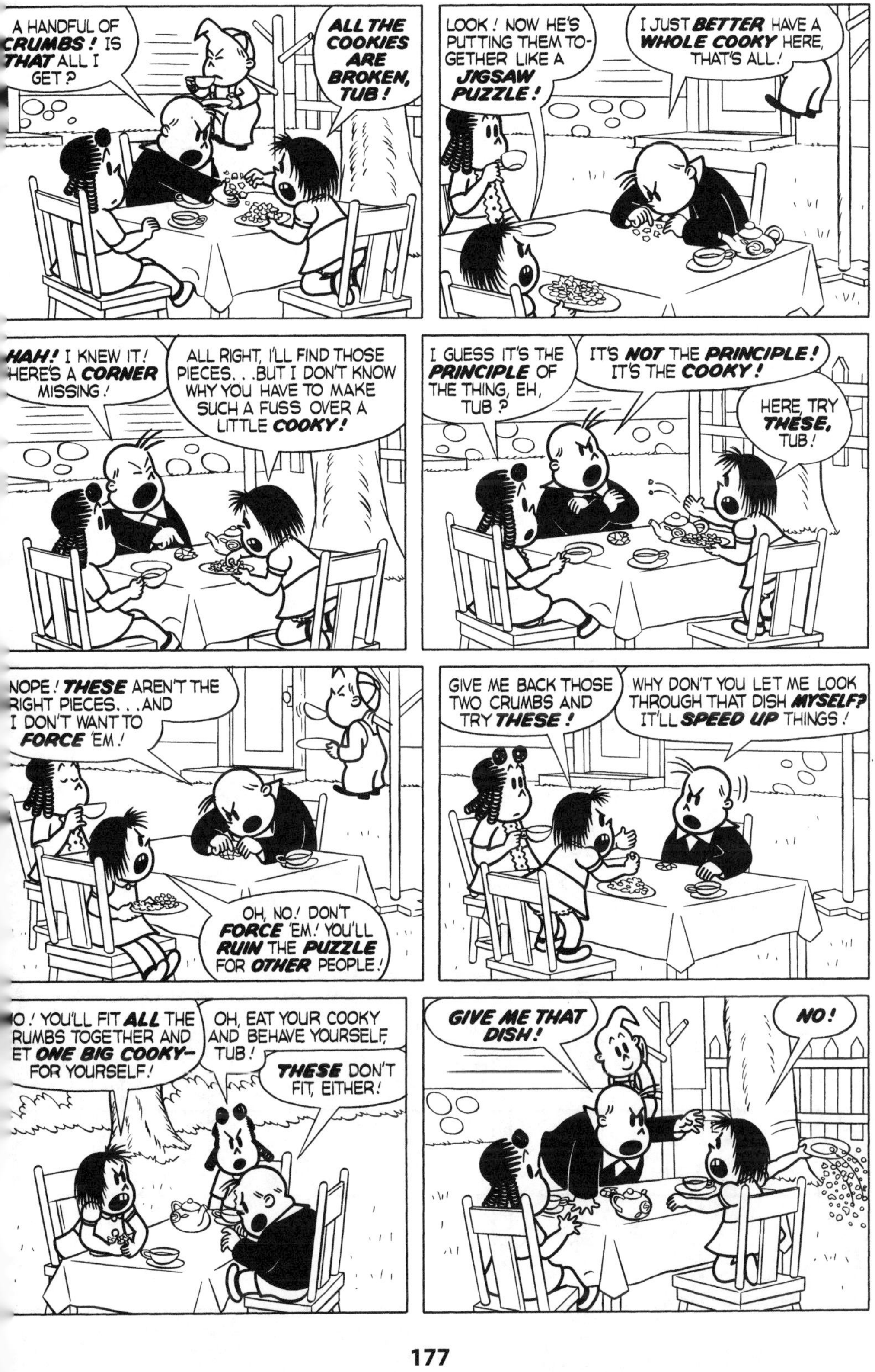
A HANDFUL OF CRUMBS! IS THAT ALL I GET?
ALL THE COOKIES ARE BROKEN, TUB!
LOOK! NOW HE'S PUTTING THEM TOGETHER LIKE A JIGSAW PUZZLE!
I JUST BETTER HAVE A WHOLE COOKY HERE, THAT'S ALL!
HAH! I KNEW IT! HERE'S A CORNER MISSING!
ALL RIGHT, I'LL FIND THOSE PIECES. . .BUT I DON'T KNOW WHY YOU HAVE TO MAKE SUCH A FUSS OVER A LITTLE COOKY!
I GUESS IT'S THE PRINCIPLE OF THE THING, EH, TUB?
IT'S NOT THE PRINCIPLE! IT'S THE COOKY!
HERE, TRY THESE, TUB!
NOPE! THESE AREN'T THE RIGHT PIECES. . .AND I DON'T WANT TO FORCE 'EM!
OH, NO! DON'T FORCE 'EM! YOU'LL RUIN THE PUZZLE FOR OTHER PEOPLE!
GIVE ME BACK THOSE TWO CRUMBS AND TRY THESE!
WHY DON'T YOU LET ME LOOK THROUGH THAT DISH MYSELF? IT'LL SPEED UP THINGS!
O! YOU'LL FIT ALL THE RUMBS TOGETHER AND ET ONE BIG COOKY— FOR YOURSELF!
OH, EAT YOUR COOKY AND BEHAVE YOURSELF, TUB!
THESE DON'T FIT, EITHER!
GIVE ME THAT DISH!
NO!

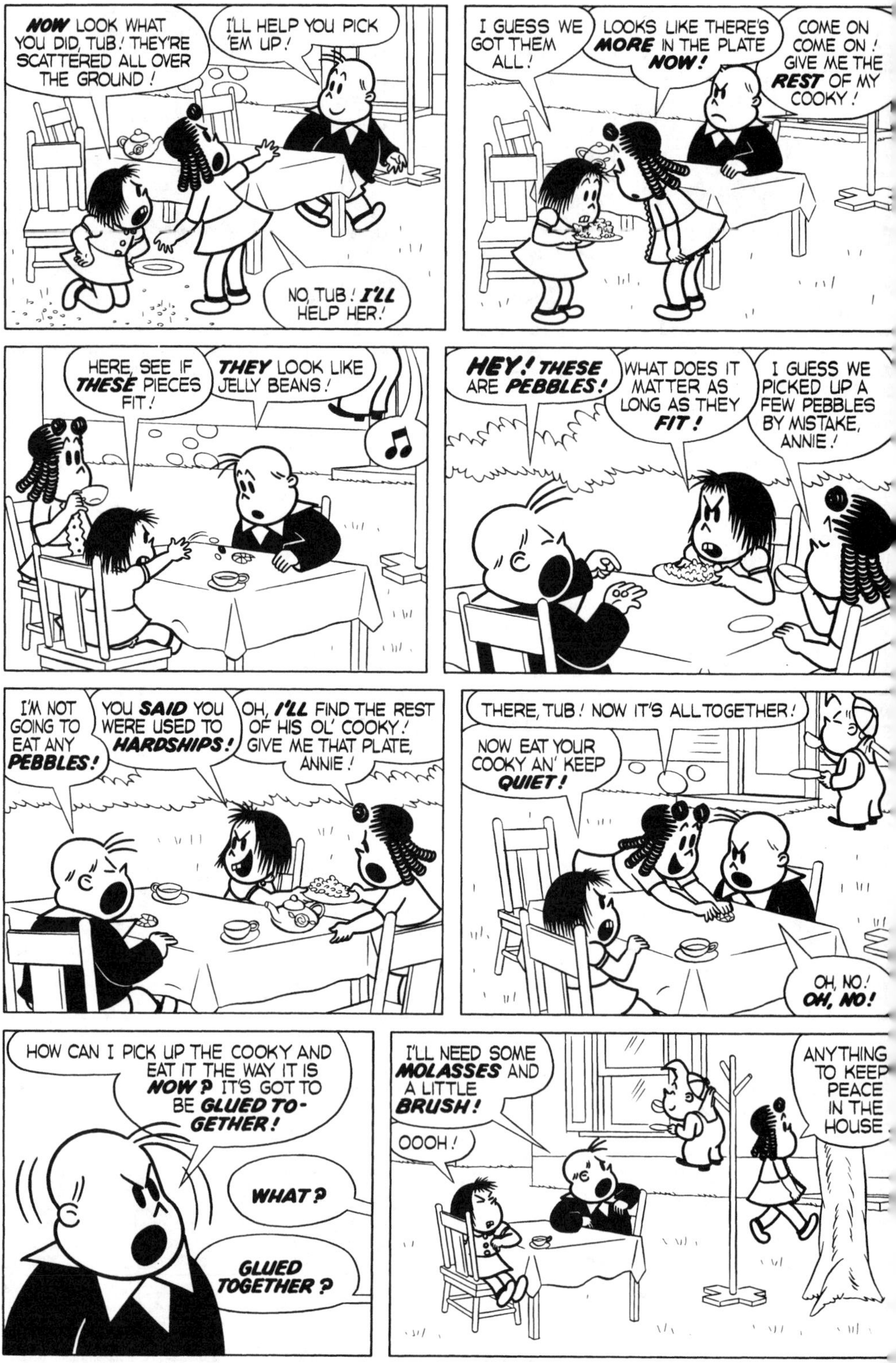
NOW LOOK WHAT YOU DID, TUB! THEY'RE SCATTERED ALL OVER THE GROUND!
I'LL HELP YOU PICK 'EM UP!
NO, TUB! I'LL HELP HER!
I GUESS WE GOT THEM ALL!
LOOKS LIKE THERE'S MORE IN THE PLATE NOW!
COME ON COME ON! GIVE ME THE REST OF MY COOKY!
HERE, SEE IF THESE PIECES FIT!
THEY LOOK LIKE JELLY BEANS!
HEY! THESE ARE PEBBLES!
WHAT DOES IT MATTER AS LONG AS THEY FIT!
I GUESS WE PICKED UP A FEW PEBBLES BY MISTAKE, ANNIE!
I'M NOT GOING TO EAT ANY PEBBLES!
YOU SAID YOU WERE USED TO HARDSHIPS!
OH, I'LL FIND THE REST OF HIS OL' COOKY! GIVE ME THAT PLATE, ANNIE!
THERE, TUB! NOW IT'S ALL TOGETHER!
NOW EAT YOUR COOKY AN' KEEP QUIET!
OH, NO! OH, NO!
HOW CAN I PICK UP THE COOKY AND EAT IT THE WAY IT IS NOW? IT'S GOT TO BE GLUED TO-GETHER!
WHAT?
GLUED TOGETHER?
I'LL NEED SOME MOLASSES AND A LITTLE BRUSH!
OOOH!
ANYTHING TO KEEP PEACE IN THE HOUSE.

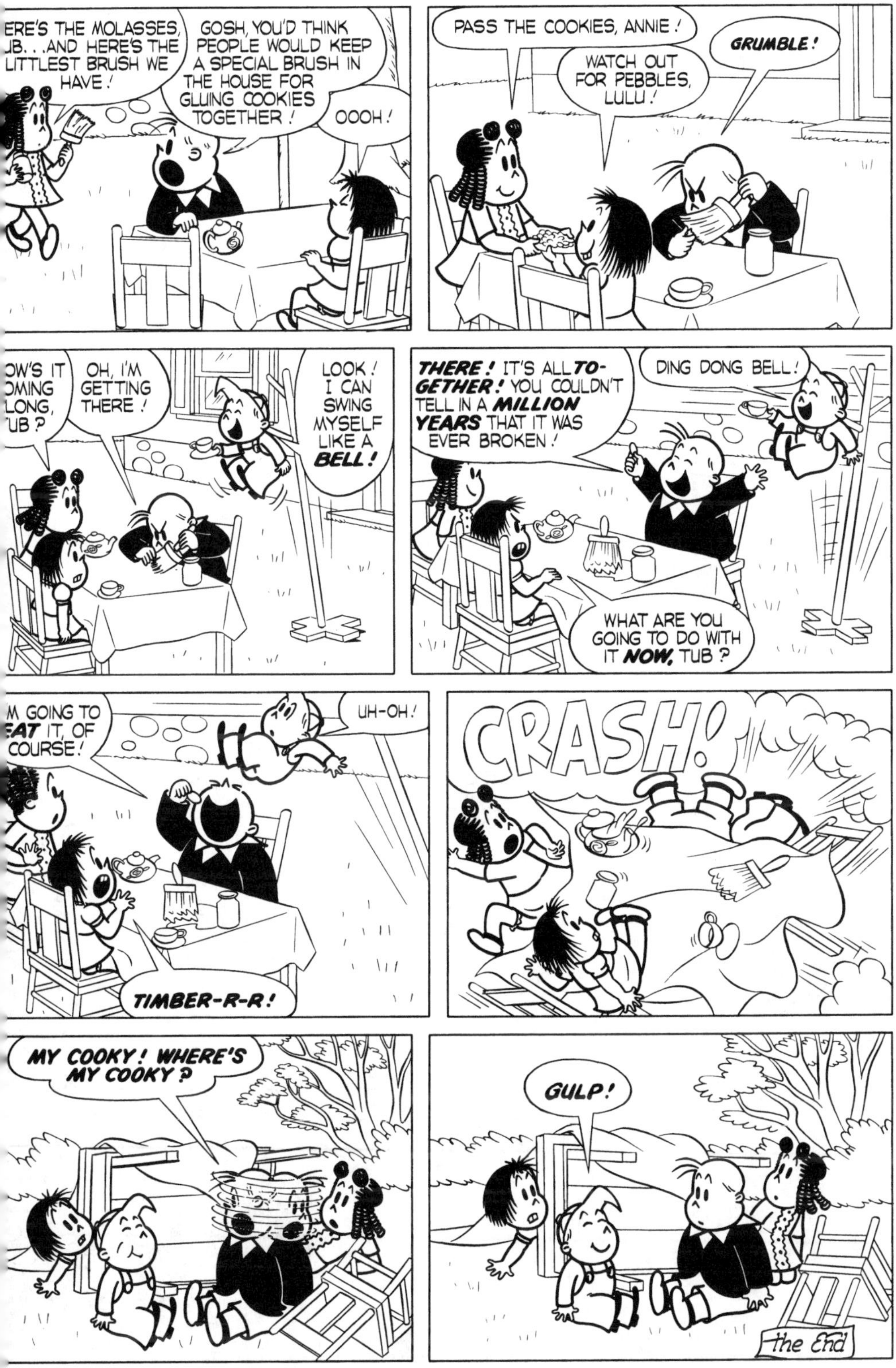

ERE'S THE MOLASSES, JB. . .AND HERE'S THE LITTLEST BRUSH WE HAVE!
GOSH, YOU'D THINK PEOPLE WOULD KEEP A SPECIAL BRUSH IN THE HOUSE FOR GLUING COOKIES TOGETHER!
OOOH!
PASS THE COOKIES, ANNIE!
WATCH OUT FOR PEBBLES, LULU!
GRUMBLE!
OW'S IT OMING LONG, UB?
OH, I'M GETTING THERE!
LOOK! I CAN SWING MYSELF LIKE A BELL!
THERE! IT'S ALL TOGETHER! YOU COULDN'T TELL IN A MILLION YEARS THAT IT WAS EVER BROKEN!
DING DONG BELL!
WHAT ARE YOU GOING TO DO WITH IT NOW, TUB?
M GOING TO EAT IT, OF COURSE!
UH-OH!
TIMBER-R-R!
CRASH!
MY COOKY! WHERE'S MY COOKY?
GULP!
the End

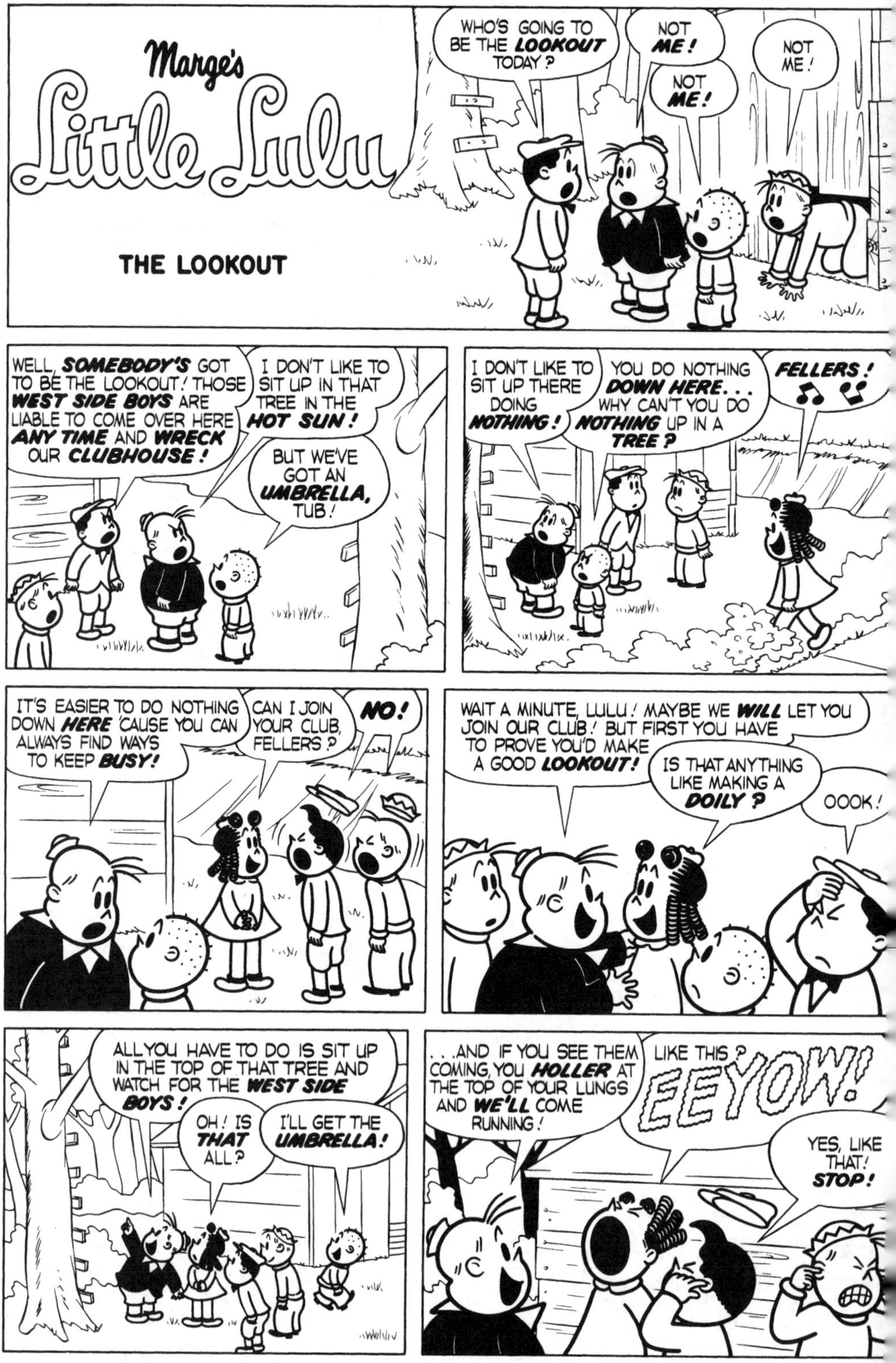
Marge's
Little Lulu
THE LOOKOUT
WHO'S GOING TO BE THE LOOKOUT TODAY?
NOT ME!
NOT ME!
NOT ME!
WELL, SOMEBODY'S GOT TO BE THE LOOKOUT! THOSE WEST SIDE BOYS ARE LIABLE TO COME OVER HERE ANY TIME AND WRECK OUR CLUBHOUSE!
I DON'T LIKE TO SIT UP IN THAT TREE IN THE HOT SUN!
BUT WE'VE GOT AN UMBRELLA, TUB!
I DON'T LIKE TO SIT UP THERE DOING NOTHING!
YOU DO NOTHING DOWN HERE... WHY CAN'T YOU DO NOTHING UP IN A TREE?
FELLERS!
IT'S EASIER TO DO NOTHING DOWN HERE 'CAUSE YOU CAN ALWAYS FIND WAYS TO KEEP BUSY!
CAN I JOIN YOUR CLUB, FELLERS?
NO!
WAIT A MINUTE, LULU! MAYBE WE WILL LET YOU JOIN OUR CLUB! BUT FIRST YOU HAVE TO PROVE YOU'D MAKE A GOOD LOOKOUT!
IS THAT ANYTHING LIKE MAKING A DOILY?
OOOK!
ALL YOU HAVE TO DO IS SIT UP IN THE TOP OF THAT TREE AND WATCH FOR THE WEST SIDE BOYS!
OH! IS THAT ALL?
I'LL GET THE UMBRELLA!
...AND IF YOU SEE THEM COMING, YOU HOLLER AT THE TOP OF YOUR LUNGS AND WE'LL COME RUNNING!
LIKE THIS?
EEYOW!
YES, LIKE THAT! STOP!

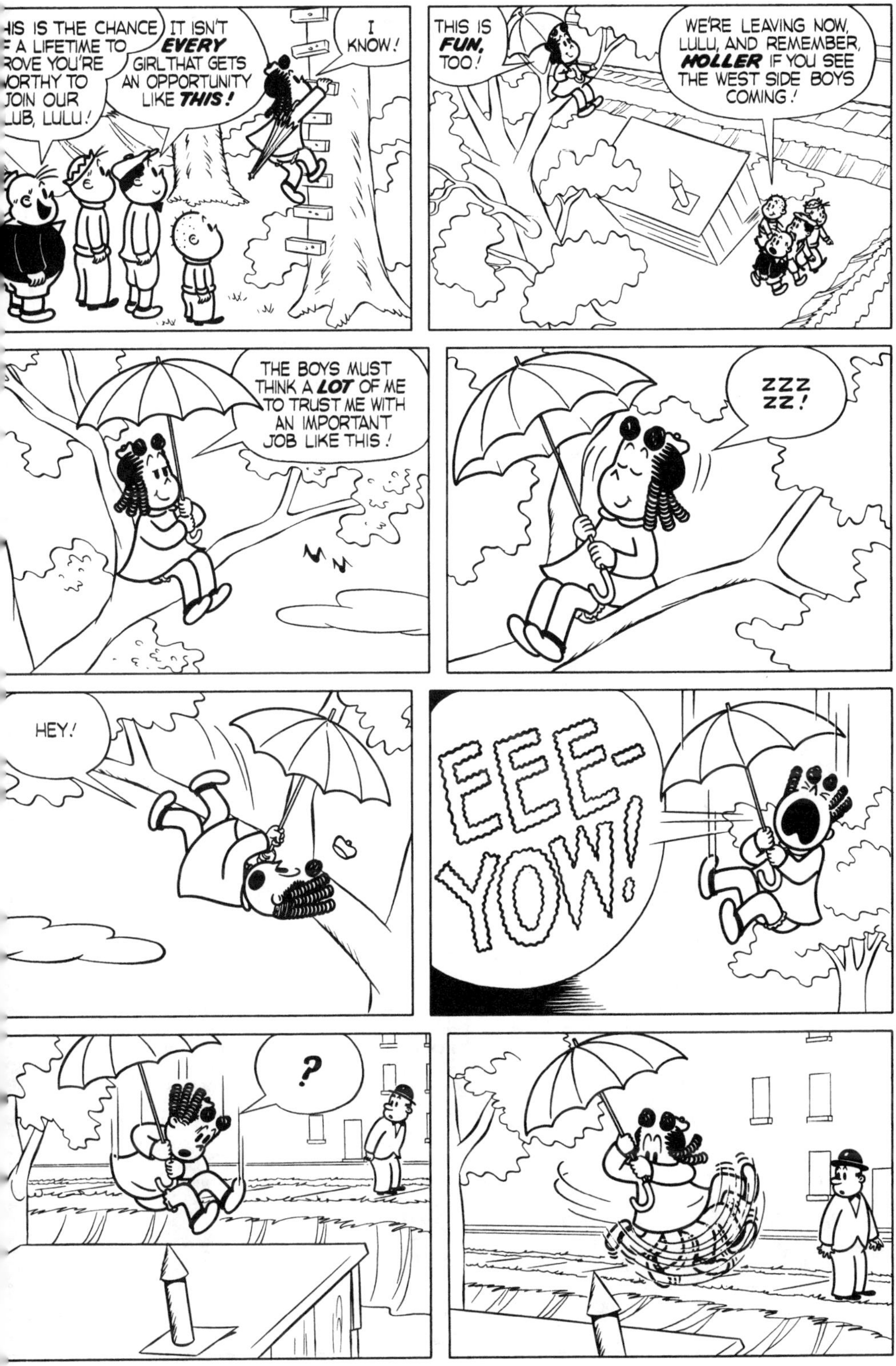

HIS IS THE CHANCE F A LIFETIME TO ROVE YOU'RE ORTHY TO JOIN OUR LUB, LULU!
IT ISN'T EVERY GIRL THAT GETS AN OPPORTUNITY LIKE THIS!
I KNOW!
THIS IS FUN, TOO!
WE'RE LEAVING NOW, LULU, AND REMEMBER, HOLLER IF YOU SEE THE WEST SIDE BOYS COMING!
THE BOYS MUST THINK A LOT OF ME TO TRUST ME WITH AN IMPORTANT JOB LIKE THIS!
ZZZ ZZ!
HEY!
EEE-YOW!
?

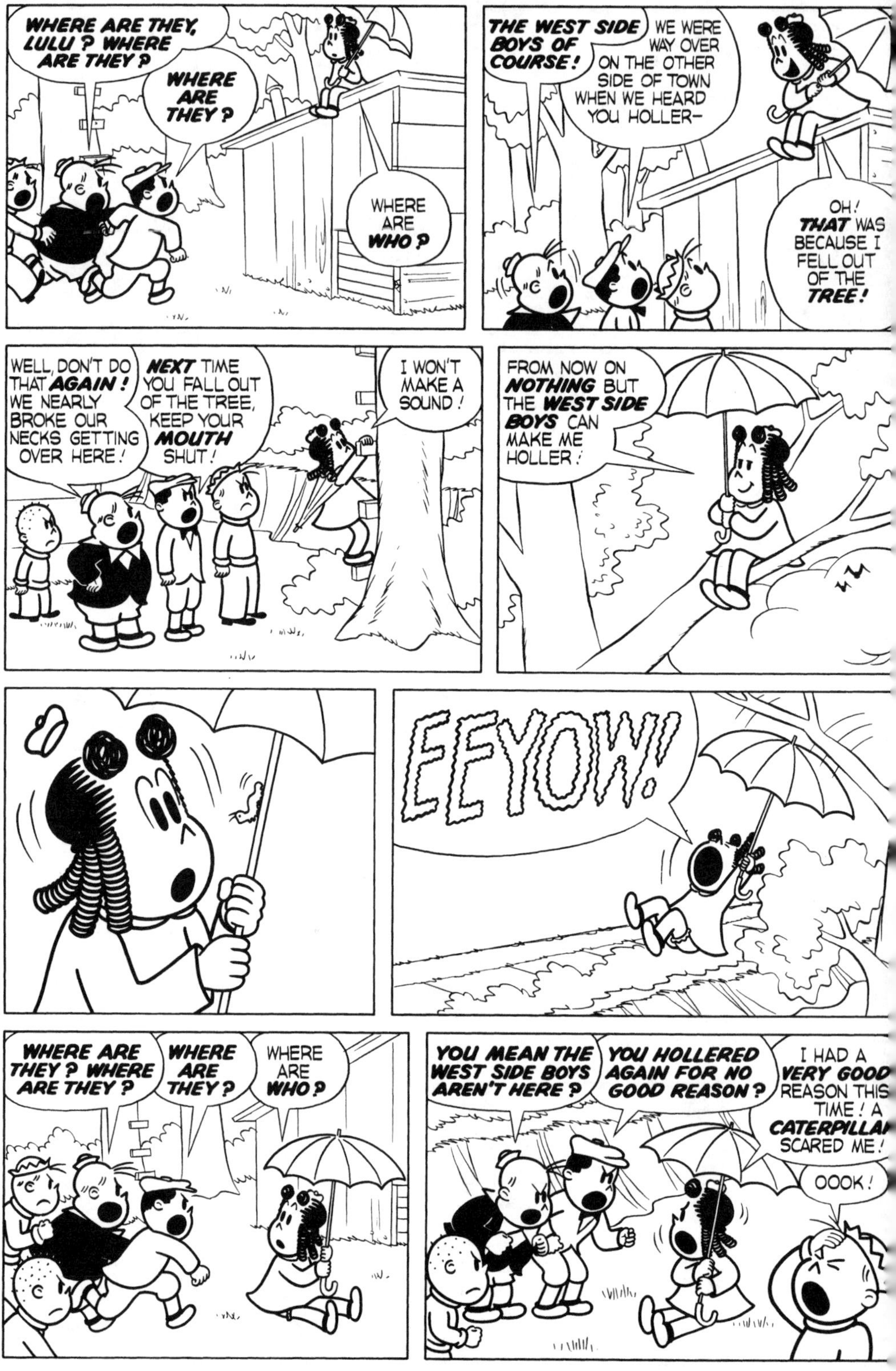
WHERE ARE THEY, LULU ? WHERE ARE THEY ?
WHERE ARE THEY ?
WHERE ARE WHO ?
THE WEST SIDE BOYS OF COURSE !
WE WERE WAY OVER ON THE OTHER SIDE OF TOWN WHEN WE HEARD YOU HOLLER–
OH! THAT WAS BECAUSE I FELL OUT OF THE TREE!
WELL, DON'T DO THAT AGAIN ! WE NEARLY BROKE OUR NECKS GETTING OVER HERE!
NEXT TIME YOU FALL OUT OF THE TREE, KEEP YOUR MOUTH SHUT!
I WON'T MAKE A SOUND!
FROM NOW ON NOTHING BUT THE WEST SIDE BOYS CAN MAKE ME HOLLER!
EEYOW!
WHERE ARE THEY ? WHERE ARE THEY ?
WHERE ARE THEY ?
WHERE ARE WHO ?
YOU MEAN THE WEST SIDE BOYS AREN'T HERE ?
YOU HOLLERED AGAIN FOR NO GOOD REASON ?
I HAD A VERY GOOD REASON THIS TIME! A CATERPILLA SCARED ME!
OOOK!

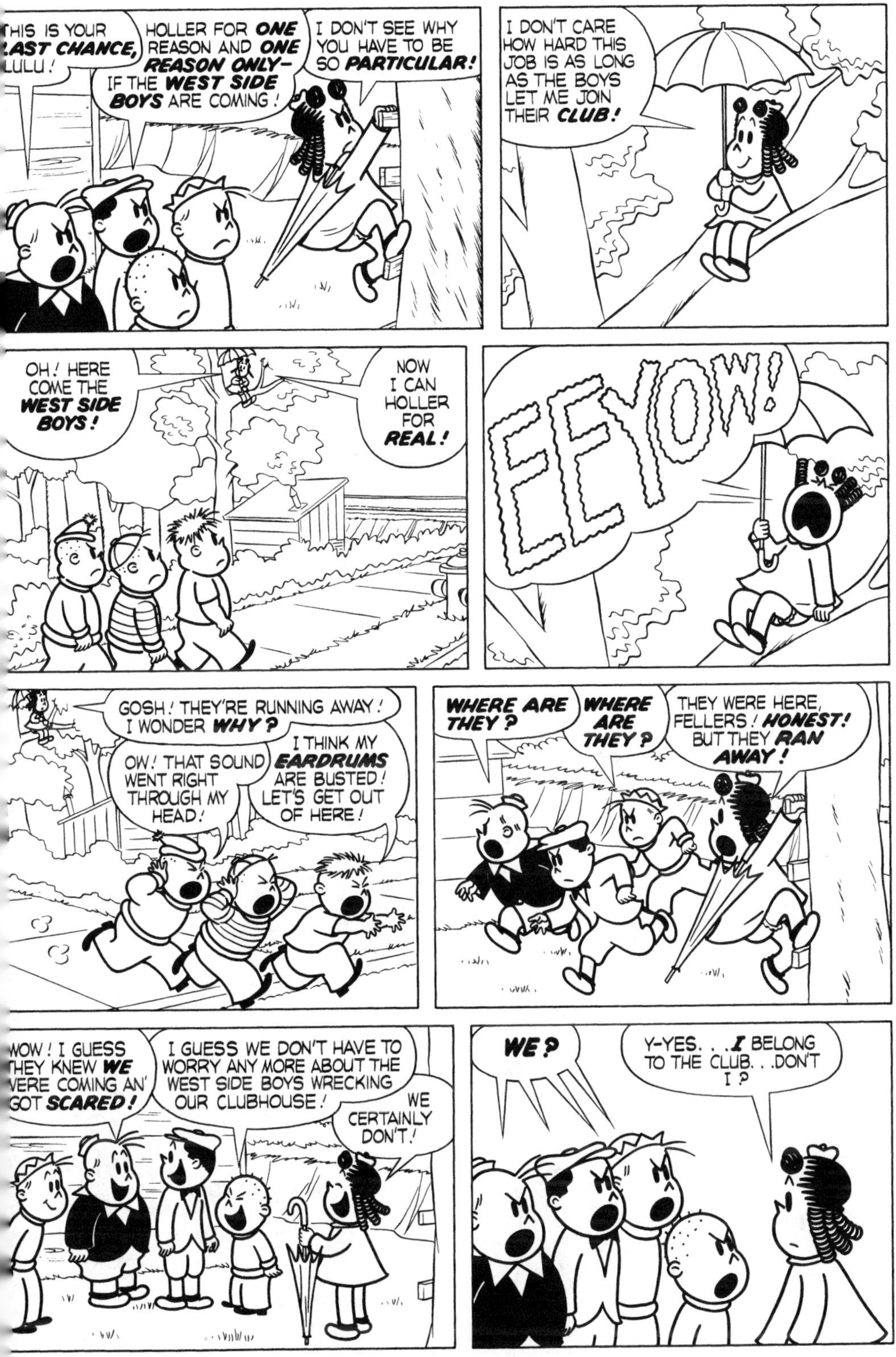

THIS IS YOUR LAST CHANCE, LULU!
HOLLER FOR ONE REASON AND ONE REASON ONLY— IF THE WEST SIDE BOYS ARE COMING!
I DON'T SEE WHY YOU HAVE TO BE SO PARTICULAR!
I DON'T CARE HOW HARD THIS JOB IS AS LONG AS THE BOYS LET ME JOIN THEIR CLUB!
OH! HERE COME THE WEST SIDE BOYS!
NOW I CAN HOLLER FOR REAL!
EEYOW!
GOSH! THEY'RE RUNNING AWAY! I WONDER WHY?
OW! THAT SOUND WENT RIGHT THROUGH MY HEAD!
I THINK MY EARDRUMS ARE BUSTED! LET'S GET OUT OF HERE!
WHERE ARE THEY?
WHERE ARE THEY?
THEY WERE HERE, FELLERS! HONEST! BUT THEY RAN AWAY!
WOW! I GUESS THEY KNEW WE WERE COMING AN' GOT SCARED!
I GUESS WE DON'T HAVE TO WORRY ANY MORE ABOUT THE WEST SIDE BOYS WRECKING OUR CLUBHOUSE!
WE CERTAINLY DON'T!
WE?
Y-YES. . .I BELONG TO THE CLUB. . .DON'T I?

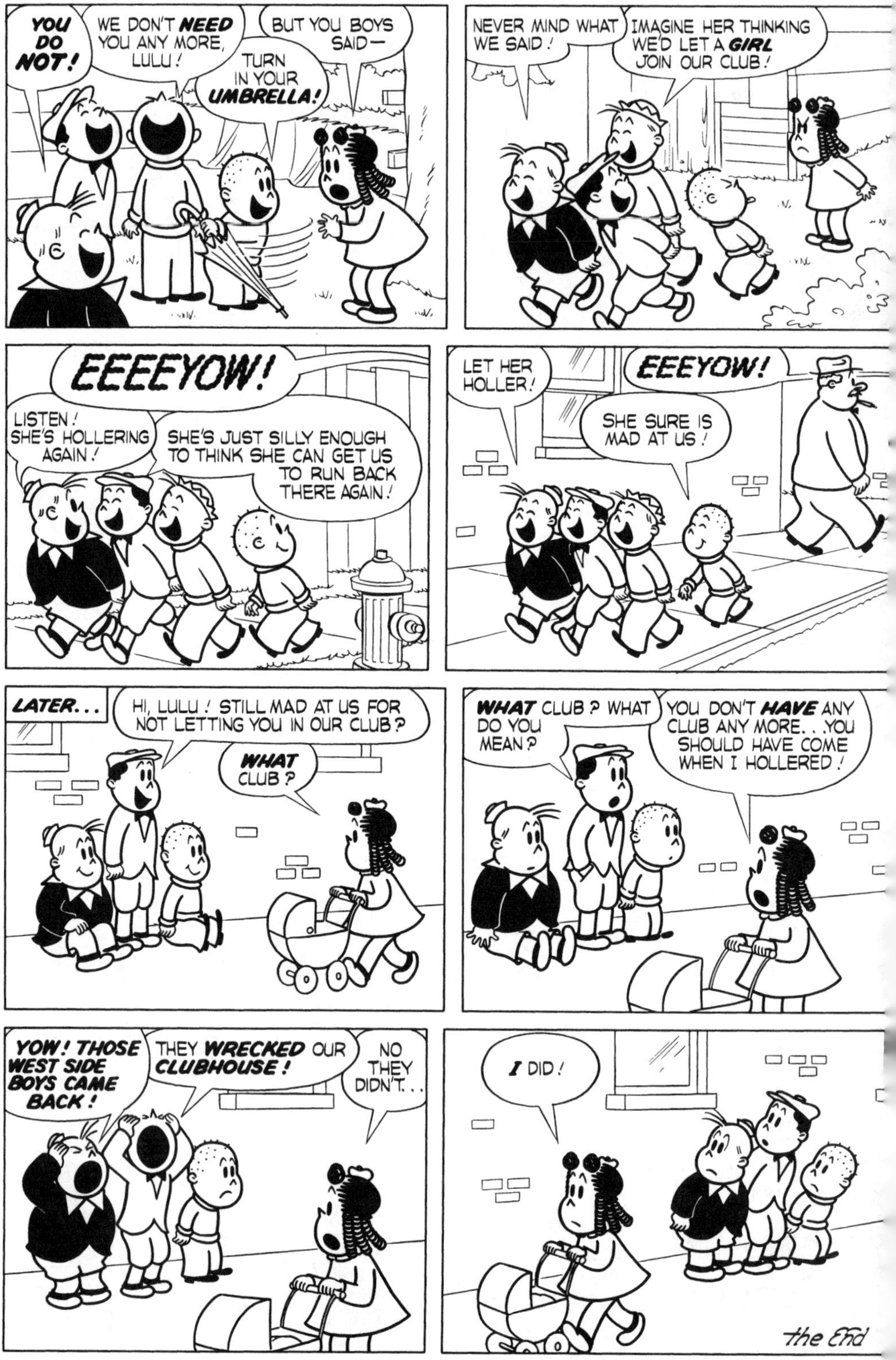
YOU DO NOT!
WE DON'T NEED YOU ANY MORE, LULU!
BUT YOU BOYS SAID—
TURN IN YOUR UMBRELLA!
NEVER MIND WHAT WE SAID!
IMAGINE HER THINKING WE'D LET A GIRL JOIN OUR CLUB!
EEEEYOW!
LISTEN! SHE'S HOLLERING AGAIN!
SHE'S JUST SILLY ENOUGH TO THINK SHE CAN GET US TO RUN BACK THERE AGAIN!
LET HER HOLLER!
EEEYOW!
SHE SURE IS MAD AT US!
LATER...
HI, LULU! STILL MAD AT US FOR NOT LETTING YOU IN OUR CLUB?
WHAT CLUB?
WHAT CLUB? WHAT DO YOU MEAN?
YOU DON'T HAVE ANY CLUB ANY MORE...YOU SHOULD HAVE COME WHEN I HOLLERED!
YOW! THOSE WEST SIDE BOYS CAME BACK!
THEY WRECKED OUR CLUBHOUSE!
NO THEY DIDN'T...
I DID!
the End

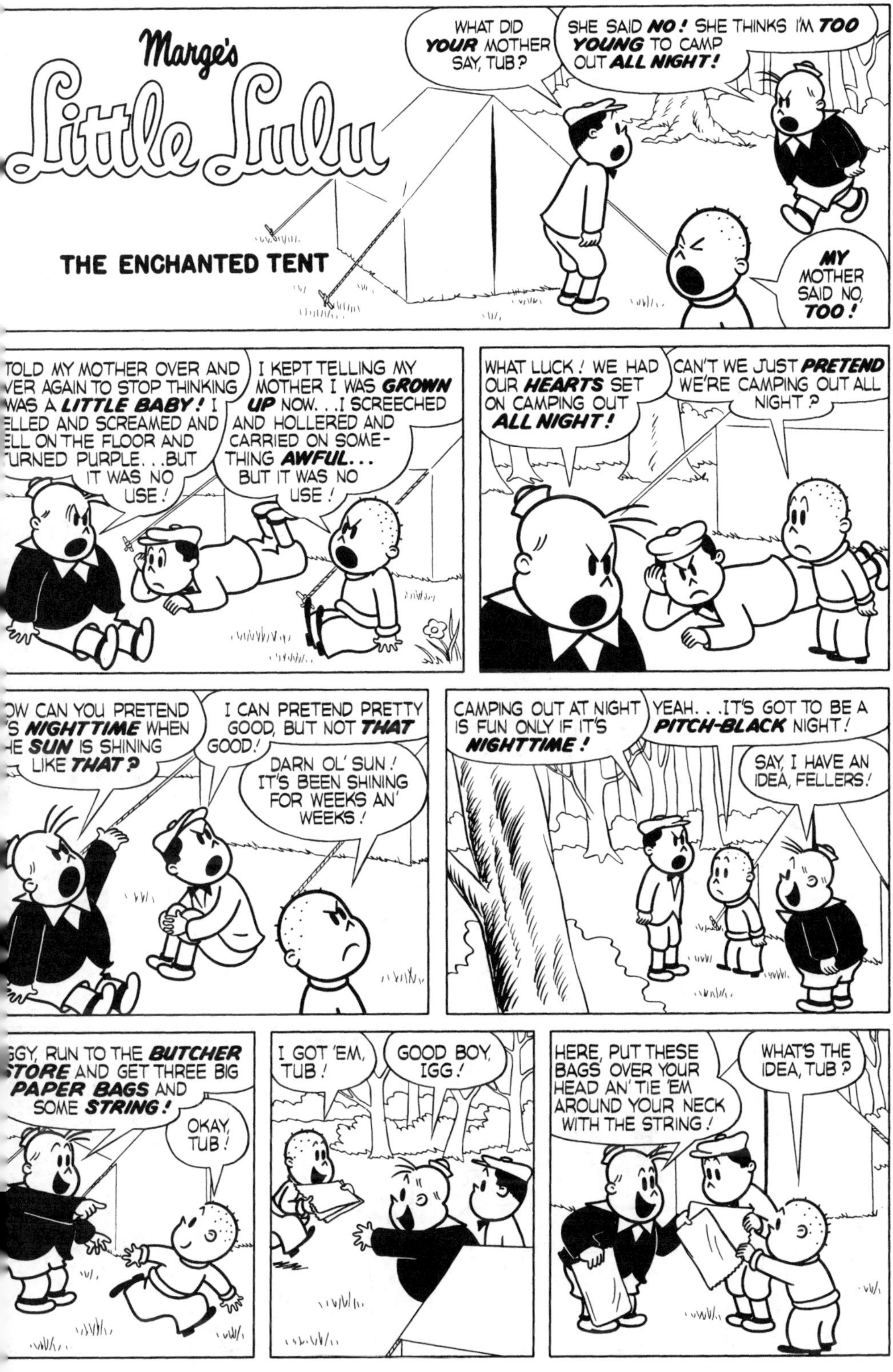
Marge's Little Lulu
THE ENCHANTED TENT
WHAT DID YOUR MOTHER SAY, TUB?
SHE SAID NO! SHE THINKS I'M TOO YOUNG TO CAMP OUT ALL NIGHT!
MY MOTHER SAID NO, TOO!
TOLD MY MOTHER OVER AND VER AGAIN TO STOP THINKING WAS A LITTLE BABY! I ELLED AND SCREAMED AND ELL ON THE FLOOR AND URNED PURPLE. . .BUT IT WAS NO USE!
I KEPT TELLING MY MOTHER I WAS GROWN UP NOW. . .I SCREECHED AND HOLLERED AND CARRIED ON SOME-THING AWFUL. . . BUT IT WAS NO USE!
WHAT LUCK! WE HAD OUR HEARTS SET ON CAMPING OUT ALL NIGHT!
CAN'T WE JUST PRETEND WE'RE CAMPING OUT ALL NIGHT?
OW CAN YOU PRETEND 'S NIGHTTIME WHEN HE SUN IS SHINING LIKE THAT?
I CAN PRETEND PRETTY GOOD, BUT NOT THAT GOOD!
DARN OL' SUN! IT'S BEEN SHINING FOR WEEKS AN' WEEKS!
CAMPING OUT AT NIGHT IS FUN ONLY IF IT'S NIGHTTIME!
YEAH. . .IT'S GOT TO BE A PITCH-BLACK NIGHT!
SAY, I HAVE AN IDEA, FELLERS!
GGY, RUN TO THE BUTCHER STORE AND GET THREE BIG PAPER BAGS AND SOME STRING!
OKAY, TUB!
I GOT 'EM, TUB!
GOOD BOY, IGG!
HERE, PUT THESE BAGS OVER YOUR HEAD AN' TIE 'EM AROUND YOUR NECK WITH THE STRING!
WHAT'S THE IDEA, TUB?

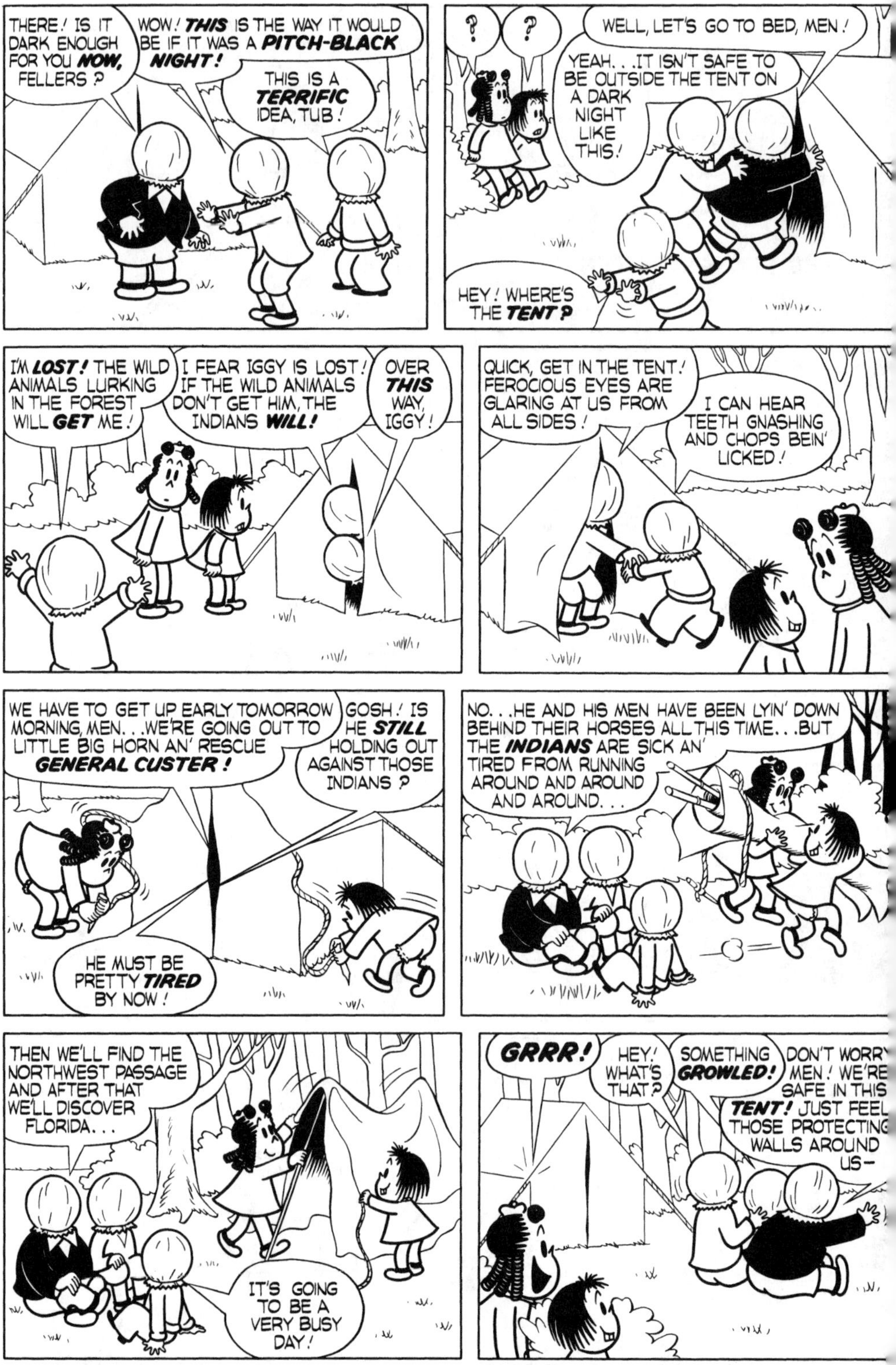
THERE! IS IT DARK ENOUGH FOR YOU NOW, FELLERS?
WOW! THIS IS THE WAY IT WOULD BE IF IT WAS A PITCH-BLACK NIGHT!
THIS IS A TERRIFIC IDEA, TUB!
?
?
WELL, LET'S GO TO BED, MEN!
YEAH. . .IT ISN'T SAFE TO BE OUTSIDE THE TENT ON A DARK NIGHT LIKE THIS!
HEY! WHERE'S THE TENT?
I'M LOST! THE WILD ANIMALS LURKING IN THE FOREST WILL GET ME!
I FEAR IGGY IS LOST! IF THE WILD ANIMALS DON'T GET HIM, THE INDIANS WILL!
OVER THIS WAY, IGGY!
QUICK, GET IN THE TENT! FEROCIOUS EYES ARE GLARING AT US FROM ALL SIDES!
I CAN HEAR TEETH GNASHING AND CHOPS BEIN' LICKED!
WE HAVE TO GET UP EARLY TOMORROW MORNING, MEN. . .WE'RE GOING OUT TO LITTLE BIG HORN AN' RESCUE GENERAL CUSTER!
GOSH! IS HE STILL HOLDING OUT AGAINST THOSE INDIANS?
HE MUST BE PRETTY TIRED BY NOW!
NO. . .HE AND HIS MEN HAVE BEEN LYIN' DOWN BEHIND THEIR HORSES ALL THIS TIME. . .BUT THE INDIANS ARE SICK AN' TIRED FROM RUNNING AROUND AND AROUND AND AROUND. . .
THEN WE'LL FIND THE NORTHWEST PASSAGE AND AFTER THAT WE'LL DISCOVER FLORIDA. . .
IT'S GOING TO BE A VERY BUSY DAY!
GRRR!
HEY! WHAT'S THAT?
SOMETHING GROWLED!
DON'T WORRY MEN! WE'RE SAFE IN THIS TENT! JUST FEEL THOSE PROTECTING WALLS AROUND US—

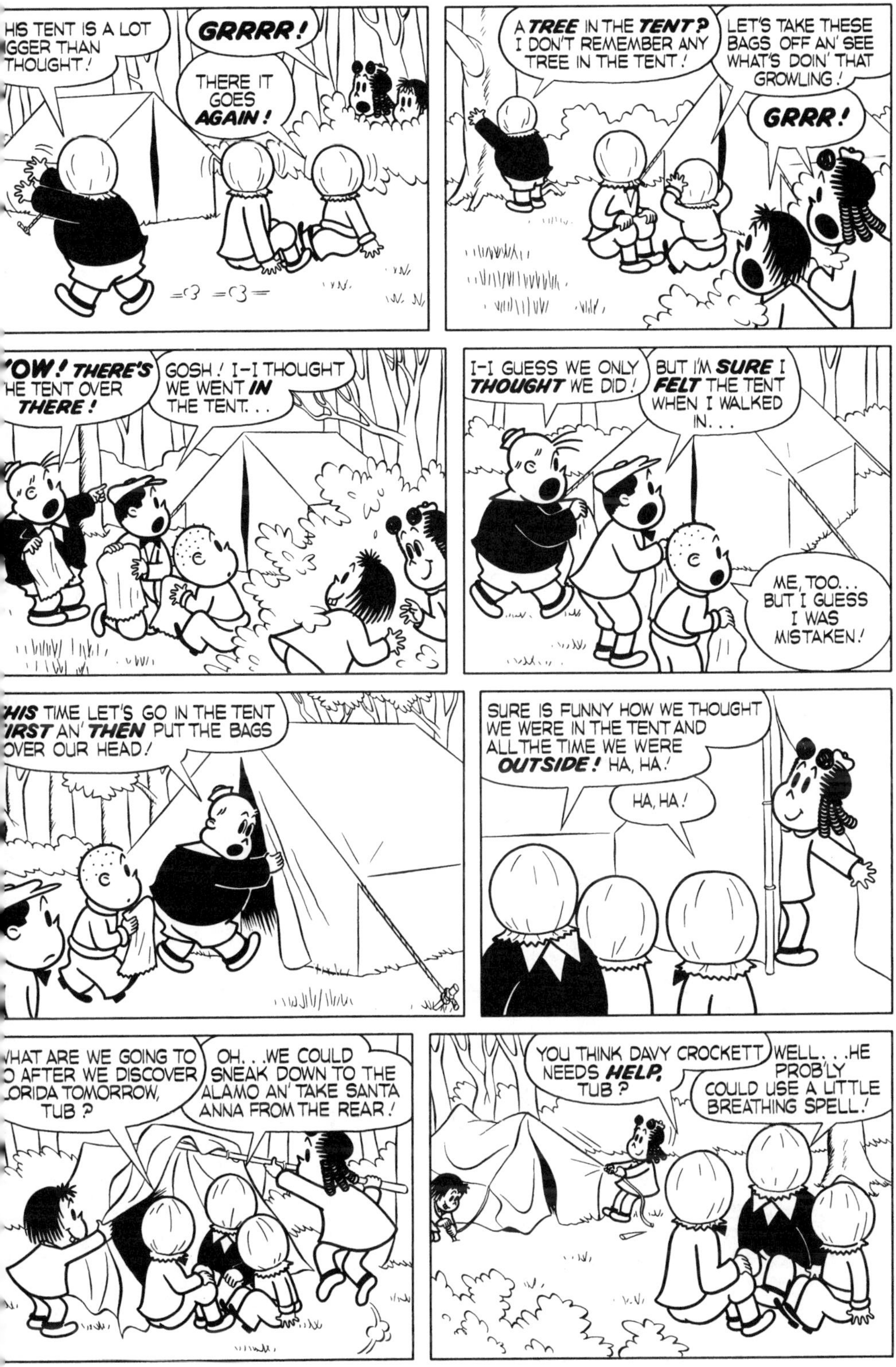
HIS TENT IS A LOT
GGER THAN
THOUGHT!
GRRRR!
THERE IT GOES AGAIN!
A TREE IN THE TENT? I DON'T REMEMBER ANY TREE IN THE TENT!
LET'S TAKE THESE BAGS OFF AN' SEE WHAT'S DOIN' THAT GROWLING!
GRRR!
'OW! THERE'S HE TENT OVER THERE!
GOSH! I-I THOUGHT WE WENT IN THE TENT...
I-I GUESS WE ONLY THOUGHT WE DID!
BUT I'M SURE I FELT THE TENT WHEN I WALKED IN...
ME, TOO... BUT I GUESS I WAS MISTAKEN!
HIS TIME LET'S GO IN THE TENT IRST AN' THEN PUT THE BAGS OVER OUR HEAD!
SURE IS FUNNY HOW WE THOUGHT WE WERE IN THE TENT AND ALL THE TIME WE WERE OUTSIDE! HA, HA!
HA, HA!
VHAT ARE WE GOING TO O AFTER WE DISCOVER LORIDA TOMORROW, TUB?
OH...WE COULD SNEAK DOWN TO THE ALAMO AN' TAKE SANTA ANNA FROM THE REAR!
YOU THINK DAVY CROCKETT NEEDS HELP, TUB?
WELL...HE PROB'LY COULD USE A LITTLE BREATHING SPELL!

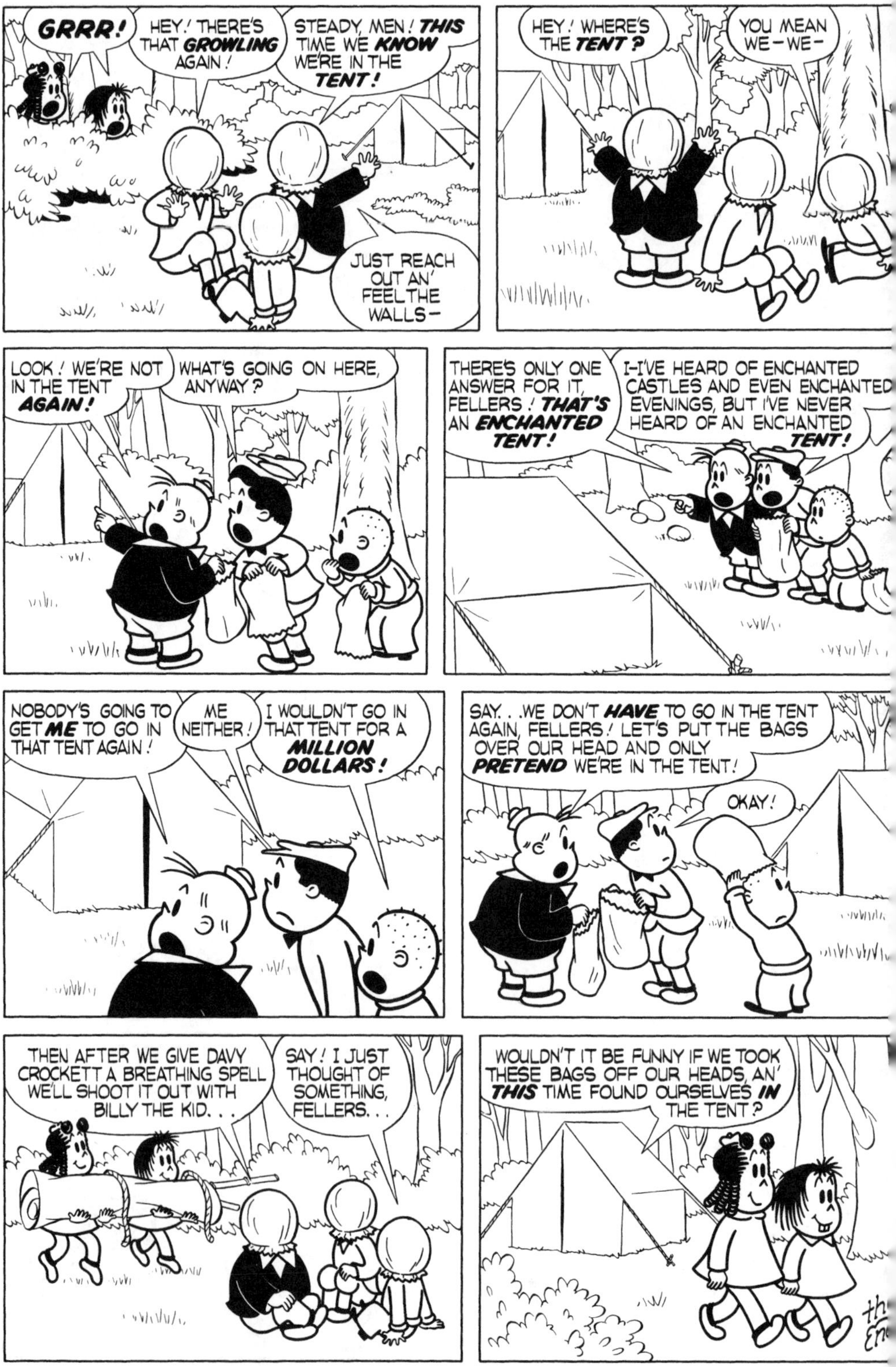
GRRR!
HEY! THERE'S THAT GROWLING AGAIN!
STEADY, MEN! THIS TIME WE KNOW WE'RE IN THE TENT!
JUST REACH OUT AN' FEEL THE WALLS—
HEY! WHERE'S THE TENT?
YOU MEAN WE—WE—
LOOK! WE'RE NOT IN THE TENT AGAIN!
WHAT'S GOING ON HERE, ANYWAY?
THERE'S ONLY ONE ANSWER FOR IT, FELLERS! THAT'S AN ENCHANTED TENT!
I-I'VE HEARD OF ENCHANTED CASTLES AND EVEN ENCHANTED EVENINGS, BUT I'VE NEVER HEARD OF AN ENCHANTED TENT!
NOBODY'S GOING TO GET ME TO GO IN THAT TENT AGAIN!
ME NEITHER!
I WOULDN'T GO IN THAT TENT FOR A MILLION DOLLARS!
SAY...WE DON'T HAVE TO GO IN THE TENT AGAIN, FELLERS! LET'S PUT THE BAGS OVER OUR HEAD AND ONLY PRETEND WE'RE IN THE TENT!
OKAY!
THEN AFTER WE GIVE DAVY CROCKETT A BREATHING SPELL WE'LL SHOOT IT OUT WITH BILLY THE KID...
SAY! I JUST THOUGHT OF SOMETHING, FELLERS...
WOULDN'T IT BE FUNNY IF WE TOOK THESE BAGS OFF OUR HEADS, AN' THIS TIME FOUND OURSELVES IN THE TENT?

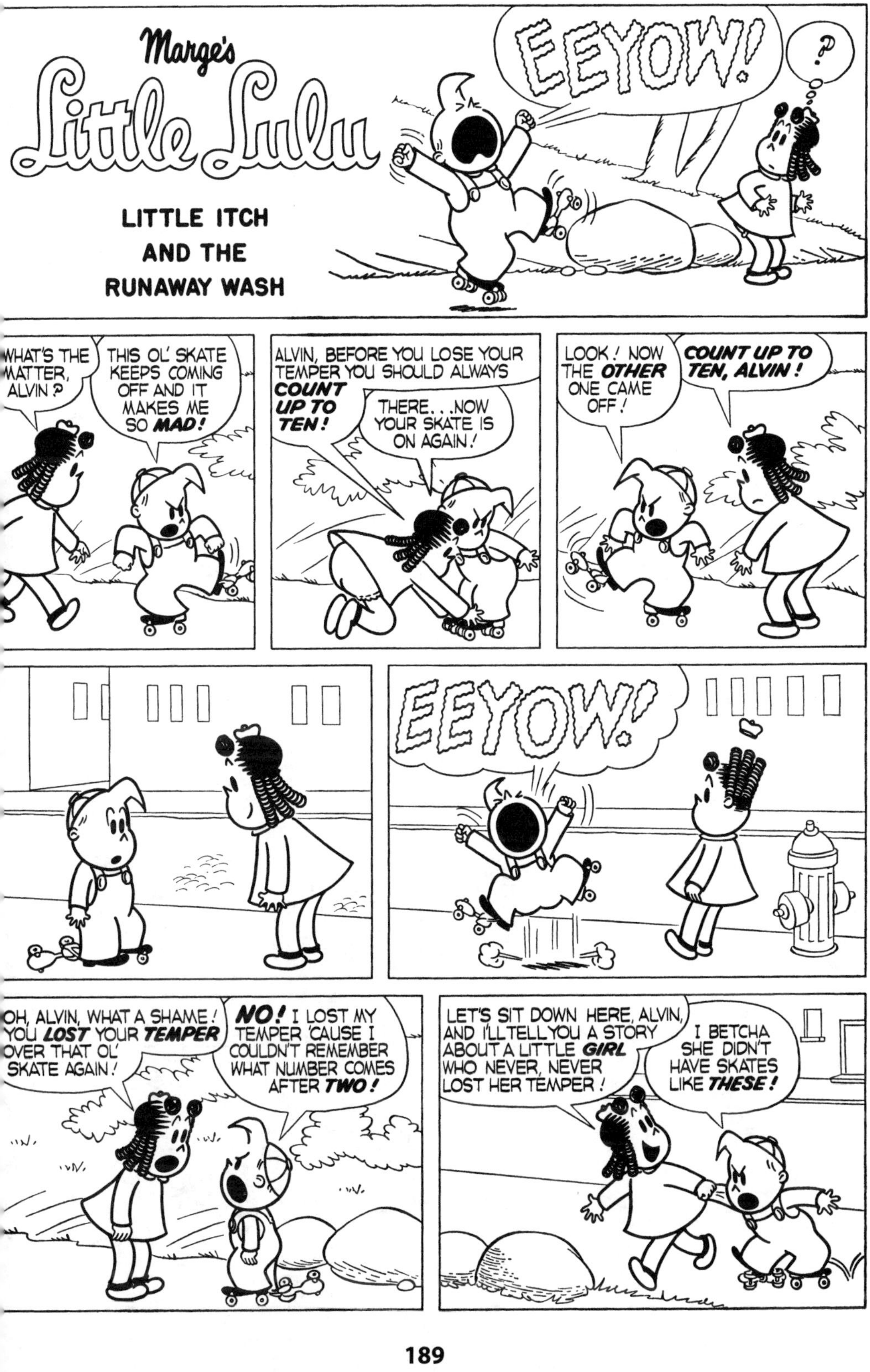
Marge's Little Lulu
LITTLE ITCH AND THE RUNAWAY WASH
EEYOW!
?
WHAT'S THE MATTER, ALVIN?
THIS OL' SKATE KEEPS COMING OFF AND IT MAKES ME SO MAD!
ALVIN, BEFORE YOU LOSE YOUR TEMPER YOU SHOULD ALWAYS COUNT UP TO TEN!
THERE...NOW YOUR SKATE IS ON AGAIN!
LOOK! NOW THE OTHER ONE CAME OFF!
COUNT UP TO TEN, ALVIN!
EEYOW!
OH, ALVIN, WHAT A SHAME! YOU LOST YOUR TEMPER OVER THAT OL' SKATE AGAIN!
NO! I LOST MY TEMPER 'CAUSE I COULDN'T REMEMBER WHAT NUMBER COMES AFTER TWO!
LET'S SIT DOWN HERE, ALVIN, AND I'LL TELL YOU A STORY ABOUT A LITTLE GIRL WHO NEVER, NEVER LOST HER TEMPER!
I BETCHA SHE DIDN'T HAVE SKATES LIKE THESE!

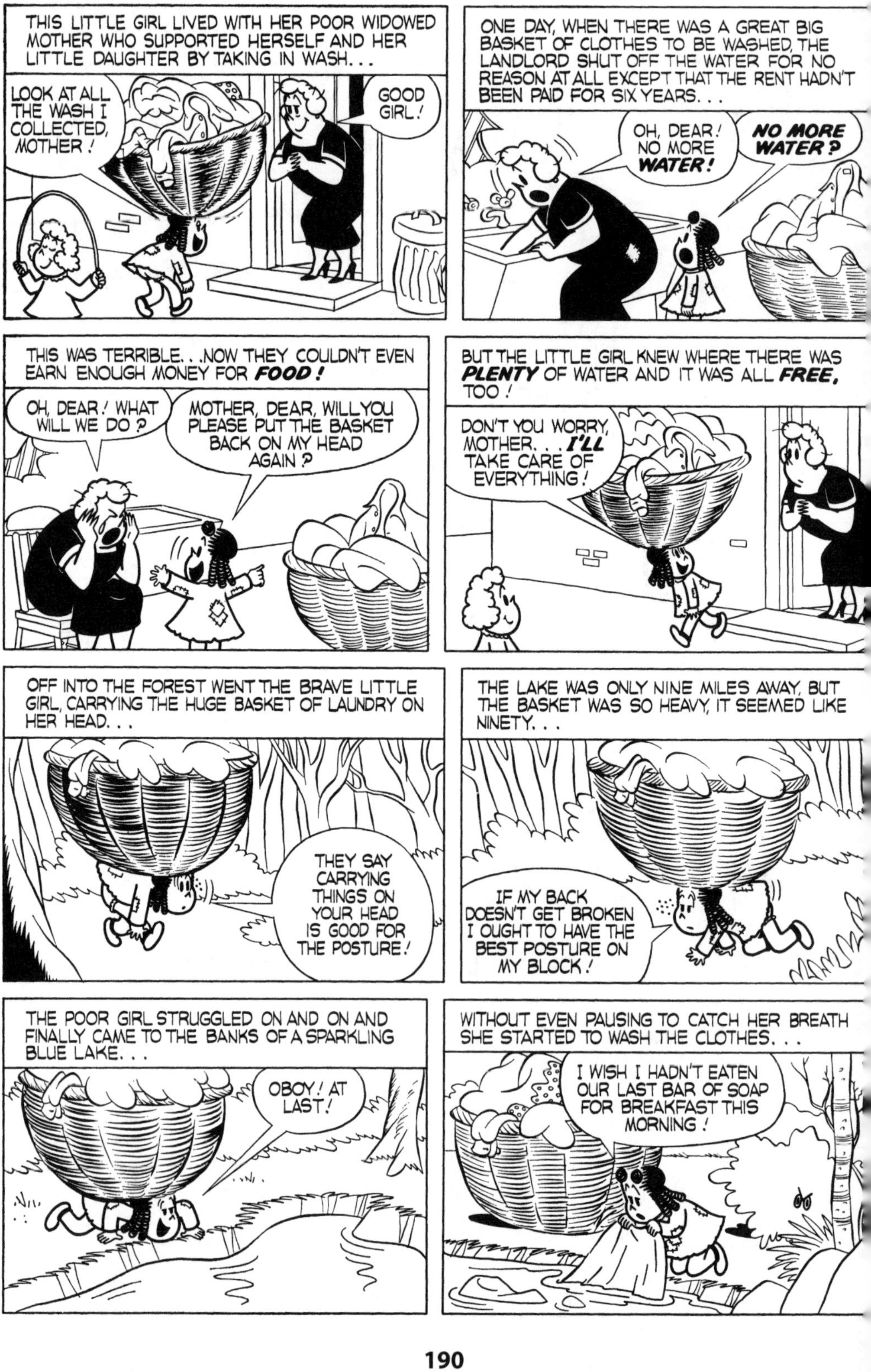
THIS LITTLE GIRL LIVED WITH HER POOR WIDOWED MOTHER WHO SUPPORTED HERSELF AND HER LITTLE DAUGHTER BY TAKING IN WASH...
LOOK AT ALL THE WASH I COLLECTED, MOTHER!
GOOD GIRL!
ONE DAY, WHEN THERE WAS A GREAT BIG BASKET OF CLOTHES TO BE WASHED, THE LANDLORD SHUT OFF THE WATER FOR NO REASON AT ALL EXCEPT THAT THE RENT HADN'T BEEN PAID FOR SIX YEARS...
OH, DEAR! NO MORE **WATER!**
NO MORE WATER?
THIS WAS TERRIBLE...NOW THEY COULDN'T EVEN EARN ENOUGH MONEY FOR **FOOD!**
OH, DEAR! WHAT WILL WE DO?
MOTHER, DEAR, WILL YOU PLEASE PUT THE BASKET BACK ON MY HEAD AGAIN?
BUT THE LITTLE GIRL KNEW WHERE THERE WAS **PLENTY** OF WATER AND IT WAS ALL **FREE,** TOO!
DON'T YOU WORRY, MOTHER...**I'LL** TAKE CARE OF EVERYTHING!
OFF INTO THE FOREST WENT THE BRAVE LITTLE GIRL, CARRYING THE HUGE BASKET OF LAUNDRY ON HER HEAD...
THEY SAY CARRYING THINGS ON YOUR HEAD IS GOOD FOR THE POSTURE!
THE LAKE WAS ONLY NINE MILES AWAY, BUT THE BASKET WAS SO HEAVY, IT SEEMED LIKE NINETY...
IF MY BACK DOESN'T GET BROKEN I OUGHT TO HAVE THE BEST POSTURE ON MY BLOCK!
THE POOR GIRL STRUGGLED ON AND ON AND FINALLY CAME TO THE BANKS OF A SPARKLING BLUE LAKE...
OBOY! AT LAST!
WITHOUT EVEN PAUSING TO CATCH HER BREATH SHE STARTED TO WASH THE CLOTHES...
I WISH I HADN'T EATEN OUR LAST BAR OF SOAP FOR BREAKFAST THIS MORNING!

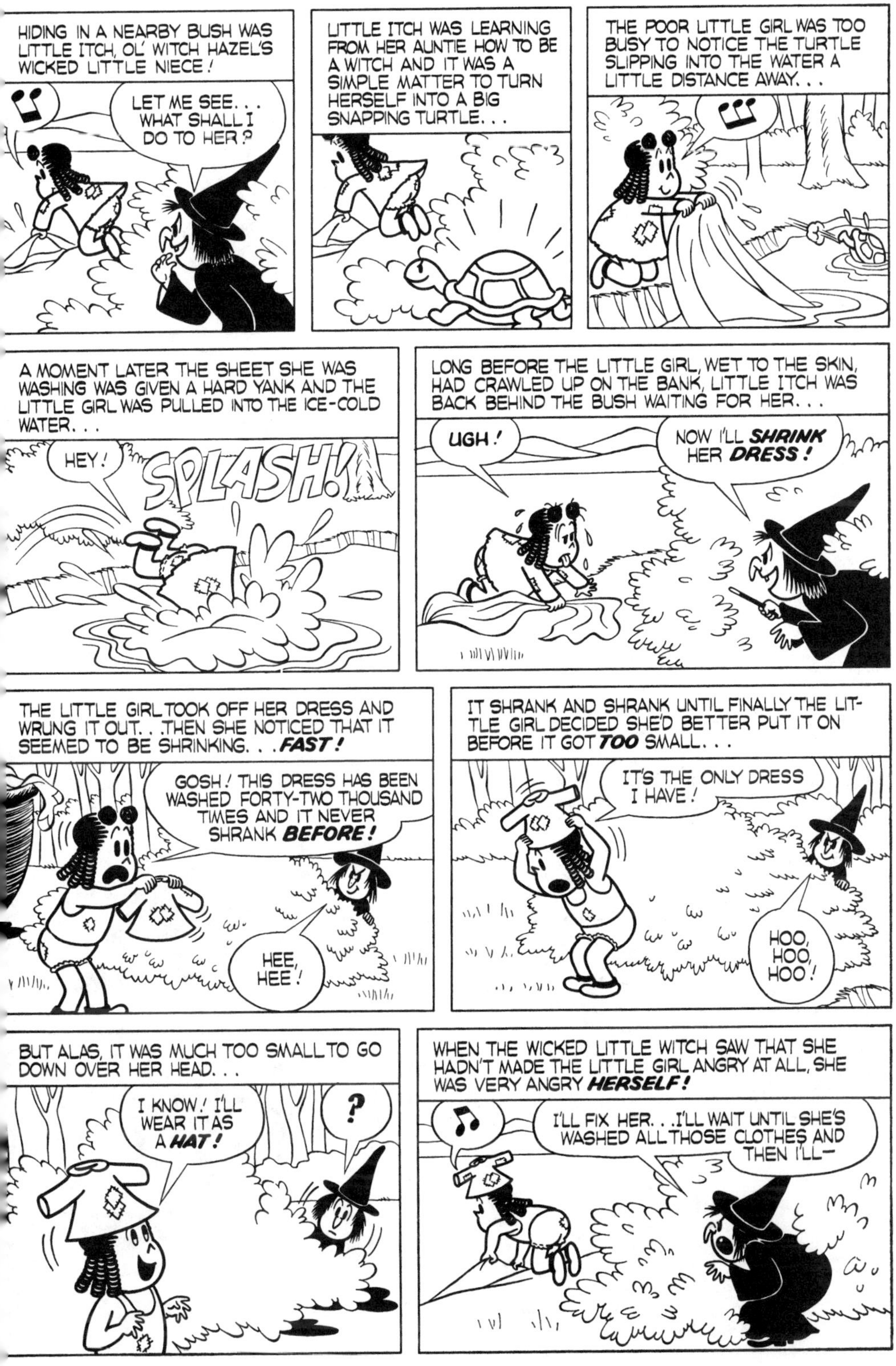
HIDING IN A NEARBY BUSH WAS LITTLE ITCH, OL' WITCH HAZEL'S WICKED LITTLE NIECE!
LET ME SEE... WHAT SHALL I DO TO HER?
LITTLE ITCH WAS LEARNING FROM HER AUNTIE HOW TO BE A WITCH AND IT WAS A SIMPLE MATTER TO TURN HERSELF INTO A BIG SNAPPING TURTLE...
THE POOR LITTLE GIRL WAS TOO BUSY TO NOTICE THE TURTLE SLIPPING INTO THE WATER A LITTLE DISTANCE AWAY...
A MOMENT LATER THE SHEET SHE WAS WASHING WAS GIVEN A HARD YANK AND THE LITTLE GIRL WAS PULLED INTO THE ICE-COLD WATER...
HEY!
SPLASH!
LONG BEFORE THE LITTLE GIRL, WET TO THE SKIN, HAD CRAWLED UP ON THE BANK, LITTLE ITCH WAS BACK BEHIND THE BUSH WAITING FOR HER...
UGH!
NOW I'LL SHRINK HER DRESS!
THE LITTLE GIRL TOOK OFF HER DRESS AND WRUNG IT OUT...THEN SHE NOTICED THAT IT SEEMED TO BE SHRINKING...FAST!
GOSH! THIS DRESS HAS BEEN WASHED FORTY-TWO THOUSAND TIMES AND IT NEVER SHRANK BEFORE!
HEE, HEE!
IT SHRANK AND SHRANK UNTIL FINALLY THE LITTLE GIRL DECIDED SHE'D BETTER PUT IT ON BEFORE IT GOT TOO SMALL...
IT'S THE ONLY DRESS I HAVE!
HOO, HOO, HOO!
BUT ALAS, IT WAS MUCH TOO SMALL TO GO DOWN OVER HER HEAD...
I KNOW! I'LL WEAR IT AS A HAT!
?
WHEN THE WICKED LITTLE WITCH SAW THAT SHE HADN'T MADE THE LITTLE GIRL ANGRY AT ALL, SHE WAS VERY ANGRY HERSELF!
I'LL FIX HER...I'LL WAIT UNTIL SHE'S WASHED ALL THOSE CLOTHES AND THEN I'LL—

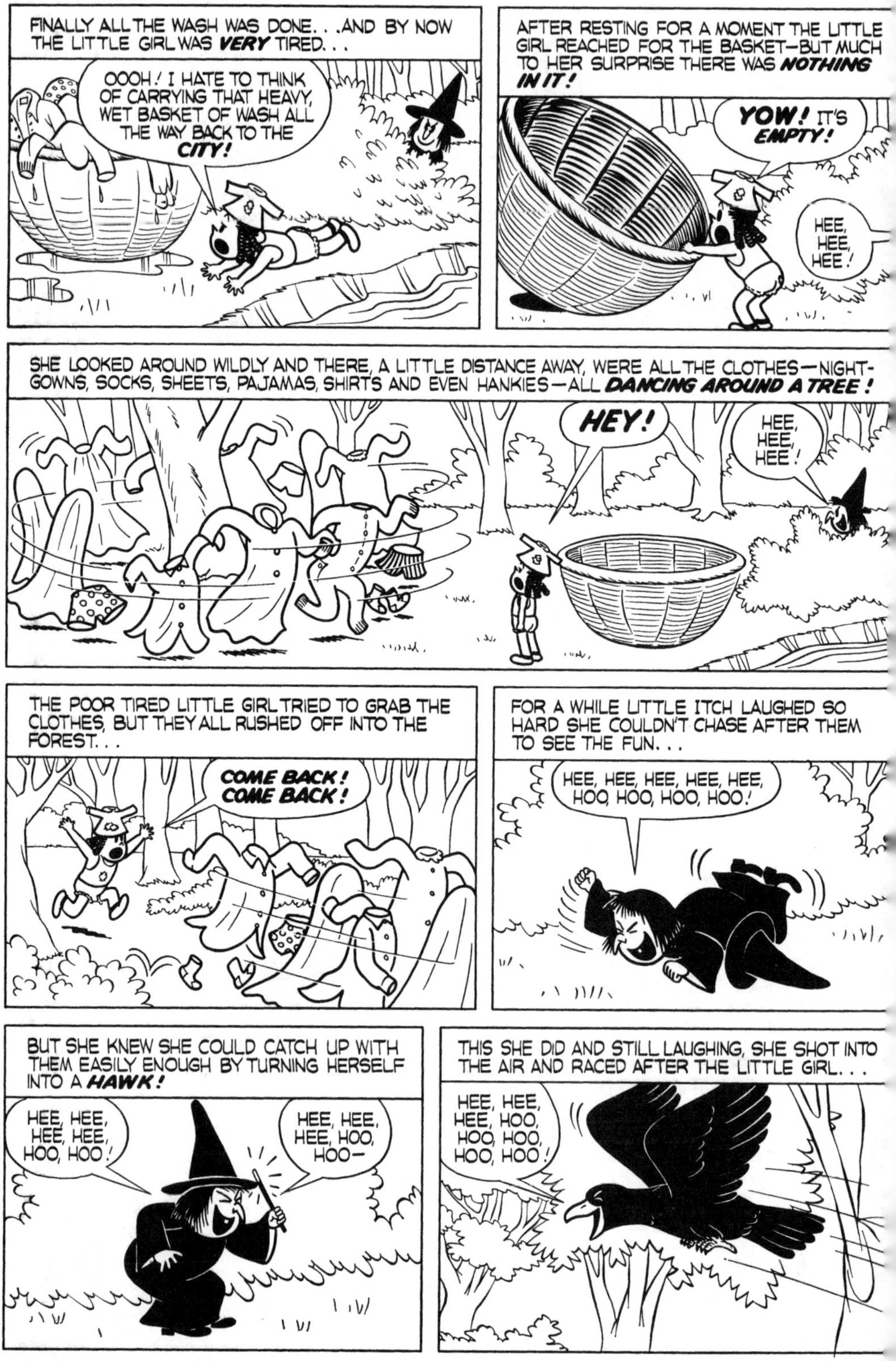
FINALLY ALL THE WASH WAS DONE. . .AND BY NOW THE LITTLE GIRL WAS VERY TIRED. . .
OOOH! I HATE TO THINK OF CARRYING THAT HEAVY, WET BASKET OF WASH ALL THE WAY BACK TO THE CITY!
AFTER RESTING FOR A MOMENT THE LITTLE GIRL REACHED FOR THE BASKET—BUT MUCH TO HER SURPRISE THERE WAS NOTHING IN IT!
YOW! IT'S EMPTY!
HEE, HEE, HEE!
SHE LOOKED AROUND WILDLY AND THERE, A LITTLE DISTANCE AWAY, WERE ALL THE CLOTHES—NIGHT-GOWNS, SOCKS, SHEETS, PAJAMAS, SHIRTS AND EVEN HANKIES—ALL DANCING AROUND A TREE!
HEY!
HEE, HEE, HEE!
THE POOR TIRED LITTLE GIRL TRIED TO GRAB THE CLOTHES, BUT THEY ALL RUSHED OFF INTO THE FOREST. . .
COME BACK! COME BACK!
FOR A WHILE LITTLE ITCH LAUGHED SO HARD SHE COULDN'T CHASE AFTER THEM TO SEE THE FUN. . .
HEE, HEE, HEE, HEE, HEE, HOO, HOO, HOO, HOO!
BUT SHE KNEW SHE COULD CATCH UP WITH THEM EASILY ENOUGH BY TURNING HERSELF INTO A HAWK!
HEE, HEE, HEE, HEE, HOO, HOO!
HEE, HEE, HEE, HOO, HOO—
THIS SHE DID AND STILL LAUGHING, SHE SHOT INTO THE AIR AND RACED AFTER THE LITTLE GIRL. . .
HEE, HEE, HEE, HOO, HOO, HOO, HOO, HOO!

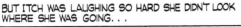

BUT ITCH WAS LAUGHING SO HARD SHE DIDN'T LOOK WHERE SHE WAS GOING. . .

HEE, HEE, HEE, HOO, HOO, HOO, HOO!

SHE SMACKED RIGHT INTO A TREE AND JAMMED HER HEAD IN A SQUIRREL HOLE!

HOO—

UNFORTUNATELY FOR HER, THE SQUIRREL WAS HOME AT THE TIME. . .AND HE WAS A SQUIRREL WHO DIDN'T LIKE HAWKS AT ALL. . .

YOWK! OWK! OORK!

MEANWHILE, THE LITTLE GIRL WAS STILL CHASING THE RUNAWAY WASH. . .

STOP! COME BACK!

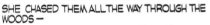

SHE CHASED THEM ALL THE WAY THROUGH THE WOODS—

STOP!

?

AND INTO TOWN. . .

STOP!

. . .AND WOULD YOU BELIEVE IT, [AL]VIN, ALL THOSE CLOTHES RAN [S]TRAIGHT TO THE PEOPLE WHO [O]WNED THEM, ALL CLEAN AND DRY, [A]ND ALL THE LITTLE GIRL HAD TO [D]O WAS COLLECT THE MONEY FOR WASHING THEM!

[N]O!

NO, WHAT?

NO, SIR!

NO, SIR, WHAT?

NO, SIR, I DON'T BELIEVE IT!

the End

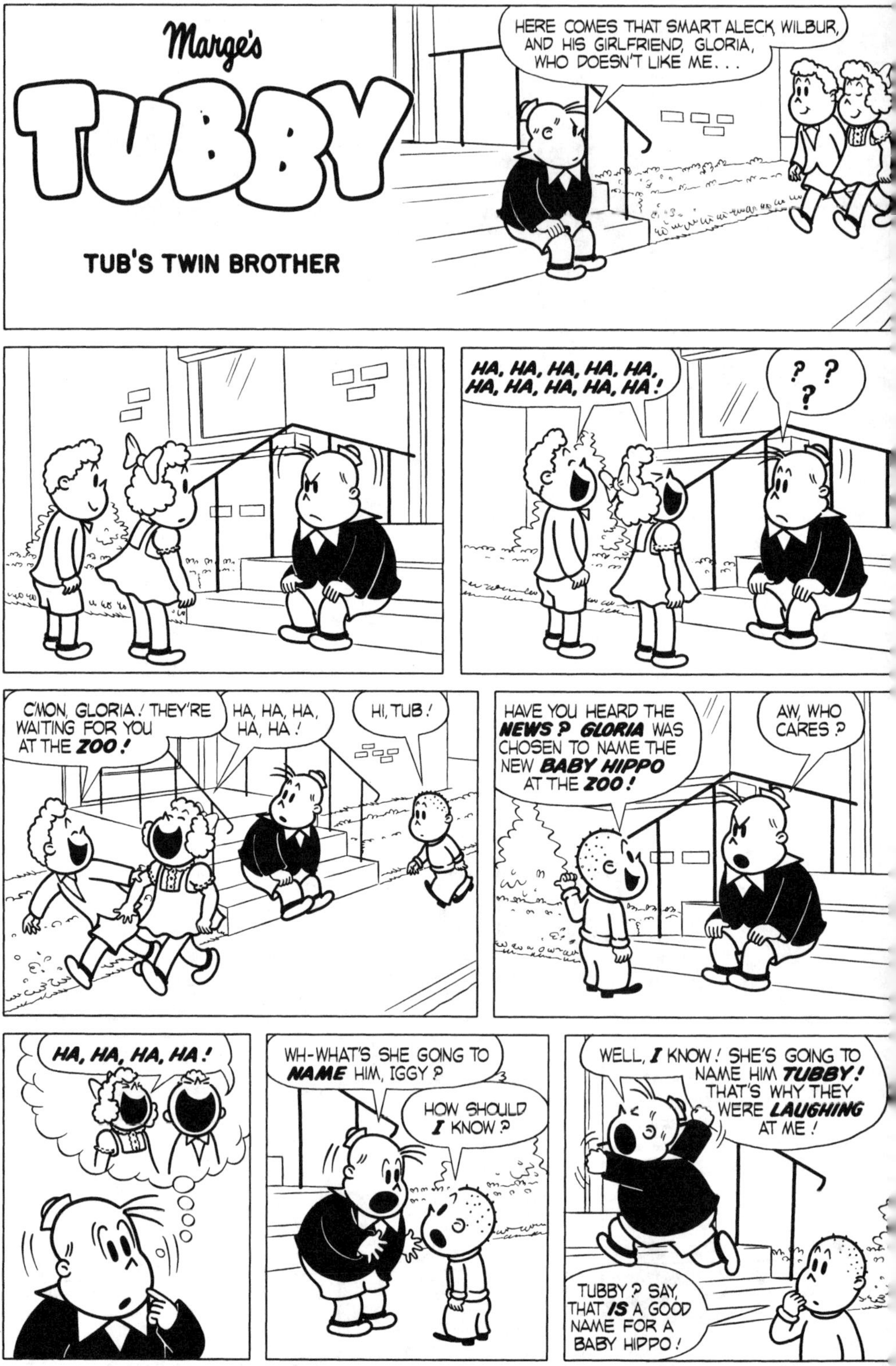
Marge's
TUBBY
TUB'S TWIN BROTHER
HERE COMES THAT SMART ALECK WILBUR, AND HIS GIRLFRIEND, GLORIA, WHO DOESN'T LIKE ME...
HA, HA, HA, HA, HA, HA, HA, HA, HA, HA!
? ? ?
C'MON, GLORIA! THEY'RE WAITING FOR YOU AT THE ZOO!
HA, HA, HA, HA, HA!
HI, TUB!
HAVE YOU HEARD THE NEWS? GLORIA WAS CHOSEN TO NAME THE NEW BABY HIPPO AT THE ZOO!
AW, WHO CARES?
HA, HA, HA, HA!
WH-WHAT'S SHE GOING TO NAME HIM, IGGY?
HOW SHOULD I KNOW?
WELL, I KNOW! SHE'S GOING TO NAME HIM TUBBY! THAT'S WHY THEY WERE LAUGHING AT ME!
TUBBY? SAY, THAT IS A GOOD NAME FOR A BABY HIPPO!

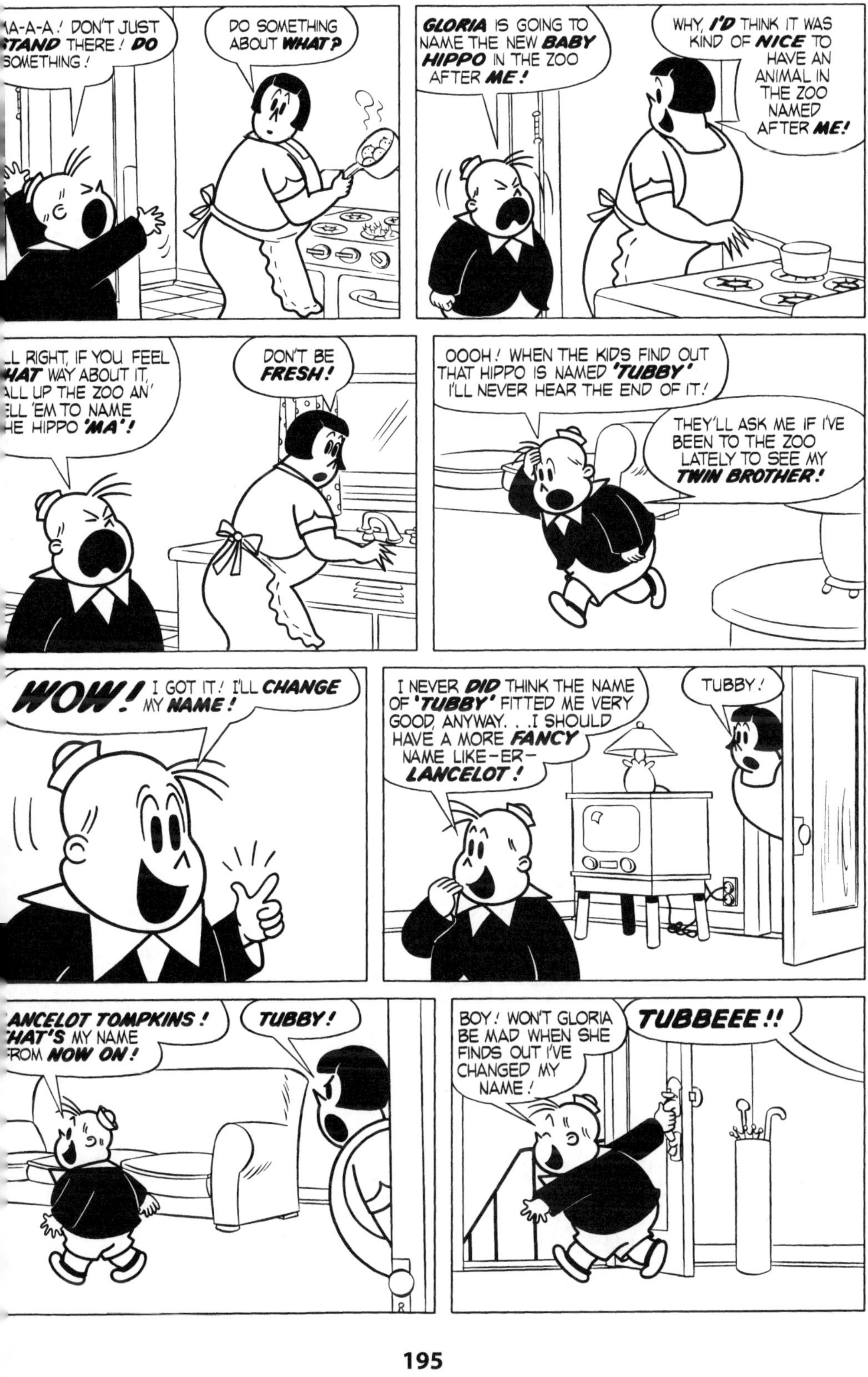

A-A-A! DON'T JUST TAND THERE! DO SOMETHING!
DO SOMETHING ABOUT WHAT?
GLORIA IS GOING TO NAME THE NEW BABY HIPPO IN THE ZOO AFTER ME!
WHY, I'D THINK IT WAS KIND OF NICE TO HAVE AN ANIMAL IN THE ZOO NAMED AFTER ME!
LL RIGHT, IF YOU FEEL HAT WAY ABOUT IT, ALL UP THE ZOO AN' ELL 'EM TO NAME HE HIPPO 'MA'!
DON'T BE FRESH!
OOOH! WHEN THE KIDS FIND OUT THAT HIPPO IS NAMED 'TUBBY' I'LL NEVER HEAR THE END OF IT!
THEY'LL ASK ME IF I'VE BEEN TO THE ZOO LATELY TO SEE MY TWIN BROTHER!
WOW! I GOT IT! I'LL CHANGE MY NAME!
I NEVER DID THINK THE NAME OF 'TUBBY' FITTED ME VERY GOOD, ANYWAY. . .I SHOULD HAVE A MORE FANCY NAME LIKE-ER- LANCELOT!
TUBBY!
ANCELOT TOMPKINS! HAT'S MY NAME ROM NOW ON!
TUBBY!
BOY! WON'T GLORIA BE MAD WHEN SHE FINDS OUT I'VE CHANGED MY NAME!
TUBBEEE!!

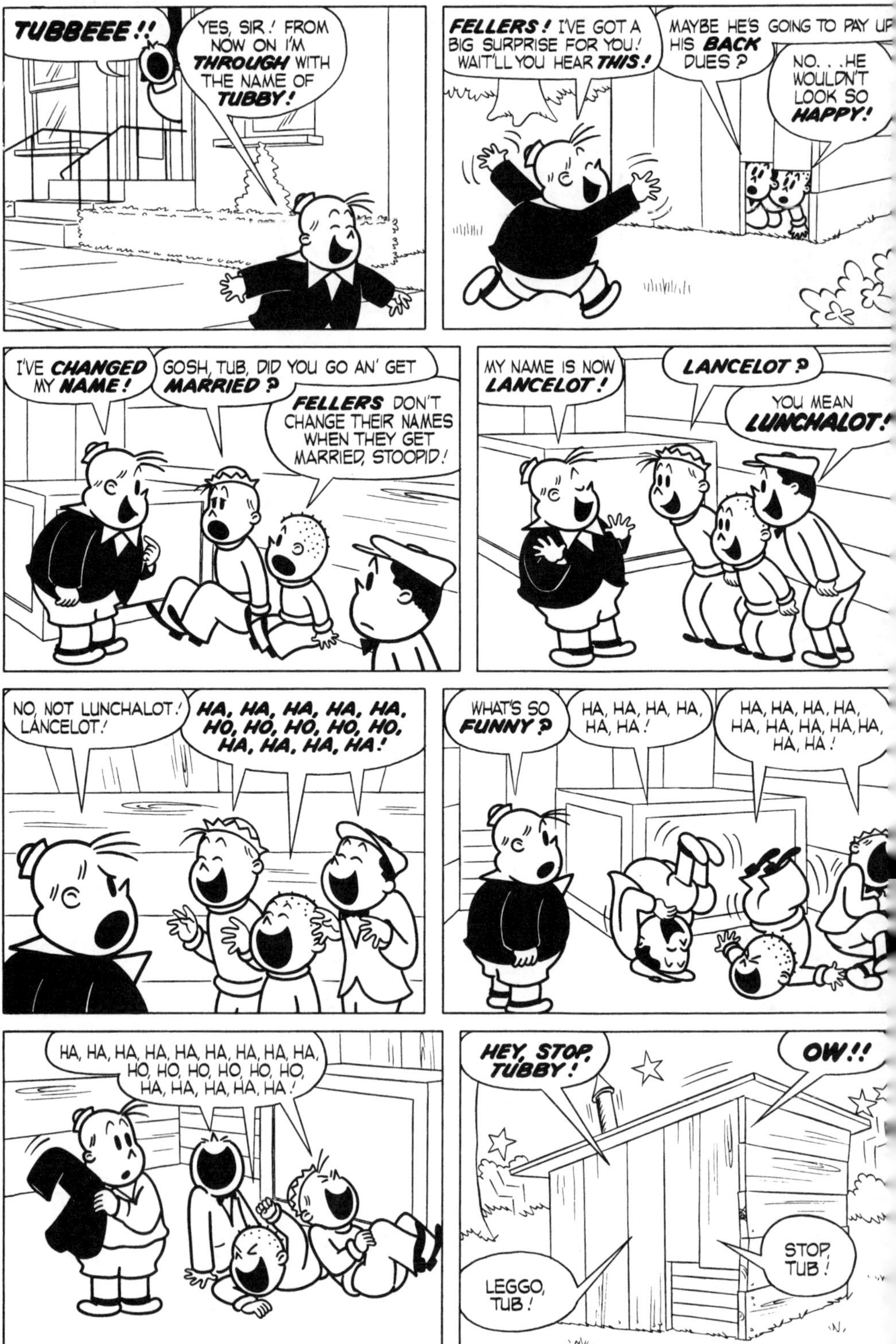
TUBBEEE!!
YES, SIR! FROM NOW ON I'M THROUGH WITH THE NAME OF TUBBY!
FELLERS! I'VE GOT A BIG SURPRISE FOR YOU! WAIT'LL YOU HEAR THIS!
MAYBE HE'S GOING TO PAY UP HIS BACK DUES?
NO. . .HE WOULDN'T LOOK SO HAPPY!
I'VE CHANGED MY NAME!
GOSH, TUB, DID YOU GO AN' GET MARRIED?
FELLERS DON'T CHANGE THEIR NAMES WHEN THEY GET MARRIED, STOOPID!
MY NAME IS NOW LANCELOT!
LANCELOT?
YOU MEAN LUNCHALOT!
NO, NOT LUNCHALOT! LANCELOT!
HA, HA, HA, HA, HA, HO, HO, HO, HO, HO, HA, HA, HA, HA!
WHAT'S SO FUNNY?
HA, HA, HA, HA, HA, HA!
HA, HA, HA, HA, HA, HA, HA, HA, HA, HA, HA!
HA, HA, HA, HA, HA, HA, HA, HA, HA, HO, HO, HO, HO, HO, HO, HA, HA, HA, HA, HA!
HEY, STOP, TUBBY!
OW!!
LEGGO, TUB!
STOP, TUB!

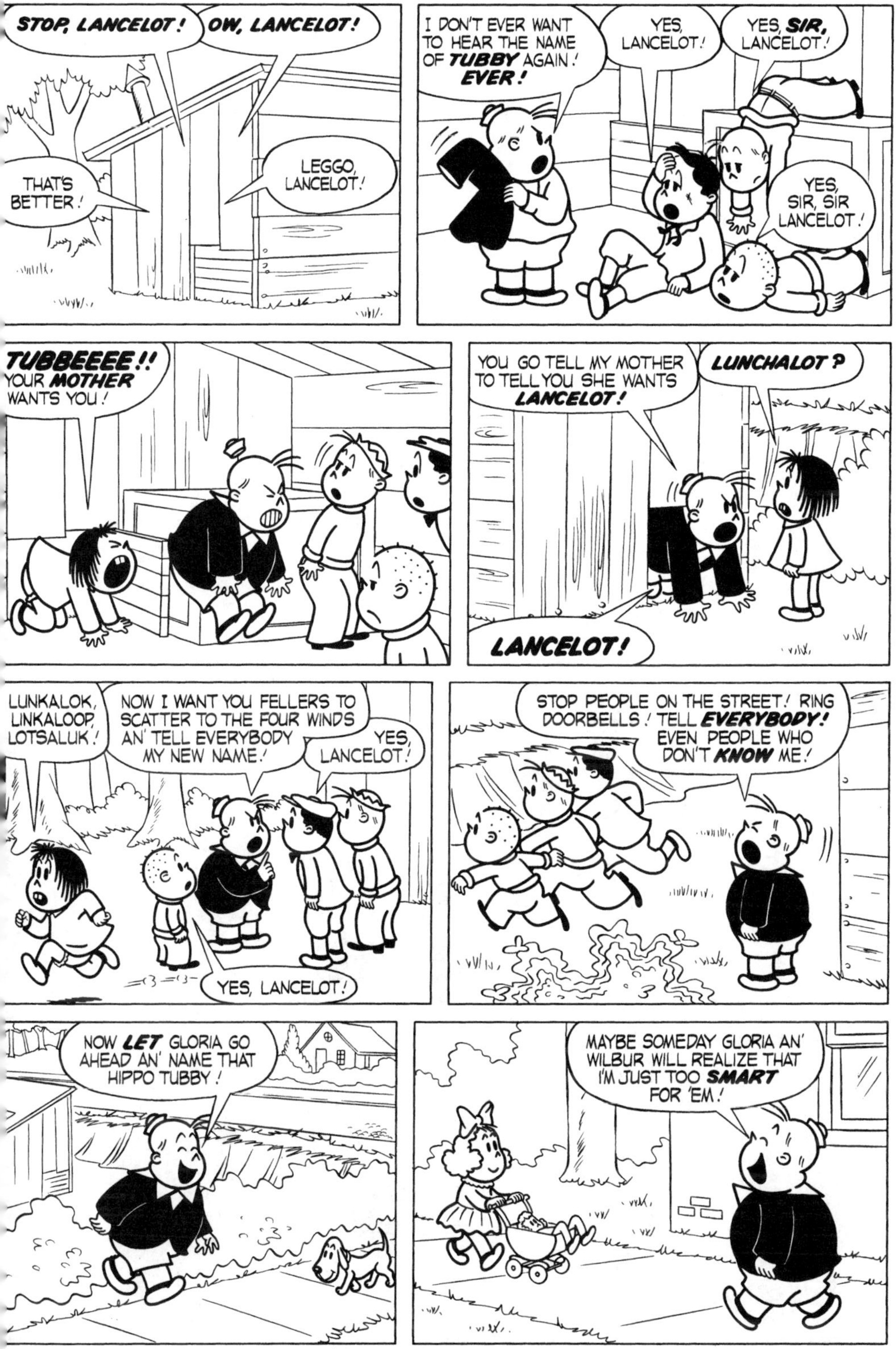
STOP, LANCELOT!
OW, LANCELOT!
THAT'S BETTER!
LEGGO, LANCELOT!
I DON'T EVER WANT TO HEAR THE NAME OF TUBBY AGAIN! EVER!
YES, LANCELOT!
YES, SIR, LANCELOT!
YES, SIR, SIR LANCELOT!
TUBBEEEE!! YOUR MOTHER WANTS YOU!
YOU GO TELL MY MOTHER TO TELL YOU SHE WANTS LANCELOT!
LUNCHALOT?
LANCELOT!
LUNKALOK, LINKALOOP, LOTSALUK!
NOW I WANT YOU FELLERS TO SCATTER TO THE FOUR WINDS AN' TELL EVERYBODY MY NEW NAME!
YES, LANCELOT!
YES, LANCELOT!
STOP PEOPLE ON THE STREET! RING DOORBELLS! TELL EVERYBODY! EVEN PEOPLE WHO DON'T KNOW ME!
NOW LET GLORIA GO AHEAD AN' NAME THAT HIPPO TUBBY!
MAYBE SOMEDAY GLORIA AN' WILBUR WILL REALIZE THAT I'M JUST TOO SMART FOR 'EM!

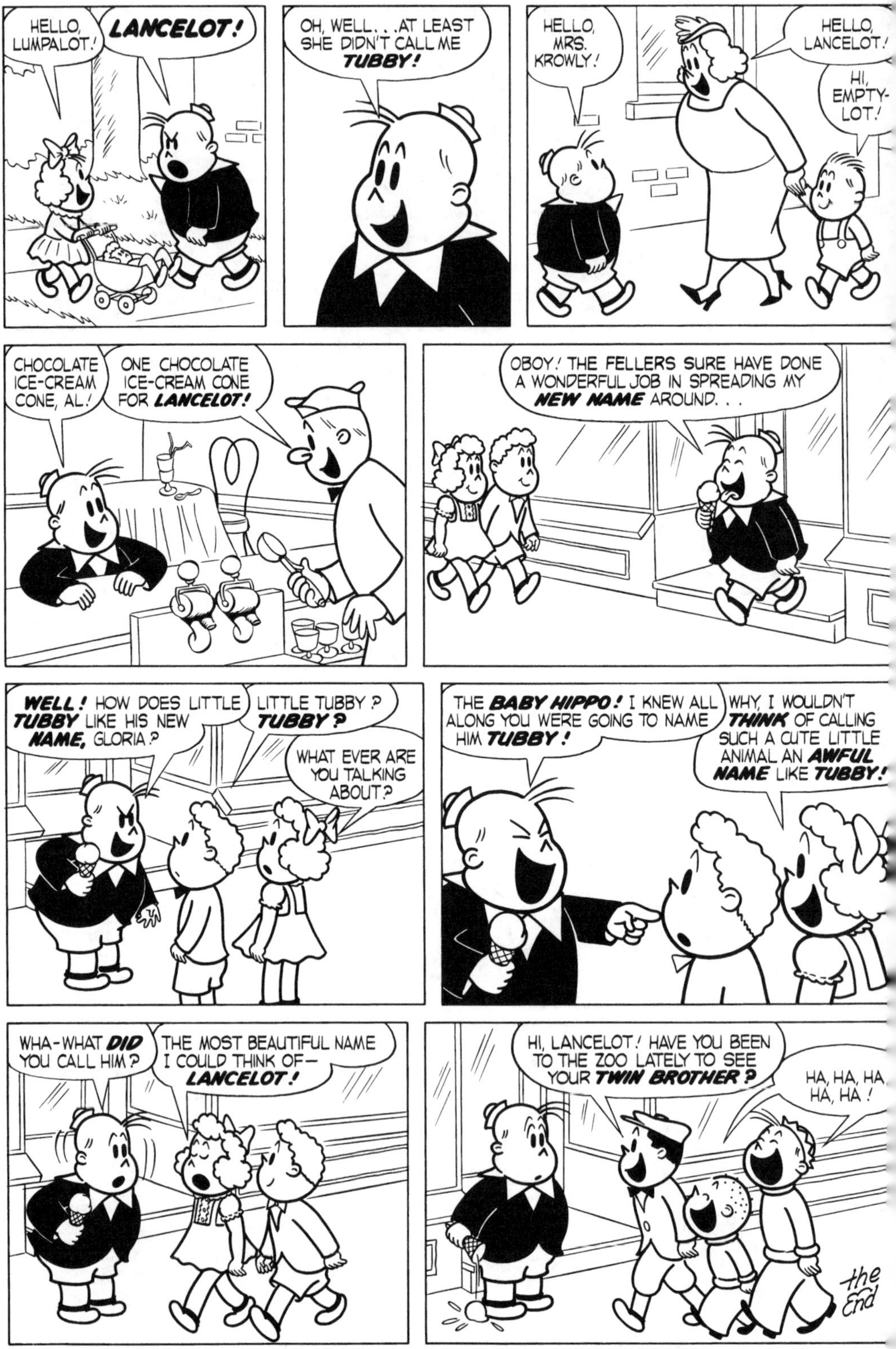
HELLO, LUMPALOT!
LANCELOT!
OH, WELL. . .AT LEAST SHE DIDN'T CALL ME TUBBY!
HELLO, MRS. KROWLY!
HELLO, LANCELOT!
HI, EMPTY-LOT!
CHOCOLATE ICE-CREAM CONE, AL!
ONE CHOCOLATE ICE-CREAM CONE FOR LANCELOT!
OBOY! THE FELLERS SURE HAVE DONE A WONDERFUL JOB IN SPREADING MY NEW NAME AROUND. . .
WELL! HOW DOES LITTLE TUBBY LIKE HIS NEW NAME, GLORIA?
LITTLE TUBBY? TUBBY?
WHAT EVER ARE YOU TALKING ABOUT?
THE BABY HIPPO! I KNEW ALL ALONG YOU WERE GOING TO NAME HIM TUBBY!
WHY, I WOULDN'T THINK OF CALLING SUCH A CUTE LITTLE ANIMAL AN AWFUL NAME LIKE TUBBY!
WHA-WHAT DID YOU CALL HIM?
THE MOST BEAUTIFUL NAME I COULD THINK OF— LANCELOT!
HI, LANCELOT! HAVE YOU BEEN TO THE ZOO LATELY TO SEE YOUR TWIN BROTHER?
HA, HA, HA, HA, HA!
the End

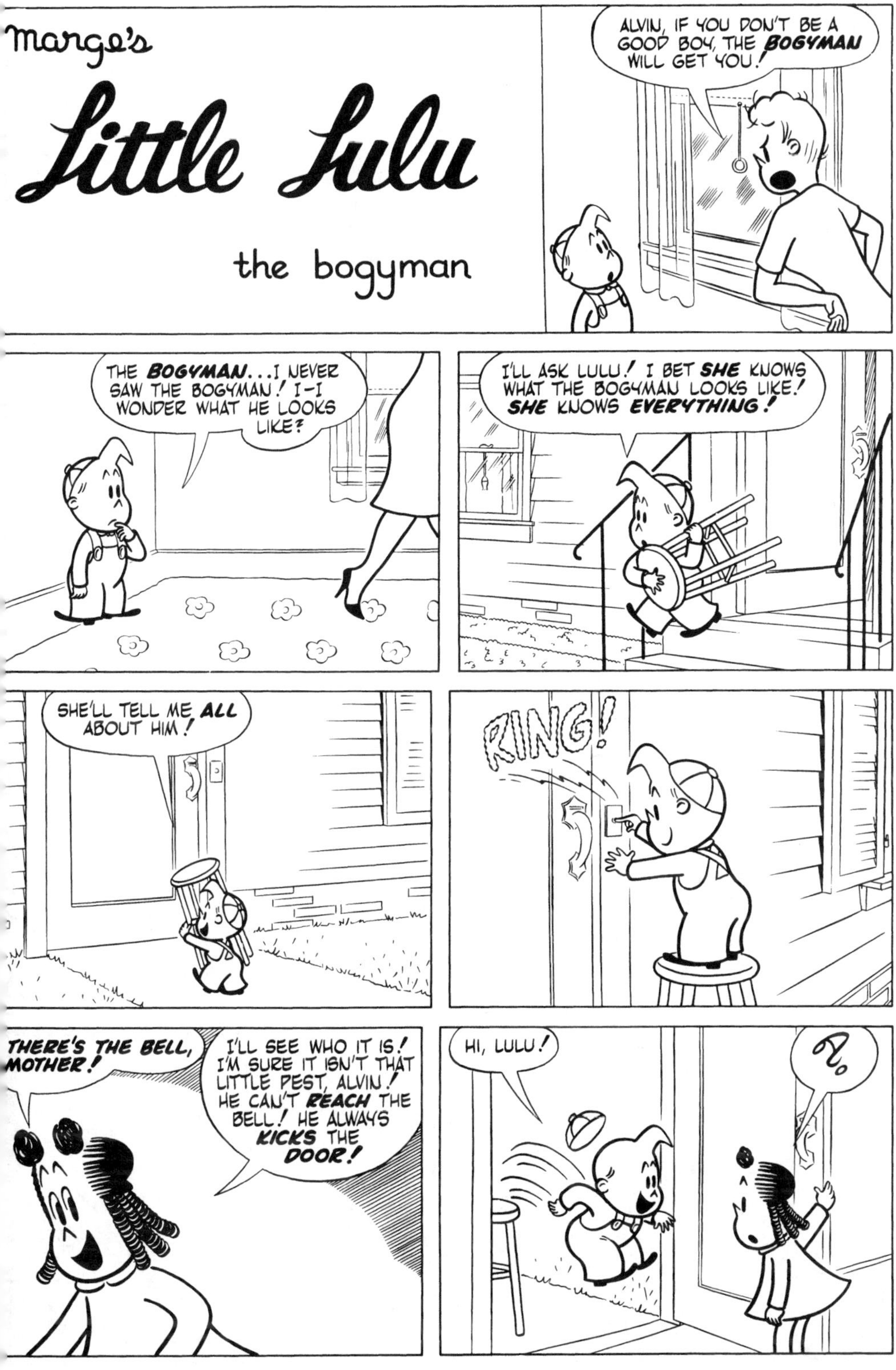

Marge's
Little Lulu
the bogyman
ALVIN, IF YOU DON'T BE A GOOD BOY, THE BOGYMAN WILL GET YOU!
THE BOGYMAN...I NEVER SAW THE BOGYMAN! I-I WONDER WHAT HE LOOKS LIKE?
I'LL ASK LULU! I BET SHE KNOWS WHAT THE BOGYMAN LOOKS LIKE! SHE KNOWS EVERYTHING!
SHE'LL TELL ME ALL ABOUT HIM!
RING!
THERE'S THE BELL, MOTHER!
I'LL SEE WHO IT IS! I'M SURE IT ISN'T THAT LITTLE PEST, ALVIN! HE CAN'T REACH THE BELL! HE ALWAYS KICKS THE DOOR!
HI, LULU!

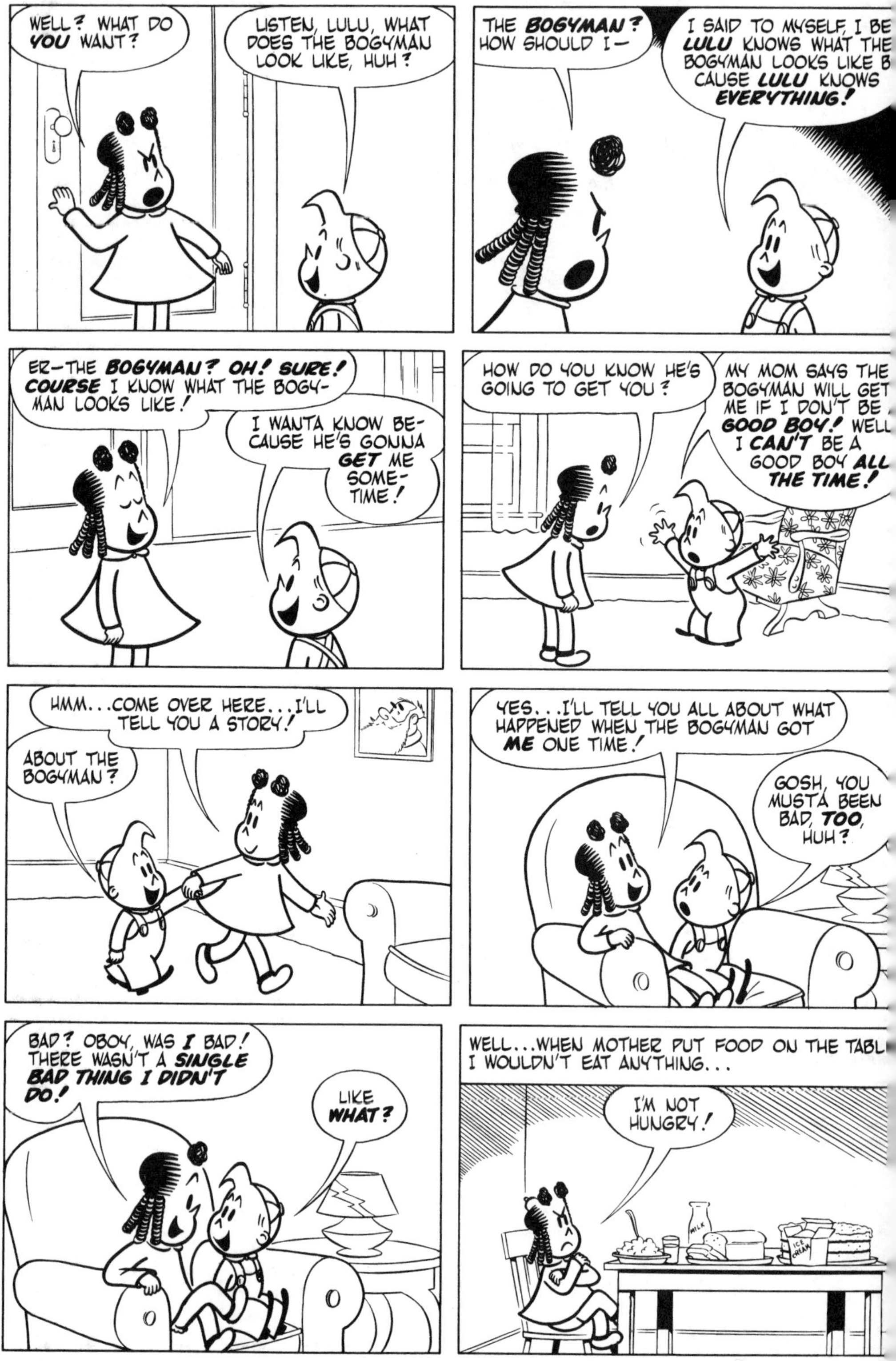
WELL? WHAT DO YOU WANT?
LISTEN, LULU, WHAT DOES THE BOGYMAN LOOK LIKE, HUH?
THE BOGYMAN? HOW SHOULD I—
I SAID TO MYSELF, I BE LULU KNOWS WHAT THE BOGYMAN LOOKS LIKE B CAUSE LULU KNOWS EVERYTHING!
ER—THE BOGYMAN? OH! SURE! COURSE I KNOW WHAT THE BOGYMAN LOOKS LIKE!
I WANTA KNOW BECAUSE HE'S GONNA GET ME SOMETIME!
HOW DO YOU KNOW HE'S GOING TO GET YOU?
MY MOM SAYS THE BOGYMAN WILL GET ME IF I DON'T BE GOOD BOY! WELL I CAN'T BE A GOOD BOY ALL THE TIME!
HMM...COME OVER HERE...I'LL TELL YOU A STORY!
ABOUT THE BOGYMAN?
YES...I'LL TELL YOU ALL ABOUT WHAT HAPPENED WHEN THE BOGYMAN GOT ME ONE TIME!
GOSH, YOU MUSTA BEEN BAD, TOO, HUH?
BAD? OBOY, WAS I BAD! THERE WASN'T A SINGLE BAD THING I DIDN'T DO!
LIKE WHAT?
WELL...WHEN MOTHER PUT FOOD ON THE TABL
I WOULDN'T EAT ANYTHING...
I'M NOT HUNGRY!
MILK
ICE CREAM

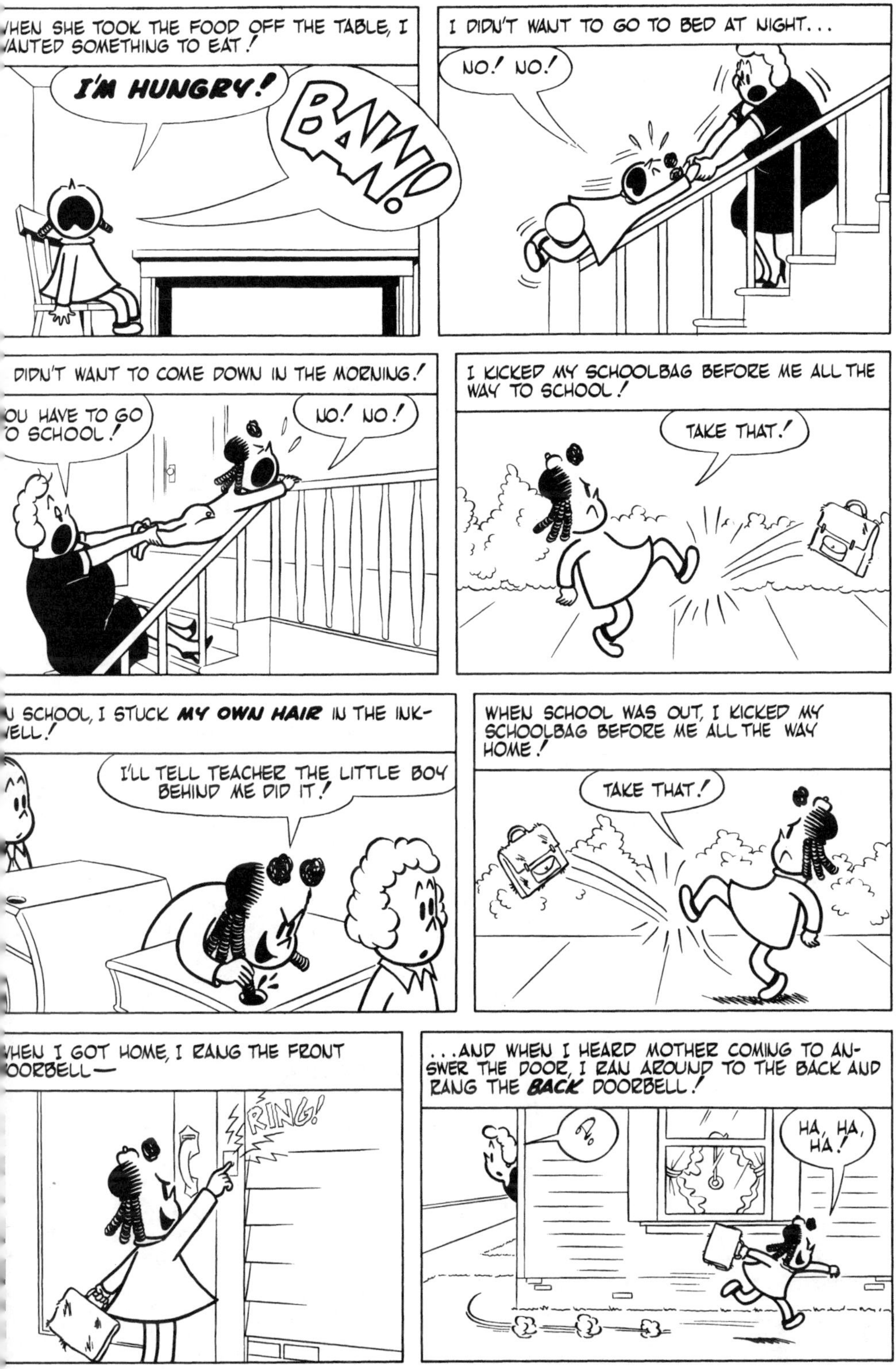
HEN SHE TOOK THE FOOD OFF THE TABLE, I ANTED SOMETHING TO EAT!
I'M HUNGRY!
BANG!
I DIDN'T WANT TO GO TO BED AT NIGHT...
NO! NO!
DIDN'T WANT TO COME DOWN IN THE MORNING!
OU HAVE TO GO O SCHOOL!
NO! NO!
I KICKED MY SCHOOLBAG BEFORE ME ALL THE WAY TO SCHOOL!
TAKE THAT!
SCHOOL, I STUCK MY OWN HAIR IN THE INK-ELL!
I'LL TELL TEACHER THE LITTLE BOY BEHIND ME DID IT!
WHEN SCHOOL WAS OUT, I KICKED MY SCHOOLBAG BEFORE ME ALL THE WAY HOME!
TAKE THAT!
HEN I GOT HOME, I RANG THE FRONT OORBELL—
RING!
...AND WHEN I HEARD MOTHER COMING TO ANSWER THE DOOR, I RAN AROUND TO THE BACK AND RANG THE BACK DOORBELL!
?
HA, HA, HA!

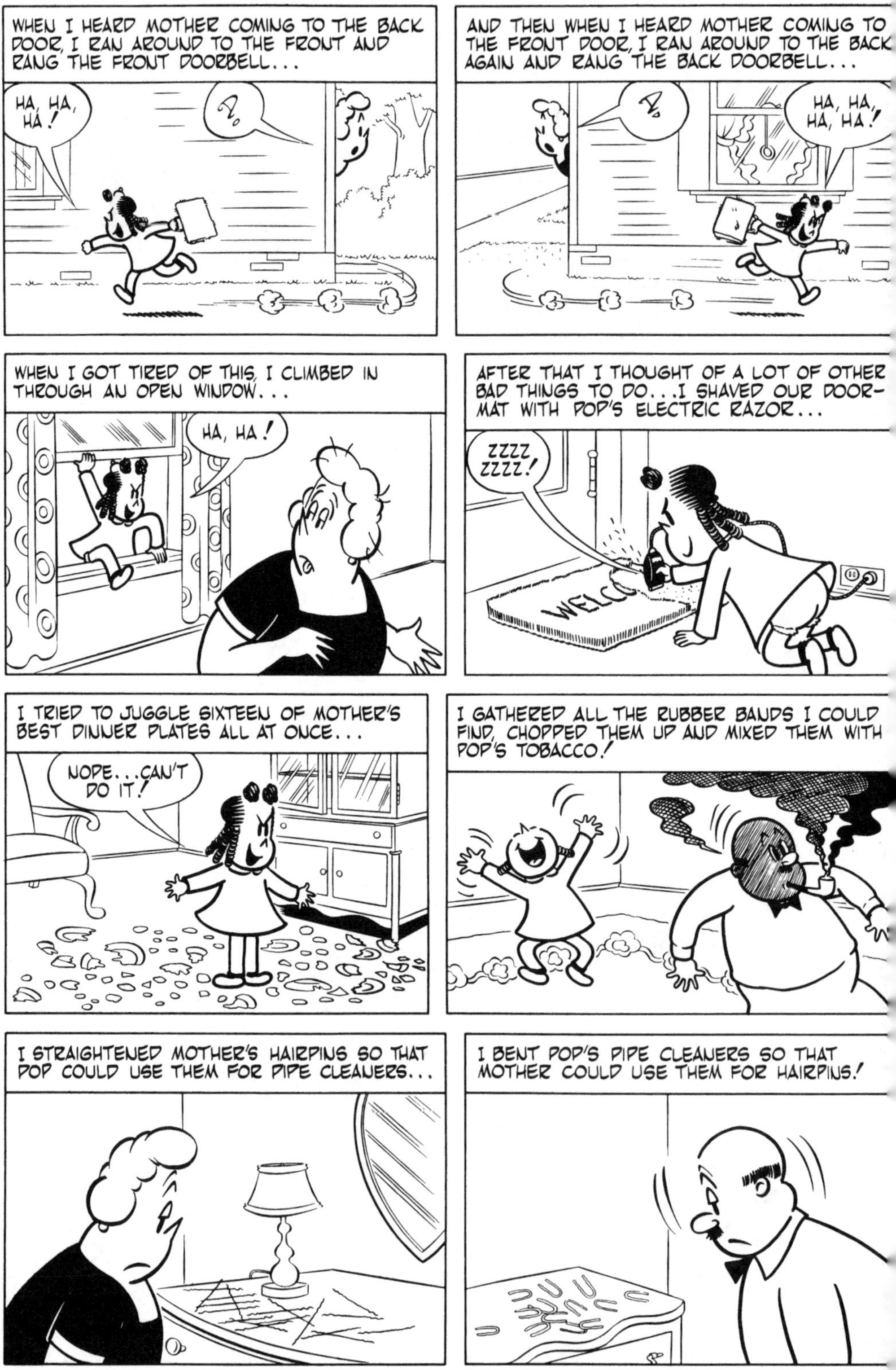
WHEN I HEARD MOTHER COMING TO THE BACK DOOR, I RAN AROUND TO THE FRONT AND RANG THE FRONT DOORBELL...
HA, HA, HA!
AND THEN WHEN I HEARD MOTHER COMING TO THE FRONT DOOR, I RAN AROUND TO THE BACK AGAIN AND RANG THE BACK DOORBELL...
HA, HA, HA, HA!
WHEN I GOT TIRED OF THIS, I CLIMBED IN THROUGH AN OPEN WINDOW...
HA, HA!
AFTER THAT I THOUGHT OF A LOT OF OTHER BAD THINGS TO DO...I SHAVED OUR DOOR-MAT WITH POP'S ELECTRIC RAZOR...
ZZZZ ZZZZ!
I TRIED TO JUGGLE SIXTEEN OF MOTHER'S BEST DINNER PLATES ALL AT ONCE...
NOPE...CAN'T DO IT!
I GATHERED ALL THE RUBBER BANDS I COULD FIND, CHOPPED THEM UP AND MIXED THEM WITH POP'S TOBACCO!
I STRAIGHTENED MOTHER'S HAIRPINS SO THAT POP COULD USE THEM FOR PIPE CLEANERS...
I BENT POP'S PIPE CLEANERS SO THAT MOTHER COULD USE THEM FOR HAIRPINS!

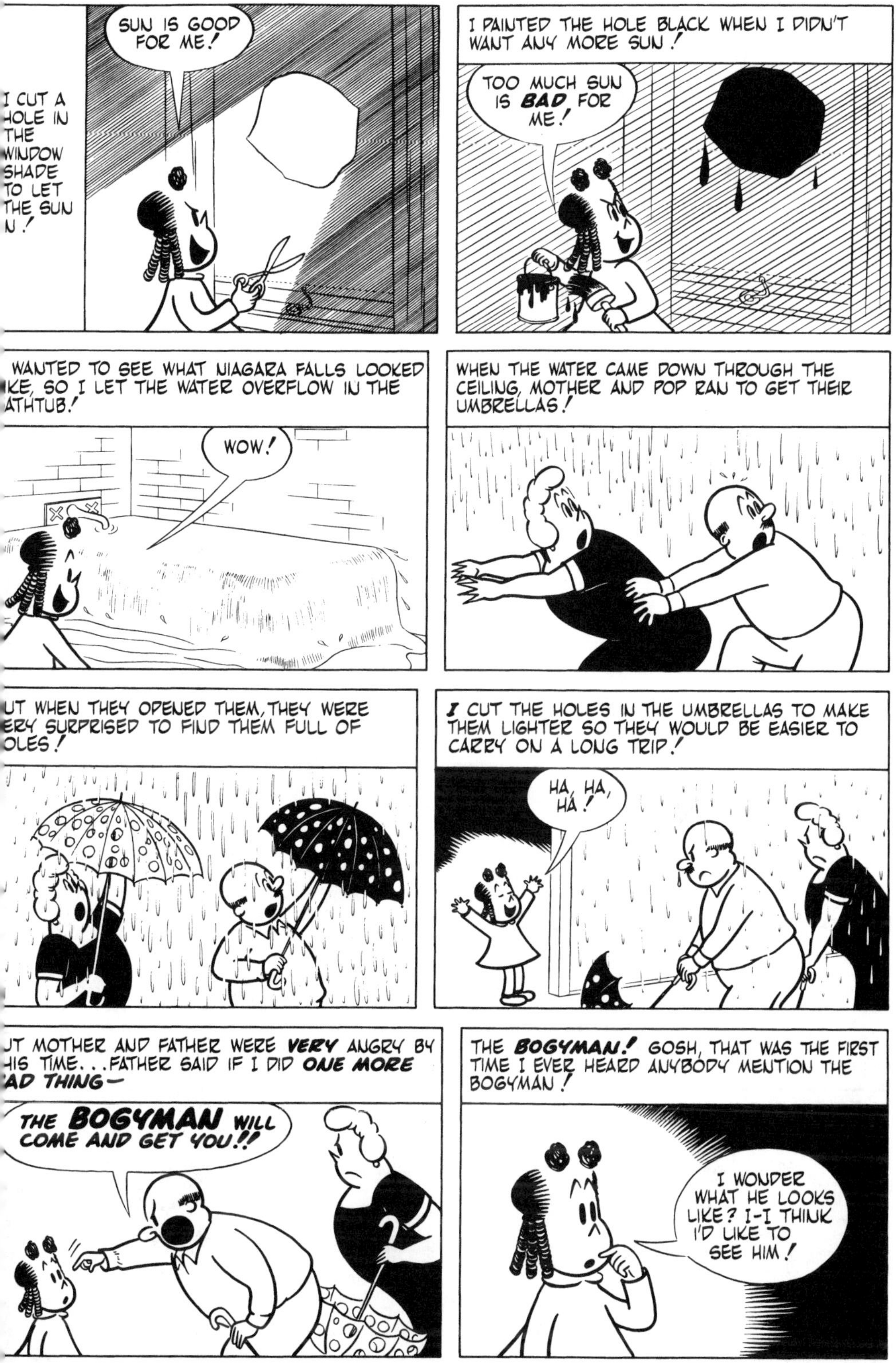
I CUT A
HOLE IN THE WINDOW SHADE TO LET THE SUN
N!
SUN IS GOOD FOR ME!
I PAINTED THE HOLE BLACK WHEN I DIDN'T WANT ANY MORE SUN!
TOO MUCH SUN IS BAD FOR ME!
WANTED TO SEE WHAT NIAGARA FALLS LOOKED
KE, SO I LET THE WATER OVERFLOW IN THE
ATHTUB!
WOW!
WHEN THE WATER CAME DOWN THROUGH THE CEILING, MOTHER AND POP RAN TO GET THEIR UMBRELLAS!
UT WHEN THEY OPENED THEM, THEY WERE
ERY SURPRISED TO FIND THEM FULL OF
OLES!
I CUT THE HOLES IN THE UMBRELLAS TO MAKE THEM LIGHTER SO THEY WOULD BE EASIER TO CARRY ON A LONG TRIP!
HA, HA, HA!
UT MOTHER AND FATHER WERE VERY ANGRY BY
HIS TIME. . .FATHER SAID IF I DID ONE MORE
AD THING—
THE BOGYMAN WILL COME AND GET YOU!!
THE BOGYMAN! GOSH, THAT WAS THE FIRST TIME I EVER HEARD ANYBODY MENTION THE BOGYMAN!
I WONDER WHAT HE LOOKS LIKE? I-I THINK I'D LIKE TO SEE HIM!

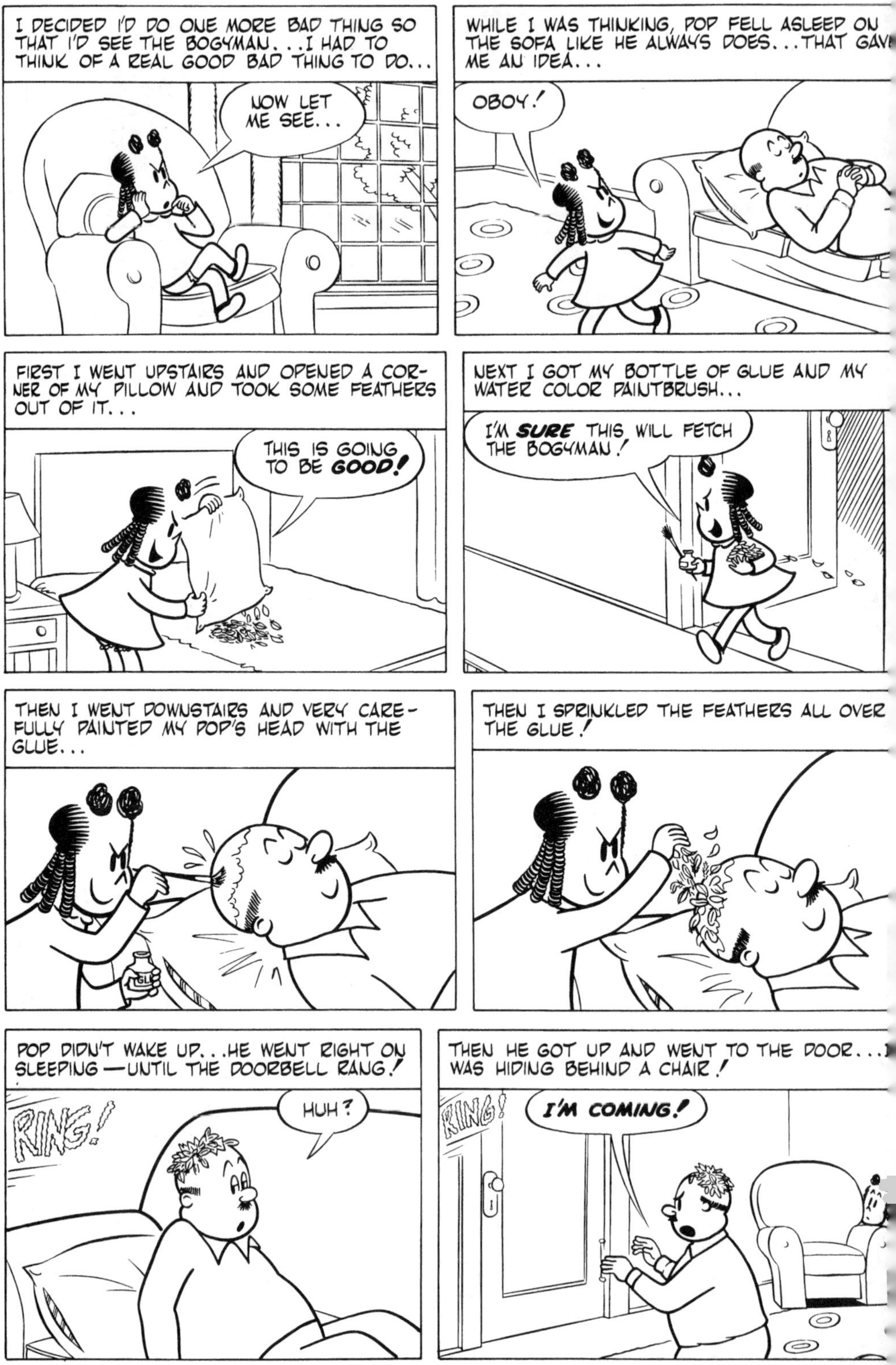
I DECIDED I'D DO ONE MORE BAD THING SO THAT I'D SEE THE BOGYMAN. . . I HAD TO THINK OF A REAL GOOD BAD THING TO DO. . .
NOW LET ME SEE. . .
WHILE I WAS THINKING, POP FELL ASLEEP ON THE SOFA LIKE HE ALWAYS DOES. . . THAT GAV
ME AN IDEA. . .
OBOY!
FIRST I WENT UPSTAIRS AND OPENED A CORNER OF MY PILLOW AND TOOK SOME FEATHERS OUT OF IT. . .
THIS IS GOING TO BE GOOD!
NEXT I GOT MY BOTTLE OF GLUE AND MY WATER COLOR PAINTBRUSH. . .
I'M SURE THIS WILL FETCH THE BOGYMAN!
THEN I WENT DOWNSTAIRS AND VERY CAREFULLY PAINTED MY POP'S HEAD WITH THE GLUE. . .
THEN I SPRINKLED THE FEATHERS ALL OVER THE GLUE!
POP DIDN'T WAKE UP. . . HE WENT RIGHT ON SLEEPING—UNTIL THE DOORBELL RANG!
RING!
HUH?
THEN HE GOT UP AND WENT TO THE DOOR. . . I
WAS HIDING BEHIND A CHAIR!
RING!
I'M COMING!

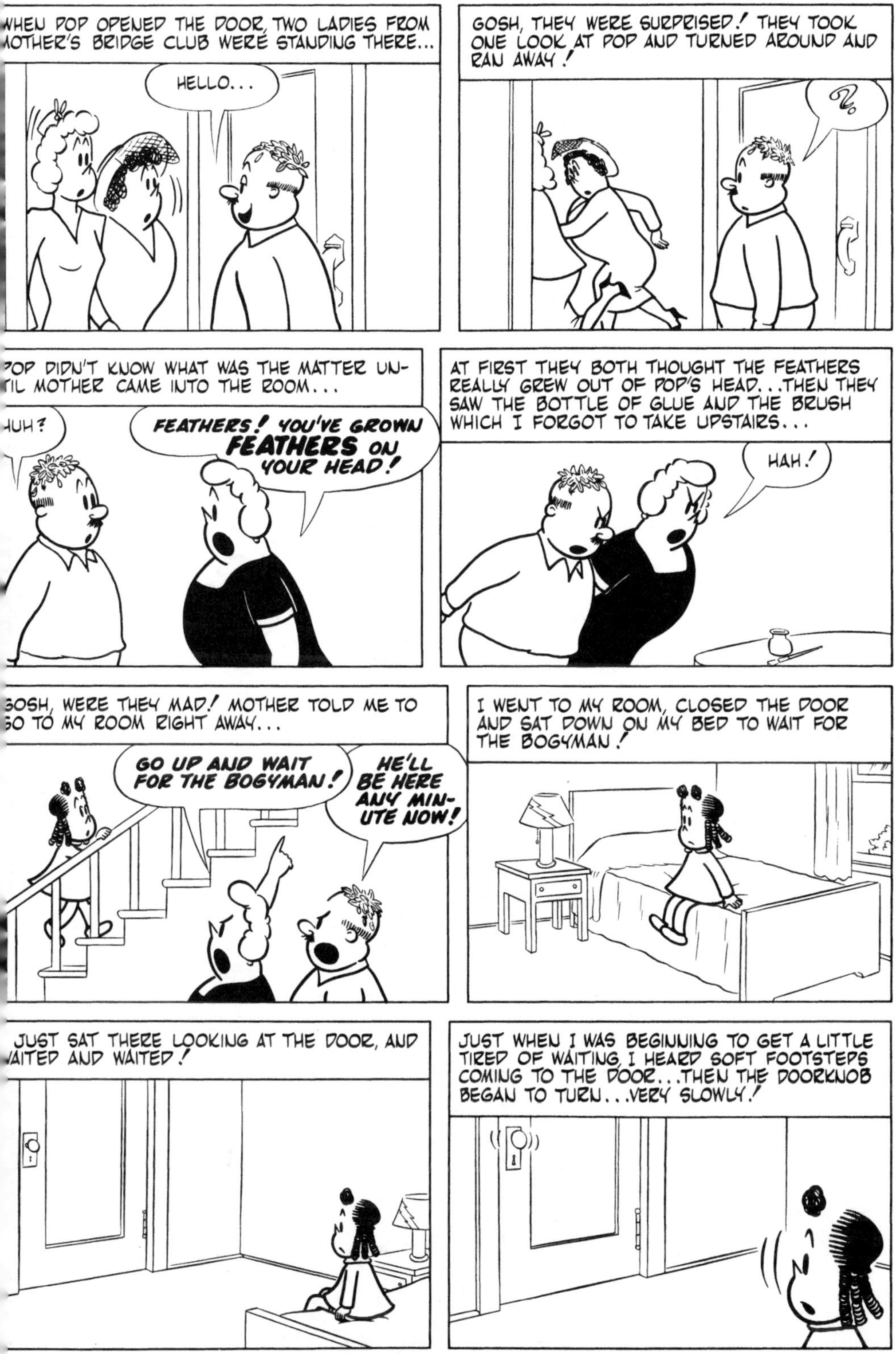
WHEN POP OPENED THE DOOR, TWO LADIES FROM MOTHER'S BRIDGE CLUB WERE STANDING THERE...
HELLO...
GOSH, THEY WERE SURPRISED! THEY TOOK ONE LOOK AT POP AND TURNED AROUND AND RAN AWAY!
?
POP DIDN'T KNOW WHAT WAS THE MATTER UNTIL MOTHER CAME INTO THE ROOM...
HUH?
FEATHERS! YOU'VE GROWN FEATHERS ON YOUR HEAD!
AT FIRST THEY BOTH THOUGHT THE FEATHERS REALLY GREW OUT OF POP'S HEAD...THEN THEY SAW THE BOTTLE OF GLUE AND THE BRUSH WHICH I FORGOT TO TAKE UPSTAIRS...
HAH!
GOSH, WERE THEY MAD! MOTHER TOLD ME TO GO TO MY ROOM RIGHT AWAY...
GO UP AND WAIT FOR THE BOGYMAN!
HE'LL BE HERE ANY MINUTE NOW!
I WENT TO MY ROOM, CLOSED THE DOOR AND SAT DOWN ON MY BED TO WAIT FOR THE BOGYMAN!
I JUST SAT THERE LOOKING AT THE DOOR, AND WAITED AND WAITED!
JUST WHEN I WAS BEGINNING TO GET A LITTLE TIRED OF WAITING, I HEARD SOFT FOOTSTEPS COMING TO THE DOOR...THEN THE DOORKNOB BEGAN TO TURN...VERY SLOWLY!

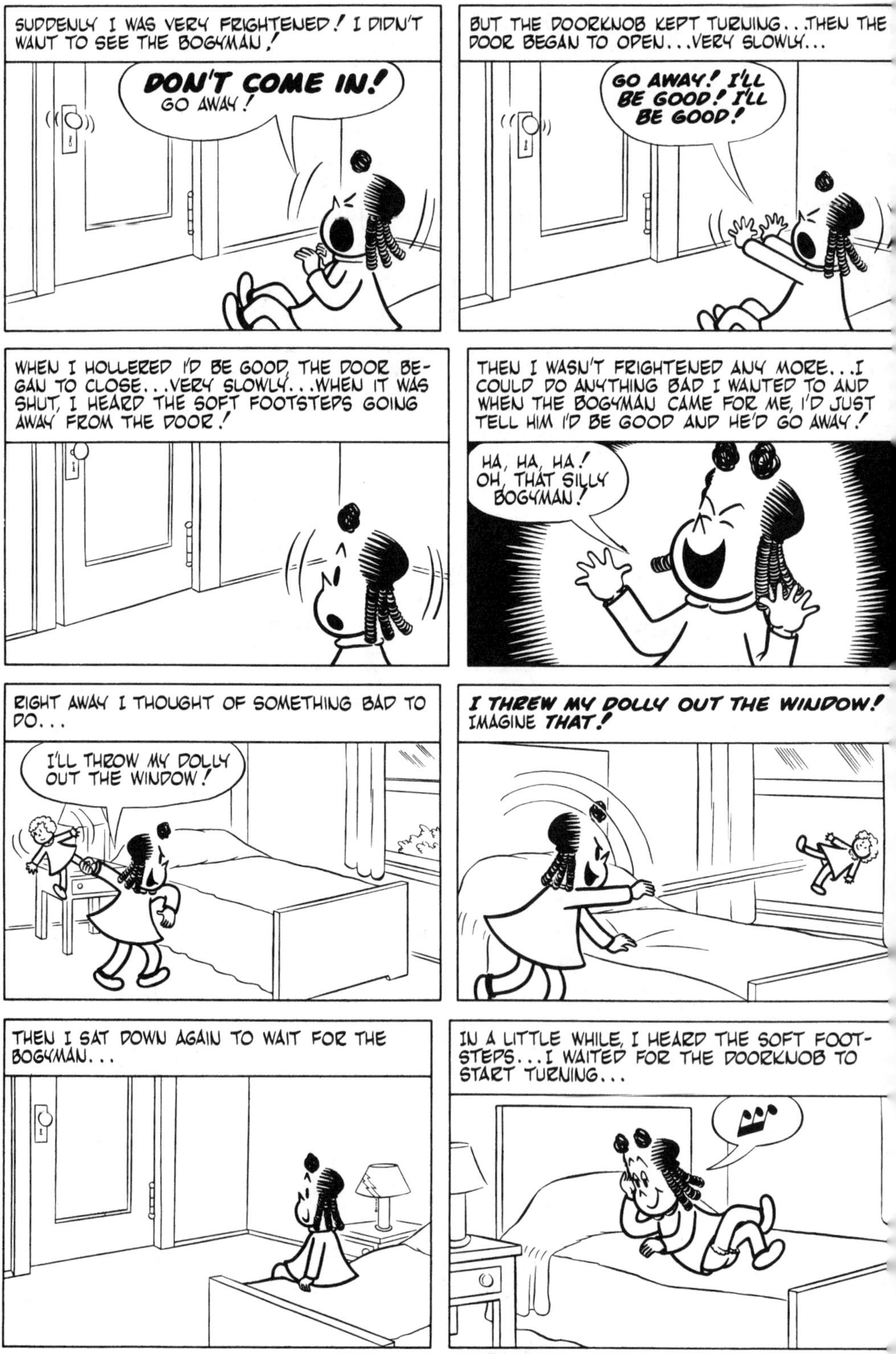
SUDDENLY I WAS VERY FRIGHTENED! I DIDN'T WANT TO SEE THE BOGYMAN!
DON'T COME IN! GO AWAY!
BUT THE DOORKNOB KEPT TURNING...THEN THE DOOR BEGAN TO OPEN...VERY SLOWLY...
GO AWAY! I'LL BE GOOD! I'LL BE GOOD!
WHEN I HOLLERED I'D BE GOOD, THE DOOR BEGAN TO CLOSE...VERY SLOWLY...WHEN IT WAS SHUT, I HEARD THE SOFT FOOTSTEPS GOING AWAY FROM THE DOOR!
THEN I WASN'T FRIGHTENED ANY MORE...I COULD DO ANYTHING BAD I WANTED TO AND WHEN THE BOGYMAN CAME FOR ME, I'D JUST TELL HIM I'D BE GOOD AND HE'D GO AWAY!
HA, HA, HA! OH, THAT SILLY BOGYMAN!
RIGHT AWAY I THOUGHT OF SOMETHING BAD TO DO...
I'LL THROW MY DOLLY OUT THE WINDOW!
I THREW MY DOLLY OUT THE WINDOW! IMAGINE THAT!
THEN I SAT DOWN AGAIN TO WAIT FOR THE BOGYMAN...
IN A LITTLE WHILE, I HEARD THE SOFT FOOTSTEPS...I WAITED FOR THE DOORKNOB TO START TURNING...

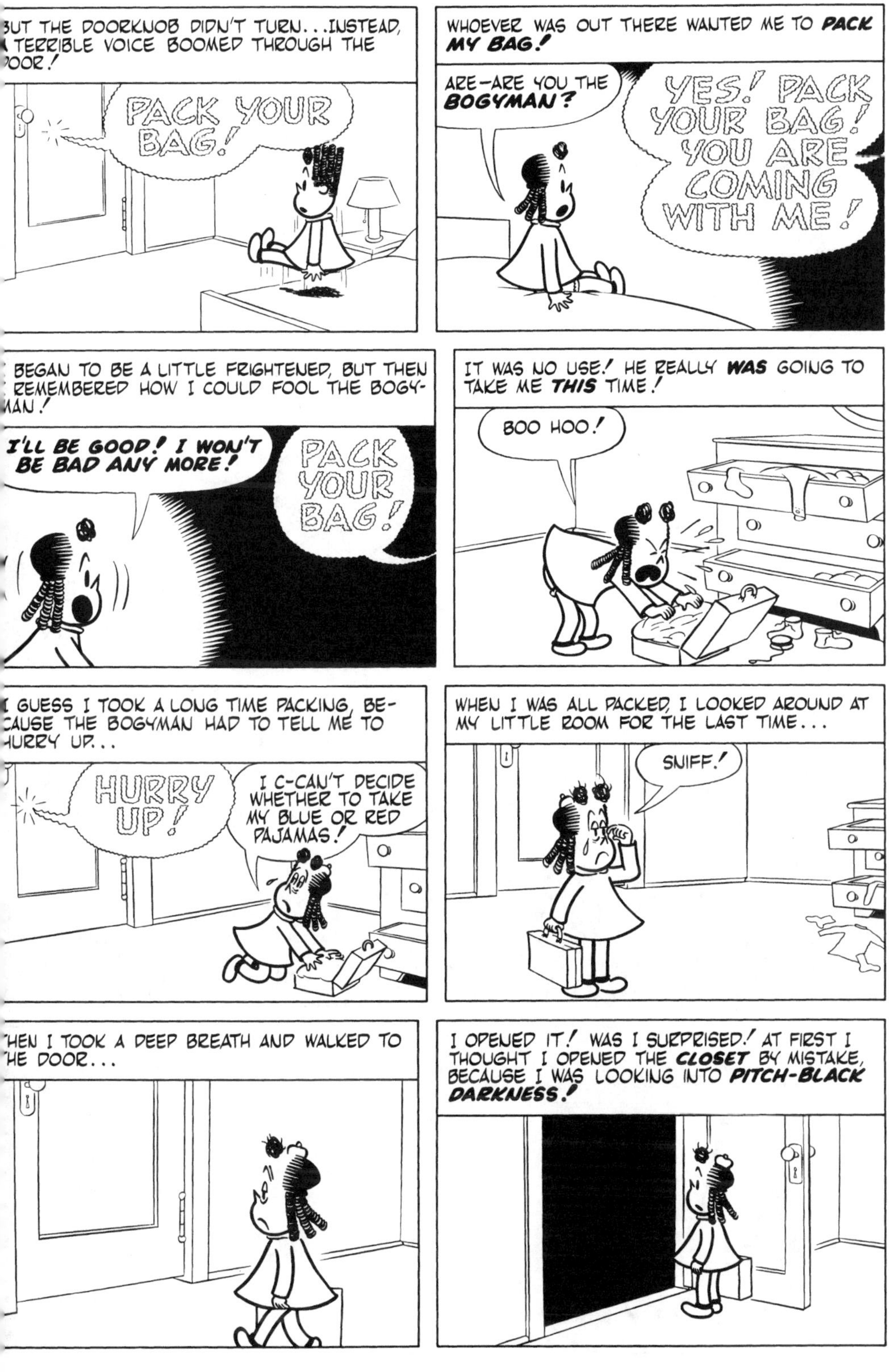
BUT THE DOORKNOB DIDN'T TURN...INSTEAD, A TERRIBLE VOICE BOOMED THROUGH THE DOOR!
PACK YOUR BAG!
WHOEVER WAS OUT THERE WANTED ME TO PACK MY BAG!
ARE—ARE YOU THE BOGYMAN?
YES! PACK YOUR BAG! YOU ARE COMING WITH ME!
I BEGAN TO BE A LITTLE FRIGHTENED, BUT THEN I REMEMBERED HOW I COULD FOOL THE BOGYMAN!
I'LL BE GOOD! I WON'T BE BAD ANY MORE!
PACK YOUR BAG!
IT WAS NO USE! HE REALLY WAS GOING TO TAKE ME THIS TIME!
BOO HOO!
I GUESS I TOOK A LONG TIME PACKING, BECAUSE THE BOGYMAN HAD TO TELL ME TO HURRY UP...
HURRY UP!
I C-CAN'T DECIDE WHETHER TO TAKE MY BLUE OR RED PAJAMAS!
WHEN I WAS ALL PACKED, I LOOKED AROUND AT MY LITTLE ROOM FOR THE LAST TIME...
SNIFF!
THEN I TOOK A DEEP BREATH AND WALKED TO THE DOOR...
I OPENED IT! WAS I SURPRISED! AT FIRST I THOUGHT I OPENED THE CLOSET BY MISTAKE, BECAUSE I WAS LOOKING INTO PITCH-BLACK DARKNESS!

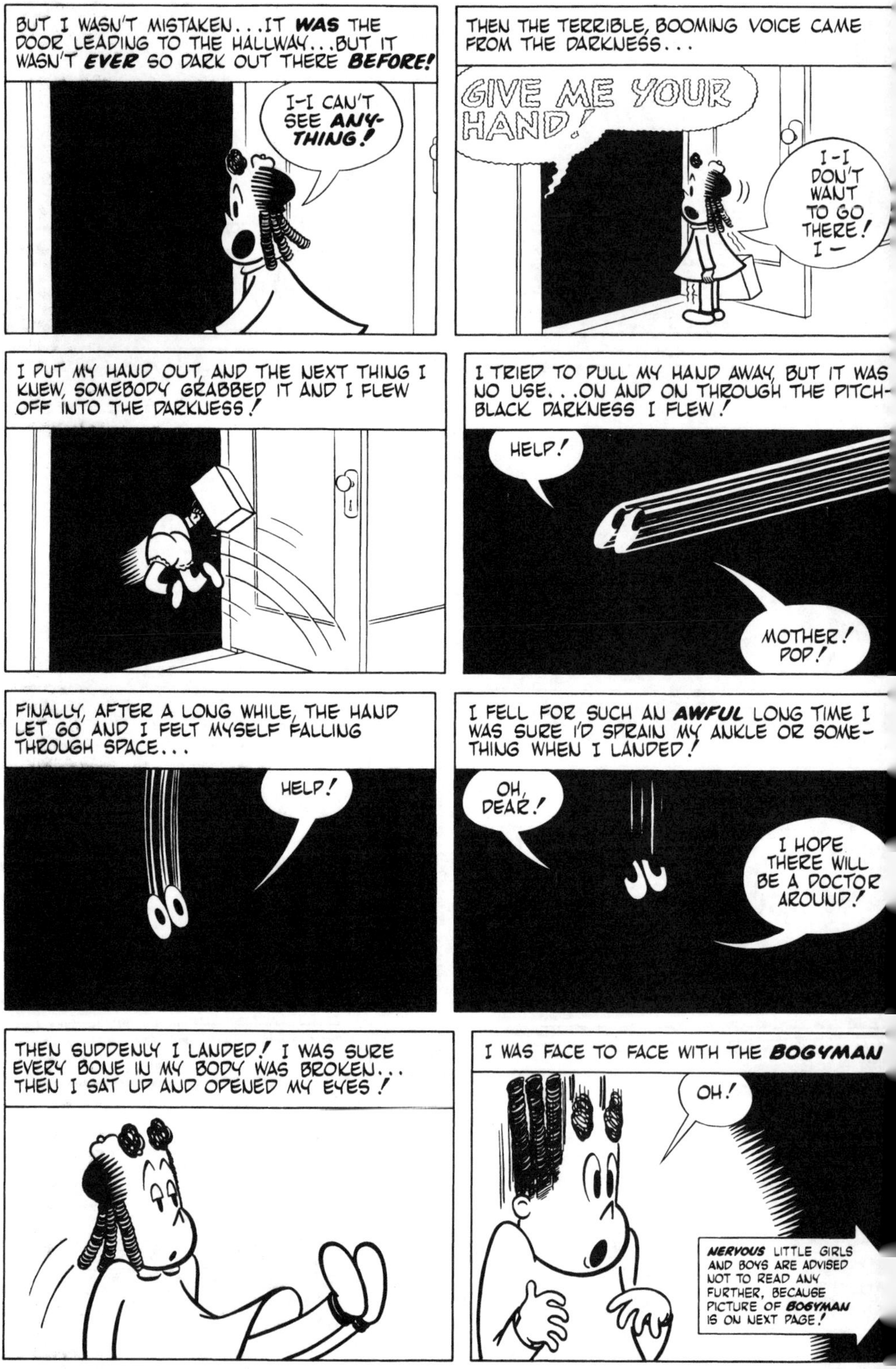
BUT I WASN'T MISTAKEN...IT WAS THE DOOR LEADING TO THE HALLWAY...BUT IT WASN'T EVER SO DARK OUT THERE BEFORE!
I-I CAN'T SEE ANY-THING!
THEN THE TERRIBLE, BOOMING VOICE CAME FROM THE DARKNESS...
GIVE ME YOUR HAND!
I-I DON'T WANT TO GO THERE! I—
I PUT MY HAND OUT, AND THE NEXT THING I KNEW, SOMEBODY GRABBED IT AND I FLEW OFF INTO THE DARKNESS!
I TRIED TO PULL MY HAND AWAY, BUT IT WAS NO USE...ON AND ON THROUGH THE PITCH-BLACK DARKNESS I FLEW!
HELP!
MOTHER! POP!
FINALLY, AFTER A LONG WHILE, THE HAND LET GO AND I FELT MYSELF FALLING THROUGH SPACE...
HELP!
I FELL FOR SUCH AN AWFUL LONG TIME I WAS SURE I'D SPRAIN MY ANKLE OR SOME-THING WHEN I LANDED!
OH, DEAR!
I HOPE THERE WILL BE A DOCTOR AROUND!
THEN SUDDENLY I LANDED! I WAS SURE EVERY BONE IN MY BODY WAS BROKEN... THEN I SAT UP AND OPENED MY EYES!
I WAS FACE TO FACE WITH THE BOGYMAN
OH!
NERVOUS LITTLE GIRLS AND BOYS ARE ADVISED NOT TO READ ANY FURTHER, BECAUSE PICTURE OF BOGYMAN IS ON NEXT PAGE!

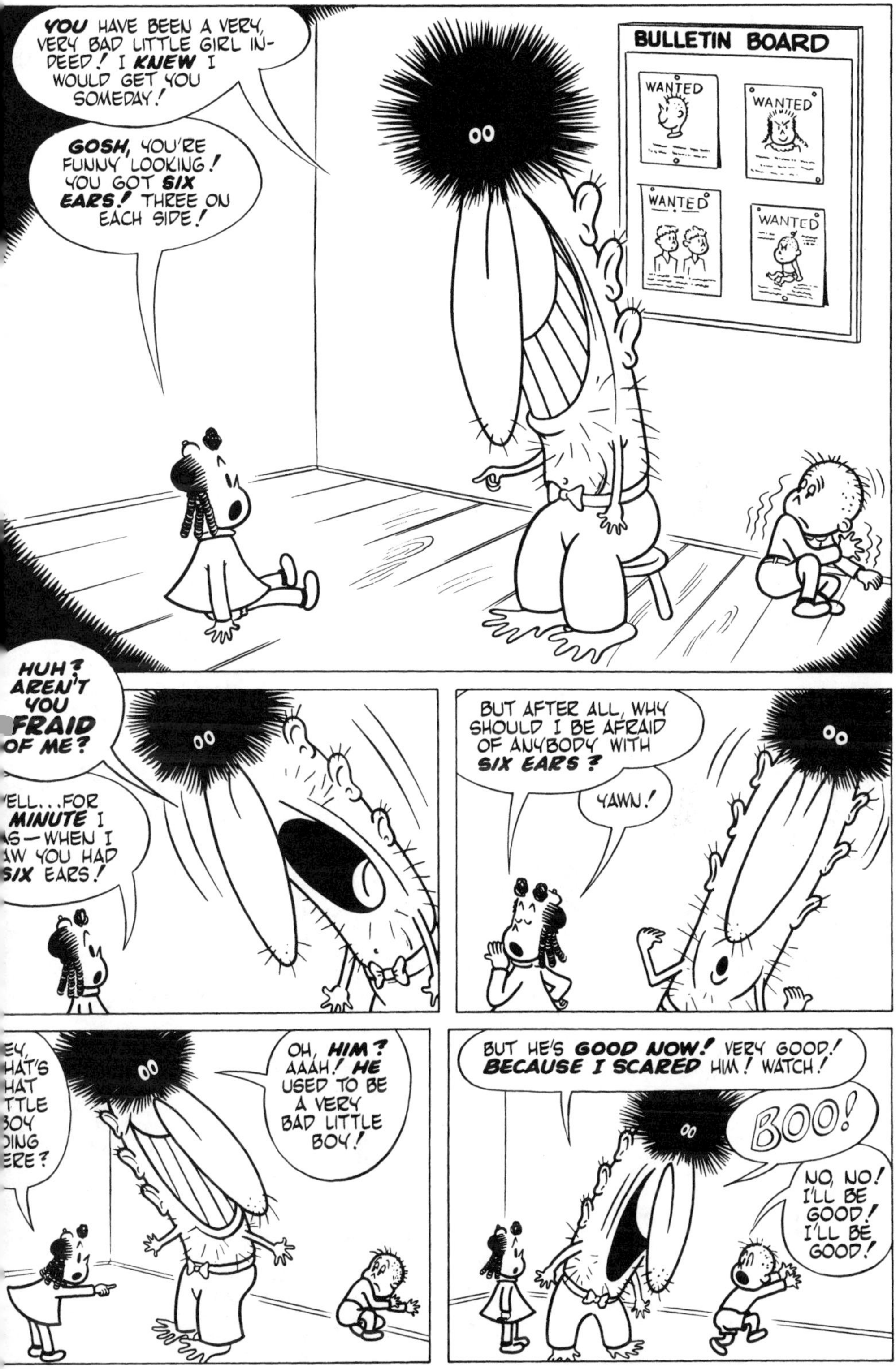
YOU HAVE BEEN A VERY, VERY BAD LITTLE GIRL INDEED! I KNEW I WOULD GET YOU SOMEDAY!
GOSH, YOU'RE FUNNY LOOKING! YOU GOT SIX EARS! THREE ON EACH SIDE!
BULLETIN BOARD
WANTED
WANTED
WANTED
WANTED
HUH? AREN'T YOU FRAID OF ME?
ELL...FOR MINUTE I S—WHEN I AW YOU HAD SIX EARS!
BUT AFTER ALL, WHY SHOULD I BE AFRAID OF ANYBODY WITH SIX EARS?
YAWN!
EY, HAT'S HAT TTLE BOY DING ERE?
OH, HIM? AAAH! HE USED TO BE A VERY BAD LITTLE BOY!
BUT HE'S GOOD NOW! VERY GOOD! BECAUSE I SCARED HIM! WATCH!
BOO!
NO, NO! I'LL BE GOOD! I'LL BE GOOD!

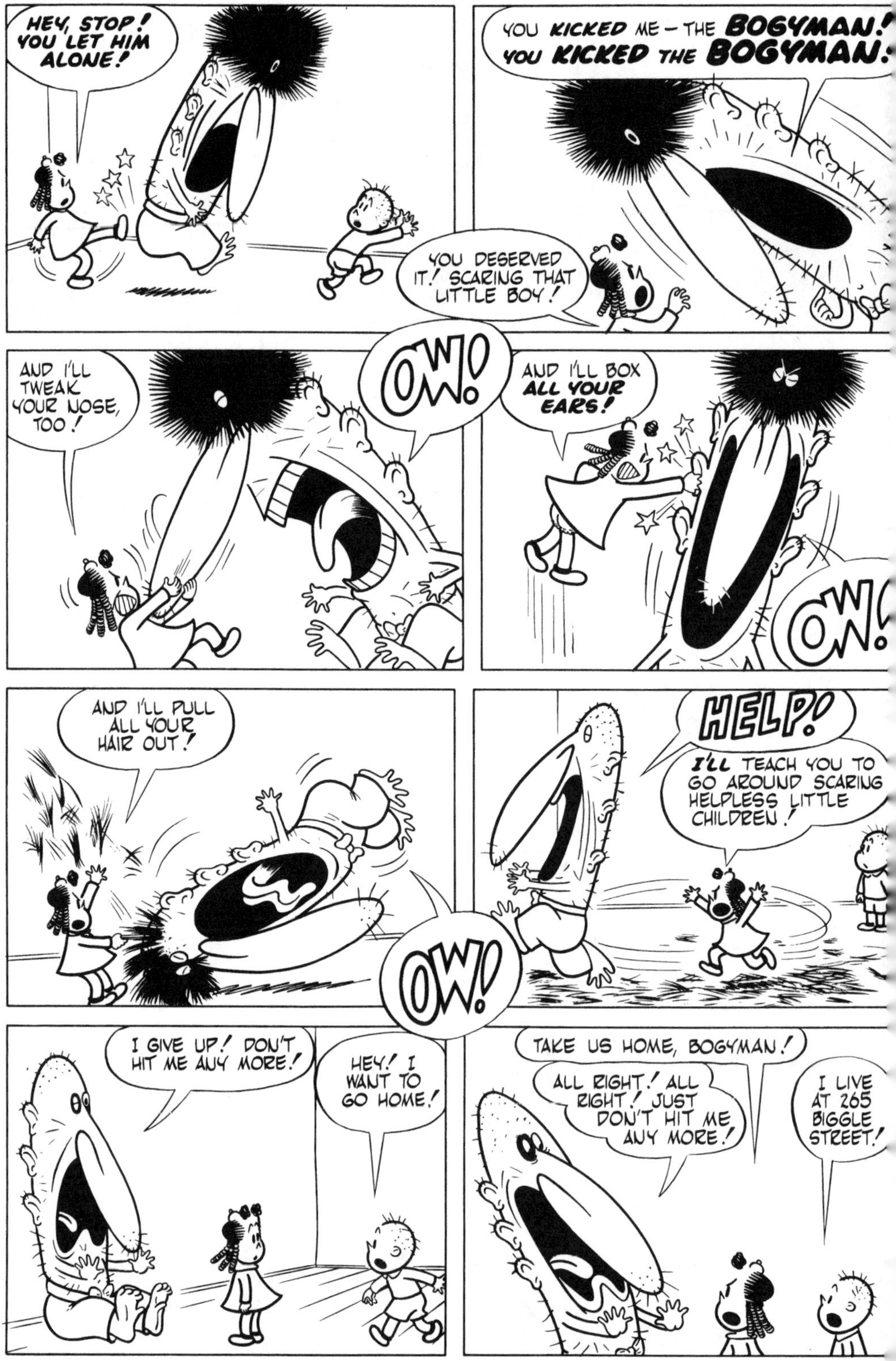
HEY, STOP! YOU LET HIM ALONE!
YOU KICKED ME – THE BOGYMAN! YOU KICKED THE BOGYMAN!
YOU DESERVED IT! SCARING THAT LITTLE BOY!
AND I'LL TWEAK YOUR NOSE, TOO!
OW!
AND I'LL BOX ALL YOUR EARS!
OW!
AND I'LL PULL ALL YOUR HAIR OUT!
OW!
HELP!
I'LL TEACH YOU TO GO AROUND SCARING HELPLESS LITTLE CHILDREN!
I GIVE UP! DON'T HIT ME ANY MORE!
HEY! I WANT TO GO HOME!
TAKE US HOME, BOGYMAN!
ALL RIGHT! ALL RIGHT! JUST DON'T HIT ME ANY MORE!
I LIVE AT 265 BIGGLE STREET!

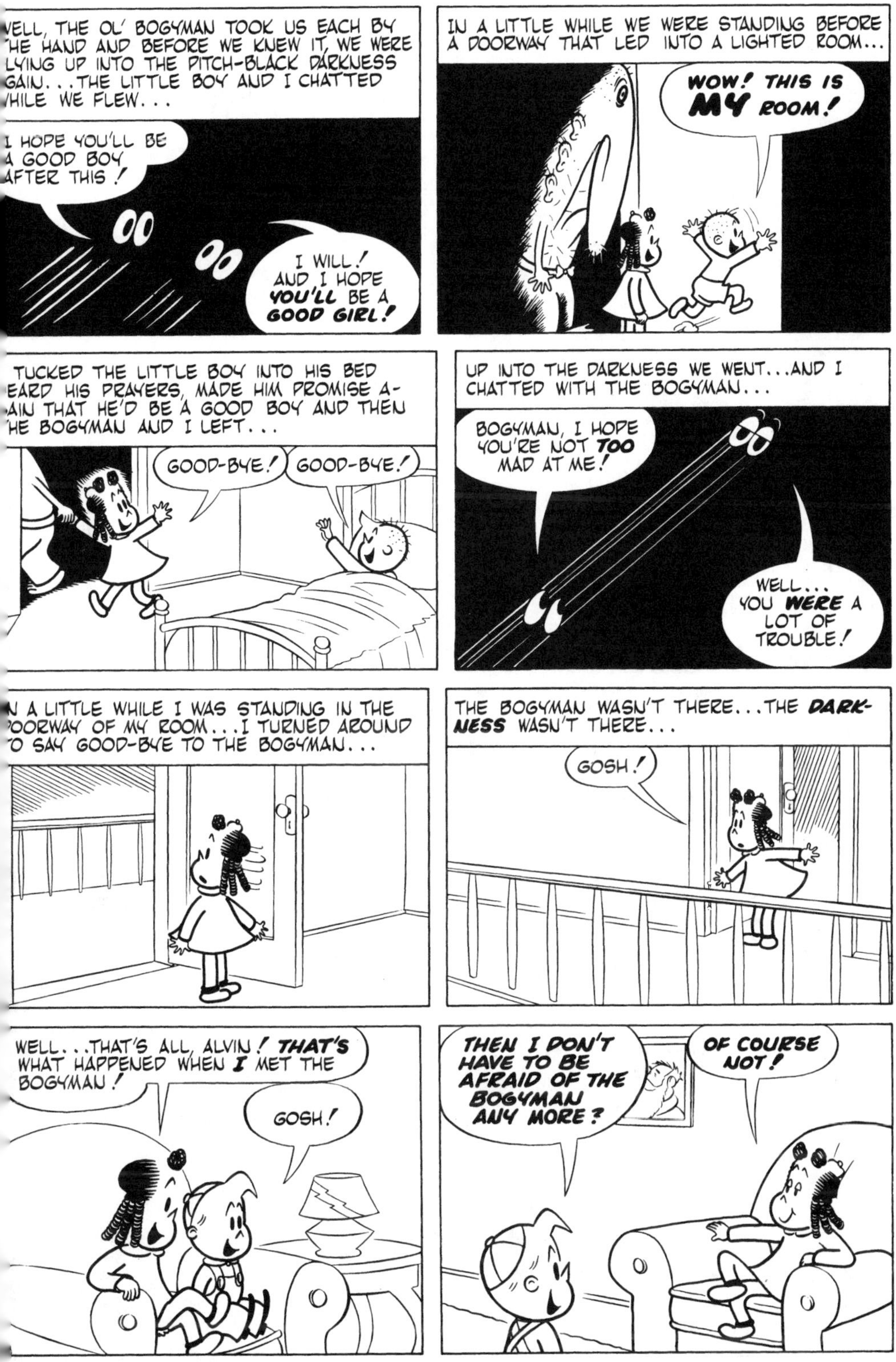

VELL, THE OL' BOGYMAN TOOK US EACH BY HE HAND AND BEFORE WE KNEW IT, WE WERE LYING UP INTO THE PITCH-BLACK DARKNESS GAIN. . . THE LITTLE BOY AND I CHATTED HILE WE FLEW. . .
I HOPE YOU'LL BE A GOOD BOY AFTER THIS!
I WILL! AND I HOPE YOU'LL BE A GOOD GIRL!
IN A LITTLE WHILE WE WERE STANDING BEFORE A DOORWAY THAT LED INTO A LIGHTED ROOM...
WOW! THIS IS MY ROOM!
TUCKED THE LITTLE BOY INTO HIS BED EARD HIS PRAYERS, MADE HIM PROMISE A- AIN THAT HE'D BE A GOOD BOY AND THEN HE BOGYMAN AND I LEFT. . .
GOOD-BYE!
GOOD-BYE!
UP INTO THE DARKNESS WE WENT. . . AND I CHATTED WITH THE BOGYMAN. . .
BOGYMAN, I HOPE YOU'RE NOT TOO MAD AT ME!
WELL. . . YOU WERE A LOT OF TROUBLE!
N A LITTLE WHILE I WAS STANDING IN THE OORWAY OF MY ROOM. . . I TURNED AROUND O SAY GOOD-BYE TO THE BOGYMAN. . .
THE BOGYMAN WASN'T THERE. . . THE DARK- NESS WASN'T THERE. . .
GOSH!
WELL. . . THAT'S ALL, ALVIN! THAT'S WHAT HAPPENED WHEN I MET THE BOGYMAN!
GOSH!
THEN I DON'T HAVE TO BE AFRAID OF THE BOGYMAN ANY MORE?
OF COURSE NOT!

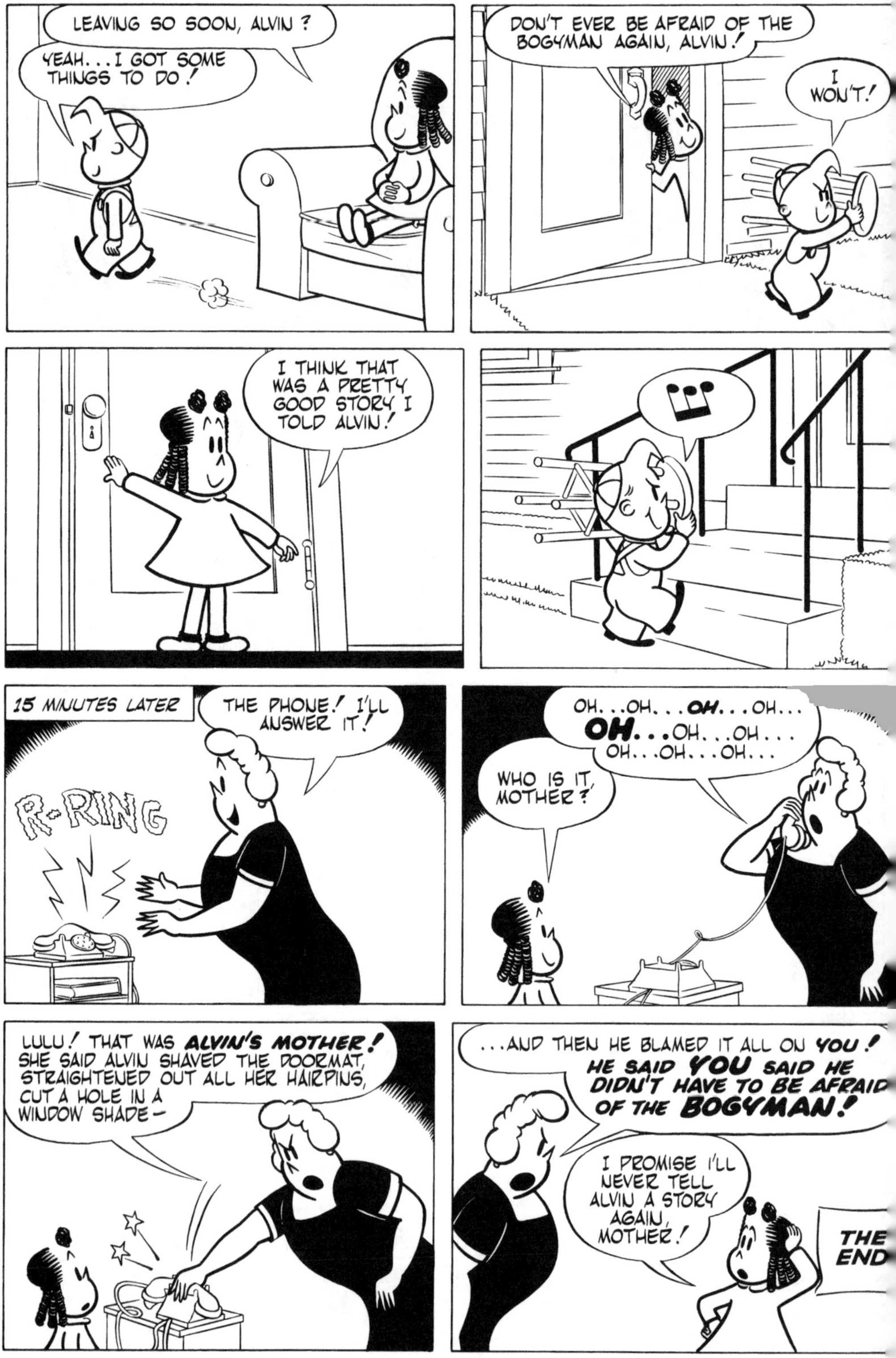
LEAVING SO SOON, ALVIN ?
YEAH...I GOT SOME THINGS TO DO!
DON'T EVER BE AFRAID OF THE BOGYMAN AGAIN, ALVIN!
I WON'T!
I THINK THAT WAS A PRETTY GOOD STORY I TOLD ALVIN!
15 MINUTES LATER
THE PHONE! I'LL ANSWER IT!
R-RING
OH...OH...OH...OH... OH...OH...OH... OH...OH...OH...
WHO IS IT, MOTHER?
LULU! THAT WAS ALVIN'S MOTHER! SHE SAID ALVIN SHAVED THE DOORMAT, STRAIGHTENED OUT ALL HER HAIRPINS, CUT A HOLE IN A WINDOW SHADE—
...AND THEN HE BLAMED IT ALL ON YOU! HE SAID YOU SAID HE DIDN'T HAVE TO BE AFRAID OF THE BOGYMAN!
I PROMISE I'LL NEVER TELL ALVIN A STORY AGAIN, MOTHER!
THE END

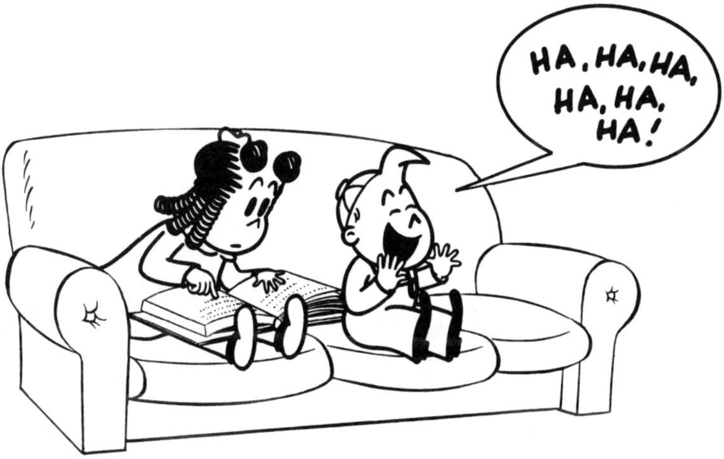
HA, HA, HA, HA, HA, HA!

Little Lulu®

Look For Makoto Kobayashi's

What's Michael?

At Your Bookstore Today!

Volume One: Michael's Album
ISBN-10: 1-56971-247-6
ISBN-13: 978-1-56971-247-4
Price: $5.95

Volume Two: Living Together
ISBN-10: 1-56971-248-4
ISBN-13: 978-1-56971-248-1
Price: $5.95

Volume Three: Off the Deep End
ISBN-10: 1-56971-249-2
ISBN-13: 978-1-56971-249-8
Price: $5.95

Volume Four: Michael's Mambo
ISBN-10: 1-56971-250-6
ISBN-13: 978-1-56971-250-4
Price: $5.95

Volume Five: Michael's Favorite Spot
ISBN-10: 1-56971-557-2
ISBN-13: 978-1-56971-557-4
Price: $8.95

Volume Six: A Hard Day's Life
ISBN-10: 1-56971-744-3
ISBN-13: 978-1-56971-744-8
Price: $8.95

Volume Seven: Fat Cat in the City
ISBN-10: 1-56971-914-4
ISBN-13: 978-1-56971-914-5
Price: $8.95

Volume Eight: Show Time
ISBN-10: 1-56971-972-1
ISBN-13: 978-1-56971-972-5
Price: $8.95

Volume Nine: The Ideal Cat
ISBN-10: 1-59307-120-5
ISBN-13: 978-1-59307-120-2
Price: $8.95

Volume Ten: Sleepless Nights
ISBN-10: 1-59307-337-2
ISBN-13: 978-1-59307-337-4
Price: $8.95

Volume Eleven: Planet of the Cats
ISBN-10: 1-59307-525-1
ISBN-13: 978-1-59307-525-5
Price: $9.95

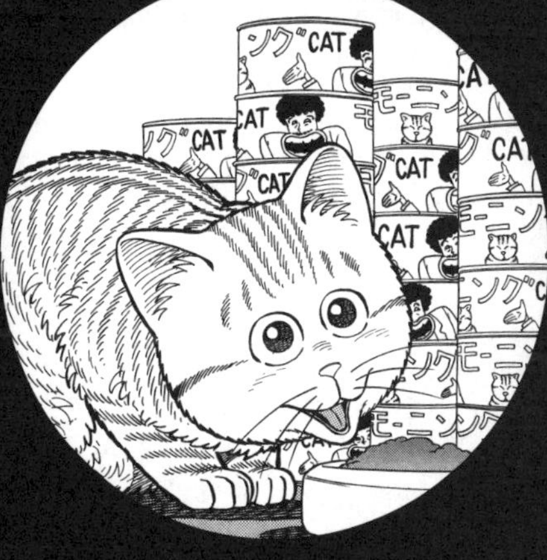

What's Michael? Michael is a cat. A cat who is inexplicably attracted to the smell of raw fish, yet horribly repulsed by the smell of toothpaste. In short, Michael is a cat like any other cat. *What's Michael?* is an amusing look at the lives of cats, written and illustrated by manga master Makoto Kobayashi. In these books you'll find answers to some of the burning "cat" questions that you've been dying to have answered, such as: Do cats always land on their feet? Do cats make good detectives? Are cats better pets than dogs? And the often-asked but seldom-answered, why do cats dance? Of course, there are more than just cats in *What's Michael?* These stories show us how people interact (and often make idiots of themselves) in the presence of felines. These tales allow us to look in on the lives of cats and the people who love (and hate) them.

Available at your local comics shop or bookstore
To find a comics shop in your area, call 1-888-266-4226

DARK HORSE MANGA

For more information or to order direct:
On the web: darkhorse.com
E-mail: mailorder@darkhorse.com
Phone: 1-800-862-0052
Mon.-Fri. 9 A.M. to 5 P.M. Pacific Time

Looking for something new to read?

CHECK OUT THESE ALL-AGES TITLES FROM DARK HORSE BOOKS!

Join Usagi Yojimbo in his hare-raising adventures of life and death. Watch as he faces assassins, medicine peddlers, bat ninjas, and more, in this twenty-volumes-and-counting epic! This is a story of honor and adventure, a masterful adaptation of samurai legend to sequential art. Dark Horse is proud to present this Eisner award–winning and internationally acclaimed tour de force by master storyteller Stan Sakai!

It's amazing how many comics fans who grew up admiring Spiderman, Batman, and Nick Fury still retain warm places in their hearts for Casper the Friendly Ghost. Now Dark Horse is delighted to participate in the revival of Casper, who remains among the most beloved of cartoon and comic book icons. *Harvey Comics Classics Volume 1: Casper* contains over one hundred of Casper's very best stories, from the beginning of the Harvey series in 1952 through the classic years of the mid-1960s.

Just how much trouble can a toy animal really cause? Find out in this funny, unsettling, and utterly endearing series written and drawn by Tony Millionaire! Follow along with mischievous sock monkey Uncle Gabby and bumbling bird Drinky Crow as they try to find a home for a shrunken head, try their hands at matchmaking, hunt salamanders and butterflies, tackle home repairs, face off against creatures from the deep, and try to get to heaven. Delights! Happy endings and random destruction are guaranteed! Check out any of the amazing Sock Monkey stories already out and about, or hop on board for the latest Sock Monkey yarn, *The Inches Incident.*

Find out more about these and other great Dark Horse all-ages titles at darkhorse.com!